Criminal Justice Administration

Strategies for the 21st Century

Clyde L. Cronkhite
Doctor of Public Adminstration
University of Southern California

Professor
Western Illinois University
Macomb, Illinois

JONES AND BARTLETT PUBLISHERS
Sudbury, Massachusetts
BOSTON   TORONTO   LONDON   SINGAPORE

Jones and Bartlett Publishers
World Headquarters
40 Tall Pine Drive
Sudbury, MA 01776
978-443-5000
info@jbpub.com
www.jbpub.com

Jones and Bartlett Publishers Canada
6339 Ormindale Way
Mississauga, Ontario L5V 1J2
Canada

Jones and Bartlett Publishers International
Barb House, Barb Mews
London W6 7PA
United Kingdom

Jones and Bartlett's books and products are available through most bookstores and online booksellers. To contact Jones and Bartlett Publishers directly, call 800-832-0034, fax 978-443-8000, or visit our website www.jbpub.com.

Production Credits
Chief Executive Officer: Clayton Jones
Chief Operating Officer: Don W. Jones, Jr.
President, Higher Education and Professional Publishing: Robert W. Holland, Jr.
V.P., Sales and Marketing: William J. Kane
V.P., Design and Production: Anne Spencer
Publisher—Public Safety Group: Kimberly Brophy
Acquisitions Editor: Jeremy Spiegel
Associate Managing Editor: Janet Morris
Production Supervisor: Jenny L. Corriveau
Associate Production Editor: Jamie Chase
Director of Marketing: Alisha Weisman
Manufacturing and Inventory Coordinator: Amy Bacus
Composition: Publishers' Design and Production Services, Inc.
Interior Design: Anne Spencer
Cover Design: Kristin E. Ohlin
Chapter Opener Image: © Masterfile
Cover Image Photo: Column © Ron Chapple/ThinkStock/Alamy Images
Cover Image Photo: Selahattin Bayram/ShutterStock, Inc.
Printing and Binding: Malloy, Inc.
Cover Printing: Malloy, Inc.

Library of Congress Cataloging-in-Publication Data
Cronkhite, Clyde L.
  Criminal justice administration : strategies for the 21st century / Clyde L. Cronkhite.
    p. cm.
  Includes bibliographical references and index.
  ISBN-13: 978-0-7637-4111-2
  ISBN-10: 0-7637-4111-6
  1. Criminal justice, Administration of—United States.   I. Title.
  KF9223.C76 2008
  364.973—dc22
                                                              2007022554

6048
Printed in the United States of America
11 10 09 08 07   10 9 8 7 6 5 4 3 2 1

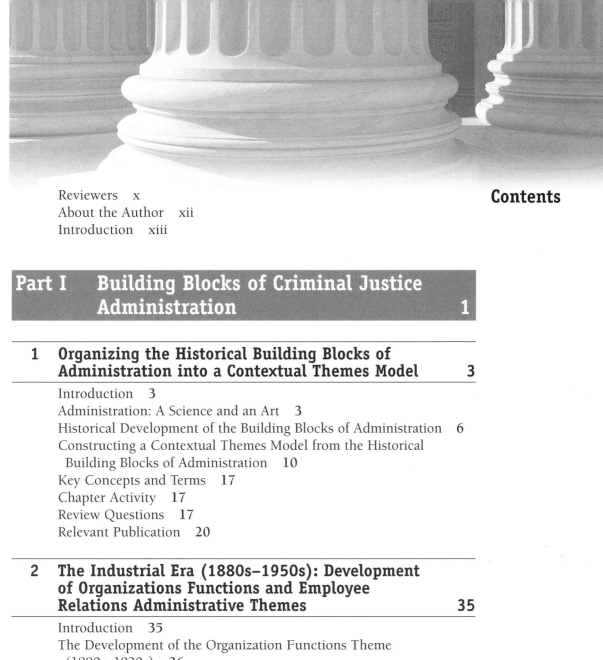

Contents

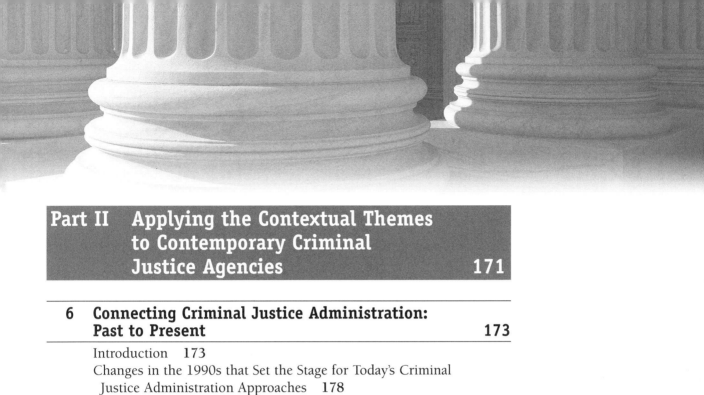

Part III Applying Contextual Themes of Administration to Future Criminal Justice Issues   333

11 Applying Client-Oriented Service to the Administration of Criminal Justice Agencies   335

12 Criminal Justice Administration and Diversity in the 21st Century   369

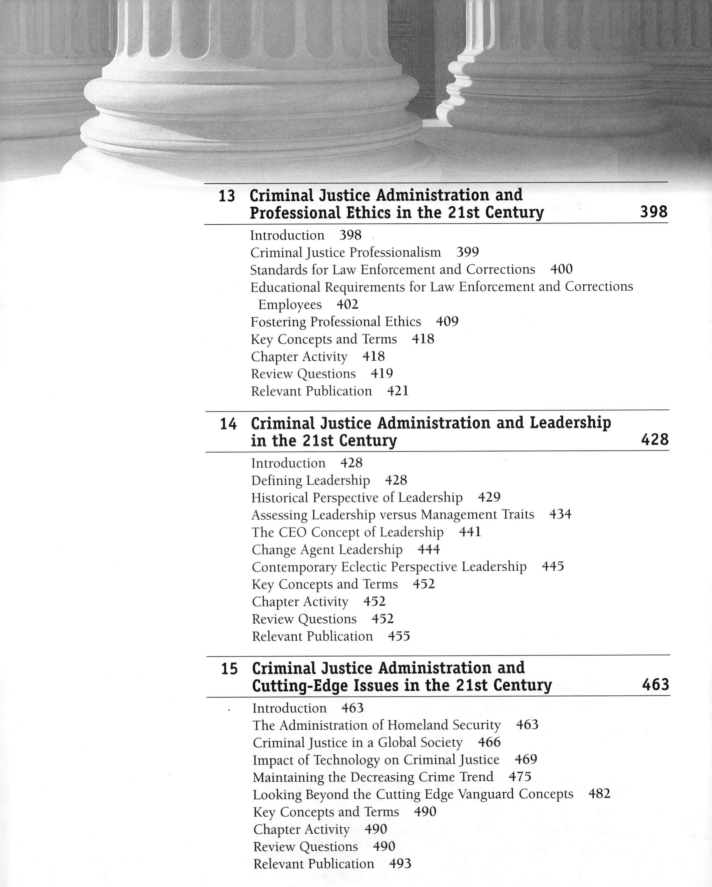

Appendices

Reviewers

Ross Clayton, PhD
Dean Emeritus
Department of Public Administration
University of Southern California
Los Angeles, California

Terry M. Mors, EdD
Professor/Graduate Coordinator/Assistant Chair
Department of Law Enforcement and Justice Administration
Western Illinois University
Macomb, Illinois

Darrell L. Ross, PhD
Chair and Professor
Department of Law Enforcement and Justice Administration
Western Illinois University
Macomb, Illinois

William L. Tafoya, PhD
Professor
College of Criminal Justice and Forensic Sciences
University of New Haven
West Haven, Connecticut

To all the criminal justice practitioners and administrators who have helped me throughout my career and to all my students who are the future of our profession.

Dedication

To my wife and partner in life, Patricia.

To my mother, Evelyn, and children, Pamila, Caren, and Carl, who are my inspiration.

To my grandchildren, John, Carrie, Evan, Tendra, and Jaydan, who are my future.

About the Author

Clyde Cronkhite is a professor and former Chair of the Department of Law Enforcement and Justice Administration at Western Illinois University (WIU). He was also a faculty member and Director of the Center for Administration of Justice at the University of Southern California (USC). He has served in all law enforcement ranks (officer through deputy chief with the Los Angeles Police Department and Chief of Police of the Santa Ana Police Department in California). Dr. Cronkhite was also Corporate Chief of Security for Columbia Finance in Beverly Hills. He received his doctorate and master degrees in public administration from USC. In addition to teaching and writing, he also lectures and consults regarding criminal justice issues (http://www.clcconsultants.com).

Criminal justice administration is at the very heart of the American way of governing and the American way of life. Those who oversee criminal justice agencies are charged with certain responsibility important to public quality of life. As set forth in the Preamble to the U.S. Constitution, the public is guaranteed "justice" and "domestic tranquility." The criminal justice system plays a vital role in maintaining these guarantees. Criminal justice administrators take an oath of office that obligates them to administrate public resources efficiently and effectively. This text is meant to assist in the performance of this noble task.

Introduction

This text brings together the extensive spectrum of concepts of administration for criminal justice teachers, students, and practitioners. The content is presented in a style and format that allows educators to customize the material to meet the specific needs of both undergraduate and graduate courses. Those studying or teaching public and political administration will find the contents relevant to all fields of public service. The text blends historic administrative themes and concepts with future trends. From this perspective, practitioners and academics can develop strategies to enhance the future of administration in Law Enforcement, in the Courts and in Corrections. The text is intended for:

Students. Many criminal justice students will be the criminal justice administrators of tomorrow. Even for those who do not follow this career path, understanding the concepts that guide their employers will be of benefit. Many administrative concepts apply to all levels of criminal justice practice, and knowledge of these concepts can enhance the practitioner's career.

Faculty. The text is specifically calculated to enable faculty to teach the subject in most every classroom environment. The design allows for each chapter to provide the information base for each week of a regular semester (or grouped for other course schedules). The author, as a professor, has "field-tested" the material in the classroom and customized it to fit the needs of both faculty and students.

Administrators. When the author was an administrator, he often hoped for a reference text that could assist in carrying out the daily task of administrators. This text was written with this concept in mind and should be of particular use to criminal justice administrators as well as to administrators in other public fields.

Those preparing to become administrators. The material in this text is arranged in a manner that will enable the thousands of criminal justice practitioners who are studying for promotional examinations to have access to required information. Many of the subjects in the text are relevant to all field of public administration as well as business administration.

Those interested in criminal justice and the American way of life. The text brings together the history of criminal justice and social changes in America. Starting in the years when the individual rights guaranteed by the U.S. Constitution were not applied to some minorities, to today's mandate that requires the criminal justice system to protect the individual rights of all people, the text tells the story of the evolution of justice in America from a criminal justice administration perspective.

Academics and practitioners have voiced concerns that there is a need to bring together the many theories and concepts of administration into a structure that facilitates learning and application. This text introduces the Contextual Themes Model of criminal justice administration as just such a structure. The Contextual Themes Model is meant to provide a framework based on the historical development of public and business administration themes, theories, and concepts. It should serves as a reminder for criminal justice students, practitioners, and academics of the variety of theoretical tools that can be applied to contemporary issues. Themes and concepts are extracted from the many milestone books and articles that form the contextual development of public and business administration. These themes and concepts are blended into a model that is meant to facilitate learning and application.

In a recent issue of *Scientific American*, an article titled "The Expert Mind" studies how experts in various fields assimilate major amounts of data into forms that they can apply. The article documents that people can contemplate only five to nine items at a time. But by "packing hierarchies of information into *chunks*, they get around this limitation." This concept is called the "chunk theory." By identifying concepts by key terms that can be placed into five to nine categories, large amounts of information can be mentally retained. The Contextual Themes Model applies this concept.

The historical evolution of administration offers five major themes: (1) Organization Functions, (2) Employee Relations, (3) Open Systems, (4) Social Equity, and (5) Client-Oriented Service. By connecting the many concepts of administration to key terms and then placing them under the appropriate themes, a method of retaining these concepts for application is presented. Readers are encouraged to check the Compendium of Criminal Justice Themes and Related Key Concepts for a review of the concepts that they should be familiar with on completion of this text. Using the Contextual Themes Model, readers should be able to apply a variety of administrative concepts to a given situation. In writing a class paper, for example, the student should be able to think through the five themes

and bring to mind various key concepts that they can apply to a given situation (e.g., the creation of a police Vice Squad or a Community-Based Probation Unit). In this same manner, the practicing administrator should be able to recall and apply various concepts to contemporary criminal justice challenges.

The text is divided into three parts. In Part I, the Contextual Themes Model is developed by examining the historical building blocks of criminal justice administration and organizes them into the five evolutionary themes. The major milestone writings that document important administrative concepts are then reviewed within the context of their related themes. Part II takes the administrative concepts from Part I, using the first four contextual themes, and applies them to the practice of contemporary criminal administration. Part III discusses the application of the administrative concepts in the future, with the definition of the future being "from this moment on." From this perspective, Part III begins with the application of the fifth contextual theme, as it is the contemporary administrative theme that is "leading us into the future." Part III goes on to discuss "cutting-edge" criminal justice administrative issues. The text then concludes with the previously mentioned Compendium of Criminal Justice Themes and Related Key Concepts. The Compendium organizes the key concepts discussed throughout the text, under appropriate themes, for use by students in applying to class assignments. Additionally, the Compendium should be useful to practicing administrators as well as those preparing to be administrators.

Building Blocks of Criminal Justice Administration

I

This text is divided into three parts. Here, in Part I, the history of criminal justice administration is the subject of study. As discussed in the introduction, in order to successfully practice the art of administration, one must have mastered the science of administration. The science of administration involves the study of past practices and concepts. By studying the past, one can experience vicariously what others have practiced and thereby develop an understanding of the various administrative approaches available for application in today's environment. Chapter 1 provides some basic definitions and introduces the Contextual Themes Model that will be used throughout this book. Chapters 2 through 4 explore the past 100 years of administrative practices and concepts that formed the building blocks of the Contextual Themes Model. Chapter 5 provides examples of how the Contextual Themes Model concepts apply to one field of criminal justice, that of law enforcement. Part II applies administrative concepts to contemporary criminal justice challenges, and Part III focuses on the future.

Organizing the Historical Building Blocks of Administration into a Contextual Themes Model

■ Introduction

It is appropriate to begin by establishing an understanding of the main theme of this book—criminal justice administration. Criminal justice administration is the task of overseeing the fulfillment of the public mission for criminal justice agencies. It is the task of executive officers, managers, and supervisors to establish a structure and environment that provides employees with a clear sense of their responsibilities. Additionally, administrators must ensure that these responsibilities are carried out efficiently and effectively. Administration includes the concepts of leadership and management. The purpose of this text is to provide an understanding of the theories and concepts that those who administrate draw on in order to fulfill their responsibilities successfully.

■ Administration: A Science and an Art

A metaphor that may help to understand the difference between science and art is the process of learning to play a musical instrument. To play a musical instrument well, one must first learn to read music and play the various notes and chords that make a melody. This requires study and the learning of the concepts and theories relating to music that have evolved over many centuries. This process can be viewed as the science of music. The process can be a tedious and demanding endeavor of repeated practicing; of playing musical notes and scales that separately may not sound like music. If one continues this pursuit of the science of music, one will, ideally, no longer have to concentrate on individual notes and scales. Rather, one will be able to play combinations of notes and scales to create music. This is where the science of music becomes art.

Dwight Waldo (1955) stated in *The Study of Public Administration* that the word "**administration**" has two usages. One involves the study or intellectual inquiry of the discipline. The science of administration therefore can be viewed as studying the facts that have been gleaned from research and past practices. It can be viewed as somewhat quantitative as well as based on concepts and theories that have evolved over time. Waldo defined the other usage of administration as the activity or actual practice of overseeing a public organization. This is the art of administration and can be considered to occur when one has internalized those facts relating to the discipline and is able to convert them to the practice of overseeing the accomplishment of organizational missions and goals.

Often, the administrator must coordinate and direct the members of an organization within a time frame that does not provide for step-by-step consideration of the concepts and theories that have been studied. But if he or she has mastered the scientific phase of administration, and has internalized the related concepts and theories, then he or she is able to conceptualize more appropriate approaches to achieve desired results. The difference between the **science** and **art** of administration can be defined in the following way:

Science = the study of concepts and theories

Art = the converting of concepts and theories into practice

Administration is the creation of synergy. Synergy can be defined as the combed action of energies that results in an outcome that exceeds the individual energies. A more understandable example might be the coordination of the physical abilities of two people to push an object (a vehicle, for example) that neither of the two can push individually. This is why organizations are formed and why administrators are given the responsibility of combining and coordinating the activities of employees. A well-administrated organization can produce much greater results than can the members of the organization acting individually. Synergy can be viewed as:

Properly combining 1 + 1 can equal more than 2.

The Major Responsibilities of Administrators

Dwight Waldo (1955) wrote that administrators are held accountable for two major responsibilities. One is to achieve the social or public mission of the organization. The other is to satisfy the needs of employees. Accomplishment of both these goals requires a combination of management and leadership skills. These skills can best be acquired by those who have scientifically studied related theories and concepts and who can artfully apply them to current and future challenges. An objective of this book is to provide the reader with a level of understanding of how to apply concepts and theory to practice. The two major responsibilities of the administrator are:

1. Accomplishment of the mission
2. Satisfaction of employee needs

Basic Administrative Terms

In discussing administration, a number of terms have been used. Although these terms will be discussed in more detail later in this text, they are briefly defined here to provide a basic understanding of administration.

Organization is the grouping of two or more people and the coordination of their efforts to achieve common goals and objectives.

Management is making appropriate use of resources (people and equipment) to achieve organizational goals and objectives as efficiently and effectively as possible. It may be referred to as the technical aspects of administration (planning, organizing, directing, and coordinating) and does not necessary involved leadership.

Leadership is the process of getting people to work willingly toward a common goal. It involves inspiring and motivating people.

Missions and **goals** are often used interchangeably, and are the very broad statements that establish the overall philosophy and direction of an organization. They are sometimes called "value statements."

Objectives are measurable and time-bound components of an organization's overall mission. For example, a mission may be to rehabilitate those in the corrections system and prevent them from continuing a life of crime when released back into society. An objective would be to reduce the recidivism rate by 15% (measurable) over the next year (time-bound).

Efficient and **effective** often are used interchangeably; however, they have different meanings. Being efficient means making the best use of resources. Being effective means achieving the desired goals and objectives. One can be achieved without the other. For example, administrators may have their personnel working at maximum capacity but are unable to achieve goals and objective because they have not been provided ample resources. Conversely, an objective relating to reducing burglaries might be achieved without efficient use of resources. The objective may be accomplished because the prime perpetrator of the burglaries is arrested by another agency. A successful administrator is both efficient and effective.

To provide a better understanding of how these basic terms relate to administration, the following statements are offered:

Missions and goals are usually established by executive officers, whereas objectives are developed by mid-managers and supervisors.

Objectives are a means by which executive officers can hold supervisors and managers accountable for contributing to the missions and goals.

Efficiency may be said to be a better measure of management ability, whereas effectiveness is better associated with leadership.

■ Historical Development of the Building Blocks of Administration

The history of administrative practices provides a foundation of knowledge with which today's criminal justice administrators must be familiar if they are to be successful. What follows is a brief review to provide the reader with the basis for understanding these building blocks of administration. Subsequent chapters will expand on this brief review. The building blocks of administration are the components of the **Contextual Themes Model**, which will be used throughout this text. The Contextual Themes Model is meant to provide the reader with a method of understanding the multitude of administrative theories and concepts available in overseeing contemporary criminal justice agencies. Five contextual themes are identified from the three historical eras (**Figure 1–1**). These themes are the building blocks of the Contextual Themes Model.

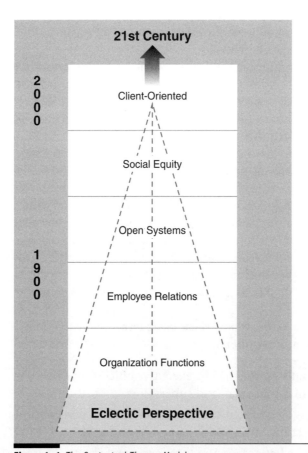

Figure 1–1 The Contextual Themes Model.

The Industrial Era (1880s–1950s)

Development of Organization Functions Theme

During the first half of the Industrial Era, literature analyzed and described the basic functions of bureaucratic organizations. It included the establishment of management principles and organization functions that guide the administration of public agencies. The public administration approach during this period was that under the U.S. Constitution, public representatives were elected and public agencies carried out the directions of elected officials.

In "The Study of Administration," Woodrow Wilson (1887) described public administration as the business end of government. He wrote, "Representatives of the people are the proper ultimate authority in all matters of government and administration is merely the clerical part of government."

Wilson's work was an outgrowth of the reform movement of the time. This movement resulted in the passage of the first federal civil service reform legislation, the Pendleton Act of 1883. The Pendleton Act began a process of replacing the "spoils system" with a federal personnel system based on merit. This reform movement was a result of public disappointment with the blatant political abuse and corruption that had prevailed since the 1820s.

It can be seen in Wilson's writings that the theme of the time for public administration was centered on creating efficient organizations to carry out the public interest as interpreted by elected officials. This period emphasized rationalism, efficiency, and productivity through established rules, laws, and scientific principles. These subjects were of major concern to public administrators in the early 1900s.

Sometimes called "classical organization theories," the **Organization Functions** theme viewed public agencies as social systems in which power and authority flowed from the top downward through a hierarchy and accountability flowed from the bottom upward. The mission or goals of an organization could be divided into specific tasks. Tasks were assigned and delegated downward through a superior/subordinate relationship wherein employees were held accountable for efficiently achieving desired goals. The concentration of writings relating to this theme was published from 1887 to the late 1930s.

Development of the Emphasis on Employee Relations Theme

Although the previous period centered on how the bureaucratic structure controlled efforts of employees, the emerging interest began to consider the quality of life of individuals within the organization. How employees were motivated to achieve work tasks led to the development of the **Employee Relations** theme.

This shift in theme was promoted by research in furtherance of a theory of the Organization Functions period, Taylor's theory of scientific management. Elton Mayo and F. J. Roethlisberger investigated how physical factors contributed to production at the Western Electric Company's Hawthorne plant in Chicago. They discovered that the social environment and attention given to workers had a more pronounced effect on productivity than the physical environment had.

Even though the Hawthorne Experiments took place in the late 1920s and early 1930s, the findings were not published until the 1940s. Following the private sector lead, the public sector interest in efficiency broadened to include employees and how to motivate them to be more productive.

This "humanism" approach took the position that workers would produce more if they gained job satisfaction. Job satisfaction related to democratic participation by workers in decision making. It was a supervisory approach that was less autocratic, more trusting, and emphasized concern for the "team members'" welfare.

Although under the Organization Functions approach employees were thought to gain fulfillment from attaining organization goals, the humanist approach focused on integrating individual and organization goals toward employee self-actualization. One school of thought in this category (sometimes called "neoclassical" theories) dealt with the idea of power as a human relations concept. The boss could give orders, but the informal organization had the power to determine to what extent employees would obey.

The Civil Rights Era (1960s–1970s)

Development of the Open Systems Theme

Following the Employee Relations period, public administration scholars began to broaden their view to include those influences outside the organization, that is, influences that had some impact on the internal operations of an organization. This shift in theme happened as the public sector became more aware that, in order to be more efficient, there must be concern and interaction with elements outside the boundaries of public agencies. Again, the public sector followed the private sector.

There was a move away from the "closed system" theory, which held that an organization was analogous to a physical system (such as a machine) and essentially was insulated from its own environment. The closed system approach related to the previous two development periods that centered on the inner workings of the organization (functions and employees).

The **Open Systems** period marked the beginning of the view that organizations are part of a larger environment. An organization has a greater purpose than mere survival and reaches beyond itself much as human beings do. From the Open Systems perspective, the essential parts of an organization or administrative system are input, throughput, output, and feedback.

Input is interaction in the system emanating from the environment (such as the energies of citizens who become employees.) Throughput is the transformation of environmental factors (such as supplies and other resources) into output. Output is the interaction initiated by the system (such as a product or service) that leaves the boundaries of the system. Feedback can alert the organization to output mistakes so that they can be corrected at the input or throughput stages.

A Commitment to Social Equity Theme

Social equity became more of a concern to scholars of public administration in the 1970s. This theme shift began with the "New Public Administration" movement, which was inaugurated in 1968 when Dwight Waldo sponsored a conference for young public administrators at the Minnowbrook Conference site in Syracuse, New York. This is the only theme in the Contextual Development of Public Administration Model that seems to have developed entirely from within the public sector.

The products of this conference (often referred to as the "Minnowbrook Perspective" or "Minnowbrook Papers") were published in 1971 as *The New Public Administration: The Minnowbrook Perspective*. These papers emphasized social needs—particularly the problems of urbanism and violence.

Earlier periods of public administration had addressed two questions of public policy:

1. Can better service be offered with available resources?
2. Can the level of service be maintained while spending less?

The Social Equity period, however, added a third question: Do the services enhance social equity? From this perspective, administrators should understand the ethical framework on which government is based, and should be advocates for the disadvantaged.

Proponents of social responsibility said that the public servant should impress on higher-level policy makers the basic values of democracy and should actively advance the cause of social justice. An attendant role should be to increase citizen participation as a means of gaining more direct involvement of the disadvantaged and minorities.

Some who held this view even foresaw a political system in which elected officials would speak for the majority, whereas the courts and public administrators would speak for the disadvantaged and minorities.

The Transition to the 21st-Century Era (1980–)

Advancement of the Client-Oriented Service Theme

Once the focus moved outside the organization and toward more social responsibility, attention shifted to people-participation and the resulting impact that the public (the clients of public service) had on input, output, and feedback. In some ways, it was a return to the constitutional theme of the late 1700s, which focused on the sovereignty of the people and local rule.

For example, Vincent Ostrom said that public administrators should concentrate their services on individual consumers of public goods and services, and should not take their entire direction from "political masters." He wrote that although public agencies were obligated to respect government authority (public officials), they were not mere "obedient servants" (Ostrom, 1974, p. 110). Norton Long, in 1949, probably best predicted the coming of this theme shift when he wrote:

> *The theory that agencies should confine themselves to communicating policy suggestions to the executive and legislature, and refrain from appealing to their clientele and the public, neglects the failure*

> *of the parties to provide either a clear-cut decision as to what they should do or an adequately mobilized political support for a course of action. The bureaucracy under the American political system has a large share of responsibility for the public promotion of policy and even more in organizing the political basis for its survival and growth. (Long, cited in Stillman, 1988, p. 93)*

In contrast to the earlier Woodrow Wilson years, when public managers were considered administrators of political centralized power, this **Client-Oriented Service** view recognized the need to allow public agencies to have more decentralized responsibilities in serving the public. Public managers began to interact directly with the public, and to respond more as private corporation managers would respond to their customers while following the policies of a board of directors (in public agencies, the elected officials equated to a board of directors and the public to the shareholders).

Within the concept of public participation are what some scholars refer to as "public choice" and "marketplace" theories. These theories take the position that public agencies should compete to provide the public with goods and services instead of acting as monopolies under the influence of organized pressure groups and political factions.

The basis of this school of thought is that the free-enterprise market system is dependent on individual customer support, and our government agencies should be as well. Accordingly, because the citizen is a consumer of government goods and services, administrative responsiveness to citizens needs should be increased by creating a market system for government activities. The distinctive characteristic of this view is its primary unit of analysis, namely, the self-interested individual seeking to maximize utility through the exercise of rational choice.

■ Constructing a Contextual Themes Model from the Historical Building Blocks of Administration

The task of the administrator can be compared to a once popular juggling act in which the performer would spin a series of china plates on wooden poles. In order to keep all of the plates spinning, the **juggler** often had to energize several plates simultaneously while maintaining an awareness of the velocity and balance of all the plates. The successful administrator, like the juggler, must often attend to several challenges at one time while maintaining an awareness of the variety of all potential problems within a given area of public responsibility.

A premise of this text is that the history of public and business administration can provide a structure to serve as a guide for criminal justice administrators in handling current and future multi-task challenges. The history of administration provides a set of building blocks that criminal justice administrations can use as guides in overseeing current and future tasks.

It was Alfred Korzybski, the father of General Semantics, who stated that the essence of knowledge is structure (Korzybski, 1958, pp. 21–28). It follows that for criminal justice administrators to benefit from the historical development of public and business administration, a structure is required, one that will define and connect relative themes and concepts so they can be applied to contemporary issues. It was the absence of such structure that led Charlesworth (1968) and Waldo (1980) to conclude throughout their writings that the volumes of public administration literature notwithstanding, uncertainty remains regarding definition, scope, and methods of verification essential to establishing public administration as a legitimate and respectable field of study.

Richard J. Stillman II wrote, "More than three decades ago, Dwight Waldo said that public administration suffered from a definite identity crisis, or as Vincent Ostrom termed it 'an intellectual crisis.' Ostrom wrote that he was persuaded that the major task for the future was "to lay new foundations for the study of public administration" (Ostrom, 1974, 5). More recently, Nicholas Henry called the dilemma "a paradigmatic quandary" (Stillman, 1991, p. vii). The Contextual Themes Model is offered as a means of resolving this dilemma.

The Contextual Themes Model is meant to provide a framework based on the historical development of public and business administration themes, theories, and concepts. It should serve as a reminder for criminal justice practitioners and academicians of the variety of theoretical tools that can be applied to contemporary issues. Themes and concepts are extracted from the many milestone books and articles that form the contextual development of public and business administration. **Appendix 1** lists the articles from which the building blocks of administration emanate. The result is a structure intended to provide the reader with a means of conceptualizing and applying past themes and practices to current and future administrative challenges (**Figure 1–2**). It also is meant to serve as a reminder that administrative approaches are ever evolving in response to changing social, political, and economic changes.

Just as with the development of scientific principles (Asimov, 1972, p. 1), the development of administration themes is a process whereby new and more current ideas are constantly updating older ones. It is through this process that theories and concepts are built and refined, leading to enhanced understanding and management of public sector challenges.

A structure that will facilitate understanding should provide a mechanism for connecting and making understandable seemingly disjointed concepts and theories. Such a structure also should be based on a commonly understood model. The well-known **Hierarchy of Human Needs**, provided by Abraham H. Maslow, serves as a comparison for the Contextual Themes of Public Administration Model (**Figure 1–3**). Maslow showed how these basic needs—physiological, safety, love, esteem, and self-actualization—were interrelated by arranging them into a hierarchy (Maslow, 1943, pp. 89–100). In describing his model, Maslow wrote:

> *The most proponent goal will monopolize consciousness and will tend of itself to organize with recruitment of the various capacities of the organism. The less proponent needs are minimized, even for-*

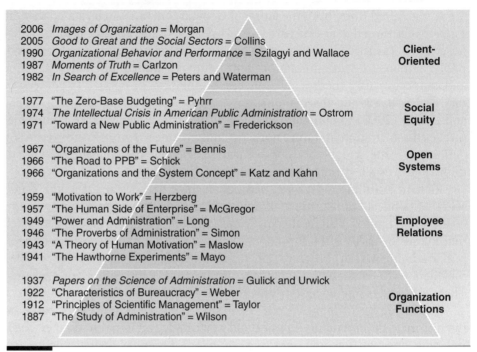

2006 *Images of Organization* = Morgan
2005 *Good to Great and the Social Sectors* = Collins
1990 *Organizational Behavior and Performance* = Szilagyi and Wallace
1987 *Moments of Truth* = Carlzon
1982 *In Search of Excellence* = Peters and Waterman

Client-Oriented

1977 "The Zero-Base Budgeting" = Pyhrr
1974 *The Intellectual Crisis in American Public Administration* = Ostrom
1971 "Toward a New Public Administration" = Frederickson

Social Equity

1967 "Organizations of the Future" = Bennis
1966 "The Road to PPB" = Schick
1966 "Organizations and the System Concept" = Katz and Kahn

Open Systems

1959 "Motivation to Work" = Herzberg
1957 "The Human Side of Enterprise" = McGregor
1949 "Power and Administration" = Long
1946 "The Proverbs of Administration" = Simon
1943 "A Theory of Human Motivation" = Maslow
1941 "The Hawthorne Experiments" = Mayo

Employee Relations

1937 *Papers on the Science of Administration* = Gulick and Urwick
1922 "Characteristics of Bureaucracy" = Weber
1912 "Principles of Scientific Management" = Taylor
1887 "The Study of Administration" = Wilson

Organization Functions

Figure 1–2 Contextual Themes Model and Key Milestones.

> *gotten or denied. But when a need is fairly well satisfied the next proponent (higher) need arises to dominate the conscious life and to serve as the center of organization or behavior, since gratified needs are not active motivators. (Maslow, 1943, p. 91)*

In Maslow's hierarchal system, if one is at a higher level and if a previously satisfied level is threatened, one's primary focus is often redirected to that lower goal. For example, if one is at the "self-actualization" level and loses their job, then they immediately regress to the "physiological" and "safely" level and become concerned with how they are going to provide for their basic needs. We will see that the same dynamics occur in the Contextual Themes of Public Administration Model.

It should be acknowledged at this point that Maslow's work has been criticized as having little empirical support (Williams, 1980). Nevertheless, the hierarchy remains today as a well-known model of motivation. One of the reasons for the endurance of Maslow's model is that it is logical and easy to understand.

A review of the development of public administration during the past 150 years reveals an interesting correlation with Maslow's Human Needs Model. As previously reviewed in this chapter, the history of administrative theory provides five themes:

1. Establishment of Organization Functions (beginning in the 1880s): a focus on efficiency.

2. Emphasis on Employee Relations (beginning in the 1940s): a focus on human relations within the organization.

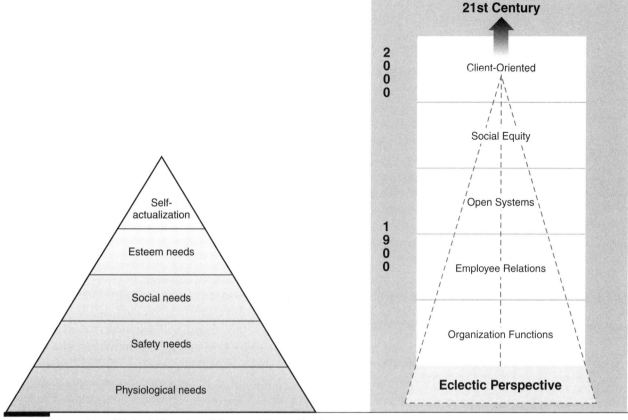

Figure 1–3 Comparison of Maslow's Hierarchy and Contextual Themes Model.

3. Development of an Open Systems outlook (beginning in the 1960s): a focus on input, output, feedback relating to the external environment of the organization.

4. Commitment to social equity (becoming a focal point in the 1970s): protect the individual rights of the public as well as employees.

5. Movement to Client-Oriented Service (became a central theme in the 1980s and continued into the 21st century): a focus on the interest of, and gaining and maintaining the trust of, the public.

A challenge for public administration in the 21st century is to recognize the relevance of these historical themes to current issues. This requires an **Eclectic Perspective**, that is, an understanding of the past themes and related concepts and the ability to tailor and apply them to current situations. The Eclectic Perspective allows one to "mix and match" various administrative concepts to meet given contemporary situations. The tabulated milestone building blocks in Appendix 1 are associated with the five numbered themes and, as indicated by asterisks, are reminders of the need for an Eclectic Perspective.

During the Open Systems period, in 1966, Allen Schick wrote about "The Road to PPB: The Stages of Budget Reform"; and in 1977, during the Social Equity period, Peter Pyhrr wrote about "The Zero-Base Approach to Government Budgeting." In both cases, the focus of public administration was temporarily diverted to a previous contextual theme because of a downturn in the economy. Reductions in budgets forces public administrators to return their attention to the efficiency interests of the Organization Functions period.

Maslow's Needs Hierarchy was later modified by Clayton P. Alderfer, in his ERG theory. Alderfer condensed the Maslow hierarchy into three needs categories: Existence, Relatedness, and Growth. Two changes that the ERG theory made to the Needs Hierarchy should be noted. First, Maslow's hierarchy theory was based on a satisfaction-progression approach in that a movement to a higher level need would occur once a lower need had been satisfied. The ERG theory, by contrast, incorporated not only a satisfaction-progression component but also a frustration-regression approach. Frustration-regression describes the situation in which a higher-order need remains unsatisfied, or frustrated, and greater importance or desire is placed on the next lower need. The second change is closely related to the first. Unlike Maslow's approach, the ERG theory indicates that more than one need may be operative at any one time (Landy, 1976, p. 301).

These two changes, particularly the latter, are important in understanding the Contextual Themes Model of Public Administration. As the history of public administration has progressed through evolutionary phases, earlier themes remain important and function as building blocks that support and serve as a foundation for developing new themes, theories, and concepts.

For example, Elton Mayo's Hawthorne Experiment at the Western Electric plant was intended to study Frederick Taylor's Scientific Management Theory of the Organization Functions period. Mayo's study was motivated by an established Organization Functions theory and resulted in the discovery of yet another theory that moved the attention of private, as well as public, administration to a new theme.

It should be understood that when interest develops in a new theme, the themes of earlier periods remain important. Today's public administrator must attend to all the themes developed in the previous periods, as they provide a contextual guide when current and future public sector issues are confronted.

This approach postulates a contextual understanding based on historical themes. Samuel Bois, clinical psychologist, wrote that "Humankind's ability to know phenomena is limited and the rational mind acknowledges its limitations. Postulating is at best approximating. No formulation is one hundred percent valid" (Bois, 1978, p. 166).

For example, the historical periods of the Contextual Themes Model of Public Administration are divided by the boundaries of decades. In reality, theme shifts may and do occur at any time, although these shifts conveniently can be identified with decades.

To make allowance for "unpatterned" shifts, the following chapters in Part I are divided into Theme Milestones and Transition Milestones. The Theme Milestones are those works that make major contributions to the theme of the period. The Transition Milestones are contributions made during the time frame of each period but are not exclusively consistent with the major theme of the period. The

Transition Milestones are those works that point the way to or enhance theories and concepts of other periods.

There have been other ways of categorizing and understanding the development of public administrative theories. Harmon and Mayer, for example, categorized public administration theories into: (1) Baseline Organization Theory; (2) Neo-Classical Theories; (3) Systems Theory; (4) Later Human Relations Theory; (5) Market Theories; (6) Interpretive and Critical Theories; and (7) Theories of Emergence (Harmon & Mayer, 1986, p. 67).

Dwight Waldo provided a framework for understanding public administration theories through a comparative analysis of political science, cultural anthropology, sociology, psychology, economics, business administration, and other disciplines (1956, pp. 49–57). He also provided insight into mechanisms for understanding the context of public administration when he defined the difference between what he called "maps and models." "By maps I mean a conceptual scheme for organizing and classifying models or theories of organization; map is honestly metaphorical and implies no claim of precision. By model I mean a conceptual pattern for defining and organizing the phenomena of organization" (Waldo, a 1963 speech as cited in Etzioni, 1969, p. 8).

Ira Sharkansky compared American public administration to that of other countries (1970, pp. 14–31). David Rosenbloom (1989) examined the theories and concepts of public administration from managerial, political, and legal perspectives. Jeffrey D. Straussman (1990) correlated the functions of government: taxing, governmental budgeting, public personnel, unions and collective bargaining, intergovernmental management, and the law and courts.

A review of these themes illustrates how theories are enhanced and changed with experience and time. The Contextual Themes Model is an evolutionary structure that is meant to be expanded and built on in the future. The titles of the themes for each level should serve as reminders of the numerous milestone concepts and theories that are products of each historical period. They should serve as reminders of the many administrative tools that can be incorporated into the task of overseeing current and future criminal justice agencies.

Focusing on these themes illustrates how theories are enhanced and changed with experience and time. The intent of this text is to provide a historical perspective from which insight and intuitive action may be generated and applied to current and future public sector issues. Alfred Korzybski suggested that man is a "time-binder," as distinguished from other animals that he labeled as "space-binders." He defined time-binding as having "the capacity to summarize, digest, and appropriate the labors and experiences of the past, . . . the capacity of which man is at once the inheritor of bygone ages and trustee of posterity" (Korzybski, 1958, p. 59). It may be concluded from this that past theories and concepts are essential components of today's Eclectic Perspective administration.

The importance of this epistemological aspect of public administration was supported by William J. Williams when he wrote:

> *The epistemological profile is an instrument for bringing history into*
> *a contemporary evolution and cultural science, in order to enable us*

to go beyond the macroscopic in finding direction and postulating new meanings. It can be used to facilitate understanding of individuals, groups, nations, international situations, institutions and systems. It is theory and therapy. It is a matter of moving from descriptive (history) to history in action; from what was, what is, to what might be. (Williams, 1980, p. 40)

Albert Einstein was quoted as saying that he had "always believed that the invention of concepts and the building of theories upon them was one of the great creative properties of the human mind" (World Book Dictionary, 1979, p. 429). Public administrators should contemplate the writings of Williams and Einstein, and they should apply and enhance the theories and concepts that are the legacy of the history of public administration.

The Contextual Themes Model should be used as a reminder of the themes, and related theories and concepts, that are the products of the history of public administration. The ability to energize several of these themes simultaneously, and to be continually aware of all the themes, is important in confronting contemporary criminal justice issues. Using the Contextual Themes Model as a management and "academic prompter" is consistent with Dwight Waldo's definition of the two usages of public administration.

As an "area of intellectual inquiry," the Contextual Themes Model can be used as a structure for assimilating knowledge. The model furnishes a structure for categorizing theories and concepts for a clearer understanding of the volumes of public administration literature. In the same way that McGregor's Theory X and Theory Y and Maslow's Needs Hierarchy (discussed in Chapter 2) assist in the study of motivational theory, the five building blocks themes in the Contextual Themes Model are intended to organize the theories of public administration into key terms that serve as reminders of detailed concepts.

The Contextual Themes Model provides a structure for acknowledging the contextual development of American public administration themes and their eclectic application to criminal justice issues in the 21st century. In this model, the Eclectic Perspective is a "lens" through which past themes, theories, and concepts are modulated to focus on current and future issues. It represents an understanding that all of the themes compose a spectrum of theories that are useful in today's environment.

In taking this perspective, it is understood that many of the theories and concepts developed during the past 100 years play a role in the administration of contemporary criminal justice agencies, and that the importance placed on any given theme depends on the present social, economic, and political environment. Within the Eclectic Perspective can be included what some call "theories of emergence," as well as the works of scholars such as Karl Weick (1979) and Frederick Thayer (1981), who asserted that rationality and the discovery of "truth" often happen after the fact. Retrospective learning allows for the reconsideration of contextual themes and their related theories and concepts as a guide to alternatives for the future.

KEY CONCEPTS AND TERMS

- Administration—Both a science and an art
  - Science = the study of concepts and theories
  - Art = the converting of concepts and theories into practice
- Basic administrative terms
  - Organization
  - Management
  - Leadership
  - Missions
  - Goals
  - Objectives
  - Efficient
  - Effective
- Historical development of the building blocks of administration
  - The Industrial Era (1880s–1950s)
    - Organization Functions theme
    - Employee Relations theme
  - The Civil Rights Era (1960s–1970s)
    - Open Systems theme
    - Social Equity theme
  - The Transition to the 21st-Century Era (1980–)
    - Client-Oriented theme
    - Eclectic Perspective
- Constructing a Contextual Themes Model from historical building blocks of administration
  - Maslow's Hierarchy of Human Needs Model
  - "Juggler" metaphor

CHAPTER ACTIVITY

Explore the Internet for advertisements for criminal justice administrative positions. Review the qualifications and job descriptions for these positions and compare them with administrative responsibilities discussed in this chapter.

REVIEW QUESTIONS

1. Define public administration. How does the term administration relate to the terms of management and leadership?
2. Explain why administration is called both a science and an art. Can you relate the metaphor of playing a musical instrument (used in this chapter) and other metaphors (such as learning to play golf) to that of learning to be an administrator?

Wrap Up

3. What are the two major tasks of an administrator? How does the concept of synergy apply to these tasks?

4. Explain why efficiency may be a better measure of management skills, whereas effectiveness is better associated with leadership.

5. Explain the relationship between the contextual themes, the Eclectic Perspective, and the comparison of an administrator to a "juggler." How does the model compare to Maslow's Human Needs Hierarchy?

REFERENCES

Asimov, I. (1972). *The Realm of Science*, Vol. I. Louisville, KY: Touchtune.

Bois, S. J. (1978). *The Art of Awareness*. Dubuque, IA: William C. Brown.

Charlesworth, J. C. (Ed.) (1968). *Theory and Practice of Public Administration; Scope, Objective and Methods* (Monograph 8). Philadelphia: American Academy of Political Science.

Harmon, M. M., & Mayer, R. T. (1986). *Organization Theory for Public Administration*. Boston: Little Brown.

Korzybski, A. (1958). *Science and Sanity*. Lakewood, CT: The International Non-Aristotelian Library.

Landy, F. J. (1976). *Psychology of Work Behavior*. Homewood, IL: Dorsey Press.

Long, N. (1988). Power and Administration. In R. J. Stillman, *Public Administration*. Boston: Houghton Mifflin.

Maslow, A. H. (1943). The Theory of Human Motivation. *Psychological Review*, July, p. 50.

Ostrom, V. (1974). *The Intellectual Crisis in American Public Administration*. Mobile, AL: University of Alabama Press.

Rosenbloom, D. H. (1989). *Public Administration: Understanding Management, Politics, and Law in the Public Sector*. New York: Random House.

Sharkansky, I. (1970). *Public Administration: Policymaking in Government Agencies*. Chicago: Markham Publishing Company.

Stillman, R. J. (1988). *Public Administration*. Englewood Cliffs, NJ: Houghton Mifflin.

Stillman, R. J. (1991). *Public Administration: A Search for Themes and Direction*. New York: St. Martin's Press.

Straussman, J. D. (1990). *Public Administration*. New York: Longman.

Thayer, F. C. (1981). *An End to Hierarchy and Competition*. New York: Franklin Watts.

The World Book Dictionary (1979). Chicago: Thorndike-Barnhart Publisher.

Waldo, D. (1955) *The Study of Administration*. New York: Random House.

Waldo, D. (1956). *Political Science in the United States of America*. Paris, France: United Nations' Educational Scientific and Cultural Organization.

Waldo, D. (1969). *Theory of Organization Status and Problems*. (Speech delivered at the Annual Meeting of the American Political Science Association, New York City, 1963). Document by Amitai Etzioni, *Readings on Modern Organizations*, Englewood Cliffs, NJ: Prentice Hall Inc.

Waldo, D. (1980). *The Enterprise of Public Administration*. Novato, California: Chandler & Sharp.

Weick, K. E. (1979). *The Social Psychology of Organizing*. Reading, MA: Addison-Wesley.

Williams, J. D. (1980). *Public Administration: The Peoples' Business*. Boston: Little, Brown and Company.

Wilson, W. (1887). The Study of Administration. *Political Science Quarterly*, June 1887, pp. 197–222.

Wrap Up

■ RELEVANT PUBLICATION

The following publication is the first milestone article written about public administration. It was written by a prominent public figure who later became the 28th president of the United States. His milestone article first recognized public administration as "the clerical end of government." He set the stage for the professionalizing of public service and the direction for public administrators for many decades to come. This article marked the beginning of the public sector's focus on Organization Functions. (Reprinted from Wilson, W. (1887). The Study of Administration. *Political Science Quarterly*, June, pp. 197–222. Permission to reprint from the publisher.)

"The Study of Administration" by Woodrow Wilson

I suppose that no practical science is ever studied where there is no need to know it. The very fact, therefore, that the eminently practical science of administration is finding its way into college courses in this country would prove that this country needs to know more about administration, were such proof of the fact required to make out a case. It need not be said, however, that we do not look into college programmes for proof of this fact. It is a thing almost taken for granted among us, that the present movement called civil service reform must, after the accomplishment of its first purpose, expand into efforts to improve, not the *personnel* only, but also the organization and methods of our government offices: because it is plain that their organization and methods need improvement only less than their *personnel*. It is the object of administrative study to discover, first, what government can properly and successfully do, and secondly, how it can do these proper things with the utmost possible efficiency and at the least possible cost either of money or of energy. On both these points there is obviously much need of light among us; and only careful study can supply that light.

Before entering on that study, however, it is needful:

I. To take some account of what others have done in the same line; that is to say, of the history of the study.

II. To ascertain just what is its subject-matter.

III. To determine just what are the best methods by which to develop it, and the most clarifying political conceptions to carry with us into it.

Unless we know and settle these things, we shall set out without chart or compass.

I.

The science of administration is the latest fruit of that study of the science of politics which was begun some twenty-two hundred years ago. It is a birth of our own century, almost of our own generation.

Why was it so late in coming? Why did it wait till this too busy century of ours to demand attention for itself? Administration is the most obvious part of government; it is government in action; it is the executive, the operative, the most visible side of government, and is of course as old as government itself. It is government in action, and one might very naturally expect to find that government in action had arrested the attention and provoked the scrutiny of writers of politics very early in the history of systematic thought.

But such was not the case. No one wrote systematically of administration as a branch of the science of government until the present century had passed its first youth and had begun to put forth its characteristic flower of systematic knowledge. Up to our own day all the political writers whom we now read had thought, argued, dogmatized only about the *constitution* of government; about the nature of the state, the essence and seat of sovereignty, popular power and kingly prerogative; about the greatest meanings lying at the heart of government, and the high ends set before the purpose of government by man's nature and man's aims. The central field of controversy was that great field of theory in which monarchy rode tilt against democracy, in which oligarchy would have built for itself strongholds of privilege, and in which tyranny sought opportunity to make good its claim to receive submission from all competitors. Amidst this high warfare of principles, administration could command no pause for its own consideration. The question was always: Who shall make the law, and what shall that law be? The other question, how law should be administered with enlightenment, with equity, with speed, and without friction, was put aside as "practical detail" which clerks could arrange after doctors had agreed upon principles.

That political philosophy took this direction was of course no accident, no chance preference or perverse whim of political philosophers. The philosophy of any time is, as Hegel says, "nothing but the spirit of that time expressed in abstract thought"; and political philosophy, like philosophy of every other kind, has only held up the mirror to contemporary affairs. The trouble in early times was almost altogether about the constitution of government; and consequently that was what engrossed men's thoughts. There was little or no trouble about administration,—at least little that was heeded by administrators. The functions of government were simple, because life itself was simple. Government went about imperatively and compelled men, without thought of consulting their wishes. There was no complex system of public revenues and public debts to puzzle financiers; there were, consequently, no financiers to be puzzled. No one who possessed power was long at a loss how to use it. The great and only question was: Who shall possess it? Populations were of manageable numbers; property was of simple sorts. There were plenty of farms, but no stocks and bonds; more cattle than vested interests.

• • •

There is scarcely a single duty of government which was once simple which is not now complex; government once had but a few masters; it now has scores of masters. Majorities formerly only underwent government; they now conduct government. Where government once might follow the whims of a court, it must now follow the views of a nation.

And those views are steadily widening to new conceptions of state duty; so that, at the same time that the functions of government are every day becoming more complex and difficult, they are also vastly multiplying in number. Administration is everywhere putting its hands to new undertakings. The utility, cheapness, and success of the government's postal service, for instance, point towards the early establishment of governmental control of the telegraphs system. Or, even if our government is not to follow the lead of the governments of Europe in buying or building both telegraph and railroad lines, no one can doubt that in some way it must make itself master of masterful corporations. The creation of national commissioners of railroads, in addition to the older state commissions, involves a very important and delicate extension of administrative functions. Whatever hold of authority state or federal governments are to take upon corporations, there must follow cares and responsibilities which will require not a little wisdom, knowledge, and experience. Such things must be studied in order to be well done. And these, as I have said, are only a few of the doors which are being opened to offices of government. The idea of the state and the consequent ideal of its duty are undergoing noteworthy change; and "the idea of the state is the conscience of administration." Seeing every day new things which the state ought to do, the next thing is to see clearly how it ought to do them.

This is why there should be a science of administration which shall seek to straighten the paths of government, to make its business less unbusinesslike; to strengthen and purify its organization, and to crown its duties with dutifulness. This is one reason why there is such a science.

But where has this science grown up? Surely not on this side of the sea. Not much impartial scientific method is to be discerned in our administrative practices. The poisonous atmosphere of city government, the crooked secrets of state administration, the confusion, sinecurism, and corruption ever and again discovered in the bureaus at Washington forbid us to believe that any clear conceptions of what constitutes good administration are as yet very widely current in the United States. No; American writers have hitherto taken no very important part in the advancement of this science. It has found its doctors in Europe. It is not of our making; it is a foreign science, speaking very little of the language of English or American principle. It employs only foreign tongues; it utters none but what are to our minds alien ideas. Its aims, its examples, its conditions, are almost exclusively grounded in the histories of foreign races, in the precedents of foreign systems, in the lessons of foreign revolutions. It has been developed by French and German professors, and is consequently in all parts adapted to the needs of a compact state, and made to fit highly centralized forms of government; whereas, to answer our purposes, it must be adapted, not to a simple and compact, but to a complex and multiform state, and made to fit highly decentralized forms of government. If we would employ it, we must Americanize it, and that not formally, in language merely, but radically, in thought, principle, and aim as well. It must learn our constitutions by heart; must get the bureaucratic fever out of its veins; must inhale much free American air.

If an explanation be sought why a science manifestly so susceptible of being made useful to all governments alike should have received attention first in Europe, where government has long been a monopoly, rather than in England or the United States, where government has long been a common franchise, the reason will doubtless be found to be twofold: first, that in Europe, just because government was independent of popular assent, there was more governing to be done; and, second, that the desire to keep government a monopoly made the monopolists interested in discovering the least irritating means of governing. They were, besides, few enough to adopt means properly.

• • •

The English race . . . has long and successfully studied the art of curbing executive power to the constant neglect of the art of perfecting executive methods. It has exercised itself much more in controlling than in energizing government. It has been more concerned to render government just and moderate than to make it facile, well-ordered, and effective. English and American political history has been a history, not of administrative development, but of legislative oversight,—not of progress in governmental organization, but of advance in law-making and political criticism. Consequently, we have reached a time when administrative study and creation are imperatively necessary to the well-being of our governments saddled with the habits of a long period of constitution-making. That period has practically closed, so far as the establishment of essential principles is concerned, but we cannot shake off its atmosphere. We go on criticizing when we ought to be creating. We have reached the third of the periods I have mentioned,—the period, namely, when the people have to develop administration in accordance with the constitutions they won for themselves in a previous period of struggle with absolute power; but we are not prepared for the tasks of the new period.

Such an explanation seems to afford the only escape from blank astonishment at the fact that, in spite of our vast advantages in point of political liberty, and above all in point of practical political skill and sagacity, so many nations are ahead of us in administrative organization and administrative skill. Why, for instance, have we but just begun purifying a civil service which was rotten fully fifty years ago? To say that slavery diverted us is but to repeat what I have said—that flaws in our Constitution delayed us.

Of course all reasonable preference would declare for this English and American course of politics rather than for that of any European country. We should not like to have had Prussia's history for the sake of having Prussia's administrative skill; and Prussia's particular system of administration would quite suffocate us. It is better to be untrained and free than to be servile and systematic. Still there is no denying that it would be better yet to be both free in spirit and proficient in practice. It is this even more reasonable preference which impels us to discover what there may be to hinder or delay us in naturalizing this much-to-be desired of administration.

What, then, is there to prevent?

Well, principally, popular sovereignty. It is harder for democracy to organize administration than for monarchy. The very completeness of our most cherished political successes in the past embarrasses us. We have enthroned public opinion; and it is forbidden us to hope during its reign for any quick schooling of the sovereign in executive expertness or in the conditions of perfect functional balance in government. The very fact that we have realized popular rule in its fullness had made the task of *organizing* that rule just so much the more difficult. In order to make any advance at all we must instruct and persuade a multitudinous monarch called public opinion,—a much less feasible undertaking than to influence a single monarch called a king. An individual sovereign will adopt a simple plan and carry it out directly; he will have but one opinion, and he will embody that one opinion in one command. But this other sovereign, the people, will have a score of differing opinions. They can agree upon nothing simple: advance must be made through compromise, by a compounding of differences, by a trimming of plans and a suppression of too straightforward principles. There will be a succession of resolves running through a course of years, a dropping fire of commands running through a whole gamut of modifications.

In government, as in virtue, the hardest of hard things is to make progress. Formerly the reason for this was that the single person who was sovereign was generally either selfish, ignorant, timid, or a fool,—albeit there was now and again one who was wise. Nowadays the reason is that the many, the people, who are sovereign have no single ear which one can approach, and are selfish, ignorant, timid, stubborn, or foolish with the selfishness, the ignorances, the stubbornness, the timidities, or the follies of several thousand persons,—albeit there are hundreds who are wise. Once the advantage of the reformer was that the sovereign's mind had a definite locality, that it was contained in one man's head, and that consequently it could be gotten at; though it was his disadvantage that that mind learned only reluctantly or only in small quantities, or was under the influence of someone who let it learn only the wrong things. Now, on the contrary, the reformer is bewildered by the fact that the sovereign's mind has no definite locality, but is contained in a voting majority of several million heads; and embarrassed by the fact that the mind of this sovereign also is under the influence of favorites, who are none the less favorites in a good old-fashioned sense of the word because they are not persons but preconceived opinions; *i.e.*, prejudices which are not to be reasoned with because they are not the children of reason.

Wherever regard for public opinion is a first principle of government, practical reform must be slow and all reform must be full of compromises. For wherever public opinion exists it must rule. This is now an axiom half the world over, and will presently come to be believed even in Russia. Whoever would effect a change in a modern constitutional government must first educate his fellow-citizens to want *some* change. That done, he must persuade them to want the particular change he wants. He must first make public opinion willing to listen and then see to it that it listen to the right things. He must stir it up to search for an opinion, and then manage to put the right opinion in its way.

The first step is not less difficult than the second. With opinions, possession is more than nine points of the law. It is next to impossible to dislodge them. Institutions which one generation regards as only a makeshift approximation to the realization of a principle, the next generation honors as the nearest possible approximation to that principle, and the next worships as the principle itself. It takes scarcely three generations for the apotheosis. The grandson accepts his grandfather's hesitating experiment as an integral part of the fixed constitution of nature.

Even if we had clear insight into all the political past, and could form out of perfectly instructed heads a few steady, infallible, placidly wise maxims of government into which all sound political doctrine would be ultimately resolvable, *would the country act on them?* That is the question. The bulk of mankind is rigidly unphilosophical, and nowadays the bulk of mankind votes. A truth must become not only plain but also commonplace before it will be seen by the people who go to their work very early in the morning; and not to act upon it must involve great and pinching inconveniences before these same people will make up their minds to act upon it.

And where is this unphilosophical bulk of mankind more multifarious in its composition than in the United States? To know the public mind of this country, one must know the mind, not of Americans of the older stocks only, but also of Irishmen, of Germans, of Negroes. In order to get a footing for new doctrine, one must influence minds cast in every mould of race, minds inheriting every bias of environment, warped by the histories of a score of different nations, warmed or chilled, closed or expanded by almost every climate of the globe.

• • •

II.

The field of administration is a field of business. It is removed from the hurry and strife of politics; it at most points stands apart even from the debatable ground of constitutional study. It is a part of political life only as the methods of the counting-house are a part of the life of society; only as machinery is part of the manufactured product. But it is, at the same time, raised very far above the dull level of mere technical detail by the fact that through its greater principles it is directly connected with the lasting maxims of political wisdom, the permanent truths of political progress.

The object of administrative study is to rescue executive methods from the confusion and costliness of empirical experiment and set them upon foundations laid deep in stable principle.

It is for this reason that we must regard civil service reform in its present stages as but a prelude to a fuller administrative reform. We are now rectifying methods of appointment; we must go on to adjust executive functions more fitly and to prescribe better methods of executive organization and action. Civil service reform is thus but a moral preparation for what it is to follow. It is clearing the moral atmosphere of official life by establishing the sanctity of public office as a public trust, and, by making the service unpartisan, it is opening the way for making it businesslike. By sweetening its motives it is rendering it capable of improving its methods of work.

Let me expand a little what I have said of the province of administration. Most important to be observed is the truth already so much and so fortunately insisted upon by our civil service reformers; namely, that administration lies outside the proper sphere of *politics*. Administrative questions are not political questions. Although politics sets the tasks for administration, it should not be suffered to manipulate its offices.

This is distinction of high authority; eminent German writers insist upon it as of course. Bluntschli, for instance, bids us separate administration alike from politics and from law. Politics, he says, is state activity "in things great and universal," while "administration, on the other hand," is "the activity of the state in individual and small things. Politics is thus the special province of the statesman, administration of the technical official." "Policy does nothing without the aid of administration"; but administration is not therefore politics. But we do not require German authority for this position; this discrimination between administration and politics is now, happily, too obvious to need further discussion.

There is another distinction which must be worked into all our conclusions, which, though but another side of that between administration and politics, is not quite so easy to keep sight of; I mean the distinction between *constitutional* and administrative questions, between those governmental adjustments which are essential to constitutional principle and those which are merely instrumental to the possibly changing purposes of a wisely adapting convenience.

One cannot easily make clear to every one just where administration resides in the various departments of any practicable government without entering upon particulars so numerous as to confuse and distinctions so minute as to distract. No lines of demarcation, setting apart administrative from non-administrative functions, can be run between this and that department of government without being run up hill and down dale, over dizzy heights of distinction and through dense jungles of statutory enactment, hither and thither around "its" and "buts," "whens" and "howevers," until they become altogether lost to the common eye not accustomed to this sort of surveying, and consequently not acquainted with the use of the theodolite of logical discernment. A great deal of administration goes about *incognito* to most of the world, being confounded now with political "management," and again with constitutional principle.

Perhaps this case of confusion may explain such utterances as that of Niebuhr's: "Liberty," he says, "depends incomparably more upon administration than upon constitution." At first sight this appears to be largely true. Apparently facility in the actual exercise of liberty does depend more upon administrative arrangements than upon constitutional guarantees; although constitutional guarantees alone secure the existence of liberty. But—upon second thought—is even so much as this true? Liberty no more consists in easy functional movement than intelligence consists in the ease and vigor with which the limbs of a strong man move. The principles that rule within the man, or the constitution, are the vital springs of liberty or servitude. Because dependence and subjection are without chains, are lightened by every easy-working device of considerate, paternal government, they are not thereby transformed into liberty. Liberty cannot live apart from constitutional principle; and no administration, however perfect and liberal its methods, can give men more than a poor counterfeit of liberty if it rest upon illiberal principles of government.

A clear view of the difference between the province of constitutional law and the province of administrative function ought to leave no room for misconception; and it is possible to name some roughly definite criteria upon which such a view can be built. Public administration is detailed and systematic execution of public law. Every particular application of general law is an act of administration. The assessment and raising of taxes, for instance, the hanging of a criminal, the transportation and delivery of the mails, the equipment and recruiting of the army and navy, etc., are all obviously acts of administration; but the general laws which direct these things to be done are as obviously outside of and above administration. The broad plans of governmental action are not administrative; the detailed execution of such plans is administrative. Constitutions, therefore, properly concern themselves only with those instrumentalities of government which are to control general law. Our federal Constitution observes this principle in saying nothing of even the greatest of the purely executive offices, and speaking only of that President of the Union who was to share the legislative and policy-making functions of government, only of those judges of highest jurisdiction who were to interpret and guard its principles, and not of those who were merely to give utterance to them.

This is not quite the distinction between Will and answering Deed, because the administrator should have and does have a will of his own in the choice of means for accomplishing his work. He is not and ought not to be a mere passive instrument. The distinction is between general plans and special means.

There is, indeed, one point at which administrative studies trench on constitutional ground—or at least upon what seems constitutional ground. The study of administration, philosophically viewed, is closely connected with the study of the proper distribution of constitutional authority. To be efficient it must discover the simplest arrangements by which responsibility can be unmistakably fixed upon officials; the best way of dividing authority without hampering it, and responsibility without obscuring it. And this question of the distribution of authority, when taken into the sphere of the higher, the originating functions of government, is obviously a central constitutional question. If administrative study can discover the best principles upon which to base such distributions, it will have done constitutional study an invaluable service. Montesquieu did not, I am convinced, say the last word on this head.

To discover the best principle for the distribution of authority is of greater importance, possibly, under a democratic system, where officials serve many masters, than under others where they serve but a few. All sovereigns are suspicious of their servants, and the sovereign people is no exception to the rule; but how is its suspicion to be allayed by *knowledge?* If that suspicion could but be clarified into wise vigilance, it would be altogether salutary; if that vigilance could be aided by the unmistakable placing of responsibility, it would be altogether beneficent. Suspicion in itself is never healthful either in the private or the public mind. *Trust is strength* in all relations of life; and, as it is the office of the constitutional reformer to create conditions of trustfulness, so it is the office of the administrative organizer to fit administration with conditions of clear-cut responsibility which shall insure trustworthiness.

And let me say that large powers and unhampered discretion seem to me the indispensable conditions of responsibility. Public attention must be easily directed, in each case of good or bad administration, to just the man deserving of praise or blame. There is no danger in power, if only it be not irresponsible. If it be divided, dealt only in shares to many, it is obscured; and if it be obscured, it is made irresponsible. But if it be centred in heads of the service and in heads of branches of the service, it is easily watched and brought to book. If to keep his office a man must achieve open and honest success, and if at the same time he feels himself entrusted with large freedom of discretion, the greater his power the less likely is he to abuse it, the more is he nerved and sobered and elevated by it. The less his power, the more safely obscure and unnoticed does he feel his position to be, and the more readily does he relapse into remissness.

Just here we manifestly emerge upon the field of that still larger question,—the proper relations between public opinion and administration.

To whom is official trustworthiness to be disclosed, and by whom is it to be rewarded? Is the official to look to the public for his need of praise and his push of promotion, or only to his superior in office? Are the people to be called in to settle administrative discipline as they are called in to settle constitutional principles? These questions evidently find their root in what is undoubtedly the fundamental problem of this whole study. That problem is: What part shall public opinion take in the conduct of administration?

The right answer seems to be, that public opinion shall play the part of authoritative critic.

But the *method* by which its authority shall be made to tell? Our peculiar American difficulty in organizing administration is not the danger of losing liberty, but the danger of not being able or willing to separate its essentials from its accidents. Our success is made doubtful by that besetting error of ours, the error of trying to do too much by vote. Self-government does not consist in having a hand in everything, any more than housekeeping consists necessarily in cooking dinner with one's own hands. The cook must be trusted with a large discretion as to the management of the fires and the ovens.

In those countries in which public opinion has yet to be instructed in its privileges, yet to be accustomed to having its own way, this question as to the province of public opinion is much more readily soluble than in this country, where public opinion is wide awake and quite intent upon having its own way anyhow. It is pathetic to see a whole book written by a German professor of political science for the purpose of saying to his countrymen, "Please try to have an opinion about national affairs"; but a public which is so modest may at least be expected to be very docile and acquiescent in learning what things it has *not* a right to think and speak about imperatively. It may be sluggish, but it will not be meddlesome. It will submit to be instructed before it tries to instruct. Its political education will come before its political activity. In trying to instruct our own public opinion, we are dealing with a pupil apt to think itself quite sufficiently instructed beforehand.

The problem is to make public opinion efficient without suffering it to be meddlesome. Directly exercised, in the oversight of the daily details and in the choice of the daily means of government, public criticism is of course a clumsy nuisance, a rustic handling delicate machinery. But as superintending the greater forces of formative policy alike in politics and administration, public criticism is altogether safe and benificent, altogether indispensable. Let administrative study find the best means for giving public criticism this control and for shutting it out from all other interference.

But is the whole duty of administrative study done when it has taught the people what sort of administration to desire and demand, and how to get what they demand? Ought it not to go on to drill candidates for the public service?

There is an admirable movement towards universal political education now afoot in this country. The time will soon come when no college of respectability can afford to do without a well-filled chair of political science. But the education thus imparted will go but a certain length. It will multiply the number of intelligent critics of government, but it will create no competent body of administrators. It will prepare the way for the development of a sure-footed understanding of the general principles of government, but it will not necessarily foster skill in conducting government. It is an education which will equip legislators, perhaps, but not executive officials. If we are to improve public opinion, which is the motive power of government, we must prepare better officials as the *apparatus* of government. If we are to put in new boilers and to mend the fires which drive our governmental machinery, we must not leave the old wheels and joints and valves and bands to creak and buzz and clatter on as the best they may at bidding of the new force. We must put in new running parts wherever there is the least lack of strength or adjustment. It will be necessary to organize democracy by sending up to the competitive examinations for the civil service men definitely prepared for standing liberal tests as to technical knowledge. A technically schooled civil service will presently have become indispensable.

I know that a corps of civil servants prepared by a special schooling and drilled, after appointment, into a perfected organization, with appropriate hierarchy and characteristic discipline, seems to a great many very thoughtful persons to contain elements which might combine to make an offensive official class,—a distinct, semi-corporate body with sympathies divorced from those of a progressive, free-spirited people, and with hearts narrowed to the meanness of a bigoted officialism. Certainly such a class would be altogether hateful and harmful in the United States. Any measures calculated to produce it would for us be measures of reaction and of folly.

But to fear the creation of a domineering, illiberal officialism as a result of the studies I am here proposing is to miss altogether the principle upon which I wish most to insist. That principle is, that administration in the United States must be at all points sensitive to public opinion. A body of thoroughly trained officials serving during good behavior we must have in any case: that is a plain business necessity. But the apprehension that such a body will be anything un-American clears away the moment it is asked, What is to constitute good behavior? For that question obviously carries its own answer on its face. Steady, hearty allegiance to the policy of the government they serve will constitute good behavior. That *policy* will have no taint of officialism about it. It will not be the creation of permanent officials, but of statesmen whose responsibility to public opinion will be direct and inevitable. Bureaucracy can exist only where the whole service of the state is removed from the common political life of the people, its chiefs as well as its rank and file. Its motives, its objects, its policy, its standards, must be bureaucratic. It would be difficult to point out any examples of impudent exclusiveness and arbitrariness on the part of officials doing service under a chief of department who really served the people, as all our chiefs of departments must be made to do.

• • •

The ideal for us is a civil service cultured and self-sufficient enough to act with sense and vigor, and yet so intimately connected with the popular thought, by means of elections and constant public counsel, as to find arbitrariness or class spirit quite out of the question.

III.

Having thus viewed in some sort the subject-matter and the objects of this study of administration, what are we to conclude as to the methods best suited to it—the points of view most advantageous for it?

Government is so near us, as much a thing of our daily familiar handling, that we can with difficulty see the need of any philosophical study of it, or the exact point of such study, should it be undertaken. We have been on our feet too long to study now the art of walking. We are a practical people, made so apt, so adept in self-government by centuries of experimental drill that we are scarcely any longer capable of perceiving the awkwardness of the particular system we may be using, just because it is so easy for us to use any system. We do not study the art of governing: we govern. But mere unschooled genius for affairs will not save us from sad blunders in administration. Though democrats by long inheritance and repeated choice, we are still rather crude democrats. Old as democracy is, its organization on a basis of modern ideas and conditions is still an unaccomplished work. The democratic state has yet to be equipped for carrying those enormous burdens of administration which the needs of this industrial and trading age are so fast accumulating. Without comparative studies in government we cannot rid ourselves of the misconception that administration stands upon an essentially different basis in a democratic state from that on which it stands in a non-democratic state.

After such a study we could grant democracy the sufficient honor of ultimately determining by debate all essential questions affecting the public weal, of basing all structures of policy upon the major will; but we would have found but one rule of good administration for all governments alike. So far as administrative functions are concerned, all governments have a strong structural likeness; more than that, if they are to be uniformly useful and efficient, they *must* have a strong structural likeness. A free man has the same bodily organs, the same executive parts, as the slave, however different may be his motives, his services, his energies. Monarchies and democracies, radically different as they are in other respects, have in reality much the same business to look to.

It is abundantly safe nowadays to insist upon this actual likeness of all governments, because these are days when abuses of power are easily exposed and arrested, in countries like our own, by a bold, alert, inquisitive, detective public thought and a sturdy popular self-dependence such as never existed before. We are slow to appreciate this; but it is easy to appreciate it. Try to imagine personal government in the United States. It is like trying to imagine a national worship of Zeus. Our imaginations are too modern for the feat.

But, besides being safe, it is necessary to see that for all governments alike the legitimate ends of administration are the same, in order not to be frightened at the idea of looking into foreign systems of administration for instruction and suggestion; in order to get rid of the apprehension that we might perchance blindly borrow something incompatible with our principles. That man is blindly astray who denounces attempts to transplant foreign systems into this country. It is impossible: they simply would not grow here. But why should we not use such parts of foreign contrivances as we want, if they be in any way serviceable? We are in no danger of using them in a foreign way. We borrowed rice, but we do not eat it with chopsticks. We borrowed our whole political language from England, but we leave the words "king" and "lords" out of it. What did we ever originate, except the action of the federal government upon individuals and some of the functions of the federal supreme court?

We can borrow the science of administration with safety and profit if only we read all fundamental differences of condition into its essential tenets. We have only to filter it through our constitutions, only to put it over a slow fire of criticism and distill away its foreign gases.

● ● ●

Let it be noted that it is the distinction, already drawn, between administration and politics which makes the comparative method so safe in the field of administration. When we study the administrative systems of France and Germany, knowing that we are not in search of *political* principles, we need not care a peppercorn for the constitutional or political reasons which Frenchmen or Germans give for their practices when explaining them to us. If I see a murderous fellow sharpening a knife cleverly, I can borrow his way of sharpening the knife without borrowing his probable intention to commit murder with it; and so, if I see a monarchist dyed in the wool managing a public bureau well, I can learn his business methods without changing one of my republican spots. He may serve his king; I will continue to serve the people; but I should like to serve my sovereign as well as he serves his. By keeping this distinction in view,—that is, by studying administration as a means of putting our own politics into convenient practice, as a means of making what is democratically politic towards all administratively possible towards each,—we are on perfectly safe ground and can learn without error what foreign systems have to teach us. We thus devise an adjusted weight for our comparative method of study. We can thus scrutinize the anatomy of foreign governments without fear of getting any of their diseases into our veins; dissect alien systems without apprehension of blood-poisoning.

Our own politics must be the touchstone for all theories. The principles on which to base a science of administration for America must be principles which have democratic policy very much at heart. And, to suit American habit, all general theories must, as theories, keep modestly in the background, not in open argument only, but even in our own minds,—lest opinions satisfactorily only to the standards of the library should be dogmatically used, as if they must be quite as satisfactory to the standards of practical politics as well. Doctrinaire devices must be postponed to tested practices. Arrangements not only sanctioned by conclusive experience elsewhere but also congenial to American habit must be preferred without hesitation to theoretical perfection. In a word, steady, practical statesmanship must come first, closet doctrine second. The cosmopolitan what-to-do must always be commanded by the American how-to-do-it.

Our duty is, to supply the best possible life to a *federal* organization, to systems within systems; to make town, city, county, state, and federal governments live with a like strength and an equally assured healthfulness, keeping each unquestionably its own master and yet making all interdependent and cooperative, combining independence with mutual helpfulness. The task is great and important enough to attract the best minds.

This interlacing of local self-government with federal self-government is quite a modern conception. It is not like the arrangements of imperial federation in Germany. There local government is not yet, fully, local *self*-government. The bureaucrat is everywhere busy. His efficiency springs out of *esprit de corps*, out of care to make ingratiating obeisance to the authority of a superior, or, at best, out of the soul of a sensitive conscience. He serves, not the public, but an irresponsible minister. The question for us is, how shall our series of governments within governments be so administered so that it shall always be to the interest of the public officer to serve, not his superior alone but the community also, with the best efforts of his talents and the soberest service of his conscience? How shall such service be made to his commonest interest by contributing abundantly to his sustenance, to his dearest interest by furthering his ambition, and to his highest interest by advancing his honor and establishing his character? And how shall this be done alike for the local part and for the national whole?

If we solve this problem we shall again pilot the world. There is a tendency—is there not?—a tendency as yet dim, but already steadily impulsive and clearly destined to prevail, towards, first the confederation of parts of empires like the British, and finally of great states themselves. Instead of centralization of power, there is to be wide union with tolerated divisions of prerogative. This is a tendency towards the American type—of governments joined with governments for the pursuit of common purposes, in honorary equality and honorable subordination. Like principles of civil liberty are everywhere fostering like methods of government; and if comparative studies of the ways and means of government should enable us to offer suggestions which will practicably combine openness and vigor in the administration of such governments with ready docility to all serious, well-sustained public criticism, they will have approved themselves worthy to be ranked among the highest and most fruitful of the great departments of political study. That they will issue in such suggestions I confidently hope.

The Industrial Era (1880s–1950s): Development of Organizations Functions and Employee Relations Administrative Themes

2

■ Introduction

The Industrial Era began in the latter part of the 1900s with the recognition that public administration was a *business*, that is, the business of implementing public policy. There was a public outcry for efficiency in government and an end to the corruption that plagued public agencies for most of the 1900s. Public administrators were forced to look for better methods of running their public businesses, so they looked to the private sector for answers.

Efficient and effective management was the pursuit of the era. Criminal justice administrators sought better techniques by which to organize their agencies. The pursuit of "professional" Organization Functions was the theme that led public administrators into the 20th century. After several decades of development in the early 20th century, a new theme began to materialize. Attention moved from the organization structure to the employees who performed the work within the organization. Employee Relations became the new theme with the emphasis on how to get more productivity out of the workers.

The focus was still on efficiency and effectiveness, but results were to be achieved through employees who were motivated to be more productive. How to get employees motivated was the driving question. What follows is a discussion of these developing two themes. The study of the development of these themes provides valuable information about the supporting concepts that administrators draw on in successfully overseeing today's criminal justice agencies.

It is important to understand that past doctrines are not necessarily replaced by new and more current discoveries. What has occurred, and is occurring, is an evolutionary building and enhancing of past concepts and theories. Public administrators did not embrace Open Systems, Social Equity, and Client-Oriented themes without first establishing sound principles of Organization Functions, and fair Employee Relations methods.

The Organizations Functions concepts are as crucial in supporting public administration as the skeletal system is to the human body. However, without the Employee Relations theme and related concepts, organizations could not survive in today's environment. Both of these themes are vital in administrating criminal justice agencies today.

■ The Development of the Organization Functions Theme (1880s–1930s)

This period formed the foundation on which public administration is structured in the United States. Although concepts and theories developed during this period are sometimes criticized, they remain, through updating and enhancing, a solid basis from which today's criminal justice administration gains its support. For example, the bureaucratic organization system exalted during this period remains a fulcrum of public institutions. When asked, most of today's public employees would identify their organization as a bureaucracy, with the principles of hierarchical interlocking responsibilities and controls that were developed during this founding period.

Current bureaucratic organizations vary greatly from extremely rigid (such as military departments) to relatively flexible agencies (such as citizen's committees and community groups). Even Warren Bennis (1967, p. 27), who proclaimed "an end to bureaucracy in 25 years," more recently stated that certain forms of bureaucracy are necessary. In *The Public Administration Dictionary*, Chandler and Plano (1988, p. 191) wrote, "Despite the possibility of abuse, the hierarchical principle remains a key to governmental operations in the United States on all levels and provides the means by which a democratic society can keep its bureaucrats accountable."

Historical Setting for the Period (1880s–1930s)

This period was preceded by almost a century of government corruption and political trauma. Several events exemplify the mood of the times. In 1832, Senator William Marcy, in a Senate debate, gave title to the "spoils system" by proclaiming that politicians "see nothing wrong in the rule, that to the victor belongs the spoils of the enemy." In 1881, President James Garfield was assassinated by a deranged office seeker.

The period begins just after the passage of the 1883 Pendleton Act, which created the United States Civil Service Commission. The Act was aimed at replacing the "spoils system" with a federal personnel system based on merit. It was the result of public disappointment with political abuse and corruption that had prevailed since the 1820s.

World War I and the Great Depression had a major impact on both the public and private sector. The industrial revolution and the union movement were significant contributors to economic and social changes. Louis Brandeis (1910), an associate of Frederick Taylor, popularized the term "scientific management" in testimony before the Interstate Commerce Commission. He argued that railroad rate increases of the day should be denied because the railroads could save millions of dollars by applying "scientific management methods." Additionally, the proliferation of the automobile caused the need for highways, traffic regulation, licensing, and insurance.

The Sixteenth Amendment to the U.S. Constitution legislated the first permanent federal income tax in 1913, and in 1920 the Retirement Act created the first federal service pension system. In 1933, President Franklin D. Roosevelt began the "New Deal," and in 1935 Social Security became a reality. These are a few of the events that provided the environment for the development of the following milestones in public administration.

Organization Functions Theme Milestones

From the 1880s until the 1930s there were many contributors to this theme. The important contributions of each are discussed in this section.

1887: Woodrow Wilson, "The Study of Administration"

Woodrow Wilson was an educator, public administrator, and the twenty-eighth president of the United States. He was the first to say, in "The Study of Administration," that public administration should be a "self-conscious" field. This essay, published in the June 1887 *Political Science Quarterly*, is regarded as the beginning of public administration as a specific field of study. Wilson's essay came just after the 1883 Pendleton Act, which created the U.S. Civil Service Commission and focused political interest on how government should be administered. The Act began a process of replacing the "spoils system" with a federal personnel system based on merit. It was the result of public disappointment with the blatant political abuse and corruption that had prevailed since the 1820s.

Wilson contributed two major concepts that reflected the values of this period. First, Wilson made a major distinction between politics and administration. Administration should be separate from traditional partisan politics. He wrote that public administration "is removed from the hurry and strife of politics . . . administrative questions are not political questions." Wilson viewed public administration as the business end of government. He saw public administrators carrying out the directions of elected officials with little involvement in the political arena. Wilson said, "Representatives of the people are the proper ultimate authority in all matters of government and administration is merely the clerical part of government" (Wilson, cited in Altshuler, 1977, p. 2). Second, he emphasized running public agencies in an efficient and economical manner. He advocated conducting government activities like businesses with the use of established administrative principles. Wilson wrote, "This is why there should be a science of administration which shall seek to straighten the paths of government, to make its business less un-businesslike, to strengthen and purify its organization" (Wilson, cited in Shafritz & Hyde, 1987, p. 12). The full text of Wilson's essay is reprinted in Chapter 1.

1890: Frank J. Goodnow, *Politics and Administration*

Frank Goodnow was a founder and the first president of the American Political Science Association. His book *Politics and Administration* was an extension of Wilson's work, with a more carefully argued examination of the politics-administration dichotomy. He presented a number of dilemmas involving political and administrative functions that supplemented traditional concerns with separation of powers. He described the distinction between politics and administration as "the expression of the will of the state and the execution of that will."

In his later chapters, however, he differentiated the functions of administration, some of which he thought should be subject to political control, whereas he felt that others should be free of politics. He concluded that certain kinds of offices should be politically appointed and removable, whereas others should be protected by civil service tenure.

Goodnow's work is a good example of how one person can add to the milestone concept of another.

1916: Frederick W. Taylor, *Principles of Scientific Management*

Frederick Taylor was a mechanical engineer who is considered to be the "father of scientific management." His work serves as one of many examples of how the public sector drew on knowledge developed in the private sector. In fact, all five administrative themes rely heavily on theories from other disciplines, with the exception of Social Equity (discussed in Chapter 3).

With Woodrow Wilson's cry for a "science of administration," Taylor's "scientific management" approach became a natural focus for the public sector. Taylor's public sector popularity came in 1912 when he presented his ideas to a Special Committee of the House of Representatives that was investigating methods of improving government.

Taylor based his efforts on the premise that there was "one best way" of accomplishing any given task. He sought to increase productivity by discovering the fastest, most efficient, and least fatiguing job methods. The Organization Functions period fed on this notion. Where there is "one best way" to accomplish a production task, then there also must be "a one best way" to accomplish each task in social organizations.

Taylor's works supported efforts in government to replace "rule of thumb" management with management that was based on measuring productivity and the division of labor. He conceptualized people as extensions of machines and sought to increase productivity by providing workers with the right tools, training, and support to do the job.

Today, "scientific management" often is described as having a dehumanizing effect. Even so, Taylor's "time and motion" approach is to be found in many plan-

ning functions for developing employee training and supportive work environments. The public sector learned much from Taylor about maximizing skills of
employees and replacing traditional methods of work accomplishment with systematic, more scientific methods of measuring and managing.

1918: William F. Willoughby, *The Movement for Budgetary Reform in the States*

William F. Willoughby also authored *Principles of Public Administration* (1927).
He was a principal advocate of the legislative-administrative position. From the
1910s through the 1930s, this was a major issue among students of government
who were concerned with the relationship of administration to the executive and
legislative powers.

His opinion distinguished between the presidential power to "take care that
the laws be faithfully executed" (Article II, Section 4, of the U.S. Constitution)
and actual execution of them, which, he held, was legally under the direction of
Congress. The opposing school of thought identified executive and administrative as virtually synonymous terms embodying the execution of orders by the
Chief Executive.

Willoughby's writing identified developments leading to the creation of budget systems in state government. He argued for budget reforms that would (1)
advance and provide for popular control, (2) enhance legislative cooperation, and
(3) ensure efficiency. His work was yet another contribution to defining and explaining organization functions important to administrating public agencies.

1922: Max Weber, *Characteristics of Bureaucracy*

Weber was a German sociologist, known as the father of the bureaucratic model
of organization theory. His *Characteristics of Bureaucracy* was translated into
English in 1946, when it received its greatest attention. However, his concepts
were widely discussed in other English publications starting in the 1920s.

Weber identified organizational components that could withstand intrusion
of a ruling class. He wrote that the public interest could best be served by impersonal, rule-based, efficient merit systems, with justice and management based
on rational law. He perceived the key to getting things accomplished organizationally to be a matter of rationalizing behavior and getting each unit to carry
out official goals.

His theories were based partly on his own experience of the Prussian military, the German civil service, and large German corporations. His ideas reached
the United States through leaders in the field of sociology, who first translated
his works and later criticized the consequences of bureaucracy.

His ideas on legal-rational authority closely paralleled the Principles of Classical Organization theory developed during this period in the United States. Both
employed administrative regulations and established fixed jurisdictional areas of
responsibility as part of a systematic division of labor. Both emphasized efficiency.
Both used authority to give the commands required for the discharge of duties.

Weber insisted that human beings who made up bureaucratic organizations
should be stripped of their human differences for efficiency's sake, and this

became a controversial component of both Weber's theory and practice in the United States. Each involved a hierarchical structure and levels of graded authority in an ordered system of superiors and subordinates. Both included officials who were full-time, career employees, with thorough and expert training, and who were selected on the basis of technical qualifications.

Weber wrote that bureaucracy was the most efficient form of large-scale organization. His "ideal type" of bureaucracy became a means by which to measure public organizations, both in theory and in practice. Because his works became a special resource for the "closed systems" approach to management, his writings were later used as analytical frameworks for those who advocated a more open systems approach as developed in the third period of the Contextual Themes Model.

1926: Leonard D. White, *Introduction of the Study of Public Administration*

Introduction of the Study of Public Administration was the first textbook in the field of public administration. White was a political scientist and historian at the University of Chicago and Chairman of the U.S. Civil Service Commission.

Woodrow Wilson provided the rationale for public administration to be an academic discipline, and White articulated the details. He wrote, "Public administration is, then, the execution of the public business: the goal of administrative activity is the most expeditious, economical, and complete achievement of public programs" (White, cited in Shafritz & Hyde, 1987, p. 58).

Public administration is "the management of men and materials in the accomplishment of the purposes of the state. Administration is, of course, bound by the rules of administrative law, as well as by the prescriptions of constitutional law; but within the boundaries thus set, it seeks the most effective accomplishment of public purposes" (White, cited in Shafritz & Hyde, 1987, p. 56).

White considered the study of public administration to be unitary. He held that it was an art but could become a science in the future, and that administration was the heart of government. He emphasized management but avoided the politics-administration dichotomy on which Wilson and Goodnow focused.

He also wrote about how the morale of public administrators was directly related to their prestige. White believed that favorable public opinion enabled administrators to have increased public support and compliance which increased their job efficacy and morale.

1937: Luther Gulick and Lydall Urwick, *Papers on the Science of Administration*

This text made its mark in the history of public administration by providing detailed descriptions of what Gulick and Urwick believed to be principles or laws by which administration was governed. Gulick was a professor of Municipal Science and Administration at Columbia University. He also served as Director of the Institute of Public Administration at Columbia and as a member of the President's Committee on Administrative Management (the Brownlow Committee).

Gulick and his British colleague Lyndall Urwick published a collection of papers in this book that became the "bible" for Organization Functions.

Gulick and Urwick condensed the duties of an administrator into the acronym **POSDCORB**. Each letter stands for one of the major functions of administrators: *planning*, *organizing*, *staffing*, *directing*, *coordinating*, *reporting*, and *budgeting*. They also defined the four ways of organizing work as (1) *purpose* served; (2) *process* used; (3) *persons or things* dealt with; and (4) the *place* in which work is accomplished.

Included in their publication was work of Henri Fayol (1841–1925). Fayol was a French industrial engineer who believed that administrative functions could be documented and taught as principles of administration. He defined general principles of administration as:

1. Unity of Command, in which each employee receives orders from one superior only: sometimes referred to as the "one boss rule."

2. The Scalar Principle, in which a chain of command reflects an organization pyramid. Orders and information are communicated through "official channels."

3. Span of Control, that recognizes that there is a limit to the number of subordinates a supervisor can effectively oversee, generally set at a maximum of 12.

4. Centralization, in which the organization is administered from the top down. Ultimate responsibility is at the top of the organization and cannot be delegated.

5. Responsibility, by which executives can delegate authority and commensurate responsibility but never the ultimate responsibility. Each level can hold the subordinate level responsible when commensurate authority is delegated to that level.

These "principles" of administration were later criticized by Herbert A. Simon, in his now famous article "The Proverbs of Administration" (1946; described in the next section of this chapter). Simon said that these so-called principles were in fact proverbs because they had never been tested empirically. His writings pointed out that these "principles" cannot be relied on as "concrete and without flaw."

Even though the definitions of Gulick and Urwick were criticized, they remain useful guides to which criminal justice administrators should give attention.

Gulick's and Urwick's ideas are more closely aligned with Weber's bureaucratic model than with Taylor's scientific management because of their concern for perfection of the organization and management rather than the productivity of workers. Their work served as advice to President Franklin Roosevelt and as a basis for the reorganization of the executive branch during this period. Their principles also served as substance for contrast with the emerging humanistic employee relations views.

Transitional Milestones of the 1880s through the 1930s

Most periods within the development of public administration contain milestones by scholars that are harbingers of emerging themes. Within these writings are concepts that led to the development of the theories that form the basis of subsequent themes of public administration. Several such milestones pertain to this period.

1926: Mary Parker Follett, *The Giving of Orders*

Mary Parker Follett's writings were definitely a harbinger of the Employee Relations theme. Her work, even though written in 1926, did not have significant impact for some years to come. She assessed the reaction of workers to direction and the value of gaining cooperation rather than the use of coercion.

Follett was an administrative theorist who spent much of her life writing and lecturing on the development of management as a profession. She stressed the value of participatory management and said that workers were more responsive to peers than to management pressure. She focused on the interaction of labor and management and its impact on productivity. She distinguished between linear management and circular behavior. She said that orders would not take the place of training, and that efforts to unite and integrate personnel were essential to the carrying out of orders.

Her work pointed academic study beyond the executive to the role of workers and laid a basis for rethinking some of the concepts of the period. She was a founding contributor to the period of Employee Relations and her work demonstrates how an ensuing period in the contextual development of public administration themes begins to emerge even before the current period is fully developed.

1938: Chester I. Barnard, *Functions of the Executive*

Chester Barnard was an executive and administrative theorist. During his long career, he served as president of New Jersey Bell Telephone, president of the United Service Organization, president of the Rockefeller Foundation, and chairman of the National Science Foundation. He saw organizations as cooperative systems, and he wrote about the existence of both a formal and an informal system within organizations. He believed that one of the executive's functions was to maintain the dynamic equilibrium between the needs of the organization and the needs of the employees.

He presented a challenge to the scientific management movement by arguing that informal organizations were "necessary to the operation of formal organizations." The informal organization provides a means of communication, of cohesion, and of protecting the integrity of the individual against certain effects of the formal organization (Barnard, cited in Shafritz & Hyde, 1987, p. 97).

Barnard's work served as a bridge from the Organization Functions period to the Employee Relations period.

Organization Functions Period Summary

In summary, today's criminal justice agencies could not operate without these basic principles—from local police agencies to federal criminal justice departments, all function with bureaucratic concepts that were created during this period. Although Weber's "ideal bureaucracy" has been tempered with more flexible approaches, the basic concepts remain as a structural foundation for contemporary public organizations.

All contemporary criminal justice agencies, from county sheriff's departments to the United States Secret Service, are involved in POSDCORB. Although the concept of POSDCORB has been expanded to PAFHRIED (Policy Analysis, Financial management, Human Resources management, Information technology management, and External Relations—see Chapter 7), the basic theories developed during this period remain important to current and future criminal justice administrators.

The transition to the next theme did not occur suddenly. In fact, the Employee Relations movement was put in motion by the Hawthorne experiments that started in the late 1920s. The results of these experiments, however, were not published until the early 1940s, when they became part of the theme shift that led to administrators focusing on methods of motivating employees to be more productive. The Hawthorne experiments and the other milestone works of the next period are discussed in the following section.

■ The Development of Employee Relations (1940s–1950s)

The next period in the contextual development of public administration centered on Employee Relations. This new focus did not mean an abandonment of interest in Organization Functions. It meant only that the fundamentals of Organization Functions were well established. The theories and concepts of the previous 50 years set a solid foundation for the next step. Although Organization Functions continued to be important, the attention of public administration scholars and practitioners turned to motivating employees.

The interest of public administrators continued to follow the direction set by Woodrow Wilson over 50 years earlier. As described in an earlier section of this chapter, Wilson's statement that the "representatives of the people are the proper ultimate authority in all matters of government and administration is merely the clerical part of government" continued to be the guiding philosophy for the public sector.

The emphasis was still on effectiveness and efficiency. The focus on Employee Relations was merely an extension of the pursuit of efficiency and more productivity. In fact, the Employee Relations movement began from an investigation into the applicability of the Taylorian theory of "scientific management" at the Western Electric Company (Hawthorne plant in Chicago) during the late 1920s and early 1930s.

Historical Setting for the Period

World War II had a major impact on public administration. The impact can be seen in the growth of federal employees, as outlined by Rosenbloom (1989, p. 35):

Year	Federal Employees
1931	609,746
1941	1,437,682
1951	2,482,666

Much of the increase in employees was to be found in the armed services. However, many defense-related functions also grew, causing an increase in government employees at most levels of government. Government defense became one of the largest employers in the public sector.

Another factor caused by the war was an increase of women in both the private and public workforces. Additionally, as jobs became more plentiful, competition to hire and retain personnel required more attention to the job satisfaction of employees. Growing union power also required private and public managers to be more sensitive to employee rights and relations.

In 1946, the Employment Act created the Council of Economic Advisors. This council asserted that it was the policy of the federal government to maintain full employment. The same year, the Administrative Procedure Act standardized many federal government administrative practices.

In 1947, the National Security Act created the Department of Defense and President Harry S. Truman's Executive Order launched the federal government's loyalty program designed to remove subversives from the government.

In 1953, the Department of Health, Education and Welfare (HEW) was created, and in 1955 the AFL-CIO was formed by the merger of the American Federation of Labor and the Congress of Industrial Organizations, which gave employees more representation in the public and private sector. In 1959, New York City became the first major city to allow for collective bargaining with its employee unions and Wisconsin was the first state to enact a comprehensive law governing public sector labor relations. These, along with the global "cold war" and the impact of new technology, were a few of the events that set the stage for further development in public administration.

Employee Relations Theme Milestones

1941: Elton Mayo, "The Hawthorne Experiments"

The "Hawthorne Experiments" were the subjects of an article by F. J. Roethlisberger in 1941 and were later described by Elton Mayo in his 1945 book, *The Social Problems of an Industrial Civilization*. The actual experiments were conducted from 1927 through 1932 by Roethlisberger and Mayo. Of the two, Mayo is best remembered and is frequently identified as the "father of human relations" because of his leadership in conducting the Hawthorne studies and other investigations of people at work. He began his study of psychopathology in Scotland and later became an Associate Professor of Industrial Research at Harvard.

The site of the experiments was Western Electric Company's Hawthorne plant in Chicago. The purpose of the investigation was to determine the basis of productivity among workers. Mayo and Roethlisberger began with the Taylorian "scientific management" approach (described in the previous section) by enhancing physical factors that they hypothesized related to human productivity.

For example, they sought to demonstrate the effect of illumination on work by improving candle power. Productivity went up. To validate their work, they had a control group in which illumination remained unchanged. The productivity of the control group also went up. In fact when they diminished light, productivity by the primary group went up. What they discovered was that the social environment was having a much more pronounced affect on productivity than the physical environment. The researchers concluded that the operative influences were both the workers' opportunity to function as a small group and the workers' psychological payoffs that came from their being the objects of attention in the experiments.

The investigation found that (1) level of production is set by social norms and not by physiological capabilities, (2) noneconomic rewards and sanctions significantly affect behavior of workers and largely limited effects of economic incentive plans, and (3) often workers do not act or react as individuals but as *members of groups*. The study set an early direction for participative management theories and was a major milestone for the Employee Relations movement.

1943: Abraham H. Maslow, "A Theory of Human Motivation"

Abraham Maslow's Human Needs Hierarchy is one of many examples of the public sector adopting theories from other disciplines. Maslow was a professor and chaired the Department of Psychology at Brandeis University. Although he was a prolific writer and published several books, he is best remembered for his Human Needs Theory, which, although criticized, has been popular in public administration education as well as in practice. He asserted that humans have five goals or needs arranged in a hierarchy. The five needs, starting from the bottom level, are:

1. Physiological needs. Here he listed the basic needs for sustaining human life—food, water, clothing, shelter, sleep, and sexual satisfaction. He said that until these needs are satisfied to the degree necessary to maintain life, other needs will not motivate people.

2. Security, or safety, needs. Here he placed the needs that provide protection from physical danger and the fear of loss of a job, property, clothing, food, or shelter.

3. Acceptance or love needs. He wrote that because people are social beings, they need to belong, to be affiliated with and accepted by others.

4. Esteem needs. Maslow said that once people begin to satisfy their need to belong, they want to be held in esteem both by themselves and by others. This kind of need produces such satisfactions as power, prestige, status, and self-confidence.

5. Need for self-actualization. He regarded this as the highest need in his hierarchy.

This level is based on one's desire to become all that one is capable of becoming: to maximize one's potential and to accomplish that which provides personal satisfaction.

Maslow wrote that when subordinate categories are threatened, the interest and motivation to achieve the higher needs diminishes. He said that he did not want to give the false impression that a need must be satisfied 100% before the next need emerges. He pointed out that:

> . . . most members of our society who are normal, are partially satisfied in all their basic needs and partially unsatisfied in all their basic needs at the same time. A more realistic description of the hierarchy would be in terms of decreasing percentages of satisfaction as we go up the hierarchy of prepotency. For instance, if I may assign arbitrary figures for the sake of illustration, it is as if the average citizen is satisfied perhaps 85 percent in his physiological needs, 70 percent in his safety needs, 50 percent in his love needs, 40 percent in his self-esteem needs, and 10 percent in his self-actualization needs. (Maslow, cited in Shafritz & Hyde, 1987, p. 146)

What public administrators learned from Maslow was that work should satisfy the workers' needs at whatever level they may be because satisfied employees are more productive. If workers seek social activity, then the organization should provide opportunities for it. If they seek self-esteem or self-actualization, then they will need some control over their jobs and an opportunity to participate in decision making. The following summary of Maslow's Human Needs Hierarchy lists specific factors that organizations can provide to satisfy each level of need (Szilagyi & Wallace, 1983, p. 86).

Maslow's Human Needs theory has been criticized for not being supported by solid research. For example, D. T. Hall and K. E. Nougaim (1968, pp. 12–35) found little support for Maslow's theory in a study of managers at AT&T. E. E. Lawler and J. L. Suttle found some evidence for a two-step hierarchy (security needs must be satisfied before other needs become motivators), and C. P. Alderfer (1972) developed a revision of Maslow's theory (ERG theory, for Existence Relatedness, and Growth) based on actual research (both are discussed in Szilagyi & Wallace, 1983, pp. 88, 91). Despite the criticism, Maslow's hierarchy of needs remains an easy-to-understand identification of the needs of people that can serve as a reminder of how public managers must be sensitive to the personal needs of their employees. **Table 2–1** applies Maslow's Human Needs theory to the organizational setting.

1957: Chris Argyris, "The Individual and Organization: Some Problems of Mutual Adjustment"

Chris Argyris was a member of the faculty of the Harvard Business School and served as consultant to many major firms throughout the world. He is a recognized author in organizational employee relations and a major contributor to the evolution of Employee Relations theories.

His 1957 publication was influenced by Maslow's work. He wrote that there were incongruities between mature people and the formal organizations for which they worked. He said that human personalities grow toward independence,

Table 2–1	Maslow's Human Needs Hierarchy as Applied to the Organization	
General Factors	**Needs Levels**	**Factors that Organizations Can Provide**
1. Growth 2. Achievement	Self-actualization	1. Challenging 2. Creativity 3. Advancement in work 4. Achievement in work
1. Recognition 2. Status 3. Self-esteem 4. Self-respect	Ego, Status, Esteem	1. Job title 2. Merit pay increase 3. Peer/Supervision 4. Work itself 5. Responsibility
1. Companionship 2. Affection 3. Friendship	Recognition	1. Quality of supervision 2. Compatible work group 3. Professional friendships
1. Safety 2. Security 3. Competence 4. Stability	Safety and Security	1. Safe working conditions 2. Fringe benefits 3. Salary increases 4. Job security
1. Air 2. Food 3. Shelter 4. Sex	Physiological	1. Heat and air conditioning 2. Base salary 3. Cafeteria 4. Working conditions

multiple behaviors, and interests. Human beings are different from one another and jobs need to be adjusted to fit the person, not the reverse.

Argyris criticized the structured principles developed during the Organization Functions period. He saw organizations as centering on specializations that he found to inhibit self-actualization because specialization requires the use of only a few abilities. He saw overreliance on the chain of command as a cause of employees becoming passive and not reacting unless directed by superiors. He wrote that the span of control principles provide for too much supervision and overdependence of employees on their supervisors.

He described how he saw rewards that were provided for individual performance running counter to group participation. He pointed out that employees were getting paid for their dissatisfaction at work and using wages to provide satisfaction outside the organization. He was not against organizations, but advocated that organizations must be altered to accommodate for the individualities of employees.

1957: Douglas M. McGregor, "The Human Side of Enterprise"

Douglas McGregor's experiences ranged from service station attendant (1928) to president of Antioch College (1948). His teaching spanned the fields of psychology and industrial management. He taught at Harvard, MIT, and Antioch. His **Theory X** and **Theory Y** concepts and his contributions to the then new field of organization development (OD) made him one of the best-known behavioral theorists during this period.

McGregor also challenged the universal principles of organization and management established in the Organization Functions period as discussed in the previous chapter. Influenced by Maslow, he presented two theories about employee motivation, Theory X and Theory Y, which reflect different perceptions of people and management. Theory X represents the predominant perceptions of the prior Organization Functions period and Theory Y, the essence of the concepts developed during the Employee Relations period.

Theory X holds that people are passive, dislike responsibility, and are indifferent to the needs of the organization. This theory encompasses a set of propositions (developed during the Organization Functions period) that view management's task as harnessing human energy to organizational requirements. This theory supports the beliefs that (McGregor, cited in Shafritz & Hyde, 1987, pp. 256–262):

- It is management's responsibility to organize the elements of a productive enterprise in the interests of economic ends.
- The behavior of employees must be directed, motivated, controlled, and modified to fit the needs of the organization or they will be passive organizational goals.
- The worker basically lacks ambition, is inherently self-centered, gullible, and resistant to change.
- To gain compliance from employees, management must be "firm" but "fair."

Theory Y embodies a position that does not necessarily disagree with Theory X beliefs about workers' behavior but blames this behavior on the practices of industrial organizations, and management's philosophy, policy, and practice. Theory Y holds that:

- Management's responsibility involves organizing the elements of productive enterprise in the interest of economic ends (which does not differ with Theory X).
- Employees have become passive to organizational needs because of their experiences in organizations.
- Management should allow employees to recognize and develop motivational characteristics.
- Management's task is to allow people to achieve their own goals by directing their own best efforts toward organizational objectives.
- Workers respond best to "management by objectives" rather than "management by control."

A major difference between these theories is that Theory X places major emphasis on external control of human behavior, whereas Theory Y places reliance on self-control and self-direction. The management environment that supports Theory Y is one that places confidence in human capacities and is directed toward organizational objectives rather than toward the preservation of personal power and control.

Under the Theory Y approach, motivation of employees toward the objectives of the organization follows the Maslow "human needs" hierarchy. The "human needs" hierarchy level of employees must be assessed by management and appropriate satisfaction provided within the organization environment. The organization must provide for physiological, safety, social, ego, and self-fulfillment needs in order to gain desired productivity.

McGregor's Theory Y enlarged the view of motivation, and indicated that a management that stresses lower-end needs will fail over time to achieve desired results. When a worker's physiological and safety needs are satisfied, their behavior is motivated by social needs. When social needs are satisfied, egoistic needs become motivators. Egoistic needs are, however, divided into two kinds: (1) those that relate to self-esteem, and (2) those that relate to one's reputation. Unlike lower needs, these needs are rarely satisfied. McGregor's work formed the basis on which Herzberg built his "two-factor theory."

1959: Frederick Herzberg, *The Motivation to Work*

The Motivation-Hygiene theory, also called Two-Factor theory, was developed by Frederick Herzberg in 1959. Herzberg was then a psychologist at Case Western Reserve University in Cleveland. He conducted experiments in motivation with 200 engineers and accountants, finding that certain maintenance needs had to be met before the workers could begin to be motivated. He defined the maintenance factors as (1) company policy and administration, (2) technical supervision, (3) interpersonal relations with supervisor, (4) interpersonal relations with peers, (5) interpersonal relations with subordinates, (6) salary, (7) job security, (8) personal life, (9) work conditions, and (10) status. Herzberg called these maintenance factors "dissatisfiers." He meant that these factors could not motivate but, if they were lacking, they would cause dissatisfaction. He identified motivational factors as (1) achievement, (2) recognition, (3) advancement, (4) the work itself, (5) the possibility of growth, and (6) responsibility. These factors he called "satisfiers," factors that could motivate and bring about employee dedication to the organization (Herzberg, Mausner, & Snyderman, 1959).

Transitional Employee Relations Milestones

The transitional milestones during the Employee Relations period focused on both the past and future periods.

1945: Paul Appleby, *Big Democracy*

Paul Appleby, in *Big Democracy* (1945), and in *Policy and Administration Policy* (1949), asserted that theoretical insistence on an apolitical government administrative process was against the "grain of the American way." In contrast to the earlier writings of Woodrow Wilson, Appleby was one of those to begin the move toward the belief that politics was not separate from public administration.

He wrote that the two are not separate because bureaucrats create legislation by making rules, by interpreting the law, and by determining the rights of citizens. He described public administrators as "supplementary lawmakers" who nevertheless operate under constraints such as (1) the intentions and mood shifts of Congress, (2) the judicial implications of policy implementation and the possible responses of the courts, (3) accountability to the public and interest groups, and (4) pressure to cooperate and coordinate with other government agencies.

In essence, Appleby said "government is politics." His work shows a beginning of a trend that led to the development of Open Systems, Social Equity, and Public Participation themes.

1947: Robert Dahl, "The Science of Public Administration"

Robert Dahl believed that a science of administration should be created that recognized the complexities of human behavior, dealt with normative values, and took into account the social setting. He wrote, "In an attempt to make the science of public administration analogous to the natural sciences, the laws or putative laws are stripped of normative values, of the distortions caused by the incorrigible individual psyche, and of the presumably irrelevant effects of the cultural environment" (Dahl, p. 135).

Dahl said that studies should be comparative because cultural factors make a difference. His work documents a refocusing from Organization Functions to Employee Relations and the beginning of a move toward a more Open System thinking.

1947: John Gaus, *The Ecology of Public Administration*

John Gaus can be credited with introducing the public sector to the idea of "ecology." Gaus was a Harvard professor and one of the early pioneers of public administration. He elaborated on ecology in a series of lectures at the University of Alabama in 1945. These lectures were later published in *Reflections of Public Administration* in 1947.

Gaus said that ecology "deals with all interrelationships of living organisms and their environment" and "an ecological approach to public administration builds . . . quite literally from the ground up; from the elements of a place—soil, climate, location, for example—to the people who live there—their numbers and ages and knowledge, and the ways of physical and social technology by which from the place and in relationships with one another, they get their living."

He also wrote that the task of public administration "is one of discovery of the causes of problems, of the communication of possible remedies, of the organization of citizens, of the formulation of law. It is the task, in short, of politics." In the conclusion to this section of his book, he wrote, "The task will be more fruitfully performed if the citizen, and his agents in public offices, understand the ecology of government" (Gaus, 1947, p. 19). Gaus was a forerunner of the Open Systems period.

1949: Norton Long, "Power and Administration"

Norton Long, in his *Public Administration Review* article, dealt with the ramifications of executive power and responsibility. He stressed the significance of prestige and the possible outcome of sacrificing employees to this end. Long is well known for his statement, "The lifeblood of administration is power." Even so, he pointed out, it is the most overlooked topic in theory and the most dangerous to overlook in practice.

Long believed that public administrators take their direction only from their political bosses. Long wrote:

> *The theory that agencies should confine themselves to communicating policy suggestions to executive and legislature, and refrain from appealing to their clientele and the public, neglects the failure of the parties to provide either a clear-cut decision as to what they should do or an adequately mobilized political support for a course of action. The bureaucracy under the American political system has a large share of responsibility for the public promotion of policy and even more in organizing the political basis for its survival and growth. (Long, 1949, p. 259)*

Long argued that a great deal of the public administrator's time must be devoted to "mustering on their own" power through public support or "accept the consequences in frustration—a course itself not without danger." He blamed this situation on the political parties' failure to protect and provide appropriate leadership for public agencies. Long pointed the way toward Open Systems and Public Participation perspectives.

1949: Hoover Commission, First Report

The First Commission on Organization of the Executive Branch of Government was a Republican response to World War II and the New Deal. The Republican Party captured Congress in 1947 and set about to reduce what they perceived as an oversized bureaucracy.

The commission, named for its chairman, former president Herbert Hoover, established five goals to pursue: (1) find ways to cut government costs, (2) eliminate duplication and overlap, (3) consolidate similar functions, (4) abolish unnecessary functions, and (5) define and limit executive branch activities. The latter goal was in response to the fact that, although there was a Republican majority in Congress, the president, Harry Truman, was a Democrat.

The commission avoided questions of policy and tried to deal with philosophical issues concerning the roles that government should and should not be undertaking. It concentrated on antiquated processes and structural questions. Of the 273 recommendations that were adopted, performance budgeting is probably best remembered. The commission declared that "the whole budgetary concept of the Federal Government should be refashioned by the adoption of a budget based upon functions, activities and projects," and be designated the "performance budget." Other important recommendations reduced the president's span of control, delegated preaudit responsibilities from the General

Accounting Office to the line departments, and strengthened the power of the departmental secretaries (Chandler, 1988, p. 193).

1955: Hoover Commission, Second Report

This second report pursued policy matters and government functions that competed with private enterprise. Among the programs recommended for termination were crop loans, housing loans, and use of interdepartmental committees for coordination purposes. The commission also recommended the abandonment of foreign aid agencies and accrual accounting rather than cash flow accounting for federal budgeting.

The report made recommendations to limit presidential appointments of political executives to fill top federal positions. It proposed a new upper-echelon administrative class called "senior civil service," politically neutral career managers who would be transferable from one post to another. By the time that the report was published, however, Congress was back in Democratic hands and only 64% of the 314 recommendations for reorganization of the federal government were implemented. Housing, educational, and crop-supporting loans continued (Chandler, 1988, p. 194).

Both the First and Second Hoover Commission Reports provide evidence of the continuation of emphasis on Organization Functions at the federal level during the period, which saw the development of the Employee Relations theme.

Employee Relations Period Summary

Just as Woodrow Wilson's first article on public administration formed a point of departure for the Organization Functions period, so did Mayo's research for the period of Employee Relations. Argyris, McGregor, and Herzberg took Maslow's concepts and developed them into more comprehensive theories of motivation and organizational behavior.

Herzberg's "satisfiers" are supportive of McGregor's Theory Y and also support the top levels of Maslow's Hierarchy of Human Needs. Herzberg's "dissatisfiers" can be compared with McGregor's Theory X and Maslow's lower human needs. When employees are at lower levels of human needs, they may be responsive to Theory X management and interested more in the "dissatisfiers." Conversely, if they are at the higher human needs level, Theory Y approaches are motivating approaches required to keep them satisfied.

This was the time of World War II and the postwar period. Jobs were plentiful and employees could find work elsewhere if they were dissatisfied with their treatment in a given organization. Employers had to focus more on the "motivators" in order to attract and retain needed employees in the competitive job market that was developing.

As can be seen from the backgrounds of the major contributors to this period, development of the theories "in good currency" was not occurring in the public sector. The research and innovation was in the private sector. However, public administration was finding itself also in a competitive job market and was forced to follow the successful practices of the business world.

The theories that had their beginning during this era are paramount in administrating today's public agencies. Whether a municipal personnel department or the national Department of Social Security Administration, the bureaucratic structure, with evolutional mortifications, remains intact. Ninety-plus percent of all public agencys' budgets support employees' salaries. Employees are not only the most costly component of public agencies but also the most important. Motivating employees to achieve public missions effectively and efficiently was, is, and will always be of prime importance to criminal justice administrators.

As can be seen by the Transitional Milestones, the theme shift to the Open Systems period had its beginning in literature written during the two decades before it took hold in public administration. One of the factors that caused public administrators to awaken to the Open Systems outlook was the national effort to "put a man on the moon" by end of the 1960s. The cybernetic, multi-agency, systems approach of the aerospace industry and its successful use in space exploration captured the imagination of the public, as well as the private sector. The impact on the public sector will be explored in the next chapter as the development of the Open Systems and Social Equity themes are examined.

KEY CONCEPTS AND TERMS

- Organization Functions
  - POSDCORB—planning, organizing, staffing, directing, coordinating, reporting, and budgeting
    1937, "Notes on the Organization," Luther Gulick
  - Principles of Bureaucratic Organizations
    1922, "Characteristics of Bureaucracy" Max Weber
  - Scientifically finding the best way to do the job
    1912, "Principles of Scientific Management," Frederick Taylor
  - Public service as the business of the government
    1887, "The Study of Administration," Woodrow Wilson
- Employee Relations
  - Maintenance vs. satisfying factors
    1959, *Motivation to Work*, Frederick Herzberg, B. Mausner, and B. Snyderman
  - Altering organizations to fit individual needs
    1957, "The Individual & Organization," Chris Argyris
  - Theory X and Theory Y
    1957, "The Human Side of Enterprise," Douglas McGregor
  - Hierarchy of Human Needs
    1943, "A Theory of Human Motivation," A. H. Maslow
  - Motivating employees to increase productivity
    1941, "The Hawthorne Experiments," Elton Mayo

CHAPTER ACTIVITY

Select a current criminal justice agency (through publications, the Internet, or an on-site visit). Compare the "principles" of the bureaucratic organization structure discussed in this chapter with contemporary practices. Do you think all, most, or none of these "principles" are being followed today? Additionally, you may take the same approach with some of the Employee Relations concepts discussed in this chapter.

REVIEW QUESTIONS

1. What fields of enterprise did most of the concepts come from in the development of Organization Functions and Employee Relations themes? What major improvements did these two themes bring to criminal justice administration?
2. What was the public and political motivation behind the passage of the 1883 Pendleton Act? How does this act relate to today's civil service practices?

3. The metaphor of the human skeleton and internal organs was used in this chapter. How do Organization Functions and Employee Relations relate to this metaphor?

4. What major research is credited with the beginning of the Employee Relations theme? What Organization Functions concept was the intended subject of this research?

5. How do the concepts of Maslow, McGregor, and Herzberg compare? Do you see any areas of conflict between these concepts?

REFERENCES

Alderfer, C. P. (1972). *Existence, Relatedness, and Growth*. New York: Free Press.

Altshuler, A. (1977). "The Study of American Public Administration." *The Politics of the Federal Bureaucracy*. New York: Harper & Row.

Appleby, P. (1945). *Big Democracy*. New York: Alfred A. Knopf.

Argyris, C. (1957). The Individual and Organization: Some Problems of Mutual Adjustment. *Administrative Science*, 21(3), pp. 1–24.

Bennis, W. (1967). *The Functions of the Executive*. Cambridge, MA: Harvard University Press.

Chandler, R., & Plano, J. (1988). *The Public Administration Dictionary*. Santa Barbara, CA: ABC-CLIO.

Dahl, R. (1947). The Science of Public Administration. *Public Administration Review*, 7, pp. 1–11.

Follett, M. (1926). *The Giving of Orders: Scientific Foundations of Business Administration*. Baltimore: Williams & Wilkins Co.

Gaus, J. (1947). *The Ecology of Public Administration*. Mobile, AL: University of Alabama Press.

Gaus, J. (1947). *Reflections of Public Administration*. Mobile, AL: University of Alabama Press.

Goodnow, F. J. (1900). *Politics and Administration: A Study in Government*. New York; London: Macmillan.

Gulick, L., & Uruick, L. (1937). *Papers on the Science of Administration*. New York: Russell & Russell.

Hall, D. T., & Nougaim, K. E. (1968). An Examination of Maslow's Needs Hierarchy in an Organizational Setting. *Organizational Behavior and Human Performance*, Englewood Cliffs, NJ: Prentice Hall.

Herzberg, F., Mausner, B., & Snyderman, B. (1959). *The Motivation to Work*, (2nd ed.). New York: Wiley.

Long, N. (1949). Power and Administration. *Public Administration Review*, 9, pp. 257–264.

Maslow, A. (1943). A Theory of Human Motivation. *Psychological Review*, 50, pp. 370–396.

McGregor, D. M. (1957). The Human Side of Enterprise. *Management Review*. November, pp. 112–134.

Wrap Up

Mayo, E. (1945). *The Social Problems of an Industrial Civilization*. Boston: Division of Research, Graduate School of Business Administration, Harvard University.

Rosenbloom, D. (1989). *Public Administration: Understanding Management, Politics, and Law in the Public Sector*. New York: Random House.

Shafritz, J. M., & Hyde, A. C. (1987). *Classics of Public Administration*. Chicago: Dorsey Press.

Simon, H. A. (1946). The Proverbs of Administration. *Public Administration Review, 6*.

Szilagyi, A., & Wallace, M., Jr. (1983). *Organizational Behavior and Performance*, (3rd ed.). Glenview, IL: Scott, Foresman and Company.

Taylor, F. W. (1916). "Principles of Scientific Management," *Bulletin of the Taylor Society*. Society for Advancement of Management, December, pp.13–23.

Weber, M. (1946). Bureaucracy. *Essays in Sociology* by Gerth and Mills (translated from 1922 German original article). New York: Oxford University Press.

White, L. (1926). *Introduction of the Study of Public Administration*. New York: Macmillan.

Willoughby, W. (1918). *The Movement for Budgetary Reform in the States*. New York: D. Appleton and Company.

Wilson, W. (1887). The Study of Administration, in J. Shafritz & A. C. Hyde, *Classics of Public Administration*. Chicago: Dorsey Press.

■ RELEVANT PUBLICATION

An article that sets the stage for this period is Max Weber's writing about *bureaucracy*. Although Weber wrote this milestone article in 1922 in German (and it was not translated into English until 1946) it was widely referred to during this period by administrators through translations. Weber, known as "the father of bureaucracy," expressed the principles upon which the *Organization Functions* concepts are founded. Today, although considered more as guides than principles, Weber's offerings are basic to most all criminal justice agencies. (From Weber, M. (1922). Bureaucracy. *Essays in Sociology*. Translated and edited by H. H. Gerth and C. Wright Mills. Copyright 1946 by Oxford University Press, Inc. Renewed copyright 1973 by Hans H. Gerth. Reprinted by permission of the publisher.)

"Bureaucracy" by Max Weber

1. Characteristics of Bureaucracy

Modern officialdom functions in the following specific manner:

I. There is the principle of fixed and official jurisdictional areas, which are generally ordered by rules, that is, by laws or administrative regulations.

1. The regular activities required for the purposes of the bureaucratically governed structure are distributed in a fixed way as official duties.

2. The authority to give the commands required for the discharge of these duties is distributed in a stable way and is strictly delimited by rules concerning the coercive means, physical, sacerdotal, or otherwise, which may be placed at the disposal of officials.

3. Methodical provision is made for the regular and continuous fulfilment of these duties and for the execution of the corresponding rights; only persons who have the generally regulated qualifications to serve are employed.

In public and lawful government these three elements constitute 'bureaucratic authority.' In private economic domination, they constitute. bureaucratic 'management.' Bureaucracy, thus understood, is fully developed in political and ecclesiastical communities only in the modern state, and, in the private economy, only in the most advanced institutions of capitalism. Permanent and public office authority, with fixed jurisdiction, is not the historical rule but rather the exception. This is so even in large political structures such as those of the ancient Orient, the Germanic and Mongolian empires of conquest, or of many feudal structures of state. In all these cases, the ruler executes the most important measures through personal trustees, table-companions, or court-servants. Their commissions and authority are not precisely delimited and are temporarily called into being for each case.

II. The principles of office hierarchy and of levels of graded authority mean a firmly ordered system of super- and subordination in which there is a supervision of the lower offices by the higher ones. Such a system offers the governed the possibility of appealing the decision of a lower office to its higher authority, in a definitely regulated manner. With the full development of the bureaucratic type, the office hierarchy is monocratically organized. The principle of hierarchical office authority is found in all bureaucratic structures: in state and ecclesiastical structures as well as in large party organizations and private enterprises. It does not matter for the character of bureaucracy whether its authority is called 'private' or 'public.'

When the principle of jurisdictional 'competency' is fully carried through, hierarchical subordination—at least in public office—does not mean that the 'higher' authority is simply authorized to take over the business of the 'lower.' Indeed, the opposite is the rule. Once established and having fulfilled its task, an office tends to continue in existence and be held by another incumbent.

III. The management of the modern office is based upon written documents ('the files'), which are preserved in their original or draught form. There is, therefore, a staff of subaltern officials and scribes of all sorts. The body of officials actively engaged in a 'public' office, along with the respective apparatus of material implements and the files, make up a 'bureau.' In private enterprise, 'the bureau' is often called 'the office.'

In principle, the modern organization of the civil service separates the bureau from the private domicile of the official, and, in general, bureaucracy segregates official activity as something distinct from the sphere of private life. Public monies and equipment are divorced from the private property of the official. This condition is everywhere the product of a long development. Nowadays, it is found in public as well as in private enterprises; in the latter, the principle extends even to the leading entrepreneur. In principle, the executive office is separated from the household, business from private correspondence, and business assets from private fortunes. The more consistently the modern type of business management has been carried through the more are these separations the case. The beginnings of this process are to be found as early as the Middle Ages.

It is the peculiarity of the modern entrepreneur that he conducts himself as the 'first official' of his enterprise, in the very same way in which the ruler of a specifically modern bureaucratic state spoke of himself as 'the first servant' of the state. The idea that the bureau activities of the state are intrinsically different in character from the management of private economic offices is a continental European notion and, by way of contrast, is totally foreign to the American way.

IV. Office management, at least all specialized office management—and such management is distinctly modern—usually presupposes thorough and expert training. This increasingly holds for the modern executive and employee of private enterprises, in the same manner as it holds for the state official.

V. When the office is fully developed, official activity demands the full working capacity of the official, irrespective of the fact that his obligatory time in the bureau may be firmly delimited. In the normal case, this is only the product of a long development, in the public as well as in the private office. Formerly, in all cases, the normal state of affairs was reversed: official business was discharged as a secondary activity.

VI. The management of the office follows general rules, which are more or less stable, more or less exhaustive, and which can be learned. Knowledge of these rules represents a special technical learning which the officials possess. It involves jurisprudence, or administrative or business management.

   The reduction of modern office management to rules is deeply embedded in its very nature. The theory of modern public administration, for instance, assumes that the authority to order certain matters by decree—which has been legally granted to public authorities—does not entitle the bureau to regulate the matter by commands given for each case, but only to regulate the matter abstractly. This stands in extreme contrast to the regulation of all relationships through individual privileges and bestowals of favor, which is absolutely dominant in patrimonialism, at least in so far as such relationships are not fixed by sacred tradition.

2. The Position of the Official

All this results in the following for the internal and external position of the official:

I. Office holding is a 'vocation.' This is shown, first, in the requirement of a firmly prescribed course of training, which demands the entire capacity for work for a long period of time, and in the generally prescribed and special examinations which are prerequisites of employment. Furthermore, the position of the official is in the nature of a duty. This determines the internal structure of his relations, in the following manner: Legally and actually, office holding is not considered a source to be exploited for rents or emoluments, as was normally the case during the Middle Ages and frequently up to the threshold of recent times. Nor is office holding considered a usual exchange of services for equivalents, as is the case with free labor contracts. Entrance into an office, including one in the private economy, is considered an acceptance of a specific obligation of faithful management in return for a secure existence. It is decisive for the specific nature of modern loyalty to an office that, in the pure type, it does not establish a relationship to a *person*, like the vassal's or disciple's faith in feudal or in patrimonial relations of authority. Modern loyalty is devoted to impersonal and functional purposes. Behind the functional purposes, of course, 'ideas of culture-values' usually stand. These are *ersatz* for the earthly or supra-mundane personal master: ideas such as 'state,' 'church,' 'community,' 'party,' or 'enterprise' are thought of as being realized in a community; they provide an ideological halo for the master.

The political official—at least in the fully developed modern state—is not considered the personal servant of a ruler. Today, the bishop, the priest, and the preacher are in fact no longer, as in early Christian times, holders of purely personal charisma. The supra-mundane and sacred values which they offer are given to everybody who seems to be worthy of them and who asks for them. In former times, such leaders acted upon the personal command of their master; in principle, they were responsible only to him. Nowadays, in spite of the partial survival of the old theory, such religious leaders are officials in the service of a functional purpose, which in the present-day 'church' has become routinized and, in turn, ideologically hallowed.

II. The personal position of the official is patterned in the following way:

1. Whether he is in a private office or a public bureau, the modern official always strives and usually enjoys a distinct social esteem as compared with the governed. His social position is guaranteed by the prescriptive rules of rank order and, for the political official, by special definitions of the criminial code against 'insults of officials' and 'contempt' of state and church authorities.

   The actual social position of the official is normally highest where, as in old civilized countries, the following conditions prevail: a strong demand for administration by trained experts; a strong and stable social differentiation, where the official predominantly derives from socially and economically privileged strata because of the social distribution of power; or where the costliness of the required training and status conventions are binding upon him. The possession of educational certificates—to be discussed elsewhere—are usually linked with qualification for office. Naturally, such certificates or patents enhance the 'status element' in the social position of the official. For the rest this status factor in individual cases is explicitly and impassively acknowledged; for example, in the prescription that the acceptance or rejection of an aspirant to an official career depends upon the consent ('election') of the members of the official body. This is the case in the German army with the officer corps. Similar phenomena, which promote this guild-like closure of officialdom, are typically found in patrimonial and, particularly, in prebendal officialdoms of the past. The desire to resurrect such phenomena in changed forms is by no means infrequent among modern bureaucrats. For instance, they have played a role among the demands of the quite proletarian and expert officials (the *tretyj* element) during the Russian revolution.

Usually the social esteem of the officials as such is especially low where the demand for expert administration and the dominance of status conventions are weak. This is especially the case in the United States; it is often the case in new settlements by virtue of their wide fields for profitmaking and the great instability of their social stratification.

2. The pure type of bureaucratic official is *appointed* by a superior authority. An official elected by the governed is not a purely bureaucratic figure. Of course, the formal existence of an election does not by itself mean that no appointment hides behind the election—in the state, especially, appointment by party chiefs. Whether or not this is the case does not depend upon legal statutes but upon the way in which the party mechanism functions. Once firmly organized, the parties can turn a formally free election into the mere acclamation of a candidate designated by the party chief. As a rule, however, a formally free election is turned into a fight, conducted according to definite rules, for votes in favor of one of two designated candidates. . . . [pp. 196–200]

3. Normally, the position of the official is held for life, at least in public bureaucracies; and this is increasingly the case for all similar structures. As a factual rule, *tenure for life* is presupposed, even where the giving of notice or periodic reappointment occurs. In contrast to the worker in a private enterprise, the official normally holds tenure. Legal or actual life-tenure, however, is not recognized as the official's right to the possession of office, as was the case with many structures of authority in the past. Where legal guarantees against arbitrary dismissal or transfer are developed, they merely serve to guarantee a strictly objective discharge of specific office duties free from all personal considerations. In Germany, this is the case for all juridical and, increasingly, for all administrative officials.

Within the bureaucracy, therefore, the measure of 'independence,' legally guaranteed by tenure, is not always a source of increased status for the official whose position is thus secured. Indeed, often the reverse holds, especially in old cultures and communities that are highly differentiated. In such communities, the stricter the subordination under the arbitrary rule of the master, the more it guarantees the maintenance of the conventional seigneurial style of living for the official. Because of the very absence of these legal guarantees of tenure, the conventional esteem for the official may rise in the same way as, during the Middle Ages, the esteem of the nobility of office rose at the expense of esteem for the freemen, and as the king's judge surpassed that of the people's judge: In Germany, the military officer or the administrative official can be removed from office at any time, or at least far more readily than the 'independent judge,' who never pays with loss of his office for even the grossest offense against the 'code of honor' or against social conventions of the salon. For this very reason, if other things are equal, in the eyes of the master stratum the judge is considered less qualified for social intercourse than are officers and administrative officials, whose greater dependence on the master is a greater guarantee of their conformity with status conventions. Of course, the average official strives for a civil-service law, which would materially secure his old age and provide increased guarantees against his arbitrary removal from office. This striving, however, has its limits. A very strong development of the 'right to the office' naturally makes it more difficult to staff them with regard to technical efficiency, for such a development decreases the career-opportunities of ambitious candidates for office. This makes for the fact that officials, on the whole, do not feel their dependency upon those at the top. This lack of a feeling of dependency, however, rests primarily upon the inclination to depend upon one's equals rather than upon the socially inferior and governed strata. The present conservative movement among the Badenia clergy, occasioned by the anxiety of a presumably threatening separation of church and state, has been expressly determined by the desire not to be turned 'from a master into a servant of the parish.'

4. The official receives the regular *pecuniary* compensation of a normally fixed *salary* and the old age security provided by a pension. The salary is not measured like a wage in terms of work done, but according to 'status,' that is, according to the kind of function (the 'rank') and, in addition, possibly, according to the length of service. The relatively great security of the official's income, as well as the rewards of social esteem, make the office a sought-after position, especially in countries which no longer provide opportunities for colonial profits. In such countries, this situation permits relatively low salaries for officials.

5. The official is set for a '*career*' within the hierarchical order of the public service. He moves from the lower, less important, and lower paid to the higher positions. The average official naturally desires a mechanical fixing of the conditions of promotion: if not of the offices, at least of the salary levels. He wants these conditions fixed in terms of 'seniority,' or possibly according to grades achieved in a developed system of expert examinations. Here and there, such examinations actually form a character *indelebilis* of the official and have lifelong effects on his career. To this is joined the desire to qualify the right to office and the increasing tendency toward status group closure and economic security. All of this makes for a tendency to consider the offices as 'prebends' of those who are qualified by educational certificates. The necessity of taking general personal and intellectual qualifications into consideration, irrespective of the often subaltern character of the educational certificate, has led to a condition in which the highest political offices, especially the positions of 'ministers,' are principally filled without reference to such certificates. . . . [pp. 202–204]

6. Technical Advantages of Bureaucratic Organization

The decisive reason for the advance of bureaucratic organization has always been its purely technical superiority over any other form of organization. The fully developed bureaucratic mechanism compares with other organizations exactly as does the machine with the nonmechanical modes of production.

Precision, speed, unambiguity, knowledge of the files, continuity, discretion, unity, strict subordination, reduction of friction and of material and personal costs—these are raised to the optimum point in the strictly bureaucratic administration, and especially in its monocratic form. As compared with all collegiate, honorific, and avocational forms of administration, trained bureaucracy is superior on all these points. And as far as complicated tasks are concerned, paid bureaucratic work is not only more precise but, in the last analysis, it is often cheaper than even formally unremunerated honorific service.

Honorific arrangements make administrative work an avocation and, for this reason alone, honorific service normally functions more slowly—being less bound to schemata and being more formless. Hence it is less precise and less unified than bureaucratic work because it is less dependent upon superiors and because the establishment and exploitation of the apparatus of subordinate officials and filing services are almost unavoidably less economical. Honorific service is less continuous than bureaucratic and frequently quite expensive. This is especially the case if one thinks not only of the money costs to the public treasury—costs which bureaucratic administration, in comparison with administration by notables, usually substantially increases—but also of the frequent economic losses of the governed caused by delays and lack of precision. The possibility of administration by notables normally and permanently exists only where official management can be satisfactorily discharged as an avocation. With the qualitative increase of tasks the administration has to face, administration by notables reaches its limits—today, even in England. Work organized by collegiate bodies causes friction and delay and requires compromises between colliding interests and views. The administration, therefore, runs less precisely and is more independent of superiors; hence, it is less unified and slower. All advances of the Prussian administrative organization have been and will in the future be advances of the bureaucratic, and especially of the monocratic, principle.

Today, it is primarily the capitalist market economy which demands that the official business of the administration be discharged precisely, unambiguously, continuously, and with as much speed as possible. Normally, the very large, modern capitalist enterprises are themselves unequalled models of strict bureaucratic organization. Business management throughout rests on increasing precision, steadiness, and, above all, the speed of operations. This, in turn, is determined by the peculiar nature of the modern means of communication, including, among other things, the news service of the press. The extraordinary increase in the speed by which public announcements, as well as economic and political facts, are transmitted exerts a steady and sharp pressure in the direction of speeding up the tempo of administrative reaction towards various situations. The optimum of such reaction time is normally attained only by a strictly bureaucratic organization.*

Bureaucratization offers above all the optimum possibility for carrying through the principle of specializing administrative functions according to purely objective considerations. Individual performances are allocated to functionaries who have specialized training and who by constant practice learn more and more. The 'objective' discharge of business primarily means a discharge of business according to *calculable rules* and 'without regard for persons.'

'Without regard for persons' is also the watchword of the 'market' and, in general, of all pursuits of naked economic interests. A consistent execution of bureaucratic domination means the leveling of status 'honor.' Hence, if the principle of the free-market is not at the same time restricted, it means the universal domination of the 'class situation.' That this consequence of bureaucratic domination has not set in everywhere, parallel to the extent of bureaucratization, is due to the differences among possible principles by which polities may meet their demands.

---

*Here we cannot discuss in detail how the bureaucratic apparatus may, and actually does, produce definite obstacles to the discharge of business in a manner suitable for the single case.

The second element mentioned, 'calculable rules,' also is of paramount importance for modern bureaucracy. The peculiarity of modern culture, and specifically of its technical and economic basis, demands this very 'calculability' of results. When fully developed, bureaucracy also stands, in a specific sense, under the principle of *sine ira ac studio*. Its specific nature, which is welcomed by capitalism, develops the more perfectly the more the bureaucracy is 'dehumanized,' the more completely it succeeds in eliminating from official business love, hatred, and all purely personal, irrational, and emotional elements which escape calculation. This is the specific nature of bureaucracy and it is appraised as its special virtue.

The more complicated and specialized modern culture becomes, the more its external supporting apparatus demands the personally detached and strictly 'objective' *expert*, in lieu of the master of older social structures, who was moved by personal sympathy and favor, by grace and gratitude. Bureaucracy offers the attitudes demanded by the external apparatus of modern culture in the most favorable combination. As a rule, only bureaucracy has established the foundation for the administration of a rational law conceptually systematized on the basis of such enactments as the latter Roman imperial period first created with a high degree of technical perfection. During the Middle Ages, this law was received along with the bureaucratization of legal administration, that is to say, with the displacement of the old trial procedure which was bound to tradition or to irrational presuppositions, by the rationally trained and specialized expert. . . . [pp. 214–216]

10. The Permanent Character of the Bureaucratic Machine

Once it is fully established, bureaucracy is among those social structures which are the hardest to destroy. Bureaucracy is *the* means of carrying 'community action' over into rationally ordered 'societal action.' Therefore, as an instrument for 'societalizing' relations of power, bureaucracy has been and is a power instrument of the first order—for the one who controls the bureaucratic apparatus.

Under otherwise equal conditions, a 'societal action,' which is methodically ordered and led, is superior to every resistance of 'mass' or even of 'communal action.' And, where the bureaucratization of administration has been completely carried through, a form of power relation is established that is practically unshatterable.

The individual bureaucrat cannot squirm out of the apparatus in which he is harnessed. In contrast to the honorific or avocational 'notable,' the professional bureaucrat is chained to his activity by his entire material and ideal existence. In the great majority of cases, he is only a single cog in an ever-moving mechanism which prescribes to him an essentially fixed route of march. The official is entrusted with specialized tasks and normally the mechanism cannot be put into motion or arrested by him, but only from the very top. The individual bureaucrat is thus forged to the community of all the functionaries who are integrated into the mechanism. They have a common interest in seeing that the mechanism continues its functions and that the societally exercised authority carries on.

The ruled, for their part, cannot dispense with or replace the bureaucratic apparatus of authority once it exists. For this bureaucracy rests upon expert training, a functional specialization of work, and an attitude set for habitual and virtuoso-like mastery of single yet methodically integrated functions. If the official stops working, or if his work is forcefully interrupted, chaos results, and it is difficult to improvise replacements from among the governed who are fit to master such chaos. This holds for public administration as well as for private economic management. More and more the material fate of the masses depends upon the steady and correct functioning of the increasingly bureaucratic organizations of private capitalism. The idea of eliminating these organizations becomes more and more utopian.

The discipline of officialdom refers to the attitude-set of the official for precise obedience within his *habitual* activity, in public as well as in private organizations. This discipline increasingly becomes the basis of all order, however great the practical importance of administration on the basis of the filed documents may be. The naive idea of Bakuninism of destroying the basis of 'acquired rights' and 'domination' by destroying public documents overlooks the settled orientation of *man* for keeping to the habitual rules and regulations that continue to exist independently of the documents. Every reorganization of beaten or dissolved troops, as well as the restoration of administrative orders destroyed by revolt, panic, or other catastrophes, is realized by appealing to the trained orientation of obedient compliance to such orders. Such compliance has been conditioned into the officials, on the one hand, and, on the other hand, into the governed. If such an appeal is successful it brings, as it were, the disturbed mechanism into gear again.

The objective indispensability of the once-existing apparatus, with its peculiar, 'impersonal' character, means that the mechanism—in contrast to feudal orders based upon personal piety—is easily made to work for anybody who knows how to gain control over it. A rationally ordered system of officials continues to function smoothly after the enemy has occupied the area; he merely needs to change the top officials. This body of officials continues to operate because it is to the vital interest of everyone concerned, including above all the enemy.

During the course of his long years in power, Bismarck brought his ministerial colleagues into unconditional bureaucratic dependence by eliminating all independent statesmen. Upon his retirement, he saw to his surprise that they continued to manage their offices, unconcerned and undismayed, as if he had not been the master mind and creator of these crea-tures, but rather as if some single figure had been exchanged for some other figure in the bureaucratic machine. With all the changes of masters in France since the time of the First Empire, the power machine has re-mained essentially the same. Such a machine makes 'revolution,' in the sense of the forceful creation of entirely new formations of authority, tech-nically more and more impossible, especially when the apparatus controls the modern means of communication (telegraph, et cetera) and also by virtue of its internal rationalized structure. In classic fashion, France has demonstrated how this process has substituted *coups d'état* for 'revolutions': all successful transformations in France have amounted to *coups d'état*.

11. Economic and Social Consequences of Bureaucracy

It is clear that the bureaucratic organization of a social structure, and es-pecially of a political one, can and regularly does have far-reaching eco-nomic consequences. But what sort of consequences? Of course in any individual case it depends upon the distribution of economic and social power, and especially upon the sphere that is occupied by the emerging bu-reaucratic mechanism. The consequences of bureaucracy depend therefore upon the direction which the powers using the apparatus give to it. And very frequently a crypto-plutocratic distribution of power has been the result.

In England, but especially in the United States, party donors regularly stand behind the bureaucratic party organizations. They have financed these parties and have been able to influence them to a large extent. The breweries in England, the so-called 'heavy industry,' and in Germany the Hansa League with their voting funds are well enough known as political donors to parties. In modern times bureaucratization and social leveling within political and particularly within state organizations in connection with the destruction of feudal and local privileges, have very frequently ben-efited the interests of capitalism. Often bureaucratization has been carried out in direct alliance with capitalist interests, for example, the great his-torical alliance of the power of the absolute prince with capitalist interests. In general, a legal leveling and destruction of firmly established local struc-tures ruled by notables has usually made for a wider range of capitalist ac-tivity. Yet one may expect as an effect of bureaucratization, a policy that meets the petty bourgeois interest in a secured traditional 'subsistence,' or even a state socialist policy that strangles opportunities for private profit. This has occurred in several cases of historical and far-reaching importance, specifically during antiquity; it is undoubtedly to be expected as a future development. Perhaps it will occur in Germany.

The very different effects of political organizations which were, at least in principle, quite similar—in Egypt under the Pharaohs and in Hellenic and Roman times—show the very different economic significances of bureaucratization which are possible according to the direction of other factors. The mere fact of bureaucratic organization does not unambiguously tell us about the concrete direction of its economic effects, which are always in some manner present. At least it does not tell us as much as can be told about its relatively leveling effect socially. In this respect, one has to remember that bureaucracy as such is a precision instrument which can put itself at the disposal of quite varied—purely political as well as purely economic, or any other sort—of interests in domination. Therefore, the measure of its parallelism with democratization must not be exaggerated, however typical it may be. Under certain conditions, strata of feudal lords have also put bureaucracy into their service. There is also the possibility—and often it has become a fact, for instance, in the Roman principate and in some forms of absolutist state structure—that a bureaucratization of administration is deliberately connected with the formation of *estates*, or is entangled with them by the force of the existing groupings of social power. The express reservation of offices for certain status groups is very frequent, and actual reservations are even more frequent. The democratization of society in its totality, and in the *modern* sense of the term, whether actual or perhaps merely formal, is an especially favorable basis of bureaucratization, but by no means the only possible one. After all, bureaucracy strives merely to level those powers that stand in its way and in those areas that, in the individual case, it seeks to occupy. We must remember this fact—which we have encountered several times, and which we shall have to discuss repeatedly: that 'democracy' as such is opposed to the 'rule' of bureaucracy, in spite and perhaps because of its unavoidable yet unintended promotion of bureaucratization. Under certain conditions, democracy creates obvious ruptures and blockages to bureaucratic organization. Hence, in every individual, historical case, one must observe in what special direction bureaucratization has developed.

The Civil Rights Era (1960s–1970s): Development of Open Systems and Social Equity Themes

3

■ Introduction

The 1960s and 1970s saw a shift from the postwar public's domestic safety concerns to a fear of government control and a concern for individual rights. Peace marches and "make love, not war" demonstrations were common. The criminal justice system, particularly the police, became the target of many civil rights groups. Criminal justice administrators often found themselves in the "crossfire" between the public and elected officials. Public administrators were still accustomed to functioning under the concept that public agencies were to follow the dictates of their elected officials. However, the volatile social and political conditions of the time caused criminal justice administrators to begin paying more attention to what was going on around them and to the constitutional commitments of their oaths of office. They sometimes found that the elected officials to whom they reported were giving directives that were not in keeping with constitutional guarantees. Some governors in southern states, for example, were taking strong stands against desegregation. This was the era that prompted the Open Systems and Social Equity themes of public administration.

■ Development of an Open Systems Outlook (1960s)

In the 1960s, as the Employee Relations approach continued to grow, a major administration refocusing occurred. During this period, changes occurred that caused public administrators to be more concerned with their environment. This was a significant departure from the traditional "closed system" approach of the earlier years.

The closed system approach had been set by Woodrow Wilson in 1887 when he wrote that "administration is merely the clerical part of government and representatives of the people are the proper ultimate authority in all matters of government" (see Chapter 2).

Wilson's view caused public administrators to look for most of their direction to come from elected officials even though Wilson's real intent was to protect public administrators from the politics. Outside of this one source (elected officials), administrators managed their agencies as closed systems with little concern for the social and intergovernmental environment that was outside the boundaries of their organizations.

In the previous era, Chester Barnard began to encourage public managers to look beyond the immediate borders of the organization's chain of command. But his writings only incidentally began a departure from the closed systems view and then only from the perspective of a few chief executives. During the second period, the move to deemphasize the formal organization structure advanced slightly with the findings of the Hawthorne Experiments, and their recognition of the role of informally organized groups within the larger organization.

It was not until after World War II, however, that the importance of this shift in thinking began to materialize. The system theorists began to describe the interactions of large-scale social units as intimately connected with a larger social world. Organizations of a scope and complexity not experienced before were being created to resolve the problems of postwar America.

A transdisciplinary movement called "general systems theory" emerged from the work of the biologist Ludwig von Bertalanffy. He formulated a generalized scientific language and methodology that could be used in the "formulation of principles that are valid for 'systems' in general, whatever the nature of their component elements and the relations or 'forces' between them" (von Bertalanffy, 1968, p. 37).

Scientific explanations, von Bertalanffy argued, were necessary in solving the complexity and interdisciplinary nature of practical problems of all kinds. Identifying principles of scientific explanation common to all kinds of systems could make it possible to use the knowledge from more highly understood systems to explore the less-understood ones. Systems, however, are most understandable in terms of their interplay among constituent systemic elements and their relationship with the larger environment.

The search for guiding principles resulted in several concepts that form the basis of the system outlook. For example, the distinction between open and closed systems was established. The closed system metaphor depicts a self-contained entity in which the functioning of the component parts and their interrelationships are the primary objects of interest.

Bureaucracy had been viewed in this manner before this period. Max Weber, for instance, described the characteristics of the ideal-typical bureaucracy in a closed system context. Frederick Taylor's discussion of "scientific management principles" assumed a stable closed system with little concern for a changing "open" environment.

Following the lead of von Bertalanffy, the **Open Systems** theory of the 1960s marked the beginning of the view that public organizations are part of a larger environment. Public administrators began to see a need for direct feedback about the elements of the environment that had an impact on the internal operations of their agencies. **Figure 3–1** provides an Open Systems model of public agencies (developed from Sharkansky, 1970, p. 5).

Historical Setting for the Open Systems Period

The 1960s was a period of social change energized by the interest in the systems approach. Newly inaugurated President John F. Kennedy set the tone for the period with his 1961 commitment to put a man on the moon by the end of the decade. The National Aeronautics and Space Administration (NASA) would achieve that feat in 1969. The cybernetic approach of aerospace technology spread into many other fields including the public sector. President Lyndon Johnson's Great Society program also brought an unprecedented degree of social intervention and change.

The direction, and much of the energy for social change during the 1960s, emanated from the federal government. However, implementation of these changes was usually at the state and local government levels. This fostered "creative federalism," which forced planning and decision making among all levels of government. Implementation of the mandates by any given public agency could not be achieved without close interaction with the relevant elements in their environment.

Some of the direction for this period came from President Kennedy's executive orders that "affirmative action" be used to implement the policy of nondiscrimination in employment by the federal government (1961) and that the

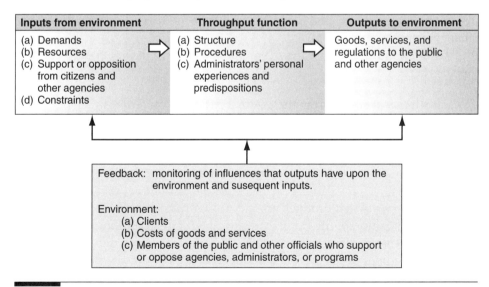

Figure 3–1 Open System View of Public Agencies.

unionization of federal workers be encouraged (1962). In 1963, Martin Luther King Jr. delivered his "I have a dream" speech at a civil rights march in Washington, D.C., and President Kennedy was assassinated. In 1964, the Civil Rights Act was created to prohibit discrimination on the basis of race, color, religion, sex, or national origin in most private sector employment. In 1968, Martin Luther King Jr. and Senator Robert F. Kennedy were assassinated, and Richard M. Nixon was elected president of the United States.

Open Systems Theme Milestones

1966: Daniel Katz and Robert Kahn, "The Social Psychology of Organizations"

Katz and Kahn expressed an application of Open Systems theory in general to organizations in particular, and provided a systems framework for how organizations operate. They established that the purpose of an organization can be determined by examining its inputs, throughputs, and the outputs. This, they emphasized, was more nearly accurate than trying to define the purpose by seeking what the agency executives listed as the organizational objectives.

Katz and Kahn asserted that all social systems are open systems in that they gain their input of energies from the outside environment, convert these energies to outputs through a process of internal functions, and return the energies to the environment where they energize additional inputs. This view helped to establish organizational boundaries by observing the inputs, processes, and outputs and asking what is system-controllable and what is not. Behavior outside the controllable components is not part of the organizational system.

Katz and Kahn disclosed the defect in using a closed system approach to managing. The closed system approach does not consider the outer environment to which organizations must react and can lead to failure. Open systems import energies from their environment that foster growth and survival. The open systems view allows for planning and flexibility to change in order to conform to an ever-changing environment.

According to Katz and Kahn (1966, pp. 23–27), common characteristics of open systems are:

- *Importation* of energy from the external environment. There are maintenance inputs (energy inputs that sustain the system) and productive inputs (energy imports that are processed to yield productive outputs).
- *Throughputs* or functions that transform the energy to a product or service.
- *Outputs* are the services or products produced and submitted to the environment.
- *Cycles of events* that produce an output that furnishes the source of energy for the repetition of the cycle by energizing inputs back into the system.
- *Negative entropy* that repels or slows the natural law that moves toward disorganization or death. An open system is able to do this by importing more energy than it expends.
- *Information inputs*, *negative feedback*, and a *coding process* that guides systems on how to manage the throughput to create the desired outputs.

- *Steady* or *homeostatic state* that allows for continual adjustments that preserve the system and stabilize the outputs.
- *Differentiation* that causes a system to grow and improve through an evolutionary process.
- *Integration* and *coordination* that causes the system parts to work in a complementary and output oriented manner.
- *Equifinality*, which allows systems to be flexible enough to take a variety of paths, depending on changing conditions, and produce the same desired outputs.

Katz's and Kahn's work is considered the most comprehensive documentation of the application of systems theory to organizations. They considered the Open Systems theory a framework, "a meta-theory, a model in the broadest sense of that overused term." Their objective was to develop a framework for organizational analysis that permits integration of several levels of theoretical approaches, from the micro (individual) level up through the macro (organization in its environment) level.

1966: Morton Grodzins, *An American System: A New View of Government in the United States*

Morton Grodzins connected the Open Systems approach to governmental agencies with several colorful metaphors and concepts. He developed the concept of "marble-cake" federalism to describe the cooperative and more open system relationships among various levels of government that resulted in an overlapping of activities. This was in contrast to the more traditional view of "layer-cake" federalism that held that the three levels of government were disconnected and operated as separate closed systems.

He observed that with tens of thousands of tax-levying governmental entities, the process of "federal governance" was very complex. "Government by chaos and cooperation," as he called it, demanded a special understanding of the complexities and overlapping functions of the interacting three levels of government.

His overall assessment was that open systems that shared functions could and did work in intergovernmental programs. His work pointed out that the essence of successful public management is the acknowledgment of the interaction of all levels of government plus the understanding and proper assessment of the social, political, and economical environment in which public agencies operate.

1967: James D. Thompson, *Organizations in Action*

James Thompson extended the open systems work of Katz and Kahn in two directions. Thompson argued for a reinstatement of the closed system concept on the grounds that organizations must and do employ a combination of both open and closed systems. A closed system can work where the environment is stable and controllable. It also can be a successful structure for a unit or division, which is within an organization but is somewhat isolated from the outer environment. Organizational environments, however, are increasingly dynamic and unstable.

The Open Systems approach is required at higher levels in an organization and in most organizational interactions with a dynamic environment. Thompson linked the idea of rationality to the means by which organizations strive for efficiency and survival, and in doing so provided for an acceptance of open and closed senses of rationality.

Thompson tested nearly 100 propositions about how organizations and individuals act in particular circumstances using the open system framework. He concluded that an open system approach must be used to determine and monitor overall organizational goals. However, once the goals are set, it is possible for the "technical core" level of the organization to perform the designated tasks in a closed system environment. Thompson saw open-system strategies of boundary-spanning activities and closed-system strategies of efficiency-maximizing as being performed by different sectors or levels of the organization.

1967: Warren Bennis, "Organizations of the Future"

In his 1967 *Personnel Administration* article, Warren Bennis predicted an "end to bureaucracy in the next 25 to 50 years" (Bennis, cited in Shafritz & Hyde, 1987, p. 325). Bennis wrote that organizational formats and structures were inadequate to cope with increasing demands, technological changes, participatory management, and the increasingly professional workforce. He indicated that bureaucracy was right for the past but now was vulnerable to the dynamics of the current and future changing environment. He said that for bureaucratic structures to be functional at all they must be less rigid, take into consideration human factors, and be reduced in size.

Bennis was one of the first to state that organizations in the future would rely on significantly different ideas of the nature and worth of human behavior, power, and organizational form. He provided an integration of themes, human factors, and the Open Systems theory. His work made public managers more aware of the necessity to link organizations to their environments and the public they serve.

Transition Milestones

The transition milestone works produced during this period exemplified how environmental conditions can cause a retreat to earlier levels and pointed the way to future themes.

1966: Allen Schick, "The Road to PPB: The Stages of Budget Reform"

Allen Schick gave a description of the U.S. history of budgetary theory from its early emphasis on accounting and control to planning, programming, and budgeting (PPB; a budgeting system mandated for all federal agencies in 1965 and for the federal government in 1969).

Schick indicated that although PPB portended a radical shift in the central function of budgeting (to strategic planning), it was anchored in a tradition a half-century old. PPB was predicated on the planning function and commanded a high level of centralization.

Schick's work presents a good example of what Maslow called "proponent goals" in his Human Needs Model. In Chapter 1, the Contextual Development of Public Administration Model was metaphorically compared to Maslow's model, in that when the study and practice of public administration is focused on a particular theme and a previously satisfied theme is threatened, the focus is redirected to that previously satisfied theme.

Schick's milestone article provides an example of retreat to the basic Organization Function theme during a period of attention to the Open Systems outlook. With the concerns over Vietnam and the economy, the focus of the period was temporarily diverted to an earlier period's emphasis of efficiency through better planning and budgeting.

By the end of this period, PPB, which had been a mandatory system for all federal agencies and widely adopted by state and local jurisdictions, was considered to be unusable in its original format. Nevertheless, PPB's influence as a major rational process remains. Where it is still in use, however, it will be found to be much different from the original system.

In 1969, Aaron Wildavsky provided a critical review of PPB in a *Public Administration Review* article. He documented the demise of the popularity of this budgeting approach. Wildavsky denounced PPB as unworkable and demonstrated how its planning and analytical functions were contradictory to the essential nature of budgeting.

1967: Anthony Downs, *Inside Bureaucracy*

Anthony Downs presented an analysis of American bureaucracy (based upon a systems approach) and developed propositions to aid in predicting behavior of bureaus and bureaucrats. He introduced a recognition of life cycles of bureaus associated with growth and stagnation.

In this work, Downs expanded on Weber's "ideal-type" bureaucracy by suggesting that two new elements be added to Weber's definition. First, organizations are large; "any organization in which the highest ranking members know less than half of the other members can be considered large." Second, most of the organization's output cannot be "directly or indirectly evaluated in any markets external to the organization by means of voluntary 'quid pro quo' transactions" (Downs, 1967, p. 6).

Downs attempted to explain the characteristics of government agencies, why they change and how they survive. He argued that organizations that are deprived of market conditions (not subjected to public choice) become more hierarchical, rule-oriented, and are more prone to stagnate. Downs's concept of life cycles had a great influence on subsequent organization theories. Not only would organizational environments differ, but organizational responses could be predicated on their own stages of development at different times in their life cycle.

1968: Dwight Waldo, "Public Administration in a Time of Revolution"

Dwight Waldo predicted continuing and revolutionary changes because of growth in government, the civil rights movement, public employee and student militancy, and manipulation of "client groups" (Waldo, 1968, p. 363).

He cited exponential increases in scientific-technological enterprise, growing reaction against science and technology, the generation gap, and revolution of morals as factors to which public administration had a responsibility to help society adjust. Waldo was setting the stage for the next theme in the Contextual Development of Public Administration: the commitment to Social Equity.

1969: Herbert Kaufman, "Administrative Decentralization and Political Power"

Herbert Kaufman analyzed national trends in administrative structures, particularly the then current pressure for decentralization. He described the pressure from segments of the population that believed the bureaucratic system was not delivering its fair share of benefits to the public.

Kaufman saw that a modern, highly complex society needed new modes of representation to involve the public and ensure responsive administration. Even though he saw the need, he recognized that the implications of this might be considerably beyond the capacities of public administration in the 1960s. His work pointed the way for theories and concepts developed in the following two periods.

1969: Theodore J. Lowi, *The End of Liberalism: Ideology, Policy, and the Crisis of Public Authority*

Theodore Lowi described a "crisis of public authority" arising from over-decentralization and the dominating role of interest groups. He indicated that "corruption of modern government began with the emergence of interest group liberalism as a public philosophy." He wrote that such philosophy and practice corrupted democracy by rendering government impotent, limited government ability to achieve justice, and weakened its ability to live by democratic power.

Lowi asserted that public authority was parceled out to private interest groups, resulting in a weak, decentralized government incapable of long-range planning. These interest groups operate to promote private goals and not to promote the public interest. Consequently, government would become a "holding company of interest" and not an institution capable of making hard choices among conflicting values. Lowi gave an indictment of the administrative process in which agencies charged with regulation are seen as basically protectors of those being regulated. He contributed to setting the stage for the next period: the period of commitment to Social Equity.

Open Systems Period Summary

As Deil Wright later wrote in 1983, we function in a "picket fence" intergovernmental relation environment (Wright, cited in Stillman, 1988, p. 114). No major public administrative function is achieved without interplay and coordination between at least two or three levels of government. For example, if a county mental health agency wants to expand its services it will undoubtedly have to gain the support of the state and federal health/welfare agencies as well as the political backing of all three levels of government. This requires an open systems outlook.

Today it is important for criminal justice administrators to have an open systems outlook that includes insight into international, as well as local, state, and national issues. The world market economy, the influx of people from Pacific Rim countries, and global information technology are just a few of the current additions to the public administrator's "juggling act" ("juggling act" was used metaphorically in Chapter 1 to describe the multifaceted aspects of today's public administration).

In 1968, Dwight Waldo called together at a conference many public administration forward-thinkers. At this conference, the foundation for a "new public administration" was established. The results were published in the early 1970s and served as the main thrust of the next theme shift. It was a shift to more concern about social equity, which is the subject of the following section.

■ A Commitment to Social Equity (1970s)

The 1970s marked another shift in the direction of public administration. This period differed from all the other periods in the development of public administration theories and concepts in that the theme originated with public administrators rather than originating in the private sector. Concentration on Organization Functions, Employee Relations, Open Systems, and, later, Client-Oriented Service in the public sector came as a result of developments in the private sector.

Commitment to **social equity**, however, developed out of concerns of public administration academicians and practitioners in the mid-1960s and 1970s. These concerns resulted in a shifting of public administration away from a commitment just to efficiency and good administrative practices to a position that also included a concern for social equity.

Social equity was the principle on which was based the "new public administration" movement of the early 1970s. "Social Equity is a normative standard that makes equity in the delivery of public services the criterion for judging the value of administrative policy" (Chandler & Plano, 1988, p. 33).

Previously, public administration had centered on two questions of public policy: (1) Can better service be offered with available resources? and (2) Can the level of services be maintained while spending less? The "new public administration" added a third question: Do the services enhance social equity? (Frederickson, 1971, p. 426).

The real beginning for this period came in 1968 when Dwight Waldo, having noted that public administration was "in a time of revolution," called a conference of forward-thinking academics in public administration. The conference was held at Syracuse University's Minnowbrook conference site. The products of the conference were published in 1971 under the title *Toward a New Public Administration: The Minnowbrook Perspective.*

The theme of this period was somewhat a delayed reaction to the turbulent events of the previous decade. The political climate engendered by the civil rights movement, the U.S. involvement in the Vietnam War, and the assassination of Martin Luther King Jr. all played a part in shaping this theme. Ethical neutrality by public administrators (which had been the public management philosophy under the 80-year-old Woodrow Wilson prescription of allegiance to the elected official) came under fire. The concept that public administrators were merely the "clerical end of government" was no longer acceptable to these "young Turks" of public administration.

The "new public administration" called for proactive administrators with a feeling of social responsibility to replace the traditional impersonal, neutral bureaucrats. H. George Frederickson, in "Toward a New Public Administration" (from the Minnowbrook conference), went so far as to say that he saw the day coming when public administration and the courts would represent the disadvantaged and minorities, whereas the elected officials would stand for the majority.

One result of this was the realization that public organizations could no longer rely solely on the existing political apparatus when responding to the rapidly changing needs and requirements of the public at large.

Another development was the beginning of the formation of a more client-oriented public organization that set the stage for the Movement to Foster Public Client-Oriented Service (the next period in the contextual development of public administration, discussed in Chapter 4). This development drew its inspiration from two sources: the first was the citizen participation movement created in part by the War on Poverty, and the second was the client-employee humanistic approach reflected in the Minnowbrook emphasis on equity and social justice for the public and public employees alike.

Some say that the "minnowbrookers" went too far in advocating a move away from political accountability. Many of today's scholars agree that the movement may have been too extreme. Most, however, agree that the "new public administration" movement forced the discipline to recognize that the most important challenges of public administration cannot always be reduced to political accountability. Public administrators, too, have a moral if not legal responsibility to ensure social equity for all people.

Historical Setting for the Social Equity Period

The decade became what many considered an era of resource scarcity dominated by "cutback management." Although the 1960s, while being traumatic, seemed a time of optimism and growth, the 1970s followed with retrenchment and pessimism.

During this period, many of the public administration ideals were jolted by the failure of a number of the Great Society programs, the Watergate debacle, the first resignation of a president, and the growing fiscal crisis that devastated many state and local governments.

The concentration of power and control in the executive branch had been the direction for public administration. Now Watergate provided a chilling lesson about what could happen if such centralized power was abused. The public administration "profession" reacted by conducting its own review of Watergate.

In response to a request from the Senate Select Committee on Presidential Campaign Activities, a special panel of the National Academy of Public Administration examined the situation. The panel, chaired by Frederick C. Mosher, produced a report called *Watergate Implications for Responsible Government*. The report detailed the Nixon administration's abuses of administrative power. It called for educational institutions to direct more attention on public sector ethics.

The panel concluded that more detailed and effective codes of conduct and standards for public employees were needed. The real significance of the report was the responsibility it placed on public administration to institutionalize ethical values that provided guidance for policy making regardless of political actions.

Public sector efforts were aimed at reshaping public administration to adapt to the turbulence of the era. Additional efforts were made to meet the concerns raised about the practices developed during the Organization Functions period (Chapter 2) that were now being contrasted to theories developed during the Employee Relations period by contributors such as Chris Argyris and Douglas McGregor (Chapter 2) plus the issues raised in the Open Systems period by Katz and Kahn and Warren Bennis.

Some significant events of the times were the Postal Reorganization Act of 1970, which made the U.S. Postal Service a public corporation within the executive branch and allowed for the collective bargaining over wages by postal employee unions. That same year, Hawaii became the first state to allow state and local government employees the right to strike and the Occupational Safety and Health Administration (OSHA) was created.

In 1972, the Equal Employment Opportunity Act prohibited discrimination by public sector employers. In 1974, Gerald Ford became president and granted former president Nixon a full pardon for all possible crimes. Proposition 13, requiring reductions in local property taxes, was voted into law in California in 1978, signaling a tax revolt that spread across the nation.

Social Equity Theme Milestones

1971: Dwight Waldo, *Towards a New Public Administration: The Minnowbrook Perspective*

Dwight Waldo introduced the "New Public Administration" school of thought in this publication. His book brought together the products of the Minnowbrook conference. In September 1968, Waldo (then a Professor of Humanities at Syracuse University and Editor of the *Public Administration Review*) sponsored a conference in which forward-thinking public administrators were encouraged to consider new approaches.

Proceedings of the conference were published in *Towards a New Public Administration: The Minnowbrook Perspective*, which remains the key work in understanding this school of thought. The new public administration thinking centered on social equity with less interest in administrative efficiency and economic use of resources. The idea of a more humane bureaucracy gained influence in the 1970s with such programs as Affirmative Action and Equal Employment Opportunity hiring and promotion.

The new public administration movement was partly a response to the "new political science movement" (which was occurring simultaneously and aimed at ridding political science of its emphasis on behavioralism). The new public administration was a move of independence from both political science and administrative science.

During the 1960s, public administration was being forced out of the political science field. This removal from the academic political science organizations was exemplified by the elimination of public administration as an organizing category at the annual meeting of the American Political Science Association in 1967. Dwight Waldo wrote, "Many political scientists not identified with Public Administration are indifferent or even hostile; they would sooner be free of it." He pointed out that public administration had become a "second-class citizen" in political science.

Public administration was not faring much better in the field of administrative science. The technical approach of systems analysts and economists dominated administrative science in the 1960s (fueled by the Open Systems movement). Waldo and his followers felt that the sense of the public interest should be a central theme of public administration and could best be preserved by separation from the political and administrative sciences.

Waldo's formation of the Minnowbrook Conference and his publication of the thinking generated at the conference established a new theme in public administration and a more autonomous approach to servicing the public.

1971: H. George Frederickson, "Toward a New Public Administration"

George Frederickson's article was inspired by the Minnowbrook conference and was published in Dwight Waldo's book. Frederickson emphasized the refocusing of public administration toward social responsibility efforts and advocated that public sector managers should become "change agents."

He called for proactive public administrators to promote "second generation behavioralism" that would be more normative and sensitive to public needs. He wrote, as he stated at the conference, that the new movement was "in alignment with good, or possibly God" and should become public administration's "holy grail."

Frederickson wrote, "New Public Administration seeks not only to carry out legislative mandates as efficiently and economically as possible but to both influence and execute policies which more generally improve the quality of life for all." He also wrote:

> . . . New Public Administration, in its search for changeable structures, tends therefore to experiment with or advocate modified bureaucratic-organizational forms. Decentralization, sensitivity training, organization development, responsibility expansion, confrontation and client involvement are all essentially counter bureaucratic notions that characterize New Public Administration. (p. 75)

Frederickson foresaw a political system in which elected officials would speak for the majority, and the courts and public administrators would be protective of the interests of the disadvantaged minorities. He felt that public administrators must concentrate on current problems of social equity such as urban poverty, widespread narcotics use, and high crime.

1971: Todd R. LaPorte, "The Recovery of Relevance in the Study of Public Organization"

Todd LaPorte probably best summarized the overall concept of the Minnowbrook conference in one paragraph:

> *Our primary normative premise should be that the purpose of public organization is the reduction of economic, social, and psychic suffering and the enhancement of life opportunities for those inside and outside the organization. Translated into more detailed sentiments, this statement means that public organizations should be assessed in terms of their effect on the production and distribution of material abundance in efforts to free all people from economic deprivation and want. Furthermore, it means that public organizations have a responsibility to enhance social justice by freeing their participants and the citizenry to decide their own way and by increasing the probability of shared political and social privilege. Finally, it means that the quality of personal encounter and increasing possibilities of personal growth should be elevated to major criteria of organizational assessment. (LaPorte, 1971, p. 32)*

LaPorte linked the emerging conception of political democracy with the humanism proposal for internal organizational democracy.

1971: Frederick C. Mosher, "The Public Service in a Temporary Society"

In this article, Frederick Mosher accepted Warren Bennis's premise of the "temporary society" (one that is changing rapidly and will be transformed into another society within a relatively short span of years) but centered his interest on the impact of professionalism on modern public service. He saw professionalism as a most distinguishing feature of this public service era. The problem with professionalism that concerned Mosher was the increase in specialization and narrowing of focus caused by professionals at a time when social problems were growing and requiring a broad prospective approach. Also of concern to him was the "functional interdependence" of these professionals on one another and their evolving separation from other public sector employees.

He pointed out that "two-fifths of all professionals in this country will be employed directly or indirectly by governments." Was their allegiance to public service and its social responsibility or to their profession?

He did, however, recognize that social problems were requiring tools other than the traditional techniques associated with public administration, and that education and new approaches that could be learned from other professions were necessary.

1973: Vincent Ostrom, *The Intellectual Crisis in American Public Administration*

Vincent Ostrom added to the support for social equity while setting the stage for more interest in public participation in public administration. As a market theorist, he viewed organizations by the way individuals made decisions. He subscribed to the public choice theory that advocated that individuals are motivated by self-interest and will choose courses of action to maximize their own gain.

He proposed a theory of "democratic administration" and said that public administration could not be separated from politics because most decisions are not a matter of political indifference. He believed that public administrators must serve the individual consumers of public goods and services and must not be strictly guided by elected "masters."

Transition Milestones

1972: Aaron Wildavsky, "The Self-Evaluating Organization"

Aaron Wildavsky's article provided an insightful discussion of the difficulties of evaluating public programs in a dynamic political environment. Wildavsky is sometimes referred to as a great critic of public administration because he was constantly reminding the field of its inherent political nature and its limitation.

The problem with evaluation, he wrote, was that no matter how compelling the case for change, change was what evaluation most often emphasizes and change was what organizations disliked most. Public administrators, he said, can barely cope with everyday demands. What they strive for is stability, not change. Also someone had to support the cost of change and evaluations seldom addressed this critical issue. Finally, most public organizational strategies minimize disruption and many managers would consequently ignore changes recommended by the evaluation process.

Wildavsky's work also gives a reminder of the past level in the Contextual Development of Public Administration, the Open Systems outlook. He wrote that "the ability of any single organization to make self-generated changes is limited by the necessity of receiving support from its environment." He points out that an important activity of an evaluation is measuring the impact of the agency on the environment and of the environment on the success of an agency, in other words, evaluating the relative inputs and outputs.

1973: Jeffrey L. Pressman and Aaron Wildavsky, *Implementation*

Pressman and Wildavsky teamed up to write a classic case study of federal programs in the city of Oakland, California. Their book made the term "implementation" popular as a new emphasis of public administration. The "unabridged" title of their book in itself gives an indication of their thinking—*Implementation: How Great Expectations in Washington Are Dashed in Oakland; or Why It's Amazing that Federal Programs Work at All; This Being a Saga of the Economic Development Administration as Told by Two Sympathetic Observers Who Seek to Build Morals on a Foundation of Ruined Hopes.*

Their main point was that policy planning and analysis often does not take into account the difficulties of execution, which is another word for implementation. Their work inspired increased interest in bringing evaluation, planning, and implementation together.

1977: Howard E. McCurdy, *Public Administration: A Synthesis*

Howard McCurdy gave further support to Ostrom's public choice approach by providing examples of how this theory could be practiced in the public sector and pointed the way to the next level in the Contextual Development of Public Administration.

First, he described the "voucher system" in public education, in which parents would be given vouchers that would ensure government payment for their child's education at any school of their choice. This meant that parents could select the school that they determined could best provide the education they wanted for their children. He pointed out that schools were administered by a central bureaucracy controlled by professional educators who have a stake in maintaining a large, uniform system that promotes their interest. Consequently, school systems grow inflexible and not responsive to diverse and new demands. His solution was to put the schools into a market environment where those that produced the best education would be supported by the public and those that did not would not survive.

Another example of public choice in the public sector given by McCurdy was the Lakewood Plan. This plan is based on the experience of a residential community in Los Angeles County. Instead of creating municipal departments, this city purchased all of its services from other governments and contractors. Lakewood became the first completely "contract city" in the United States. McCurdy pointed out that the success of this experiment was based on the fact that the city officials who represented the residents were completely separated from the officials who produced the services to satisfy local demands. Lakewood officials could bargain over the public service. They could get the county of Los Angeles, nearby cities, and private vendors to bargain over who was to provide municipal services to this community.

1977: Peter Pyhrr, "The Zero-Base Approach to Government Budgeting"

Peter Pyhrr's work marked another retreat to the Organization Functions level (see Chapter 2) of the contextual development of public administration. His article spotlights a renewed emphasis on efficiency during a time of financial "belt-tightening." Pyhrr's work supports a premise of the Contextual Themes Model in that it shows a retreat to a prior theme when the principles of that theme are threatened. Here we see that during the period of major interest in Social Equity, a sudden return to earlier values as the national economy threatened public revenues. Revenue shortages were spread throughout all levels of government and were evidenced at the state level with enactments such as California's Proposition 13, which severely limited the state's tax revenue.

Zero-base budgeting required all spending for an agency or program to be justified anew each year. It altered the principle of "incrementalism" in budgeting, which assumed that the following year's budget would begin at or near the funding level of the current year's budget.

This budgeting approach had three basic elements: (1) identifying decision units, (2) analyzing decision packages, and (3) ranking the decision packages in a descending order of importance.

The purpose of this approach was to eliminate or reduce low-priority programs. It was used to shift resources within an agency to high-impact programs that might not otherwise receive funding increases, or to achieve a balanced budget. President Jimmy Carter ordered the adoption of zero-base budgeting throughout the executive branch in 1977 and it continued as the federal level form of budgeting throughout the Carter administration.

Social Equity Period Summary

The lessons learned during this period are important in administrating today's public affairs. Administrators overseeing agencies that range from county housing authority departments to the national Department of Health and Human Services have a moral and legal obligation to promote and protect social equity for both the public and their employees. This is particularly true for criminal justice administrators.

The news media provides a daily reminder of the social equity responsibilities of public agencies. Examples, from claims of police brutality to discrimination in government hiring practices, serve as indicators of the continuing concern for public agencies to provide social equity. Public administrators must ensure equal employment opportunity/affirmative action through sound merit examinations for hiring and promoting, by eliminating violations of equal protection, and by promoting greater social representation in the public sector workforce as well as providing equal public service to all people.

The theme of Social Equity, as well as the earlier period theme of an Open Systems outlook, brought public administrators into closer contact with the public. As the public sector became more directly aware of its environment and the attitudes of the public at the "grassroots" level, a growing distrust of and dissatisfaction with public service was perceived. Public complaints, civil unrest, moves to privatize public services, and tax cuts all served as indicators of dwindling public support for government.

Many private businesses also were sensing client dissatisfaction as people became more service-oriented. The theme of the private sector became "excellence in service" and "client satisfaction." A theme shift resulted first in the private sector, then in the public sector, and finally became the predominant theme in the criminal justice system. This theme shift is the subject of the next chapter.

KEY CONCEPTS AND TERMS

- Open Systems
  - Is bureaucracy outdated?
    1967, "Organizations of the Future," Warren Bennis
  - Re-focusing on Organization Functions in times of economic cutbacks
    1966, "The Road to PPB: The Stages of Budget Reform," Allen Schick
  - The need for Open Systems organizations
    1966, *The Social Psychology of Organizations*, Daniel Katz and Robert Kahn
- Social Equity
  - Refocusing on Organization Functions in times of economic cutbacks
    1977, "The Zero-Based Approach to Government Budgeting," Peter Pyhrr
  - Public sector responsibility for individual rights
    1971, "Toward a New Public Administration: The Minnowbrook Perspective," H. George Frederickson

CHAPTER ACTIVITY

Obtain access to at least one milestone publication discussed in this chapter (other than the one presented at the end of the chapter). Study the publication(s) for additional insight into this era and the conditions that created some of the concepts used by criminal justice administrators today.

REVIEW QUESTIONS

1. What social and political conditions caused the development of the Open Systems and Social Equity themes?
2. What were some of the reasons why Warren Bennis criticized bureaucratic organizations and what did he predict would happen to them?
3. Metaphors such as "Marble Cake," "Layer Cake," and "Picket Fence" have been used to describe the government in this chapter. Explain what these descriptions mean.
4. What caused Allen Schick's writing on reforming budget approaches to become a milestone during the Social Equity period?
5. Earlier contextual themes focused on efficiency and effectiveness and sound financial practices. How did the Social Equity theme differ from this focus when it came to human rights?

REFERENCES

Bennis, W. (1967). Organizations of the Future. *Personnel Administration*, September–October, pp. 17–25.

Chandler, R., & Plano, J. (1988). *The Public Administration Dictionary*. Santa Barbara, CA: ABC-CLIO.

Downs, A. (1967). *Inside Bureaucracy*. Santa Monica, CA: Rand Corporation, and Boston, MA: Little Brown and Company.

Frederickson, H. G. (1971). *Toward a New Public Administration: The Minnowbrook Perspective*. Scranton, PA: Chandler Publishing Company.

Grodzins, M. (1966). *An American System: A New View of Government in the United States*. Chicago: Rand McNally.

Katz, D., & Kahn, R. L. (1966). *The Social Psychology of Organizations*. New York: John Wiley.

Kaufman, H. (1969). Administration Decentralization and Political Power. *Public Administrative Review*, January–February, pp. 3–15.

LaPorte, T. R. (1971). The Recovery of Relevance in the Study of Public Organizations. *The New Public Administration: The Minnowbrook Perspective*. Scranton, PA: Chandler Publishing Company.

Lowi, T. J. (1969). *The End of Liberalism: Ideology, Policy, and the Crisis of Public Authority*. New York: W. W. Norton.

McCurdy, H. E. (1977). *Public Administration: A Synthesis*. Menlo Park, CA: Benjamin/Cummings.

Mosher, F. C. (1971). The Public Service in a Temporary Society. *Public Administration Review*, January–February, pp. 47–62.

Mosher, F. C. and others (1974). *Watergate: Implications for Responsible Government*. New York: Basic Books.

Ostrom, V. (1973). *The Intellectual Crisis in American Public Administration*. Mobile: University of Alabama Press.

Pressman, J. L., & Wildavsky, A. (1973). *Implementation*. Berkeley: University of California Press.

Pyhrr, P. (1977). The Zero-Base Approach to Government Budgeting. *Public Administration Review*, January–February, pp. 1–8.

Schick, Allen (1966). The Road to PPB: The Stages of Budget Reform. *Public Administration Review*, December.

Shafritz, J. M., & Hyde, A. C. (1987). *Classics of Public Administration*. Chicago: The Dorsey Press.

Sharkansky, I. (1970). *Public Administration: Policy-Making in Government Agencies*. Chicago: Markham Publishing Company.

Thompson, J. D. (1967). *Organizations in Action*. New York: McGraw-Hill.

von Bertalanffy, L. (1968). *General Systems Theory*. New York: George Braziller.

Waldo, D. (1968). Public Administration in a Time of Revolution. *Public Administration Review, 28*, pp. 362–368.

Waldo, D. (1971). *Toward a New Public Administration: The Minnowbrook Perspective*. Edited by Frank Marini. Scranton, PA: Chandler Publishing Company.

Wildavsky, A. (1969). Rescuing Policy Analysis for PPBS. *Public Administration Review, 29,* March–April, pp. 189–202.

Wildavsky, A. (1972). The Self-Evaluating Organization. *Public Administration Review,* September–October, pp. 509–520.

Wrap Up

■ RELEVANT PUBLICATION

As in the previous chapter, the era covered in this chapter also produced two administrative themes. A significant milestone that emerged as a starting point for these themes was written by Katz and Kahn, who can be credited with fostering the Open Systems Theme. Once their work made its way into the public sector, public administrators started moving away from the "closed systems" approach that had prevailed since the turn of the century. Criminal justice administrators, along with other public sector leaders, developed a broader perspective that promoted a realization of their responsibility for Social Equity.

The concepts of Katz and Kahn are described in the following article. (Katz, D. & Kahn, R. L. (1966). Organizations and the System Concept. *The Social Psychology of Organizations*. New York: John Wiley & Sons, Inc. Reprinted by permission of John Wiley & Sons, Inc.)

"Organizations and the System Concept" by Daniel Katz and Robert L. Kahn

The aims of social science with respect to human organizations are like those of any other science with respect to the events and phenomena of its domain. The social scientist wishes to understand human organizations, to describe what is essential in their form, aspects, and functions. He wishes to explain their cycles of growth and decline, to predict their effects and effectiveness. Perhaps he wishes as well to test and apply such knowledge by introducing purposeful changes into organizations—by making them, for example, more benign; more responsive to human needs.

Such efforts are not solely the prerogative of social science, however; common sense approaches to understanding and altering organizations are ancient and perpetual. They tend, on the whole, to rely heavily on two assumptions: that the location and nature of an organization are given by its name; and that an organization is possessed of built-in goals—because such goals were implanted by its founders, decreed by its present leaders, or because they emerged mysteriously as the purposes of the organizational system itself. These assumptions scarcely provide an adequate basis for the study of organizations and at times can be misleading and even fallacious. We propose, however, to make use of the information to which they point.

The first problem in understanding an organization or a social system is its location and identification. How do we know that we are dealing with an organization? What are its boundaries? What behavior belongs to the organization and what behavior lies outside it? Who are the individuals whose actions are to be studied and what segments of their behavior are to be included?

The fact that popular names exist to label social organizations is both a help and a hindrance. These popular labels represent the socially accepted stereotypes about organizations and do not specify their role structure, their psychological nature, or their boundaries. On the other hand, these names help in locating the area of behavior in which we are interested. Moreover, the fact that people both within and without an organization accept stereotypes about its nature and functioning is one determinant of its character.

The second key characteristic of the common sense approach to understanding an organization is to regard it simply as the epitome of the purposes of its designer, its leaders, or its key members. The teleology of this approach is again both a help and a hindrance. Since human purpose is deliberately built into organizations and is specifically recorded in the social compact, the by-laws, or other formal protocol of the undertaking, it would be inefficient not to utilize these sources of information. In the early development of a group, many processes are generated which have little to do with its rational purpose, but over time there is a cumulative recognition of the devices for ordering group life and a deliberate use of these devices.

Apart from formal protocol, the primary mission of an organization as perceived by its leaders furnishes a highly informative set of clues for the researcher seeking to study organizational functioning. Nevertheless, the stated purposes of an organization as given by its by-laws or in the reports of its leaders can be misleading. Such statements of objectives may idealize, rationalize, distort, omit, or even conceal some essential aspects of the functioning of the organization. Nor is there always agreement about the mission of the organization among its leaders and members. The university president may describe the purpose of his institution as one of turning out national leaders; the academic dean sees it as imparting the cultural heritage of the past, the academic vice president as enabling students to move toward self-actualization and development, the graduate dean as creating new knowledge, the dean of men as training youngsters in technical and professional skills which will enable them to earn their living, and the editor of the student newspaper as inculcating the conservative values which will preserve the status quo of an outmoded capitalistic society.

The fallacy here is one of equating the purposes or goals of organizations with the purposes and goals of individual members. The organization as a system has an output, a produce or an outcome, but this is not necessarily identical with the individual purposes of group members. Though the founders of the organization and its key members do think in teleological terms about organization objectives, we should not accept such practical thinking, useful as it may be, in place of a theoretical set of constructs for purposes of scientific analysis. Social science, too frequently in the past, has been misled by such short-cuts and has equated popular phenomenology with scientific explanation.

In fact, the classic body of theory and thinking about organizations has assumed a teleology of this sort as the easiest way of identifying organizational structures and their functions. From this point of view an organization is a social device for efficiently accomplishing through group means some stated purpose; it is the equivalent of the blueprint for the design of the machine which is to be created for some practical objective: The essential difficulty with this purposive or design approach is that an organization characteristically includes more and less than is indicated by the design of its founder or the purpose of its leader. Some of the factors assumed in the design may be lacking or so distorted in operational practice as to be meaningless, while unforeseen embellishments dominate the organizational structure. Moreover, it is not always possible to ferret out the designer of the organization or to discover the intricacies of the design which he carried in his head. The attempt by Merton to deal with the latent function of the organization in contrast with its manifest function is one way of dealing with this problem.[1] The study of unanticipated consequences as well as anticipated consequences of organizational functioning is a similar way of handling the matter. Again, however, we are back to the purposes of the creator or leader, dealing with unanticipated consequences on the assumption that we can discover the consequences anticipated by him and can lump all other outcomes together as a kind of error variance.

It would be much better theoretically, however, to start with concepts which do not call for identifying the purposes of the designers and then correcting for them when they do not seem to be fulfilled. The theoretical concepts should begin with the input, output, and functioning of the organization as a system and not with the rational purposes of its leaders. We may want to utilize such purposive notions to lead us to sources of data or as subjects of special study, but not as our basic theoretical constructs for understanding organizations.

Our theoretical model for the understanding of organizations is that of an energic input-output system in which the energic return from the output reactivates the system. Social organizations are flagrantly open systems in that the input of energies and the conversion of output into further energic input consist of transactions between the organization and its environment.

All social systems, including organizations, consist of the patterned activities of a number of individuals. Moreover, these patterned activities are complementary or interdependent with respect to some common output or outcome; they are repeated, relatively enduring, and bounded in space and time. If the activity pattern occurs only once or at unpredictable intervals, we could not speak of an organization. The stability or recurrence of activities can be examined in relation to the energic input into the system, the transformation of energies within the system, and the resulting product or energic output. In a factory the raw materials and the human labor are the energic input, the patterned activities of production the transformation of energy, and the finished product the output. To maintain this patterned activity requires a continued renewal of the inflow of energy. This is guaranteed in social systems by the energic return from the product or outcome. Thus the outcome of the cycle of activities furnishes new energy for the initiation of a renewed cycle. The company which produces automobiles sells them and by doing so obtains the means of securing new raw materials, compensating its labor force, and continuing the activity pattern.

In many organizations outcomes are converted into money and new energy is furnished through this mechanism. Money is a convenient way of handling energy units both on the output and input sides, and buying and selling represent one set of social rules for regulating the exchange of money. Indeed, these rules are so effective and so widespread that there is some danger of mistaking the business of buying and selling for the defining cycles of organization. It is a commonplace executive observation that businesses exist to make money, and the observation is usually allowed to go unchallenged. It is, however, a very limited statement about the purposes of business.

Some human organizations do not depend on the cycle of selling and buying to maintain themselves. Universities and public agencies depend rather on bequests and legislative appropriations, and in so-called voluntary organizations the output reenergizes the activity of organization members in a more direct fashion. Member activities and accomplishments are rewarding in themselves and tend therefore to be continued, without the mediation of the outside environment. A society of bird watchers can wander into the hills and engage in the rewarding activities of identifying birds for their mutual edification and enjoyment. Organizations thus differ on this important dimension of the source of energy renewal, with the great majority utilizing both intrinsic and extrinsic sources in varying degree. Most large-scale organizations are not as self-contained as small voluntary groups and are very dependent upon the social effects of their output for energy renewal.

Our two basic criteria for identifying social systems and determining their functions are (1) tracing the pattern of energy exchange or activity of people as it results in some output and (2) ascertaining how the output is translated into energy which reactivates the pattern. We shall refer to organizational functions or objectives not as the conscious purposes of group leaders or group members but as the outcomes which are the energic source for a maintenance of the same type of output.

This model of an energic input-output system is taken from the open system theory as promulgated by von Bertalanffy.[2] Theorists have pointed out the applicability of the system concepts of the natural sciences to the problems of social science. It is important, therefore, to examine in more detail the constructs of system theory and the characteristics of open systems.

System theory is basically concerned with problems of relationships, of structure, and of interdependence rather than with the constant attributes of objects. In general approach it resembles field theory except that its dynamics deal with temporal as well as spatial patterns. Older formulations of system constructs dealt with the closed systems of the physical sciences, in which relatively self-contained structures could be treated successfully as if they were independent of external forces. But living systems, whether biological organisms or social organizations, are acutely dependent upon their external environment and so must be conceived of as open systems.

Before the advent of open-system thinking, social scientists tended to take one of two approaches in dealing with social structures; they tended either (1) to regard them as closed systems to which the laws of physics applied or (2) to endow them with some vitalistic concept like entelechy. In the former case they ignored the environmental forces affecting the organization and in the latter case they fell back upon some magical purposiveness to account for organizational functioning. Biological theorists, however, have rescued us from this trap by pointing out that the concept of the open system means that we neither have to follow the laws of traditional physics, nor in deserting them do we have to abandon science. The laws of Newtonian physics are correct generalizations but they are limited to closed systems. They do not apply in the same fashion to open systems which maintain themselves through constant commerce with their environment, i.e., a continuous inflow and outflow of energy through permeable boundaries.

One example of the operation of closed versus open systems can be seen in the concept of entropy and the second law of thermodynamics. According to the second law of thermodynamics a system moves toward equilibrium; it tends to run down, that is, its differentiated structures tend to move toward dissolution as the elements composing them become arranged in random disorder. For example, suppose that a bar of iron has been heated by the application of a blowtorch on one side. The arrangement of all the fast (heated) molecules on one side and all the slow molecules on the other is an unstable state, and over time the distribution of molecules becomes in effect random, with the resultant cooling of one side and heating of the other, so that all surfaces of the iron approach the same temperature. A similar process of heat exchange will also be going on between the iron bar and its environment, so that the bar will gradually approach the temperature of the room in which it is located, and in so doing will elevate somewhat the previous temperature of the room. More technically, entropy increases toward a maximum and equilibrium occurs as the physical system attains the state of the most probable distribution of its elements. In social systems, however, structures tend to become more elaborated rather than less differentiated. The rich may grow richer and the poor may grow poorer. The open system does not run down, because it can import energy from the world around it. Thus the operation of entropy is counteracted by the importation of energy and the living system is characterized by negative rather than positive entropy.

COMMON CHARACTERISTICS OF OPEN SYSTEMS

Though the various types of open systems have common characteristics by virtue of being open systems, they differ in other characteristics. If this were not the case, we would be able to obtain all our basic knowledge about social organizations through the study of a single cell.

   The following nine characteristics seem to define all open systems.

1. Open Systems of Energy

Open systems import some form of energy from the external environment. The cell receives oxygen from the bloodstream; the body similarly takes in oxygen from the air and food from the external world. The personality is dependent upon the external world for stimulation. Studies of sensory deprivation show that when a person is placed in a darkened sound-proof room, where he has a minimal amount of visual and auditory stimulation, he develops hallucinations and other signs of mental stress.[3] Deprivation of social stimulation also can lead to mental disorganization.[4] Kohler's studies of the figural after-effects of continued stimulation show the dependence of perception upon its energic support from the external world.[5] Animals deprived of visual experience from birth for a prolonged period never fully recover their visual capacities.[6] In other words, the functioning personality is heavily dependent upon the continuous inflow of stimulation from the external environment. Similarly, social organizations must also draw renewed supplies of energy from other institutions, or people, or the material environment. No social structure is self-sufficient or self-contained.

2. The Through-Put

Open systems transform the energy available to them. The body converts starch and sugar into heat and action. The personality converts chemical and electrical forms of stimulation into sensory qualities, and information into thought patterns. The organization creates a new product, or processes materials, or trains people, or provides a service. These activities entail some reorganization of input. Some work gets done in the system.

3. The Output

Open systems export some product into the environment, whether it be the invention of an inquiring mind or a bridge constructed by an engineering firm. Even the biological organism exports physiological products such as carbon dioxide from the lungs which helps to maintain plants in the immediate environment.

4. Systems as Cycles of Events

The pattern of activities of the energy exchange has a cyclic character. The product exported into the environment furnishes the sources of energy for the repetition of the cycle of activities. The energy reinforcing the cycle of activities can derive from some exchange of the product in the external world or from the activity itself. In the former instance, the industrial concern utilizes raw materials and human labor to turn out a product which is marketed, and the monetary return is used to obtain more raw materials and labor to perpetuate the cycle of activities. In the latter instance, the voluntary organization can provide expressive satisfactions to its members so that the energy renewal comes directly from the organizational activity itself.

The problem of structure, or the relatedness of parts, can be observed directly in some physical arrangement of things where the larger unit is physically bounded and its subparts are also bounded within the larger structure. But how do we deal with social structures, where physical boundaries in this sense do not exist? It was the genius of F. H. Allport which contributed the answer, namely that the structure is to be found in an interrelated set of events which return upon themselves to complete and renew a cycle of activities.[7] It is events rather than things which are structured, so that social structure is a dynamic rather than a static concept. Activities are structured so that they comprise a unity in their completion or closure. A simple linear stimulus-response exchange between two people would not constitute social structure. To create structure, the responses of A would have to elicit B's reactions in such a manner that the responses of the latter would stimulate A to further responses. Of course the chain of events may involve many people, but their behavior can be characterized as showing structure only when there is some closure to the chain by a return to its point of origin with the probability that the chain of events will then be repeated. The repetition of the cycle does not have to involve the same set of phenotypical happenings. It may expand to include more sub-events of exactly the same kind or it may involve similar activities directed toward the same outcomes. In the individual organism the eye may move in such a way as to have the point of light fall upon the center of the retina. As the point of light moves, the movements of the eye may also change but to complete the same cycle of activity, i.e., to focus upon the point of light.

A single cycle of events of a self-closing character gives us a simple form of structure. But such single cycles can also combine to give a larger structure of events or an event system. An event system may consist of a circle of smaller cycles or hoops, each one of which makes contact with several others. Cycles may also be tangential to one another from other types of subsystems. The basic method for the identification of social structures is to follow the energic chain of events from the input of energy through its transformation to the point of closure of the cycle.

5. Negative Entropy

To survive, open systems must move to arrest the entropic process; they must acquire negative entropy. The entropic process is a universal law of nature in which all forms of organization move toward disorganization or death. Complex physical systems move toward simple random distribution of their elements and biological organisms also run down and perish. The open system, however, by importing more energy from its environment than it expends, can store energy and can acquire negative entropy. There is then a general trend in an open system to maximize its ratio of imported to expended energy, to survive and even during periods of crisis to live on borrowed time. Prisoners in concentration camps on a starvation diet will carefully conserve any form of energy expenditure to make the limited food intake go as far as possible.[8] Social organizations will seek to improve their survival position and to acquire in their reserves a comfortable margin of operation.

The entropic process asserts itself in all biological systems as well as in closed physical systems. The energy replenishment of the biological organism is not of a qualitative character which can maintain indefinitely the complex organizational structure of living tissue. Social systems, however, are not anchored in the same physical constancies as biological organisms and so are capable of almost indefinite arresting of the entropic process. Nevertheless the number of organizations which go out of existence every year is large.

6. Information Input, Negative Feedback, and the Coding Process

The inputs into living systems consist not only of energic materials which become transformed or altered in the work that gets done. Inputs are also informative in character and furnish signals to the structure about the environment and about its own functioning in relation to the environment. Just as we recognize the distinction between cues and drives in individual psychology, so must we take account of information and energic inputs for all living systems.

The simplest type of information input found in all systems is negative feedback. Information feedback of a negative kind enables the system to correct its deviations from course. The working parts of the machine feed back information about the effects of their operation to some central mechanism or subsystem which acts on such information to keep the system on target. The thermostat which controls the temperature of the room is a simple example of a regulatory device which operates on the basis of negative feedback. The automated power plant would furnish more complex examples. Miller emphasizes the critical nature of negative feedback in his proposition: *"When a system's negative feedback discontinues, its steady state vanishes, and at the same time its boundary disappears and the system termi-nates.*"[9] If there is no corrective device to get the system back on its course, it will expend too much energy or it will ingest too much energic input and no longer continue as a system.

The reception of inputs into a system is selective. Not all energic inputs are capable of being absorbed into every system. The digestive system of living creatures assimilates only those inputs to which it is adapted. Similarly, systems can react only to those information signals to which they are attuned. The general term for the selective mechanisms of a system by which incoming materials are rejected or accepted and translated for the structure is coding. Through the coding process the "blooming, buzzing confusion" of the world is simplified into a few meaningful and simplified categories for a given system. The nature of the functions performed by the system determines its coding mechanisms, which in turn perpetuate this type of functioning.

7. The Steady State and Dynamic Homeostasis

The importation of energy to arrest entropy operates to maintain some constancy in energy exchange, so that open systems which survive are characterized by a steady state. A steady state is not motionless or a true equilibium. There is a continuous inflow of energy from the external environment and a continuous export of the products of the system, but the character of the system, the ratio of the energy exchanges and the relations between parts, remains the same. The catabolic and anabolic processes of tissue breakdown and restoration within the body preserve a steady state so that the organism from time to time is not the identical organism it was but a highly similar organism. The steady state is seen in clear form in the homeostatic processes for the regulation of body temperature; external conditions of humidity and temperature may vary, but the temperature of the body remains the same. The endocrine glands are a regulatory mechanism for preserving an evenness of physiological functioning. The general principle here is that of Le Châtelier, who maintains that any internal or external factor making for disruption of the system is countered by forces which restore the system as closely as possible to its previous state.[10] Krech and Crutchfield similarly hold, with respect to psychological organization, that cognitive structures will react to influences in such a way as to absorb them with minimal change to existing cognitive integration.[11]

The homeostatic principle does not apply literally to the functioning of all complex living systems, in that in counteracting entropy they move toward growth and expansion. This apparent contradiction can be resolved, however, if we recognize the complexity of the subsystems and their interaction in anticipating changes necessary for the maintenance of an overall steady state. Stagner has pointed out that the initial disturbance of a given tissue constancy within the biological organism will result in mobilization of energy to restore the balance, but that recurrent upsets will lead to actions to anticipate the disturbance:

> *We eat before we experience intense hunger pangs. . . . energy mobilization for forestalling tactics must be explained in terms of a cortical tension which reflects the visceral-proprioceptive pattern of the original biological disequilibration . . . . Dynamic homeostasis involves the maintenance of tissue constancies by establishing a constant physical environment—by reducing the variability and disturbing effects of external stimulation. Thus the organism does not simply restore the prior equilibrium. A new, more complex and more comprehensive equilibrium is established.*[12]

Though the tendency toward a steady state in its simplest form is homeostatic, as in the preservation of a constant body temperature, the basic principle is *the preservation of the character of the system*. The equilibrium which complex systems approach is often that of a quasi-stationary equilibrium, to use Lewin's concept.[13] An adjustment in one direction is countered by a movement in the opposite direction and both movements are approximate rather than precise in their compensatory nature. Thus a temporal chart of activity will show a series of ups and downs rather than a smooth curve.

In preserving the character of the system, moreover, the structure will tend to import more energy than is required for its output, as we have already noted in discussing negative entropy. To insure survival, systems will operate to acquire some margin of safety beyond the immediate level of existence. The body will store fat, the social organization will build up reserves, the society will increase its technological and cultural base. Miller has formulated the proposition that the rate of growth of a system—within certain ranges—is exponential if it exists in a medium which makes available unrestricted amounts of energy for input.[14]

In adapting to their environment, systems will attempt to cope with external forces by ingesting them or acquiring control over them. The physical boundedness of the single organism means that such attempts at control over the environment affect the behavioral system rather than the biological system of the individual. Social systems will move, however, towards incorporating within their boundaries the external resources essential to survival. Again the result is an expansion of the original system.

Thus, the steady state which at the simple level is one of homeostasis over time, at more complex levels becomes one of preserving the character of the system through growth and expansion. The basic type of system does not change directly as a consequence of expansion. The most common type of growth is a multiplication of the same type of cycles or subsystems—a change in quantity rather than in quality. Animals and plant species grow by multiplication. A social system adds more units of the same essential type as it already has. Haire has studied the ratio between the sizes of different subsystems in growing business organizations.[15] He found that though the number of people increased in both the production subsystem and the subsystem concerned with the external world, the ratio of the two groups remained constant. Qualitative change does occur, however, in two ways. In the first place, quantitative growth calls for supportive subsystems of a specialized character not necessary when the system was smaller. In the second place, there is a point where quantitative changes produce a qualitative difference in the functioning of a system. A small college which triples its size is no longer the same institution in terms of the relation between its administration and faculty, relations among the various academic departments, or the nature of its instruction.

In short, living systems exhibit a growth or expansion dynamic in which they maximize their basic character. They react to change or they anticipate change through growth which assimilates the new energic inputs to the nature of their structure. In terms of Lewin's quasistationary equilibrium the ups and downs of the adjustive process do not always result in a return to the old level. Under certain circumstances a solidification or freezing occurs during one of the adjustive cycles. A new base line level is thus established and successive movements fluctuate around this plateau which may be either above or below the previous plateau of operation.

8. Differentiation

Open systems move in the direction of differentiation and elaboration. Diffuse global patterns are replaced by more specialized functions. The sense organs and the nervous system evolved as highly differentiated structures from the primitive nervous tissues. The growth of the personality proceeds from primitive, crude organizations of mental functions to hierarchically structured and well-differentiated systems of beliefs and feelings. Social organizations move toward the multiplication and elaboration of roles with greater specialization of function. In the United States today medical specialists now outnumber the general practitioners.

One type of differentiated growth in systems is what von Bertalanffy terms progressive mechanization. It finds expression in the way in which a system achieves a steady state. The early method is a process which involves an interaction of various dynamic forces, whereas the later development entails the use of a regulatory feedback mechanism. He writes:

> It can be shown that the primary regulations in organic systems, that is, those which are most fundamental and primitive in embryonic development as well as in evolution, are of such nature of dynamic interaction. . . . Superimposed are those regulations which we may call secondary, and which are controlled by fixed arrangements, especially of the feedback type. This state of affairs is a consequence of a general

principle of organization which may be called progressive mechaniza-
tion. At first, systems—biological, neurological, psychological or so-
cial—are governed by dynamic interaction of their components; later
on, fixed arrangements and conditions of constraint are established
which render the system and its parts more efficient, but also gradu-
ally diminish and eventually abolish its equipotentiality.[16]

9. Equifinality

Open systems are further characterized by the principle of equifinality, a
principle suggested by von Bertalanffy in 1940.[17] According to this principle, a system can reach the same final state from differing initial conditions
and by a variety of paths. The well-known biological experiments on the
sea urchin show that a normal creature of that species can develop from a
complete ovum, from each half of a divided ovum, or from the fusion product of two whole ova. As open systems move toward regulatory mechanisms
to control their operations, the amount of equifinality may be reduced.

SOME CONSEQUENCES OF VIEWING ORGANIZATIONS AS OPEN SYSTEMS

In the following chapter we shall inquire into the specific implications of
considering organizations as open systems and into the ways in which social organizations differ from other types of living systems. At this point,
however, we should call attention to some of the misconceptions which
arise both in theory and practice when social organizations are regarded as
closed rather than open systems.

The major misconception is the failure to recognize fully that the
organization is continually dependent upon inputs from the environment
and that the inflow of materials and human energy is not a constant. The
fact that organizations have built-in protective devices to maintain stability and that they are notoriously difficult to change in the direction of some
reformer's desires should not obscure the realities of the dynamic interrelationships of any social structure with its social and natural environment.
The very efforts of the organization to maintain a constant external environment produce changes in organizational structure. The reaction to
changed inputs to mute their possible revolutionary implications also results in changes.

The typical models in organization theorizing concentrate upon principles of internal functioning as if these problems were independent of
changes in the environment and as if they did not affect the maintenance
inputs of motivation and morale. Moves toward tighter integration and coordination are made to insure stability, when flexibility may be the more important requirement. Moreover, coordination and control become ends in
themselves rather than means to an end. They are not seen in full perspective

as adjusting the system to its environment but as desirable goals within a closed system. In fact, however, every attempt at coordination which is not functionally required may produce a host of new organizational problems.

One error which stems from this kind of misconception is the failure to recognize the equifinality of the open system, namely that there are more ways than one of producing a given outcome. In a closed physical system the same initial conditions must lead to the same final result. In open systems this is not true even at the biological level. It is much less true at the social level. Yet in practice we insist that there is one best way of assembling a gun for all recruits, one best way for the baseball player to hurl the ball in from the outfield and that we standardize and teach these best methods. Now it is true under certain conditions that there is one best way, but these conditions must first be established. The general principle, which characterizes all open systems, is that there does not have to be a single method for achieving an objective.

A second error lies in the notion that irregularities in the functioning of a system due to environmental influences are error variances and should be treated accordingly. According to this conception, they should be controlled out of studies of organizations. From the organization's own operations they should be excluded as irrelevant and should be guarded against. The decisions of officers to omit a consideration of external factors or to guard against such influences in a defensive fashion, as if they would go away if ignored, is an instance of this type of thinking. So is the now outmoded "public be damned" attitude of businessmen toward the clientele upon whose support they depend. Open system theory, on the other hand, would maintain that environmental influences are not sources of error variance but are integrally related to the functioning of a social system, and that we cannot understand a system without a constant study of the forces that impinge upon it.

Thinking of the organization as a closed system, moreover, results in a failure to develop the intelligence or feedback function of obtaining adequate information about the changes in environmental forces. It is remarkable how weak many industrial companies are in their market research departments when they are so dependent upon the market. The prediction can be hazarded that organizations in our society will increasingly move toward the improvements of the facilities for research in assessing environmental forces. The reason is that we are in the process of correcting our misconception of the organization as a closed system.

Emery and Trist have pointed out how current theorizing on organizations still reflects the older closed system conceptions. They write:

In the realm of social theory, however, there has been something of a tendency to continue thinking in terms of a "closed" system, that is, to regard the enterprise as sufficiently independent to allow most of its problems to be analyzed with reference to its internal structure and without reference to its external environment. . . . In practice the system theorists in social science . . . did "tend to focus on the statics of social structure and to neglect the study of structural change." In an attempt to overcome this bias, Merton suggested that "the concept of dysfunction, which implied the concept of strain, stress and tension on the structural level, provides an analytical approach to the study of dynamics and change." This concept has been widely accepted by system theorists but while it draws attention to sources of imbalance within an organization it does not conceptually reflect the mutual permeation of an organization and its environment that is the cause of such imbalance. It still retains the limiting perspectives of "closed system" theorizing. In the administrative field the same limitations may be seen in the otherwise invaluable contributions of Barnard and related writers.[18]

SUMMARY

The open-system approach to organizations is contrasted with common-sense approaches, which tend to accept popular names and stereotypes as basic organizational properties and to identify the purpose of an organization in terms of the goals of its founders and leaders.

The open-system approach, on the other hand, begins by identifying and mapping the repeated cycles of input, transformation, output, and renewed input which comprise the organizational pattern. This approach to organizations represents the adaptation of work in biology and in the physical sciences by von Bertalanffy and others.

Organizations as a special class of open systems have properties of their own, but they share other properties in common with all open systems. These include the importation of energy from the environment, the throughput or transformation of the imported energy into some product form which is characteristic of the system, the exporting of that product into the environment, and the reenergizing of the system from sources in the environment.

Open systems also share the characteristics of negative entropy, feedback, homeostasis, differentiation, and equifinality. The law of negative entropy states that systems survive and maintain their characteristic internal order only so long as they import from the environment more energy than they expend in the process of transformation and exportation. The feedback principle has to do with information input, which is a special kind of energic importation, a kind of signal to the system about environmental conditions and about the functioning of the system in relation to its environment. The feedback of such information enables the system to correct for its own malfunctioning or for changes in the environment, and thus to maintain a steady state or homeostasis. This is a dynamic rather than a static balance, however. Open systems are not at rest but tend toward differentiation and elaboration, both because of subsystem dynamics and because of the relationship between growth and survival. Finally, open systems are characterized by the principle of equifinality, which asserts that systems can reach the same final state from different initial conditions and by different paths of development.

Traditional organizational theories have tended to view the human organization as a closed system. This tendency had led to a disregard of differing organizational environments and the nature of organizational dependency on environment. It has led also to an over-concentration on principles of internal organizational functioning, with consequent failure to develop and understand the processes of feedback which are essential to survival.

Notes

1. Merton, R. K. 1957. *Social theory and social structure*. rev. ed. New York: Free Press.
2. von Bertalanffy, L. 1956. General System theory. *General Systems*. Yearbook of the Society for the Advancement of General System Theory, 1, 1–10.
3. Solomon, P., *et al.* (Eds.). 1961. *Sensory deprivation*. Cambridge, Mass.: Harvard University Press.
4. Spitz, R. A. 1945. Hospitalism: an inquiry into the genesis of psychiatric conditions in early childhood. *Psychoanalytic Study of the Child*, 1, 53–74.
5. Kohler, W., and H. Wallach. 1944. Figural after-effects: an investigation of visual processes. *Proceedings of the American Philosophical Society*, 88, 269–357. Also, Kohler, W., and D. Emery. 1947. Figural after-effects in the third dimension of visual space. *American Journal of Psychology*, 60, 159–201.
6. Melzack, R., and W. Thompson. 1956. Effects of early experience on social behavior. *Canadian Journal of Psychology*, 10, 82–90.
7. Allport, F. H. 1962. A structuronomic conception of behavior: individual and collective. I. Structural theory and the master problem of social psychology. *Journal of Abnormal and Social Psychology*, 64, 3–30.
8. Cohen, E. 1954. *Human behavior in the concentration camp*. London: Jonathan Cape.
9. Miller, J. G. 1955. Toward a general theory for the behavioral sciences. *American Psychologist*, 10, 513–531; quote from p. 529.
10. See, Bradley, D. F., and M. Calvin. 1956. Behavior: imbalance in a network of chemical transformations. *General Systems*. Yearbook of the Society for the Advancement of General System Theory, 1, 56–65.
11. Krech, D., and R. Crutchfield. 1948. *Theory and problems of social psychology*. New York: McGraw-Hill.

12. Stagner, R. 1951. Homeostasis as a unifying concept in personality theory. *Psychological Review*, 58, 5–17; quote from p. 5.
13. Lewin, K. 1947. Frontiers in group dynamics. *Human Relations*, 1, 5–41.
14. Miller, *op. cit.*
15. Haire, M. 1959. Biological models and empirical histories of the growth of organizations. In M. Haire (Ed.), *Modern organization theory*. New York: Wiley, 272–306.
16. von Bertalanffy. 1956, *op. cit*, p. 6.
17. von Bertalanffy, L. 1940. Der organismus als physikalisches system betrachtet. *Naturwissenschaften*. 28, 521 ff.
18. Emery, F. E., and E. L. Trist. 1960. Sociotechnical systems. In *Management sciences models and techniques*. Vol. 2, London: Pergamon Press; quote from p. 84.

4

The Transition to the 21st-Century Era (1980–): Development of the Client-Oriented Service Theme and the Eclectic Perspective

■ Introduction

This chapter discusses the fifth of the five themes—**Client-Oriented Service**. This theme had its beginning several decades before the turn of the century. After going through almost three decades of adjustments, it is the theme that continues to dominate today. Additionally, this period has fostered an **Eclectic Perspective**, an approach that encourages criminal justice administrators to have a through knowledge of the evolutionary concepts of administration. With this knowledge, they will be better able to apply the most appropriate approaches to any given situation. This is where the art and science of administration unite to provide the insight that criminal justice administrators require in meeting today's and tomorrow's challenges.

■ The Client-Oriented Service Era (the 1980s)

The focus on social equity in the 1970s set the stage for the next step, a step toward more public participation in government. More attention to customizing services to the individual needs of the public (clients) has become an integral component of this movement. Another essential ingredient of this theme is for management to treat employees as they would want the customers to be treated.

This period in the contextual development of administration came about partly because of trends in the private sector and partly because of a growing concern in the public sector. The private sector discovered that as businesses grew, their decision-making levels often became too distant from the client and the changing needs of the consumer. Public administrators, having developed a sense for public feedback during the Open Systems period, detected a growing dissatisfaction toward government services by the public. For example, public opinion surveys in 1982 showed that 56% of the public felt alienated from their government (Harmon & Mayer, 1986, p. 395). Americans showed their disenchantment with public services by voting for tax cuts and by supporting the privatization of a number of public responsibilities.

The citizenry perceived a failure of the bureaucracy to meet policy needs, especially at the local level. The public, exposed to the products of the "information boom," was becoming more opinionated and critical of the decisions of elected officials and public administrators. As they were becoming more demanding of services from the business world, they also were requiring public services to be more customized to their local needs.

The emphasis on citizen participation signaled a revived interest in the doctrine of participatory democracy promoted by Thomas Jefferson. Contributing factors to this revived interest in participatory democracy were the perceived (or real) failure of the bureaucracy to meet the service needs of the public and a growing feeling that the public knew more about what they needed than did the professional administrator.

Citizen participation is distinguished from the more common methods of public participation such as voting or local interest group activity. Forms of participation include citizen committees acting as advisory groups and even governing groups such as commissions, and individual citizens serving as staff members for public entities.

The desire for more citizen participation in controlling public services raised issues of accountability, efficiency, and administrative discretion. Public administrators often found themselves in a "marketplace" environment in which they competed for tax dollars and public support. Winning public support through better and more localized services meant the possibility of more tax revenue.

This "marketplace" approach often was called "public choice economics." Supporters of public choice economics took the view that the public agencies of the day acted as monopolies and were institutionally incapable of representing the demands of individual citizens. Because the citizens are consumers of government goods and services, the responsiveness of public agencies to their needs could be enhanced by creating a market system for governmental activities based on the microeconomic theory. In this market system, the public would be given a choice between free-enterprise economics and competing services. Even though public choice economics never really caught on, it did force the public sector to be more sensitive to the individual needs of the public and provide services in a more client-oriented manner.

Toffler's Three Wave Model, as he presented it in the early 1980s, shows the major issue of interest to mankind during each of three periods of history. As Toffler put it, the major interest at any given time is about what the majority of people spend most of their waking hours concerned about. For several thousand years, it was the production of agricultural goods for personal consumption. As mankind learned to mechanize, the interest in agricultural activities shifted toward a second "wave," which created the Industrial Revolution. This period lasted several hundred years.

The "third wave" came as people learned to automate and apply new technology to industrial functions. Toffler said that the "third wave" may last only a decade or two and that its major issue would center on information and technology. Information and technology was to be the main source of employment in the 1980s as agriculture and industry had been to the earlier "waves."

As we entered the 21st century, it could be seen that information and technology had not become the major source of employment. Current U.S. Census statistics substantiate the Toffler model's depiction of the decline of agriculture and industrial employment; however, service occupations have become the main sources of employment, rather than information and technology.

Dual-occupation families require others to support their lifestyles with services that once were performed by family members. Service occupations also include specialties that today's public believe it needs to support its quality of living. The "information boom" has brought into everyone's home, through the electronic and automated media, images of more and better standards of living. Consequently, the public expects and demands better service.

Service includes many kinds of employment. Service industries include communications, transportation, vacation destinations, entertainment, health care, consulting, financial and legal assistance, and insurance providers. Service also includes the major work activities of all federal, state, county, city, and town employees, including all criminal justice services.

Toffler's model can now be viewed in retrospect. Each "wave" contains a physical element that supports the major interest of the day. Information and technology best fit in this category for the "third wave," as did land in the agricultural period and energy in the industrial period. Today, Toffler's model can be viewed as:

The Three Waves of Society in Retrospect
Major Elements of Enterprise

Historical periods	Physical elements	Human elements
Agricultural	Land	Muscle
Industrial	Energy	Hands
Service	Information/ technology	Mind

Each "wave" also includes human elements that support the major occupations of the period. In the "agricultural wave," human muscle was needed to till the land. In the "industrial wave," human hands were needed to work the conveyer-line, piecemeal work. Today, service occupations require more use of people's minds to convert information into knowledge. Successful occupations are service-orientated, make productive use of information and technology, and encourage their employees and customers to become thinking contributors to the organization's goals.

Service does not merely mean personalized, courteous assistance. If it did, self-service pumps at the automobile gas stations and cut-rate department stores would not have proliferated during this period. Service means being client-oriented and providing what people perceive they need to maintain a good quality of life and to support their chosen lifestyles.

The development of neighborhood private postal businesses serves as an example of what many people apparently perceive as service-oriented. Many people are willing to pay more for a service provided by the private sector that spares them long waits in line and is offered at hours that are more conducive to current lifestyles than those services provided by the government. The proliferation of these private businesses, in turn, has caused the government services to become more customer-oriented.

■ Historical Setting for the Period

The era began with a new president, Ronald Reagan. The Equal Employment Opportunity Commission was expanded to include sexual harassment. Sex discrimination was now prohibited by the Civil Rights Act. Employers were required to provide a place of work that was free of sexual harassment or intimidation. The Supreme Court also ruled that Congress had the authority to use racial quotas to remedy past discrimination. President Reagan fired 11,500 air controllers for going on strike in violation of federal law in 1981. In 1982, the President's Private Sector Survey on Cost Control found widespread inefficiencies in the federal government.

In 1983, the birthday of Martin Luther King Jr. was declared a national holiday. The American Society for Public Administration adopted a Code of Ethics in 1984 that made the protection of the rights of *all* people a public responsibility. The Supreme Court ruled that courts could not interfere with seniority systems to protect newly hired minority employees from layoff. In 1985, the Gramm-Rudman-Hollings Act was made law in an effort to balance the federal budget by mandating across-the-board cuts over a period of years. In 1988, George H. W. Bush was elected president. In the 1990s, Bill Clinton was elected to the presidency, signaling the beginning of a more liberal era. The economy improved and unemployment and crime dropped to a 20-year low.

The beginning years of the 21st century saw a continuing decrease in crime until 2005, when violent crime started to again rise. The national economy that had been strong during the 1990s began to falter, with increases in interest rates. The terrorist attack of September 11, 2001, followed by the "Global War on Terrorism," certainly altered the focus of public service, particularly the service of criminal justice agencies.

These are a few of the events that were occurring as the Client-Oriented Service theme took shape.

Client-Oriented Service Milestones

1982: Thomas J. Peters and Robert H. Waterman Jr., *In Search of Excellence*

Peters and Waterman studied 62 companies in the private sector, which were identified as well-managed businesses that successfully achieved their objectives. Some of the companies analyzed were IBM, 3M, McDonald's, and Delta Airlines.

Peters and Waterman identified eight interrelated criteria, or characteristics, that were common to all the companies. Each of these factors was found to be a critical part of what created excellence in these organizations. The eight characteristics are:

1. **A Bias for Action.** Companies exhibiting this established an organizational attitude for action. They had a healthy preference for doing something, anything, rather than sending a concept or question through cycles and cycles of analyses and committee reports. They created a proactive, progressive stance within the organization. "Do it, fix it, try it" was a motto coined by Peters and Waterman that exemplified this characteristic.

2. **Close to the Customer.** This attribute called for listening intently and regularly to the customer and providing quality service and reliability in response to the needs of customers. These companies established a total commitment to those they served.

3. **Autonomy and Entrepreneurship.** Innovation and practical risk-taking was found to be a common activity of people at all levels in these organizations. These agencies often divided their structures into small sections and encouraged the employees in each section to think independently and competitively.

4. **Productivity through People.** Employees were regarded as the source of quality and productivity improvements. Creating in all employees the awareness that their best efforts were essential and that they would share in the rewards of success were emphasized.

5. **Hands-On, Value-Driven.** A well-defined basic philosophy was clearly articulated to employees. These companies insisted that the executives/managers keep in touch with the organization's essential business.

6. **Sticking to the Knitting.** These businesses remained focused on what they knew best and drew their strength from it.

7. **Simple Form, Lean Staff.** These businesses were simple structural forms and systems and the corporate staffs were relatively small.

8. **Simultaneous Loose/Tight Properties.** These businesses fostered and maintained an organizational climate in which there was dedication to the central values of the company. This was combined with tolerance for all employees who accepted those values and autonomy in the workplace was encouraged.

Peters and Waterman pointed out that excellence does not mean perfection. Excellent agencies should readily admit to mistakes and ask for assistance if necessary. Constant sensitivity to the outer environment that impacts the organization, and ongoing reevaluation of the internal environment of the organization are necessary in obtaining excellence.

One major point to consider when applying Peters and Waterman's findings to the public sector is how and when the agencies were created. Most of the 62 companies examined in this work were founded on a client-oriented philosophy and many were created in recent years. The founders recruited, hired, trained, fired, and rewarded based on a client-service orientation. In contrast, public managers most often deal with long-established organizational cultures with long-standing values and customs. Consequently, employee attitude changes may take considerable time. A point to remember, however, is that the best time to implant the values of "excellence" is on those infrequent occasions when new public agencies are being created.

1984: George P. Barbour, *Excellence in Local Government*

Following the lead of Peters and Waterman, Barbour and his colleagues at the Center for Excellence in Local Government discussed the principles described in *In Search of Excellence* as they might apply to the public sector. They found that in many instances the private sector characteristic of excellence had to be modified when applied to public agencies.

Politics and its control on public resources was found to be one significant difference in applying these approaches. The Peters and Waterman theories were modified by Barbour and his colleagues to meet local government requirements:

1. Action Orientation. Excellent local government agencies identify problems and deal with them quickly, fighting through structural, political, legal, and environmental constraints that make action more difficult than in the private sector.

2. Closeness to the Citizenry. This criterion includes establishing and maintaining a variety of close links with citizens who are served by the local agency—including those who are regulated against their will. Excellent local governments listen, and are sensitive and responsive to public input.

3. Autonomy and Entrepreneurship. Develop climates conducive to conceiving ideas and doing new things to solve problems. They have a track record for implementing creative solutions, even in the face of declining resources.

4. Employee Orientation. Excellent public agencies treat employees as adult human beings.

5. Values. Defining a set of values is important to excellent public agencies. Being the best by providing the highest quality service to the community must be institutionalized. As these goals are communicated regularly and positively to employees, enthusiasm and pride result.

6. **Mission, Goals, and Competence.** Excellent local governments have evaluated their mission based on changing resources and citizen demands. They have modified goals to achieve consistent and uniform service levels.

7. **Structure.** A firm central direction is displayed, whereas antiquated bureaucratic structures have been eliminated. There are fewer management levels and smaller support staff.

8. **Political Relationships.** In addition to the characteristics found by Peters and Waterman in the private sector, public agencies must be keenly aware of local political relationships. Managers and policy makers must be "tuned in" to, and maintain a working relationship with, the political environment.

This work made the Peters and Waterman book more relevant to the public sector.

1987: Jan Carlzon, *Moments of Truth*

Jan Carlzon wrote about his approach in making the Scandinavian Airlines System (SAS) a successful client-oriented business. When Carlzon took over SAS in 1981, the company was in the midst of compiling a loss of $20 million, its second straight losing year. Morale was low, employees were being laid off, service was being substantially reduced, and the market for passenger and freight services was stagnant. Carlzon immediately set out to make SAS "the best airline in the world for the frequent business traveler." He invested $45 million to upgrade every detail of service for the business traveler, while cutting nearly as much from programs directed at tourists.

The most important change, however, was in the way in which he treated the employees and customers. His approach centered on what he called "moments of truth," which he defined as "any time a customer comes into contact with some part of the organization (employees) and they judge the quality of service in the organization." That is the moment that creates in the customer the support or nonsupport for the agency (Carlzon, 1987, p. 6).

It does no good to have service-oriented mission statements posted on every wall. What makes the difference is how the employees treat the customers in every employee-customer contact. In order for employees to provide customer-oriented contacts, they must be treated in a like manner by management. If employees are treated well by management, then they will be more likely to do the same for customers.

Carlzon believed that for SAS to improve, it had to be successful in each of its daily 50,000 "moments of truth." This meant turning the organizational chart upside down. No longer were middle managers to spend their time making sure that instructions were followed. Now, they were to support the frontline employees who had direct contact with customers, enabling them to make decisions and solve problems on the spot. Carlzon moved decision making down to the frontline and empowered frontline employees to make the decisions that tailored services to customer needs.

As a result, SAS returned to profitability the next year. Two years later, in 1983, SAS won the Air Transport World's Airline of the Year award, and in 1986 it received that magazine's Passenger Service award.

Carlzon's work stands as an example of an unsuccessful agency being turned around through a customer-oriented service approach. The "moments of truth" concept certainly has application to the public sector and consequently has made its way into the approaches being used by forward-thinking government managers.

One major distinction between the environment at SAS and that found in most public agencies related to financing. Carlzon was able to gain a commitment from his Board of Directors for millions of dollars to improve conditions for his employees. This was at a time when there were many layoffs in the air travel industry. Part of Carlzon's success can be credited to the support that he was able to obtain from his employees, who saw an immediate positive impact on their job security and benefits.

Seldom are substantial funds available in the public sector that can be used to enhance the working conditions of the employees. Judging from Carlzon's experience, however, on those rare occasions when new public resources are available that can have a positive impact on the welfare of government employees, strides can be made in changing the worker's attitudes and the organization culture. These rare occasions should be viewed as excellent opportunities to enhance public service.

More often, however, public managers will have to deal with tight budgets. Consequently, culture changes will come at a much slower pace than that experienced by Carlzon.

1989: Tom Peters, *Excellence in the Public Sector*

Peters's work is an extension of *In Search of Excellence*, but it was dedicated to the public sector. It was produced as a video and workbook rather than a textbook (video publications have become more prevalent in the dynamic and growing field of education). Peters analyzed "excellence" in five public agencies and defined the key factors that contributed to their client-oriented and employee participation management approaches.

The first case study was of the Alameda Naval Depot in California, which found ways to repair airplanes with recycled parts and saved the taxpayers $22 million. Here Peters found:

- Accountability was a function of employees feeling ownership at all levels of the organization.
- Good management was a two-way process; top-down/bottom-up policy ensured communication and efficiency.
- Trust was an integral part of successful management. Trusted employees contributed more and derived greater satisfaction from the job.
- Empowerment at all levels was a function of trust and accountability.
- There was such a thing as too many rules; overregulation did not engender efficiency.

Peters's next study involved the Department of Juvenile Justice in New York City, a public agency that was able to return 1,000 juvenile offenders to school in one year and dramatically reduce recidivism. He found the key points of success for this institution were:

- Having a clear mission that employees supported.
- Creating an atmosphere in which bad news is welcomed and rethinking is an art.
- Celebrating small "wins."
- Promoting creativity and risk-taking.
- Empowering the staff. The director's job was to provide the environment and resources to support the employees.
- Having a clear agenda and communicating the organization's vision to the employees.
- Feeling free to take ideas from elsewhere. Case management often was used in social services but was an innovation when used in a juvenile detention facility.

Peters next used the city government of Phoenix, Arizona, as a case study. Key factors found there were:

- Participative management that ensured input at all levels of city government.
- Customer service as the hallmark of a well-run city.
- Citizen input and expectations have a direct effect on the bottom line.
- Quality is a necessary focus at every level of government.
- Listening to the employees; the person closest to the job is the best resource.

The National Theatre Workshop for the Handicapped in New York City was Peters's next case study. The theater had been able to increase its budget substantially through aggressive fund-raising. The people in this public agency recognized the importance of self-definition and fiscal responsibility as the cornerstone of success in the world of nonprofit organizations. Important findings included:

- Self-definition: knowing your "niche" and concentrating on your individuality.
- Incremental growth: overexpansion is fatal to nonprofit organizations.
- The vision of the leader must be converted into a system supported and understood by all those responsible for success.

Peters's final study involved the Ochoco Forest Service in Oregon; its worker productivity increased 60% in two years with a fiscal year savings of $250,000. Here, Peters found a flattening of the organization structure with everyone contributing to "debureaucratization."

One innovation was the "Groo" award. Groo, a forestry technician land worker, proposed that every employee be given authority to give awards to fellow employees. Consequently, management gave every employee a voucher for

$25 to use for an award for anyone in the organization. In the first year, 148 awards were handed out, giving employees a new way to feel good about their jobs and to feel empowered to improve the productivity of the entire organization. Key findings included:

- If trusted and empowered, people do their jobs better and more efficiently.
- Bureaucracy can become more responsive if management listens to its online people.
- Employee freedom does not create chaos: it brings better systems at appreciable savings.

Peters's work provides a good analysis of how many of the private sector findings can be successfully applied to the public sector and how employee empowerment is essential to promoting Client-Oriented Service.

Transition Milestones

1983: Deil S. Wright, *Understanding Intergovernmental Relations*

Wright provided an approach to understanding national-state-local relationships. He assessed intergovernmental conditions during the 1960s and 1970s as an era of tension and conflict. He described intense competition among policies, programs, and funding. Wright depicted the 1980s as "calculative" and concerned with strategies to cope with severe fiscal restraints, loss of public confidence, and loss of federal support. Wright's work exemplified the need for a more Integrated Knowledge approach to solving very complex public issues while facing dwindling resources.

1986: Michael M. Harmon and Richard T. Mayer, *Organizational Theory for Public Administration*

Harmon and Mayer provide a comprehensive study of the theories that support the field of public administration. They describe how six types of current theories illuminate different aspects of public administration. The six perspectives are:

1. Baseline or neoclassical theories (that relate to the Organization Functions period and the Hierarchy of Public Administration)
2. Human relations theories (that relate to the Employee Relations period)
3. Systems theories (that relate to the Open Systems period)
4. Market or public choice theories (that relate to the Client-Oriented Service period)
5. Interpretive and critical theories (that relate to the Eclectic Perspective) and
6. Emergence theories (that relate to the future)

Harmon and Mayer, although mainly concerned with organization theory, direct attention to the need to take a more eclectic approach to the study and practice of public administration.

Client-Oriented Period Summary

An emphasis on Client-Oriented Service is very much a part of criminal justice administration today. A continuing problem is a deficiency in tax revenues to support public agencies, which relates to a deficiency in support from the public. Public support is built on public trust and satisfaction. Public trust and satisfaction can be enhanced through more participation by community members in public service. When the public takes an active role in public affairs, they are more inclined to share in the responsibility for providing the desired level of service. They also gain a more realistic perspective of the operations of public agencies and can better judge when an increase in tax revenue is justified.

An example, as described in the next chapter, is law enforcement's objective of reducing crime and providing for a safe community environment. The most effective method of achieving this objective is by improving neighborhood quality of life. This improvement can not be achieved without substantial community participation. Police departments across the nation are pursuing a more client/community-oriented approach to providing their services in an effort to gain police/community partnerships. These partnerships can increase public support of law enforcement as well as help achieve better quality of life.

The Transition Milestones described in this section provide examples of how the theories and concepts of the earlier periods in the contextual development of administration themes point the way for a more Eclectic Perspective, which is the subject of the next section.

■ The Eclectic Perspective

Within the Contextual Themes Model, the Eclectic Perspective is presented as a "lens" through which themes, theories, and concepts are focused on current and future criminal justice administrative issues. It represents an understanding that all the themes compose a spectrum of theories and concepts from which to draw in confronting contemporary issues. This perspective has been important throughout the history of criminal justice administration. However, because of the current and future multitudinous and increasingly diverse public issues (many of which are described in later chapters), this perspective is critical to the development of contemporary criminal justice administrative responses.

The Eclectic Perspective component of the Contextual Themes Model is not to be construed as the emerging theme. The next theme will probably be named in retrospect. As presented in the previous section of this chapter (discussing the inaccuracy of Toffler's Three Wave Model in predicting the future), models are best used in retrospect and the unity of the information they provide should be reflected on for direction in designing the future.

It was Karl Weick who put forth the "natural selection" theory of organizing on which he based the belief that organizational purposes and goals typically are discovered retrospectively. Organizational trend discovery, according to Weick, is largely a sense-making activity performed subsequent to action, which is usually spontaneous and unplanned (Weick, 1979, p. 194). Consequently, no claim is being made here that in the future the Eclectic Perspective concept retrospectively will be called the theme of this period.

Eclectic Perspective, rather, is the approach from which the direction for the future of criminal justice administration may best emanate. Just as information and technology have been the driving force behind the service industry, so can the Eclectic Perspective serve to help focus on the next theme in the contextual development of criminal justice administration.

The essence of an Eclectic Perspective is the understanding that most of the theories and concepts from the past serve as a reservoir of information from which to draw. The appropriate theories and concepts drawn on depend on the situation at hand. Many years ago, Mary Parker Follett pointed toward this direction of thinking with her "law of the situation" (Metcalf & Urwick, 1940, p. 65). Follett's idea was that responsible action is linked to the emergence of collective purpose, which depends on the current situation as perceived by the participants (Metcalf & Urwick, p. 65).

Each period in the contextual development provides a theme. These themes provide categories of theories and concepts that should be considered when confronting current and future criminal justice administration issues.

The Eclectic Perspective includes an understanding that the movement into a new theme period does not signal the end of the development of theories and concepts of the earlier theme(s). Rather, the theme of the new period only emphasizes the major interest of practitioners and academicians of that period. Although original theories are being developed around the major theme of the period, many theories and concepts of earlier periods are being altered and enhanced.

The Eclectic Perspective approach provides a means by which today's criminal justice administrators may select from a wide array of theories and concepts to meet current needs. This requires a type of management approach, which Fred Fiedler called "contingency leadership." Fiedler developed a contingency leadership model based on four factors that he recommended for consideration when selecting the appropriate theories and concepts to meet the needs of the current situation. They are (1) leadership style, (2) task structure, (3) group atmosphere, and (4) the leader's position of power. The first factor identifies the motivational aspects of the leader; the other three describe the situation (Fiedler, 1967, p. 37).

Szilagyi and Wallace supported the need for an Eclectic Perspective approach in their writings on "situational theories." They said that the most effective leadership approach is a dynamic and flexible process that adapts to the particular situation. They also listed four factors to consider when deciding on appropriate theories and concepts to meet the current situation. The factors are (1) managerial characteristics, (2) subordinate characteristics, (3) group structure and the nature of the task, and (4) organizational factors such as the leader's power base, established policies and whether an immediate decision must be made or whether there is a high level of tension and stress involved in the situation at hand (Szilagyi & Wallace, 1983, p. 273).

These authors, however, concluded that although an administrator's style has an important effect on subordinate behavior, the "use of positive rewards may have the strongest influence on the behavior and attitudes of employees." Rewards such as merit pay increases, bonuses, or praise may have the greatest and most permanent impact on the activities and behavior of workers, according to contemporary studies (Szilagyi & Wallace, 1983, pp. 287–288). The ability of criminal justice administrators to provide pay and bonus increases depends on financial support, thus increasing or decreasing financial support can have a bearing on the motivation of employees.

The following major milestones are contemporary works that emphasize the need for an Eclectic Perspective in meeting today's public sector challenges.

Eclectic Perspective Major Milestones

1990: Jeffrey D. Straussman, *Public Administration*

Straussman's 1990 publication is the second edition of this book. This work brings together many of the theories and practices that should be considered in meeting today's public sector challenges. Straussman points out that the public administrator can no longer easily separate the private and public sectors because they have (and will continue to) become increasingly intertwined.

The same holds true of the various levels of government. According to the author, understanding the complexity of intergovernmental and public-private associations is indispensable for effective public management in today's world (Straussman, 1990, p. ix). Straussman's description of the intertwining of private and public sector functions provides evidence that a public-private partnership approach may become a theme for the 1990s.

Included in his presentation of issues for public administrators is information on unions and collective bargaining; how information processing and the communication technology are tied to decision making; and includes a special emphasis on ethics and commitment to protecting the rights of all people. This work demonstrates the multifaceted approaches that public administrators must take to cope with the many current and future complex issues.

1991: Richard J. Stillman II, Preface to *Public Administration: A Search for Themes and Direction*

Stillman takes on the task of discussing what the scope and substance of public administrative theory is in America today. He offers a broad but definitive perspective of the field by presenting a way of looking at the principles and methods of public service that unites them with the evolving theories and concepts of the past.

By way of analyzing what is currently being taught as public administration in universities, Stillman paints a vivid picture of the Eclectic Perspective. He points out the diversity in graduate education that is necessary to meet the differing needs of the various levels of government and the many types of professions involved in public service. He gives the following example:

> *Furthermore, there are the comprehensive programs, which view pubic administration broadly as a general focus of study. Large public administration programs, housed in free-standing autonomous schools, such as at the University of Southern California, offer under one roof a wide range of public administration programs that combine a diversity of educational approaches in politics, management, and/or policy. Faculty size, institutional resources, student diversity, and even geographic diversity (in the case of USC) allow for the comprehensive program to offer students a variety of specializations within the MPA degree.*

USC's MPA, much like other MPA degrees, ostensibly aims "to provide creative, high-quality education for public sector personnel," but because USC runs public-service educational programs at three campuses (in Los Angeles, Sacramento, and Washington, DC), the USC program can draw on as well as respond to a broader type of student interests and backgrounds for an MPA degree. The USC downtown Washington Public Affairs Center offers a series of MPA classes geared directly to the functional needs of a practicing federal manager with class titles covering such topics as federal management systems; problems in R&D administration; seminar in intergovernmental management from the national perspective; public financial management; project management theory, practice and realities; acquisitions management; and defense management and national security.

These topics are more directly focused on the salient issues that confront modern federal managers working in the Nation's Capitol, and they are frequently taught by knowledgeable, well-respected practitioners from the Washington, DC, government community.

Furthermore, at times USC can supplement these instructors with regular faculty from its other two campuses and even classes at locations and times convenient for busy public managers (for example, in weekend intensives). (Stillman, 1991, pp. 160–161)

Stillman goes on to describe how those without previous public employment experience, at the Los Angeles main campus or in Sacramento, can select broader, more traditional public administrative subjects. He points out how considerable latitude for mixing and matching courses allows students to tailor programs to prepare them for the challenges that they will confront in the variety of public sector jobs to which they aspire.

1991: J. Steven Ott, Albert C. Hyde, and Jay M. Shafritz, *Public Management: The Essential Readings*

These editors assembled a number of important writings that contribute to today's Eclectic Perspective approach. In addition to current approaches to budgeting and financial management, planning and control, and administrative rationality and accountability, they present leading articles on public management in transition with insight into problems of government overmanagement, the changing responsibilities of the federal government, and the changing public/private sector relationship.

This work emphasizes that public managers must develop a research agenda to advance the management of public sector organizations and to develop critical planning, evaluation, and other management skills on a macro scale. They point out that there has been very little development of a research perspective for public management. The research that does exist is almost entirely of micro focus. It has been based on micro issues such as administration dichotomy, scientific management, management sciences, principles of management, and operations research. A major thesis of this work is that to be successful in meeting current public sector demands a much broader perspective is required. The editors wrote:

> *If public management is not to base its case solely on the values of efficiency and rationality, then what values should shape it and guide its purposes, objectives, and methods in the twenty-first century? In the early 1990s performance is perhaps the dominant theme, but it is only a theme. For all the words devoted to "excellence" in the 1980s, one can never be sure where the marketing of image and product or public relations leaves off and actual, sustained commitment to change begins.* (Ott, Hyde, & Shafritz, 1991, p. xvi)

This is the real agenda for public management; balancing political, economic, and social concerns for equity, ethics, and fairness, as well as integrating perspectives for bettering "the public good" in complex, highly diverse, competitive and inequitable environments. Public management must continue to seek ways to be proactive on behalf of humankind while avoiding administrative errors in a very chaotic world.

This book exemplifies how broad an Eclectic Perspective should be and what therefore is required of contemporary public managers.

■ Conversional Milestones

The following milestones are works that have altered, enhanced, and extended previously developed theories and concepts. For ease of understanding, they are grouped in relationship to the periods in the contextual development of administration theories. As might be expected, there are more works relating to the older theories and concepts because of the greater length of time from their inception. The greater the length of time for analysis and use by scholars and practitioners, the more there will be written to alter and enhance the original theories and concepts.

Organization Functions

1947: Herbert Simon, "The Proverbs of Public Administration"

Herbert Simon took a position of major dissent against the idea that there existed immutable principles of organization. He said that scientific studies of organizations require an understanding of the values, goals, and personalities of the inner culture.

He argued that Gulick and Urwick's POSDCORB (see Chapter 2) did not necessarily lead to efficiency. He developed a theory of rational choice and a fact/value distinction (consequences-preferences) and took a position that appropriate factual and value premises are required. "Decisions are made in the mind." Mental choices are limited because complete and absolute knowledge of all the data in a given situation is seldom available.

He advised public administrators to concentrate on behavioral issues (such as the decision to participate) and the limits of administrative rationality instead of concentrating on so-called management principles. His work is a reminder that the "principles" of the first theme of public administration can be used as guides but are not rules.

1981: Frederick C. Thayer, *An End to Hierarchy and Competition: Administration in the Post-Affluent World*

In his controversial book, Thayer proposed a radical new world based on a noncoercive theory of organization to replace contemporary theories of politics, economics, and organization. He urged the elimination of (1) political democracy, as predicated on the ideas of representation and voting; (2) economic competition; and (3) hierarchy. In place, he offered a form of social, economic, and political organization that he called "structured non-hierarchy," in which no decision is made without the agreement of all those impacted by it.

Thayer argues that existing modes of organizations are impossible to sustain and are not worth sustaining in view of the current social world. His work provides a direction from which others followed in an effort to modernize organization theories.

1981: Alberto Guerreiro Ramos, "Theory of Social Systems Delimitation: A Paradigmatic Statement"

Alberto Ramos took a less drastic position than Thayer regarding hierarchy organizations. Ramos argued that bureaucratic organizations are indispensable requirements for our material survival: the best that can be done is to attempt to limit their influence by separating them from other domains of social life.

1982: David Hampton, Charles Summer, and Ross Webber, *Organizational Behavior and the Practice of Management*

This text provides many of the updates that have been added to past theories and concepts. For example, the "hierarchy of objectives" is emphasized as the process of translating a basic organizational objective into contributing subsidiary objectives for departments within the organization. The authors quoted Peter Drucker in suggesting that organizations require objectives in every area where performance is necessary to survival. They define these objectives "as distinguished from pontification, philosophies, or vague hopes"—they are, rather, solid commitments with the following characteristics:

1. They are specific.
2. They are reality-oriented.
3. Their achievement can be verified.
4. They specify the time they will be achieved (Hampton, Summer, & Webber, 1982, pp. 373–375).

"Management by Objectives" (MBO) is described as having five key steps:

1. Supervisors must provide subordinates with a framework that reflects the purpose and objectives of the organization.
2. Subordinates then propose objectives for themselves within the provided framework.
3. Supervisors and subordinates discuss, modify, and agree on a set of objectives for subordinates.
4. Subordinates review their own progress and describe it periodically to supervisors.
5. The sequence is repeated as necessary.

The authors also described some of the difficulties that inhibited the success of MBO. (They quote from a 1974 *Fortune 500* study, which indicated that, although nearly half of the 500 largest corporations used MBO, less than 10% said that it was successful). Some of the inhibitors were burdensome procedures, lack of management support, overemphasis on results as distinguished from the processes and methods by which results are achieved, and authoritarian administration with illusory participation of subordinates.

In summary, they reported that MBO is an enhancement to planning and controlling that can improve motivation and performances by employees. However, the process is often imperfectly implemented, producing complaints of burdensome requirements, and is lacking in emphasis on the necessary cooperation that must exist between organizational units, groups and individual employees.

Chapter 9 in their book describes some of the more contemporary theories of organization design. The authors pointed out that the current organization design purposes center on achieving excellence in specializations while achieving technical coordination and human cooperation. One organizational structure that is replacing the hierarchy is the "matrix organization."

The matrix structure contravenes the universally accepted rule that workers must have only one boss. It evolved from the need for an organization choice between the project and the functional forms. With the escalating trend of complexity and uncertainty in a changing world, the need grew for multifocused management and lower-level decision making. The use of task forces and the increased flexibility of worker assignment seemed suited to a matrix design. The authors concluded by writing:

> *The matrix is a far cry from the organizations most managers have read about and idealized. Clean lines of authority; unambiguous re-*

source allocation to each problem or goal; clear boundaries sepa-
rating jobs, divisions, organizations, and loyalties are all part of that
simpler life that we need to forsake in a dynamic world of overlap-
ping and contradictory interests and goals. (Hampton, Summer, &
Webber, 1982, p. 551).

1986: Cole Graham Jr. and Steven Hays, "Management Functions and Public Administration—POSDCORB Revisited"

Graham and Hays contend that POSDCORB (Luther Gulick's 1937 acronym for planning, organizing, staffing, directing, coordinating, reporting, and budgeting) remains the most relevant statement of the functions of public managers. They acknowledge, however, that the meaning of this acronym needs to be updated. They refer to Garson and Overman (1983), who suggested a new acronym, PAFHRIER, to reflect more of the public administration issues: Policy Analysis, Financial management, Human Resources management, Information management, and External Relations. These are the issues that have emerged in the more recent theoretical and practical thinking in the field. With this acronym in mind, Graham and Hays recommend the following enhancements to Gulick's description of management:

- Expansion of the planning concept to the broader policy analysis concept.
- Expansion of the staffing concept to the broader human-resources concept.
- Expansion of the neglected reporting concept to the broader information-management concept.
- Addition of external relations as a major category.
- Dispersion of the POSDCORB categories, especially organizing, directing, and coordinating, for use as aspects of the new PAFHRIER (Graham & Hays, 1986, p. 14).

This work presents insight into how a well-known previous organization function theory can be modified and applied to today's public sector issues.

Employee Relations

1961: Rensis Likert, *New Patterns of Management*

Likert proposed the "Integrating Principle" and subsequently called it "System 4" after conducting several hundred studies of organizations. He found a number of factors that contributed to successful management.

For example, he found that high-producing managers tend to differ from mediocre and low-producing managers. They tend to foster favorable attitudes toward all aspects of the job from their workers and promote an effectively functioning social system within the organization. Measurements of performance primarily are used for self-guidance, but the highest-producing managers use all the technical resources of the classical theories of management.

The general pattern of highly motivated, cooperative workers appears to be a central characteristic of the newer management systems developed by the higher-producing managers. They more often think of employees as "human beings" instead of entities used to achieve work goals. Their attitude toward subordinates is perceived favorably by subordinates and their direction of work is characterized by employees as fair and equitable.

Successful managers employ the principle of supportive relationships, which means that all members understand and support the mission of the organization and see their job as contributing not only to the mission but to their personal worth and growth. These managers develop methods of gaining direct evidence of what subordinates think and attempt to see things through the eyes of their employees.

The use of work groups is essential in making full use of the capacities of employees. In high-producing organizations, employees view themselves as individual members of highly effective work groups with high performance goals. Linking these work groups to the overall organization is accomplished through people, whom Likert calls "linking pins," who hold overlapping group memberships.

Effective group decision making is one of the productive results of work groups. Likert, however, found that responsibility and situational requirements limit the effectiveness of group decision making and "suboptimization" is reduced when group decision making is utilized.

1964: Chris Argyris, *Integrating the Individual and the Organization*

Chris Argyris was a contemporary of McGregor and in this work describes the problem of the individual's relationship to the organization. Argyris sees tension between the individual and the organization more as a product of the formal organization's requirements for specialization and rationality than of its authoritarian management practices.

Argyris cites specialization as requiring a person to use only a few of his or her abilities. He wrote that the more specialized the task the simpler the ability required of the employee. This, he said, was counter to the human tendency to want more complex, interesting jobs. Similarly, hierarchical authority suppresses the need for autonomy and self-direction, which Argyris said characterizes mature employees. He concluded that a principal task of management is to provide job enlargement, greater employee participation in decision making, and other such practices that will help satisfy the personal needs of workers.

1966: Warren G. Bennis, *Changing Organizations*

Bennis disagreed with Argyris's optimistic vision of human nature. He sided more with what Douglas McGregor called the "tragic view," namely, that the best that one can hope for is to achieve a satisfactory resolution between the competing claims of the individual and the organization levels. Bennis faulted Argyris for advocating participative management and job enrichment practices. Bennis favored recognizing that trading, negotiating, and accommodating are necessary in gaining real integration of employee and organization goals.

Bennis wrote:

> As for my own belief, I, like Machiavelli, hold that man is both good and evil and that certain conditions in the organization will accentuate the expression of one or the other. Man's goodness and/or badness, this ambivalence, is part of the human condition and, as such, has to be considered in any theory of organization. (Bennis, 1966, p. 74)

1968: Frederick C. Mosher, *Democracy and the Public Service*

Mosher spotlighted the fact that although public institutions were to uphold the principles of democracy, adhering to such principles internally may cause results that are contrary to the public purpose of the organization. He wrote:

> There has already developed a great deal of collegian decision-making in many public agencies, particularly those which are largely controlled by single professional groups. But I would point out that democracy within administration, if carried to the fullest, raises a logical dilemma in its relation to political democracy. All public organizations are presumed to have been established and to operate for public purposes—i.e., purposes of the people. They are authorized, legitimized, empowered, and usually supported by authorities outside of themselves or broad purposes initially determined outside of themselves. To what extent, then, should insiders, the officers and employees, be able to modify their purposes, their organizational arrangements, and their means of support? It is entirely possible that internal administrative democracy might run counter to the principles and objectives of political democracy in which the organizations of government are viewed as instruments of public purpose (Mosher, 1969, p. 18)

Mosher pointed to caution when considering overreliance on participative management approaches in the public sector.

1973: Victor H. Vroom, *Organizational Dynamics*

In considering participative management approaches, Vroom developed a normative model to assist managers in deciding how much involvement employees should have in decision making. He described a set of rules for matching the manager's leadership behavior to the demands of the situation and defines the classes of outcomes that have a direct bearing on the ultimate effectiveness of decisions.

From this, he provided a seven-question decision tree to diagnose a given situation and to recommend the appropriate managerial style. The recommended management style indicates how much employee participation is needed to achieve the desired goals in the given situation. Variables of the model involve diagnostic questions about how much acceptance of the decision by subordinates is critical for effective implementation, and how much information is already available to the decision maker.

1984: A. W. McEachern, *Organizational Illusions*

McEachern reflects on and analyses many of the principles and assumptions that have governed public administration and presents them in a way that exposes how some have caused distorted thinking about modern organizations. He writes about people in the organizational setting and what really motivates them. He wrote, "Being influenced, manipulated or controlled, I would therefore argue, is not necessarily undesirable, even if you don't know it's happening. What is undesirable is being manipulated in ways you don't like or in ways that most people of a given community would consider undesirable or unethical" (McEachern, 1984, p. 6).

His views on the Eclectic Perspective processing that must be performed by today's public managers is revealed in the following:

> *True complexity arises when someone tries to explain what happens and occasionally what should happen in organizations. Max Weber's ideal-type bureaucracy must somehow be ingested in the same mouthful, so to speak, as B.F. Skinner's operant conditioning. McGregor's Theory X and Theory Y (which are not theories at all, but more like "ideal-types") must somehow be made compatible with notions of contingency theory or expectancy theory. And many others try to explain how people are motivated, how they perceive the world around them, how they learn new behavior, how they interact with one another, formally and informally, how they can lead or exercise authority over others, how power can be garnered or distributed, and how organizations can be developed or changed. (McEachern, 1984, p. 4)*

McEachern also provides a conceptual and procedural framework in which human judgments can be applied with more awareness of their relevance and of their importance in the context of specific decisions. He calls this process Multi-Attribute Desirability (MAD) analysis. This process involves seven steps:

1. Specifying the criteria or dimensions of value against which each alternative will be evaluated.
2. Prioritizing and assigning importance weights to the dimensions of value.
3. Establishing desirability functions for each dimension (specify how the raw measures—cost, for example—can be transformed into a common scale).
4. Measuring or rating each alternative of each dimension.
5. Transforming each measure into measures of desirability according to the desirability functions established in step 3.
6. Aggregating the products of the importance weights and the desirability measures across dimensions for each alternative.
7. Selecting (or recommending) the alternative with the highest weighted aggregated desirability score (McEachern, 1984, p. 62).

McEachern's work provides an update of those organization activities that involve people in the workplace and a genuine perspective of what really works and what is mere illusion.

1989: David Cherrington, *Organizational Behavior*

Cherrington's work is a gathering of later theories about the Employee Relations aspects of management. For example, he updates motivational theories by concluding that:

> Perhaps the best summary principle explaining human behavior is that people do what they expect to be rewarded for doing. This principle, which sounds much like the earlier principle of hedonism, serves as a useful foundation for analyzing motivation problems. The difference between this principle and hedonism, however, is that this principle recognizes the complexity of determining what is rewarding to the individual and it is based on more than physical gratification. (Cherrington, 1989, p. 192)

This text also points out that although research (1970) has failed to support Herzberg's claim of two separate factors (motivator-hygiene theory), his theory has been successfully applied to job redesign programs, in which significant job enrichment has occurred by focusing on the motivator factors.

In the leadership theories field, Cherrington provides four situational leadership theories (pp. 663–685). First he cites Hersey and Blanchard (1982), who developed a situational leadership model that matched combinations of task and relationship behaviors with the maturity of those being supervised. They found that as the maturity of the workers increases, the appropriate leadership styles were first: telling; second: selling; third: participating; and finally (for highly actualized workers): delegating. This approach generally corresponds to the level at which the subordinate functions on Maslow's Hierarchy of Needs. Research conducted at two universities in 1974 identified two similar leadership approaches essential to the effectiveness of a group: "production-centered" and "employee-centered." The two approaches were later formed into a matrix called the "managerial grid" by Blake and Mouton in 1978. The grid stresses concern for production on one side and concern for people on the other. Each dimension is measured on a 9-point scale, and the ideal leadership style is considered to be 9.9 to indicate a leader who is high in both dimensions. The research evidence, however, does not consistently support this conclusion.

Cherrington states that the most extensively researched situational leadership theory was Fiedler's (1967) "contingency theory" of leadership. Fiedler used a LPC (Leaders Preferred Coworker) scale. The process consists of a questionnaire with 16 semantic differential scales used to measure who the leader rates as the least preferred/most preferred coworker. This scale measures leadership orientation. The most appropriate leadership style is then determined by assessing three situational variables: the relationship between the leader and the employees (good or poor), the task (structured or unstructured), and power position of the leader (strong or weak). When these three variables created an extremely favorable or extremely unfavorable situation, the most effective leadership style was a task-oriented leader. When there were intermediate levels of favorableness, a leader with a high concern for interpersonal relationships was deemed more effective.

Vroom and Yetton (1973) developed a normative decision-making model to identify the appropriate styles that leaders should use in making decisions. The three styles are: autocratic, consultive, and group decision making. In selecting which style to use, pertinent questions are included to determine whether the leader has adequate information to make the decision alone; whether subordinates will accept the goals of the organization; whether subordinates will accept the decision if they do not participate in making it; and whether the decision will produce a controversial solution.

Cherrington wrote that one of the most popular models for selecting an appropriate leadership style was proposed by Tannenbaum and Schmidt in 1979. This model plots seven different styles of leadership along a continuum from highly autocratic to highly participative. At one end, the manager simply uses authority to make the decision and to announce it. At the other end, the manager provides an area of freedom for subordinates and permits them to function within limits to make decisions and direct their own activities. The correct leadership style, according to Tannenbaum and Schmidt, is determined by forces in (1) the manager, (2) the subordinates, and (3) the situation. This framework provides a useful way to analyze a leadership situation and to choose a successful leadership approach.

2003: Stephen P. Robbins, *Organizational Behavior*

This publication bears the same title as the previously discussed publication, but it has a different author and publisher. It appears to be a descendant of the previous text and offers a number of contemporary concepts in OB (organizational behavior). It brings into play the concepts of globalization and diversity and how they have become important elements in administrating multicultural employees. New approaches to leadership such as participative, team, and mentoring are discussed. The need for ethics, vision, and creativity in administration are also spotlighted as contemporary issues. These are subjects that will be discussed in Part III of this text as they apply to criminal justice administration.

2004: Barry M. Staw, *Psychological Dimensions of Organizational Behavior*

This is another more recent publication that the reader may review. It contains a number of articles by contemporary administrators and researchers that focus on the changing approaches to motivating employees. Several of the articles address how to maintain employee satisfaction during periods of change and approaches such as path finding and management mix, and when authoritative power is necessary. As with the previously mentioned publication, these are contemporary subjects that will be discussed in Parts II and III of this text.

Open Systems

1971: Donald Schon, *Beyond the Stable State*

As public agencies began to realize the need to function more as Open Systems, the escalating changes of the environment in which government operates captured widespread interest. Schon's work offered a view of the central problems facing Western civilization: accelerating changes that could not be absorbed by the patterns of adaptation used in the past.

Schon described the way institutions, particularly government institutions, normally responded to the threat of change. He called reaction "dynamic conservatism"—the fight to remain the same. His work was published at a time when popular views of occupations, religions, organizations, and value systems were beginning to erode.

Belief in stability is belief in unchangeability, the constancy of life, or the effort to attain such constancy. There is no longer such a condition as a stable state and not accepting this fact can be disastrous.

Schon argued that businesses, government, and social institutions must become "learning systems," decentralizing control and organizing not around their products or services but rather around functions. He said government, which he described as one of the most dynamically conservative of all institutions, must gain from the private sector experience about how to learn. "We must act before we know in order to learn," and give up pragmatic models of knowing that were workable only in relatively stable times (Schon, 1971, p. 116).

1980: Michael White, Ross Clayton, Robert Myrtle, Gilbert Siegel, and Aaron Rose, *Managing Public Systems: Analytic Techniques for Public Administration*

The work of these authors provides additional understanding about the application of systems concepts to public management. They stress that a basic strategy for applying systems concepts to the public sector is the process of separating a system into its component subsystems and exploring the relationships among these subsystems. This leads to looking for inputs and outputs, feedback loops, and the boundaries of systems and subsystems. The approach requires defining the purpose of systems and subsystems, and their relationship to other systems and subsystems, and their surroundings.

The authors define the difference between classical and systems theory: "In systems theory the emphasis and outcome of investigation are questions rather than answers; in classical theory, the tendency is for the 'principles' to be answers looking for questions" (White et al., 1980, p. 44).

This work presents a model of environmental management that can assist public administrators in decision making. Environmental management is "a system for managing human affairs so as to ensure an acceptable balance between the quality of the human environment and the quality of the natural environment" (White et al., 1980, pp. 32–44). The authors state:

> *A systems approach to environmental management requires that one view the totality of the systems environment in order to fully*

understand the various impacts or constraints that condition the decision making process. The view of environmental management as an open system creates a difficult role for the decision maker. It requires that management deal with many uncertainties and ambiguities and be concerned continuously with adapting to new and changing requirements. Management is the process that spans and links the various subsystems. In this context, management must work to reduce uncertainty but at the same time search for the flexibility necessary to respond to changing values and new demands. Management must integrate and balance the various subsystem demands and their activities. (White et al., 1980, p. 32)

1983: Andrew Szilagyi and Marc Wallace, *Organizational Behavior and Performance*

This text provides some advancements in management theories and concepts. One part of the book discusses organizational environments. The authors state, "Organizations of every type are in constant interaction with the external environment. The important components of the environment that have a direct impact on the organization include suppliers, customers, competitor government agencies, and society in general." They list environmental components as (1) economic, (2) political, (3) social, and (4) technological (Szilagyi & Wallace, 1990, pp. 625–636).

Demographic trends, changing individual needs, and cross-cultural differences are leading managers to look differently at customers and employees. The technological environment, the processes of innovation, and technology transfer are changing the ways organizations compete and are requiring a more Eclectic Perspective approach to managing public organization.

Social Equity

1981: Samuel Krislov and David Rosenbloom, *Representative Bureaucracy and the American Political System*

Krislov and Rosenbloom based their work on the constitutional aspects of public employment and considered the concept from a number of political and legal perspectives. They pointed out that the objective of representative bureaucracy can be achieved in a number of alternative methods. They also described the limitations inherent in this objective. They analyzed the personnel, administrative organization, and citizen participation issues of representative bureaucracy, and have provided a context for understanding the goals of affirmative action and equal employment opportunity.

Client-Oriented Service

1987: Tom Peters, *Thriving on Chaos*

This book, which was written in the late 1980s, serves as an extension into the 1990s for Peters's coauthored works, *In Search of Excellence* and *A Passion for Ex-*

cellence. Here he argues that the two earlier books (both advocating Client-Oriented Service) described the parameters of a relatively stable and predictable world that no longer exists. He explains the necessity of treating the customer as an appreciating asset and presents methods of measuring customer satisfaction in an unstable environment. Peters gives an example of public sector excellence:

> *Ron Hartman, general manager of Baltimore's Mass Transit Administration, offers up a fine example: Two years ago we received a series of complaints on one of our premium park-and-ride express bus lines from a suburb to downtown Baltimore. Several buses were continually late. We fixed the problem, but felt we owed the riders more for the inconvenience. One day after the service got back to normal, we took advantage of the fact that it was the Christmas season. On a cold December morning, instead of the usual bus showing up, we decorated a bus with lots of crepe paper and tinsel, stuck a Christmas tree in the fare box to offer the service free, hooked up a tape recorder playing carols, and dressed the driver like Santa Claus. We offered cookies, coffee, and candy canes as commuters boarded. We still get letters from those customers and most continue to ride with us. (Peters, 1987, p. 104)*

2001: Jim Collins, *Good to Great*

Jim Collins might be said to present a more contemporary version of Peters and Waterman's work, in that he details the results of his research of a number of contemporary companies that "make the leap from good to great." Collins says he found that, "Greatness is of a function of circumstance—Greatness, it turns out, is largely a matter of conscious choice, and discipline." He calls great leaders Level 5 executives. He describes this type of leader as "able to sustain greatness through a seemingly disparate blend of personal humility and unwavering resolve to do the right thing—for the company and not for themselves, irrespective of constraints." Collins's finding will be explored further in this text in the chapter on leadership (Chapter 14).

2005: Jim Collins, *Good to Great and the Social Sectors*

Collins can be compared with Tom Peters, who in 1989 took the approach from his *In Search of Excellence* book and applied it to the public sector. Here Collins takes his Level 5 executive concept from his *Good to Great* and applies it to the social sector. He writes about his findings in a monograph meant to be a supplement to his original book. Here, for example, he compares executives such as Sam Walton to a police chief. In an interview about this publication, he said, "He [Sam Walton] can do whatever he wants with Wal-Mart. Even in a publicly traded company, the CEO still has immense power and can make most of the decisions. But as police chief "there are points of power that are out of your control. For example, there are unions. The mayor may have a tremendous amount of power—and that is a reality in making decisions. In policing, leadership has to have a different flavor. Chiefs still have to be Level 5 leaders, but they have to be much more nuanced in how they assemble the points of power needed to get things done. This can be referred to as "legislative leadership." When you are a legislative leader like a police chief, you have to find out where the sources of power are—both visible and invisible—that you can draw upon to get things done, even if you personally don't have the raw power to make things happen (*Subject to Debate*, 2006, p. 1). Collins's findings and how they relate to the criminal justice administrator will be discussed further in Chapter 14.

2006: Gareth Morgan, *Images of Organization*

Morgan's writings can best be classified under the Eclectic Perspective category but are discussed here because they focus on how current organizations are client-oriented, how they must be prepared for change. The premise of his book is that theories of organization and management are based on implicit images or metaphors that stretch our imagination in productive ways and also in ways that can cause distortion. Scholars and practitioners can become so entrenched in an administrative paradigm that they can lose sight of the changes going around them. Morgan discussed how in describing organizations, the use of metaphor to compare it to a machine, an organism, brain, or a culture is useful but can lead to distortions. Some of Morgan's concepts will be discussed in Part III of this book.

Eclectic Perspective Summary

Using an Eclectic Perspective approach to solving criminal justice administrative issues requires consideration of many variables. In addition to considering past theories and concepts, the criminal justice administration must be able to "mix and match" appropriate approaches to today's situations. In the next chapter, the historical administrative themes and trends are focused on one criminal justice field, law enforcement. This will provide insight into how the evolution of administrative themes is similar in all criminal justice fields.

KEY CONCEPTS AND TERMS

- Client-Oriented Service
  - Importance of employee-customer contacts
    1987, *Moments of Truth*, Jan Carlzon
  - Focus on customer service
    1983, *In Search of Excellence*, Thomas Peters and Robert Waterman
- Eclectic Perspective
  - Intertwining of private and public sectors
    1990, *Public Administration*, Jeffrey Straussman
  - Public administration programs for better service
    1991, *Public Administration: A Search for Themes and Direction*, Richard J. Stillman II

CHAPTER ACTIVITY

This chapter has reviewed milestone publications as of the writing of this textbook. Research the reviews of business and public administration publications that may be more recent. Can you identify any trends that may be the milestones of the future?

REVIEW QUESTIONS

1. What caused (or forced) the public sector to become interested in Client-Oriented approaches?

2. Service, information/technology, and human minds were described as the elements of a successful enterprise. Can you give examples of how they apply to criminal justice administration?

3. The research of Peters and Waterman in the 1970s and Jim Collins in the 2000s were described in this chapter. Can you identify similarities in their approaches and findings regarding leadership?

4. A number of "transition milestones" were discussed in this chapter as they relate to contributing to changes and enhancement in contextual themes concepts. Discuss a few of these transition concepts and the impact they have had on criminal justice administration.

5. The Eclectic Perspective approach has been described as being able to "mix and match" and compared to juggling a number of china plates. Explain how this relates to the role of the contemporary criminal justice administrator.

REFERENCES

Argyris, C. (1964). *Integrating the Individual and the Organization*. New York: John Wiley.

Barbour, G. P., Jr. (1984). *Excellence in Local Government*. Washington, DC: IMCA Training Institute Publication.

Bennis, W. G. (1966). *Changing Organizations*. New York: McGraw-Hill.

Carlzon, J. (1987). *Moments of Truth*. New York: Harper & Row.

Cherrington, D. J. (1989). *Organizational Behavior*. Boston: Allyn & Bacon.

Collins, J. (2001). *Good to Great*. New York: Harper Business.

Collins, J. (2005). *Good to Great and the Social Sectors*. New York: Harper Business.

Fiedler, F. E. (1967). *A Theory of Leadership Effectiveness*. New York: McGraw-Hill.

Graham, C., Jr., & Hays, S. (1986). Management Functions and Public Administration—POSDCORB Revisited. *Managing the Public Organization*. Washington, DC: CQ Press.

Hampton, D. R., Summer, C. E., & Webber, R. A. (1982). *Organizational Behavior and the Practice of Management*. Glenview, IL: Scott, Foresman & Company.

Harmon, M. M., & Mayer, R. T. (1986). *Organization Theory for Public Administration*. Boston: Little, Brown & Company.

Krislov, S., & Rosenbloom, D. (1981). *Representative Bureaucracy and the American Political System*. New York: Praeger.

Likert, R. (1961). *New Patterns of Management*. New York: McGraw-Hill.

McEachern, A. W. (1984). *Organizational Illusions*. Redondo Beach, CA: Shale Books.

Metcalf, H. C., & Urwick, L. (1940). *Dynamic Administration*. New York: Harper & Brothers.

Morgan, G. (2006). *Images of Organization*. Thousand Oaks, CA: Sage Publications.

Mosher, F. C. (1968). *Democracy and the Pubic Service*. New York: Oxford University Press.

Ott, S. J., Hyde, A. C., & Shafritz, J. M. (eds.). (1991). *Public Management: The Essential Readings*. Chicago: Lyceum Books/Nelson-Hall.

Peters, T. J. (1987). *Thriving on Chaos*. New York: Alfred A. Knopf.

Peters, T. J. (1989). *Excellence in the Public Sector*. Boston: Enterprise Media Inc. [Video and workbook].

Peters, T. J., & Waterman, R. H., Jr. (1982). *In Search of Excellence*. New York: Warner Books.

Ramos, A. G. (1981). Theory of Social Systems Delimitation: A Paradigmatic Statement. In *The New Science of Organizations: A Reconceptualization of the Wealth of Nations* (Chapter 7). Toronto: University of Toronto Press.

Robbins, S. P. (2003). *Organizational Behavior*, (10th ed.). Upper Saddle River, NJ: Prentice Hall.

Schon, D. A. (1971). *Beyond the Stable State*. New York: W.W. Norton.

Simon, H. A. S. (1946). The Proverbs of Public Administration. *Public Administration Review*, 6 (Winter), pp. 53–57.

Staw, B. M. (2004). *Psychological Dimensions of Organizational Behavior*, (3rd ed.). Upper Saddle River, NJ: Pearson/Prentice Hall.

Stillman, R. J. (1991). *Public Administration: A Search for Themes and Direction*. New York: St. Martin's Press.

Straussman, J. D. (1990). *Public Administration*. New York: Longman.

Subject to Debate: A Newsletter of the Police Executive Research Forum (2006). Washington, DC: Police Executive, Research Forum, *20*, July, front page interview of Tom Collins.

Szilagyi, A., & Wallace, M. Jr. (1983). *Organizational Behavior and Performance*. (3rd ed.), Glenview, IL: Scott, Foresman & Company.

Thayer, F. C. (1981). *An End to Hierarchy and Competition: Administration in the Post-Affluent World*. (2nd ed.). New York: New Viewpoints.

Toffler, A. (1980). *The Third Wave*. New York: Bantam Books.

Vroom, V. H., & Yetton, P.W. (1973). *Leadership and Decision-making*. Pittsburgh: University of Pittsburgh Press.

Weick, K. E. (1979). *The Social Psychology of Organizing*. Reading, MA: Addison-Wesley.

White, M. J., Clayton, R., Myrtle, R., Siegel, G., & Rose, A. (1980). *Managing Public Systems: Analytic Techniques for Public Administration*. North Scituate, MA: Duxbury Press.

Wright, D. S. (1983). *Understanding Intergovernmental Relations*. New York: Marcel Dekker.

Wrap Up

■ RELEVANT PUBLICATION

Jan Carlzon's success as the new executive officer of a failing airline provided a blueprint for client-oriented efforts in the private as well as the public sector. His approach was well documented in his book *Moments of Truth* in 1987. Several years prior, Thomas Peters, along with Robert H. Waterman Jr., wrote *In Search of Excellence*, which is credited with fostering the "client-service" theme.

Presented here is the Foreword to Jan Carlzon's book, written by Tom Peters. This Foreword provides an insightful view of the *Client-Oriented Service* theme and demonstrates the influence of both Peters and Carlzon during this era. (Carlzon, J. (1987). *Moments of Truth—New Strategies for Today's Consumer-Driven Economy*. New York: Ballinger Publisher Company/Harper & Row Publishers, Inc. Permission to reprint by Harper Collins Publishers.)

Foreword by Tom Peters to *Moments of Truth— New Strategies for Today's Customer-Driven Economy*

Imagine that there's a loose panel in the passenger compartment of the New York to Los Angeles airplane. The panel has a sharp, protruding edge that has torn the stockings of a passenger who reports it to the nearest flight attendant. The flight attendant can't repair the panel herself because she doesn't have the proper tools. She needs help. The only thing she knows to do is file a report that will end up in an office somewhere. But the office contains only a telephone and intercom; no tools. Meanwhile, our flight attendant has delegated the problem upward in the company. To her way of thinking, she has done her job. Late that afternoon, the report will be sent to a corresponding level of another department. A half-hour later, it is placed on the desk of someone in the technical department. The technician isn't sure whether or not he can fix the problem. But he needn't worry. By now the plane is flying at 31,000 feet over Dubuque. The technician scribbles a directive on the now dog-eared form: "Repair when possible." And it will be repaired—10 pairs of torn stockings later.

Jan Carlzon's answer to this? Get rid of the horizontal barriers to communication. Turn middle managers, "hired to make sure instructions are followed," away from the role of administrator and into leaders and facilitators for the frontline people who serve the customer and market.

After all, the first 15-second encounter between a passenger and the frontline people, from ticket agent to flight attendant, sets the tone of the entire company in the mind of the customer. This is what Carlzon calls the "moment of truth."

Who is Carlzon? In late summer 1986, *Business Week* described how Sweden "became Europe's powerhouse. . . . Ten years ago it was the 'sickest of sick men.' Now it's the envy of the continent." No one better exemplifies what *Business Week* calls "the aggressive, fast-moving management style that has made winners out of many Swedish companies" than SAS's Carlzon.

At age 36, in 1978, he took over Linjeflyg, Sweden's domestic airline, thus becoming the world's youngest airline president. Following a People Express-like strategy, he slashed fares; filled seats, and achieved exceptional success in record time. His reward was the presidency of SAS in 1981. After 17 consecutive profitable years, the airline had racked up $30 million in losses in 1979 and 1980.

Employees ruefully awaited his arrival. More cost cutting and fare slashing was expected. Instead, Carlzon created "EuroClass," first-class service at coach rates, as part of his single-minded focus on the business traveler in an effort to become "the best airline for the frequent business traveler" in Europe.

In short order, punctuality became the best in Europe; remarkably, SAS returned to profitability in just a year, while the rest of the international airlines tallied a record $2 billion collective loss. By 1984, SAS had been voted *Air Transport World*'s "Airline of the Year."

To be sure, Carlzon's story in *Moments of Truth* is the saga of an extraordinary turnaround in the volatile airline business, but its general applicability knows no bounds. He argues, correctly I believe, that we are at an "historic crossroad." Our traditional (Western) competitive advantages have been badly eroded.

We are entering, Carlzon contends, a customer- and market-driven era. Wiser consumers and new competitors, from air transport to autos to semi-conductors to financial services, are turning up the heat on traditional businesses. To deal with this market-led discontinuity, we must revolutionize our organizations. Specifically, says Carlzon, the "customer-oriented company is organized for change." It will simply not survive with detached, administrative, topdown leadership.

This book is chock-a-block full of instructive stories and practical advice, describing Carlzon's activities at Vingresor (the package vacation subsidiary of SAS, where he assumed his first presidency at age 32), Linjeflyg, and SAS in particular. He began at Vingresor as an order giver, not a listener—neither to his people nor to his customers—and made every mistake in the book. By the time he got to Linjeflyg four years later he had learned many lessons; in fact, he began his second stint as top dog by calling the entire company together in a hangar and asking for help—a far cry from his barking out commands just 48 months before.

At SAS, he arrived at a time of crisis. He concluded that service and the frontline people who delivered it were the success levers. He shifted focus from the plane as physical asset to the customer. He stunned the technocrats by mothballing his big Airbuses and flagship 747s, keeping instead the older, less efficient DC-9 fleet that provided the flexibility necessary to best serve the cherished business traveler.

Carlzon and his newly energized team boldly mounted 147 service improvement projects, at a cost of about $50 million, despite the still-flowing red ink. He also cut to the bone all costs that didn't serve the airline's single-minded goal. For instance, a 40-person centralized market survey unit was disbanded—market data collection was to be done locally; that is, closer to the ultimate customer.

Carlzon charged the frontline people with "provid[ing] the service that they had wanted to provide all along." He spiffed up uniforms, transferred autonomy to the field, and encouraged people not to take "no" for an answer. For instance, in support of the business traveler, separate EuroClass check-in was desired. All the experts pooh-poohed the idea. The regulators would never permit it, given Sweden's pronounced egalitarian philosophy. Ignoring its own experts, SAS plunged ahead, and the request was approved.

Empowerment of frontline people to get on with it is one ingredient. Leadership is another. Carlzon's leadership formula (proven by him in practice) is unconventional to say the least. He slams professional management as it has evolved. He honors intuition, emotion, and showmanship. Analytic thinkers "are often disastrous decision-makers and implementers," he asserts. The analysis-bound professional manager dreams up new alternatives in order to avoid making decisions. At Carlzon's SAS, "analysis is always directed toward the overall business strategy, not toward the individual elements of that strategy."

The new leaders' tools are a clear, concise vision and consummate communication skills—with soul. There is nothing soft and squishy about it. Carlzon calls the new executive (and himself by implication) an "enlightened dictator."

Loyalty to the vision, not the details of execution, is a must—or else. People shine only if demands are sky high, he believes. Part and parcel is rigorous, honest measurement. Tough, visible goals, aimed at serving the customer and measured so as to engender unit versus unit competition, spur the process onward.

Enlightening as all this is, the best is yet to come. SAS leapt hurdle after hurdle, far ahead of schedule, between 1981 and 1984. Then the energy began to wane. After about a year's soul searching, with much dissipated momentum in its wake, Carlzon launched "the second wave." It is an ambitious program aimed at a major improvement in efficiency in order to proactively prepare for impending European airline deregulation.

The goal is worthy, but the process of achieving it profound—providing exceptional insights that go a long way toward explaining why most U.S. turnaround efforts have run aground. Carlzon acknowledges having "hot-wired" the system at the outset to breathe new life into the frontline people: They were SAS's heroes. Nothing was to get in the way of their providing superior service. Should a middle manager demur, the first line was vigorously encouraged to go around him or her, directly to the top.

To be sure, the process worked. But it does not, says Carlzon, form the base for sustained vitality. Middle management must be ignited and redirected toward serving the market, too. The initial short-circuiting of middle management, Carlzon admits, did not contain "viable alternatives to their old role as rule interpreters." "We had let our middle managers down," he now says.

The second wave's answer to achieving unheard-of efficiency is not—once more—an issue of improving physical assets. It is a people issue, through and through. The "distribution of roles is radically different"; the pyramid, that is, must be flattened once and for all.

Will Carlzon achieve a second miracle? We don't know yet. But his prescription is on the mark, I feel. From bank to boilermaker, the typical U.S. firm's response to the economic revolution engulfing us has been hardware first, people and organization second. The wisest heads, usually ignored, have warned that this was a perilous course. Automation will not save a poorly laid out factory with demotivated workers. A bigger computer will not save a bank in the volatile world of financial services, where bold new products are being launched daily.

As Carlzon suggests, our organizations must literally be turned upside down. We must learn to welcome change rather than fight it, to encourage risk-taking rather than snuff it out, to empower rather than demotivate our firstline people, and to focus outwardly on the fast-changing market rather than inwardly on Byzantine bureaucratic maneuvers. To this list Carlzon adds his brilliant analysis of the middle manager, so often ignored in the transition program—and so often the eventual dragging force that slows down the best-intended programs. He also underscores the tough-minded role of the new visionary leader: vision and trust, yes; but with loyalty, rigorous demands, and customer-focused measures.

One would hope that Carlzon's colleagues—and all managers—in the U.S. airline industry will read this book. Uncompetitive service—despite attractive prices—eventually humbled recent highflier, People Express. Merger digestion problems and frantic responses to deregulation have resulted in a generally intolerable level of service for the American business traveler—and big losses for many of the flailing airlines to boot. Only American Airlines—which has, alone among the majors, been the sole carrier to eschew sizeable acquisitions—is in the pink of health; its service still tops most charts, and its strategic use of information is plowing new ground for all service industries. With Delta as a second exception, the frequent flying customer has been left out in the greedy rush to expand at a rate that even minimum service cannot match. One suspects that many of the huge dollar losses and much pain could have been avoided if Carlzon's methodology had been applied by his American counterparts.

Moments of Truth is a book for U.S. airline executives and U.S. bankers, for U.S. textile makers and machine tool purveyors. It is a marvelous contribution to our urgent effort to fundamentally redefine our organizations for the brave new world that is upon us. It provides examples, suggestions, and, above all, a new philosophy—from someone who has been on the firing line and achieved brilliant turnaround successes in record time.

—*Tom Peters*

5

The Application of the Contextual Theme Concepts in Law Enforcement

---

■ Introduction

This chapter explores the development and application of the **contextual administrative** themes in law enforcement. Law enforcement is used as an example as it comprises the largest segment of the criminal justice system. A review of history should remind the reader that "history does repeat itself." A knowledge of past administrative methods can provide today's criminal justice administrators with the ability to "mix and match" appropriate administrative approaches to current events.

Most administrative concepts originate in the private sector and subsequently are implemented in the public sector. The evolution appears to be that concepts are generally developed in the private sector, adopted by the public sector, and then applied in specific criminal justice agencies. This is why criminal justice administrators must keep abreast of administrative development in the private sector as part of their Eclectic Perspective approach to overseeing their agencies.

Additionally, a historical law enforcement incident is reviewed to show how failure to apply and maintain these administrative theme concepts can result in malfeasance and failure. This case study is meant to illustrate the practical application of the aforementioned metaphor of the administrator as a juggler. It should serve as a reminder that the administrator must be mindful of all the contextual themes and their concepts, just as the juggler must pay attention to the spinning of all the plates.

■ Historical Application of the Contextual Administrative Themes in Law Enforcement

To establish an appropriate background for the examination of the evolution of law enforcement administration, this chapter begins with a brief review of the development of policing in America. In colonial towns during the 17th century, the task of public safety was carried out by a "watch and ward" system. Neighborhood safety was a duty shared by community members in contrast to the military enforcement of laws, which was the practice under monarchical governments.

The early settlers in America did not want law enforcement to be centrally controlled; they wanted it to be the responsibility of all citizens. If the people standing watch on a given night needed help, they could wake the sleeping residents for assistance.

In the 1800s, the daily life of the citizens became more regimented and most could no longer stand watch at night and tend to a regular job in the daytime. Consequently, citizens began to select certain people in each community to take over the night guard functions on a regular basis. Nevertheless, the concept of the shared responsibility remained because those selected to stand guard could call on any citizens when assistance was needed.

Most towns paid watchmen to walk neighborhood beats at night. In 1833, Philadelphia was the first city to establish a separate daytime force. New York followed a few years later (1844) with a night and day watch, and this became the first recognized police department (Fosdick, 1920, pp. 63–64).

As police departments began to form, many followed the guidelines set by Sir Robert Peel (Britain's Home Secretary) for the London Metropolitan Police in 1829. Peel modeled the reorganization of the Metropolitan Police after the successful British military system, and hoped to bring discipline, loyalty, and efficiency into the "ragged" ranks of London's first patrolmen (Reith, 1948, pp. 64–65).

This concept, which consolidated the crime prevention and law enforcement powers of constables and watchmen, required that the entire city be patrolled both night and day by men who were assigned to regular sectors or "beats." This model was widely emulated by newly forming American police agencies.

Further review of the evolution of policing will be provided in Chapter 6. The remainder of this section will explore the development of American law enforcement administration during the past century and the correlation of this development to the advancements of the five contextual themes.

Organization Functions

The transformation of American society from agrarian to industrialized urban centers in the early 20th century required new occupational specializations and promoted the process of professionalism in many occupations. This was more the case in the private sector. Professionalism lagged behind in law enforcement, perhaps because policing remained politically controlled. The spoils system method of selecting police officers remained deeply imbedded in local politics for many years.

Lawyers, doctors, and scientists were creating a base of knowledge, setting professional standards for admission, and developing ethical guidelines. In contrast, law enforcement had minimal control over the conditions that would facilitate developing policing as a profession.

Early American police were authorized by municipalities, and, unlike their British counterparts, had no central authority to provide a unifying direction for their existence and methods of operation. The direction for early law enforcement in the United States came from local political leaders.

City councils and mayors decided who was hired as police officers, where they were assigned, and who was to be promoted. Officers were often fired for political rather than professional reasons (Jordan, 1972). This type of administration followed the 1887 directive of Woodrow Wilson, who wrote, "Representatives of the people are the proper ultimate authority in all matters of government and administration is merely the clerical part of government" (Wilson, cited in Alshulter, 1977, p. 2).

Political control over law enforcement led to widespread corruption. For example, a broadly circulated article of this period read:

> *Every large American police department is under suspicion. The suspicion amounts to this: for-money crimes are not only tolerated but encouraged. The higher the rank of the police officer, the stronger the suspicion. Now it is only one step from the encouragement of vice, for the purposes of loot to an alliance with criminals. Indeed, in some of our large cities, the robbery of drunken men is permitted already by police on the profit-sharing plan. (Matthews, 1909, p. 1314)*

The ensuing public distrust of the police brought pressure for reform. Law enforcement responded by searching for ways to becoming more "professional" and bureaucratic. They began to adopt the teachings of Gulick, Urwick, and Fayol (see Chapter 2). For example, August Vollmer (as police chief of Berkeley, California) was first to rally police administrators to the idea of reform during the 1920s and early 1930s. It was Vollmer's protégé, O. W. Wilson, however, who, through his writings, became the principal administrative architect of police reform by bringing to law enforcement many of the organization function theories and strategies of the private sector. Vollmer and Wilson's contributions will be explored further in Chapter 6.

Wilson also took some guidance from J. Edgar Hoover, who was credited with professionalizing the Federal Bureau of Investigation and making it a prestigious law enforcement agency by following prevailing administrative concepts.

In his *Police Administration* textbook, O.W. Wilson refers to Gulick and Fayol in providing Organization Functions concepts for police administrators. He wrote:

> *Luther Gulick lists the administrative duties as planning, organizing, staffing, directing, coordinating, reporting, and budgeting; from the initial letters of these words he has coined the word "posdcorb." Henri Fayol lists the administrative duties as forecasting, planning,*

organizing, commanding, coordinating and controlling. (Wilson, 1963, p. 26)

Wilson's textbook on police administration, using many of the Organization Functions concepts, helped shape police administration strategy to rid policing of wasteful and corrupt practices. He used Frederick Taylor's "Principles of Scientific Management" (see Chapter 2) to describe the task of the police as being designed to limit discretion and to ensure efficiency. Systems were instituted to account for the time and work products of officers. Work was reduced to component parts to promote the development of expertise (Wilson, 1950, p. 27).

In some departments, control systems became so restrictive that patrol officers did little more than answer radio calls, take reports, and make arrests. Specialized work such as traffic and detective functions were performed by "experts." Bureaucratic control focused on efficiency rather than effectiveness.

Many field officers became separated from the community, just responding to calls-for-service rather than solving problems and preventing crime. These officers became disconnected from the feedback that comes from community interaction; they were isolated in their squad cars, and worked in communities they knew little about.

Employee Relations

In the 1950s and early 1960s, American law enforcement administration began to focus on Employee Relations concepts. *Municipal Police Administration*, a popular police administration book of this period, contained chapters on "Creating a Climate of Participation" and how to enhance relationships between "The Supervisor and the Individual." These chapters informed law enforcement administrators about the theories developed by Chris Argyris, Rensis Likert, Robert Tannenbaum, as well as Mary Parker Follett (International City Management Association, 1958, chs. 3 and 5).

This police administration textbook spotlighted concepts such as Likert's "Developing Patterns in Management" (p. 59) and Tannenbaum's "Participation by Subordinates in the Managerial Decision-Making Process" (p. 67). The influence of Employee Relations concepts can be seen in the following quote:

> *Motivation fuels the engine of the human personality which has perception, expectation, and aspiration as its common moving parts. The reactions it produces we call behavior. The most basic human motives from the standpoint of supervisory practice appear to be recognition, security, opportunity, and belonging. Motivation drives people toward satisfaction. If something blocks satisfaction, frustration is the result and aggression against the supervisor or others in the work group is a highly possible result. Other reactions to frustration include rationalization, sublimation, regression, and repression. (International City Management Association, 1958, p. 35)*

O. W. Wilson's 1950 *Police Administration* textbook contained a section on "Democracy in Leadership." He wrote, "The wise leader wins the support of his force to his policies, plans, and procedures before placing them into effect" (Wilson, 1963, pp. 14, 15).

Open Systems

In the 1960s and 1970s, federal grant money (Law Enforcement Assistance Administration funds) promoted innovation and a quest for better policing methods among law enforcement administrators. These funds drew the interest of the aerospace industry that had just placed a man on the moon and was looking for a means of new employment. The resulting infusion of aerospace technology into law enforcement brought a more cybernetic orientation to confronting crime problems.

The cybernetic approach helped law enforcement administrators to grasp the **Open Systems** outlook, and Katz and Kahn became well known in most police administration courses. For example, one police textbook featured a chapter titled "Police Administration and the Systems Approach" (Whisenand & Tamaru, 1970, pp. 66–86). This text stated, "Consequently, today we can see the need for an informational processing system for police bureaucracies that is interfaced with externally related information systems and simultaneously supports the decision-making processes of all participating organizations" (p. 69).

Figure 5–1 is adapted from another law enforcement textbook of that period that depicts a police department as an Open System. Cronkhite (1974, p. 7) explained the concept.

Law enforcement agencies are a system with external variables that have a bearing on their performance. These variables are shown as **inputs** in the Open System Model. The police operations are pictured as **processing** within the department, and the **outputs** are the objectives for which a police department is responsible.

The objectives, or outputs, are (1) prevention of criminality, (2) repression of crime, (3) apprehension of offenders, (3) recovery of property, (4) regulation of noncriminal conduct such as traffic and (5) maintaining public order.

These outputs must be achieved by each police agency and are used in this model to measure the effectiveness of the operation. The Control Feedback Subsystem component is structured around the cybernetic feedback model. This subsystem is shown as a means by which a police agency can evaluate how well it is accomplishing outputs and the actions it can take to alter the Inputs and Processing to produce desired outputs.

By means of an Open Systems outlook, law enforcement began to see the importance of the external environment and the benefits of evaluating inputs and outputs that related to police service. Law enforcement became more independent of political direction and more inclined to establish methods of monitoring their own environment.

The police were more sensitive to the fact that most major problems impacting the criminal justice system were external to their agencies. Providing responsive service and finding solutions to these problems required constant analysis of feedback relating to inputs and outputs that could be obtained through an Open Systems approach.

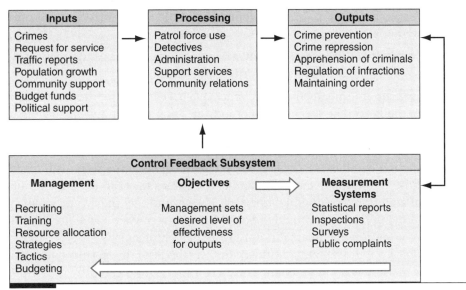

Figure 5-1 Law Enforcement as an Open System.

Social Equity

The 1960s and early 1970s found law enforcement taking the brunt of social unrest. The militant "Black Power" movement, which included groups such as the Black Panthers, resulted in battles with the police, which heightened tensions on both sides. Race riots erupted in Los Angeles, Newark, Detroit, and then nationwide in 1968 when Martin Luther King Jr. was killed.

The Vietnam War and draft protests became increasingly violent. Militant demonstrations also were held for such causes as legalizing marijuana and other drugs, sexual freedom, and equality for minorities and women. The police continually were seen in the media in riot formation.

The "New Left" materialized and demanded a variety of social changes, under the overall umbrella of social justice. To those of this movement, the police were "pigs," and were agents of establishment oppression. To the police, the New Left was made up of "hippies" and "longhairs."

The initial reaction of law enforcement to the escalating social unrest was to become more regimented and centrally controlled. However, the 1970s and 1980s saw a mellowing of enforcement tactics as more "baby boomers" became police officers. Additionally, equal opportunity hiring standards and court enforced affirmative action mandates impacted the recruiting, hiring, and promoting practices of law enforcement. The 1973 National Advisory Commission on Criminal Justice Standards and Goals set the following hiring standards, which recommended that every police agency:

1. Engage in positive efforts to employ ethnic minority group members.
2. Direct recruitment efforts toward attracting large numbers of minority applicants.

3. Research, develop, and implement specialized minority recruitment methods.

4. Ensure that hiring, assignment, and promotion policies and practices do not discriminate against minority group members.

5. Evaluate continually the effectiveness of specialized minority recruitment methods so that successful methods are emphasized and unsuccessful ones discarded (p. 329).

This period emphasized for law enforcement agencies the responsibility to protect those traditional American democratic values that call for a maximum amount of attention to individual liberties. They found that they were responsible for enforcing laws that provided Social Equity even when local elected officials and community members did not favor such enforcement.

A major law enforcement administration textbook of this period stated that the police mission was "maintenance of social order within carefully prescribed ethical and constitutional restrictions" (International City Management Association, 1969, p. 2). Another textbook stated the mission included "protecting individual rights and ensuring social justice" (International City Management Association, 1977, p. 352).

■ Client-Oriented Service

The 1970s and 1980s saw a transition in law enforcement administration toward a more community-oriented strategy. The social unrest begun in the 1960s had strained relations between the public and the police.

Public dissatisfaction with police services could be seen in ballot measures that reduced tax support for additional officers and equipment and in the privatization of some law enforcement functions. The recently acquired Open Systems posture of police administrators underscored the need for constant input and feedback from the community.

Research conducted during the 1970s indicated that information was a major factor in dealing with crime. If information about crimes and criminals could be obtained from citizens by the police and could be managed properly by police agencies, the efficiency of investigative and other police functions could be significantly increased (Pate, 1976).

The realization that law enforcement may have strayed from the early American philosophy of a shared community-police responsibility became a major topic among law enforcement academicians and practitioners. Public dissatisfaction was a reminder that law enforcement in this country was never meant to be a "standing army" that protected the citizens from crime. It was time to return to more of a community-police partnership approach.

Inherent in the change was an epistemological shift from the classical organization functions theories. The rigidity of the classical theories of management had to be tempered to facilitate the new law enforcement agenda. The classical theories of the past helped reform the nonsystematic policing of the early decades to a more respected management structure.

However, many of the classical theories could not accommodate the new demands placed on law enforcement, such as fast response, community organizing, decentralization, and problem-solving strategies. To overcome polarization between rank-and-file police and minorities, and the tendency toward polarization of police-community relations units and the rest of the department, team policing became a strategy. Team policing was described in one milestone publication in this way:

> In theory, the patrol force is reorganized to include one or more quasi-autonomous teams, with a joint purpose of improving police services to the community and increasing job satisfaction of the patrol officers. Usually the team is based in a particular neighborhood. Each team has responsibility for police services in its neighborhood and is intended to work as a unit in close contact with the community to prevent crime and maintain order (Sherman, Milton, & Kelly, 1973, p. xiv)

Team policing never really became a fully developed strategy in the United States because of financial restraints and the fear of loss of authority and control by middle and upper management in some agencies. However, the concept of closer ties with the community continued to be in vogue. Deployment of "basic patrol cars" with commitments for long-term neighborhood problem solving and increased foot patrols became prevalent.

A number of milestone writings about community policing appeared in the 1980s and early 1990s. *The New Blue Line* (Skolnick & Bayley, 1986), *Community Policing: Issues and Practices Around the World* (National Institute of Justice, 1988), and *Community Policing: A Contemporary Perspective* (Trojanowicz & Bucqueroux, 1990) were perhaps the most widely read.

These writings pointed out that community policing should be more than just a program. Community/client-oriented policing is a philosophy that provides that the police, and the public they serve, have an interdependent and shared responsibility in making their community a safe and desirable place to live and do business.

Community/client-oriented policing became known as a philosophical commitment to (1) increasing accountability to service, (3) organizing community-based crime prevention, (4) improving communication with the community, and (5) decentralizing the police authority structure.

■ Eclectic Perspective

Even though the 1980s and 1990s found law enforcement administration more community/client-oriented, these agencies were facing the challenge of increasing crime with decreasing resources. Local tax revenues, as well as federal funding, were in short supply. As a result, an awareness that a "mix and match" approach to administration was necessary to meet an unstable environment. Consequently, **Eclectic Perspective** milestones began to appear.

In *Policing Practices in the 90s: Key Management Issues*, Phyllis McDonald wrote, "In recent years there has been a new emphasis on police manuals, policies, and procedures." A reason for this is ". . . the number and dollar amounts of civil liability suits from citizens who have become more knowledgeable of their civil rights and therefore have higher expectations of fair treatment by the police" (as quoted by Fyfe, 1989, p. 37).

The call for stricter control over police conduct and the need to make more efficient use of dwindling resources caused law enforcement administrators to take a more eclectic approach to managing their agencies. Various strategies were tried that included priority management of radio calls, directed patrol, minimizing report-taking time, creating interagency crime task forces, civilianization, increasing crime prevention efforts, and more advanced use of information technology (Cronkhite, 1990, pp. 3–13).

Additionally, research was questioning a number of long-established law enforcement theories, including those described here.

Increase the number of police officers and the police budget. Increasing the number of police does not necessarily reduce the crime rate or improve the proportion of crimes solved. The same is true of budgetary expenditures for police. The most that can be said is that if there were no police there would be more crime. Once a certain threshold of coverage has been reached, added increments of money and personnel are seldom efficacious. Variations in both crime and clearance rates are best predicted by social conditions such as income, unemployment, population, income distribution, and social heterogeneity (Morris, 1981, pp. 24–41).

Random motorized patrol. This neither reduces crime nor improves chances of apprehending suspects. Moreover, it does not reassure citizens enough to relieve their fear of crime, nor does it engender greater trust in the police. Regular patrolling by foot-beat officers, by contrast, has been shown to reduce citizen fear of crime, although it has no demonstrable impact on crime itself (Kelling, 1974).

Two-person patrol cars. These are no more effective than one-person cars in reducing crime or apprehending criminals. Furthermore, injuries to police officers are not as likely to occur in one-person patrol cars (Reiss, 1971).

Saturation patrolling. This does not prevent crime; it only temporarily curtails it, largely by displacement to other areas (Biech & Kessler, 1977, pp. 8, 9).

Patrol officers encounter criminals. The kind of crime that frightens Americans most (robbery, burglary, rape, homicide) is rarely encountered by police on patrol (Biech & Kessler, 1977, pp. 25–27).

Improved response time. Improving response time to emergency calls has no effect on the likelihood of arresting suspects or on the satisfaction level of the citizen involved. A federal Law Enforcement Assistance Administration study showed that the chances of making an arrest dropped below 10% when even 1 minute had elapsed from the time when the crime was committed and the time when police arrived at the scene. Only instantaneous reaction would be effective. Response time makes little difference because victims on average wait for 4 to 5 minutes before calling the police, even when they are victims of confrontational crimes (Greenwood, 1976).

Criminal investigations. Crimes seldom are solved (in the sense of offenders being arrested and prosecuted) through criminal investigations conducted by police departments. Generally, crimes are solved because offenders are apprehended immediately or because someone identifies the offender specifically such as by name, address, or license plate number (Palen, 1975, p. 75).

In the field of supervision and leadership, police administrators have to take a more situational approach. A milestone assessment of 155 police managers by Kuykendall and Unsinger, using the Hershey and Blanchard contingency model (see Chapter 8) indicated that police managers use a variety of leadership styles, depending on the situation. They are most likely to use the "selling, telling, and participating" style, whereas the "delegating" style is used less frequently (Kuykendall & Unsinger, 1982, pp. 311–321).

Organization patterns also were changing, as Eclectic Perspective approaches were applied to traditional bureaucratic law enforcement structures. These changes were reflected in one leading policing textbook of the day:

> *Organizational theorists have tended to favor the adoption of a single organizational form for an entire organization. If, however, various organizational forms are more effective for different types of problems and tasks, and if tasks vary widely (as in any complex organization), then it is improper to suggest that a single organizational form and its attendant management style should prevail throughout the enterprise. (International City Managers Association, 1977, pp. 112–113)*

This textbook described how "contingency theory" management can be applied to law enforcement (1977, pp. 109–119). A later edition of this text describes the dynamics of organizational change for police managers (International City Management Association, 1982, pp. 79–90). These concepts will be discussed in Chapter 14.

Law enforcement changed significantly as an Eclectic Perspective view of theories and concepts of the past were revisited. Some of the strategies explored were matrix-type division of responsibilities to relate to individual neighborhood needs, institutionalizing community-oriented policing, assessing community needs, and establishing accountability (Cronkhite, 1988, pp. 94–98). These organizational changes will be discussed in Chapter 7.

The next section concentrates on contextual theme lessons from a historical law enforcement incident that can provide current direction for criminal justice administration.

■ A Case Study of the Importance of Applying and Maintaining Contextual Themes Concepts in Law Enforcement

Police administrators, as with all criminal justice administrators, exist in an ever-changing environment. Keeping abreast of past and current concepts and theories is essential if criminal justice administrators are to provide services that meet contemporary demands.

This section serves as a reminder that an awareness of all the contextual themes is important in confronting contemporary criminal justice issues. In studying administrative malfunctions, the themes can help spotlight theories and concepts, the abandonment of which may result in malfeasance. In seeking cures for this, the themes can point to theories and concepts that may need to be reinstated.

In March 1991, a police incident resulted in a national outcry against the actions of certain members of the Los Angeles Police Department (LAPD). This incident has become an example of administrative failure. A videotape (taken by a citizen) of the arrest of **Rodney King** was seen by millions of people on television. The videotape showed uniformed officers of the Los Angeles Police Department striking King numerous times, in the presence of a sergeant and with a group of other officers standing by.

This incident galvanized public demands for reform of police procedures involving the use of force. An independent commission (known as the Christopher Commission) was established to investigate and make recommendations with regard to the fundamental issues raised by this incident:

- the apparent failure to control or discipline officers with repeated complaints of excessive force,
- the concerns about the LAPD's "culture" and officers' attitudes toward racial and other minorities,
- the difficulties the public encounters in attempting to make complaints against LAPD officers, and
- the roles of the LAPD leadership and civilian oversight authorities addressing or contributing to these problems (*Christopher Commission Report*, 1991, p. vii).

The commission investigation found:

> *There is a significant number of officers in the LAPD who repetitively use excessive force against the public and persistently ignore the written guidelines of the Department regarding force. This finding is documented and confirmed from detailed analyses of documents and statistics by the Commission. Our computerized study of the complaints filed in recent years shows a strong concentration of allegations against a problem group of officers. A comparable study of the use of force reports reveals a similar concentration. Graphic confirmation of improper attitudes and practices is provided by the brazen and extensive references to beatings and other excessive uses*

of force on the MDTs [Mobil Digital Terminals in the police vehicles].
(1991, p. viii)

The Commission also found that the problem of excessive force was "aggravated by racism and bias," again strikingly revealed in the MDTs:

> *The failure to control these officers is a management issue that is at the heart of the problem. The documents and data that we have analyzed have all been available to the Department; indeed, most of this information came from that source. The LAPD's failure to analyze and act upon these revealing data evidences a significant breakdown in the management and leadership of the Department. The Police Commission, lacking investigators or other resources, failed in its duty to monitor the Department in this sensitive use of force area. The Department not only failed to deal with the problem group of officers but it often rewarded them with positive evaluations and promotions.*
>
> *Our findings drive our principal recommendations. We urge that the leadership of the LAPD go beyond rhetoric in carrying out its existing policies against excessive force. From the Chief of Police on down to the sergeants this means taking a firm stand against the "bad guys" on the force and employing all the instruments available—training, discipline, assignments, and promotion. It also means monitoring and auditing all available data—patrol car transmissions, use of force reports, and citizen complaints—and then acting on the data. We urge a comparable effort to monitor and root out the manifestations of racism and bias.*
>
> *We recommend a new standard of accountability. Los Angeles should have a Police Department whose Chief is accountable to civilian officials for the Department's performance, and where ranking officers are responsible for the conduct of those they lead (1991, pp. iii, iv).*

An analysis of this incident demonstrates how the lessons learned during the past 100 years of the development of the Contextual Administration themes are important in confronting today's criminal justice challenges. One of the many causes of the Rodney King incident may be related to a myopic focusing on just one of the contextual themes at the expense of all the others.

The emphasis on "employee empowerment" (a concept of the Client-Oriented theme), for example, without considering other themes could have been at fault. Overemphasis on "employee empowerment" at the expense of the inspection and control concepts from the Organizational Functions theme and the need for community "feedback" developed from the Open Systems theme appears to be at fault.

The Contextual Themes Model is meant to assist public administrators in maintaining an Eclectic Perspective: an awareness of the themes, and their related theories and concepts, that can be applied to current issues. An analysis of the Rodney King case demonstrates how this approach may have prevented the incident and how the Contextual Themes Model can be used to select conceptual tools that should be applied. The model serves as a guide to lessons of the past and can assist in finding causes and cures for current and future public sector issues. For example, the Rodney King incident can be analyzed using the five themes of the model.

■ Organization Functions Theme

The Christopher Commission found a "failure to analyze" data, and a need for "monitoring and auditing" (1991, p. iv). "The Inspector General should audit the disciplinary system at least annually, and forward that detailed audit to the Police Commission for its review and approval" (1991, p. 178). These recommendations point to historic administrative practices that were developed during the Organization Functions period (see Chapter 2) and later adopted by law enforcement but not followed in this incident.

In relating the commission's report to past administrative practices, it is good to remember that these practices were documented in the first law enforcement textbook, *Police Administration*, under the subject of "Inspection and Control." This text states, ". . . inspection and control are not performed exclusively by any one person, but are in process throughout the department. At each level of authority, the head must plan, direct, and control—from the chief down each successive level to the officer who performs the task" (Wilson, 1963, p. 15). This text also recommends that the Chief of Police appoint a command level inspector to audit "the integrity of the force" (Wilson, p. 16). The text also refers to Gulick in defining control:

> *"Control," states Gulick [referring to Luther Gulick's Papers on the Science of Administration (1937)], consists in seeing that everything is carried out in accordance with the plan which has been adopted, the organization which has been set up, and the orders which have been given . . . control is in a sense the consequence of command in action. Authority cannot be delegated safely without this check and hence the rule: Every delegation of authority should be accompanied by a commensurate placing of responsibility (Wilson, p. 10).*

Continuing with the commission's investigation, the report states, "The documents and data that we have analyzed have all been available to the Department; indeed, most of this information came from that source. The LAPD's failure to analyze and act upon these revealing data evidences a significant breakdown in the management and leadership of the Department" (p. iv). The commission's investigation provided an example of how Organization Functions theories that were documented years before in Wilson's *Police Administration* should have been followed in preventing this incident. Wilson states:

> *A regular and orderly system of reviewing investigation reports and other police records in order to control the work of individual offi-*

*cers is essential. A police department that relies solely upon the in-
dividual officers to follow through on cases to which they are assigned cannot give satisfactory service. A system is needed to
supervise and control all police matters that require action to ensure
that all available information at the command of the department is
brought to bear on each case, and to determine that the service ren-
dered is effective and of a high quality. A system of report review ex-
pedites the day-to-day business, catches the stray threads at proper
intervals, causes action to be instituted at a stated time in the future,
and generally aids in keeping the staff alert (1963, pp. 400–401).*

The commission also recommended ". . . a new standard of *accountability.*
Los Angeles should have a Police Department whose Chief is accountable to civilian officials for the Department's performance, and where ranking officers are responsible for the conduct of those they lead" (p. iv).

The concept of accountability was established during the period of development of Organization Functions in law enforcement. "Persons to whom authority is delegated are invariably held accountable for the use made of it and for
the failure to use it" became a founding principle for police agencies (Wilson,
1963, p. 35). Accountability of command was further defined:

*Although he may free himself of the actual performance of the tasks
involved, a superior officer cannot rid himself of an iota of responsibility for their accomplishment. He may delegate to subordinates
the authority to perform the tasks, and he may tell those subordinates
that they are responsible for a successful conclusion of the assignment; but he remains accountable for its final accomplishment (Wilson, 1963, p. 110).*

In April 1991, the *Los Angeles Daily News* printed an article about the Rodney King incident written by Terry Cooper, a professor of public administration
at the University of Southern California. Cooper reminded us of Paul Appleby's
"Morality and Administration in Democratic Government" (1952), which stated,
"The only way bureaucratic organizations can be made to function ethically is
when responsibility is maintained at each level of the hierarchy."

Cooper applied this theory to the King incident by stating, "Each public agent
from top to bottom of large-scale bureaucracies like the LAPD must be held accountable for carrying out the public's will in the face of pressures and tempta-
tions to do otherwise, or these modern machinelike organizations tend to become
self-serving and inhumane" (Cooper, 1991, p. 2).

■ Employee Relations Theme

The Christopher Commission recommended ". . . employing all the instruments
available—training, discipline, assignments, and promotion" (1991, p. iv)
and improvement in "recruitment, selection and psychological testing" (p. 110).

Directions for these functions were ingrained in law enforcement administration during the period of the development of the Employee Relations theme.

> *The selection and management of personnel is the chief's most important administrative task. A high quality of service is dependent upon his unwavering insistence upon the application of two principles: (1) the best man [written before affirmative action changes that would have made this "the best person"] must invariably be selected for appointment, promotion, and assignment; and (2) doubt in reference to appointment, promotion, or separation from service must be resolved in favor of the department.*
>
> *The chief has the further responsibility to provide a continuing and effective training program; to exercise controls that will ensure compliance with department policies, programs, and procedures and accomplishment equal to the capacity of the individual officer; and to safeguard the welfare of the members of the force. His attainment of these goals will determine in large measure his success as police chief.... His success as an administrator is dependent on his control of the members of his force. (Wilson, 1963, pp. 130–131)*

Additionally, during the period of the development of the Employee Relations theme in law enforcement, it was found that periodic rotation of officer assignments, particularly from the morning watches, is necessary to prevent the development of employee subcultures that are counterproductive to the goals of police agencies.

Officers who are developing attitudes and behavior patterns that are in conflict with agency policies and procedure tend to gravitate to substations farthest away from headquarters, as well as to the morning watch, which is often farthest from the scrutiny of command personnel. Because they are working when most other people sleep and vice versa, morning watch officers can become separated from friends and relatives outside of law enforcement. As a result, the employees on the morning watch tend to be limited to association with other employees on their watch. Over time, this can result in a myopic and sometime biased work environment. The primary officers in the Rodney King incident were assigned to the morning watch in the LAPD Foothill Substation, which is one of those farthest from headquarters.

The Rodney King incident had a psychological impact on law enforcement personnel and organizations, not only within the LAPD but also throughout the country. Some of the psychological concepts developed in response to the Employee Relations theme can be used in coping with the added stress, in improving morale, and in promoting quality service despite the added pressures of current events.

Some strategies that are supported by Employee Relations concepts were described in an article in *Western City* under the title "Coping with the Aftermath of the Rodney King Incident":

- Reaffirming a belief in the basic mission.
- Encouraging communication and dialogue.
- Demonstrating a caring about people.

- Allowing for the ventilation of frustrations.
- Ensuring fairness.
- Keeping personnel on the healthy end of the continuum.
- Reinforcing a supportive structure.
- Continuing toward goals of excellence.
- Getting issues out in the open (Barry & Cronkhite, 1991, p. 22).

Open Systems Theme

The Christopher Commission recommended ". . . an effort to monitor and root out the manifestations of racism and bias" (1991, p. iv). Racism and bias often develop from a "closed system" perspective, an "us against them" attitude.

In the 1970s, the LAPD and several other police departments initiated a program in which police recruits were assigned to live with minority community families during their academy training. This program provided an Open Systems outlook to new police officers who had not experienced life in a minority neighborhood. This program should not have been abandoned.

The commission reported, "The LAPD has an organizational culture that emphasizes crime control over crime prevention and that isolates the police from the communities and the people they serve" (1991, p. xiv). In response to the Open Systems theme, in the 1960s and 1970s law enforcement learned the advantages of cooperating with residents and other government agencies to rid neighborhoods of physical factors that contribute to crime. This "Broken Window" concept came from a study that showed that when abandoned vehicles and structures were allowed to remain, there was a natural progression of more broken windows to neighborhood deterioration to increased crime. It was learned that crime can be prevented by an Open Systems cooperation with the environment outside the police agency (Kelling, 1974). Promoting this philosophy can reduce the isolation of the police from the communities and the people they serve.

The commission said, "The LAPD remains committed, however, to its traditional style of law enforcement with an emphasis on crime control and arrests" (1991, p. xv). Under the Open Systems outlook, law enforcement recognized that its outputs not only were arrests and crime control but also crime prevention, crime repression, regulation of infractions, and maintaining order. Additionally, that success depended on the inputs of community and political support. Additionally, a feedback systems was needed to measure output accomplishments through review of reports, field inspections, review of citizen complaints, and public opinion surveys.

Many police departments have established a mission statement and measures of accountability that reflect an Open Systems outlook. For example, the Santa Ana Police Department (California) developed the slogan of "Partners with the Community" and a mission statement and measures of accountability to support its mission:

> *To ensure the safety and security of all of the people of our city by*
> *providing responsive and professional police service with compassion*

> *and concern. Our Mission is accomplished within the moral and legal standards of our community through a partnership of community and members of the department. (Cronkhite, 1988, p. 95)*

The measures of accomplishment for the mission statement ranged from crime statistics, community satisfaction surveys, analysis of citizen complaint to "biopsy" inspections of crime investigations in which victims and witnesses were re-interviewed to gain their evaluation of the quality of police service. The emphasis was on crime reduction and community support rather than on arrests. Officers were held accountable for the accomplishment of the mission statement in assigned geographical areas (Cronkhite, 1988, p. 95).

An Open Systems outlook, when applied to the Rodney King incident, would allow for a broader understanding of the causes. A prominent Los Angeles attorney and political observer (who later became mayor of Los Angeles), Richard J. Riordan, exemplified this outlook when he wrote:

> *In the future, the aftermath of the Rodney King incident may be seen as a time when Los Angeles opened up not only to the world, but to itself. The incident divided the city, or more accurately, brought into the open the huge divisions already existing. The divisions are not merely racial; they also run between the "haves" and the "have-nots."*
>
> *The "have-nots" are not only the penniless and destitute; this category also embraces the broad class of "working poor" of all races, people who permanently teeter on the brink of true, hopeless poverty, without having the education and economic opportunities necessary to pull themselves higher. For them, Police Chief Daryl Gates has become a symbol of despair, just as he is a symbol of protection for the "haves."*
>
> *Although some populists blamed racism for the King incident, cooler heads saw the immediate problem as that of an efficient, paramilitary police department suffering from a breakdown in discipline at the street level. The level of racism among the police is no more or less than among the general population. However, for the police officer to "take it to work" is not tolerable. . . . The solution to the problems in our city is nothing so simple, or so difficult, as purging the Police Department of racism. Even after a round of reforms, the principal mission of a kinder, gentler LAPD will remain the protection of law-abiding citizens from crime, not the provision of better medical care, nutrition and education for the have-nots. This is a job for the whole society. (Riordan, 1991).*

Riordan's article gives insight into the social complexities that require coordination among the police, other government agencies, and the community in seeking solutions. This requires an Open Systems approach by law enforcement as well as by other related agencies.

■ Social Equity Theme

The commission's report summarized concerns about the Police Department protection of equal rights under the laws of the nation:

> *Within the minority communities of Los Angeles, there is a widely-held view that police misconduct is common place. The King beating refocused public attention on long-standing complaints by African-Americans, Latinos and Asians that LAPD officers frequently treat minorities differently from whites, more often using disrespectful and abusive language, employing unnecessarily intrusive practices such as the "prone-out," and engaging in use of excessive force when dealing with minorities.*
>
> *The extent to which minority officers are accepted and integrated within the LAPD is a measure of the Department's responsiveness to the larger minority communities. The MDT [Mobil Digital Terminal in police vehicles] messages and other evidence suggests that minority officers are still too frequently subjected to racist slurs and comments and to discriminatory treatment by fellow officers.*
>
> *Bias within the LAPD is not limited to racist and ethnic prejudices, but embraces widespread and strongly felt gender bias as well. The Los Angeles Police Department has a well-documented prior history of discrimination against gay men and lesbians. . . . Some of the most offensive comments in the MDT transcripts reviewed by the Commission concerned lesbians and gay men. (1991, pp. 70–72)*

A commitment to Social Equity was emphasized at the Minnowbrook Conference in 1968 as part of the "New Public Administration" by Dwight Waldo and other forward-thinking public administrators. H. George Frederickson warned: "A Public Administration which fails to work for changes which try to redress the deprivation of minorities will likely be eventually used to repress those minorities (1971, p. 426).

Todd R. LaPorte wrote, "Our primary normative premise should be that the purpose of public organization is the reduction of economic, social, and psychic suffering and the enhancement of life opportunities for those inside and outside the organization" (1971, p. 32).

Robert Wasserman reminded police administrators:

> *Every resident of the community has the same rights, and these rights are protected by the Constitution. It is a primary police responsibility to ensure that the degree of protection of these rights is equal through out the community. . . . When individual rights are involved, the police have a Constitutional mandate to provide every resident with equal protection. This responsibility forms the basic fabric of the police functions (1977, p. 32).*

A number of police administration textbooks provide reminders of law enforcement Social Equity responsibilities. The duties of law enforcement are described as "maintenance of social order within carefully prescribed ethical and constitutional restrictions" (International City Management Association, 1969, p. 3) and "protecting individual rights and ensuring social justice" (International City Management Association, 1977, p. 352). These are responsibilities of law enforcement that must be ingrained in all police officers.

Institutionalizing the police mission as not merely a program, but rather a philosophy that permeates each agency. The philosophy needs to be an integral part of the selection, recruit-training, in-service training, evaluation, promotion, and reward processes.

The commission's report revealed concern about these personnel functions particularly in the area of training. The report states: "At present the curriculum [recruit training] provides only eight hours in cultural awareness training. No more than 1–1/2 [sic] hours is devoted to any ethnic group" (1991, pp. xvi, xvii). The commission went on to say, ". . . Virtually all of the Field Training Officers interviewed stated that their primary objective in training probationers is to instill good "officer safety skills" (*Christopher Commission Report*, 1991, p. xvii).

The subject of a 1991 Master of Science thesis presented to the University of Southern California's Graduate School was the training of both the Los Angeles Police Department and the Los Angeles Sheriff's Department. The writer of the thesis found:

> *The socialization of recruits at the academy level does not focus specifically on the departmental goals and objectives; they remain very much in the background. Guided by their abstract and idealistic nature, the academy exposes recruits to them in a very cursory and abstract fashion along with other features of the departmental policy, manual and ethics during the orientation or introductory brief. At that stage, recruits have faint ideas about police work and are hardly in a position to relate these principles to procedures (Ramasundaram, 1991, pp. 139–140).*
>
> *In recent years, the emphasis on articulation of goals and mission has gone up. . . . However, the treatment of goals is still idealistic rather than practical; it appears to be more for pleasing a public audience than for guiding the performance of the employees (Ramasundaram, 1991, pp. 140–141).*
>
> *Thus although field training officers are responsible for helping recruits apply the information and training they received at the academy to "real world" situations, the actual performance of most of them is contrary to what is expected of them. Most recruits find it difficult to adjust to the transition from the academy to the field training; there is a sudden switching over of socializing agencies, each preaching a different philosophy and often working at cross purposes. Recruits see little connection between what they were taught at the academy and what their field training officers are advising them. The result is a confusion in the minds of the recruits,*

which was very aptly termed as "cognitive dissonance" by one of my interviewees. It is primarily at this stage that the gains of academy training are lost. (Ramasundaram, 1991, p. 148)

The Rodney King incident symbolized the need for a commitment to Social Equity and that this commitment is crucial to the future of policing in America.

■ Client-Oriented Service Theme

The commission's report recommended a community-oriented approach, which is in support of the Client-Oriented Service theme:

> *. . . nearly two-thirds (62.9%) of the 650 officers who responded to the recent LAPD survey expressed the opinion that "increased interaction with the community would improve the Department's relations with citizens. A model of community policing has gained increased acceptance in other parts of the country during the past 10 years. The community policing model places service to the public and prevention of crime as the primary role of police in society and emphasizes problem solving, with active citizen involvement in defining those matters that are important to the community, rather than arrest statistics. Officers at the patrol level are required to spend less time in their cars communicating with other officers and more time on the street communicating with citizens. Proponents of this style of policing insist that addressing the causes of crime makes police officers more effective crime fighters, and at the same time enhances the quality of life in the neighborhood (Christopher Commission Report, 1991, pp. xiv, xv).*

It should be noted that the conditions in Los Angeles at the time were reflective of the community's loss of trust and consequential loss of support for the LAPD. In the years before the Rodney King incident, the public had passed legislation that reduced tax support for policing as well as other governmental services. As will be discussed in Chapter 11, adequate resources are required if the police are to be proactive and community-oriented.

The commission's report stated: "Of the police departments of the six largest United States cities, the LAPD has the fewest officers per resident and the fewest officers per square mile" (*Christopher Commission Report*, 1991, p. viii). Los Angeles Annual Reports substantiated that the department was reduced almost 10% in personnel between 1975 and 1985. This was partly because of the California tax initiative known as Proposition 13 and partly because of cutbacks that were decided on a local political basis.

The commission's report went on to state that community policing concepts were not foreign to the LAPD, but that this concept was deemphasized in part because of budget constraints and a reduction of the number of officers:

In the late 1960s, after the Watts Riots, Chief Tom Reddin appointed Community Relations Officers (CRO), all lieutenants, to provide liaison to neighborhood organizations. In 1970, Chief Ed Davis created "the basic car plan," a beat system in which small teams of officers had 24-hour responsibility for patrolling a relatively small area within a precinct. A new rank was created—senior lead officer (SLO)—to lead the team. The SLO coordinated the basic car team, handled his or her own patrol responsibilities, monitored conditions within his or her geographic area, organized Neighborhood Watch groups, and arranged crime-prevention meetings with the local residents. Several years later, Chief Davis instituted *team policing*, which decentralized authority by creating a number of smaller, autonomous units throughout the city. The goal of team policing was to develop closer ties with the community and to respond to concerns for the overall well-being of the area. Beginning in 1979, Chief Gates began to emphasize priorities that turned away from the team policing system and recentralized authority in headquarters, in part because of budget constraints and a reduction in the number of officers. In light of budget cuts, CRO lieutenants were eliminated; area captains were given responsibility for the work the CRO's had done. (*Christopher Commission Report*, 1991, pp. 101–102)

The Los Angeles Budget Reports showed that the elimination of the CRO position (as well as some other reductions in the Department budget) was directed by elected officials. These officials perceived that the Neighbor Watch/Team Policing program was a political effort of then Chief Davis, who had indicated he might run for mayor and in fact did run for governor of California. They viewed this program as a "grassroots" approach to getting votes.

In the late 1980s, hiring was reinstituted, bringing the number of employees to 8,450 sworn police officers, augmented by 2,000 civilian employees. This was far below the ratio of officer to citizen of most other large police departments. If the LAPD was to have enough personnel so that officers could spend . . . "less time in their cars communicating with other officers and more time on the street communicating with citizens" (*Christopher Commission Report*, 1991, p. xv), they would need additional personnel.

There must be time available for officers to interact with the public and proactively provide problem-solving policing. More officers are required to meet the time frame for this. Additional officers require further political and public support. This is an example of how community trust and support for law enforcement are needed if Client-Oriented Service is to be provided.

■ Eclectic Perspective

Within the Contextual Themes Model, the Eclectic Perspective is presented as a "lens" through which past themes, theories, and concepts are modulated to focus on current issues. It represents an understanding that all the themes compose a spectrum of theories and concepts from which to draw in confronting contemporary issues such as the Rodney King incident. This analysis of the King incident, using the five contextual themes, is a demonstration of the approach.

The 1991 *Western City* article "Coping with the Aftermath of the Rodney G. King Incident" offers some guidance from this perspective:

> ... *managers may want to view the stress resulting from the King affair as a challenge to review and improve the coping skills of their law enforcement personnel and organizations. Change most often is a product of dissatisfaction; people usually are not motivated to change unless their current status is uncomfortable. Employees become more supportive of change when they see it as a means of reducing their dissatisfaction and of improving their feelings of self-worth.*
>
> *So management should consider this situation as an opportunity to instigate change when change is needed, an ideal time to enhance the values and mission of police agencies. A renewed emphasis on ethics and a rekindling of the community-oriented policing philosophy should be viewed as essentials in enhancing the morale and professional esteem of all personnel. (Barry & Cronkhite, 1991, p. 32; the complete article can be found at the end of Chapter 8)*

Barry and Cronkhite continue with advice that relates to the Christopher Commission Report recommendation that "We urge that the leadership of the LAPD go beyond rhetoric in carrying out existing policies against excessive force" (*Christopher Commission Report*, 1991, p. iv). Barry and Cronkhite emphasize that the actions and philosophy exhibited by the leadership is much more important than the words in the mission statement:

> *The primary thrust of such a value-based management philosophy is not so much toward prohibitions which restrain officers but toward encouraging employees to weigh their actions constantly in light of the high ethical and constitutional values of their profession. All law enforcement officers are sworn to uphold state and federal constitutions as well as the traditional "Law Enforcement Code of Ethics." The value-based philosophy should be defined in an employee-accepted mission statement, which emphasizes that:*
>
> - *Recognition of individual dignity is vital in the free system of law enforcement by the Constitution. All persons have a right to be treated with as much respect as they will allow and officers have a duty to protect this right.*
> - *Ensuring the safety and security of all people by providing responsive and professional police service with compassion and concern is of prime importance in every public contact.*
> - *The move in emphasis on quantity to quality action empowers officers to select an appropriate course of action from a range of options rather than a few prescribed responses.*
> - *Making the community policing philosophy the central focus of police employees will foster closer contact between the employees*

and the public, provide more situations for positive feedback and give officers a cause that can improve their morale and enhance their feeling of self-worth. Making that commitment could turn the King incident into an opportunity to transcend to a higher level of professionalism, a quest for excellence in striving toward long-range individual and organizational goals and objectives. (Barry & Cronkhite, 1991, p. 32)

This philosophy is presented as an example of the importance of institutionalizing contextual themes concepts that are the building blocks that support today's criminal justice administration.

KEY CONCEPTS AND TERMS

- Contextual administrative themes in law enforcement
  - Private sector development of themes
  - Subsequent adoption by law enforcement
- Open Systems model
  - Inputs
  - Processing
  - Outputs
- The Rodney King Case
  - All five contextual themes relate
  - Failure to adhere to past themes
- Eclectic Perspective in law enforcement

CHAPTER ACTIVITY

The Rodney King incident was presented as a case study of how failure to institutionalize some of the contextual themes concepts can result in malfeasance. Research incidents of other criminal justice malfeasance and, by using the five contextual themes as a guide, identify administrative concepts that could have prevented these situations.

REVIEW QUESTIONS

1. This chapter begins with a statement that law enforcement lagged behind other public sector fields in pursuing "professionalism." What factors caused this to occur?

2. Give examples of how some of the five contextual themes concepts have been applied to law enforcement.

3. What were some of the long-established law enforcement theories that research dispelled during the 1980s and 1990s?

4. What were some of the contextual themes concepts that were lacking in the Rodney King case study, and how did they contribute to this incident?

5 What were some of the social, economic, and political conditions that contributed to the Rodney King incident?

REFERENCES

Alshulter, A. (1977). The Study of American Public Administration. In *The Politics of the Federal Bureaucracy*. New York: Harper & Row.

Wrap Up

Barry, R., & Cronkhite, C. (1991). Managing Police Agencies under Stress: Coping with the Aftermath of the Rodney G. King Incident. *Western City*, July Issue, pp. 21–26.

Biech, W., & Kessler, D. (1977). *Response Time Analysis*. Washington, DC: Police Executive Research Forum.

Christopher Commission Report: Report of the Independent Commission on the Los Angeles Police Department (1991). 400 South Hope Street, Los Angeles: Warren Christopher, Chair.

Cooper, T. (1991). Police Officers Receive Cues from Gates: Chief Responsible for Shaping LAPD "Culture" That Led to King Beating. *Los Angeles Daily News*, p. 2.

Cronkhite, C. (1974). *Automation and Law Enforcement*. Springfield, IL: Charles C. Thomas.

Cronkhite, C. (1988). Santa Ana's Reorganization-Matrix Community Oriented Policing. *Journal of California Law Enforcement*, April Issue, pp. 22–28.

Fosdick, R. B. (1920). *American Police Systems*. New York: The Century Co.

Frederickson, H. G. (1971). Toward a New Public Administration. In *Toward a New Public Administration: The Minnowbrook Perspective*. New York: Harper & Row.

Fyfe, J. J. (Ed.). (1989). *Police Practice in the '90's: Key Management Issues*. Washington, DC: International City Managers Association.

Greenwood, P. (1976). *The Criminal Investigation Process*. Washington, DC: Law Enforcement Assistance Administration.

International City Management Association. (1958). *Supervisory Methodism Municipal Administration*. Chicago: Institute for Training in Municipal Administration.

International City Management Association. (1969). *Municipal Police Administration*. Washington, DC: Institute for Training in Municipal Administration.

International City Management Association. (1982). *Local Government Police Management*. Washington, DC: Institute for Training in Municipal Administration.

Jordan, K. E. (1972). *Ideology and the Coming of Professionalism: American Urban Police in the 1920's and 1930's*. Unpublished Doctoral Dissertation, Rutgers University, New Jersey.

Kelling, G. (1974). *The Kansas City Preventive Patrol Experiment: A Summary Report*. Washington, DC: Police Foundation.

Kuykendall, J., & Unsinger, P. C. (1982). The Leadership Styles of Police Managers. *Journal of Criminal Justice, 2*, p. 10.

LaPorte, T. R. (1971). The Recovery of Relevance in the Study of Public Organization. In Waldo, D. (Ed.), *The New Public Administration: The Minnowbrook Perspective*, Scranton, PA: Chandler.

Matthews, F. (1909). *The Character of the American Police, The World's Work 2*. New York: Doubleday.

Morris, P. (1981). *Crime Control and the Police: A Review of Research*. London: HMSO.

National Advisory Commission on Criminal Justice Standards and Goals. (1973). *Police*. Washington, DC: Task Force on Police.

National Institute of Justice. (1988). *Community Policing: Issues and Practices around the World*. Washington, DC: Police Foundation.

Palen, J. J. (1975). *The Urban World*. New York: McGraw-Hill.

Pate, T. (1976). *Three Approaches to Criminal Apprehension in Kansas City: An Evaluation Report*. Washington, DC: Police Foundation.

Ramasundaram, A. M. (1991). *Police Academy Training: A Link between Department Goals and Field Realities*. Unpublished Master's thesis, University of Southern California, Los Angeles.

Reiss, A., Jr. (1971). *The Police and the Public*. New Haven, CT: Yale University Press.

Reith, C. (1948). *A Short History of the British Police*. New York: Oxford University Press.

Riordan, R. (1991, July 28). Perspective on Los Angeles: Rescue Plan for a City at Risk. *Los Angeles Times*, p. 2.

Sherman, L. W., Milton, C. H., & Kelly, T. V. (1973). *Team Policing: Seven Case Studies*. Washington, DC: The Police Jerome Foundation.

Skolnick, H., & Bayley, D. H. (1986). *The New Blue Line*. New York: Free Press.

Stillman, R. J. (1988). *Public Administration: Concepts and Cases*. Boston: Houghton Mifflin.

Szilagyi, A. D., & Wallace, M. J., Jr. (1983). *Organizational Behavior and Performance*, (3rd ed.). Glenview, IL: Scott, Foresman & Company.

Trojanowicz, R., & Bucqueroux, B. (1990). *Community Policing: A Contemporary Perspective*. Cincinnati: Anderson.

Wasserman, R. (1977). The Government Setting. In *Local Government Police Management*. Washington, DC: International City Management Association.

Whisenand, P. M., & Tamaru, T. T. (1970). *Automated Police Information Systems*. New York: John Wiley.

Williams, W. J. (1985). *The Miracle of Abduction*. Los Angeles: Epistemics Institute Press.

Wilson, O. W. (1963). *Police Administration*, (2nd ed.). New York: McGraw-Hill.

■ RELEVANT PUBLICATION

The following article is offered here as it relates to the police administration concepts in this chapter. It is also a fitting end to Part I as it summarizes many of the concepts presented thus far in this textbook. The article emphasizes the need for attention to the Contextual Themes of Administration in policing. It also reviews how history provides the building blocks that support the Contextual Model that is the product of the preceding chapters. (Cronkhite, C. (1995). An Eclectic Approach to Policing: Applying Past Principles to Community Policing. *Criminal Justice in America*, October/November.)

"An Eclectic Approach to Policing: Applying Past Principles to Community Policing" by Clyde Cronkhite

In law enforcement there is a tendency at times to adopt the latest concepts without reviewing some well-founded principles of the past. This does not necessarily mean that the principles of the past are best. It means that contemporary challenges require an eclectic approach: a blending of what we have learned in the past with an understanding of trends shaping future policing. This article strives to provide assistance in applying this approach.

In the 1940s and 1950s, the focus was on the principles of effectiveness and efficiency. It was the era of Dragnet and "just the facts." The aim was to be professional. Policing was devoted to such concepts as Gulick's POSD-CORB (Planning, Organizing, Staffing, Directing, COordinating, Reporting, and Budgeting), and the rules of Weber's Bureaucratic Model (Swanson et al. 1993, 87–94). This period might be called the Organization Functions period.

In the 1950s, the concepts of Maslow's Need Hierarchy, McGregor's Theory X and Theory Y, and Herzberg's Motivation-Hygiene Theory (Swanson et al. 1993, 98–108) emphasized motivating employees to be more effective and efficient. This period can be referred to as the Employee Relations period.

In the 1960s, civil rights demonstrations protested a broad spectrum of issues from the draft and sexual mores to discrimination by race or sex. This period highlighted law enforcement responsibility to guard against infringements of individual liberties. The police were responsible for enforcing laws that provided social equity even when some elected officials and community members did not favor such enforcement.

During the 1960s and 1970s, federal grant money (Law Enforcement Assistance Administration funds) promoted innovation and a quest for advanced technological support for policing. The resulting infusion of aerospace technology into the field of law enforcement brought a more cybernetic orientation to confronting crime. The cybernetic approach promoted a macro perspective, and the Open Systems Theory of Katz and Kahn became a well-known reference in many police textbooks of the day (Swanson et al. 1993, 112–115). This led to thinking about inputs, processing; and outputs and to the necessity of interaction with "outside" entities in achieving the police mission. "Open Systems" became the theme of this period.

The 1980s (and 1990s) saw a move toward a more client and community-oriented strategy. The social unrest of the previous decades had strained relations between the public and the police. Public dissatisfaction could be seen in ballot measures that reduced tax support for public police and promoted the privatization of many law enforcement functions. The concepts of *In Search of Excellence* (Peters and Waterman, 1982) were embraced by many policing agencies. Client-oriented service will likely be remembered as the theme of this period.

The history of American law enforcement appears to be one of circumrotation. In colonial towns during the seventeenth century, the task of policing was carried out by "able-bodied citizens" who in turn were assigned to watch for "fires and unruly persons." Early settlers did not want policing to be centrally controlled by the government as it had been in many countries from which they had migrated. Policing in this country was meant to be shared by community members.

As law enforcement became more formalized, we patterned our principles after England's Peelian Reform of 1829 (Swanson et al. 1993, 4). It is interesting to note the similarities between the principles established by Sir Robert Peel for British policing in the 1800s (Reith 1948, 64–65) and principles of community policing today.

For more than a century, however, as the police became more efficient and more professional they also became more distant from the public. Currently, there is an outcry for a return to those founding principles of community participation and local control of policing. In responding to this outcry, it is important to remember the basic principles inherent in policing.

The contextual themes of policing form an essential foundation that informs our future. They may be categorized as:

Contextual Themes of Policing

- Organizational Functions
- Employee and Human Relations
- Open Systems (interaction with other entities)
- Social Equity
- Client and Community-Oriented Service

The history of policing provides evidence of periods of retreat to earlier founding principles. For example, while focusing on social equity and community-oriented approaches, an economical downturn could lead to a return to organization theory that advocates efficiency and better use of decreasing resources.

Today's policing professional must attend to specific problems while maintaining an awareness of the multiplicity of potential problems. He or she must maintain an eclectic perspective whereby past themes, theories, and concepts are modulated to focus on current issues. This perspective recognizes that all themes compose a spectrum of theories and concepts from which to draw in confronting contemporary issues.

This perspective has been important throughout the history of policing. However, because of the current and future multitudinous diverse policing issues, this perspective is crucial in developing successful approaches to contemporary challenges.

Eclectic Prospective and Client-Oriented Policing

Today, while attention is centered on community-oriented policing (which is an outgrowth of the social equity and client-oriented themes), other themes should not be forgotten but used as a foundation on which to build the future of policing.

The prevailing community-oriented philosophy is committed to (1) increasing accountability to local communities, (2) reorienting patrol activities to emphasize service, (3) organizing community-based crime prevention, (4) improving communication with the community, and (5) decentralizing the police authority structure. (Barry and Cronkhite 1992, 11).

Implementing these approaches without attention to past contextual themes can result in failure. For example, one community-oriented approach is to assign patrol officers to given areas on a long-term basis. In the 1940s and 1950s many law enforcement agencies abandoned this practice in an effort to curtail corruption. Also, leaving officers on a given watch (morning watch in particular) can result in the development of employee subcultures that are counterproductive to the police mission.

Today, the community accountability benefits of long-term area assignments of patrol officers must be balanced by an application of inspection and control practices which are part of the organizational functions building block. A recent reminder comes from the 1992 Christopher Commission report that reviewed the Los Angeles Rodney King incident. It stated that there is a need for more "monitoring and auditing" as well as a need for a more community-oriented approach to policing (1991).

Another relevant aspect of the Organization Functions building block is the authority, responsibility, and accountability rule. "Empowering" employees (which is another component of community policing) does not relieve supervisors, managers, and the police executive of overall responsibility. O.W. Wilson wrote in the 1960s that:

Although he may free himself of the actual performance of the tasks involved, a superior officer cannot rid himself of an iota of responsibility for their accomplishment. He may delegate to subordinates the authority to perform the tasks, and he may tell those subordinates that they are responsible for a successful conclusion of the assignment; but he remains accountable for its final accomplishment (Wilson 1963, 110).

Additionally, to empower line-level employees and decentralize authority without applying the principles established in the employee relations building block could have disastrous results. Before officers can be empowered, they must receive proper training and indoctrination.

Law enforcement training and education must place strong emphasis on the constitutional responsibilities of the police—the historical development of community-shared police responsibilities, the ethical and moral responsibility of the police, the importance of crime prevention in achieving the police mission, and other educational tools needed for officers to be problem solvers. The percentage of police academy training that focuses on these vital components of community-oriented policing versus what is provided with regards to the technical and survival aspects of law enforcement, requires further research.

Another element of community policing is the mission statement. Mission statements are often prominently displayed in the offices of the police executives, but in actuality may not be the mission of the rank-and-file. The principles that form the employee relations theme serve as a guide for institutionalizing its mission. To institutionalize the mission, it must be converted into goals and the goals made an element of the employee reward system (Roberg 1993, 91–94).

Michael LeBoeuf described his "Greatest Management Principle" as "what gets done is what gets rewarded" (LeBoeuf 1991). The goals of community policing must be made a component of the employee selection, evaluation, and promotion process, and the awards system.

The Employee Relations principles also reflect concepts learned in the late 1930s from Elton Mayo's Hawthorne Studies (Mayo 1945). A recent police textbook relates Mayo's findings to current reorganization efforts:

Attempts to modify bureaucracy, such as team policing, may succeed temporarily in large police departments, if only because such efforts produce a Hawthorne effect. However, in large-scale organizations over time, the latent power of bureaucracy will assert itself.

The text states further that "This is not a call to abandon efforts or experimentation with alternative organizational structures in policing; it is a call for realism and reason" (Swanson et al. 1993, 123).

For many agencies, institutionalizing community policing represents a cultural change within the organization. People usually are not motivated to change unless their current status is uncomfortable. Employees become more supportive of change when they see it as a means of reducing their dissatisfaction. Changes cannot be achieved by presenting community policing as a new approach to fighting crime, as a substitute for arresting criminals, or as a conversion of officers to social workers. Law enforcement still has to make arrests, respond to emergency calls, and attend to other essential public safety functions.

It seems that most law enforcement employees are dissatisfied with their current status. Organizational change can be achieved by showing employees that working to prevent crime by enhancing ties with the community and by improving neighborhood quality of life can make their job easier and more satisfying. Employee support for change will be promoted by demonstrating that the community policing approach will result in a reduction in crime and a recapture of diminishing public support.

Organizational culture takes time to change and should not be rushed. Law enforcement leaders who have been involved in community policing changes will agree with the fact that after a decade of effort to make organizational changes, only 30 percent of their employees fully support the change. Another 20 percent will never change and the remaining 50 percent are in a "wait and see" mode.

Finally, the open systems building block is a reminder of the "broken-window" concept of George Kelling and J.Q. Wilson. They argued that community decay (e.g., broken windows, graffiti, abandoned houses, poor street lighting, and pot holes) contributes to the breakdown of community controls and to increased crime and fear of crime (Roberg and Kuykendall 1993, 120).

Perhaps police neighborhood watch meetings should be community quality of life meetings. That is, the meetings should act as a community forum that provides citizens access to officials who will work at correcting the myriad problems degradating the quality of life. The police, since they are on the front-line 24 hours a day, should promote such gatherings. Other government representatives such as local elected officials, street maintenance personnel, and urban planners should also become involved in the community process.

Successful policing will be created by those who are able to draw upon past knowledge and current trends to create solutions to the multifaceted challenges of contemporary society. As Harlan Cleveland pointed out, "For the '90s and beyond, public administration will be the art of making creative interconnections. All real-world problems are interdisciplinary, interprofessional, and international" (Cleveland 1988, 685). Hopefully the concepts outlined here will serve as a reminder of the compendium of theories and concepts available in creating a better future for all.

Bibliography

Barry, Robert, and Clyde Cronkhite. "Back to Basics," *Sheriff*, 10, April 1992.

Christopher Commission Report: Report of the Independent Commission on the Los Angeles Police Department. 400 South Hope Street, Los Angeles: Warren Christopher, Chair: July 9, 1991.

Cleveland, Harlan. "Theses of a New Reformation: The Social Fallout of Science 300 Years After Newton," *Public Administration Review*, May/June 1968.

LeBoeuf, Michael. *The Greatest Management Principle in the World*. Nightingale Conant Books on Cassette, P.O. Box 896, Lake Arrowhead, CA, 1988.

Maslow, Abraham H. "The Theory of Human Motivations," *Psychological Review*, 50, July 1943.

Mayo, Elton. *The Social Problems of an Industrial Civilization*. Boston, MA: Division of Research, Graduate School of Business Administration, Harvard University, Copyright by the President and Fellows of Harvard College, 1945.

Peters, Thomas J. and Robert H. Waterman, Jr. *In Search of Excellence*. New York: Warner Books, 1982.

Reith, Charles. *A Short History of the British Police*. New York: Oxford University Press, 1948.

Roberg, Roy R. and Jack Kuykendall. *Police & Society*. Belmont, CA: Wadsworth Publishing Company, 1993.

Swanson, Charles R., Leonard Territo, and Robert W. Taylor. *Police Administration: Structure, Processes and Behavior*, 3rd ed. New York: Macmillan Publishing Company, 1993.

Toffler, Alvin. *The Third Wave*. New York: Bantam Books, 1980.

Waldo, Dwight. *Toward a New Public Administration: The Minnow-Brook Perspective*, edited by Frank Marini. Scranton, PA: Chandler, 1971.

Wilson, O.W. *Police Administration*, 2nd ed., New York: McGraw-Hill Book Company, Inc., 1963.

Applying the Contextual Themes to Contemporary Criminal Justice Agencies

In Part II, the Contextual Themes Model of the building blocks of administration is reformatted into an Eclectic Perspective Model. The Eclectic Perspective Model is meant to remind the reader of the importance of keeping all contextual themes in mind when confronted with administrative challenges. Chapter 5 serves as a transition point for connecting the past to the present. Chapters 6 through 10 discuss how each of the first four themes of the Contextual Themes Model can be applied to contemporary criminal justice agencies. The fifth theme, Client-Oriented Service, is presented as the first chapter (Chapter 11) in Part III as the concept that is taking us into the future.

Connecting Criminal Justice Administration: Past to Present

6

■ Introduction

This chapter looks at the connection between the past and the present with the intent of establishing a plateau from which current strategies can be designed. Designing strategies requires making predictions. Predictions are most reliable when based on experiences of the past. The ancient Greeks made two important distinctions between the past and the future. First, they held that the past was completely knowable and the future, of course, was not. They thought that by looking hard enough in the right places they could "discover" the past, but that no amount of looking would enable them to "discover" the future.

Their second distinction was that the past (although discoverable) could not be changed; the future (although undiscoverable) could be changed. This assumption (that human efforts make a difference in creating the future) is the reason for exploring trends and for planning. The future is created by people who take an educated look at past and current trends, then create a realistic image of the future that they pursue.

Dr. Selwyn Enzer, Director, Pacific Rim Data Base, International Business Education Research (IBEAR), School of Business Administration, University of Southern California, has observed that the future is difficult to predict because of two kinds of uncertainties: (1) uncertainty about technological developments, natural phenomena, accidents, and other conditions over which organizations have limited or no control; and (2) uncertainty about human choice. To assist in making predictions, Enzer offers the following formula (Enzer, 1978):

> *The future equals the extension of the past,*
> *plus the uncertainty introduced by conditions not under human control,*
> *plus the uncertainty introduced by human choice.*

With Enzer's formula in mind, a brief review of some milestone directions from the past are presented to help establish a foundation for strategies for the present. We begin with two founding milestones from the distant past.

Direction from the Distant Past

1788. John Jay, John Madison, and Alexander Hamilton, *The Federalist*

More than 200 years ago, Alexander Hamilton and his associates raised a question that was not answered in the Constitution: What is the appropriate role of the federal government in the economic and social development of the nation? That question raised a second question: What is the role of public administration? Is a strong and independent or a weak and well-controlled public administration needed? Today, scholars and practitioners are still trying to answer these questions.

The federalism of the Constitution is very clear. The division and sharing of powers, however, is not as clear. Men like Hamilton seemed to use the ambiguity to further the centralization of government and its strong control over public administration. Thus, Americans have been bequeathed these uncertainties that Woodrow Wilson described as the "cardinal questions of American politics" (Wilson as quoted by Ostrom, 1987, p. xvi).

1887. Woodrow Wilson, "The Study of Administration"

Woodrow Wilson in his classic essay "The Study of Administration" wrote that administration is removed from the hurry and strife of politics and that administrative questions are not political questions. Wilson saw public administration as distinct from politics, more akin to business and business methods than to anything political. In other words, public administrators carried out the direction of the elected officials with no involvement in the political arena. Wilson proclaimed that representatives of the people are the proper ultimate authority in all matters of government and administration is "merely the clerical part of government."

As we focus on more current milestone directions, the summaries of six noteworthy authors are offered here as predictors for the immediate future based on events of the recent past.

Direction from the Recent Past

1976. Herbert Simon, *Administrative Behavior*

Simon saw the direction of the organization as being problem-facing and problem-solving. His focus was on organizational processes "related to choice of courses of action in an environment which does not fully disclose the alternatives available or the consequences of these alternatives" (Simon, 1976, p. 20).

In his formulation, organizations are neither fully closed nor fully open systems. In today's increasingly interdependent world, a closed system is probably impractical, if not impossible; a fully open system, although possible, would produce a situation in which an organization would be overwhelmed by the influx of energy and information, rendering it nearly ineffective. In this mixed view of organizations, external environments are, however, regarded as very important.

At the same time, organizations attempt to cope internally with enormously increasing uncertainty as they try to meet their public missions. Judging from this concept, Simon's direction for public agencies is to receive and screen input from all sources relevant to the accomplishment of their related missions. This points to a more direct public organization involvement with the social and political environments than was envisioned by Hamilton and Wilson.

1980. Dwight Waldo, *The Enterprise of Public Administration*

Waldo wrote that public agencies have journeyed through a time of "growth, abundance, and consensus" but that they are now headed for "decay, scarcity, and conflict" (p. 153). The challenge for the present and the foreseeable future is to do more (or at least as much) with less.

Waldo also said that public agencies will have to cope with the problems of obsolescence of knowledge, of growing union power, and, when it is appropriate, of making public policy instead of relying on the direction of elected officials. Waldo described public organizations of the future as less bureaucratic; they will be less hierarchical, authority will be less authoritarian, and there will be more flexibility and adaptability.

1980. Alvin Toffler, *The Third Wave* (revisited in retrospect)

Toffler's "three wave" model was discussed in Chapter 4. Here it will be viewed in retrospect and corrected from today's perspective. In 1980, Toffler wrote about the major issues of interest to mankind during each of his three "wave" periods of history. As Toffler put it, the major issues are what mankind has spent most waking hours thinking about. For several thousand years, it was the production of agricultural goods for personal consumption. As mankind learned to mechanize the production of agricultural goods, society moved into a second "wave," which led to the Industrial Revolution. This period lasted several hundred years.

The "third wave" came as people learned to automate and mechanize the industrial functions of the "second wave." Toffler said that the "third wave" may only last a decade or two and that its major issue would center on information and technology. Information and technology was to be the main source of employment in the 1980s as agriculture and industry had been to the earlier "waves."

By the 1990s, it could be seen that information and technology had not become the major source of employment. U.S. Census statistics substantiated Toffler's model depiction of the decline of agriculture and industrial employment. However, service occupations became the main sources of employment rather than information and technology, as Toffler had predicted. The "information boom" brought into everyone's home, through the electronic and automated media, images of more and better quality of living. Consequently, the public expected and demanded better service.

Service includes many kinds of employment, including communications, transportation, vacations, entertainment, information, health care, consulting,

Table 6–1	The Three Waves of Society in Retrospect and Elements of Successful Enterprise for the Future		
Historical periods	**Physical elements**		**Human elements**
Agricultural	Land		Muscles
Industrial	Energy		Hands
Service	Information/technology		Minds

finances, legal assistance, investment, and insurance jobs. Service also includes the major work activities of all federal, state, county, city, and town employees.

We can review Toffler's model in retrospect. Each "wave" contains a physical element that supports the major issue of the day (**Table 6–1**). Information and technology best fit in this category for the "third wave" as did land in the agricultural period and energy in the industrial period.

Each "wave" also includes human elements that support the major occupations of the period. In the "agricultural wave," human muscle was needed to till the land. In the "industrial wave," human hands were needed to work the conveyer line piece-meal work. Service occupations require more use of people's minds to convert information into knowledge. As with private businesses, today's successful criminal justice agencies are service-orientated, make productive use of information and technology, and encourage their employees to become thinking contributors to the organization goals.

The development of neighborhood private postal businesses in the 1990s serves as a good example of what the public perceive as service-oriented. Many people were willing to pay more for services provided by the private sector if these services spared them long waits in line and were offered at hours that were more conducive to current lifestyles than services that were provided by the government. The move toward customized private mail service has more recently resulted in the government mail systems becoming much more customer-oriented in an effort to compete with the private sector.

The public desire for better service is also one of the major reasons that today there are twice as many private police as public police and the public is spending more on private security than public law enforcement. Is this an indicator that the public does not think the public police can meet community service needs?

1981. Alberto Ramos, *The New Science of Organization*

Ramos articulated a need to change the "prevailing" attempts to apply the market-centered theory of organization to all forms of activity. He wrote that this approach hindered the actualization of "possible new social systems needed to overcome the basic dilemmas of our society" (Ramos, 1981, p. 52).

He saw the need for a new direction, one that he called "the new science of organization." He wrote that a "variety of social systems constitute an essential qualification of any society, which is to be responsive to its members' basic needs of production and actualization" (Ramos, 1981, p. 71). His approach also emphasized a need for public agencies to be more directly responsive to the people they serve.

1982. George Gordon, *Public Administration in America*

Gordon stated that "millions of Americans seek to reassert control over agencies of government that have major impact on their daily lives" (p. 525). He pointed out that the public administration of the future must take a direction of determining what the public wants and how satisfied they are with the services they are receiving. He said that public agencies of the future must include more citizen participation in bureaucratic decision making and must be more responsive at the local level.

1987. Vincent Ostrom, *The Political Theory of a Compound Republic*

Ostrom saw federalism as "constitutional choice" applicable to various units of government in a system where each unit is bound by enforceable rules of constitutional law. He conceptualized a system of government in which rulers are themselves subject to a rule of law. He conjectured, "The United States, snarled in a morass created by the increasing nationalism of American society, will be forced to draw back and explore ways to free itself from the central-government trap."

This brief review documents a direction for a public administration that has moved from strong centralized control and separation from politics (as Hamilton and Wilson had supported) to a more decentralized approach of responding to citizen needs (as prescribed by the more recent writings of Simon, Ramos and Ostrom).

As society becomes larger and more complex, decentralization and more responsive involvement by government at the local level to the needs of the public occurs. This direction follows the experience of the private sector, which has grown and has had to decentralize to accommodate customer demands to be more responsive.

1988. Harlan Cleveland, "Theses of a New Reformation: The Social Fallout of Science 300 Years after Newton"

In Cleveland's *Public Administration Review* article, he states, "For the 90s and beyond, public administration will be the art of making creative interconnections. All real-world problems are interdisciplinary, interprofessional, and international" (p. 685). Public managers must look beyond the confines of their own organizations and direct their operations accordingly. Public managers cannot always wait for elected officials to give direction. Often they must gain input directly from the public. They should be given the authority to act on this public input in a growing number of situations and must be held accountable for the results.

1990. Jeffrey D. Straussman, *Public Administration*

According to Straussman, the tasks of tomorrow's public managers will be both difficult and more challenging. They will need greater sensitivity to marketing approaches, with knowledge about "what will sell" to the public. They will also need the ability to innovate and to take risks, be both specialist and generalist, be cognizant of evolving societal complexity and will have to cope with scarcity (pp. 366–373).

1990. John Naisbitt and Patricia Aburdene, *Megatrends 2000*

This update of Naisbitt's original 1982 *Megatrends* article lists a number of trends for consideration of the 21st-century criminal justice administrator:

- a global economic boom,
- global lifestyles and cultural nationalism,
- the privatization of the welfare state,
- women's leadership,
- triumph of the individual,
- the rise of the Pacific Rim.

■ Changes in the 1990s that Set the Stage for Today's Criminal Justice Administration Approaches

This chapter continues with some trends of the 1990s that were considered by criminal justices leaders as they designed strategies for the future. The predictions of the 1990s are included here, as they provide insight into the creation of many of the administrative approaches that are currently used. Additionally, by comparing conditions today with the predictions of the 1990s, the reader can gain insight into the reliability of predictions that are being made today for the future.

Cultural Changes Indicators

The countries of the world were becoming global-oriented and at local levels neighborhoods in many areas were merging into single massive communities that synthesized many races and cultural backgrounds. Technological advances, particularly in communication and transportation, reduced the barriers of time and distance. Additionally, the mineral resources of China, Canada, Australia, Siberia, and the Antarctic; the manufacturing capabilities of Japan, Thailand, and South Korea; the petroleum resources of Alaska, Mexico, and Indonesia; the agricultural, aerospace, and electronic products of the United States, plus the lifting of the "iron curtain" provided a natural basis for a profitable exchange of ideas and commodities.

Accelerating advances caused the world population, particularly the residents of the Pacific Rim nations, to become more transnational and cross-cultural. As the concentration of any foreign-born group in a population increased, assimilation into the mainstream language and culture slowed. Some facts to be considered that were documented in the early 1990s by Selbert (1990, pp. 2–3) are:

> Between 1900 and 1949, the majority of immigration to the United States came from Europe (78%). From 1950 to 1980, the proportions

became: Europeans—31%; Latin Americans—36%; and Asians—21%. Through the 1980s (and continuing to increase in the 2000s) more than 80% of immigration into our country were Asian and Hispanic. Asian Americans numbered between 6 and 7 million (about 3% of the U.S. population) but became the fastest growing minority. The Asian American population grew 70% from 1980 to 1988, three times faster than blacks and twice as fast as Hispanics. According to projections from the Population Reference Bureau, Filipinos will surpass Chinese to become the largest Asian-American population group in the early part of 2000.

Black Americans numbered around 30.3 million, or 12.3% of the 1988 U.S. population, and grew by 12.7% from 1980, double the white population growth rate for the same period. Hispanic Americans approached 20 million in number (or 30 million including legal U.S. residents, according to Thomas Weyr, author of Hispanic USA). The Hispanic population, which grew by 34% between 1980 and 1988, made up over 8% of the total U.S. population in the 1990s.

Understanding the various cultures, customs, values, and languages of expanding multicultural communities emerged as a significant challenge to criminal justice administrators in the 1990s. According to Bort Meays (1985, pp. 6–7), "In the area of public transit, more than 18% of immigrants took the bus to work compared with 4.5% of all non-immigrants."

Housing needs were another area of contrast. Immigrant households tended to be larger: 26% had five or more persons compared with 14% in this range among the general population, and 83% rented, compared with 42% of other residents.

Overcrowded living conditions were a problem: 44% of immigrants in southern California lived with more than one person per room, compared to only 8% of nonimmigrants. Nearly twice as many immigrants as other residents paid too much for housing.

Immigration caused notable changes to the social and cultural fabric. These changes were apparent in the growth and density of ethnic neighborhoods, new architectural and visual features, and the expanding variety of arts, culture, and ethnic cuisines. Many immigrants preserved their ethnic identity by continuing native customs and languages, leading to differences in rates of assimilation. A growing need developed for cultural education for both new arrivals and for native-born citizens.

Impact of Information and Technology

The information boom altered public faith and employee faith in public institutions and its management, as well as in political personalities and heads of criminal justice agencies. In less complicated times, people regarded their leaders, employers, and public institutions as being in a position to make appropriate decisions because that position provided almost exclusive access to information.

The communication technology created an information explosion, and vast amounts of information became available to most everyone. Consequently, most people now have their own opinions and are more prone to "second-guess" those in authority. Employees and the public want to be involved in the decision-making processes that were once left to management, public institutions, and elected officials. It is important that criminal justice administrators consider this trend in developing strategies in the 21st century. It is the mental processing of information by people that creates knowledge and makes information a viable resource. Information must be processed through the human mind. Involving the public and as many employees as possible in the decision-making process is an important public administration challenge (Cronkhite, 1986, pp. 33–35).

Economic and Social Influences

As the turn of the century approached, one challenge for criminal justice leaders that was still prevalent despite a healthy economy was that of meeting increasing needs while still facing financial cutbacks. Although cost-cutting throughout government continued to cause cutbacks in support, the public still demanded more effective and client-oriented criminal justice services. This is a lesson for criminal justice administrators in the future, as history has shown that this situation will recur.

The struggle to be more efficient while facing cutbacks continued to force criminal justice administration to place more reliance on information technology, whereas the call for more client-oriented services was causing a community-police partnership approach to policing. Some of the social, technological, and demographic trends that were expected to impact criminal justice services were reported in *Crime Warps* in 1987:

> With the exception of Florida, birthrates at or above the national average and relatively high birth/death ratios, will sustain large crime-prone youthful populations in the Sunbelt states. (Bennett, 1987, p. 115)
>
> Those regions in which illegal Latin-American aliens concentrate—the South and West—will experience increases in violence among those groups. The violence will peak between 1990 and 2005, when the current Hispanic baby boom passes through the crime-prone ages of fourteen to twenty-four. California, Arizona, Texas, and Colorado will feel the crime surge most intensely. This violence will be offset by the aging of the other populations in those regions. (Bennett, 1987, p. 115)
>
> Racial and ethnic crimes will increase as the competition for unskilled jobs traditionally available to minorities is heightened. The disproportionately educated and socially active oriental community will grow in size and influence. As it enters the mainstream, the traditional Asian gangs and their current violence will diminish. (Bennett, 1987, p. 115)
>
> As elderly migration and aging-in-place continues to swell the populations of California, Arizona, and Florida, the serious crimes of youth will be displaced by white-collar crimes, larcenies, and domestic violence committed by the elderly. Purse snatchings, pocket

pickings, and confidence games, which victimize the elderly more than other age groups, will abound in these same states. However, since the elderly have the lowest composite rates of victimization, the overall crime rates will decline. (Bennett, 1987, p. 116)

In the 1980s there were approximately 52.6 million people in the white-collar crime-prone ages of 25 to 39. Those ten to 24 years old numbered closer to 58.4 million. As they enter the 25 to 39 age group over the next fifteen years, the additional 6 million will create a surge in cashless money crimes. However, the youngest cohorts, following behind the ten-to-twenty-four-year old group, will be a much smaller group than their predecessors. By the time the youngest group reaches twenty-five years of age in the year 2010, white-collar crime rates will begin to drop off. (Bennett, p. 159) There will be an overall decline in the number of sworn officers. However, the number of civilian workers will increase. (Bennett, p. 330) Automated surveillance, report-writing, and information systems will reduce some police functions. Among these will be fixed posts, firsthand intelligence gathering, and random patrol. (Bennett, p. 330) Physical trace evidence will become the method of choice for developing criminal cases. Confessions will become obsolete except as a form of corroboration. (Bennett, p. 331) The social service functions of police will become more community-oriented. (Bennett, p. 331)

Brown (1991, p. 22) advised criminal justice administrators that they would have to address these problems with:

- Strategic planning—a process that will enable policing agencies to influence the future.
- Multilevel perspective—for the delivery of police service that meets different needs of neighborhoods, individuals, and special interest groups.
- Awareness—of what is happening not only in the community but also within the police agency.
- Service partners—which include the community as partners in determining agency levels and types of services.
- Community resources—to assist in overcoming budget constraints.
- Development of confidence—that nurtures community support for the police.
- Demilitarization—that moves policing organizational structures away from the paramilitary model towards an appropriate corporate model that results in a flattening of the organization.
- Neighborhood policing—centralized efforts no longer will suffice; the responsibility for positive change must be spread among the participants and the beneficiaries.

Although not all of Brown's predictions have come to pass, most have. Her advice remains an important contribution to today's criminal justice administration.

As in the past, success today means keeping abreast of developing trends, theories, and concepts, and through an Eclectic Perspective, adapting past theories and concepts to contemporary issues. The remainder of this chapter will focus on connecting the past to the present, specifically in the criminal justice field.

■ Connecting the History of American Criminal Justice to the Present

Early arrivals to what we now call America came to be free and live in a democratic environment in which all individuals hoped to have equal rights. Many came from countries where a totalitarian government ruled and only the military was allowed to bear arms. Even today, most Americans cherish "the right to bear arms" as a means of every citizen maintaining independence from the development of an all-powerful government. This philosophy is at the heart of why we have over 17,000 police departments nationwide, a court system that is built around the concept of an adversarial process, and an overall criminal justice system that is structured with checks and balances to avoid any centralizing of authority. We start our exploration of the historical evolution with policing as it employs the largest number of personnel in the criminal justice system (**Figure 6–1**).

Connecting the History of Police Administration

As America grew, there was a general resistance to the formation of any type of authority. The first form of policing was the *watch and ward*. This early form of policing required all "able-bodied men" to take turns standing guard at night in

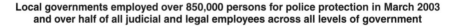

Local governments employed over 850,000 persons for police protection in March 2003 and over half of all judicial and legal employees across all levels of government

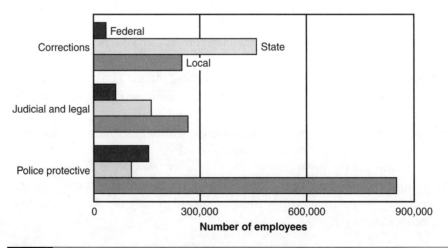

Figure 6–1 Relative Size of American Police, Courts, and Corrections.

their villages. They were not given arms but, rather, had a stick that they could pound on the ground to alert the sleeping villagers, who would unite to take care of whatever threatened their community. This was to ensure that no one authority existed but, rather, power to overcome threats to the community's well-being was formed through a joint effort in furtherance of their concept of democracy. Everyone had a share in the protection of their communities.

This system continued into the 1800s, when the workday of many people became more regimented and they could not stay awake all night standing guard and go to work the following day and be expected to perform a day's work. Because of this, the practice of appointing certain individuals to take over the "watch and ward" duties that had been rotated among the villagers was created. Men were selected to perform these duties full time so that the majority of villagers could perform jobs in what was becoming an industrial society. As a result, the *night watchman* form of policing became popular. The first fully deployed day-and-night police department was formed in New York in 1844.

The general public, however, still fearful of armed military authority, continued to provide the watchmen with only a stick to awaken their sleeping fellow citizens. This was in the spirit of continuing the practice of the power coming from a partnership of the members of the community. This philosophy of *home rule* and all citizens having control over any enforcement power prevails today and is a cornerstone of today's criminal justice system.

The watchmen were given wide powers. Although many performed their jobs well, they were generally not trained, poorly paid, and often appointed as a part of the *spoils system* (given jobs by elected officials based on favors for political support). As a result, there was widespread corruption, causing a call for reform not only for police but also for all public employees.

The Pendleton Act of 1883 (discussed in Chapter 2) resulted in and began a process of replacing the "spoils system" with a federal personnel system based on merit. This was the beginning of what is now referred to as the *civil service system*. Although this act was for federal employees, it "trickled down" to the state and local levels over the next several decades.

The call for reform and the Pendleton Act also prompted a new era in policing, often called the Professional or Legalistic Era because of the focus on standards, rules, and regulations. The major thrust of this movement was the development and application of the administrative approaches of the Contextual Themes Model, which continued through the 1900s and into the 21st century. **Table 6–2** shows the evolutionary development of policing in America and the relationship of the contextual themes as they advanced in the 1900s. Throughout the 1960s and 1970s, there was a general social backlash against the government partly promoted by growing concern over involvement in the Vietnam War. The police were called "pigs" by some radical groups, with many expressing the view that the police were "too professional" and in fact were becoming more like the authoritarian arm of the government that our forefathers had fled. There was a call for a return to the more public police partnership law enforcement of the past—without, of course, the corruption of the "watchmen" era. This resulted in the Client-Oriented approach that continued into the 21st century.

Table 6–2	Evolution of American Policing
Watch and ward	1700s
Watchman	1800s
Professionalism	1900s
Community policing • Return to Peel principles • Team policing • Community-Oriented Policing (COP) • Problem-Oriented Policing (POP)	1980s
Police Accountability to Community (PAC) • Comstat	2000s

Some of the early leaders who helped shape the "professional" approach to policing and the founding concepts of the administration that prevail today are discussed here.

Sir Robert Peel

Sir Robert Peel is remembered as the creator of what is called the first professional police department in the world, London's Scotland Yard. In 1822, Peel, a wealthy member of Parliament, was appointed to improve the London police. English citizens at first resisted the idea of a professional police department as they felt it would restrict their liberties. They were fearful of a strong police organization that might harshly enforce the law. Peel overcame this with a philosophy that "the police are the public, and the public are the police." He worked this philosophy into nine "Peel's Principles of Policing," which will be discussed in Chapter 11. These principles are considered to be the "holy grail" of policing. Additionally, Peel established 12 law enforcement organizational principles:

1. The police must be stable, efficient, and organized along military lines.
2. The police must be under government control.
3. The absence of crime will best prove the efficiency of the police.
4. The distribution of crime news is absolutely essential.
5. The deployment of police strength both by time and area is essential.
6. No quality is more indispensable to a policeman than a perfect command of temper.
7. Good appearance commands respect.
8. The securing and training of proper persons is at the root of efficiency.
9. Public security demands that every police officer be given a number.
10. Police headquarters should be centrally located and easily accessible to the people.
11. Policemen should be hired on a probationary basis.

12. Police records are necessary to the correct distribution of police strength. (Mayhall, 1985, p. 425)

Peel had a difficult time implementing these principles, but in time they proved successful, with Scotland Yard becoming the model policing agency of the day. As police departments were being developed in America in the mid-1800s, Peel's principles became the "guiding light" and remain as standards in police organizations today.

Leonhard F. Fuld

Leonhard Fuld published *Police Administration* in 1909. Although it was published several years before Frederick Taylor's "Principles of Scientific Management," Fuld's work stressed the same concept of efficiency through the selection and training of qualified personnel. He criticized the U.S. system of selecting executive personnel for political reasons and pointed out that in Europe, police administration was a respected career that attracted army officers and university graduates. He emphasized the importance that all law enforcement personnel be held to a higher code of conduct and morality than that demanded of other citizens. He was concerned about the selection and training of officers and stressed that political considerations should be eliminated in the selection of personnel (Fuld, 1909).

August Vollmer

August Vollmer is often called the "Father of Modern Police Administration." From his appointment as town marshal in Berkeley, California, in 1905 (where he later served as police chief) to his death in 1955, Vollmer was an innovator and a reformer in law enforcement. He instigated many of the early police communication concepts, from corner emergency signal lights to the first radio system in a patrol car (a "crystal set"). He fostered many scientific investigation advances such as the modus operandi concept and the use of forensics and fingerprints. He was first to put officers in automobiles for patrolling as well as forming bicycle patrols. As early as 1908, he created a "police school" and was an important force in requiring training and education for law enforcement officers. He stressed the importance of liberal, educated law enforcement officers by emphasizing the need for officers to be familiar with the mental, biological, and social sciences and the need for a broad cultural, scientific, and technical background for patrol personnel. He is also remembered for developing future police administrators from his employees and his students when he was a professor at the University of Berkeley in California. O. W. Wilson was one of his most notable followers (Douthit, 1983).

O. W. Wilson

O. W. Wilson is best known for the law enforcement textbook that set the tone for professional police administration. He published the first edition of *Police Administration* in 1950, which brought together the themes and concepts of administration and applied them to policing. The text includes some of the organization functions and employee relations concepts and approaches described thus far in this text. He served as a police practitioner and as an academician as police chief in Fullerton, California; Wichita, Kansas; and Chicago, Illinois; and he also was a professor at the University of California at Berkley. Today, the structure of most police agencies can be traced back to the teaching of Wilson (Bopp, 1977).

William Parker

William Parker became one of the most prominent law enforcement administrators in law enforcement during the mid-20th century. While coming up through the ranks in the Los Angeles police force, he obtained a law degree. He was appointed chief of his department in 1950. He was a leader in the professional/legalistic approach to law enforcement administration and reorganized the department along the lines espoused by O. W. Wilson and August Vollmer. He centralized the organization, focusing on efficiency and reducing costs and improved the recruitment, selection, and training of his officers. Under his leadership, the Los Angeles Police Department often was referred to as a "crime-fighting machine" and represented the "thin blue line" that separated the honest citizen from the criminal element. His association with Jack Webb, a well-known actor and director of that period, resulted in several popular television programs that bolstered the image of the Los Angeles Police Department, *Dragnet* and *Adam 12*. These television programs served as reminders of how the entertainment media influence public opinion. Parker fought to eliminate excessive political influence in police activities and was a very outspoken leader. He was feared by some politicians because of the civil service protection that he had helped institutionalize for police chiefs of that period (Johnson, 1981).

Connecting the History of Corrections Administration

Even though the corrections system is viewed as being last in flowcharts of the criminal justice system, it is explored here as it parallels the evolution of policing. As will be seen, both police and correction administration history predates court administration. What we call the correction system today began as the penal system, which indicates the range of changes that have occurred. These changes are outlined in **Table 6–3**.

1790–1825

The Penitentiary Era began in Pennsylvania with the Quaker philosophy of serving penance, prompting the idea of rehabilitation and deterrence. The incarceration facilities (which featured solitary confinement) were known as penitentiaries. The name came from William Penn, the Quaker leader of the time; Pennsylvania, known as the "Penn" state; and the philosophy of penance.

1825–1876

The Mass (Congregate) Era was a response to the growing prison population and the cost of solitary confinement. The Aubury System in Auburn, New York, be-

Table 6-3	Evolution of American Corrections	
Year	**Prison Era**	**Philosophy**
1790	The Penitentiary Era	Rehabilitation, deterrence
1825	The Mass (Congregate) Prison Era	Incapacitation, deterrence
1876	The Reformatory Era	Rehabilitation
1890	The Industrial Era	Incapacitation, restoration
1935	The Punitive Era	Retribution
1945	The Treatment Era	Rehabilitation
1967	The Community-based (Declaration Era)	Restoration, rehabilitation
1980	The Warehousing Era	Incapacitation
1995	The Just Deserts Era	Retribution, incapacitation, deterrence

came the new model. This era continued the penance philosophy but introduced the congregational concept in which inmates lived, ate, and worked together in enforced silence. Group activities were part of this era, and corporal punishment was included as a means of handling uncooperative prisoners. Incapacitation and deterrence were the goals of the time.

1876–1890

The Reformatory Era focused on rehabilitation and grew out of what other countries such as Great Britain and Ireland were doing at the time. A central concept of this period was that prisoners had to be provided training and incentives that would prepare them to become crime-free on release. Additionally, successful rehabilitation could not occur without supervised integration into the community, which led to the birth of *parole*. A system of graded stages required inmates to achieve educational, behavioral, and other goals before they could be released. Unfortunately, this approach "proved a relative failure and disappointment," with many inmates returning to a life of crime on release (Barnes & Teeters, 1959, p. 428).

1890–1935

The Industrial Era was yet another response to the rising cost of the growing prison population as well as to a growing concern over discipline and security in American prisons. As the United States became more industrialized, the idea of inexpensive prison labor came into play. Systems were developed to allow private businesses to contract for prison laborers. In the North, prison labor was incorporated into manufacturing, whereas in the South, prisoners were used more for agricultural work. However, as the economy began to sour and unemployment rose, workers and their labor unions began to complain about having to compete with cheap prison labor. Congress and various states reacted with legislation to regulate and curtail prisoners performing labor that competed with the manufacture of free-market goods. The *Ashurst-Sumners Act* of 1935 is credited with bringing an end to the Industrial Prison Era by prohibiting the interstate transportation and sale of prison goods when state laws forbade them. This in addition to the Depression forced most states to do away with prison labor.

1935–1945

The Punitive Era arose out of the dust of the crash of the free-market prison industry which left prison administrators with custody and institutional security as their predominant purpose. The dominant theme was that prisoners owed a debt to society and long periods of confinement were justified as repayment. Maximum-security institutions were built, the most notable being the federal penitentiary on Alcatraz Island in California. The daily treatment of prisoners shifted from efforts to rehabilitate to "do nothing" activities that often were monotonous and led many prisoners to refer to their treatment as "driving them stir-crazy."

1945–1967

The Treatment Era bloomed from the after-war euphoria that swept the nation. The approach was based on a medical model that viewed offenders as ill and needing treatment. Inmates were often referred to as "patients" and "group members" rather that prisoners. Treatment focused on the individual and included chemotherapy, sensory deprivation, neurosurgery, and behavior and aversion therapy. It was during this period that prisons began to be known as correctional institutions.

Resistance to the correctional approach surfaced in the 1970s with some prisoners refusing treatment as an infringement of their individual rights. The American Civil Liberties Union (ACLU) supported the inmates and a number of civil suits followed. The main federal funding agency, the Law Enforcement Assistance Administration (LEAA), began to be concerned about potential liability and ceased to fund treatment programs. These variables put such a squeeze on the prisons that this era came to an end in 1967. It should be noted, however, that a number of such treatment programs continue today. Those who back this approach argue that the prison system of that period was ill-equipped to provide adequate treatment and that the approach would have been successful with proper support.

1967–1980

The Community-Based Era coincided with a shift in the general mood of the American public towards individual rights and away from a concern for public safety. Advocates felt that prisons were dehumanizing and that rehabilitation could not occur in isolation. Thus, there was a movement away from institutionalization and toward the creation of programs that would integrate offenders back into the community. Halfway houses, work release programs, and conjugal visits became part of the rehabilitation process. Some prisons were closed. Many treatment institutes for the mentally ill and those addicted to drugs and alcohol were closed and funds were provided to local jurisdictions to handle inmates who heretofore had been sentenced to state facilities. Many jurisdictions took the state funding but were unable to provide proper community care. This has contributed to the current intercity "homeless" criminal justice challenge, which will be discussed in Chapter 15.

1980–1995

The Warehousing Era grew out of the public shift back toward a concern for public safety, which was generated by a dramatic increase in crime as well as a number of media stories about "soft prison conditions" and some violent crimes that were committed by prisoners serving sentences in community facilities. Increasing recidivism (the repetition of criminal behavior) rates were spotlighted by those proponents of a nothing-works doctrine with statistics showing that more than half of those serving prison sentences continued to commit crimes after their release. One key study often cited was conducted by Robert Martinson and his colleagues in 1974. They surveyed 231 research studies of correctional treatment and could not identify a single rehabilitation approach that substantially reduced recidivism (Martinson, 1974, pp. 22–54). The National Academy of Science joined the debate, stating that they "do not now know of any program or method of rehabilitation that could be guaranteed to reduce the criminal activity of released offenders" (Sechrest, White, & Brown, 1979).

1995 to the Present

The Just Deserts Era, which began in the mid-1900s and continues today, includes some aspects of the Warehousing Era but places more emphasis on individual responsibility for criminal acts rather than blaming society for not being able to prevent crime. Sometimes referred to as "you do the crime, you do the time," it includes mandatory and "zero tolerance" sentencing as well as the elimination of paroles in some states. It is a return to the Classical Theory of causes of crime, which holds that individuals are accountable for their actions. Limiting inmate privileges and increasing the discomfort of confinement are part of this movement. Some prison administrators have received national media attention by eliminating television viewing and housing prisoners in tents in hot desert climates. Proponents of this approach point out that crime has substantially declined during this era and, even though inmates may not be rehabilitated, they cannot victimize the public while they are behind bars.

As with the other fields of criminal justice, prominent figures have contributed to corrections administration.

Zebulon Reed Brockway

The beginning of the Reformatory Era of the 1870s can be traced to the first National Prison Congress, held in 1870 in Cincinnati, which resulted in the "Declaration of Principles." The declaration called for reform based on the Irish system of that time and was documented in a paper written by **Zebulon Brockway**. Brockway started as a prison employee and worked his way up to warden in Detroit. His presentation of the paper at the congress resulted in him being recognized as a leader in correctional administration. He said that the central aim of the prison system should be protection of society against crime, and not to punish criminals. He was a champion of indeterminate sentencing, in which prisoners could be rewarded for good behavior by early release, thus giving prison authorities more control over inmates. He developed vocational training programs and put prisoners to work at 34 major trades. Brockway was known for his personal contact with his prisoners. Records indicate that he spoke to nearly 50 convicts a day and was referred to as "friend, minister, and prison master." He served as warden for 20 years and fought hard against the oncoming Punitive Era (Torsten, 1976, pp. 32–50).

Mary Belle Harris

Mary Belle Harris became superintendent at the Blackwell's Island Institution for Women in 1914 at the age of 39. She found the facilities depressingly grim and recommended that they be demolished. There she put her rehabilitative philosophy to work, which differed from the Industrial Era emphasis on incapacitation and restoration. She created many new approaches to handling inmates including open lines of communication with prisoners, exercise yards, gardening, and a library. She subsequently served in a number of other correctional administration positions. As superintendent for the State Home for Girls in Trenton, New Jersey, she introduced a "credit card" system whereby at the end of the day inmates received a pay or credit loss based on their behavior. As superintendent of the Federal Industrial Institution for Women at Alderson, West Virginia, she arranged housing of inmates in cottages rather than cells, offered vocational and educational classes, and provided religious services and entertainment (Harris, 1942).

John Augustus

The concept of probation can be traced back to **John Augustus**. Even though Augustus may not be considered an administrator, he is noted here because probation is part of the corrections system and he contributed to its beginning. In the mid-1880s, while working as a shoemaker in Boston, John Augustus took a sentenced prisoner to his home from court. He wrote that when in court one morning he heard a man charged with being a common drunk tell the judge that if he did not have to go to jail he would "never taste intoxicating liquors." Augustus bailed him out and started the first recorded program of probation, which he continued for over 18 years with many types of offenders. Augustus voluntarily performed a number of duties that are associated with probation today. He investigated each case, kept detailed records of each person's progress, and made reports to the judge. He was not always viewed favorably by the police and prosecutors and only was able to continue with financial help from friends (Abadinsky, 1987, p. 118).

Alexander Maconochie

Parole is another component of the corrections system, and its conception can be attributed to **Alexander Maconochie**. Maconochie became superintendent of the British penal colony on Norfolk Island near Sydney, Australia, in 1840. There he was first to initiate a program to "punish them for their past but to train them for the future." He promoted open-ended (indeterminate) sentences and included allowing inmates early release under close supervision. He began writing and speaking about this approach and motivated Walter Crofton (who was the director of the Irish Penal System in the 1850s) to start a process whereby prisoners were allowed a "ticket of leave," which was a conditional early release under police supervision. Zebulon Brockway copied this procedure when he became superintendent of the Elmira Reformatory in New York in 1876. This was the beginning of the parole system in the United States (Abadinsky, 1987, p. 18).

Connecting the History of Court Administration

In 1790, the Constitution of the United States established that judicial power "shall be vested in One Supreme Court, and in such inferior courts as the Congress may from time to time ordain and establish" (Constitution of the United States of American, Article III). Even with this early beginning, the milestones of court administration did not begin to materialize until the mid-1900s, decades later than police administration and even centuries after corrections. Court administration as we know it today grew out of the organization developments of the 1940s.

A major factor in the development of professional court administration was the Administrative Office of the United States Courts Act, passed by Congress in 1939, that placed efficient services as a goal and cultivated modern management methods within the court system. As with other reforms in the justice system, the movement started at the federal level and "trickled" down to state and local courts over the next few decades.

As with other professions such as the medical profession, practitioners in the legal system are educated in the purposes and technicalities of their professions. Their education rarely involves administration. Consequently, specially educated administrative positions began to materialize in the mid-1900s. Although there had been some previous movement to hire business administrators in the federal system, the first state court administrator was appointed by New Jersey in 1949. By the early 1960s, approximately 30 people could be identified as serving as court administrators. By 1979, the number had grown to 70 and by the 1980s there were 2000–3000 nationwide and a number of universities began to offer courses and degrees in the subject (Peak, 1998, p. 63). Today, most courts of any size have court administrators. The tasks of most state court administrators today include:

- Preparation, presentation, and monitoring of the budget
- Analysis of case flows and backlogs to determine where additional personnel, such as judges, prosecutors, and others, are needed
- Collection and publication of statistics describing the operation of state courts
- Providing efforts to streamline the flow of cases
- Service as a liaison between state legislatures and the court system
- Development and coordination of requests for federal and other outside funding

- Management of state court personnel, including promotions for support staff and the handling of retirement and other benefits packages for court employees
- Creation and coordination of plans for the training of judges and other court personnel (in conjunction with local chief judges and supreme court justices)
- Administrative review of payments to legal counsel for indigent defendants. (Scalia, 2002, p. 1)

The recent history of sentencing practice offers some evidence of how, as with the other two criminal justice fields, the courts have had to conform to social, political, and economical trends. American sentencing has always included retribution, incapacitation, deterrence, rehabilitation, and restoration as goals; however, which of these goals predominates at any given time (as with police and correction trends) can be linked to external conditions. For example, the courts focused on probation, parole, and indeterminate sentences during the Community-Based Treatment Era in the 1990s. With the shift to the Warehousing Era in the 1980s and the Just Deserts Era in the 1990s (and continuing into the 21st century), determinate, mandatory, and "three strikes and you're out" sentencing became common in most courts.

Several court reformers need mentioning here, as they were instrumental in creating the trends that established court administration as it exists today.

Arthur T. Vanderbilt

The Institute of Judicial Administration at New York University of Law was established by **Arthur T. Vanderbilt** in 1952 and he served as its president until 1957. The institute is known internationally for improving administration, particularly in the court system. His most important publication on court reform was Minimum Standards of Judicial Administration in 1949, an important guide for court administrators. Vanderbilt emphasized the need for the courts to use sound business administration principles. He also criticized judges and lawyers for allowing the problem of delays and congestion in the courts to become, as he called it, "chronic." Just before his death in 1957, he reflected on the progress made in the previous two decades by writing:

> *Thus today, twenty years after the creation of the Administrative Office of the United States Courts and ten years after the establishment of the first state Administrative Office of the Courts in New Jersey, a total of fifteen states have given their courts some form of administrative assistance to help the courts manage their own business better. No longer is an administrative organization within the judicial establishment both rare and suspect . . . looked upon as novel experiments. (Vanderbilt, 1957, p. 155)*

A. Leo Levin

A. Leo Levin, as a law professor at the University of Pennsylvania in the mid-1900s, contributed to court administration through his support and promotion of research in the field. During his 50-year career, he wrote many books and articles on court administration issues. In 1977, he became the director of the Federal Judicial Center (FJC) and took a firsthand look at court practices by touring the many U.S. district and circuit courts. He enlisted the services of educators, researchers, and automation specialists to improve the managing of the courts. He believed several factors stood in the way of advancements and named them as: "A rather narrow conception of the field and . . . a failure to appreciate the intellectual challenge, the value judgments, and the ultimate significance to litigants and to society inherent in resolving issues of 'mere administration'" (Wheeler, 1979, pp. 134–135).

Levin believed that court administration policies should determine the number of personnel needed, define the scope of the rule-making power, provide guidelines for budgeting, and generally provided a judicial system structure (Levin, 1981, p. 229).

Edward B. McConnell

Edward B. McConnell, educated in both law and business administration at Harvard, served as president of the National Center for State Courts and chairman of the National Conference of Court Administrative Officers. In his 1984 article titled "The Golden Future," he observed that a number of problems of the court during the previous 25 years, especially in calendar congestion and delays, "still plagued them." He predicted that the courts would delegate more authority and responsibility to judges and court administrators and these components of the court would become more professional.

McConnell agreed with Vanderbilt and Levin that business management techniques should be applied to the courts. However, he differed somewhat in that he felt that the relationship of court administrators and judges should be close but not mutually exclusive, stating, "The concept that judges should stick to judging and managers to managing is counterproductive." He further wrote, "Judges have the organizational power but lack the operational knowledge, and the court managers have the knowledge but lack the power. The team approach merges these strengths." Even though he stressed the team approach, he conceded that such a relationship could be threatening to judges. He believed that the judges and court administrations should:

- foster good relations between the courts and the legislative and executive branches of government
- educate the public about the role, structure and operations of the court
- improve the quality of service to the public by reducing cost and delays, holding court at more convenient times and places and having court personnel reflect the racial composition and gender of their communities (McConnell, 1991).

No matter what administrative role one plays in the criminal justice system, knowledge of the history of administration in other fields (and the concepts and principles that come from it) can help in coordinating with the other agencies so that the overall system can best serve the public.

KEY CONCEPTS AND TERMS

- General Concepts
  - Names and milestones
    - 1788, John Jay, John Madison, and Alexander Hamilton, *The Federalist*
    - 1887, Woodrow Wilson, "The Study of Administration"
    - 1976, Herbert Simon, *Administrative Behavior*
    - 1980, Dwight Waldo, *The Enterprise of Public Administration*
    - 1980, Alvin Toffler, *The Third Wave* (revisited in retrospect)
    - 1981, Alberto Ramos, *The New Science of Organization*
    - 1982, George Gordon, *Public Administration in America*
    - 1987, Vincent Ostrom, *The Political Theory of a Compound Republic*
    - 1988, Harlan Cleveland, "Theses of a New Reformation: The Social Fallout of Science 300 Years after Newton"
    - 1990, Jeffrey D. Straussman, *Public Administration*
    - 1990, John Naisbitt and Patricia Aburdene, *Megatrends 2000*
- History of American Criminal Justice: Concepts and Names
  - **Police**
    - Pendleton Act 1883
    - Professionalism
    - Sir Robert Peel
    - Leonhard Fuld
    - August Vollmer
    - O. W. Wilson
    - William Parker
- **Corrections**
  - Changes in Approaches
    - 1790–1825, The Penitentiary Era
    - 1825–1876, The Mass (Congregate) Era
    - 1876–1890, The Reformatory Era
    - 1890–1935, The Industrial Era
    - 1935–1945, The Punitive Era
    - 1945–1967, The Treatment Era
    - 1967–1980, The Community-Based Era
    - 1980–1995, The Warehousing Era
    - 1995–present, The Just Deserts Era
    - Zebulon Reed Brockway
    - Mary Belle Harris
    - John Augustus
    - Alexander Maconochie
- **Courts**
  - Administrative concepts trailed other branches
    - Arthur T. Vanderbilt
    - A. Leo Levin
    - Edward B. McConnell

CHAPTER ACTIVITY

Review the predictions in this chapter from the 1990s to the 21st century. Research and compare the predictions with current conditions. How accurate were these predictions? Your answer should provide you with some insight into the reliability of predictions being made today about the future.

REVIEW QUESTIONS

1. At the beginning of this chapter, Dr. Selwyn Enzer was quoted as stating, "The future is the extension of the past, plus the uncertainty introduced by conditions not under human control, plus the uncertainty introduced by human choice." Can you think of any "conditions not under human control" and "uncertainties introduced by human choice" that may impact the future of criminal justice administration?

2. The Elements of a Successful Enterprise were listed as "service, information, and technology, and involvement of the minds of employees and the public." Give examples of how these elements apply to today's administration of criminal justice.

3. List some of the contributions made by Leonhard Fuld, August Vollmer, O. W. Wilson, and William Parker to police administration. Who wrote the first police administration textbook?

4. Discuss some of the contributions that Zebulon Brockway, Mary Belle Harris, John Augustus, and Alexander Maconochie made to correctional administration. Who is credited with starting the concepts of probation and parole?

5. Why do you think court administration did not begin until many years after it developed in law enforcement and corrections? What role did Arthur Vanderbilt, A. Leo Levin, and Edward McConnell play?

REFERENCES

Abadinsky, H. (1987). *Probation and Parole: Theory and Practice* (3rd ed.). Englewood Cliffs, NJ: Prentice Hall.

Barnes, H. E., & Teeters, N. (1959). *New Horizons in Criminology* (3rd ed.). Englewood Cliffs, NJ: Prentice Hall.

Bennett, G. (1987). *Crime Warps: The Future of Crime in America.* New York: Anchor Books.

Bopp, W. H. (1977) *O.W. Wilson and the Search for a Police Profession.* Port Washington, NY: Kennikat Press.

Cleveland, H. (1988). Theses of a New Reformation: The Social Fallout of Science 300 Years after Newton. *Public Administration Review*, May/June, pp. 42–54.

Wrap Up

Cronkhite, C. (1984). 21st Century Cop. *Centurion: A Police Lifestyle Magazine,* Number III, April, pp. 28–48.

Cronkhite, C. (1986). Management Trends in a Changing World. *Western City,* May, pp. 33–35.

Douthit, N. (1983). August Vollmer. In C. B. Klockars (Ed.), *Thinking about Police: Contemporary Readings.* New York: McGraw-Hill.

Enzer, S. (1978). Presentation made at the Los Angeles Police Department Staff Officers Annual Retreat.

Fuld, L. F. (1909). *Police Administration.* New York: G. P. Putnam.

Gordon, G. (1942). *I Knew Them in Prison.* New York: Viking.

Gordon, G. (1982). *Public Administration in America.* New York: St. Martin's Press.

Jay, J., Madison, J. & Hamilton, A. (1788). *The Federalist.* New York: The Heritage Press.

Johnson, D. R. (1981). *American Law Enforcement.* St Louis: Forum Press.

Lane, F. S. (Ed.). (1990). *Current Issues in Public Administration.* New York: St. Martin's Press.

Levin, L. A. (1981). Research in Judicial Administration: The Federal Experience. *26 New York Law Review,* Winter, pp. 237–241.

Martinson, R. (1974). What Works: Questions and Answers about Prison Reform. *Public Interest,* No. 4, pp. 139–153.

Mayhall, P. D. (1985). *Police-Community Relations and the Administration of Justice* (3rd ed.). New York: John Wiley & Sons.

McConnell, E. B. (1991). What Does the Future Hold for Judges? *Judges Journal, 30,* Summer, pp. 13–14.

Meays, B. (1985). Strategic Management and Population Change. *Public Management,* August, pp. 10–13.

Naisbitt, J., & Aburdene, P. (1990). *Megatrends 2000.* New York: Avon Books.

Ostrom, V. (1987). *The Political Theory of a Compound Republic.* Lincoln: University of Nebraska Press.

Peak, K. J. (1998). *Justice Administration.* Upper Saddle River, NJ: Prentice Hall.

Ramos, A. G. (1981). *The New Science of Organization.* Toronto: University of Toronto Press.

Scalia, J. *Federal Pretrial Release and Detention.* Retrieved in 2002 from http: //www.ojp.usdoj.gov/bjs/pub/pdf/frpd96.pdf

Sechrest, L., White, S., & Brown, E. (Eds.). (1979). *The Rehabilitation of Criminal Offenders: Problems and Prospects.* Washington, DC: National Academy of Science.

Selbert, R. (1990). *Future Scan.* Santa Monica, CA: Bank of America.

Simon, H. (1976). *Administrative Behavior.* New York: The Free Press.

Straussman, J. D. (1990). *Public Administration.* New York: Longman Group.

Toffler, A. (1980). *The Third Wave.* New York: Bantam Books.

Torstein, E. (1976). *The Reformers: An Historical Survey of Pioneer Experiments in the Treatment of Criminals.* New York: Elsevier.

Vanderbilt, A. T. (1957). *Improving the Administration of Justice: Two Decades of Development.* Cincinnati, OH: College of Law, University of Cincinnati.

Waldo, D. (1980). *The Enterprise of Public Administration.* Novato, CA: Chandler & Sharp.

Wheeler, R. (1979). Judicial Reform: Basic Issues and References. *8 Policy Studies Journal*, pp. 8–10.

Wilson, W. (1887). The Study of Administration. *Political Science Quarterly*, June, pp. 197–218.

Wrap Up

■ RELEVANT PUBLICATION

The following article is presented to provide insight into how law enforcement administrators prepared for the transition into the 21st century. (Cronkhite, Clyde. (1984). *Centurion: A Police Lifestyle Magazine*, Number III, April.)

"21st Century Cop" by Clyde Cronkhite

The job of police officer in the 2000s may be hardly recognizable to today's cop. As we move completely into the Computer Age, crime may become mostly electronic theft, requiring investigators with high-tech expertise. More and more people may live in small, walled communities with their own private police. The cop on the beat may patrol by means of jet backpack flight equipment. Cities will become even more multinational, and officers will be able to tie in to "language banks" of translators via their wrist radios.

These predictions and more are brought to you by Forum 2000, the Los Angeles Police Department's volunteer future-watchers, headed by Deputy Chief Clyde L. Cronkhite, commanding officer of the LAPD Support Services Bureau. Part of his responsibilities deal with planning for the LAPD.

He received his Master of Public Administration degree from the University of Southern California and is author of the textbook Automation and Law Enforcement, *contributing author of the book* Computers in Local Government *and author of numerous articles on police and management subjects. He lectures and consults on "Future Management" for criminal justice agencies in Canada and the United States.*

Today we hear much talk about cutbacks, reduced resources and managing with less. Working with these realities is necessary, but sometimes depressing. It is true that we may have to deal with reduced resources for some years to come—but in the overall history of our society, this may be but a short period. As we look back 10 to 15 years from now, we will probably reflect on this period as a time of reevaluation and refinement—a time of adjustment to meet economic and cultural changes.

Conversely, looking into the future can be an exciting and invigorating experience. It can provide the motivation necessary to guide us through trying times. It is for this reason that nearly 100 people affiliated with the Los Angeles Police Department participate in a volunteer program called Forum 2000. They meet monthly and brainstorm with such notable futurists as Professor Selwyn Enzer of the USC Center for Future Research and Mr. Hank Koehn, Vice President in charge of Future Research, Security Pacific National Bank.

From this forum are emerging concepts and ideas that provide images of what future law enforcement may look like. One pattern being studied by the forum comes from Alvin Toffler's *The Third Wave* and John Naisbitt's current best seller, *Megatrends*. These books point out that we are entering a new "wave" of society based on information and technology. To put this new "wave" into proper perspective, it is helpful to review the previous social "waves."

The "first wave" is described as a society that was based on agricultural activities and took thousands of years to play itself out. During this "wave" mankind drew energy from "living batteries" such as human and animal power, sun, wind, water and wood, all of which were renewable.

The "second wave" was based on industrial production and drew energy from irreplaceable sources such as coal, gas and oil.

Today, we are moving into the "third wave," a society that will depend on technology and information systems to compensate for dwindling worldwide resources. We in law enforcement are capitalizing on this trend and making use of technology and automated information to meet our challenge of managing with fewer resources.

Law Enforcement Enters the Third Wave

Let's explore some examples of how law enforcement is currently using technology to make the transition into the "third wave."

Instant Cops

In the past, officers have had to detain people as long as 20 to 30 minutes while clerical personnel searched manual warrant files. Now it takes seconds to determine if a person is wanted or a vehicle or property is stolen. This rapid response comes through automated access to local, state and national law enforcement files. This reduces inconvenience to citizens and saves valuable field time for officers.

The growing use of remote out-of-vehicle radios, in-vehicle mobile digital terminals and computer-aided communication are more examples of how technology is assisting field operations.

The Electronic Sherlock Holmes

As the workloads of detectives increase, automated systems are needed to correlate large amounts of informational clues. LAPD's Automated Field Interview System (AFIS), for example, links daily observations made by field officers with crimes investigated by detectives. Other systems can sift through thousands of crime and arrest reports, correlating incidents by *modus operandi* (MO) patterns.

Automated Police Managers

Computerized information on calls-for-service, officer-initiated activity, traffic accidents and crime trends can now assist police managers to more economically deploy personnel. Better use and better training of personnel can be provided with automated data on such items as language skills, occupational experiences, hobbies, physical fitness, shooting proficiency and training achievements. Additionally, video communication is growing in use in academy and roll call training. Also, computerized shooting simulators are assisting in training officers when and when not to use deadly force.

Mini-Computers for the New Centurions

Today, mini-computers are within the financial reach of most police agencies. Mini-computers have the capabilities of larger computer systems of a decade ago. A growing number of small law enforcement agencies are using mini-computers to supply most of their automation needs. Larger police agencies are beginning to use mini-computers as replacements for their area station filing systems.

Transitional Challenges for Law Enforcement

As we advance into the future, many immediate challenges face us:

- Chances are that financial restraints will remain with us for the next five to eight years. City tax bases will continue to erode as those who "have" move to the suburbs and those who "have not" move into the central cities. The division between the haves and the have-nots will probably grow as those educated in the advancing technology capitalize on this knowledge and those without it become less employable.
- Law enforcement will have to look more to private businesses for contributions. Additionally, special-assessment taxing of people who want increased police service and are willing to pay for it will become commonplace. The Federal government may be approached to set up low-interest loans so police agencies can implement long-range cost reduction programs. Automation that would reduce personnel costs but would take several years to pay for itself through saved salaries is one example of what these loans could promote. The courts could increase fines for white-collar crimes and channel this revenue back to law enforcement to offset the dwindling tax dollar.
- Police officers will have to understand the various values and customs of the many nationalities that make up our communities. Shrinking tax dollars will curtail the growth of police departments and consequently adversely affect affirmative action hiring. Police agencies will have to recruit more minority and female police reserves and volunteers to offset this trend.
- Police managers will be placing more emphasis on crime prevention and community involvement and will take a more active role in city planning. New police programs will have to be tailored to the community's

desire for more "get tough" approaches, more public input and say-so in police activities, and more defined measurements of success for public evaluation.
- Internally, new means of motivation and reward will have to be developed as budget constraints slow upward mobility for employees. Emphasis on professional service as now found in the medical and legal fields may be a growing trend in police work. As employees become more interested in their personal time and off-duty activities, police departments may have to increase their "4-10" type deployment (longer hours worked but more days off) in order to compete with other occupations. Additionally, as the general public becomes more interested in jobs that affect the quality of life, law enforcement should look for ways of spotlighting this aspect of police work.

Law Enforcement in the 2000's

Based on some of the forecasts of futurists, let's take a look at what the state of the police may be after we have fully made the transition into the "third wave."

- The job of a police officer in the 2000's may be hardly recognizable to those of us employed in 1984. Advances in technology will assist the police officer in many tasks, while the state of the criminal justice system may prove to be more challenging than ever before.
- Budget restraints will probably cause a major reevaluation of the priorities of our duties. Local police departments may be handling police work of major importance only. Social service agencies and crisis intervention teams may be called in to handle many of the domestic disputes and other social problems currently handled by local police departments.
- Many communities may be walled. The people living in these small neighborhoods may contract for private police protection, which will reduce the workload of municipal agencies.
- The crime picture in the 2000's will have changed. White-collar crime and computer crime may be rampant, requiring a new form of investigative expertise. As a result of the rising age of the population, violent crimes against elderly persons will increase. Property-related crimes may be less of a problem than in 1984 due to more sophisticated prevention systems. Such devices as burglar alarms that, when activated, seal off the entire location, turning it into a detention tank until responding officers arrive, may reduce burglaries.
- Criminal activity will focus on a different type of valuable. Crime has always centered on what society holds valuable. In the agricultural "first wave," gold, cattle and horse thefts were the crimes of the day. In

the industrial "second wave," the almighty dollar has been the focus of robberies and other monetary crimes. In the future, money may all but disappear as more and more of our bank accounts become electronic. Very few people may carry cash, thereby reducing purse-snatching, pickpocketing and street robbery. The emphasis will be on theft by electronic technology. The computer terminal may become the "booster box" of the future.

- Police officers will be assisted in the identification of criminal suspects through various technological advances. Against popular opinion, all citizens may be required to carry a national identification card. Failure to do so will probably constitute a crime. Police agencies internationally will share data on criminals. Systems may be designed for which a single fingerprint will be sufficient to retrieve an individual's complete criminal history, description and photo. This information may be obtainable from an optic screen in the police car. Holographic, or 3-D, photography may be used for mug photos. Satellite photography will probably be used to assist in some criminal investigations.

- Police communications systems in the 2000's will be far superior to the current technology. The 911 system will be fully implemented. Current hand-held radios may be replaced by watch-size wrist radios. The location of these radios, and the officers wearing them, may be automatically tracked. This will enhance officer safety and management control by keeping the supervisors apprised of officers' locations. Mobile digital terminals, which are currently being installed in police vehicles, may be reduced in size to hand-held terminals, allowing officers immediate computer access from any location. Officers may carry compact video recorders that will provide a record of criminal actions in some arrest situations.

- Countries of the "Pacific Rim" (countries ringing the Pacific Ocean) will become a "community" of nations. Technological advances, particularly in communication and transportation, will reduce the barriers of time and distance. Cities will become even more transnational and cross-cultural, with the Hispanic and Asian communities making up large portions of the population. Officers will probably have access, via their wrist radios, to centralized "language banks" of translators.

- Computers may be in nearly every home. People who request police service may do so via their computer terminals and may even be able to communicate directly with the terminal in their local police car. Many of the crime reports we now take by telephone may be taken by computer. The victim's terminal will display a format for the reporting of a minor crime.

- With computers in more homes, more people may be working at home. Futurists predict that 70 percent of today's office clerical work could be accomplished on a home computer. More people working at home could reduce daytime residential burglaries and traffic on the streets. Also, people may move less often because they can just dial into another computer instead of relocating to the site of a new job. Less movement may increase the cohesiveness of local neighborhoods, which also could result in less community crime. The "cabin fever" resulting from working at home may, however, result in more domestic crime.

- The arsenal of weapons available in the 2000's may be substantially larger than now. Most officers will carry weapons like the Taser, a non-lethal electronic dart gun already in use in a number of police departments. Field supervisors may drive vehicles equipped with a vast array of non-lethal weapons, including water bombs, nets, bean-bag guns, and the like.

- Police vehicles will be specially designed to fit police needs. A major manufacturer may market a utilitarian vehicle designed solely as a police car. It will have no unnecessary frills such as chrome strips, deluxe interior, etc. The rear seat will be a plastic bench. Roll bars, light bars, cages and necessary electronic equipment will be built in. Energy conservation may require engines that alternate from fuel to batteries as officers alternate from pursuit to normal patrol. Private cars may have a factory-installed "kill" switch that can be activated by depressing a button in a nearby police vehicle. This may virtually eliminate vehicular pursuits.

- In the 2000's the number of foot patrols may increase. Foot beat officers may be aided in making their rounds by the use of Moped-type vehicles and jet "backpack" flight equipment. This will increase mobility while still retaining the personal touch. Hybrids of ultralite aircraft will facilitate aerial patrol at less cost than helicopters and fixed-wing planes.

- Lasers may also help police officers do their job in the 2000's. Laser "radar-guns" may track speeders. Lasers may also be attached to weapons as sighting devices and be used to enhance latent fingerprint discovery techniques.

- Citizen involvement may become even more important in the 2000's. Neighborhood Watch may be better organized, with most people participating in many neighborhoods. There may be more emphasis on peacekeeping and crime prevention.

- The courts may continue to frustrate police officers. Warrants may be required for most misdemeanor arrests and searches. Search and seizure rules may be stricter. However, on the bright side, conviction rates may go up due to technological advances that will aid officers. Also, police officers and witnesses may not be required to appear in court. Testimony may be taken and transmitted by home computer/video systems. This could substantially speed up the court process.

- Convicted criminals will still be given prison sentences. The need for more prisons may be resolved by turning coastal islands into a series of penal colonies with varying degrees of security. The theory of rehabilitation may be forsaken. Penal colonies may be pleasant, humane societies that will be self-sufficient, and society may lose some of its guilt about locking up criminals.

- Society in the 2000's will provide new challenges to police officers and police managers. Hopefully, technology will advance faster than problems increase, and police departments will be able to provide better service to their constituents.

Looking Toward the Future

Of course, some of these projections for the future are highly speculative. They do, however, provide useful images in preparing to meet the future. As a runner soon learns, you don't win races by looking down at your feet. You win by looking forward and setting your sights on what's ahead. We in law enforcement are looking ahead, and what we see makes being a part of the police profession an exciting and challenging experience.

> *"The greater thing in this world is not so much where we stand as in what direction we are going."*
>
> —*Thomas Jefferson*

Applying Organization Functions Concepts to the Administration of Contemporary Criminal Justice Agencies

7

■ Introduction

As discussed in Chapter 2, the Organization Functions concepts form the base from which today's criminal justice administration gains its support. The human body could not function without a skeleton to support the many other body components. So it is with criminal justice administration, which cannot be successful without the Organization Functions providing support for all the other themes. As stated in Chapter 1, Organization Functions involve the managing of an organization, in comparison to leadership, which relates more to Employee Relations concepts that are discussed in the next chapter.

Summaries of key concepts from Chapter 2 (as well as their authors) are brought forward here as a beginning point for the application phase of this text. The key historic Organization Functions concepts to remember are:

- POSDCORB
  1937, "Notes on the Organization," Luther Gulick
- Principles of Bureaucratic Organizations
  1922, "Characteristics of Bureaucracy," Max Weber
- Scientifically find the best way to do the job
  1912, "Principles of Scientific Management," Frederick Taylor
- Public Administration is a *profession* that responds to elected officials who represent the public
  1887, "The Study of Administration," Woodrow Wilson

Using organizational concepts as a starting point, this chapter will explore their application to today's criminal justice agencies as well as introducing some more current concepts in the category of Organization Functions. Organization Functions became important when public administration began to be considered as a profession and to be compared to business administration. This occurred in 1887 when Woodrow Wilson wrote in "The Study of Administration" that public administration should be separated from politics and that public administrators should carry out the directions of elected officials with little involvement in the political arena (Wilson, 1887).

Even though Wilson tied public administrators to their elected official, the civil service laws created during that period served to protect the executive officers of public agencies from political hiring and firing, thereby somewhat insulating them from political influence. In recent times, there has been a growing concern that some public agencies have become too removed from the influence of the elected representatives of the people. To some extent, this has promoted a return to political involvement in the hiring and firing of criminal justice administrators. The long-term civil service protection is being replaced with short-term contracts that hold criminal justice department heads more accountable to elected officials.

■ Evolutionary Modifications to the Original Organization Functions Concepts

The "closed systems" view of Wilson certainly has been modified during and subsequent to the Open Systems era. In 1966, Katz and Kahn asserted that all social systems are open systems, in that they gain their input of energies from the outside environment, convert these energies into outputs through a process of internal functions, and return the energies to the environment, where they energize additional inputs (Katz & Kahn, 1966).

In the Social Equity era, H. George Frederickson wrote that the "New public administration seeks not only to carry out legislative mandates as efficiently and economically as possible, but to both influence and execute policies which more generally improve the quality of life for all." Frederickson foresaw a political system in which "elected officials would speak for the majority, and the courts and public administrators would be protective of the interest of the disadvantaged minorities" (1971, p. 75). During this same period, Vincent Ostrom proposed a theory of "democratic administration," stating that public administrators must serve the individual consumer of public goods and services must not be strictly guided by elected officials (Ostrom, 1974.)

During the transition into the Client-Oriented era, George P. Barbour converted the *In Search of Excellence* work of Peters and Waterman regarding "Closeness to the Citizenry" (Peters & Waterman, 1982) to the public sector by writing that this criterion included public agencies establishing and maintaining a variety of close links with citizens and by being sensitive and responsive to public input (Barbour, 1984).

Additionally, old concepts have been integrated into current approaches. For example, Frederick Taylor's *Scientific Management* concept that there is "a best way to perform any given task and the job of the administrator is to scientifically find the one best way" still prevails today. Taylor's recommendations are found today in time and motion studies, approaches to maximizing skills of employees and replacing traditional methods of assessing work accomplishments with systematic and more scientific methods of measuring and managing.

■ Basic Concepts for Today's Application

We begin the discussion of the application process with the acronym **POSDCORB** (planning, organizing, staffing, directing, coordinating, reporting, budgeting) suggested by Gulick and Urwick (Gulick & Hyde, 1937, pp. 1–45). Planning is the first administrative activity that must be accomplished before any of the other activities are put into motion. There must be some thinking ahead when designing an agency, or in deciding the future direction of an existing agency, by executive officers. Even when becoming an administrator, one must plan for promotion.

POSDCORB is a classic model that describes the major functions of an organization and how they should be applied. More recently, it has been expanded to POSTBECPIRT (planning, organizing, staffing, training, budgeting, equipment, coordination, public information, reporting, directing) for policing (Holcomb, 1961, p. 77). The original terms will be discussed here, however, and the others will be covered in subsequent chapters.

Planning involves preparing for the future, both short and long range. Planning ranges from the first-line supervisor, who plans the daily activities of their personnel, to the top executive, who plans the long-range goals involved in accomplishing the organization's mission. Plans can be *reactive* (immediate reactions to a crisis that just occurred), *contingent* (prepared in advance for unusual situations), *operational* (for routine activities such as daily allocation of personnel), or *strategic* (long-range plans that lead to the accomplishment of the overall mission).

Organizing is the arrangement of tasks into subsystems to achieve the goals and objectives. It involves the division of labor, which will be discussed later in this chapter. It deals with creating a formal structure to facilitate the work of the enterprise. The desired end result is to have a structure that facilitates the coordination of all activity toward the accomplishment of the agency's mission, in the most efficient and effective manner. The "principles" of bureaucracy established by Max Weber are all part of establishing an organization.

Staffing involves the selecting, hiring, and training of employees and will be discussed in the next chapter as part of the Employee Relations theme.

Directing is communicating orders in writing and orally that channel the efforts of the employees toward the achievement of *goals and objectives*. It involves establishing policies, procedures, and rules that guide employees in performing their tasks. Plans cannot result in success unless they are communicated to those given the responsibilities of carrying them out. From the top executive, who communicates the strategic plans throughout the agencies, to the supervisors, who tell their employees what to do and how to do it, directions are necessary at every level of the organization.

Coordination includes overseeing the work of all employees for which an administrator is responsible so that work efforts complement one another, friction between activities is eliminated, and a synergistic combination of activities results. In also includes coordination of internal efforts with outside entities that have an "open systems" impact on the achievement of the organizational goals.

Reporting involves keeping essential information flowing throughout the organization both orally and in writing. It certainly involves directing but also must include feedback that allows information to go up and across, as well as down, in an organization. It also involves the communication of important information to those outside the organization with whom coordination and support is important.

Budgeting entails financial planning that ensures the funds necessary to carry out organizational activities and, once a budget is approved, making sure that operational activities are conducted within the approved plan. Normal financial planning consist of two types: **line-item budgets**, which include all those items that are needed yearly to operate the agency, and **capital budgets**, which involve large items such as a new building for which financing commitment is required for more than one year.

Planned Program Budgeting Systems (PPBS)

Planned Program Budgeting Systems (PPBS) is a type of budgeting that Allen Schick proposed during the Open Systems era (Schick, 1966). His approach is a reminder of how administrators must refocus to basic Organization Functions during economic decline, which was the case in the mid-1960s. Schick spotlighted three developments that influence budgeting in public agencies:

1. Economic analysis—macro and micro—has an increasing part in the shaping of fiscal and budgetary policy.
2. The development of new informational and decisional technologies has enlarged the applicability of objective analysis to policy making.
3. There has been a gradual convergence of planning and budgetary processes (Schick, 1966).

PPBS basically forces the entities within an organization to set and be accountable for measurable objectives and to provide information as to how these objectives converge to achieve the overall goals of the agency. In many cases, the documentation required in this approach made it unworkable. However, the basic idea of integrated financial accountability is interwoven into today's budgeting. Often, some form of PPBS is required when agencies request funds for a new program or to enlarge the size of the agency. PPBS requires that program objectives and methods of measuring achievements be defined.

Zero-Based Budgeting

Zero-Based budgeting, first introduced by Peter Pyhrr in 1977, is yet another reminder of how administrators must turn their attention to basics during periods of decreasing financial support (Pyhrr, 1977). The mid-1970s saw a nationwide tax revolt that resulted in a dynamic decrease in public financing. Pyhrr's approach required agencies to create and justify a new budget each year. The line-item budget was eliminated and every item required to run an agency had to be justified anew. This type of budgeting also "died of its own weight," especially as the economy improved; however, Zero-Based Budgeting can be expected to resurface during periods of economical downturn. During these periods, agencies are often directed to prepare "what if" budgets detailing what they would do if their budgets were reduced by 5%, 10%, or 20%, and how essential programs would continue to function under such reductions. Additionally, *sunset clauses* requirements were ushered in during this period. These "clauses" require a set time by which the requesting agency must prove the worth of the funding or the financing will be discontinued.

■ "Principles" of Bureaucracy

As discussed in Chapter 2, Max Weber is known as the "father of the bureaucratic model." "Bureaucracy" (first published in German in 1922 and translated into English in 1946) still provides a basic understanding of today's hierarchical organizational structures. Although his concepts and theories are sometimes criticized, they remain, through updating and enhancing, a solid platform from which criminal justice administration functions today.

Bureaucratic organizations vary substantially from rigid (such as military departments) to more flexible agencies (such as citizen's committees and community groups). Even Warren Bennis, who in 1967 proclaimed "an end to bureaucracy in 25 years," has more recently stated that certain forms of it are necessary (Bennis, 1967). In 1988, Chandler and Plano wrote that "despite the possibility of abuse, the hierarchical principle remains a key to governmental operations in the United States on all levels and provides the means by which a democratic society can keep its bureaucrats accountable" (Chandler & Plano, 1988).

It also should be remembered that Herbert Simon cautioned that what Weber called *principles* should be regarded as "proverbs" or guides because "in applying them over time, room for variations and enhancement must be allowed" (Simon, 1946). It is with these historical thoughts in mind that the applications of the basic concepts are discussed. In 1929, Fayol documented Weber's concepts of bureaucracy in *Industrial and General Management* (Fayol, 1929).

Fayol's Principles of Management

1. *Division of Work. Work specialization can increase efficiency with the same amount of effort. However, there is a limit to how much work should be specialized.*

2. *Authority and Responsibility. Authority includes both the right to command the power to require obedience; one cannot have authority without responsibility.*

3. *Discipline. Discipline is necessary for an organization to function effectively; however, the state of the disciplinary process depends on the quality of its leaders.*

4. *Unity of Command.* An employee should receive orders from one superior only.

5. *Unity of Direction.* There should be one manager and one plan for a group of activities that have the same objective.

6. *Subordination of Individual Interest to General Interest.* The interests of one employee or group of employees should not take precedence over those of the organization as a whole.

7. *Remuneration of Personnel.* Compensation should be fair to both the employee and the employer.

8. *Centralization.* The proper amount of centralization or decentralization depends on the situation. The objective is to pursue the optimum utilization of the capabilities of personnel.

9. *Scalar Chain.* The scalar chain, or hierarchy of authority, is the order of rank from the highest to the lowest levels in the organization; it defines the path of communication. Besides this vertical communication, horizontal communication should also be encouraged, as long as the managers in the chain are kept informed.

10. *Order.* Materials and human resources should be in the right place at the right time; individuals should be in jobs or positions most suited for them.

11. *Equity.* Employees should be treated with kindness and justice.

12. *Stability of Personnel Tenure.* An employee needs time to adjust to a new job and reach a point of satisfactory performance; high turnover should be avoided.

13. *Initiative.* The ability to conceive and execute a plan (through initiative and freedom) should be encouraged and developed throughout all levels of the organization.

14. *Esprit de Corps.* Since "union [unity] is strength," harmony and teamwork are essential to effective organizations.

Source: Adapted from Fayol, H. (1929). *General and Industrial Management* (trans. by C. Storrs). London: Pitman & Sons.

Authority and Responsibility

Authority and responsibility are the first concepts to be discussed. The top executive officers of criminal justice agencies must have received authority and responsibility from some higher power if they are to carry out the mission of their agency. The chief of police or sheriff, for example, will take an oath of office upon being appointed to their position. As will be discussed in Chapter 10, the United States is a *republic* form of government wherein the majority rule by vote or through their elected officials. When the heads of criminal justice agencies take the oath, they are given "police power" from the people to carry out the will of the majority regarding the services of their agencies.

This is a critical issue for administrators to understand. The chief executive, on taking the oath of office, is responsible for the conduct and efforts of everyone in their agency. For example, after the New York terrorist attack of September 11, 2001 (during the U.S. Senate hearings regarding the government's response to the attack), there was a motion to fire the director of the Federal Bureau of Investigation (FBI) because the FBI failed to prevent the disaster. Fortunately, the Senate did not follow through on the motion because the then FBI director had only held that office for several weeks. In 2006, the head of the Federal Emergency Management Agency (FEMA) was forced to resign because of failures of that agency to properly handle the hurricane disaster in the New Orleans area. Every year, police chiefs and correction wardens lose their jobs because of the failure of their employees to properly carry out the public missions of their agencies. It was O. W. Wilson who further defined police executive accountability:

> *Although he may free himself of the actual performance of the tasks involved, a superior officer cannot rid himself of an iota of responsibility for their accomplishment. He delegates to subordinates the authority to perform the tasks, and he may tell those subordinates that they are responsible for a successful conclusion of the assignment; but he remains accountable for its final accomplishment.* (Wilson, 1963, p. 35)

Once chief executives have received the overall authority and responsibility for their agencies, they may delegate certain tasks to lower-level personnel. However, they always retain the overall accountability for the agency. As delegation occurs down the chain, each lower-level administrator must be given the appropriate power to command. They must be able to apply both positive and negative discipline, as needed, so that they can accomplish the tasks for which they are being held responsible. They, in turn, are held accountable to their higher-level administrators. As shown in **Figure 7–1**, there is an increase in responsibility, power, and salary for individuals as they advance up the administrative hierarchy. Conversely, there are larger numbers of personnel at the lower levels of the pyramid where the mission of the organization is actually carried out.

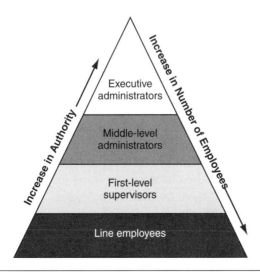

Figure 7–1 Organization Pyramid of Hierarchical Levels.

Unity of Command and Unity of Direction

Unity of command and **unity of direction** are related to authority and responsibility. Basically, these concepts mean that employees should receive direction from and be responsible to just one person. These concepts (as with other principles) have been altered over time, but the basic approach remains. For example, an employee who is officially assigned to one supervisor might work on a special task force for another supervisor. However, when it comes to the overall responsibility and evaluation of the employee, the assigned superior officer is responsible. (Comments of the taskforce supervisor should be included in the employee's evaluation.)

Control is another concept that comes into play in holding employees responsible. Gulick and Hyde defined "control" in *The Science of Administration*, and their definition was described by O. W. Wilson as an important component of police administration:

> *Control consists in seeing that everything is carried out in accordance with the plan which has been adopted, the organization which has been set up, and the orders which have been given . . . control is in a sense the consequence of command in action. Authority cannot be delegated safely without this check and hence the rule: Every delegation of authority should be accompanied by a commensurate placing of responsibility. (Wilson, 1963, pp. 109–110)*

Inspection and Control

Inspection and control are often used together because in order for administrators to have control over what their employees are doing they must have some way of assessing the activities of the employees. To inspect or to have firsthand observation of employee activities is the most common method of control. At every level of an organization, administrators have employees reporting directly to them. The chief executive has the administrators at the next level of the organization reporting to him or her as well as support personnel. This extends down to the first-line supervisor, who directs the daily activity of the line employees. Each level of administrators must inspect and evaluate the performances of their employees. This is referred to as *line inspection*, meaning the inspection of those directly in the line of supervision (directly reporting to) of every administrator.

In larger departments, there often exist "Inspection and Control" entities that inspect the activities of employees who do not directly report to those doing the inspecting. These are special units or divisions that report directly to the chief executive or another high-level administrator. These types of inspections are called *staff inspections*, and the observations of the inspectors are reported to the high-level administrators to which they are assigned.

The author (as a captain of police) served in such a capacity for the then chief of police in what was called a "duty chief" position. The assignment was for the duty chief to be in the "field" during the hours when the chief of police was not officially available and to observe firsthand how field personnel were performing. Except in emergencies, observations made when in this position were only reported back to the chief of police, who would discuss them with the next level in command. Any need for corrections would be communicated down through the chain of command for appropriate action. In this manner, the chief of police could assess how directions that he was providing were actually being carried out. The experience of being present when the chief gave directions, then hearing the interpretation of these directions at precinct roll call the following day, was quite revealing. The weakness of directives being altered and misinterpreted as they progress down through the chain of command caused the chief to implement a televised broadcast of him giving important directives for viewing at roll call by line officers.

Span of Control

Span of control is still another concept connected with control. It refers to the number of subordinates who report to any one administrator. This concept recognizes that there is a limit to the number of employees that a supervisor can be assigned and expected to properly manage. In 1937, Gulick and Hyde wrote, "No superior can supervise directly the work of more than five or, at the most, six subordinates whose work interlocks" (pp. 52–53).

For years, the military listed seven employees as the appropriate number. Over time, however, it has been recognized that there is no set number. The number of employees depends on the complexities of the jobs each employee is assigned and their work location in relation to the supervisor. For example, a supervisor may be assigned a larger number of employees if the employees are all doing the same type of work (say filing documents) and are all located in one room with the supervisor. However, if each employee is responding to a variety of work tasks and the employees are spread out in different geographical areas (patrol officers, for example), then fewer employees may be assigned to a supervisor. Additionally, a lesser number of employees should be assigned to a supervisor if the employees are new to the job or have been involved in some type of misconduct, in which case closer supervision is needed. It is the responsibility of administrators to determine the appropriate span of control for their employees.

Division of Work

Division of work is important to any administrator who supervises two or more persons, which include all administrators except those in a "one-person" agency. This concept acknowledges that there is a limit to the work that any one person can do efficiently and that some type of delegation is often required. This requires administrators to determine a proper balance between too much work and not enough. Remember, the basic responsibility of an administrator, as discussed in Chapter 1, is to ensure the *effective and efficient accomplishment of the mission and to providing a work environment that satisfies the needs of the employee.*

The division of work can be divided into two categories, vertical division and horizontal division.

Vertical Division of Labor

Vertical division of labor is the separation of functions into hierarchical levels based on authority and responsibility. It is sometimes referred to as division by rank, and supports the **scalar chain** and unity of command concepts. The three general levels of administration are:

> *Executive Administrators* are responsible for setting the mission and overall goals of the agencies (e.g., chiefs of police; wardens, chief probation officers, and their next level of command).
>
> *Middle Administrators* are responsible for establishing objectives that support directions from above and coordinating their execution (e.g., police captain and lieutenants, and prison division commanders).
>
> *First-Line Supervisors* are responsible for overseeing the day-to-day activities of line employees and carrying out the directions of those at a higher level (e.g., police sergeants and parole supervisors).

Horizontal Division of Labor

Horizontal division of labor is the assignment of work to individuals or units that have the same rank and authority and are on the same level in the hierarchy. At the top of the organization, the first order of horizontal division is to divide work into three general categories: operations, support/auxiliary, and administration/staff functions (**Figure 7–2**).

Operations personnel perform the major tasks that accomplish the mission of the agency, usually on a 24-hour-a-day basis. This is the largest part of an agency and usually is comprised of approximately 80% of the personnel (e.g., police patrol officers/detective, parole/probation officers, bailiffs, and custodial officers).

Support/Auxiliary personnel are responsible for supporting the day-to-day activities of the operations personnel and usually comprise approximately 15% of the department. Whereas most operations personnel are "sworn" (have powers of arrest), the support or auxiliary personnel are often "civilians" and not given "peace officer" status. Examples of functions that come under this category are recordkeeping, communication, property, and vehicle maintenance.

Administrative or Staff are personnel removed from the line functions with the responsibility to prepare for the future and assist the executive officers with their responsibilities. They usually comprise 5% of the employees and are involved in such functions as planning; budgeting; the recruitment, selection, and

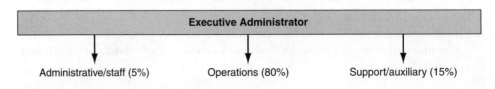

Figure 7–2 Horizontal Division of Labor.

training of personnel; and inspections and administration of discipline (e.g., Human Resources and Financial Planning personnel).

It might help to understand the reason for this type of division of labor by comparing the responsibilities of the executive officer with a military general's responsibilities in fighting a war. The general would deploy most of his or her personnel to fighting the battle (operations personnel). However, to win the war, the general must have support or auxiliary personnel manufacturing the ammunition, maintaining the equipment, and feeding the battlefield solders. Additionally, the general must have administrative or staff personnel assisting in the planning of battle strategies, recruiting, and training solders to replace casualties and the wounded, and obtaining the financial support necessary to win the war. So it is with the criminal justice administrator.

Additional guides for division of labor are listed here to assist in further refinement of work assignments.

Task assignments involves grouping related activities into division, or units. For example, police Operations can be divided into patrol and detective work. Detective work may be divided into "crimes against person" and "crimes against property."

Clientele division of labor relates to the "customers" or types of categories of persons for which employees are responsible. For example, local jailers or probation/parole officers may be separated into divisions that deal with felonies and others with misdemeanors. The police often have separate units that deal with juveniles and vice/narcotic offenders, for example.

Area means separating work into territories such as patrol precincts and parole or probation state or county districts.

Time is the division of labor by time of day and day of the week. Any function that requires 24-hour-a-day deployment will need to be divided into weekly and monthly assignments that provide for daily divisions of work often called day, night, and morning watches.

Specialization is a consideration in which there is a real need to fix responsibility for a particular function or a need for specially trained personnel who are capable of handling a unique task. For example, some personnel may be removed from the patrol function to concentrate on traffic violations and accidents. In a detective division, certain personnel may be deployed to sex or narcotic crimes. When dividing work by specialties, some disadvantages must be considered. A major consideration is that those not assigned to the specialized task will decrease their efforts in that activity. For example, if a special traffic unit is implemented, the regular patrol officers may cease to look for traffic violations and even resist the taking of traffic reports. Another consideration is that specialization will fragment employee efforts to achieve the overall mission of the agency. The author, while an investigative division commanding officer, found detectives protecting prostitutes from arrest by vice officers because the prostitutes were acting as informants for the detectives. When the author developed a special crime prevention unit, patrol officers were noted to lose interest in the prevention aspects of their job, often referring interested citizens to the "crime prevention unit."

The concepts of bureaucracy are important in holding chief administrative personnel *accountable* to their governing power. In the private sector, a chief administrator is held accountable to the shareholders for the success of the organization through the organization's board of officers. In the public sector, chief administrative officers are held accountable to the public for the success of their agency's mission through the elected officials to which they report.

◾ Contemporary Modifications to Organization Functions

Organization Charts are useful in showing formal organization structures. They also display both the horizontal and vertical division of labor as well as the scalar chain of command. As previously mentioned, the formal bureaucratic organization structure often has been criticized for its inflexibility and mechanistic characteristics. Called the "paramilitary model," it is questionable whether it is applicable to criminal justice agencies, as their employees are not soldiers but are given a wide range of discretion. For example, patrol officers seldom work in groups; rather, most of their work is done individually or in pairs. Only in extreme emergencies such as riots or other unusual occurrences do they respond as a paramilitary unit.

Criticism of the bureaucratic models has been documented in a study by Franz and Jones. In this study that compared police employees working in a paramilitary structure with other government employees working in a more flexible, organic organization, they found that police employees perceived (1) greater problems with communications, (2) lower levels of morale and organizational performance, and (3) greater amounts of distrust of management (Franz & Jones, 1987, p. 161). This subject will be discussed further in the next chapter, as an Employee Relations concept.

Mechanistic versus organic organization structures should be compared; the older bureaucratic structure (mechanistic) becoming more popular with the more flexible bureaucratic model (organic), which is favored today (**Table 7–1**).

Mechanistic structures exemplify the old bureaucratic organization, which is characterized by a rigid design with many rules and regulations, centralized control and decision making, and strict hierarchical channels of communication. Directions and interaction is vertical and terms such as superior and subordinate personnel are used. Is there a need for such a structure today? If the following situations exist, the answer is "yes":

1. Employees are relatively inexperienced and unskilled.
2. Employees have strong needs for security and stability.
3. The technology is relatively stable and involves standardized materials and a programmable task.
4. The environment is fairly calm and relatively simple (Porter, Lawler, & Hackman, 1975, p. 272).

Table 7–1	Characteristics of Mechanistic and Organic Systems

Organizational characteristics	Mechanistic	Organic
Division of work	Narrow, specialized tasks	General tasks
Performance of tasks	Specific, unless changed by managers	Adjustable, although there is interaction with others involved in the task
Communication	Mainly vertical	Vertical and horizontal
Communication content	Instructions and decisions issued by superiors	Information and advice
Decision making	Mainly centralized	Mainly decentralized
Span of control	Narrow	Wide
Levels of authority	Many	Few
Quantity of formal rules	Many	Few
Position-based authority	High	Low

Source: Adapted from T. Burns & G. M. Stalker (1961). *The Management of Innovation*, pp. 119–122. London: Tavistock. R. M. Howser & J. W. Lorsch (1967). "Organizational Inputs." In J. A. Seiler (Ed.), *Systems Analysis in Organizational Behavior*. Homewood, IL: Irwin.

Additionally, the mechanistic type of structure may be appropriate if there is a need for strong control and close supervision, as when misconduct and corruption has to be eliminated from an organization entity. As mentioned in earlier chapters, the modes of policing have evolved from the watchman to the professional/legalistic, to the client-oriented style of today. It should, however, be acknowledged that some law enforcement agencies are still operating in the watchman or professional/legalistic mode. The classical mechanistic system was the model of preference during the professional/legalistic era and there are situations that require a return to the more rigid form of administration.

Organic systems, however, are better able to facilitate today's criminal justice administration. Organic systems work best in the following situations:

1. Employees have relatively high skills that are widely distributed.
2. Employees have high self-esteem and strong needs for achievement, autonomy, and self-actualization.
3. The technology is rapidly changing, nonroutine, and involves many nonprogrammable tasks.
4. The environment is relatively dynamic and complex (Porter, Lawler, & Hackman, 1975, p. 272).

Today's communities certainly fit the situation in number 4, as they are "relatively dynamic and complex." This is why today's criminal administration involves the delegation of more discretion to employees and the recruitment of educated and motivated employees who are better able to cope with changing cultural and technology situations.

Tall and flat hierarchical structures, shown in **Figure 7–3**, relate to mechanistic and organic organization designs.

Tall structures are associated with many hierarchical levels, long chains of command, and small spans of control allowing closer supervision and control. This structure is associated with the mechanical organization and embodies the classic principles of bureaucracy.

Flat structures broaden the span of control, reduce hierarchical levels, and allow for more discretion and less supervision. It also shortens the scalar chain, therefore speeding communications and decision making. This form is most often associated with the organic system.

Realistically, many departments today are both organic and mechanistic in nature. An agency that may be considered organic may have the need for some subdivisions to operate more mechanically if one of the four situations previously listed calls for such an approach. For example, if corruption is discovered within an entity within an agency, a more mechanistic approach may be needed to ensure tighter supervision and control.

Matrix structures are becoming more prevalent. In the latter part of the 1980s, the author, as chief of police of the Santa Ana Police Department, was involved in a reorganization that resulted in a "three-dimensional" organizational structure. (A more extensive discussion of this reorganization can be found in the "Related Publication" at the end of Chapter 11.) This reorganization, called **"Matrix Community-Oriented Policing (MiCOP),"** arranged the department into specialized forces capable of confronting problems from different perspectives (see **Figure 7–4**). MiCOP represents a three-dimensional organizational structure approach in which many functions interacted to share responsibilities in resolving neighborhood problems (Swanson, Ternto, & Taylor, 1993, pp. 154–155).

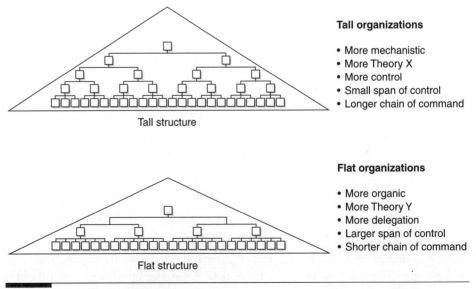

Tall organizations

- More mechanistic
- More Theory X
- More control
- Small span of control
- Longer chain of command

Tall structure

Flat organizations

- More organic
- More Theory Y
- More delegation
- Larger span of control
- Shorter chain of command

Flat structure

Figure 7–3 Tall and Flat Organizational Structures.

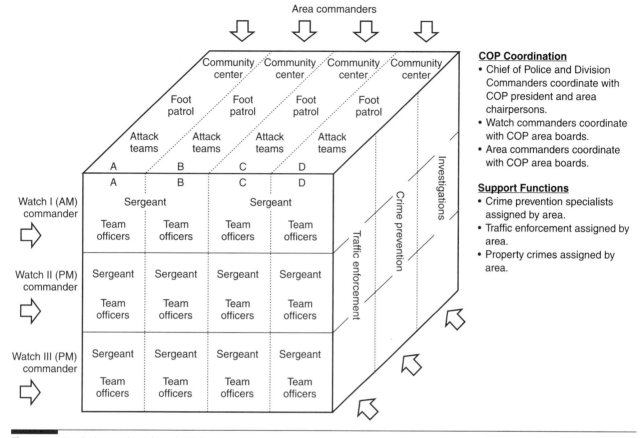

Figure 7–4 Matrix Community-Oriented Policing Organization Structure (Santa Ana P.D. Reorganization; refer to the Relevant Publication in Chapter 11).

With the development of the Employee Relations, Open Systems, Social Equity and Client Oriented themes, the basic bureaucratic structure remained but with many enhancements and customizations. These changes will be discussed in subsequent chapters as we explore the application of these evolving themes and concepts. Developing an Eclectic Perspective provides insight into these evolutionary changes and enables administrators to apply the most appropriate concepts to a given situation.

Examples of Contemporary Applications

Law enforcement will serve here as the prime example of the application of the Organization Functions theme concepts. Today, police number more than 850,000 in the United States and make up the largest segment of the criminal justice system. Additionally, most police administration applications are similar to applications in the administration of the courts and corrections.

At the executive level, tasks must be divided among a number of entities in all but the smallest of agencies. Using the three major divisions of labor, most police agencies are divided as discussed in the following sections.

Operations

Operations make up 70 to 80% of the department. In law enforcement agencies, patrol normally comprises 60 to 70% of the department and detectives about 10 to 20% of the department. The division of these two functions relates to the task that each performs. In smaller departments, all of the personnel below the rank of captain are devoted to operations functions. In a slightly larger department, these functions are called "Field Services." In correctional institutions, this division of labor is often called "Prison & Jail Operations" (see **Appendix 2A, Appendix 2B**, and **Appendix 2C** for examples of these three organization types).

Patrol

This function involves the personnel who carry out the general mission of the agency. Patrol may be divided by:

Time. Patrol officers are assigned to various times of the day, often called watches or shifts. Traditionally, officers are assigned to eight-hour shifts, commonly called day, night, and morning watches. More recently, a number of agencies have done 10–12 hour shifts with officers having more days off each deployment period.

Areas. Depending on the size of the agencies, patrol officers may be divided into geographic divisions, often called precincts or stations, which are decentralized from the main headquarters. Below is a typical deployment formula for assigning personnel to various precincts. The percentage of officers assigned to each precinct equates to the percentage of the factors in the formula as calculated from census track statistics.

Patrol Deployment Formula

- Calls for Service
- Crime
- Traffic Accidents
- Property Loss
- Population
- Street Miles
- Population Density

Specialization. Depending on local needs, some patrol officers may be designated as Traffic Officers to concentrate on traffic enforcement, direction, and accidents. Task forces are sometimes required for special needs such as drunk driving enforcement (DUI), and special weapons and tactics (SWAT).

Detective or Investigator

These assignments usually occur in agencies of 25 or more. Small departments may designate an officer to work part-time on investigative activities. Detectives are responsible for follow-up investigations of the more serious crimes (most preliminary investigations are conducted by patrol officers) and preparing cases for court often based on arrests made by patrol officers.

Table 7–2	Detective Deployment Formula		
	Crime only	**Arrest only**	**Complaints**
Homicide	38.1	12.0	67.9
Robbery	3.3	5.6	10.9
Burglary	1.9	3.5	8.3
Auto theft	0.8	2.9	6.6

Time. Detectives are most often assigned during regular business hours when the court is open but sometimes have night watches. Many often have some detective "on call" during non-business hours.

Area. As with patrol, if the jurisdiction is large enough, precinct stations are developed and detectives are assigned usually according to workload studies. **Table 7–2** shows a typical detective deployment formula that is developed from time and motion studies. Often, however, very specialized detective work such as homicide investigations remain centralized in one division at headquarters.

Specialization. As a detective division expands, further division of labor will be required. The first separation usually occurs by dividing crime investigation into (1) crimes against persons (murder, robbery, assault) and (2) crimes against property (burglaries and thefts).

Clientele. Assigning detectives to specialize in cases involving juveniles would fall into this category of division of labor. Forming special vice, narcotic, or gang details might fall within this category, as well as specialization.

Auxiliary or Staff

These positions refer to those functions that support the operations personnel but are not considered to be directly carrying out the mission of the agency. These functions comprise approximately 15% of an agency and in law enforcement are generally performed by civilian employees as opposed to those "sworn" and trained to enforce the law as are most operations personnel. Division of labor generally is by task.

Communications. This is the entity that receives calls from the public and dispatches police personnel. Often called the "9-1-1" function after the nationwide number to call for emergency service, it functions as the first contact most people have with the police department. Current efforts to reduce the workload for police personnel have caused the creation of innovative ways to handle public needs without sending a patrol car, such as taking minor crime reports over the telephone. Consequently, for a growing number of callers, communication personnel are the only contact they have with the police department. As discussed in the next chapter, the public often forms their opinion of law enforcement from their first contact, so it is important for administrators to realize that communication personnel have a significant impact on the reputation of their agency. With the continual advancements in Command and Control technology, administrators must keep abreast of current technological trends.

Recordkeeping. This entity is responsible for classifying, filing, and indexing criminal records that must be considered confidential and protected from misuse. Today, many of these records are automated and many of the employees must be technologically trained. In addition to supporting criminal justice personnel with information, the Freedom of Information Act (1974) allows citizens to access their own records and places certain restrictions on recordkeeping of personal information by which the Records Division must abide.

Jail. Most police departments have some type of arrestee-holding facilities. Larger departments have jail divisions for the temporary custody of unarraigned misdemeanor and felony prisoners. Police departments have many of the administrative challenges that are traditionally in the correction system. Jail employees also must be concerned with the feeding and medical attention of prisoners as well as ensuring their custody.

Property Control. This is the entity that has custody of evidence as well as recovered lost property. Court proceedings require that evidence be inventoried and protected from contamination. Additionally, some property is of high value and must be protected from theft. Also, provisions must be made for perishable property to be preserved and often property must be maintained for many years.

Vehicle Maintenance. Because operational personnel must be highly mobile, the purchasing and maintenance of vehicles is an important function. Personnel in this function need to be specially trained in the skills necessary for these assignments.

Crime Laboratory. With the development of DNA and other forensic technology, the crime laboratory has become an increasingly important part of police work. Placing it outside the chain-of-command of operation's administrators is important, so that there is no suspicion that laboratory personnel are pressured to falsify their findings by those responsible for the solving of crime. Employees in these functions most often have special education in the various fields of science and are not law enforcement officers. Because of the cost of these personnel and the scientific equipment, crime laboratories often are consolidated at a district, state, or federal level by local law enforcement agencies. This function also may be considered a specialization.

Building Maintenance. Police stations must be clean and maintained. Some agencies have their own custodial personnel and building repair personnel. Generally, however, for most police agencies, these task are provided by other governmental (or private) agencies that provide these services for a number of public facilities.

Administrative or Staff Functions

These are the functions that rely on planning ahead and involve approximately 5% of the department. They involve those activities that are generally thought of as being the direct responsibility of the chief of police and other top executive administrators. In fact, in smaller agencies, these activities are performed by the top executives. Again, these functions are divided by task and also specialization.

Budgeting. Ensuring the financial support for the future of the agency ultimately is the responsibility of the chief of police. In larger departments, however, personnel are designated to support the chief in planning, implementing, and controlling the budget.

Planning and Research. Larger departments have personnel assigned to these functions full time. They develop both long- and short-range plans as directed and often are responsible for the department manual and the writing of department policies, procedures, and rules.

Inspection and Control. Another function for which all administrators are responsible, but in larger agencies certain personnel are assigned to conduct staff inspections for the chief of police to provide for proper control.

Internal Affairs. This is another function that is a responsibility of all administrators (ensuring proper employee conduct). Special entities may be established to assist the chief in overseeing the overall conduct of department personnel, including the investigation of major accusations of misconduct.

Human Resources. This involves the recruitment, selection, and training of future employees.

Personnel are "the lifeblood" of the organization. Frederick Taylor (1916), in "The Principle of Scientific Management," stressed the importance of choosing the right person for each job. The subdividing of labor within this function is usually made on the basis of the tasks of recruitment/selection and training.

Recent Trends in Organization Functions

In 2006, Garth Morgan wrote, "We are shifting from a world dominated by bureaucratic-mechanistic principles into an electronic universe where new organizational logics are required. The intense theoretical and practical innovation is part of the transition and, given the fluid, self-organizing nature of a world dominated by electronic media, is likely to remain so." He goes on to describe the task of today's administrators: "This poses enormous challenges for any person wishing to stay abreast of new developments and cope with the flux in a positive way. Managers have to get beneath the surface and understand what is happening at a deeper level. Instead of being buffeted by the latest theories and trends, they need to be able to develop and take their own position" (Morgan, p. 364). Taking "their own position" required the ability to "mix and match" concepts from the five themes of the Contextual Themes Model and develop approaches that are customized for current situations. Some of criminal justice **Eclectic Perspective approaches** that should be considered include:

- enhance bureaucracy to allow for more flexibility
- promote (client) community involvement
- emphasize methods of preventing crime and disorder
- provide consultative supervision that gains employment input in making policies and final decisions
- make use of modern budget and accounting systems
- consider the art of administration as much as, if not more than, the science thereof

The organizational concepts discussed here have involved many law enforcement examples. Most of these concepts apply to court and corrections administration as well. These and other contemporary approaches to Organization Functions will be discussed in subsequent chapters.

KEY CONCEPTS AND TERMS

- POSDCORB
  - Line-item, Capital, PPBS, and Zero-Based budgeting
- "Principles" of Organization
  - Authority and responsibility
  - Unity of command and unity of direction
  - Scalar Chain
  - Span of control
  - Division of work
    - Vertical
    - Horizontal
    - Additional Guides
      - Task assignments
      - Clientele
      - Area
      - Time
      - Specialization
  - Mechanistic (tall) versus organic (flat) structures
  - Matrix Community-Oriented Policing (MiCOP) organization structure

CHAPTER ACTIVITY

Select the Web site of a criminal justice agency in which you are interested. Review the organization chart and related functions. Compare what has been discussed in this chapter to the criminal justice agency that you have selected.

REVIEW QUESTIONS

1. How did the Open Systems, Social Equity, and Client-Oriented themes alter the view that public "representatives of the people are the proper ultimate authority in all matters of government and administration is merely the clerical part of government," as put forth by Woodrow Wilson in 1887?

2. Give some examples of how the concepts of Max Weber, Fredrick Taylor, and Luther Gulick can be applied today.

3. Planned Program Budgeting Systems (PPBS) and Zero-Based Budgeting were products of the Open Systems era. Why did the importance of budgeting become a critical issue during this period?

4. The example of the duties of a military general was discussed for comparison in this chapter. How do these duties relate to the Organization Functions responsibilities of a criminal justice administrator?

5. Imagine that you are a criminal justice administrator and have been assigned to develop and implement a criminal justice entity of your choice (for example, a new correctional institution). What Organization Functions would you consider in fulfilling this assignment?

REFERENCES

Barbour, G. P. (1984). *Excellence in Local Government*. Washington, DC: IMCA Training Institute Publication.

Bennis, W. (1967). *The Functions of the Executive*. Cambridge, MA: Harvard University Press.

Chandler, R., & Plano, J. (1988). *The Public Administration Dictionary*. Santa Barbara, CA: ABC-CLIO.

Fayol, H. (1929). *Industrial and General Management*. C. Storrs (trans.). London: Pitman & Sons.

Franz, V., & Jones, D. M. (1987). Perceptions of Organizational Performance in Suburban Police Departments: A Critique of the Military Model. *Journal of Police Science and Administration*, 15, pp. 23–29.

Frederickson, H. G. (1971). Toward a New Public Administration. In *Toward a New Public Administration: The Minnowbrook Perspective*. Scranton, PA: Chandler.

Gulick, L., & Hyde, A. C. (1937). *Papers on the Science of Administration*. New York: Russell & Russell.

Holcomb, R. L. (Ed.). (1961). *Municipal Police Administration*. Chicago: International City Management Association.

Katz, D., & Kahn, R. (1966). Organizations and the System Concept. In *The Social Psychology of Organizations*. New York: John Wiley & Sons.

Morgan, G. (2006). *Images of Organization*. Thousand Oaks, CA: Sage.

Ostrom, V. (1974). *The Intellectual Crisis in American Public Administration*. Mobile: University of Alabama Press.

Peters, T. J., & Waterman, R. H., Jr. (1982). *In Search of Excellence*. New York: Warner Books.

Porter, L. W., Lawler, E. E., & Hackman, J. R. (1975). *Behavior in Organizations*. New York: McGraw-Hill.

Pyhrr, P. (1977). The Zero-Base Approach to Government Budgeting. *Public Administration Review*, January/February, pp. 1–8.

Schick, A. (1966). The Road to PPB: The Stages of Budget Reform. *Public Administration Review*, December, pp. 243–258.

Simon, H. (1946). The Proverbs of Public Administration. *Public Administration Review*, pp. 53–67.

Swanson, C. R., Territo, L., & Taylor, R. W. (1993). *Police Administration: Structures, Processes, and Behavior*. New York: Macmillan.

Taylor, F. W. (1916). Principles of Scientific Management. *Bulletin of the Taylor Society*. New York. Society for Advancement of Management.

Weber, M. (1922). Bureaucracy. *Essays in Sociology* by H. Gerth and C. Wright Mills (trans.). New York: Oxford University Press.

Wilson, O. W. (1963). *Police Administration* (2nd ed.). New York: McGraw-Hill.

Wilson, W. (1887). The Study of Administration. In *Classics of Public Administration*. Chicago: The Dorsey Press.

Wrap Up

■ RELEVANT PUBLICATION

The Relevant Publication for this chapter is one that resulted from a period of economical decline. The reduction in public financing caused by the economical decline and tax reducing legislation caused criminal justice administrators to resort to "cut-back" and "doing-more-with-less" management approaches. This included a refocusing on Organization Functions concepts that could make the most *efficient* use of existing resources. Earlier chapters in this textbook provided insight into how often "history repeats itself." When economical declines occur, administrators have to refocus on *efficiency*. Approaches in this article should provide the Eclectic Perspective Administrator with concepts to be applied in these situations. (Gladis, Stephen D. (1990). *Police Personnel*. Amherst, MA: Human Resources Development Press, pp. 3–14).

"Facing Increasing Crime with Decreasing Resources" by Clyde Cronkhite

Combating increasing crime with static or decreasing resources is a challenge for today's police administrators. This challenge requires us not only to work harder but also to work smarter to reach our mutual goal of providing a safe and comparatively crime-free environment for the public we serve. We can more effectively meet this challenge by sharing our experience—by sharing information about what works and what does not.

In California, we have experienced a substantial reduction in tax revenue due to Proposition 13, which was approved by our voters in 1978. This proposition limits property tax to 1 percent of market value. The results for the Los Angeles Police Department (LAPD) has been the loss of approximately 1,000 civilian and sworn personnel, a 10-percent reduction in our department's personnel strength. Because of this, we have been forced to manage with less, to experiment, and to research what other agencies have found successful.

Police Resources

In the broadest terms, our resources as police managers are personnel, equipment, and information.

Personnel is, of course, our largest and most important resource in meeting the crime threat. Because personnel constitutes 80–95 percent of our budgets, when budget cuts occur, they usually result in personnel reductions. However, there are methods by which remaining personnel resources can be stretched to take up the gap.

Team Policing

In the 1970's, LAPD, as well as many other police agencies, adopted team policing, which was effective in reducing crime. While crime was rising nationwide, LAPD was able to stabilize and reduce major crime from 1971 through 1977, the years the department was organized around team policing.

However, with the loss of over 10 percent of our personnel in the last 5 years, it has been determined that the department can no longer afford this concept. Combining patrol, detective, and traffic functions into geographical teams resulted in administrative overhead and inflexibility of personnel assignments. Additionally, many of the community meetings that are fundamental to team policing were being conducted on an overtime basis and were paid from overtime funds that no longer exist. Even so, a minimum number of basic field units assigned to set geographic areas are still maintained.

Neighborhood watch meetings are held on an "as needed" basis with citizen volunteers so that officers are removed from field patrol for only a short period of time. The remainder of the field force is assigned where the workload determines they are needed.

Uniform Deployment Formula

To make the maximum use of available field officers, departments experiencing cutbacks are having to rely more on formulas that usually include calls for service, crime, traffic accidents, property loss, population, street miles, and population density. In the LAPD, a number of patrol officers are "reshuffled" every deployment period (28 days) according to this formula. Each geographic area is evaluated on the above factors. and manpower deployed where the formula shows they are most needed.

Priority Management of Radio Calls

Several contemporary studies (particularly those of Kansas City, MO, and Syracuse, NY) indicated immediate response to all requests for service is not cost-effective. Consequently, a number of police agencies are now providing immediate response only to requests involving serious crimes in progress or where there is a present threat of death or serious injury. Other responses to calls for service are delayed and scheduled when sufficient radio units are available. In some cases, low priority requests are made on an appointment basis during nonpeak work hours.

In Los Angeles, under a program called System to Optimize Radio Car Manpower (STORM), a specifically deployed small percentage of radio units handle, on a scheduled basis, a large percentage of noncritical, low priority calls for service, e.g., barking dogs, loud radios, etc. Other radio units, therefore, remain available for immediate response to critical calls. Additionally, on all calls where a delay in dispatching occurs, a call-back is made to determine if the citizen still requests a police unit when one becomes available. This has reduced dispatching radio units when they are no longer needed. STORM provides the LAPD with the equivalent of approximately 56 officers in additional field time.

Some agencies, including the San Diego, Calif., Police Department (SDPD), have worked with their city council to establish a prioritized list of activities performed by radio units. By forming an agreement between the city council and the police department as to the desired activities to be performed, appropriate response times, how long each activity should take, and how much available patrol time should exist, they have established the basis for manpower requirements. If requests for service from the public increase, then the city council must provide funding for additional personnel or recognize that response time will increase and lower priority activities will not be handled. By this method, the council directly shares in the responsibility for proper service to the community.

Some agencies have strict control over the number of units responding to a dispatched call. Units other than those assigned are not allowed to respond. Additionally, units many not go "out to the station" unless approval is received from the dispatcher. To facilitate this procedure, field sergeants must announce their location by radio periodically so nearby units can meet them for crime report approval in the field. Also, approval for booking is often given by telephone when jail facilities are located some distance from the approving watch commander.

Directed Patrol

Creation of additional patrol time alone does not ensure more police productivity. The Kansas City preventive patrol experiment called into question two widely accepted hypotheses about patrol: (1) that visible police presence prevents crime by deterring potential offenders, and (2) that the public fear of crime is diminished by such police presence. Many police departments, such as South Central, Conn., Kansas City, Mo., and Wilmington, Del., have found that to be productive, use of "free patrol time" must be directed rather than used reactively. They provide directed patrol by:

1. Identifying through crime analysis the places and times crimes are occurring and are likely to occur in the future;

2. Preparing written directions describing in detail the way problem areas are to be patrolled; and

3. Activating these patrol directions through watch commanders and field supervisors and assuring concentrated effort toward specific crime problems.

Expanded Use of One-Officer Radio Units

The San Diego Police Department conducted a comparative study of 22 one-officer and 22 two-officer units to determine the difference in terms of performance, efficiency, safety, and officer attitudes. Although the two-officer units cost 83 percent more to field than one-officer units, the study found that one-officer units performed as well and were substantially more effective. Additionally, the study reported that one-officer units had better safety records.

Motorcycle Response for Congested Areas

Response time to priority calls in congested areas can be enhanced by assigning motorcycle units to respond to nontraffic as well as traffic calls for service in congested areas during peak traffic hours. Because of their maneuverability in heavy traffic, they can respond faster than radio cars.

"Call A Cop First" Program

Studies have shown that many people call someone else (a friend, employer, spouse) before they notify the police of a crime. James Elliot, in his book *Interception Patrol*[1] found that in 70 percent of crime-related service calls, citizens waited 10 or more minutes before notifying the police.

Other studies (such as those conducted by the National Advisory Commission on Criminal Justice Standards and Goals) have determined the success of solving a crime is greatly increased if the police arrive within several minutes after the event, or better yet, while it's occurring. In response to these findings, a campaign to remind the public of the importance of "calling a cop first" can be productive. Radio, television, and billboard advertisements (sponsored by local businesses and the media), wherein the chief of police, mayor, or entertainment personalities make the appeal, can be instrumental in spreading the word. More productive use of officers' radio time can result.

Eliminate "Property Damage Only" Traffic Accident Investigations

Some police agencies have found it necessary to cease taking most "property damage only" traffic accident reports. This practice has saved the Los Angeles Police Department the equivalent of approximately 20 officers in field time. Units are only dispatched to the scene of such accidents to eliminate traffic hazards and verify that a correct exchange of information has been made between involved parties, but no reports are taken.

---

[1]James Elliot, *Interception Patrol* (Springfield, Ill.: Charles C. Thomas, 1973).

Increased Use of Search Dogs and Mounted Crowd Control

Besides using specially trained dogs for bomb and narcotics searches, these animals can be a great manpower saver when searching for suspects in large areas such as warehouses, department stores, and outdoor field searches. In a 2-month study of LAPD's program, a team of dogs engaged in 165 searches, apprehended 54 suspects, and saved time equivalent to that of 11 officers per month.

Likewise, a few officers on horseback can provide crowd control equivalent to that of many officers on foot. LAPD has recently returned to the use of horses—something we learned from our Canadian colleagues many years ago.

Minimizing Report-taking Time

Many agencies are being forced to reevaluate their telephonic reporting procedure. It may be found that some agencies must limit their onscene investigation to those incidents where the suspect is still at the scene or very recently left, where recoverable evidence may be present, or where the nature of the crime or incident requires immediate response, e.g., violent or potentially violent crimes against persons and major traffic accidents. The San Diego Police Department now handles a monthly average of 45 percent of its calls for service telephonically with no adverse community feedback.

With cutbacks confronting many agencies, an evaluation of reporting requirements could be in order. Information required on reports that is "nice to know" may no longer be affordable and could be eliminated. Arrest, crime, evidence, and booking reports may have to be combined. The Los Angeles Police Department and Los Angeles County Sheriff's Department use a consolidated booking form packet which contains eight other reports, including a standardized front sheet for the arrest report. The information from the booking form is transferred by carbon paper to the other report forms. Also, some agencies are using "incident reports" to record only statistical information for minor crimes where little or no information is available that may lead to the apprehension of the suspect.

Followup time can be saved by allowing victims of theft-related crimes to list additional property taken (which was not included on the original crime report) on a separate report which is mailed to the police station. Use of this form eliminated the necessity of detectives having to complete followup investigation reports to list the additional items stolen.

Interagency Crime Task Force

Criminals do not often confine their activities to one jurisdiction. Combining investigative efforts with surrounding police agencies can often reduce duplication in investigations involving multi-occurrence crime trends.

Detective Case Assignments

Many police departments, including Rochester, N.Y., Long Beach, Calif., and Los Angeles, Calif., are having detective supervisors classify cases to allow detectives to focus their immediate efforts on the more serious, solvable cases. The procedure of the Los Angeles Police Department includes detective supervisors classifying and assigning cases as follows:

Category 1: Require Followup Investigations
Cases that have significant investigative leads and/or circumstances which require a followup investigation. A followup investigative report is generally due within 10 working days.

Category 2: Additional Investigation Required
Cases that do not have significant leads initially but which, with additional investigation, may provide significant leads. A followup report is required within 30 days. If significant leads are discovered, the case is reclassified to category 1.

Category 3: No Citizen Contact Required
In cases that do not contain apparent leads in the initial report, detectives are expected to investigate when category 1 and 2 cases have been handled. These cases are reviewed by detectives and their supervisors to ensure knowledge of crime trends in their areas of responsibility. Detectives are not required to routinely contact category 3 victims.

Cases that involved in-custody arrestees are, of course, given top priority.

The positive impact of classifying cases is further complemented through the use of a form given victims by uniformed officers when crime reports are made. This form informs victims that a detective will not contact them unless additional information is required. This strategy thus tends to reduce the number of phone calls to detectives from curious victims only wishing to know how things are going on their case.

Detective Deployment Formula

A number of agencies have developed "work units" for the time it takes a detective to handle a crime, arrest, complaint, or petition filing. The average time to complete these work units varies and are established by periodic surveys. Detective staffing can be determined by calculating this information with the number of crimes in each geographic area and applying the percentage of work load in each area. Los Angeles, for example, uses this system to redeploy detectives semiannually.

Detective Complaint Officer

Significant timesaving may be achieved by having only one detective file cases with the prosecuting agency. This practice can eliminate wasted hours spent by detective personnel traveling to, and waiting for, available filing deputies. Other agencies have been fortunate enough to have district attorney and/or city attorney staff assigned to their police stations.

Another aid in the area of filing cases is to construct a filing manual that details what is required for successful prosecution for various types of cases. This can save investigative time often used to obtain additional information which the prosecutor found missing in police reports.

Oncall Court System

Significant officer time is expended in court waiting for cases to be heard. Many agencies have made arrangements with their local courts to have officers placed on call. This provides for more officers in the field and reduces overtime which often has to be paid back in the form of days off. Police personnel usually have to be assigned at court to coordinate notifying officers when they are needed. The return in manhours saved, however, is usually worth more than the manpower expended. LAPD, for example, estimates that their oncall system saves the equivalent of over 100 officers in field time annually.

Civilian Personnel

Most departments are expanding the replacement of sworn personnel with civilians, particularly in the areas of records, laboratory, traffic direction, jail, communications, property, supply, front desk, detective aide, and traffic reports. Persons trained to perform these auxiliary and support functions require less salary (and usually less pension benefits), and therefore, can provide savings that should be used to provide more field officers.

Manpower Supplements

Use of citizen volunteers, student workers, explorer scouts, and the like is even more important as personnel cutbacks occur. LAPD has created a reserve officer program that involves three types of reservists. First, there are the traditional reserve line officers who receive extensive training and are qualified to work in radio cars. There are also technical reserve officers who require less training and work the desk, community relations, investigative followup, and other such jobs. Specialist reserve officers are volunteers who have special talents useful to the department, such as chemists, technical writers, and computer system analysts, and are only required to receive several days of training.

Many departments are using volunteers to file reports, fill out telephonic crime reports (after officers determine what type of report should be taken), and conduct crime prevention training. LAPD has found that advertising in local newspapers is a successful method of recruiting volunteers.

As manpower continues to be reduced, some agencies are exploring the possibility of store security and campus police handling more police functions in their jurisdictions. This includes preliminary investigations, completion of appropriate reports, and the transportation of arrestees.

Increased Crime Prevention Efforts

A common tendency of police organizations in contending with budget cuts is to regard crime prevention personnel as nonessential. Thus, the reduction or elimination of a crime prevention staff is considered an appropriate economy measure. A more productive approach, however, may be to use these individuals as leverage in making the best use of available manpower. A few crime prevention personnel involved in an effective program can prevent crimes that would require the work of many officers.

In meeting today's management challenge, many police administrators are finding that economical crime prevention efforts are most effectively applied through programs involving volunteers. Under the direction and supervision of crime prevention officers, volunteers can:

1. Conduct crime prevention meetings in the selected target areas;
2. Conduct security surveys of residences in the target areas;
3. Distribute crime prevention literature in the target areas; and
4. Conduct an identification program that assists residents in marking their property for later identification if stolen and recovered.

Through these programs, a few officers can use the assistance of volunteers to amplify crime prevention efforts.

Even a large crime prevention staff can contact only a small percentage of the public. Television, radio, and the printed media, however, communicate daily with a very large segment of the population. By using the news media, a department can capitalize on the concept of manpower leverage (obtaining a comparatively large result through a process that amplifies the efforts of a small amount of manpower).

A recent U.S. Department of Justice National Crime Survey found that over half of the burglaries nationwide were committed against unlocked dwellings. If the public could be reminded of this fact through the news media, many crimes could be prevented. The chief of the Los Angeles Police Department, for example, recently made a number of 30-second video-taped messages on crime prevention. The videotapes show various crimes in progress. The chief is "chroma keyed" (superimposed) over the crime scene activity as he tells how these crimes can be prevented. These messages have been aired by many television stations in Los Angeles County.

Another idea is to obtain the services of motion picture, television, and sports celebrities in making television and radio crime prevention messages. Many well-known personalities are willing to volunteer their services. The idea is to make these public service messages "grab" the interest of the viewer or listener long enough to get the crime prevention message across.

The victim of a crime is likely to be more receptive to crime prevention suggestions than other persons. His or her experience as the victim causes the realization that "it can happen to me." The uniform police officer taking the crime report is usually the first law enforcement representative to contact the victim. This officer is in an ideal position to provide the victim with suggestions on how to prevent a recurrence of the crime. Field officers should be given special crime prevention training and handout material for these victim/officer contacts.

Crime prevention efforts can be greatly enhanced by the enactment of local ordinances that require "target hardening" construction in residential and business structures. It should be part of a police administrator's crime prevention program to encourage the enactment of this type of legislation.

Arrangements should be made for building permits to be reviewed by crime prevention personnel to ensure proper construction that will prevent crime. Another idea is to encourage insurance companies to give reduced rates on structures that have built-in crime prevention-type construction.

Task Force Organizations

As personnel reductions occur, there is a tendency to reduce planning and staff personnel in order to maximize the number of officers assigned to field duties., The resulting reduction of planning and administrative functions can cause great harm to the future of law enforcement. One approach to this dilemma is to form a planning committee composed of all top managers. The planning entities are reduced to a minimum number of experts. As the planning committee determines needs for planning and other administrative research, task forces are appointed.

The task force members are selected from areas of the agency that have the experience needed for the particular task. They are assigned to the experts from the planning entities and return to their regular duties when the task is completed. This type of organization reduces the number of personnel permanently assigned to staff functions, yet provides for planning activities on an "as needed" basis.

Equipment

Reduced finances also cause a cutback in equipment, requiring judicious use of existing equipment. Additionally, the purchase of certain manpower-saving equipment may be cost-effective in coping with reduced personnel.

Nonlethal Weapons

There is a growing need for effective nonlethal weapons because of the increase in violent mentally disturbed individuals and violent drug users. These persons do not respond usually to normal police restraints. Nonlethal weapons are needed to reduce the manpower required for incarceration of these persons. Additionally, they are needed to prevent officer injury which often reduces available manpower. Prime examples are the tazer gun and chemical irritants.

The tazer gun is now carried by all LAPD field supervisors. It shoots two barbs on electrical lines 15 feet, uses a low amperage, high voltage (50,000 volts at 7 amps) that pulsates at 28–30 pulses a minute and immediately totally incapacitates 80 percent of suspects. It causes no lasting effects, even on persons with pacemakers, and is usually effective on PCP suspects.

Chemical irritants are also carried by all LAPD field officers. They can be used up to 15 feet and cause vertigo, disorientation; and inability to act in 70 percent of cases. They have no lasting adverse effects; but may not be effective against persons under the influence of PCP.

Vehicle Deployment Formulas

Cost-effective deployment of automobiles, like the appropriate deployment of personnel, can be an effective "economizer" of existing equipment. The following vehicle formulas are based solely on personnel deployed and their vehicle requirements. The use of these formulas requires an honest look by management into vehicle needs vs. vehicle wants. For example, the factors in the formulas reflect different requirements for different assignments, ranging from officers who do not require a vehicle to officers requiring a vehicle 100 percent of the time. These types of formulas can ensure that personnel have vehicles readily available, thereby reducing down time or idle time waiting for transportation. (See figs. 1 and 2.)

Leasing vs. Buying Equipment

Some agencies are finding that funds are no longer available for the outright purchase of equipment and the building of police facilities. Leasing is often a way of avoiding the initial cash outlay and a means of surviving temporary cutbacks.

Hand-held Radios

Many police agencies, including Los Angeles, Calif., Seattle, Wash., and Chicago, Ill., have equipped their officers with out-of-car radios so that they are in constant contact. The cost of the radios has been more than compensated for by the added ability to call officers from nonpriority calls (such as report taking) to priority calls (such as robbery). As an alternative, some departments do not show their units "off the air" until they arrive at the scene rather than when the call is broadcast. This is accomplished by officers notifying the dispatcher when they have arrived and are exiting their vehicles.

Information

Alvin Toffler states in his newest book, *The Third Wave*,[2] that we are moving from an industrial society to a global society, which uses data to compensate for dwindling resources. Police administrators must capitalize on this trend and make use of information, particularly automated information, in meeting the challenge of the crime threat with less resources. We in law enforcement can make good use of automation in helping us to become more effective. Automated information can provide more rapid police response to citizen calls and faster access to information that assists uniformed officers to perform their jobs more effectively.

Figure 1
This formula is used by the LAPD to assign black-and-white radio cars to its 18 stations.

$V = .5 (n)(m)(d)(r)(a) + .5L$.
V = Number of vehicles required in the patrol fleet.
m = Maintenance factor (1.10) based on repair statistics.
d = Deployment factor (1.25) for variations in day-of-week deployment. This factor considers a 25-percent variation between weekends (heavy deployment) and weekdays (light deployment).
r = Standard relief factor (1.6).
a = Watch deployment factor (.45) for variations in number of personnel assigned to the heavy watch and light watch.
n = Total uniformed field forces including sergeants minus nonfield positions (desk, bail auditor, etc.).
L = Sergeants' cars on heavy watch.

---

[2]Alvin Toffler, *The Third Wave*, 2d ed. (New York City: Bantam Books, 1981).

Figure 2

This formula is used by LAPD to distribute plain vehicles.

$$V = (N + .2F + .5G + 5T + .75P + R) - B \, M$$

V = Total vehicles recommended for each entity by formula.

N = Personnel who do not need a vehicle, such as detective desk personnel.

F = Nonfield fixed-post personnel, such as staff workers. They receive one vehicle to five personnel.

G = Field fixed-post personnel, such as noncaseload-carrying detective supervisors. They receive one vehicle for every two personnel.

T = Personnel working two-man units on a full-time basis, such as narcotics and personnel investigators. One vehicle is provided for every two personnel.

P = Personnel carrying a full caseload, such as field detectives. The ratio is three vehicles to four personnel.

R = Personnel working one-man units and require a vehicle 100 percent of the time, such as narcotics investigators, supervisors.

B = Average number of pool vehicles used per day.

M = Maintenance factor of 1.05 as established by repair statistics.

The Automated Want and Warrant System

In the past, officers have had to detain persons in "field situations" as long as 20 to 30 minutes while clerical personnel searched manual warrant files at the station house. Now it takes only seconds to determine if a person is wanted or a vehicle or other property is stolen. This rapid response comes through automated access to local, state, and national law enforcement files. This reduces inconvenience to innocent citizens and saves valuable field time for officers.

The Emergency Command Control Communications System

These computerized communications systems provide "instant cops" by:

1. Remote out-of-vehicle radios for every field officer that make officers available for response to citizen needs at all times;

2. Mobile digital terminals in patrol cars that provide field officers direct access to computerized information; and

3. Computer-aided dispatching of police units that provide faster police response to citizen calls for service.

The Electronic Sherlock Holmes

Two law enforcement systems are examples of how automation is used to communicate essential information and to reduce the time it takes detectives to conduct criminal investigations:

1. Automated Field Interview Systems—These systems link the thousands of daily observations made by field officers with crimes investigated by detectives. The computer connects suspects by location, description, vehicle, and activity to reported crimes.

2. Modus Operandi (MO) Correlation Systems—These computer programs process large volumes of data from crime and arrest reports and correlate incidents that may have been committed by the same suspect. By linking these reports through MO patterns, a conglomerate of information can often be compiled that provides valuable assistance in identifying crime perpetrators.

The Automated Police Manager

There are systems that assist police managers to use police personnel more effectively.

1. Automated Deployment of Available Manpower Programs—By computerizing information on calls-for-services from citizens, activity initiated by officers on patrol, and crime trends, these systems predict how many police cars should be assigned each area of the city by day-of-the-week and hour-of-the-day. They also give police managers information on the timeliness and effectiveness of patrol services in each neighborhood.

2. Computerized Traffic System—This system compares when and where traffic accidents are occurring and the causes with when and where officers are issuing traffic citations and for what violations. The comparisons are used to deploy traffic officers and evaluate their effectiveness.

3. Crime Statistics Systems—Through computer analyses of all crime and arrest reports, crime trends are reported weekly, monthly, quarterly, and yearly.

4. Training Management Systems—Officers' personal data, such as language skills, special occupational experiences, hobbies, physical fitness, training examinations, shooting proficiency scores, etc., are maintained in computer files so that training needs can be assessed and personnel talents and abilities can be properly used. Additionally, video communication is being extensively used in academy training and at daily training sessions. Computerized shooting simulators are also assisting in training officers when and where not to use firearms.

Microcomputer and Electronic Word Processors

Computers are following the trend of many mechanical and electronic devices that have proved to be helpful to mankind. Mass production is increasing their availability while decreasing their cost. Already the cost of minicomputers is within the financial reach of most police agencies. Today's minicomputers have the capabilities of larger computer systems of a decade ago.

Small law enforcement departments should consider purchasing minicomputers to supply most of their automation needs, and large police agencies should be evaluating minicomputers as replacements for their precinct station filing systems. In the near future, each commanding officer may be able to have a small computer for his use and the use of his personnel.

Word processing computer terminals should replace typewriters in most police agencies in the future as they are now doing in private industry. Crime reports should be "typed" on terminals. Computer systems can strip off information and send teletype messages, plus extract and transmit appropriate information for detectives, prosecutors, and the courts. Additionally, information for statistical and management purposes can automatically be transmitted to appropriate files. Much of the duplication that now occurs can be eliminated. After the information is once entered into the computer, the computer can take care of the manipulation of information that now is often done by many persons. These types of systems have already been put to use in some police agencies, but it will be some time before they are a common police tool.

Much of the processing time now consumed in the pyramid organization structures of police departments for correspondence, research projects, budget requests, and activity reports can be reduced by word processing systems. Currently, these documents are sent up the chain of command and returned for retyping when corrections or changes are desired by persons higher up in the organization. Often, they are completely retyped a number of times before they reach the chief of police. With a computerized word processing system, they can be entered on a terminal once and stored. When changes are necessary, the text is recalled on a terminal screen and only that portion to be changed is redone. When finally approved, the computer prints out a final report. Likewise, the text of routine correspondence can be kept in computer storage. When required, it can be called up on a terminal screen and appropriate names and text changes made to "personalize" the letter before being printed for signature.

The Future of Law Enforcement—Something to Look Forward To

When we talk about cutbacks, reduced resources, and managing with less, we often do so with a pessimistic air. We are going to have to deal with reduced resources for some years to come, but in the overall history of our societies, this will be but a short period. As we look back 10 to 15 years from now, we will probably reflect on this period as a period of reevaluation and refinement—refinements to meet economic and cultural changes. Review of our histories discloses many periods of reduction—a time for cleansing the systems, removing excess fat, firming up our objectives, and assuring that they meet the expectations of the public we serve. It is indeed a time of challenge, a challenge that we should look forward to with optimism, for the future holds for us an exciting opportunity to make constructive changes through legislation that can strengthen the judicial system and through innovative uses of our shrinking police resources. As professional law enforcement officers, we can help provide a safe environment where our citizens can exercise their individual freedoms with a minimum of disruption. And together, we can stem the rising crime with decreasing resources.

8

Applying Employee Relations Concepts to the Administration of Contemporary Criminal Justice Agencies

■ Introduction

In Chapter 7, Organization Functions were compared to the human skeleton. Employee Relations can be compared to the internal organs of the body. As the skeleton supports the operation of the internal organs of the body, and one component by itself does not support life, so it is with the themes of Organization Functions and Employee Relations within an organization.

The employees are often referred to as the "lifeblood" of an organization. They are the most important part of any agency and more than 90% of budgets go to support personnel. Employees, however, must have an efficient environment in which to work and that is why Organization Functions are so important. In Chapter 2, historical milestones that relate to Employee Relations were explored and the following summary points are brought forward:

- Maintenance versus satisfaction factors
  1957, *Motivation to Work*, Fredrick Herzberg
- Organizations need to be altered to fit individual needs
  1957, *The Individual & Organization*, Chris Argyris
- Theory X and Theory Y
  1957, "The Human Side of Enterprise," Douglas McGregor

- Hierarchy of human needs applied to organizations
  1943, "A Theory of Human Motivation," A. H. Maslow
- Organizational guides, not principles
  1941, "The Proverbs of Public Administration," Herbert Simon
- Motivated employees increases productivity
  1941, "The Hawthorne Experiments," Elton Mayo

First, it is important to reflect on Herbert Simon's admonition that what is often referred to as "principles" with regard to administration should be considered proverbs or guides; this is because the main ingredients of an organization are people, and people widely vary in their makeup. Although physical sciences are well defined, psychology and the scientific research regarding dealing with people are much less exacting. Therefore, Eclectic Perspective administrators must be knowledgeable of the principles, and also must use them as guides rather than absolute rules.

Mayo's "Hawthorne Experiments" remind us of the evolving concepts of administration. Mayo started his experiments to test the validity of some of the Organization Functions principles. What he found was that the manner of interacting with employees has much to do with productivity.

Employees were considered an important part of organizations long before the Employee Relations era. However, it was not until Mayo's experiments that the administrative milestones began to focus on employee motivation as a means of increasing productivity. During the Operation Functions era, Frederick Taylor emphasized the need to find the right person for each job. Fayol defined "Esprit de Corps" as "harmony and teamwork that are essential to effective organizations."

The Organization Functions concepts regarding employees relate more to the management of personnel rather than to employee motivation. In this chapter, we bring together these Employee Relations concepts as a means of integrating them into the "building block" model. The purpose of this text is to bring the many administrative concepts and theories together into a structure that makes them more understandable and more available for application. Today's administrator should think of a given contextual theme (e.g., Employee Relations) and be able to recall a list of related key terms that bring the appropriate concepts and theories to mind so that they may be applied to a given situation. This is the Eclectic Perspective approach to administration and brings us to a function for which all administrators are responsible, that of **supervision**.

■ Supervision

Every administrator from the top executive to the first-line supervisor who has one or more employees reporting to her or him must supervise. Supervision is getting the assigned tasks accomplished through one's immediate employees, and it involves both management and leadership skills. Supervision includes the following functions:

- *Ensuring employees are properly prepared to do the job*. This includes recruiting and selecting the right people to do the job, ensuring that they are properly trained.
- *Ensuring that employees are motivated*. Employees must be motivated to accomplish the assigned task. One of the two overall responsibilities of all administrators (discussed in Chapter 1) is to satisfy the needs of the employees. This does not necessarily mean to make employees happy all the time, because happy employees are not necessarily productive employees. Making sure that employees gain satisfaction from their assigned tasks is the essence of **motivation**.
- *Providing employees with proper direction*. Proper direction allows employees to understand what they are to do and feel confident they have the support of their employer. This is accomplished through good oral and written communications and through a relationship that instills trust.
- *Providing inspection and control*. Periodic inspection allows the supervisor to see that the tasks that have been delegated to employees are properly achieved. This does not mean "standing over" the employee at all times and watching their activities. It does mean assessing each employee and keeping them motivated to accomplish the desired tasks while applying the proper amount of inspection and control.
- *Providing proper discipline*. Providing appropriate discipline is a delicate part of a supervisor's job. This involves both positive activities (rewards such as oral/written commendations to desirable assignments and promotions) and negative actions (punishment such as oral/written reprimands to termination).
- *Evaluating employee performance*. Employees need feedback as to how they are performing. This should be done orally as a matter of routine and periodically (usually at 6- to 12-month intervals) in writing. Written evaluations should always be discussed with the employee and should lead to a two-way discussion between the supervisor and the employee.

■ Employee Hiring and Training

This chapter continues with two major elements from the Employee Relations period, including more recent enhancements: (1) employee hiring and training and (2) employee motivation.

Hiring

In the 1800s, during what is sometimes called the "political era," many criminal justice employees were selected because of who they knew politically and what support they or their families had given to certain elected officials. This process was commonly known as the "spoils system." With the reforms that followed the 1883 Pendleton Act and the advent of the Organization Functions era, the professionalism/legalistic approach to hiring became common practice. This "civil service" approach entailed defining what abilities and attributes an employee had to have for a given job, establishing relative testing methods, hiring qualified candidates, and then ensuring that they had the proper training to do the job. Today, these practices are still followed but have been enhanced with Affirmative Action and Equal Employment Opportunity legislation that grew out of the Social Equity era. Hiring can be divided into the processes of **recruiting and selecting**.

Recruiting qualified candidates is an important part of the hiring process. As will be discussed in Chapter 12, hiring a fair representation of the community for which a criminal justice agency serves is certainly a requirement for today's criminal justice administrator. Having a ratio of employees at parity with the cultural mix of the community is a desirable goal. Having employees who can truly understand the needs of the community because they are, in race and culture, a fair representation of the people they serve, is an important element in providing more community-oriented services. (See Figure 12–6 for a comparison between police hiring ratios and the percentages of minority races in the general population. Figure 12–7 illustrates that women, who account for about 51% of the general population, comprise less than 15% of police personnel.)

In 1971, the U.S. Supreme Court provided standards in *Griggs v. Duke Power Company* governing when hiring practices legally could be considered as having a negative impact on minority hiring. At the time, a number of public agencies were not heeding the affirmative action guidelines and the federal government, backed by court action, was imposing minority hiring quotas that, when not met, would restrict federal funding. Fortunately, today most departments comply with Equal Employment Opportunity Standards and, hopefully, quota requirements are a thing of the past.

Affirmative action guidelines are not meant to force the hiring of unqualified employees just because they are of a protected class (minorities and females). Affirmative action is meant to guide agencies in making amends for the discriminating practices that were prevalent in our country from its inception. A basic concept of affirmative action is that if two candidates *equally* qualify for a job, the one from the protected class is to be hired. The quota systems of the past were criticized for providing restrictions that could result in the hiring of persons not qualified for the job. This was unfair to communities, including those most populated by minorities, in that the practice could result in poor public service. Today's criminal justice administrators have an obligation to provide the best public service possible and to hire employees that fairly represent the communities they serve. This can be accomplished by targeting recruiting efforts toward prospective candidates that are needed to meet this obligation.

The author, when chief of police, approached the need to hire more females by targeting prospective candidates. After serving several years as a security director for a large private corporation and recalling the many qualified women who worked as clerical personnel in that private sector, I was provided with motivation regarding recruiting. In these private corporations, many of the female clerical employees, although receiving comparatively low salaries, were compelled to buy costly apparel that was common in the corporate environment. A program was implemented that established recruitment booths near locations where the clerical personnel went for lunch. Signs stating "How would you like a salary of $38,000 [the yearly salary for that police department at the time] and not have to be concerned with what you wear to work—we will supply you a uniform" were displayed as part of the approach. This approach also could apply to any other uniformed job, such as being corrections employees.

College and university campuses offer ideal locations for recruiting, as many provide periodic job fairs. If the local candidate pool is not adequate, recruitment personnel may have to be sent to other geographical areas. Having a competitive salary and benefit package is important in attracting the best candidates. Checking Web sites of comparable agencies can help. For example, "the blue line" Web site provides an analysis of the "top 150" hiring police departments by comparing salaries and benefits and local cost-of-living information.

Presenting candidates with information about career benefits, including salaries, is also important. As chair of a university criminal justice department, the author was sometimes confronted by parents of prospective criminal justice students who said they would prefer that their sons or daughters pursued careers that offered better salary opportunities. In response, they were shown Web sites of agencies such as the Los Angeles Police Department that post salaries for each rank. Such Web sites show that the starting salaries are very competitive with salaries in other professions and that middle and upper managers can make salaries that range in the $100,000 to $300,000 level. The author, because of his experience in both the public and private sector, could provide examples of how criminal justice employment could provide an exciting and personally satisfying career that many private sector jobs could not.

Selection Process

Selection is the next step in the hiring process. Our form of government provides checks and balances over the actions of the executive branch (law enforcement and corrections) by the judicial and legislative branches in protecting the rights of the public. The following landmark legislative acts must be considered by criminal justice administrators in the selection and supervision of employees.

The Civil Rights Act (Title VII, 1964) and its subsequent amendments (42 U.S.C. 2000e) establish federal policy requiring fair employment standards in both the public and private sectors. It prohibits employment discrimination based on race, color, religion, sex, and national origin and has been extended to protect against "hostile work environment" claims based on sexual, racial, or religious harassment.

The Fair Labor Standards Act (U.S.C. 203 et seq.) provides minimum pay and overtime provisions. It contains special provisions for public safety employees in agencies that operate 24 hours per day, 7 days a week. For them, overtime must be paid for work in excess of 43 hours in a 7-day period or 171 hours in a 28-day cycle. Public safety employees may accrue a maximum of 480 hours of compensatory time, which is not used as leave time and must be paid for on termination at the employee's final rate of pay or an average pay for the last three years, whichever is highest.

The Americans with Disabilities Act (42 U.S.C. 12112) is aimed at providing hiring practices that ensure that otherwise qualified candidates with disabilities are tested as employees without disabilities. Therefore, job applications and questions during job interviews cannot refer to disabilities. However, if the candidate has a disability that causes them not to be able to perform well on a job-related test (such as a physical agility test), they can be excluded from the hiring pool.

Judicial rulings of the U.S. Supreme Court concerning employee selection with which administrators must be familiar are as follows:

Albemarle Paper Company v. Moody (1975) held that agencies can require hiring standards that restrict more minorities and females from hiring if it can be proven that the hiring requirements are *job-related*. This has caused criminal justice agencies to become much more involved in researching exactly what the job requires of an employee and setting appropriate testing procedures to show that the candidate has the ability to acquire, with proper training, the ability to perform the job.

Davis v. City of Dallas (1985) ruled that the Dallas police department did not discriminate in requiring candidates to have a certain level of college education. The Court ruled that a college education was a bona fide occupational qualification (BFOQ), paving the way for police departments to require a college degree. Unfortunately, most departments still do not have this requirement.

The selection process steps are discussed later in this chapter (and summarized in **Figure 8–1**). For economical reasons, the least expensive process is first. The steps then progress to the most expensive last so that as the expense of the various procedures increase the number of candidates to be tested decrease. The purpose should be to identify the most desirable candidates in the most economical manner.

Application Form. This should identify candidates who have the basic requirements for the job. Generally, only about 50 to 60% of those who apply will meet the requirements so it is important to create an application form that asks the proper questions. Some of the questions that can be asked on an application include:

Age. The *Age Discrimination in Employment Act* (U.S.C. 623) generally prohibits unequal treatment of applicants based on their age and the courts have ruled that youth is not a BFOQ. However, most police and correction agencies restrict the

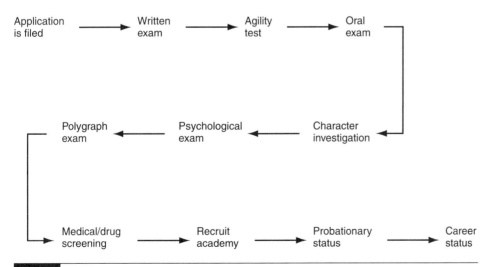

Figure 8–1 Hiring Process Flow Chart.

hiring age to between 21 and 38 years of age. Although "youth" can not be used in applications, age can be used as a BFOQ as it relates to laws relating to carrying firearms and entering businesses where alcohol is sold. Also, if an agency can show that hiring after a certain age will result in only a limited number of physically active years of service, then a maximum age may be used.

Height and Weight. As with age requirements, height and weight standards have changed over the years. Minimum height requirements have been challenged successfully as discriminating against females and minorities. In *Vanguard Justice Society v. Hughes* (1979), for example, the court ruled that a 5'7" height requirement excluded 95% of the female population but only 32% of the male population and was, therefore, evidence of sex discrimination. This and other rulings have caused most agencies to use a standard of weight in proportion to height and rely upon the physical agility test to determine if the candidate can physically perform job-related tasks.

Education. In the case of *Davis v. City of Dallas* (1985), the Court ruled that police departments can require a college education. Even though the need for educated employees can be traced back to August Vollmer (as discussed in Chapter 6), most agencies still do not have this as a hiring requirement. However, a growing number of agencies do require college education for promotions. Empirical research has shown that college-educated employees are less authoritative and have more acceptance of minorities (Weiner, 1976, pp. 450–457), receive fewer citizen complaints (Cascio, 1977, pp. 89–96), are less likely to expose their agencies to civil liability suits (Carter & Sapp, 1989, pp. 157–166), and are less likely to use excessive force (Worden, 1994, pp. 31–60). The 2006 August issue of *Police Chief* magazine features a number of research articles on why police chiefs agree with these earlier findings (*Police Chief*, 2006).

Residency. Even though the courts have rules that agencies can require employees to live within their jurisdiction (*McCarthy v. Philadelphia Civil Service Commission*, 1976), many departments do not have such a requirement. However, in the spirit of a community-oriented service, this requirement may need to be considered.

Written Examination. This is not to test what the candidates know about the job but, rather, to determine their general intelligence (reading, vocabulary, mathematical, reasoning, and logic skills). The written examination is the prime means of determining these skills and is usually an objective type of test that can be scored by a computer. Because most criminal justice agencies do not require a college education, the written examinations are designed to test for a high school-level education. If the hiring agency does require a college degree, there is nothing to restrict the written examination from being raised to a higher level. This written examination generally focuses on the following areas:

- **Reading comprehension.** This is often done by providing several sentences or a paragraph to read, then presenting candidates with objective questions to determine if they understand what they have read. Some agencies send out reading material before the examination and then ask questions about this material during the examination.

- **Observation and Memory.** Candidates are often shown a picture that involves several people doing various things, as well as a number of surrounding items. The candidate is asked to observe and memorize what is in the picture, which is then removed. He or she is then asked questions to determine what they remember.
- **Computing Skills.** General mathematical and analytical skills are tested with objective questions that are usually found on a high school-level examination.
- **Judgment and Decision-Making Abilities.** Although candidates are not required to possess detailed information about the job (only to have the ability to be trained), questions that test for an acceptable level of intellectual maturity are permissible.

Oral Interview. The oral interview is to determine communications skills, interpersonal styles, decision-making ability, ability to control emotions, appearance, and ability to think under pressure. The interview board may be composed of members of the community as well as personnel from the hiring agency. Some agencies have a subsequent interview between the chief executive officer and the candidate, just before hiring. All candidates must be asked the same questions, but individualized questions that relate to the candidates' statements or responses are permissible. Candidates are usually given an opportunity to make an opening and closing statement and then respond to questions from the board to determine the sought-after skills. A growing number of agencies have a candidate handwrite a one-page response to a question before the interview so that their ability to communicate in writing can be evaluated. One of Sir Robert Peel's Organizational Principles states that "good appearance commands respect" and appearance and demeanor can be evaluated during this process.

Physical Agility Examination. This examination is becoming increasingly important for law enforcement personnel as affirmative action restrictions are applied to selection practices. The *Albemarle Paper Company v. Moody* case held that agencies can require hiring standards that restrict more minorities and females from hiring if it can be empirically proven that the hiring requirements are job-related. Agencies must be prepared to prove that all items tested for are BFOQ related. If candidates are required to run a certain distance, do a required number of push-ups and jump a certain height, these requirements must be bona fide tests of on-the-jobs tasks that employees will be required to do. For example, the author, when captain of a police training division, had to reduce the height of the barrier that candidates had to climb over from 6 feet to 5 feet because a lawsuit determined that the city had an ordinance prohibiting any fence over 5 feet.

Many agencies are moving from "power tests" to actual field-related exercises that can more easily be justified as job-related. For example, pushing a vehicle is something a police officer must be able to do if necessary for public safety. A male candidate might use his upper-body strength to move the vehicle by placing his hands on the bumper and pushing. A female candidate, with less upper-body strength, might accomplish the same task by sitting on the bumper and using her legs to push the vehicle. Both would accomplish the task, thereby passing the examination, but by using different strength approaches.

Psychological Examination. This exam is often an objective type that can be computer-graded. Interviews by a trained psychologist are preferred but often cost-prohibitive. The purpose of this phase is to ensure that candidates are not suffering from some personality disorder and are emotionally stable. Two forms that have been found to be reliable are the Minnesota Multiphase Personality Inventory (MMPI) and the California Personality Inventory (CPI). Special qualities sought for criminal justice employees are high moral character, incorruptibility, well adjusted, able to carry out stressful and hazardous tasks, and logical but not impulsive or overly aggressive. This examination can "raise flags" that background investigators can explore during that phase of the selection process.

Character or Background Investigation. The background investigation is probably the most important phase of the selection process. It can be costly; therefore, it is better left for candidates who have passed most of the other phases. This phase should be conducted by trained investigators and be more than a record search and telephone calls to references. References given by candidates should only be starting points that lead to interviews with persons who have been closely associated with the candidates and reach back as far as 10 years. For example, college roommates, fellow workers, and neighbors should be interviewed. All persons interviewed must be guaranteed that what they state will be confidential and not available to candidates. Often a "critic" of the candidate may surface, but a single person's opinion should always be corroborated. Any "flags" coming from the psychological phase should be investigated. Additionally, many of the same qualities that are desirable in the psychological phase should be sought in this phase; such as incorruptibility, honesty, not overly aggressive but able to aggressively respond when required, and no alcohol or other drug problems.

Medical Examination. The medical exam should include drug testing. As with tests for required abilities and skills, the medical examination can exclude only candidates for job-related problems. Good general health can be proven to be job-related especially for those jobs that involve shift work, hours of inactivity with sudden demands for physical strength, and exposure to periodic high-stress situations. Being overweight and having certain ailments at the hiring stage can be proven to lead to later inability to do the job and early retirement.

Polygraph Examination. The polygraph test is still used by a majority of large police agencies as part of the selection process even though its use has been ruled unacceptable in criminal trials. Most candidates have "a conscience" and react to a polygraph examination in a more reliable manner than a "hardened criminal." Departments that use polygraphs often use them to check on possible drug use and in response to questionable areas discovered during other phases such as during background investigations. To date, there has been no court action that prohibits the use of this device in the selection process.

Assessment Center Testing. This is a selection process that certainly is not new (begun in World War II) but has become more popular in recent years. It involves job-like situations that candidates have to simulate while being evaluated by specially trained assessors. Candidates are involved in a number of situations ranging from structured interviews, simulated situational testing, leaderless group discussions with other candidates, and individual psychological interviews. There are a growing number of private companies that provide this service for both private and public institutions. A companion growing service is companies that supply "industrial actors": professional actors that act the part of irate citizens, city council members, and other roles that are used in simulating job-related situations. Currently, this type of process is more prevalent in the selection of chief executives and not for entry-level hiring because of the cost involved. Professor Frank Hughes makes a case for why the benefits outweigh the cost for selecting personnel, particularly managers (Hughes, 2006, pp. 106–111). He points out that one of the "greatest challenges facing law enforcement administrators in the 21st century is to identify qualified individuals for entry-level positions and for promotion" and that assessment centers can greatly help in meeting this challenge.

Lateral Transfers Hiring. This is another growing trend that has both positive and negative aspects. First, for agencies that want to reduce training costs, hiring an employee already trained by another agency can certainly do this. Some training should be required to customize the employee's performance to the requirements of the hiring agency. The negative aspects come into play due to the agency losing the employee after having invested in their training (average cost for training entry-level employees is more than $50,000). Consequently, many agencies now require new employees to sign 4- to 5-year contracts that require them to reimburse the hiring agency for the cost of training if they leave before the contracted number of years.

Training

After candidates have been screened and the most qualified have been hired, the training phase begins. **Training** can be defined as instructing an employee on how to do a job. **Education**, in contrast, is the process of providing a general body of knowledge on which an employee can create the best way to accomplish the job. In the first chapter of this text, the science of administration was likened to studying the facts. Here we can equate training to studying or learning the facts. The art of administration is described as converting the facts into practice and actually applying them to job-related tasks. Here we can equate education to the conceptualizing of a body of knowledge so that knowledge can be practiced in a productive manner.

Employees who have jobs of a limited nature can be trained simply to perform the specific job. Employees who perform complicated tasks of a varied nature and are given wide discretion must be educated in the body of knowledge related to the tasks that they are required to perform.

With client-oriented service, most criminal justice tasks are complicated and require a wide range of discretion. It follows that those who perform these tasks should be educated. Unfortunately, as previously discussed, most law enforcement and corrections agencies do not require a college degree. Therefore, most criminal justice employees can be required to perform at only a high school level of knowledge. In reality, training (instruction on how to do the job) is all that most criminal justice agencies have time and funds to provide. Enlightened criminal justice administrators must make up for this deficiency by encouraging and promoting "off-duty" education among their employees. This can be done through increased pay for acquiring education, rewarding through assignments and promoting those who obtain college level education, and by making it a hiring requirement whenever possible.

With the realization that training is still the main method of preparing employees to perform their jobs, administrators must make the best of the situation. Law enforcement leads the way in required training; all U.S. states except Hawaii have state law enforcement training and standards boards. **Appendix 3A and Appendix 3B** provide examples of the basic training requirements for police officers. These boards set the requirements for basic police training in their respective states as well as some states setting standards for all police ranks. Additionally, a number of states provide standards for specialized tasks such as criminal investigation and for promotion to the various ranks.

Corrections agencies follow the practice of law enforcement, with most states having state corrections boards and a growing number establishing training standards for correctional employees (**Appendix 3C**). Corrections administrators in states without boards that set training standards would do well to consult with those states that do. The study of administration only began to materialize as an important subject many years after it was established in the police and corrections fields. Because many judges do not care to perform administrative tasks, the position of court administrator is a growing profession. Most court administrators are hired to oversee the business end of the courts because of their administrative education. Most have business or public administration degrees and some universities are now offering specific degrees in court administration.

One of the duties of court administrators is to provide training for court employees as well as some introductory training for new judges. Some judges who do perform administrative duties as well as their legal duties have some business training from law schools providing related classes. Most judicial officers, however, do not have this education and obtained their position because of their legal accomplishments.

Of the three criminal justice branches, law enforcement has the most developed training standards. Most states require police officers to have from 400 to 600 hours of basic training, with some agencies requiring up to 1,000 hours (**Table 8-1**). Additionally, a growing trend is to provide more situational training wherein recruits learn through simulated exercises.

There are two schools of thinking when it comes to how to train: the **Behavioral** and the **Gestalt** approaches. Behavioral theorists believe that learning

| Table 8-1 | Training Requirements for New Recruits in Local Police Departments by Size of Population Served in the United States, 2003 |

| | New officer recruits[a] | | | | | | | | Non-probationary officers, in service | |
| | Academy | | | Field | | | | | | |
Population served	Total	State-mandated	Other required	Total	State-mandated	Other required		State-mandated	Other required
All sizes	628	588	40	326	147	179		24	23
1,000,000 or more	1,016	689	327	513	153	360		23	7
500,000 to 999,999	920	588	332	561	104	456		20	18
250,000 to 499,999	950	620	330	652	200	452		20	14
100,000 to 249,999	815	642	173	624	253	371		24	23
50,000 to 99,999	721	657	64	598	268	330		18	32
25,000 to 49,999	702	657	46	527	210	317		21	28
10,000 to 24,999	672	642	30	442	164	279		20	31
2,500 to 9,999	630	597	32	314	151	162		28	25
Less than 2,500	577	542	35	199	106	93		23	16

[a]Computations of average number of training hours required exclude departments not requiring training.

Source: U.S. Department of Justice, Bureau of Justice Statistics. (2003). Local Police Departments, NCJ 210118: p. 9.

is a function of stimulus and response (S-R), often referred to as "trial and error." What works is what we continue to do, what doesn't is what we cease to do. The Gestalt theorists, by contrast, do not subscribe to the stimulus-response approach but, rather, maintain that learning is more cognitive. Here we can relate the behavioral approach more to training and the Gestalt theory to education. Both should be involved in preparing criminal justice employees to perform their required duties but, as previously stated, training or the behavioral approach is most commonly used.

Recruit Training Academies

Recruit Training Academies usually provide police training. Many states now provide centralized police training academies for officers hired by agencies without their own training facilities. Larger agencies typically have their own academies. A review of the requirements in most states reveals that, generally, just the minimum task training for the essential basic tasks are being provided. Consequently, Eclectic Perspective administrators would do well to provide additional training and education (beyond the basic requirements) to meet their agencies' requirements.

It is now common practice to not "swear in" the new employees until they have successfully completed their recruit training. This practice is to avoid having to provide the injury and disability retirement benefits provided to "sworn" law enforcement officers.

Recruit training has often been called a cross between "boot camp" and "law school." It is the "boot camp" aspect that has drawn criticism as efforts are made to make law enforcement more community-oriented and less military. The question is asked as to why recruits have to undergo "stress training." They are not military solders performing as squads but, rather, most often work alone and are given considerable discretion in how they perform their duties. The author, having been a commanding officer of a police training academy, recommends that some military and stress training is necessary. Although a small part of their duty, police officers musts be prepared to become part of a semimilitary unit in times of unusual occurrences (riots, terrorists attacks, earthquake, and fires, for example) and response to centralized commands. Additionally, stress training allows instructors (and the recruit) to know the strength and weaknesses of the recruit, which is crucial in evaluating whether they are capable of performing their duties.

The recruit training curriculum, however, must rely most on training (and hopefully, some education) that will prepare law enforcement personnel to perform their duties with discretion and in a community-oriented manner. What is called the **andragogy** approach (as contrasted with **pedagogy**, or one-way transfer of information) of learning is recommended as it stresses analytical and conceptual skills and promotes mutual involvement of instructor and student (Knowles, 1970, pp. 38–39).

Again, encouraging recruits to pursue college education is extremely important, especially because it is not an employment requirement for most agencies. Arrangement with local colleges and universities to give credit towards a degree for recruit training can provide some incentive. Additionally, general education proficiency tests are given in some academies and recruits are required to take college remedial courses if they have deficiencies. This causes recruits to become involved in taking college courses.

Because of the cost of recruit training and the time involved, a growing number of law enforcement agencies are requiring candidates to obtain the required basic training at local colleges that provide this type of program, or at state academies. Those interested in becoming police officers must pay for the training and obtain basic training certification before being considered as a candidate for hiring. If new hires are trained at others than the hiring agency (including a state academy), criminal justice administrators would do well to provide additional training at their own facilities. This training should introduce the new employees to those concepts and tasks unique to the hiring agency (mission statement, special rules and procedure, and local cultural information, for example).

Probationary Training

Probationary training is an essential part of the hiring process. Remember that one of the founding principles of policing was Sir Robert Peel's proclamation that police officers should serve a probationary period. Today, most agencies require a 1-year probationary period after recruit training. The difference between being "on probation" and "having completed probation" is the requirement for termination.

During the probation period, the employee can be terminated by the hiring authority without presenting the employee with a great deal of documentation as to why they are not being retained. (If the terminated employee takes civil action to regain their job, the firing agency must be prepared to provide documented evidence as to why the terminated employee could not adequately perform required duties.) However, after the employee completes probation, the terminating agency must *provide evidence that the employee cannot perform required tasks before termination takes place*. The probationary period only provides administrators more latitude in terminating employees.

The probation period is the phase where the actual performance of the employee can be evaluated. It is one thing to pass examinations in the academy and another to apply what one has been taught to actual performance. Two components of this phase require mentioning. If criminal justice administrators are to require quality work, they need to assign probationary employees to a *training officer*. Those agencies that do not have such a position run the risk of civil liability for not providing adequate training in situations where employees cause civil damage. Agencies with these positions select well-seasoned employees and give them special training as to their duties, and usually provide additional pay. The author, as a police administrator, was involved in analyzing the required tasks of a police officer. More than 200 tasks (called Terminal Performance Objectives, or TPO) were established and incorporated into recruit training. Training officers were then required to ensure that each probationary officer could actually perform these tasks (TPO) before the completion of the probation period.

The second essential component of this phase is the *Probation Evaluation Form*. You can see an example of such a form that is completed by training officers, usually on a monthly basis, in **Appendix 4**. It is important that the training officer discuss his or her evaluation with the probationer and that the probationer sign that the Probation Evaluation Form has been discussed. This documentation is not only important in preparing the probationer for permanent employment but also as documentation in case civil action results from termination.

Ongoing Employee Training

Ongoing employee training is necessary, as the criminal justice field is ever changing. Remember that it is a responsibility of every supervisor to ensure that employees are properly prepared to do the job. This is a continuing responsibility. This sometimes requires supervisors to personally provide individual or group training to their assigned employees. Many state law enforcement training and standards boards provide *advance training courses* and require police officers to periodically attend these classes. These training courses are intended to provide employees with the latest information pertaining to their assigned duties.

If such training is not available or there are training needs that are unique to an individual agency, criminal justice administrators must provide such training. Additionally, they must set up training schedules to ensure that required periodic training is provided for each employee. Training for special types of tasks also must be provided for duties such as special weapon teams, K-9 duty, horse patrol, handling of handicapped prisoners, protection in court from violent defendants, and specialized probation and parole approaches. Additionally, when personnel are promoted, training that prepares them for their new role is essential. A number of state boards prescribe, and some provide, promotional training for ranks up through police chief.

Employee Evaluation

Employee evaluation is a training tool as well as an evaluation process. Evaluation is an important task of every supervisor. This applies to first-line supervisors all the way up to the top executive. Every person that has employees reporting to them must periodically conduct evaluations. There are various types of forms that are used, from force choice, scales, and narrative. Regardless of the form used, the following items need to be covered:

1. Appraisals must focus on performance standards as identified by a job analysis.
2. Performance standards must have been communicated to and understood by the employees.
3. Ratings should be based on specific clearly defined dimensions.
4. The rating dimensions should be behaviorally anchored and these ratings should be supported by objective, observable behaviors.

5. Abstract dimensions such as loyalty or honesty should be avoided unless they can be defined in actual observable behavior.

6. Rating scale anchor statements should be logical and brief.

7. The appraisal systems and the ratings of the individual raters must be reliable and valid.

8. Any system should contain an appeal mechanism for employees who disagree with their ratings (Cascio & Bernardin, 1981, pp. 211–212).

The following items need to be avoided:

1. *Halo effect*, where the employees are judged on one factor that the rater deems important, and this one factor affects all the other evaluation categories.

2. *Central tendency*, where the supervisors are too reticent to rate either high or low, resulting in all employees receiving average evaluations.

Evaluations for regular employees are usually given every 6 or 12 months. Probationary employees are usually evaluated monthly. It is important for the evaluation form to be reviewed and discussed with the employee. It is an opportunity for the supervisor to orally discuss his or her observations of the employee's performance. The periodic evaluations should be no surprise to the employee, because the supervisor should have been having periodic guiding sessions with the employee. A good practice is to make and discuss an evaluation form midway through the rating period, then destroy it after informing the employee that this is how he or she would be evaluated at that time. This gives the employee an opportunity to make improvements, if needed, before the formal evaluation report is made.

◼ Employee Motivation

Abraham Maslow's Human Needs Hierarchy has become a standard manner of understanding human **motivation** (Maslow, 1943). Even though Maslow admitted that his theory was never scientifically proven, it is such a compelling visual presentation of human nature that it has passed the test of time. Maslow's list has been converted into the needs of employees in the workplace. He described how humans can be at one level (self-esteem or self-actualization) and an event outside of the job such as a divorce can cause them to refocus on lower levels (physiological or security). It is a task of supervision to continually understand the motivational status of employees to ensure that they perform positively in the workplace. Chris Argyris put forth the idea that organizations need to be altered to fit individual needs (Argyris, 1957). McGregor's Theory X and Theory Y (**Table 8–2**) has become a standard as to the two extremes of getting the job done (McGregor, 1957). Theory X relates to traditional, hierarchical management as established during the Organization Functions era. It is based on management

Table 8–2 McGregor's Theory X and Theory Y	
Theory X (tradition, hierarchical management)	**Theory Y (humanist, participatory management**
1. Management is responsible for organizing the elements of productive enterprise—money, materials, equipment, and people—in the interests of economic ends.	1. Management is responsible for organizing the elements of productive enterprise—money, materials, equipment, and people—in the interests of economic ends.
2. With respect to people, this is a process of directing their efforts, motivating them, controlling their actions, and modifying their behavior to fit the needs of the organization.	2. People are not by nature passive or resistant to organizational needs. They have become so as a result of experience and organization.
3. Without this active intervention by management, people would be passive, even resistant, to organizational needs. They must therefore be persuaded, rewarded, punished, and controlled. Their activities must be directed. Management consists of getting things done through other people.	3. The motivation, the potential for development, the capacity for assuming responsibility, and the readiness to direct behavior toward organizational goals are all present in people. Management does not put them there. It is a responsibility of management to make it possible for people to recognize and develop these human characteristics for themselves.
4. The average person is by nature indolent—he works as little as possible. He lacks ambition, dislikes responsibility, and prefers to be led. He is inherently self-centered, indifferent to organizational needs. He is by nature resistant to change. He is gullible, not very bright, and the ready dupe of the charlatan and the demagogue.	4. The essential task of management is to arrange organizational conditions and methods of operation so that people can achieve their own goals best by directing their own efforts toward organizational objectives. This is a process of opportunities, releasing potential, removing obstacles, encouraging growth, and providing guidance.
5. Management is by control.	5. Management is by objectives.

Source: Adapted from McGregor. (November 1957). "The Human Side of Enterprise." *Management Review.*

control and, in the extreme, theorizes that the average person is passive and lacks ambition. The old saying that "the flogging will continue until morale improves" exemplifies this approach in a somewhat humorous manner. Theory Y describes the approach of the Employee Relations era and advocates inspiring employees to accomplish organizational objectives. It supports Maslow's theory of determining the human needs status of employees and providing a work environment that encourages satisfaction through achievement of objectives. In the extreme, it envisions employees as willing and capable of high job performance if only given the chance.

It is important to view these two theories as extremes and that the Eclectic Perspective administrators should be able to "mix and match" as called for in a given situation. In today's Client-Oriented Service environment, Theory Y is certainly most desirable. However, if taken to its extreme, a "country club" management style can develop that is ineffective in preventing misconduct. ("Country Club Management" will be further discussed in Chapter 14.)

It must be remembered that a basic responsibility of administrators is to implement controls to make sure that things are being performed as planned. The administrator must be aware of employee shifts in the needs within Maslow's Human Needs concept. Maslow's concept does not support that a person will always perform at their best if just given the chance.

The author, as an administrator, can recall times when employees who were motivated and self-actualized suddenly became less interested in the job because of the emotional impact of a non-job-related event. One incident comes to mind in which a highly dedicated patrol officer suddenly abandoned his patrol area to check on his wife, who he thought was having an affair (and she was—with another police officer). This situation, if not detected, could have resulted in a failure of the officer to be available to perform required duties. The practice of inspection and control brought this situation to light. Checking on even the best of employees is a sound practice and should not be considered as negative. It provides the opportunity to evaluate performances and commend for jobs "well done."

The author, therefore, advocates a "**big Y, little x**" approach. This means supporting employees toward a self-actualized state where maximum discretion is encouraged but having "checks and balance" controls that ensure the continual desired level of productivity.

Frederick Herzberg's Hygiene/Motivators approach to job satisfaction adds another level to the concepts of motivation (Herzberg, 1975). Herzberg considered the lower levels of Maslow's Human Needs not as motivating factors but, rather, as "hygiene" or maintenance factors. These are levels of need that must be satisfied before employees are motivated, but satisfaction of these levels does not necessarily result in motivation. Job security, working conditions, and good salaries are benefits that employee unions usually pursue. They are certainly conditions administrators should ensure but administration also involves ensuring job motivation. Herzberg pointed out that job motivation comes from fostering the higher levels of Maslow's hierarchy by providing opportunities for occupational growth and advancement, performance recognition, and tasks that support a feeling of accomplishment.

Figure 8–2 shows the Herzberg factors and how they affect job motivation. **Table 8–3** compares Maslow, McGregor, and Herzberg's theories and shows how they interrelate. A point to be made is that in times when unemployment is high, agencies can often get away with X Theory approaches and only provide "Hygiene Factors" benefits. Under these economical conditions, employees are often "just happy to have a job" that provides them with the lower levels of Maslow's Human Needs. However, when employment is high and agencies seek the best and most qualified employees, Theory Y and Motivating Factors must be provided to keep workers from seeking employment elsewhere.

The **Greatest Management Principle (GMP)**, developed by Dr. Michael LeBoeuf, is a concept that should be considered by criminal justice administrators (LeBoeuf, 1986). "What gets rewarded is what gets done," is what LeBoeuf says motivates employees. His concept is that if administrators want employees to perform in a manner that supports the mission and goals, employees must be

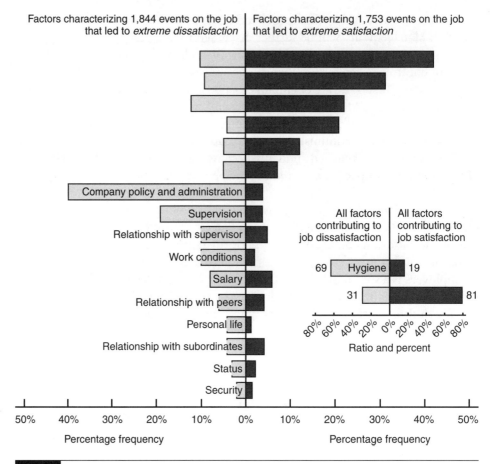

Figure 8–2 Herzberg's Factors Affecting Job Attitudes.

rewarded for such efforts. For example, a police chief may put forth a mission statement that calls for a community-oriented approach. However, if employees are rewarded solely for the number of arrests and traffic citations that they make, then the mission will not be supported by the employees. As a consultant, the author has found the GMP to be a very important point in changing the direction of criminal justice agencies.

Table 8–3	Herzberg, Maslow, and McGregor Comparison
Herzberg **Two-Factor Theory**	**Maslow** **Needs Hierarchy**	**McGregor** **Theories X and Y**
Motivators	Self-actualization, ego, status, esteem, social	Theory Y
Maintenance factors	Safety and security, physiological	Theory X

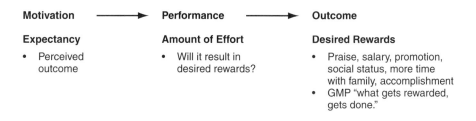

Figure 8–3 Expectancy (Vroom) and Reward (Leboeuf) Concepts Interrelated.

Motivation is defined as a "force within an individual that initiates, directs, and sustains a particular behavior" (Roberg, Kuykendall, & Norah, 2002, p. 1860). Motivation is a personal quality. Administrators must determine what motivates each of their employees, find ways of bringing together the desired performance with what motivates each employee, and reward accordingly. It must be realized that some tasks are "boring" and that these tasks do not normally result in job satisfaction. If these tasks cannot be eliminated or automated, then motivating rewards must be found for "just doing them."

Victor Vroom's **Expectancy Theory** provides insight into what constitutes reward. His theory rests on two assumptions (Vroom, 1964):

1. Individuals have cognitive expectations about what outcomes are likely to result from their behavior.

2. Individuals have preferences among these outcomes.

Figure 8–3 shows how Vroom's Expectancy Theory and Leboeuf's GMP interrelate. Rewards may range from praise, salary, to feeling of accomplishment or acceptance. One form of reward that all supervisors have access to is praise. Praise, where justified, is rewarding to most employees. For one employee, having a job that provides more time with his or her family might be rewarding, while with others the possibility of promotion and/or a salary increase will be a stronger motivating factor. The author, when responsible for the auxiliary/services functions of a police department, found that many of the civilian employees had children and were often late in reporting to work because of their child care responsibilities. By providing "flex-time" (the 8-hour shift started whenever they arrived within an hour of their official reporting time), the negative aspects of being "tardy" were reduced and employee retention and production was increased. This approach, of course, cannot apply to jobs where definite reporting times are required, such as with 9-1-1 communications personnel.

Paul Hersey and Kenneth Blanchard (1977) provided the concept of a Situational Approach to motivation, which supports the Eclectic Perspective emphasized throughout this text (**Figure 8–4**). With a new employee, an instructions style (1.) is required. This is somewhat like McGregor's Theory X approach, in that the employee needs close supervision and instruction as to how to do the job. After the employee becomes familiar with the job, a coaching approach (2.) is more appropriate. The supervisor needs to "sell" the employee on why the job is important and that good performance will result in job satisfaction.

**Hersey and Blanchard's Situational
Leadership Model**

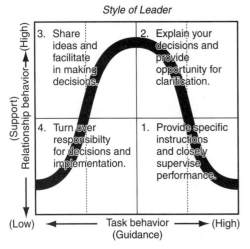

Maslow's Hierarchy of Needs

Figure 8-4 Hersey and Blanchard's Situational Leadership Model Compared with Maslow's Hierarchy of Needs.

As the employee becomes more "mature" in the job, a more supportive approach (3.) is called for. In this mode, the supervisor is there to support and encourage the employee when needed. An employee who is "self-actualized," according to Maslow's hierarchy, will react best to a delegation style (4.) of supervision—one in which the employee can be left to function on their own. This style might be likened to McGregor's Theory Y; however, a "Big Y and a little x" combination is the most productive approach in most cases. Some inspection and control is appropriate even with the best performing employees, as administrators have ultimate responsibility for the performance of their employees.

William Ouchi's Theory Z received much interest in the 1980s. Theory Z provided a model that combined many of the concepts of the period. It emphasized employee job security, participatory decision making, group responsibility and teamwork, increased product and service quality, broader career paths, and a greater concern for employee's work and family welfare (Ouchi, 1981). Ouchi developed his model from what several of his contemporaries, such as Joseph Juran and W. Edwards Demming, were implementing in Japan. Japanese industries have followed this model for decades as a successful method of motivating employees. The ideas of Ouchi, Juran, and Demming have been synthesized into a management model called Total Quality Management (TQM). TQM will be discussed in the next chapter as an example of an Open Systems approach.

■ Discipline

Discipline is discussed here as a separate element of the Employee Relations concepts. Discipline is both negative and positive. The definition of discipline is a state in which an organization's members behave in ways that best serve its goals and purposes. A "well-disciplined" organization is a desirable state. **Positive**

discipline involves those activities discussed thus far in this chapter relating to motivation. They are those administrative activities that encourage and inspire employees to achieve organizational goals.

Negative discipline, conversely, relates to punishment and might be considered as what is necessary when positive discipline fails. Unfortunately, there is a small percentage of personnel who become involved in misconduct. The misconduct of a few tarnishes the reputation of all criminal justice employees, and it must be prevented through positive means when at all possible. However, when misconduct does occur, fair and proper negative discipline must be applied. Thus, criminal justice administrators must be familiar with the concepts related to negative discipline.

When should a personnel complaint of misconduct be investigated? The guiding rule is that it should be investigated if the allegation, if true, would constitute misconduct. Misconduct is usually defined within the written policies, procedures, and rules of an agency. **Figure 8–5** shows the various categories of police misconduct as a "Slippery Slope." Starting with the lower levels of misconduct, which more employees are likely to confront, and progressing to the worst type, which very few employees even consider.

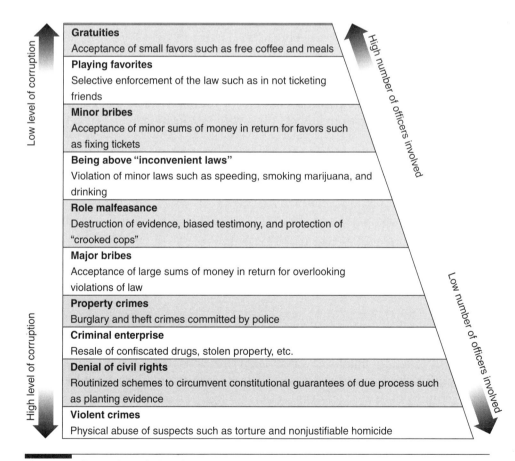

Figure 8–5 Slippery Slope of Misconduct.

Serious misconduct involving committing crimes and denying civil rights are seldom disputed as wrongful acts. It is the lesser "evils" that are more often difficult to establish as wrongdoings. The act of taking a free meal or a free cup of coffee should be considered a gratuity and therefore prohibited by the oath that most police officers swear to upon employment. The officers' Code of Ethics (see **Chapter 13**) states, "Officers will refuse to accept any gifts, presents, subscriptions, favors, gratuities, or promises that could be interpreted as seeking to cause the officer to refrain from performing official responsibilities honestly and within the law" (International Association of Chiefs of Police, 1989). To eliminate any doubt, criminal justice administrators should prohibit such conduct in their internal policies. The taking of free "anything" detracts from the professional aspects of the job and can lead to other misconduct further down the slippery slope.

Who investigates misconduct? In most cases, it is investigated by the supervisor of those accused of misconduct. Therefore, the investigation of misconduct complaints is a part of every supervisor's job. Large agencies will have Internal Affairs entities, but they usually investigate the most serious of the misconduct cases. Immediate supervisors must take part in the punishment of their employees even if investigated by another entity. Of course, the chief executives should have the "final word" in all disciplinary matters, as they are ultimately held responsible.

Investigation of allegations of misconduct should support one of the following dispositions:

- Sustained, the allegation is true
- Exonerated, the allegation is not true
- Not Sustained, the allegation cannot be proven as sustained or exonerated
- Justified, the allegation did occur but with justification.

If the allocation is sustained, one (or more) of the following forms of **punishment** should follow:

- Warning (Oral Reprimand)
- Written Reprimand
- Relinquishment of Accumulated Overtime
- Suspension without Pay
- Termination
- Criminal Prosecution

Some agencies include demotion as a form of punishment, but the author does not recommend this as appropriate. Demoted employees can result in conflicts and "festering" employee-supervision situations that are counterproductive to administrative goals. If the misconduct is serious enough to consider demotion, termination is a better disposition.

An area of conflict that sometime arises between administration and labor involves "not sustained" complaints. This disposition is to be avoided if at all possible but often occurs because the only evidence is one person's word against another. Labor organizations usually take a position that this disposition should be treated as a "not guilty" verdict, and no mention of the incident should be filed in the employee's record. Administrators often take the position that because it was not proven that the employee did not commit misconduct a record should be kept in case a pattern of such complaints develops. In the spirit of prevention, administrators should be able to provide preventive supervision at the point that any indication of undesirable conduct appears. A number of "not sustained" allegations of misconduct can provide indications of need for preventative supervision.

An **Employee Bill of Rights** exists in most states for police officers and must be considered in conducting personnel investigations. Criminal justice employees are protected under the Bill of Rights of the U.S. Constitution, as are other citizens. However, labor organizations have promoted the officers' bills of rights. This bill exists because most criminal justice employees perform within a hierarchical authoritarian structure that could result in employees giving up their rights because of commands from their superiors.

Police Officer's Bill of Rights

When any police officer is under investigation and subjected to interrogations, which could lead to punitive action, the interrogation will be conducted under the following conditions. These rights do not apply to an interrogation in a normal course of duty, which might involve counseling, instruction, or informal verbal admonishments.

1. *The interrogation will be conducted at a reasonable hour, preferably when the _____ (police officer) is on duty or during normal waking hours, unless the seriousness of the investigation requires otherwise. If the interrogation takes place during off-duty time, the officer will be compensated in accordance with regular department procedures.*

2. *The persons to be present at the interrogation must be identified in advance, and the officer will not be interrogated by more than two investigators at one time.*

3. *The police officer will be informed of the charges against him or her prior to any interrogation.*

4. *The interrogation will be for a reasonable period of time.*

5. *The police officer under interrogation will not be subjected to any offensive language or threats of punitive action, except that an officer refusing to respond to questions or submit to interrogation will be informed that failure to answer questions that are directly related to the investigation may result in punitive action. There will be no promise or reward offered as an inducement to answer any question.*

6. *The interrogation may be recorded by either the persons conducting the interrogation and/or the officer under investigation. The officer in question is entitled to written or recorded copies of the interrogation if additional action is contemplated by the department or if there is to be a continuing investigation.*

7. *If prior to or during the interrogation, it is decided he or she may be charged with a criminal offense, the officer will immediately be informed of his or her constitutional rights.*

8. *If a formal written statement of charges is filed against a police officer by the department, the officer has a right to request that a representative of his or her choice be present during any interrogation.*

Source: Adapted from the California Government Code, Section 3303.

■ Grievance Procedures

Grievance procedures are commonplace in most agencies today. Administrators must be aware of these procedures and respond appropriately. They allow for any employee to orally complain about personnel matters to their immediate supervisor. If the employee feels the supervisor does not satisfy their complaint, he or she can file the complaint with the supervisor in writing. Once done, the supervisor must respond in writing in a designated time period. If the employee still is not satisfied, they may follow the same procedure with the next level in the hierarchy, all the way up to the top executive officer if necessary.

■ Employee Stress

Employee **stress** is another area of Employee Relations for which administrators should have concern. First, it should be realized that stress can be good and bad. Most people seek some activities that cause positive stress, which excites and often is needed to "win the game." Indeed, there are a number of sporting activities that exists because people like "**good stress**." This, in fact, is one of the many benefits of criminal justice work—that of exciting and challenging activities. However, it is "**bad stress**," or distress, that can lead to avoidance of work or create a feeling of being overwhelmed by events. It is true that shift work and constant exposure to emotional situations can cause negative stress in some people.

Most studies regarding police officers find that administrative policies and procedures cause more stress than "on the street" activities. Lack of communication or miscommunication and lack of consistency by supervisors are often examples given by employees. Most officers find the majority of their "street duties" exciting and most do not consider the possibility of danger as stressful; those who do usually are terminated during the probation period (Niederhoffer, 1974; Stratton, 1984). The author, as a criminal justice administrator and consultant, has found this to be true relating to employee stress and suicide. It is true that police officers commit suicide more often than those in most other professions. However, most suicides are committed with handguns, and all officers have ready access to handguns because of their duties. The author has observed this to be more of a cause than the duties that officers perform. Most officers who commit suicide do so because of emotional traumas that are not directly related to the job, such as domestic problems.

As with many other occupations, administrative practices and personal domestic problems are the main cause of negative stress. However, domestic problems can be caused by the on-the-job "police personality." Police officers have to be able to separate themselves from the emotionality of many of the "on-the-street" problems they are called on to resolve. In doing so, they can develop an "emotional shield" that separates them from the people they have been called upon to help. Some degree of this is necessary in order to take charge of emotional situations. However, they can become so emotionally callused that they do not express feeling such as love and compassion toward their loved ones when off duty.

Additionally, the impact of media criticism, political interference, and court actions may cause some officers to become cynical. Cynicism and emotional callousness are conditions to which administrators should be sensitive. They should encourage employees to live a well-balanced and healthy life, which should include many nonemployment interests and activities.

KEY CONCEPTS AND TERMS

- Supervision
- Employee hiring: recruiting and selecting
- Training versus education
- Behavioral versus Gestalt
- Andragogy approach versus pedagogy approach
- Employee evaluations

- Motivation
  - "Big Y, little x" Theory
  - Greatest Management Principle (GMP)
  - Expectancy Theory
  - Z Theory

- Discipline
  - Positive versus negative
  - Employee Bill of Rights

- Stress
  - Good versus bad

CHAPTER ACTIVITY

Interview a person currently employed in the criminal justice system. Find out what motivates them to perform well and what *Employee Relations* approaches they desire from their administrators.

REVIEW QUESTIONS

1. The 1883 Pendleton Act was meant to do away with the "spoils system" in the hiring of public employees. Do you think there is any favoritism in public hiring today?

2. What selections and hiring approaches do you think would be most useful today in attracting criminal justice employees?

3. What is the difference between negative and positive discipline? Give examples of each.

4. Do you think there is more stress in criminal justice jobs than in other professions? Give examples of both positive and negative stress.

5. Imagine that you are a criminal justice administrator and have been assigned to develop and implement a criminal justice entity of your choice (for example, a Special Weapons Assault Team). What Employee Relations concepts would you consider in fulfilling this assignment?

REFERENCES

Argyris, C. (1957). The Individual and Organization: Some Problems of Mutual Adjustment. *Administrative Science Quarterly*, June, pp. 1–24.

Barry, R. J., & Cronkhite, C. L. (1991). Managing Police Agencies under Stress: Coping with the Aftermath of the Rodney G. King Incident. *Western City*, July, pp. 21–24.

Carter, D. L., & Sapp, A. D. (1989). The Effect of Higher Education on Police Liability Implications for Police Personnel Policy. *American Journal of Police*, pp. 8–10.

Cascio, W. F. (1977). Formal Education and Police Officer Performance. *Journal of Police Science and Administration*, pp. 21–25.

Cascio, W. F., & Bernardin, J. (1981). Implications of Performance Appraisal Litigation for Personnel Decisions. *Personnel Psychology*, pp. 9–11.

Hersey, P., & Blanchard, K. H. (1977). *Managing Organizational Behavior*. Englewood Cliffs, NJ: Prentice Hall.

Herzberg, F. (1975). One More Time: How Do You Motivate Employees? In *Business Classics: Fifteen Key Concepts for Managerial Success*. Cambridge, MA: Harvard University Press.

Knowles, M. S. (1970). *The Modern Practice of Adult Education: Andragogy versus Pedagogy*. New York: Associated Press.

LeBoeuf, M. (1986). *Greatest Management Principle in the World*. Available from the Illinois Law Enforcement Media Resource Center, LE87210V. [videotape].

Maslow, A. (1943). A Theory of Human Motivation. *Psychology Review*, 50, pp. 370–396.

McGregor, D. M. (1957). The Human Side of Enterprise. *Management Review*. November, pp. 20–27.

Niederhoffer, A. (1974). *Behind the Shield*. Garden City, NY: Doubleday.

Ouchi, W. (1981). *How American Business Can Meet the Japanese Challenge*. Reading, MA: Addison Wesley.

The Police Chief: The Professional Voice of Law Enforcement. (2006, August). Alexandria, VA: International Association of Chiefs of Police, Inc.

Roberg, R. R., Kuykendall, J., & Novah, K. (2002). *Police Management*. Los Angeles: Roxbury.

Stratton, J. (1984). *Police Passages*. Sandusky, OH: Gellon.

Vroom, V. (1964). *Work and Motivation*. New York: Wiley.

Weiner, N. L. (1976). The Educated Policeman. *Journal of Police Science and Administration*, pp. 78–79.

Worden, R. E. (1994). The 'Causes' of Police Brutality: Theory and Evidence on Police Use of Force. *And Justice for All*, pp. 175–179.

■ RELEVANT PUBLICATION

The concluding Employee Relations issue in this chapter was *stress*. The Relevant Publication for this chapter is about stress but also includes a number of methods to help motivate people. It was written in response to an infamous police incident, the Rodney King case (discussed in Chapter 5). The Eclectic Perspective Administrator should find a number of concepts that remain important today and that will continue to be so in the future (Barry, R. & Cronkhite, C. (1991). Managing Police Agencies Under Stress: Coping with the Aftermath of the Rodney G. King Incident. *Western City*, July, pp. 21–24).

"Managing Police Agencies Under Stress: Coping with the Aftermath of the Rodney G. King Incident" by Robert J. Barry and Clyde L. Cronkhite

The videotaped use of force by officers of the Los Angeles Police Department in the now-infamous Rodney G. King case has brought intense scrutiny to police agencies everywhere. The resulting furor has had a psychological impact on law enforcement personnel and organizations, not just within the L.A.P.D., but throughout the country.

Negative, and somewhat distorted, media coverage of this unfortunate event has brought about a perception by administrators, supervisors and line officers of a lack of support on the part of a public that harbors negative attitudes toward law enforcement. This perception of the event by law enforcement personnel is causing increased stress upon individual officers and their organizations. In some cases this has created unhealthy working environments, including the erosion of physical and psychological well being, hypertension, heart disease, alcohol and drug abuse, high rates of absenteeism and low levels of trust, morale, productivity and depression. Such situations can be dysfunctional to the organization, to the community it serves, and to individual officers.

Our purpose with this article is to suggest some psychological strategies and tactics for law enforcement personnel to use in coping with the added stress and some short- and long-term strategies law enforcement managers can use to improve morale and maintain the quality of work in their organizations despite the added pressure of current events.

Authorities conclude that law enforcement stressors fall into four distinct categories. Law enforcement administrators should consider how these four categories of stressors impact their personnel.

I. External Stressors To The Organization include frustrations with courts, prosecutors, public defenders, corrections, lack of public support, negative or distorted media coverage, interactions with outside administrative bodies, lack of resources, and more.

II. Internal Stressors To The Organization include a hierarchical structure, lack of resources, strict policies and procedures, poor training and/or equipment, lack of recognition, poor economic benefits and working conditions, excessive case loads and paper work, favoritism, unfair discipline and so forth.

III. Stressors In Law Enforcement Work Itself include rigors of shift work; role conflicts, exposure to the miseries of life, street brutality, boredom, panic, fear, responsibility for protecting other people, the fragmented nature of most law enforcement jobs, work overloads and the pressure that comes from being the "conscience of society."

IV. Stressors Confronting The Individual Officer including the possibility of injury and death; fears regarding job competence, individual success and personal safety; the necessity to conform; the possible need to take a second job to make ends meet; altered social status in the community because of the individual's occupation; and family responsibilities.

During this period of doubt and introspection all personnel should be aware that regardless of the media myths about the glamour of a law enforcement career, police officers routinely see the worst manifestations of human behavior. The sum total of these experiences can lead officers to depression, despair, discouragement and doubts about their mission and their own self-worth.

The traditional method of dealing with job-related stress has been to help personnel increase their coping skills and introduce them to stress management techniques. Such strategies include eating a good diet; getting adequate exercise and sleep; reduced use of alcohol, caffeine, and nicotine; use of relaxation techniques; and avoiding self-medication. It also is wise to be sure to schedule personal and family time; to develop and maintain a social life away from law enforcement; to make time for friendship, recreation, and hobbies. Officers—and their managers—also are well-advised to exercise patience; to be gentle with themselves and to avoid taking things too seriously or too personally. Law enforcement personnel must realize they do not have to become vicarious victims while policing our modern society.

When officers sense they are under attack, they may counter attack, compromise, or withdraw, on a conscious level, but on an unconscious level they will employ one or more defense mechanisms to protect their self-esteem and their egos. Defense mechanisms are psychological functions that protect the ego from internal and external threats, conflicts, doubts, impulses and all manner of hurts and bruises. Understanding how such "self-defense" mechanisms work can help managers recognize when their personnel are experiencing stress and develop strategies for limiting the toll stress can take on an organization.

The process by which defense mechanisms are integrated is based on the individual's perception of a stressor. For any event to be stressful, it first must be perceived as being stressful.

First, an individual perceives a problem. Then he or she analyzes it and decides upon a solution. That first step, perception, is a very important variable and can be manipulated to meet the individual's needs. How each individual perceives a situation largely dictates his or her psychological response.

If we do not perceive a situation to be stressful, it is not a problem.

Defense mechanisms allow officers to change their perceptions of any situation. According to several authorities, including Dr. Lawrence Blum and Dr. Michael Mantell, two noted pyschologists who are consultants to numerous law enforcement organizations in Orange and San Diego counties, those defense mechanisms utilized most frequently by officers include:

Isolation of Affect—The individual divorces the situation or incident from its emotional connotation. This process protects the self from the violence of the street but may play havoc with family ties and cause emotional isolation.

"Sick" Humor—Many professionals—doctors, lawyers, coroners, athletes—use "gallows" humor to protect their self-images in stressful circumstances. In law enforcement, it is usually very controlled and expressed by senior patrol officers only within earshot of fellow officers who are directly involved, but not to non-law enforcement personnel. Speaking the unspeakable and being understood by fellow officers releases guilty feelings and pain. The intent of this kind of humor is not to be funny but to allow the ventilation of frustrations. Engaging in "sick" humor acts as a safety valve.

Displacement—The officer displaces or transfers an emotional feeling from an internal object to a substitute external object. He may blame the problem on another person or go home and "kick the dog."

Repression—This is a primary self-defense mechanism. If a problem is causing stress, it may automatically, effortlessly, and involuntarily be relegated to the unconscious area of our mind. We "put it out of our minds." Officers continually deal with vocational stress by repression. They also are victimized by this defense mechanism when crime witnesses repress valuable information to protect their sanity.

Rationalization—Officers may make an effort to justify, or attempt to modify, otherwise unacceptable situations, or incidents, into ones that are more tolerable, or acceptable. Officers frequently use this strategy to convince themselves that a decision or behavior is acceptable.

Projection—This defense is in play when one blames others for one's own faults. For example, an officer may blame others for her own lack of success in investigations rather than face the fact that she, herself, conducted an incomplete investigation.

Defense mechanisms are used on a daily basis by everyone to protect their fragile egos and self-image—that picture of ourselves, without which it is difficult to function in a healthy, productive, manner. However, such defenses can become counter-productive if used to excess, in a habitual manner, for the wrong reason, at the wrong time, and in the wrong place.

They can also lead to additional stress and long-range psychological "burnout."

The challenge facing law enforcement administrators over the Rodney King incident is to realize the crucial nature of their roles in helping their subordinates develop coping strategies that enhance their ability to perform their duties in an appropriate manner. Administrators must attempt to improve the organizational environment as well as their management and leadership styles to meet this challenge.

Those law enforcement organizations with a strong sense of police-community cooperation will easily weather this storm of protest. *Community Policing: A Contemporary Perspective* (1990), Robert Trojanowicz and Bonnie Bucqueroux; and *Community Policing: Issues And Practices Around The World*, National Institute of Justice, describe how administrators in: Detroit, Houston, Newport News, Newark, as well as Santa Ana and Oakland in California, have instituted the philosophical concepts of community-oriented policing to cope with similar stressful problems.

Law enforcement leaders committed to developing a healthy work environment should consider implementing several management strategies to cope with the fall-out of the King case.

- **Determine the specific effect on the organization.**
  Self examination of an agency includes select interviews with all levels of employees, organizational inspections, surveys and audits, quality circles, active listening, exhibiting interest in the problem, then taking active steps to reduce the stress caused by the issue.
- **Re-affirm a belief in the basic mission.**
  An honest mission statement serves to define the purpose and intent of the organization, allowing personnel to view their self-worth and understand their true value to the great majority of the community. In times of adversity it is essential for all personnel to re-affirm their commitment to the organization's basic mission.
- **Live the organizational values.**
  Law enforcement organizations have been fashioned after the autocratic quasi-paramilitaristic model. More recently progressive managers understand that personnel reach higher levels of productivity and good mental health if pressed towards excellence by management through values. These organization values determine what both individuals and organizations consider to be appropriate and inappropriate conduct and behavior.
- **Encourage communication and dialogue.**
  Law enforcement organizations that encourage freedom of communications have a decided advantage in times of stress or crisis. Ideas, insights, thoughts and emotions may be openly exchanged, therefore, numerous problems can be resolved or avoided. Methods of encourag-

ing open communications, include advisory groups, open door sessions, retreats, surveys, task forces, employee councils, administrators' visits to roll calls, union meetings and an understanding of the concept of active listening.

- **Demonstrate a caring about people.**

True caring includes trust, pride and a sense of community. Administrators should nurture these principles in an effort to improve the working environment where personnel are trusted; have pride in themselves, their performance, their organizations and their communities; and enjoy working. Such a workplace climate should be relatively free of negative influences.

- **Ventilate frustrations.**

Most psychotherapy includes the concept of ventilation, to verbalize emotions and "get it off your chest" rather than to internalize the problem, brood, and let it accumulate. Administrators must actively support this notion of ventilating emotions and understanding the necessity of showing concern.

- **Ensure fairness.**

Administrators have the responsibility for developing fairness in the organization. Unfair disciplinary factors including favoritism, emphasis on negative discipline, external pressure, undue length of time of process, lack of written criteria or guidelines, poor policies and procedures. Efforts must also be made to eliminate unfair performance ratings and promotional practices. A fair work place is a good place to work.

- **Develop skills in "active listening."**

People can listen faster than one can talk. Therefore, listening can become boring. The ability of an administrator to actively listen is a skill that must be developed. Active listening improves ability to communicate effectively. Some techniques include preparing to listen, being patient, resisting distractions, paying strict attention, refraining from interrupting, controlling emotions and judging content as well as delivery. The last word is: listen.

- **Keep personnel on the healthy end of the continuum.**

Administrators should constantly strive to develop programs which reduce organizational stress on personnel as well as support programs to assist all personnel in coping with individual stress. The overall objective is to make the organization a healthy work place.

- **Reinforce a supportive structure.**

Law enforcement managers must recognize the critical role they play in reducing stress. Caring about people includes providing adequate wages and benefits, job security, training, education, and opportunities for promotion, personal growth and career development. A caring organization is family-like and supportive by nature.

- **Continue towards goals of excellence.**
  Law enforcement organizations must not allow a single incident such as the Rodney King affair to cause them to deviate from their long-range goals of excellence in law enforcement. Considering the community as customer will gain public support, increase citizen satisfaction, enhance police services and reduce citizen complaints.
- **Get the issue out in the open.**
  Verbalizing the issue will enable law enforcement personnel to open a line of dialogue and debate, which will lead to solutions, a healthy work place and higher morale. Dodging or avoiding the issue allows it to lie unattended and, like some insidious cancer, endanger the organization and its personnel.

While the preceding strategies can help officers cope with stress in the short term, managers may want to view the stress resulting from the King affair as a challenge to review and improve the coping skills of their law enforcement personnel and organizations. Change most often is a product of dissatisfaction; people usually are not motivated to change unless their current status is uncomfortable. Employees become more supportive of change when they see it as a means of reducing their dissatisfaction and of improving their feelings of self-worth.

So management should consider this situation as an opportunity to instigate change where change is needed, an ideal time to enhance the values and mission of police agencies. A renewed emphasis on ethics and a rekindling of the community-oriented policing philosophy should be viewed as essentials in enhancing the morale and professional esteem of all personnel.

The primary thrust of such a value-based management philosophy is not so much toward prohibitions which restrain officers but toward encouraging employees to weigh their actions constantly in light of the high ethical and constitutional values of their profession. All law enforcement officers are sworn to uphold state and federal constitutions as well as the traditional "Law Enforcement Code of Ethics."

The value-based philosophy should be well defined in an employee-accepted mission statement which emphasizes that:

—Recognition of individual dignity is vital in the free system of law established by the Constitution. All persons have a right to be treated with as much respect as they will allow and officers have a duty to protect this right.

—Ensuring the safety and security of all people by providing responsive and professional police service with compassion and concern is of prime importance in every public contact.

The move in emphasis on quantity to quality action empowers officers to select an appropriate course of action from a range of options rather than a few prescribed responses. For example, by establishing that the measure of success for all employees is not the quantity of work (number of arrests, citations and such) but rather the positive impact they have on:

—Preventing and reducing crime and traffic accidents (which can be measured statistically); and

—Community satisfaction and support (which can be measured by community surveys and public commendations and complaints).

The focus must be on innovation and problem solving rather than only on reactive responses to calls-for-service.

Equally valuable to police administrators who wish to improve morale is the philosophy of community-oriented policing. This philosophy provides that police officers, and the public they serve, have an interdependent and shared responsibility in making their communities safe and desirable places to live and conduct business. Rather than playing out an "us versus them" attitude (which is exacerbated in times of negative media coverage), community-oriented policing focuses on building a partnership between the officers and the community. It provides opportunities for employees to come into contact with community members during "non-call-for-service" situations and creates positive feedback that can overcome the effects of negative or distorted publicity.

The philosophical commitment to community policing recognizes that good neighborhood quality of life is of paramount importance in reducing crime and can best be achieved through a partnership between the police and the community. This philosophy is demonstrated not so much by programs as it is by the policies and practices that are designed and employed to accomplish:

- an increased accountability to local communities;
- reoriented patrol activities to emphasize service;
- community-based crime prevention;
- improved communication with the community; and
- decentralized police authority.

This philosophy must become an integral part of the selection, recruit training, in-service training, evaluation, promotion and reward process. The philosophy must permeate the entire organization and be accepted by every employee, not just by those in command. It can be institutionalized by becoming the theme of the personnel selection, training, reward and reinforcement policies and practices.

Making the community policing philosophy the central focus of police employees will foster closer contact between the employees and the public, provide more situations for positive feedback and give officers a cause that can improve their morale and enhance their feelings of self-worth. Making that commitment could turn the King incident into an opportunity to transcend to a higher level of professionalism, a quest for excellence in striving toward long-range individual and organizational goals and objectives.

9

Applying Open Systems Concepts to the Administration of Contemporary Criminal Justice Agencies

■ Introduction

The human body is an open system, as it depends on life-supporting substances from the surrounding environment in order to exist. Humans could not live without food, water, air, and other elements from outside the body. So it is with organizations, and this is why Open Systems concepts are important.

Woodrow Wilson's description of public organizations inferred that they were closed systems. Administrators were to be concerned only with carrying out the directions of the representatives of the people through the internal operations of the organization. They were not encouraged to work directly with the public, who certainly were part of their environment. Public administrators were to provide a proper organization structure wherein motivated employees would efficiently and effectively achieve the wishes of elected officials. Public administrators managed their agencies as closed systems with little concern for the social and intergovernmental environment that was outside the boundaries of their organizations.

In the 1960s, as Organization Function and Employee Relations concepts continued to be enhanced, a major shift in administrative interest occurred. An outlook developed, which held that public administrators had to be more directly concerned with their environment. This was a significant departure from the emphasis of the previous 70 years. However, this was not a sudden change. It developed, as with other changes in administrative approaches, over time. The roots of its development can be found decades earlier. For example, in 1938, Chester Barnard encouraged public administrators to look beyond the immediate borders of their organizations and encouraged a more open systems view (Barnard, 1938). His writings only incidentally began a departure from the closed systems view. In the Employee Relations development period, the Hawthorne Experiments recognized the role of informally organized groups within the larger organization. However, it was not until the end of World War II that this shift in thinking started to crystallize. System theorists began to describe the interactions of social units with a larger social world. Organizations were created to resolve the problems of postwar America.

In Chapter 3, historical milestones that relate to Open Systems concepts were described and the following summaries of key points are brought forward to interact with the applications discussed in this chapter. Key historic Open Systems concepts to remember are:

- Bureaucracy is outdated (or is it?)
  1967, "Organizations of the Future," Warren Bennis
- Re-focusing on organization functions
  1966, "The Road to PPB: The Stages of Budget Reform," Allen Schick
- The need for Open Systems organizations
  1966, *The Social Psychology of Organizations*, Daniel Katz and Robert Kahn

First, the forewarning from Warren Bennis that bureaucracy was outdated, was based partly on the closed system concept of the past. As discussed in Chapter 7, Bennis' predictions that the bureaucratic structure would not exist in 25 years, certainly has not come to pass. However, for bureaucracy to survive it has had to become more interconnected with the environment; *open systems* approaches have had to be implemented.

Schick's writings about budget reform (as discussed in Chapter 7) is a reminder that even while focused on one contextual theme, attention to the others is required. During this period when much attention was being paid to developing Open Systems concepts, a troubled economy caused a refocusing to Organization Functions concepts. This is why Eclectic Perspective administrators must have a grasp of all the contextual themes and be prepared to eclectically apply the best mix of administrative approaches to the situation at hand.

Contemporary Open Systems Concepts

Even though it was Ludwig von Bertanlanffy who formulated the original Open Systems concept, Katz and Kahn are remembered as major contributors to it being applied in the public sector (see Chapter 3). They listed nine characteristics of an open system (Katz & Kahn, 1966): (1) environmental awareness and importation of energy and resources, (2) conversion of energy into goods and services, (3) outputs, (4) cyclical character of processes, (5) negative entropy, (6) feedback, (7) functional steady state or dynamic homeostasis, (8) movement toward growth and expansion, and (9) equifinality.

More recently, the "**Principles of Open Systems**" were defined by Gareth Morgan:

- **Homeostasis:** an open system seeks a steady state through self-regulation based on feedback.
- **Negative entropy:** an open system sustains itself by importing energy from its environment.
- **Requisite variety:** the internal regulatory mechanisms of an open system must be as diverse as the environment with which it is trying to deal.
- **Equifinality:** in an open system there may be many different ways of achieving any particular goal.
- **System evolution:** the capacity of an open system to evolve depends on an ability to move to more complex forms of differentiation and integration (Morgan, 1997, pp. 40–41).

One of the terms that came from Max Weber's original "principles" of bureaucracy (see Chapter 2) was that of the rational organization. Weber defined rational organizations as tightly organized structures that are best able to deal with conditions that are stable and predictable. The closed system approach could exist under these conditions, and it should be acknowledged that some agencies still function as such. However, in today's ever-changing social, political, and economical environment, the "nonrational" open systems approach is best suited for survival.

It might be said that all things are systems. This means they have *inputs*; they *process* these inputs, and produce *outputs*. Take an air conditioning system, for example. Air is the input. The heating and cooling system processes the input and dispenses it as a comfortable output (at least that is the goal). An objective is established, say, a temperature of 72 degrees as the desired output. In order for the system to be successful, it must have a feedback component. In the case of an air conditioning system, the thermostat continually measures the output and compares it with the objective. If the output is 68 degrees, the processing unit is so informed and the heat is increased until the desired temperature is achieved. Conversely, if the output is 80 degrees, the cooling unit is activated until the temperature of the output decreases to the desired temperature.

As with most administrative concepts, the open systems approach applies to all levels in an organization. **Figure 9–1** illustrates how this concept is used in viewing the environmental sources that influence behavior at the organizational, group and individual levels. Today's administrator must have an understanding of the ways in which the accomplishment of goals and objectives depends on elements outside of the organization.

Total Quality Management (TQM) is based on an Open Systems approach that focuses on the customer and their demand for quality products and services.

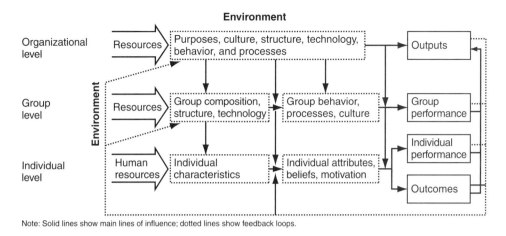

Figure 9-1 Open Systems Approach to Diagnosing Individual and Group Performance.

This approach also was the beginning of the movement toward the fifth contextual theme, Client-Oriented Service (discussed in Chapter 11). TQM encompasses:

1. Creating a constancy of purpose and commitment of purpose and commitment toward the continuous improvement of all processes, products, and services.

2. Use of systems and scientific thinking.

3. Development and use of effective leadership instead of management by control.

4. Generating an environment where people can be creative, take risks, and experience pride of workmanship, accomplishment, and self-fulfillment.

5. Creating an organization of honest and open communication, both vertical and horizontal.

6. Be customer-oriented (Greebler-Schepper, 1990, p. 7).

TQM is customer-oriented and focuses on the client as part of the Open Systems environment. It emphasizes the importance of quantitative methods as well as human resources in striving for continuous improvement in products and services. It is a good example of how one concept often promotes the beginning of a movement toward another theme.

Deming's Fourteen Points for the Transformation of Management further promoted the open systems approach in the 1980s. It is referred to here to illustrate how the Open Systems concepts, developed in the private sector, eventually moved into the public sector, then into criminal justice administration. It is a reminder that criminal justice administrators need to keep abreast of business administration trends. It is interesting to note that although W. Edwards Deming developed his concepts for American industries, they did not become widely recognized until he was invited to apply them in Japan.

Deming (along with Joseph Juran) was invited to teach statistical quality control techniques to the Japanese to help revitalize their industries following World War II. In the postwar era, "made in Japan," was a sign of cheaply made and poor quality products. Deming focused the Japanese industry on the open system's idea that it was the quality that the client wanted that was most important. Deming's attention to the environment and the customer helped Japan become a world leader in the production of many global products. Even after his death, he is still revered today in Japan, with a Deming Award given yearly to an outstanding industry in that country.

Deming's concepts revolved around 14 principles, listed here.

Deming's Fourteen Points for the Transformation of Management

1. *Create consistency of purpose toward improvement of product and service.*
2. *Adopt the new philosophy of concern for quality.*
3. *Cease dependence on mass inspection to achieve quality; build quality into the product in the first place.*
4. *End the practice of awarding business on the basis of price alone. Move toward a single supplier for any one time and build a long-term relationship of loyalty and trust.*
5. *Constantly improve the system of production and service so that quality and productivity improve and costs decrease.*
6. *Institute training on the job.*
7. *Institute leadership. The aim of supervision should be to help people and machines do a better job.*
8. *Drive out fear, so that everyone may work effectively for the company.*
9. *Break down barriers between departments so that people work as a team.*
10. *Eliminate slogans, exhortations, and targets for the work force. Such exhortations only create adversarial relationships, as the major causes of low quality and productivity can be traced to the system and thus lie beyond the power of the work force.*
11. *Eliminate work standards (quotas) and numerical goals (MBO). Instead, substitute leadership and the processes for improvement.*
12. *Remove barriers that rob workers of the right to take pride in their work, including abolishment of individual performance appraisals and annual merit or ranking systems. Instead, change the emphasis from sheer numbers to quality.*
13. *Institute a vigorous program of education and self-improvement.*
14. *Take action to accomplish the transformation. Put everybody in the organization to work on the transformation.*

Source: Adapted from Deming, W. E. (1986). *Out of the Crisis.* Cambridge, MA: MIT.

■ Open Systems and the Criminal Justice System

The Open Systems approach to a public agency was displayed in Figure 3–1. Figure 5–1 illustrated how this approach applies to a police department. Just as those figures were used to show how a private sector administrative concept can be applied to criminal justice agencies, Deming's Fourteen Principles serve here to show how they can be applied to criminal justice administration.

Quality Management's Fourteen Principles Adapted for Police Departments

1. *Develop a constant commitment toward the improvement of officer behavior and the services provided to the community, and to discovering the relationship between what the police do (outputs) and the results (outcomes) obtained.*

2. *Adopt a philosophy of management that is based on a belief in the desirability of change in order to adapt to the changing community environment in which the police function.*

3. *Change supervisory and management practices designed to monitor officers whose behavior is inappropriate and to emphasize practices that ensure that officers will not engage in such behavior before they get the opportunity to do so. In other words, prevention is more important than detection. This change requires an in-depth understanding of the organizational and environmental processes that "cause" both good and bad officer behavior.*

4. *Determine the type of department activities and officer behavior that will result in developing a long-term relationship of loyalty and trust with a substantial majority of members of the community. [The authors do not believe that it is possible for the police, by the very nature of their work, to satisfy or meet the expectations of all members of a community.]*

5. *Constantly work on police systems and processes in order to improve quality, obtain better results, and sustain a long-term relationship of loyalty and trust with the community.*

6. *Make a commitment to training of all kinds, particularly on-the-job training, to give officers the needed intellectual and technical skills and to show them exactly how to do a good job.*

7. *Emphasize leadership more than management. One purpose of leadership is to help police officers do a better job.*

8. *Work toward the elimination of fear—fear of the mistakes associated with innovation and fear of punishment for those mistakes—so that everyone can concentrate on doing a good job rather than worrying about the consequences of making a mistake. To a substantial degree this also applies to officer behavior. [The authors believe that both the organization and the community must be more forgiving of officer mistakes that are not intentionally illegal or malicious.]*

9. *Break down any barriers that exist between departmental functions (e.g., patrol and investigations) so that there will be more teamwork in problem solving.*

10. *Do not expect or exhort workers to accomplish things that cannot be accomplished because this only creates an adversarial relationship between management and workers. Often, the failure to accomplish what managers want is the result of a system failure or is related to something in the police environment, both of which are outside the control of the individual officer.*

11. *Eliminate quotas, numerical targets, and management by objectives. Instead, substitute leadership to ensure that service—in terms of quality and quantity—will be achieved. In many police departments, it is usually possible for a well-qualified, hard-working officer to accomplish more and do it better than any performance measure might determine.*

12. *Give back to the worker, supervisor, and manager the right to be proud of their work and the service they provide. The quality of the service must become more important than the number of services. The police and the community must have a clear understanding of what constitutes quality service.*

13. *Make a strong commitment to the education and improvement of each employee.*

14. *Involve everybody in the transformation of the police department because it is everyone's responsibility to ensure that total quality management is implemented.*

Source: Adapted from Deming, W. E. (1986). *Out of the Crisis.* Cambridge, MA: MIT.

Today, the goals (or missions) of a criminal justice agency are established in relationship to an agency's environment, particularly the needs of the public. For example, a parole agency's goal may be to return those that have been imprisoned to society as law-abiding citizens. An objective (previously defined as a commitment that is time-bound and quantifiable) of a given unit of parole officers might then be to improve their service by reducing recidivism by a certain percentage during the coming year. Parole administrators can then establish a feedback system that allows them to measure parolees who are rearrested as a means of control.

A "Big Y, little x" parole administrator would place major efforts on motivating employees to achieve this objective. However, they would not wait until the year is up to measure whether the objective was met. They would establish feedback that allows them to know about their employees' progress. If feedback discloses that progress is not being made toward the objective, the administrator would find out why. In this example, perhaps internal factors such as high caseload assignments are at fault. Maybe external conditions such as lack of employment or education opportunity for parolees are factors. An Open Systems outlook might then cause the administrator to generate efforts outside the agency such as pursuing an increase in tax revenue. Some criminal justice agencies have a history of acting as a closed system. For example, according to Jim L. Munro, "many correctional organizations have such a history" (Munro, 1977, p.

621). This limits the organizations' outlook to only the structural boundaries of the official organization. Closed systems institutions experience communication difficulties with the outside world and often limit the information they provide other agencies and the public. Historically, this has contributed to political alienation and fragmentation of services (Munro, p. 631).

Progressive corrections administrators now recognize that their agencies must interact with other criminal justice agencies as well as society in general. They realized that their goals are related to political, social, and economic conditions. For example, the proposed closing of a prison may be caused by reduced government funds. However, it also might be politically resisted because the local economy could depend on the prison remaining open.

Today's conditions call for a more "nonrational system" approach, which means that criminal justice administrators must recognize that they exist in an unpredictable environment and that organizations have to be more open to surrounding conditions.

Because state judges, prosecutors, and public defenders often are elected, they need to be responsive to the public they serve. For example, the police may feel they have enough evidence to convict an arrestee and request a court trail. However, prosecutors may feel the evidence is not strong enough to guarantee a conviction and refuse to file a complaint fearing that losing a case may impact them politically.

Viewing all of the components of the criminal justice systems as interrelated is significant. Police, court, and corrections administrators must understand how the other components contribute to and conflict with each agency's success. **Figure 9–2** provides an overview of the interconnection of each component as their mutual "clients" are moved through the system. Therefore, each agency can be considered a subsystem within the overall criminal justice system. This view assumes that the various parts work together by design to achieve the overall mission of the social product that we call *justice*. This perspective has been called the **consensus model** and envisions all the component parts striving toward the common goal by harmoniously moving cases and people through the system. In reality, this is not a reality!

The **conflict process model** takes the opposite view. It views the component parts functioning primarily to serve their own interest. This theoretical perspective sees justice more as a product of conflicts among agencies that ultimately serves to protect individual rights. The responsibility of the criminal justice system to keep a balance between public safety and individual rights will be explored in Chapter 10. Here, we can compare the consensus model as focusing mainly on public safety, whereas the conflict model is more concerned with individual rights.

Herbert Packer (1968) referred to these opposing views of the criminal justice system with slightly different terms. One he called the **crime-control model**, which emphasizes the efficient arrest and conviction of offenders. The other he called the **due process model**, which places the emphasis on individual rights.

An Open Systems perspective allows the administrator to realize that, although desirable, a "steady state" is often not obtainable. Support for community

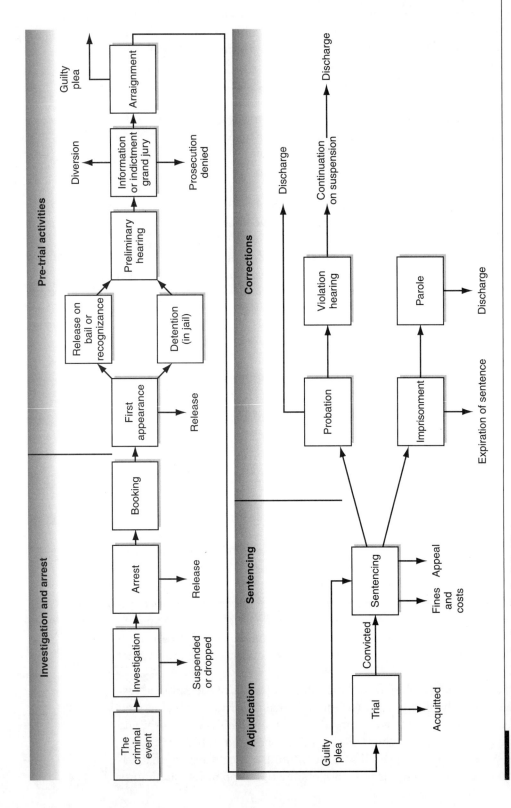

Figure 9–2 The Criminal Justice System in the United States.

safety versus individual rights can shift from one extreme to the other. These shifts impact who gets elected and the elected officials who are appointed to criminal justice positions. Those elected and appointed can further affect this balance. Successful criminal justice administrators keep abreast of these shifts and take appropriate actions to compensate for those shifts that may impact the goals of their agencies. Appropriate actions might mean having to alter goals or mount a campaign to change public opinion.

Figure 9–3 provides a perspective of the common progress, or lack of progress, of arrestees through the criminal justice system. Starting with 100 arrests by the police, on an average, only 20 adults are imprisoned. This graphically illustrates how the consensus and conflict actions of the various agencies can impact the overall results. Even though criminal justice agencies have a diversity of functions (police, courts, and corrections), and serve at various levels (local, state, and federal), they are linked by laws and procedures so as to be considered a system. The police are most concerned with arrest and conviction. The courts are concerned with ensuring that guilt is proven beyond a reasonable double and that the rights of defendants are protected. Corrections is most concerned with carrying out the court-ordered punishment and providing corrective measures that reduce recidivism.

The author, as a police administrator, oversaw a large drug arrest operation. Over a 6-month period, more than 7,000 arrests were made. What was not considered was the impact that a large number of arrests would have on the prosecutors, public defenders, and courts. The outcome was an overloading of the systems. This resulted in many arrestees being released without prosecution because the system could not accommodate the volume within the required constitutional time limits.

Members of the court system often are accused by "crime control" advocates of being "too soft on criminals," when the real cause may be lack of public funds necessary to support full prosecution of criminals. Surveys have found that 90% of all criminal cases prepared for trial are eventually resolved through plea bargaining (Bureau of Justice Statistics, 2003). Public safety advocates often point to this fact as evidence that criminals are not getting the sentences they deserve. In reality, even if no more than half the cases were plea negotiated, the system would "crash" because of the volume of cases that would go to trial.

Corrections administrators also often find themselves confronted with opposing public and political views regarding individual rights and public safety. For example, mandatory and "three strikes and you're out" sentencing legislation may require maximum-length sentences for offenders. At the same time, individual rights advocates may be filing civil action for overcrowded prison conditions.

Jim Collins stated, "Most people in the social sector face some very serious systemic constraints. They may face limits in funding and constraints on their decisions. As a result, if you're in the social sector, you have to deal with what are sometimes really oppressive constraints. The ability to confront the constraints is what's critical. If we ignore the restraints—try to pretend that they are not there—it's like a rock climber who's trying to pretend that gravity isn't there.

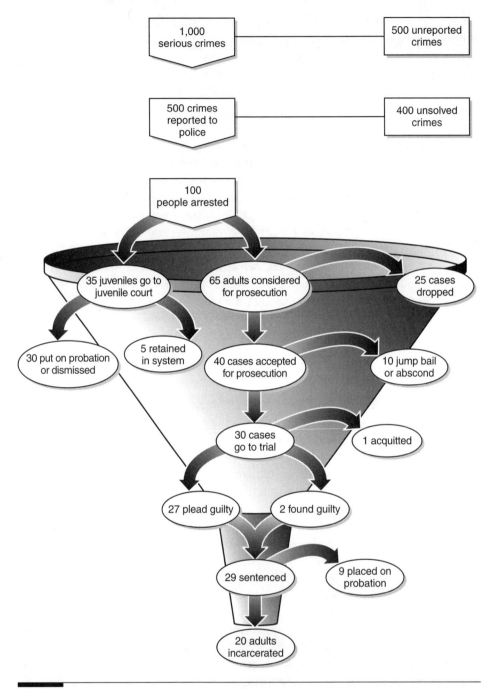

Figure 9-3 The Criminal Justice "Funnel."

But on the other hand, if you say that gravity will prevent you from making any progress, that's equally debilitating" (2006, p. 3).

The truth is that public taxes do not provide for a justice system that can fully handle today's crime volume. There are some things criminal justice administrations just have to accept and make the best of what they have. Otherwise, they will need to promote public support for additional funding.

■ Open Systems Concepts and Establishing Justice and Insuring Domestic Tranquility

The Preamble of the United States Constitution reads:

> *We the People of the United States, in order to form a more perfect union, establish justice, insure domestic tranquility, provide for the common defense, promote the general welfare, and secure the blessings of liberty to ourselves and our posterity, do ordain and establish this Constitution for the United States of America.*

As will be discussed in the next chapter, various governmental agencies are given police power to ensure these conditions. The criminal justice system is given the responsibility to "establish justice" and "ensure domestic tranquility." Within the open systems view, it is important that criminal justice administrators realized that the fulfillment of these overall responsibilities requires coordination between criminal justice agencies. It also involves coordination with, and enlisting the aid of, many "outside" agencies. The obtainment of these constitutional prescribed conditions should be the goal of all the components of the criminal justice system. The achievement of these conditions requires an open systems approach within the criminal justice system; that is, cooperation between the subsystems.

Here, crime prevention, coordination with private police, reducing crime committed by juveniles, and professional treatment programs are discussed as examples of open systems approaches in achieving these conditions. Open systems, or "thinking outside the box," enables criminal justice administrators to look for ways to achieve goals by involving resources outside their organization.

■ Crime Prevention as an Open Systems Approach

Criminal justice administrators often give crime prevention a low priority. A common tendency in contending with budget cuts is to reduce crime prevention assignments so as to increase "crime fighting" resources. The reduction or elimination of crime prevention staff is often considered an appropriate economical measure. A more productive approach, however, may be to use crime prevention approaches as leverage in making the best use of available personnel. A few crime prevention staff involved in an effective crime prevention program can prevent crimes that would require the work of many personnel.

Alfonso Lenhardt, Chief Executive Officer of the National Crime Prevention Council points to the "$428 billion yearly cost of crime" and the importance of prevention in his article titled "The Economics of Prevention: Reducing Cost and

Crime." He states that prevention does indeed save money and recommends that criminal justice administrators document the cost-benefit ratio of crime prevention efforts and use these facts in building community and government support for prevention programs that work (Lenhardt, 2006).

In meeting contemporary challenges, progressive criminal justice administrators are finding that crime prevention efforts are most effectively applied through an open systems approach that involves resources outside of their agencies. Examples of such approaches are:

- Involving the media to convey crime prevention suggestions to the public.
- Preventing victims from becoming victims again.
- Crime prevention specialist programs composed of volunteer citizens.
- Local legislation and review of building permits to ensure that new construction includes building designs that prevent crime.

Enlisting the aid of the news media in providing crime prevention tips can be a productive effort. Even a large crime prevention staff can contact only a small percentage of the public. Television, radio, newspapers, and the Internet, however, communicate daily with a very large segment of the population. By using the media, criminal justice administrators can capitalize on the concept of personnel leverage (obtaining a comparatively large result through a process that multiplies the efforts of a small number of employees).

Many crimes can be prevented by simply informing the public of how to prevent them. For example, most burglaries involve unlocked dwellings. If the public could be reminded of this through the media, a great many crimes could be prevented.

Radio and television stations are required by the Federal Communications Commission (FCC) to provide a certain amount of listening and viewing time for public service announcements. Criminal justice administrators can make use of this time for crime prevention purposes.

Another idea is to obtain the services of noted celebrities in making media prevention messages. Many well-known personalities are willing to volunteer their services. The idea is to make these messages "grab" the interest of the listener or viewer long enough to get the crime prevention message across.

Preventing crime victims from becoming victims again can be another useful approach. Patrol officers are often thought of as crime fighters whose main function is to apprehend criminals. However, most research shows that patrol officers seldom encounter crimes in progress (Biech & Kessler, 1977, pp. 25–77; Kelling & Pate, 1980). As an undercover police officer, the author can remember seeing how many crimes went on in the presence of a passing patrol car. Traditionally, patrol officers have not considered crime prevention an important part of their jobs. However, if police officers are not very successful at catching criminals in the act, shouldn't crime prevention be a part of their efforts to reduce crime?

Realistically, most people are not concerned with crime prevention techniques until they become the victim of crime. What member of the criminal justice system is most often first to come in contact with the victim? The patrol officer responding to the victim's reporting of a crime is the person who usually makes first contact. Often, the patrol officer just takes a report and goes on to the next call-for-service. However, an Open Systems approach would be to have patrol officers take time to help victims from becoming victims again by suggesting related crime prevention approaches. For example, for the victim of a burglary, suggestions about deadbolt locks, increased outdoor lighting, and removal of shrubbery that could hide intruders would be appropriate. At the same time as the officer is providing useful crime prevention information, he or she is building citizen-police trust. Police administrators should consider that the extra time the officer spends with the victim can ultimately result in less crime and more public support.

Establishing a Crime Prevention Specialist Volunteer Program is another way to use "outside" resources. Innovative criminal justice administrators have found that by enlisting the aid of specially trained volunteers, crime prevention efforts can be expanded without reducing the number of officers on patrol. The growing number of senior citizens who want to get involved in meaningfully activities should be considered as likely volunteers. The author, as a police administrator, was involved in such a program that recruited more than 600 such volunteers in the Los Angeles area.

The media can be of assistance in recruiting volunteers. Screening of applicants is necessary to ensure that reliable people are selected. Training and coordination can be provided by regular crime prevention specialists. The Los Angeles Police Department has made some of the volunteers "Reserve Officer Specialist," a special reserve officer classification requiring much less training than regular reserve officers who perform patrol duties. Volunteer crime prevention specialist can:

- Conduct crime prevention meetings as part of Neighborhood Watch programs.
- Conduct Operation Identification Programs that assists residents in marking property for later identification if stolen.
- Conduct security surveys of residences.
- Distribute crime prevention information.

This is an example of the way in which people outside the formal organization can be used to help achieve agency goals.

Fostering crime prevention through legislation and review of building permits is yet another useful method of crime prevention. By enacting local ordinances that require "target hardening" construction in residential and business structures, the opportunity for crime to occur can be reduced. Such requirements as deadbolt locks, entry doors equipped with viewers so occupants can see who is outside, and windows and sliding doors equipped with special locks are just a few requirements that can prevent many illegal entries. Additionally, arrangements should be made for building permits to be reviewed by crime prevention personnel to ensure proper construction that will prevent crime. Another idea is to encourage insurance companies to give reduced rates on structures that have built-in crime prevention construction. Gaining the public's assistance in preventing crime should be a component of the eclectic perspective criminal administrator's approach to reducing crime. The news media, volunteers, the police officers on the beat and legislation are effective Open Systems tools in meeting contemporary challenges.

Another approach, called the **Crime Triangle**, involves viewing a crime problem as three elements: victim, offender, and location/opportunity (Bureau of Justice Assistance, 1993, p. 3). Viewing a crime in this manner provides a better understanding of the relationship between these elements, suggests where more information is needed, and what approach may be most practical. Usually, the three elements must be present before a crime can occur: an offender (someone who is motivated to commit the crime), a victim (a desirable and vulnerable target must be present), and a location (the victim and offender must both be in the same place at the same time). By removing one or more of these elements, the crime may be prevented.

■ Coordination with Private Police as an Open Systems Approach

Private security personnel often are overlooked by law enforcement in establishing crime prevention programs. From an open systems approach, however, the private police can be a valuable extension of public police resources. **Figure 9–4** shows how there are more than twice as many private security personnel as there are public law enforcement officers. The author, having been a private security director, saw how most private businesses of any size developed or are developing their own private security. A growing number of private business executives are of the opinion that the public police cannot provide adequate service. Consequently, many develop their own security forces.

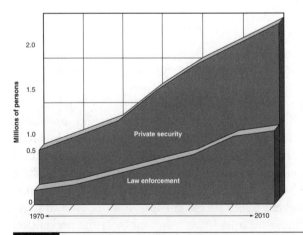

Figure 9–4 Comparison of the Number of Private versus Public Police.

Law enforcement administrators would be wise to promote coordination between patrol officers and security officers. Security officers should be considered as resources that can extend the efforts of the public police. Many police departments enlist the aid of citizens through neighborhood watch programs. Why not do the same with private security personnel? Security officers can be trained to make crime and arrest reports relating to incidents in the businesses where they are employed, thus saving a patrol officer's time. They can be alerted to criminals operating in the area and act as additional "eyes and ears" for the public police. Many calls-for-service to the public police can be handled by properly trained security officers, thereby providing more available time for patrol officers.

When a new business, manufacturing plant, entertainment theme park, or other enterprise is introduced into a municipality, are more public police funded to handle the increase in policing demands? Seldom, if ever! Open Systems police administrators should work to get local legislation that requires an appropriate number of security officers to be hired by new businesses. An additional requirement should be that the concerned police department be involved in the selection and training of the private security personnel.

Figure 9–5 shows the general responsibilities of the author as a private security director. These responsibilities can provide insight into the scope of private police activities that coincide with the public police. For example, "Electronic Date Security" is a growing private security specialty that public criminal investigators can make use of in their investigation of computer crimes. Developing strong ties with local security agencies should be a part of the open systems criminal justice administrators approach to accomplishing their public responsibilities.

Figure 9–5 Typical Private Security Responsibilities.

■ Reducing Youth Crime as an Open Systems Approach

The author, as a criminal justice administrator responsible for a police juvenile division, conducted research on the common causes of juvenile crime. Most juvenile delinquents were found to be subject to one or more of the following factors:

- No one at home when they came home from school
- No central interest in life and a feeling of disenfranchisement with society
- A contributing mental, physical, or physiological ailment
- A failure of the juvenile justice system to take appropriate action to prevent continuing delinquency

A closed systems reaction would probably be "all these factors are beyond the control of the inter-workings of a police agency." An Open Systems approach ("thinking outside the box"), however, would include the realization that in achieving the goal of domestic tranquility, juvenile delinquency is of prime importance and outside assistance may be required. **Figure 9–6** charts the action (or

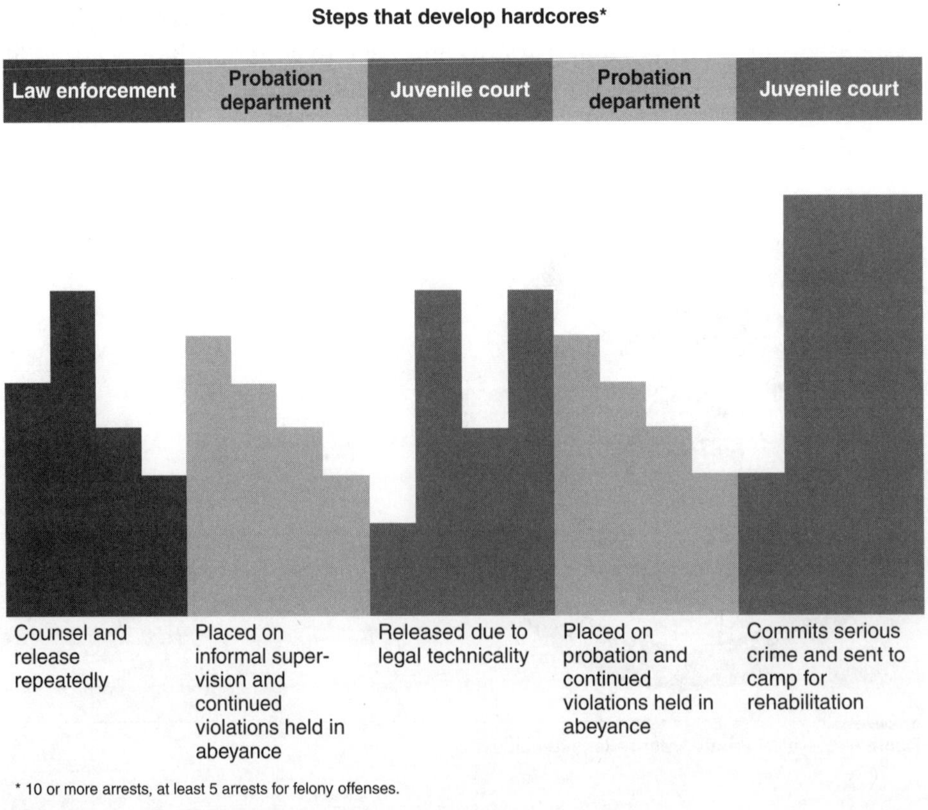

Steps that develop hardcores*

Law enforcement	Probation department	Juvenile court	Probation department	Juvenile court

| Counsel and release repeatedly | Placed on informal supervision and continued violations held in abeyance | Released due to legal technicality | Placed on probation and continued violations held in abeyance | Commits serious crime and sent to camp for rehabilitation |

* 10 or more arrests, at least 5 arrests for felony offenses.

Figure 9–6 Juvenile Justice System Inactions.

rather inaction) of the juvenile justice system with "hard core" juvenile offenders. The author first constructed this chart in the 1970s. Recent research in several metropolitan cities finds that the chart is still accurate and that these juveniles grow up to be habitual criminals (*Chicago Tribune*, 2006, p. 3).

In Figure 9–6, each arrest of an average offender is displayed as a step, from left to right. The progression from the juvenile's first arrest to his/her 10th or 20th should have been an uphill climb (many of those studied had more than 30 or more arrests). There should have been a number of positive actions that would have deterred or prevented the youth from continuing their delinquency. As depicted in the chart, this was not the case.

The child's first arrest was a positive step, but when "counseled and released" several times, they began to learn that no action would be taken against them for their acts. The term "counsel and release" is used by law enforcement to describe the process of talking to the juvenile and their parents for usually less than a half-hour with the hope of preventing continued delinquent behavior. This process can be successful with beginning minor offenders, but to repeat the process on subsequent arrests only reinforces what the child had often learned at home and in school—no real action is taken when they committed delinquent acts.

After several arrests, the police would file an application for petition with the probation department, hoping that this would result in stronger action. The probation department would then proceed to place the young offender in an "informal supervision" status, often with an overworked probation officer who could not provide any real supervision. In many cases, the youth would be arrested three and four more times while under "informal supervision" and then sent on to juvenile court, again in hopes of some positive action.

Juvenile court, also overloaded, would set up another "counseling and informal supervision process." Finally, when the then "hardcore" juveniles committed the big crime, the court would sentence them to a detention facility for "rehabilitation." The truth of the matter was that it was too late for rehabilitation. The "system" had waited too long. Most state youth authority and probation departments have good programs but they are ineffective with the hardcore offenders who are often sent to them. Their programs have been developed to handle young people much less set in their delinquency.

As stated previously, open systems administrators must realize that the criminal justice system will probably never be properly financially supported and will always be overloaded. Overloaded or not, the responsibilities to reduce and prevent crime remains the same. Realizing this, a program shown in **Figure 9–7** should be implemented. A coordinated approach should be developed in which all the components of the juvenile justice systems work together to attack the common causes of juvenile delinquency at the earliest point of contact. Realizing that the best chance for reducing delinquency is with beginning offenders, the police should institute policies to restrict "counseling and releasing" and require juvenile officers to take positive steps for first-time arrestees.

For example, to help with the "no one at home when they came home from school" issues, the police may instigate a "big brother and sister" program. They might enlist the aid of the local fire departments to become part of the program.

Steps to prevent hardcores*

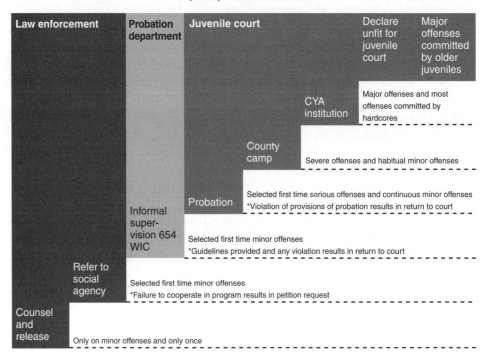

| Law enforcement | Probation department | Juvenile court | | Declare unfit for juvenile court | Major offenses committed by older juveniles |

CYA institution — Major offenses and most offenses committed by hardcores

County camp — Severe offenses and habitual minor offenses

Probation — Selected first time serious offenses and continuous minor offenses
*Violation of provisions of probation results in return to court

Informal supervision 654 WIC — Selected first time minor offenses
*Guidelines provided and any violation results in return to court

Refer to social agency — Selected first time minor offenses
*Failure to cooperate in program results in petition request

Counsel and release — Only on minor offenses and only once

* 10 or more arrests, at least 5 arrests for felony offenses

Figure 9–7 Juvenile Justice System Positive Actions.

In Los Angeles, first-time offenders were assigned to report to a local fire station after school where a fireman or firewoman became their "big brother or sister."

"Counsel and release" and "informal supervision" should be replaced with the juvenile offender and their parents selecting a community program of interest. Arrangements should then be made that assured that the juvenile will become actively involved in the selected program. The youth and their parents should be required to periodically report back for assessment to the police, probation or court officer who establishes these requirements. If there are indications that positive progress is not being made, then the youth can be sent to the next step in the system. Additionally, the assistance of the medical and psychological professionals should be enlisted to provide treatment for those in need.

The Federal Office of Juvenile Justice and Delinquency Prevention has announced that a proper juvenile justice system for the 21st century must ensure that effective juvenile justice interventions are swift, certain, consistent, and appropriate. To meet these objectives, an effective juvenile justice system must:

- Include a mechanism for comprehensively assessing a juvenile when he or she enters the system, in order to determine both the risk to the community and appropriate interventions and sanctions.
- Have the capacity to provide a range of treatment services, from family counseling to outpatient drug treatment to out-of-home care.

- Incorporate increasingly severe sanctions and enhanced treatment services when a juvenile fails to respond to interventions (Office of Juvenile Justice and Delinquency Prevention, 2000).

■ Biochemistry, Nutrition, and Genetic Factors in Reducing Crime as an Open Systems Approach

In Chapter 6, the historical support for and the support against rehabilitation of criminals was discussed. Support for genetic and psychological causes of crime was popular for periods in the past. However, in recent times, "warehousing" and "just deserts" for criminals has been the theme of the criminal justice system. With current (and hopefully future) advancements in **biochemistry**, **genetics**, and **nutrition**, it may be time for criminal justice administrators to consider a more open systems view of these fields.

As mentioned in the previous discussion of youthful offenders, one of the factors common to delinquents is "contributing mental, physical or physiological ailments." Research also has found evidence of these conditions in adult offenders. Therefore, any manner of treating ailments that may reduce crime should be of interest to Open Systems criminal justice administrators. The police should be alert to these conditions and see that treatment is provided at the earliest possible point of contact. The courts should consider treatment as part of probation and parole. Corrections, perhaps, has the best opportunity to apply appropriate treatment as they deal with a "captive audience." Treatment may have to be voluntary for inmates, but early release rewards may be a viable incentive.

Research into factors that may contribute to criminal behavior reveals some promising results, suggesting that treatment for biochemical and genetic deficiencies could be an effective approach to controlling criminal behavior. A number of research findings are included here as most criminal justice administrators are seldom provided with such information. Hopefully, some of these findings will promote more criminal justice administrators to see this approach as yet another approach of facilitating their goals. Even if criminal justice administrators do not become directly involved in the treatment approach, they can be instrumental in promoting additional efforts in this area.

Vitamin deficiencies have been linked to delinquent behavior. It has been found that disruptive children consume insufficient levels of vitamins B3 and B6 than do nonproblem youths (Hoffer, 1975, p. 229). Adding these vitamins to the deficient diets of children reduces unruly behavior and improves school performances.

Allergic reactions to common foods are reported as a cause of violent behavior in some cases. Foods such as citrus fruit, milk, chocolate, corn, eggs, and wheat produce allergic reactions in sensitive individuals, leading to a swelling of the brain. Such allergies can reduce the functioning of the learning process during childhood, and may contribute to delinquency. Brain swelling also can impede the higher faculties and reduce the sense of morality and contribute to impulsive behavior (Hoffer, 1975, p. 8). Food additives, such as monosodium glutamate (a flavor enhancer), artificial flavorings and dyes are hypothesized to be related to violent behavior (Schauss, 1980, p. 72).

A number of scientists believe that a neurotransmitted serotonin is important in controlling impulses. They have found that abnormal levels of serotonin caused an inability to control desires and lead to aggression and violence (Touchette, 1994; Unis, 1997; New, 1997; Moffitt, 1998).

Dr. Forest Tennant (1992) has conducted extensive research into the relationship between self-esteem and biochemical balance. People with high self-esteem have a better level of serotonin, a phenolicamine neurotransmitter found in the brain, blood serum, and gastric mucosa. Tenant states that people are more motivated when their serotonin function is stimulated. He also suggests that children with abnormal levels of serotonin are more inclined to take drugs and become gang members. Among those who used illegal drugs such as heroin and cocaine, an abnormal change in serotonin level was found. This causes the brain to recognize some drugs as a replacement for serotonin, causing the body to cease manufacturing serotonin and this becomes an important factor in addiction.

Dr. Paul Boccumini (1992) provided clinical evidence that linked nutritional and neurochemical deficiencies to juvenile alcohol and drug use. He focused on the relationship of nutrition/diet, on allergic responses, and on heavy metals intake to deviate behavior. These diet deficiencies result in "self-medication" through the use of drugs and alcohol, which deadens and inhibits the neurochemical/neurotransmitters. A balanced diet enriched with a vitamin/mineral supplement can bring body chemistry back into balance, thereby reducing deviate behavior according to Boccumini.

Studies indicate that up to 75% of young offenders have some sort of learning disability. In 1991, males represented 80–90% of the cases that came to the attention of the youth justice system in the United States. Boys with severe learning disabilities were more than twice as likely to engage in delinquent activities as boys not so affected (Henteleff, 1998).

Ellis and Walsh (1997) provide a summary of gene research and criminal behavior. They point out that explanations for criminal behavior are likely to involve complex interactions between learning and genetic, hormonal, and neurochemical factors. They state that evolutionary theories of criminal behavior propose that people vary in their genetic dispositions toward criminality and that it does appear that genes contribute to variations in criminal behavior.

It is not being suggested here that these research findings be used to mitigate criminal sentences but rather as approaches to prevention recidivism. Certainly, they should be considered as a part of the open systems approach to preventing and reducing crime.

■ Coordinating Community Interaction as an Open Systems Approach

The Related Publication at the end of this chapter describes another Open Systems approach that criminal justice administrators should consider. The **community partnership approach** discussed here involves not only the neighborhood members but also other elements of a criminal justices agency's environment. The publication outlines how criminal justice administrators, elected officials, academicians, and concerned citizens may be united in a partnership that can result in enhancing community quality of life (domestic tranquility) and reducing crime. In this example, committee members meet periodically and use a set of 22 "Community Wellness Indicators" to assess crime and quality of life issues in their community. When an assessment indicates the development of a possible problem, a task force is created to find solutions. These task forces recommended solutions that can be implemented by the committee to counteract situations before they become major problems.

At the end of the 20th century and the beginning of the 21st century, crime rates began to decrease. The economy, changing demographics, public demand to "get hard on crime," and many other factors are thought to have contributed to this decline. Some think these factors are outside the purview of a criminal justice agency. However, if criminal justice administrators are to see this decline continue, they must support the efforts of those who are having a positive impact on these factors.

Wrap Up

KEY CONCEPTS AND TERMS

- Principles of Open Systems
  - Homeostasis
  - Negative entropy
  - Requisite variety
  - Equifinality
  - System evolution
- Example of Open Systems concepts
  - Nonrational open systems view can be related to the organic organization and the "rational" closed systems with the mechanistic organization
  - Total Quality Management (TQM)
  - Deming's Fourteen Points for the Transformation of Management
  - Consensus Model versus Conflict Process Model
  - Crime-Control Model versus Due Process Model
- Constitution requirement to "establish justice and ensure domestic tranquility" requires an Open Systems approach
- Crime prevention as an Open Systems approach
  - Media to convey crime prevention suggestions to the public
  - Preventing victim from becoming victim again
  - A crime prevention specialist program composed of volunteer citizens
  - Local legislation and review of building permits to ensure that new construction includes building designs that prevent crime
  - Crime Triangle
- Other Open Systems approaches
  - Coordination with private police
  - Reducing youth crime
  - Biochemistry, nutrition, and genetic factors in reducing crime
  - Coordinating community efforts

CHAPTER ACTIVITY

Interview an employee in the criminal justice system. Ask them what entities outside of their organization they have to consider and coordinate with when performing their duties.

REVIEW QUESTIONS

1. Early in this chapter, it was stated that "all things might be considered as Open Systems." The traditional air conditioning systems was given as an example of the concepts of input, processing, output, and feedback. Can you think of other examples?

2. Describe how the conflict and consensus models discussed in this chapter apply to viewing criminal justice as a system.

3. In this chapter, lack of adequate public financing for the criminal justice system was discussed as a factor in criminal justice administrators not being able to achieve their goals. Do you think that this situation will change in the future?

4. Crime prevention, juvenile justice approaches, research into biochemical links to crime, and community outreach programs were discussed as *Open Systems* concepts to be considered by criminal justice administrators. Can you think of others?

5. Imagine that you are a criminal justice administrator and have been assigned to develop and implement a criminal justice entity of your choice (for example, a Crime Prevention Program). What Open Systems concepts would you consider in fulfilling this assignment?

REFERENCES

Barnard, C. (1938). *The Functions of the Executive*. Cambridge, MA: Harvard University Press.

Biech, W., & Kessler, D. (1977). *Response Time Analysis*. Washington, DC: Police Executive Research Forum.

Boccumini, P. (1992). The Relationship of Diet/Nutrition Metal Toxicity to Juvenile Substance Abuse. *Effective Prevention and Intervention Approaches for Youth Substance Abuse*. Los Angeles, Center for the Administration of Justice, University of Southern California Publication.

Bureau of Justice Assistance. (1993). *Comprehensive Gang Initiative: Operations Manual for Implementing Local Gang Prevention and Control Programs*. Washington, DC: U.S. Department of Justice.

Bureau of Justice Statistics. (2003). *The Prosecution of Felony Arrest*. Washington, DC: U.S. Government Printing Office.

Cronkhite, C. (2005). Fostering Community Partnerships that Prevent Crime and Promote Quality of Life. *FBI Law Enforcement Bulletin*, May, pp. 7–10.

Ellis, L., & Walsh, A. (1997). Gene-Based Evolutionary Theories in Criminology. *Criminology*, 25, pp. 229–261.

Greebler-Schepper, C. (1990). *Total Quality Management: The Road to Continuous Improvement*. Lucerne, CA: TQM Plus.

Henteleff, J. (1998). Special Needs Children and the Youth Justice System. *Crime Times*, 4, p. 3.

Hoffer, A. (1975). The Relation of Crime to Nutrition. *Humanist in Canada*, July, p. 8.

Hoffer, A. (1978). Children with Learning and Behavior Disorders. *Journal of Orthomolecular Psychiatry*, January, pp. 35–39.

Katz, D., & Kahn, R. L. (1966). *The Social Psychology of Organizations*. New York: Wiley.

Kelling, G., & Pate, A. (1980). *The Kansas City Preventative Patrol Experiment: A Summary Report*. Washington, DC: Police Foundation.

Lenhardt, A. E. (2006). The Economics of Prevention: Reducing Costs and Crime. *The Police Chief: The Professional Voice of Law Enforcement*. Washington, DC: The Official Publication of the International Association of Chiefs of Police, Inc. July, pp. 1–13.

Moffitt, T. (1998). Whole Blood Serotonin Relates to Violence in an Epidemiological Study. *Biological Psychiatry*, 43, pp. 465–447.

Morgan, G. (1997). *Images of Organization* (2nd ed.). Thousand Oaks, CA: Sage.

Munro, J. L. (1977). Towards a Theory of Criminal Justice Administration: A General Systems Perspective. *Public Administration Review*, November/December, pp. 621–631.

New, A. S. (1997). *Psychiatry Research*, 69, pp. 17–26.

Office of Juvenile Justice and Delinquency Prevention. (2000). *Juvenile Justice in the 21st Century*. Washington, D.C.: Department of Justice.

Packer, H. (1968). *The Limits of Criminal Sanction*. Stanford, CA: Stanford University Press.

Roberg, R. R., Kuykendall, J., & Novak, K. (2001). *Police Management*. Los Angeles: Roxbury.

Schauss, A. (1980). *Diet, Crime & Delinquency*. Berkeley, CA: Parker House.

Tennant, F. (1992). Identifying the Teenage Drug User: Essence of Prevention. *Effective Prevention and Intervention Approaches for Youth Substance Abuse*. Los Angeles: Center for the Administration of Justice, University of Southern California Publication.

Touchette, N. (1994). Key Factors in Violent Behavior. *Journal of NIH Research*, February, p. 7.

Unis, A. S., Cook, J. H., Vincent, D. K., Gjerde, B., & Perry, B. D. (1997). Neurotransmitted Serotonin and Abnormal Impulses. *Biological Psychiatry*, 42, pp. 553–559.

Wrap Up

■ RELEVANT PUBLICATION

This publication is a prime example of an Open Systems project that unites the public with criminal justice agencies as well as other professionals in a common goal of providing "domestic tranquility" and the reduction of crime. (Cronkhite, C. (2005). "Fostering Community Partnerships That Prevent Crime and Promote Quality of Life." *FBI Law Enforcement Bulletin*, May, pp. 7–10.)

"Fostering Community Partnerships That Prevent Crime and Promote Quality of Life" by Clyde Cronkhite

During the past decade, crime has decreased in urban areas, but, subsequently, some rural communities have experienced an increase because offenders have been forced away from large cities.[1] This trend threatens the quality of life in many suburban and rural areas. Therefore, a growing number of townships are taking a proactive posture against this movement by focusing on community-based crime prevention programs, which unite communities in the fight to thwart the spread of crime.

The Challenge

McDonough County, Illinois, is in the western part of the state with a population of approximately 40,000 and includes Macomb, a university town of 20,000 residents plus 12,000 college students.

Although Macomb offers a family friendly atmosphere with a low crime rate, harbingers of gang and drug activities surfaced, perhaps from an influx of individuals seeking a haven from the increased law enforcement efforts in larger cities. Drug arrests began to occur and evidence of graffiti appeared. Therefore, citizens of Macomb decided to handle these problems by drawing from their community-based, crime prevention program experiences. Macomb's results may serve as a model for other cities confronting similar trends.

The Concept

Many of today's crime prevention approaches are based on an experiment conducted in a New Jersey community years ago, which spotlighted the importance of maintaining neighborhoods to keep communities relatively

---

[1] Dr. Michael Hazlett, Western Illinois University, Department of Law Enforcement and Justice Administration, "Community Quality of Life 1993–1994," *Community Wellness Factor Report*.

crime free.[2] The broken windows theory holds that such issues as street maintenance and lighting, limits on the number of families living in a single dwelling, and control of absentee landlord rentals reduce crime. Additionally, attention to minor infractions that erode well-kept, safe environments, such as loud music, abandoned cars, and graffiti, can prevent the spread of gang violence, drug abuse, and other criminal conduct. Macomb applied the broken windows concept in a rural environment by forming community partnerships that result in a continuous focus on quality-of-life issues.

The Approach

In early 1994, Macomb formed a Crime and Quality of Life Advisory Committee, changing the name in 1996 to Community Quality of Life Committee and expanding the purview to include all of McDonough County. The committee seeks "to support efforts that contribute to the excellence of our community and to monitor and give advice regarding maintaining and enhancing community quality of life, including the prevention and reduction of crimes that adversely impact our neighborhoods."[3]

Community Wellness Indicators

- Population size, density, age, ethnicity, and education
- Single parent families
- Births by mothers under 18 years of age
- Poverty, welfare, unemployment, and rental and unoccupied property rates
- Per capita income
- Retail and wholesale sales
- Property tax assessment
- Tax revenues
- Ratio of police officers and firefighters per 1,000 residents
- Index crimes
- Arrest index
- Traffic accidents
- Emergency room admissions
- Calls for emergency services
- Reports of school confrontation and truancy

---

[2] For more information on this topic, see Frank Perry, "Repairing Broken Windows: Preventing Corruption Within Our Ranks," *FBI Law Enforcement Bulletin*, February 2001, 23–26; and J.Q. Wilson and G. Kelling, "The Police and Neighborhood Safety: Broken Windows," *The Atlantic Monthly*, March 1982, 29–38.

[3] The mission statement is restated in the minutes of the first Crime and Quality of Life Advisory Committee (CQLAC) meeting each year. These minutes are kept by the current CQLAC chair, Mr. Bill Jacob, Executive Director, McDonough County Housing Authority, 322 West Piper Street, Macomb, Illinois 61455.

The committee recruited concerned citizens who have a responsibility for quality of life and criminal justice academicians from the local university, as well as other community leaders. Several committee members, such as the fire chief, sheriff, mayor, school superintendent, executive director of the housing authority, and the local state senator, were selected because their positions have the responsibility and authority to provide a prospering neighborhood.

The major responsibility of the advisory committee involves developing a method for measuring the quality of life in the community, setting a baseline, and monitoring its status. To complete this task, a criminal justice research specialist (a member of the committee) and graduate assistants from the local university's department of law enforcement and justice administration analyzed 26 years of crime trends in Macomb and McDonough County, comparing them with eight contiguous counties and totals for the state of Illinois. They selected "community wellness" indicators (e.g., poverty and welfare rates, per capita income, single parent families, births by mothers under 18 years of age, truancy violations, and emergency room admissions) from their research.

The committee meets at least four times a year, and members review these indicators. Then, they publish a community "report card" or "wellness report." Any indication that the community is adversely affected requires recommendations for combating the negative factors before they become substantial problems.

As a result of the crime trend analysis, committee members noted early signs of substance abuse and gang involvement in the crime trends. As a result, the committee formed a youth task force that meets monthly. The task force determines the extent of the problem, confirms what is being done about the issue, recognizes any unnecessary duplication of services, decides the need for additional action and what it should be, and recommends steps that advisory committee members should take.

The school superintendent and a local religious leader oversee the youth task force. Several of the advisory committee members, such as the police chief and director of the housing authority, serve on the task force as well. Additionally, persons who deal daily with youth problems comprise part of the task force, along with an individual from the university who is an expert in substance abuse problems.

Task force members have made several recommendations, such as school dress codes, truancy enforcement, a youth teen center, and ordinances to restrict alcohol and tobacco use by minors to combat the growing crime trend. At the youth center, teens socialize in a nonalcoholic environment and participate in an annual film festival. Also, the task force uses the local cable television channel and area newspapers to alert parents about gangs and substance abuse among teens.

Task force members collected information about nearly 100 community activities available to youths and conveyed it to parents and teen through the local media and a Web site. They also made the information available to practitioners who deal with young people in trouble. Members encouraged police officers to divert underage offenders to these community activities, rather than counseling and releasing them.

Additionally, when rental property inhabited by students around the local university began to deteriorate, the task force recommended an adopt-a-street program, which made various university student organizations responsible for preserving quality of life in their own neighborhoods. This program, implemented throughout the police department, has proven successful.

Recognition Days

The advisory committee recommended spotlighting people who and activities that enhance well-maintained communities. This evolved into a yearly event held each September and includes exhibits and demonstrations by most county public safety agencies. Local schools bring students to the event where thousands of community members meet police, fire, emergency, and rescue officers. Community members have the opportunity to thank these public employees and have their pictures taken with them, pet the police dogs, climb the fire equipment, sound the police siren, and perform other such activities. The celebration includes a supplement in the local newspaper that commends and provides photographs of members of the county public safety agencies. The committee gives awards to individual agencies, as well as to citizens who contribute to a safe community. This yearly event fosters communication and trust between the public safety agencies and the community and promotes awareness of the relationship between public safety and community quality of life. During the past 10 years, nearly 100 citizens and organizations have been honored for their contributions to local quality of life.

Conclusion

As crime, particularly drug use and gang violence, seeps into smaller communities, some townships are implementing procedures to deter its spreading. The crime prevention and quality-of-life effort in McDonough County, Illinois, seeks to prevent this ever-increasing threat. An advisory committee oversees the program and promotes cooperation and coordination among the various entities that have a responsibility for ensuring a flourishing community.

The committee established and continually monitors community wellness indicators. When these indicators disclose the beginning signs of activities that adversely will impact quality of life, committee members create task forces to recommend remedies. Then, these solutions are implemented through the committee and aim to prevent community infections before they become serious.

When this project began in the early 1990s, crime had begun its downward trend across the country.[4] However, in Macomb, Illinois, as in many smaller communities, crime was on the rise. After the implementation of this program, crime has decreased and quality of life has become a hallmark of the community.

Anyone involved in resolving social problems realizes that no perfect solutions exist. However, insightful, preventative activities can inhibit and even preclude many adverse conditions that result in the deterioration of community quality of life and the increase of crime. The approach taken by McDonough County may serve as a useful model to other localities working to prevent crime and preserve a nurturing community.

---

[4]U.S. Department of Justice, Federal Bureau of Investigation, *Crime in the United States*, 1992 (Washington, DC, 1993).

10

Applying Social Equity Theme Concepts to the Administration of Contemporary Criminal Justice Agencies

■ Introduction

The theme of Social Equity is the only theme that is unique to the public sector. This is not to say that social equity is not of concern in the private sector. Affirmative Action guidelines and Equal Employment Opportunity legislation have made it of concern to all enterprises. However, when it comes to what entities are responsible for ensuring and enforcing social equity, it now rests squarely with the public sector. Until the 1970s, the public sector had a history of following the will of the public and their elected officials regardless of social rights guaranteed by the U.S. Constitution. Slavery, and later segregation, was enforced by the criminal justice system—under the same U.S. Constitution that exists today. Even as the public sector struggled to become "professional" and follow sound business practices, administrators continued to follow Woodrow Wilson's directions from 1887. However, as the Open Systems concepts gradually took hold, a different view began to emerge. The theme shift began with the milestone concepts discussed in Chapter 3. The key historic Social Equity concepts to remember are:

- Refocusing on Organization Functions
  1977, "The Zero-Based Approach to Government Budgeting," Peter Pyhrr
- Public sector's responsibility for individual rights (even at the cost of efficiency)

1971, "Toward a New Public Administration: The Minnowbrook Perspective," H. George Frederickson

Peter Pyhrr reminded us that even though the main focus of the period may be on one theme, administrators must be mindful of concepts created in previous periods. In the late 1970s, the economy took a downward turn and with it so did pubic funding. Public administrators were forced to review their organization functions approaches (mainly budgeting) and find ways to continue public services with less funding.

However, the pivotal milestone publication during this period was H. George Frederickson's recording of the results of the Minnowbrook Conference. Dwight Waldo, who promoted the conference in 1968, noted that public administration was "in a time of revolution, and there was a need to define the role of public administration." The result was a "new public administration" that called on proactive administrators to become the guardians of individual rights for the citizens they served and for their employees. H. George Frederickson went so far as to say that he saw the day coming "when public administration and the courts would represent the disadvantages and minorities, while the elected officials would stand for the majority" (Frederickson, 1971). Even though it can now be seen that public administration has not gone as far as Frederickson forecasted, his milestone publication did promote a move toward more independence from elected officials and more concern for social equity. Norton Long had signaled the move for more political independence back in 1949 when he wrote:

> *The theory that agencies should confine themselves to communicating policy suggestions to executive and legislature, and refrain from appealing to their clientele and the public, neglects that failure of the parties to provide either a clear-cut decision as to what they should do or an adequately mobilized political support for a course of action. (1949, p. 259)*

This does not mean that public service is not influenced by politics. In 1974, Vincent Ostrom, although supporting the Social Equity theme, proposed a more "democratic administration" and said public administration could not be separated from politics since most decisions were "not a matter of political indifference" (Ostrom, 1974). Politics, as differentiated from partisan politics, embodies the concept of public government, and as Woodrow Wilson said, elected officials are the best representatives of the people. In fact, most chief public administrators are appointed and terminated by elected officials.

■ Social Equity—At What Cost?

During the early development of public administration, the emphasis had been on efficiently and effectively carrying out the directions of elected officials. The Open Systems and the Social Equity period provided public administrators more freedom to carry out their public mission without as much direction from elected officials.

The new Social Equity theme produced an additional element—that even if it cost more, individual rights must be protected. The author can recall as a police administrator, having public pressure to rid communities of street drug deals that were interfering with "domestic tranquility." There were even suggestions of "strong arming" the dealers by members of the community. Violating the rights of the drug dealers might have been the most expedient and economical way to rid the community of this problem. However, the duty to protect individual rights, even for the worst of criminals, is now very much a public administration responsibility. It may take longer and cost more to accomplish the mission by ensuring Social Equity, but that is an important responsibility of all public employees.

The responsibility to protect individual rights did not begin to become a part of the **oath of office** for most public employees until the 1970s. As discussed in Chapter 13, now when criminal justice employees swear to the oath upon employment they take on the equal responsibility of providing public safety and protecting individual rights. For example, the FBI Core Value statement includes:

> *Rigorous obedience to constitutional principles ensures that individually and institutionally we always remember that constitutional guarantees are more important than the outcome of any single interview, search for evidence, or investigation. Respect for the dignity of all whom we protect reminds us to wield law enforcement powers with restraint and to recognize the natural human tendency to be corrupted by power and to become callous in its exercise. Fairness and compassion ensure that we treat everyone with the highest regard for the constitution, civil and human rights. Personal and institutional integrity reinforce each other and are owed to the Nation in exchange for the sacred trust and great authority conferred upon us (www.fbi.gov).*

This dual responsibility separates our justice system from those of many other countries. This is why the responsibility of the courts is to ensure not only that the guilt of the defendant be proven beyond a reasonable doubt, but also that the defendant's rights are protected. Under the Exclusionary Rule, evidence of the guilt of the defendant (no matter how damning) will not be admitted if it is obtained in violation of the **Bill of Rights**. It is often said that our court systems "would rather have a 100 criminals go free than to convict one innocent person." Protection of this unique form of justice (when compared to many other countries) is an important responsibility of all criminal justice administrators.

■ Social Equity and the Republic Form of Government

It is important that public administrations realize that we function within a **republic form of government**. We often refer to our government as a democracy. However, in a true democracy, everyone could do as they individually chose to do. If everyone could do as they chose, there would be social chaos. For example, if everyone could drive motor vehicles as they individually chose, drivers could not anticipate what other drivers were going to do. There would be no assurance that drivers would stop at a red light or stop sign; that they would drive on a designated side of the road and at a safe speed. In order for drivers to have maximum freedom of movement in a society of many vehicles, each driver has to give up certain freedoms. This is the republic form of government. This is why when we pledge allegiance to the flag of the United States we say, "I pledge allegiance to the flag of the United States of America and to the *republic* for which it stands."

Figure 10–1 illustrates how, in our republic form of government, it is not the individual but the *majority* that rule. Through the vote of the majority, or the actions of officials elected by the majority, laws are passed by which all citizens must abide for maximum freedom in a society made up of many individuals. Thus, the people (the majority) decreed that acts ranging from murder to petty theft interfere with the common good and make such acts against the law. They legislated that citizens must stop their motor vehicles at stop signs and wear seat belts while traveling in a motor vehicle. So, in a republic form of government, the people agree to give up some of their individual freedoms for the common good of all.

The founders of our country were fearful of any one central entity having power over the majority. In fact, many early settlers came to this country to escape central power governments that suppressed individual freedoms. However, as the country grew, it became apparent that everyone had to give up a little of their individual freedoms to provide for a society were people could peacefully coexist. Thus, the U.S. Constitution was created. The Constitution is meant to provide a balance between individual rights for everyone and the common good of all citizens. Even though all people have to give up some of their liberties to coexist, everyone is ensured certain rights, no matter who they are or what they do. This is why the Bill of Rights is so important to our form of government.

Still fearful of control by centralized power, the founders established the three branches of government to ensure "checks and balances" over the power that is

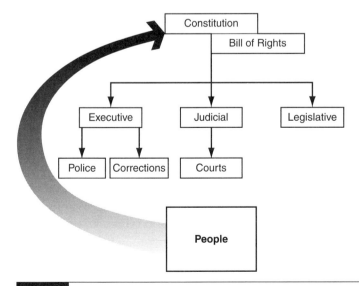

Figure 10–1 Republic Form of Government.

given to public employees to enforce the will of the majority. The executive branch is given the power to enforce the laws, but the legislative branch passes laws and also appoints many members of the executive branch. The courts have the power to exclude evidence of guilt if individual rights are violated, and to enact procedural laws that govern how members of the executive branch enforce the laws. The courts can dictate civil sanctions against members of the executive branch for violations of the Bill of Rights.

When employees take their oath of office and administrators are sworn in to oversee criminal justice agencies, they are promising to carry out the will of the majority in our country. Even if they personally disagree with a law or regulation, they are committed to enforcing the will of the people.

One area of concern relates to majority representation. Recent elections find many people not voting. Criminal justice practitioners are committed to enforcing the laws that are representative of the will of the majority. This is why it is important for criminal justice administrators to encourage everyone to vote. How they vote is not as important as that they do vote. As mentioned in previous chapters, the criminal justice system has never had the personnel to fully enforce the law. The people of our country do not want their police to be an army that has the military strength to force the majority to do what they do not want to do. So it is important that those in the criminal justice system have the support and cooperation of the majority. If the majority does not take advantage of the republic form of government's basic right, the right to vote, then members of the criminal justice system can end up enforcing laws that are not truly supported by the majority. This will make their enforcement responsibilities difficult, if not impossible.

Additionally, it often takes time to remove laws no longer supported by the majority. Because criminal justice agencies are never equipped to enforce all laws, criminal justice administrators have to decide where their limited resources are to be deployed. In using this discretion, it is important for criminal justice administrators to be sensitive to the concerns of the communities they serve. This has become even more important in recent years with the implementation of client-oriented service concepts, as will be discussed in the next chapter.

Figure 10–2 shows the delicate balance between individual rights and public order that the Constitution is meant to ensure. Criminal justice administrators need to be aware that support for these two positions by the majority is never static. Where public support is at any given time is reflected in how the majority vote, who they elect, and who elected officials appoint. After World War II, the majority was concerned with reestablishing domestic tranquility, and public order.

During the late 1960s and the 1970s, there was a shift toward individual rights. There was a reaction to the Civil Rights movement, involvement in the Vietnam War, and the Watergate scandal. **Figure 10–3**, which displays the crime picture for the past century, shows the **procedural rulings** of a more liberal Supreme Court that was concerned with protecting individual rights. With the public's awareness of the rising crime in the 1980s, the mood shifted back to more support for public rights. The "war on crime" and "get tough with criminals" became the cry of a more conservative public and their elected officials. Many pointed to the procedural rulings of the Supreme Court during the 1960s and

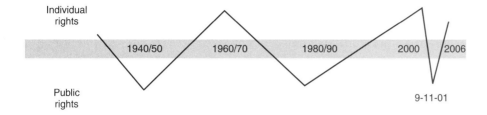

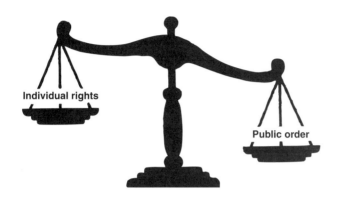

Figure 10–2 Balance of Public Order and Individual Rights.

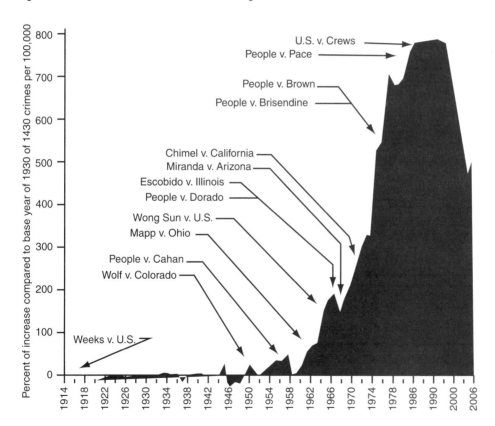

Figure 10–3 The History of Crime Rates and Procedure Laws.

1970s as contributing to the rise in crime by "tying the hands of the police." Interestingly, as crime went down in the 1990s and into the 21st century, these procedural restrictions continued to exist.

As we entered the 21st century, crime continued to decline and the mindset again began shifting back toward concern for individual rights. One indicator of this shift is the support or opposition of the public for capital punishment. During the individual rights movement of the 1960s and 1970s, the Supreme Court (reflecting the mood of the majority) declared a nationwide moratorium on all capital punishment. As crime increased in the 1980s and 1990s, capital punishment was back in "full swing."

The number of executions and their increases and decreases as the mood of the public shifted between support and opposition to the death penalty are provided by the U.S. Bureau of Justice Statistics (**Figure 10–4**). At the beginning of the 21st century, opposition to the death penalty grew, and the governor of Illinois enacted a moratorium on executions with a number of other states following. An abrupt change occurred immediately after the terrorist attack of September 11, 2001. The passage of the Patriot Act followed and opposition to capital punishment became a "weak and distant cry." Several years later, as the impact of September 11 began to fade, concern for individual rights again began to grow—particularly in regard to the Patriot Act (to be covered further in this chapter under the topic of Social Equity and Homeland Security).

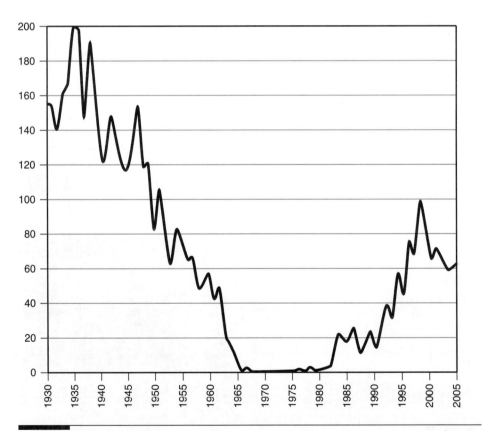

Figure 10–4 History of Executions.

Because the criminal justice system is a major representative of government and is given the task of enforcing laws and regulations, it often serves as a focal point for public concerns about the government in general. This holds true particularly with the police carrying out their duty of keeping the peace at public demonstration (ranging from protest marches to riots). Protecting the balance between public safety and individual rights is a prime responsibility of all criminal justice agencies. The administrator who leads his or her agency toward one extreme or the other within this balance is doing a disservice to the public that they serve as well as their employees.

■ Social Equity and "Us vs. Them" Mentality

Again, it is important to remember that although the Constitution was established to provide "liberty for all," in reality it has only been since the 1970s (the Social Equity Era) that it can be said that an overall government effort is being made to provide equal rights *to all people*. It was this same Constitution and the government (and the criminal justice system) that enforced slavery. After slavery was outlawed, segregation was enforced. After segregation was banned, it remained supported by local governments in some areas of the country. The author can recall, as a police officer in the early 1960s, being asked by his sergeant if he minded working with a "Negro" officer. It was not until the mid-1960s that police departments were forced to integrate. It has been a recent development for the oath of office to require that criminal justice employees swear to protect individual rights as well as provide for public safety. It is of paramount importance that criminal justice administrators instill in all employees sensitivity to this responsibility.

How did slavery, segregation, and discrimination exist in a country devoted to the Bill of Rights? What the author termed the "**us vs. them mentality**" was at fault. Throughout history, human beings seem to separate themselves from certain other humans, perhaps as a means of satisfying a need to feel better than some others. Even the previously mentioned FBI Code of Values recognizes "the natural human tendency to be corrupted by power and to become callous in its exercise." This reminds us that those in power, if not controlled, can misuse that power particularly when it comes to how we treat others.

It is obvious that the framers of our Constitution applied the Bill of Rights to "us" (meaning the majority) but not to some other groups (them). After slavery was abolished segregation prevailed. There were separate eating, residing, and traveling areas for "them" to separate "them" from "us." During World War II, African Americans could fight for our country but only in segregated units. They could be musicians and sports figures and provide entertainment for the majority, but they could not even enjoy the same hotel swimming pools.

What is deemed ethical is not always moral. Ethics is what a society (or segments of a society) deems to be "right." In World War II, many of those in Germany who committed genocide in the Holocaust felt that what they were doing was ethical because it was declared "right" by their government. They committed acts against others ("them") that they certainly believed to be unethical if committed against their loved ones and those they considered "us."

Police officers can sometimes develop cynical subcultures that allow for violating the rights of "them" because they are "low-life criminals" and "scum bags." Prison guards can come to consider inmates as "them." Title 43, U.S. Code, Section 1983 provides for civil action by states:

> *Every person who, under color of any statute, ordinance, regulation, custom, or usage of any State or Territory, subjects, or causes to be subjected, any citizen of the United States or any other person within the jurisdiction thereof to the deprivation of any rights, privileges, or immunities secured by the Constitution and laws, shall be liable to the party injured in an action of law, suit in equity, or other proper proceeding for redress.*

Title 18, U.S. Code, Section 242 goes one step future and makes it criminal by adding the word *willful*. Therefore, if individual rights are violated by criminal justice employees for any reason, punitive action can result. This also applies to administrators for not providing proper training or supervision that may prevent employees from violating rights. For example, in *City of Canton v. Harris* (1989), the U.S. Supreme Court ruled that a failure to train properly can create municipal liability when there is deliberate indifference to the rights of citizens.

If rights are violated willfully, then the criminal justice employee can be punished criminally. In the Rodney King case, for example, after the officers were found not guilty in California for the crime of aggravated assault they were tried at a federal level and found guilty of willfully violating King's rights, resulting in prison sentences. The City of Los Angeles was ruled civilly liable at a cost of $40,000,000.

In 1994, after the Rodney King incident, laws were passed that gave the federal government, specifically the Department of Justice, the authority to investigate and compel police departments to initiate safeguards against racial bias and excessive force activities. For example, after the 2001 Cincinnati police shooting of Timothy Thomas, an unarmed black teenager, the U.S. Attorney General stepped in and required the police department to initiate certain practices to prevent a future recurrence.

Subsequently, there were at least 12 local police departments that the Justice Department investigated for patterns and practices of racial discrimination or brutality (Roane, 2001, 28). In several cases (the Los Angeles Police Department being one), the Justice Department obtained consent decrees from the involved police departments, whereby certain remedial action was to be taken before Justice Department oversight was discontinued. Most criminal justice scandals involving violations of human rights can be traced to the "us versus them" mentality. This is why criminal justice administrators must provide the leadership and control that prevents this attitude from developing.

■ Social Equity and Homeland Security

The September 11, 2001 attacks on the World Trade Center and the Pentagon by international terrorists provide a prime example of how the public mood can shift (at least for period of time) as a result of a single event.

Terrorism and **Homeland Security** are now a major concern within the criminal justice system, specifically law enforcement. The War on Terrorism has caused the redeployment of many client-oriented service resources to Homeland Security efforts. The Preamble to the Constitution gives the police a responsibility to "ensure domestic tranquility." Protecting the public from terrorist crimes certainly falls within this responsibility. Criminal justice administrators must be mindful of their other major responsibility, that of protecting individual rights and ensuring social equity.

With the War on Terrorism came the Patriot Act of the United States, which extends government powers when it comes to investigating acts of terrorism. This legislation had general public support in the aftermath of the September 11 attack. However, as the years passed without another attack occurring within the United States, the mood of at least a vocal number of the public shifted from support for public safety back toward protection of individual rights.

Key Provisions of the U.S. Patriot Act

- *Allows law enforcement to conduct searches with delayed notifications—the so-called sneak-and-peek provision.*
- *Provides that law enforcement can use roving wiretaps to track any telephone that a terrorist suspect might use.*
- *Expands the range of crimes traceable by electronic surveillance.*
- *Reduces legal barriers in information sharing between intelligence and criminal investigation officers.*
- *Makes harboring a terrorist a crime.*
- *Creates new tools for investigating international money-laundering.*
- *Increases penalties for conspiracy relating to terrorism.*
- *Makes it easier to obtain search warrants relating to terrorist activity including for the monitoring of Internet, e-mail, and computer billings.*
- *Gives the Attorney General the authority to detain foreign terrorist suspects—but formal proceedings must start within a week.*
- *Provides more federal agents to patrol U.S. borders.*

Source: Office for State and Local Domestic Preparedness Support, Office of Justice Programs, U.S. Department of Justice. Retrieved from http://www.ojp.usdoj.gov/odp/docs

Civil rights advocates fear that government actions of preventing terrorism can endangering constitutional rights (particularly those granted under the Fourth Amendment) concerning search and seizure protections (Worth, 2005). Some local police departments are being accused of violating First Amendment rights of protesters. For example, during the 2004 Republican National Convention in New York City, the New York Civil Liberties Union accused the police of stifling political protest by "falsely arresting protesters and bystanders on trumped-up charges relating to terrorism" (Jacobs, 2005).

History can provide guidance for today's criminal justice administrators. In the 1930s and 1940s, before and during World War II, law enforcement (lead by the Federal Bureau of Investigation) began to take an active role in domestic intelligence gathering when it came to protecting citizens against the "enemy." The balance of public opinion leaned toward public rights during and for a period after World War II. The public wanted protection from the enemy during the war and against the subversive element during the subsequent Cold War.

Most law enforcement agencies of any size developed intelligence operations to gather information to protect the public against the "enemy" and the "subversives." Without definitive guidelines, law enforcement engaged in collecting information on those they personally selected as possible enemies. Civil rights leaders, some elected officials, and celebrities that "might be leaning towards the left," and even those some judged to be involved in immoral behavior, were included in these lists.

During the 1960s and 1970s, public opinion shifted toward individual rights. This shift was caused by disenchantment with the Vietnam War and a growing distrust of the government. Local police often stood between the disagreeing factions at demonstrations, some of which generated into riots. Law enforcement, being one of the most visible representatives of government, became the main target for civil rights groups. The intelligence files of the FBI, as well as those of many other law enforcement agencies, came under fire. Those elected to public office (and those appointed by those elected) tended to reflect the mood of the general public. This included judges who made rulings in the 1970s that caused law enforcement to cease intelligence operations and to destroy intelligence files.

The author, as a police administrator during this period, was involved in the mandatory dismantlement of police intelligence functions where some police officers were disciplined for hiding, instead of destroying, intelligence files they personally deemed important. This resulted in an absence of domestic intelligence gathering by law enforcement during the latter part of the 20th century. Police investigation could focused only on activities where there was reasonable belief to believe criminal activity was involved.

As mentioned, September 11 resulted in a dynamic shift in public and political interest in domestic intelligence. Many people questioned why law enforcement had not been able to gather intelligence information that would have prevented this attack. Post–September 11, Homeland Security plans called for law enforcement to take an active role in the War on Terrorism. In response, the International Association of Chiefs of Police (IACP), the National Sheriff's Association (NSA), the National Organization of Black Law Enforcement Executives (NOBLE), the Major Cities Chiefs Association, and the Police Foundation joined together in 2004 to conduct a project to provide guidelines as to how state and local law enforcement are to respond. Four guiding documents resulted:

- Intelligence-Led Policing: The New Intelligence Architecture
- Threat Assessment: Fundamentals and Guidelines
- Multijurisdictional Partnerships for Meeting Regional Threats
- Engaging the Private Sector to Promote Homeland Security

These documents, along with the International Association of Chiefs of Police (IACP) report "Post-9/11 Policing: The Crime Control-Homeland Security Paradigm" are available at the IACP Web site. These documents can assist the Eclectic Perspective criminal justice administrator in overseeing the task of preventing domestic terrorism.

Additionally, the criminal justice administrator will do well to remember the historical shifts in public support for criminal justice activities when it comes to intelligence gathering and other Homeland Security activities. History forecasts that if public safety measures go too far "to the right" and the responsibility to protect individual rights is diminished, trust and support for the criminal justice system will suffer and law enforcement activities will be curtailed. As local law enforcement takes a more active role in Homeland Security, police administrators must remember that preserving the constitutional balance between public safety and individual rights is of prime importance in maintaining public trust. Concepts from the Social Equity era serve as a reminder of this key responsibility.

■ Social Equity and Racial Bias in the Criminal Justice System

Is there bias in the criminal justice system? One has only to tour the courtrooms of most large cities in the United States to observe that an uneven number of defendants are minorities. Although African Americans make up about 12% of the population, they account for a much larger percentage of the arrests (**Table 10–1**) and of those imprisoned (**Table 10–2**). Is this a sign of **racial bias**? If so, one also could say that the system is biased against men. Men make up a little less than half the population but account for over 90% of arrests.

Table 10–1 **Arrests in the United States by Race**		
	White (%)	**Black (%)**
Murder and non-negligent manslaughter	49.1	48.6
Forcible rape	65.1	32.7
Robbery	42.2	56.3
Aggravated assault	63.3	34.3
Burglary	69.6	28.5
Larceny–Theft	69.3	28.0
Motor vehicle theft	62.8	34.8
Drug abuse violations	64.7	33.9

Source: Federal Bureau of Investigation, Department of Justice Uniform Crime Reporting Program. "Crime in the United States 2005." (2005). Retrieved from http://www.fbi.gov/ucr/05cius/data/table_43.html

Table 10–2	African American Imprisonment
	Percentage Black
Prisoners	46 [2001]
Jail inmates	40 [2005]
Probationers	31 [2000]
Death row inmates	42 [2004]

Sources:

1) The National Probation Data Survey, National Prisoner Statistics, Survey of Jails, Census of Jail Inmates, and The National Parole Data Survey. "Jail Inmates: Bureau of Justice Statistics Correctional Surveys." Retrieved from http://www.ojp.usdoj.gov/bjs/glance/tables/jailracetab.htm

2) U.S. Department of Justice, Office of Justice Programs, Capital Punishment. "Death row inmates." Retrieved from http://www.ojp.usdoj.gov/bjs/pubalp2.htm#pjmidyear

Crimes are committed by persons of all races, yet a disproportionate number of minorities come to the attention of the criminal justice system. How do we explain these race-based disparities? Some authors maintain that the reason for the disparities is a result of differential treatment within the criminal justice system. Marvin D. Free Jr., as an example, argues that African Americans are underrepresented as criminal justice professionals resulting in their being overrepresented in arrests and imprisonments. He states that some white police officers are more prone to arrest blacks than whites, arrest blacks without sufficient evidence to support criminal charges, and overcharge in criminal cases involving black defendants (Free, 1996, p. 3).

Others take a different point of view. William Wilbanks claims that although the criminal justice system may have been racist in the past, and although it may continue to exist in some areas, the system today is relatively objective in its processing of criminal defendants. He bases this on some studies that have examined the possible existence of discrimination from arrest to parole (Wilbanks, 1987, p. 2). The U.S. Department of Justice National Crime Victimization Survey samples more that 50,000 households each year. Consistently, this survey shows the percentage of offenders described by victims as being black, which is generally consistent with the percentage arrested (U.S. Department of Justice, 2006).

Most of those who argue about the bias of the criminal justice system do recognize the fact that the criminal justice system deals with a high rate of minorities. Many, however, acknowledge that it may be a product of social discrimination (for example, discrimination in employment, housing, and education) that might lead to a life of crime. John Hagan and Ruth D. Peterson research points to higher crime rates among minorities because of (1) concentrated poverty, (2) joblessness, (3) family disruption, and (4) racial segregation (Hagan & Peterson, 1995).

The author, as a practitioner and academician, has observed firsthand the advancements and failures of efforts to rid the criminal justice system of discrimination. This will be discussed further under the topics of servicing multicultural communities and professional ethics (see Chapters 12 and 13). Until the early

1960s, most police departments institutionalized discrimination in the ranks. A female could not be assigned to patrol duty and could only be promoted to the supervisory level in assignments such as juvenile investigation and female jail duties. In many departments, black officers were not allowed to work with white officers. It took many court rulings and federal pressure to change this to the "unisex" and nondiscriminating hiring and promoting practices of today.

■ Racial Profiling

Despite positive changes, there remain areas of concern for criminal justice administrators. *Racial profiling* is one such area. The landmark 2000 study of the New Jersey State Police found that 73% of all drivers stopped on the New Jersey Turnpike were African American, despite making up less than 14% of drivers on the road—a rate that is 27 times greater than what would be expected by random chance. Additionally, although 78% of people stopped and searched on the southern portion of the Jersey Turnpike were African American and Hispanic, police were twice as likely to discover evidence of illegal activity in cars driven by whites relative to blacks; and whites were five times more likely to be in possession of drugs, guns, or other illegal items in comparison to Latinos (Wise, 2003, p. 93).

Similar results were found in other studies. On a particular stretch of Interstate 95 in Florida, known for being a drug trafficking route, African Americans and Latinos constitute only 5% of drivers but 70% of those stopped by highway patrol officers. Only 9 drivers out of 1,100 stopped were ticketed for any violation, let alone arrested for possession of illegal contraband (Wise, 2003, p. 92). These studies have caused many states to enact requirements for law enforcement officers to record relative information in connection with all police stops so administrators can take corrective action if warranted. To assist, the Police Executive Research Forum has published *Racially Biased Policing: A Principled Response*, to help in providing guidelines (Police Executive Research Forum, 2001).

Criminal justice administrators should be mindful that "profiling" is an important part of police work. When police officers gain descriptions of suspects during criminal investigations and communicate descriptions to other officers, they are profiling. These descriptions usually include the sex, age, race, height, weight, eye and hair color, and any other distinguishing characteristics. These "profiles" are important for "reasonable suspicion" and "probable cause" justifications to stop and question and to arrest (elements of law that all officers must be training to understand). "Racial profiling" would better be termed *prejudicial profiling*. If stops are based purely on race, then it is "racial profiling." However, if an officer thinks that most college students are carrying drugs and conducts stops based on age, that is prejudicial profiling. Criminal justice administrators must ensure their personnel are well schooled about this issue and must implement proper controls to detect and prevent prejudicial profiling.

Marvin D. Free Jr.'s statement about minorities being underrepresented as criminal justice professionals brings up another area of concern. If police officers, corrections officers, court attorneys, and judges come from white backgrounds and have little previous exposure to people of other races and ethnic backgrounds, prejudiced views can develop. For example, a young white person who has had no previous association with African Americans is hired by a large city police department and assigned to an area of the city with a largely black population. More than likely, this area will have more crime than the white area in which the new patrol officer grew up. The officer may come to the erroneous conclusion that the area in which he or she now works has more crime, and most of the population is black, therefore blacks commit more crime. This same conclusion could occur with employees in Corrections and the Courts dealing with offenders that are mostly minorities.

Criminal justice administrators must ensure that employees are mindful that, 100 years ago, these inner city, poor areas that are now mostly African American or Hispanic also were the areas of most of the crime. Who populated these poor areas then? It was the Italians, Irish, Polish, and other ancestors of today's white population. It was the earlier immigrating European population, trying to gain a "foothold" in our county, who were the poor. From this perspective, it can be deduced that it is not race but poverty that breeds crime (this was pointed out previously by John Hagan and Ruth D. Peterson).

Additionally, poor areas with higher crime rates have more victims of crime—victims who need police protection and assistance. Criminal justice administrators must ensure that their employees have this perspective and realize that most people who live in these areas are not criminals but, rather, community members to whom the Constitution promises "domestic tranquility." The Eclectic Perspective criminal justice administrator realizes that working to eliminate poverty (and the lack of education and employment that comes with it) is perhaps our most promising approach to reducing crime.

Matthew B. Robinson offers some "food for thought" for criminal justice administrators in his book *Justice Blind?* **Table 10–3** summarizes what he describes as **sources** of bias in criminal justice. His **recommendations** include:

Recommendations for the Police

- Reallocate policing resources to better assist victims
- Increase educational qualifications to a minimum of a Bachelor's degree
- Develop mandatory multicultural educational efforts within police academies
- Outlaw the use of police profiling based on race and ethnicity
- Develop police-community partnerships where they are needed most, inner-city, high-crime areas

Recommendations for the Courts

- Reallocate resources so that they are more equitable, particularly defense attorneys
- Increase representation by racial and ethnic minorities in courtroom workgroups
- Return sentencing discretion to judges (eliminate mandatory sentencing laws)
- Structure bail to be based on how much the accused can afford and assess bail outcomes to ensure bail does not discriminate against any group or persons

Table 10–3	Sources of Bias in the American Criminal Justice System				
Law	**Media**	**Police**	**Courts**	**Corrections**	**Other**
Legislators not representative	Owned by large corporations	Discretion	Demographics of courtroom workgroups	Probation	War on drugs
Most people do not vote	Run for profit	Profiling	Power of prosecutor	Incarceration	Poverty
Voters not representative	Inaccurate reporting	Location by place	Charging	Death penalty	Income inequality
Money drives politics (PACS, wealthy donors)	Focus on street crime	Focus on street crime	Bail and preventative detention		Unemployment
	Focus on violent, bizarre crimes		Plea bargaining		
	No context provided		Voir dire		
	Rely on police, prosecutors for info		Private attorneys		
			Expert witnesses		
			Mandatory sentencing		
			Drug crimes		

Source: Robinson, M.R. (2005). *Justice Blind?* (2nd ed.). Upper Saddle River, NJ: Pearson/Prentice Hall. Reprinted by permission of the publisher.

- Insist the indigent clients be given quality counsel by creating incentives to represent poor clients.
- Encourage citizens to participate in jury duty by providing adequate financial compensation

Recommendations for Corrections
- Increase the use of intermediate sanctions as cost-effective alternatives to prison
- Insist on educational and vocational skill development as a criterion for release
- Provide more resources for probation and parole offices to reduce caseloads and increase supervision (Robinson, 2004, pp. 396–404)

KEY CONCEPTS AND TERMS

- Constitutional guarantees
  - Republic form of government
  - Bill of Rights
  - Procedural rulings
  - Oath of office
- "Us vs. them" mentality
- Homeland security
- Racial bias in the criminal justice systems
  - Sources
  - Recommended remedies

CHAPTER ACTIVITY

Check the mission and/or value statements of various criminal justice agencies on the Internet. Can you find social equity concepts within these statements?

REVIEW QUESTIONS

1. How does the Organization Functions concept of efficiency and cost-effective use of resources conflict with the Social Equity mandate to protect individual rights no matter the cost? Can you give examples of situations that may occur today that exemplify this conflict?

2. Explain the difference between our republic form of government and a true democracy. How does this impact the role of the criminal justice administrator?

3. How is the history of the Social Equity theme important in the current Homeland Security efforts? How does Homeland Security relate to the balance between public safety and individual rights?

4. Is "profiling" a form of discrimination? Why was "prejudicial profiling" suggested in this chapter as a more proper term than "racial profiling"?

5. Imagine that you are a criminal justice administrator and have been assigned to develop and implement a criminal justice entity of your choice (for example, a Personnel and Training Division). What Social Equity concepts would you consider in fulfilling this assignment?

REFERENCES

Frederickson, H. G. (1971). Toward a New Public Administration. *Toward a New Public Administration: The Minnowbrook Perspective*. Scranton, PA: Chandler.

Free, M. D., Jr. (1996). *African-Americans and the Criminal Justice System*. New York: Garland.

Hagan, J., & Peterson, R. D. (1995). *Crime and Inequality*. Stanford, CA: Stanford University Press.

Jacobs, A. (2005). Banner-Bearing Protester at Convention Is Acquitted. *New York Times*. Retrieved June 24, 2007 from http://www.nytimes.com

Long, N. (1949). Power and Administration. *Public Administration Review, 9*, Autumn, p. 259.

Ostrom, V. (1974). *The Intellectual Crisis in American Public Administration*. Alabama: University of Alabama Press.

Police Executive Research Forum. (2001). *Racially Biased Policing: A Principled Response*. Washington, DC.

Roane, K. R. (2001). Policing the Police Is a Dicey Business: But the Feds Have a Plan To Root Out Racial Bias. *U.S. News and World Report*, April, p. 30.

Robinson, M. (2004). *Justice Blind: Ideals and Realities of American Criminal Justice*. Upper Saddle River, NJ: Pearson-Prentice Hall.

Wilbanks, W. (1987). The Myth of a Racist Criminal Justice System. *Criminal Justice Research Bulletin*, 3, No. 5, p. 18.

Wise, T. (2003). Racial Profiling and Its Apologists. *Criminal Justice* (27th ed.). Guildford, CT: McGraw-Hill/Dushkin.

Worth, R. E. (2005). Privacy Rights Are at Issue in New Policy on Searches. *New York Times*. Retrieved July 22, 2006 from http://www.nytimes.com

■ RELEVANT PUBLICATION

The subject of this chapter was Homeland Security, from a Social Equity perspective. Law enforcement is being called on to take a more active role in the "War on Terrorism." In response, the International Association of Chiefs of Police (IACP), the National Sheriff's Association (NSA), the National Organization of Black Law Enforcement Executives (NOBLE), the Major Cities Chiefs Association, and the Police Foundation joined together to conduct a project to help position state and local law enforcement in how to respond. Here, the Executive Summary of the resulting report is presented to provide insight into how the *Social Equity* theme is being integrated into today's policing role in Homeland Security. ("Post-9/11 Policing: The Crime Control-Homeland Security Paradigm." (2005). Retrieved at http://www.theiacp.org.)

"Executive Summary Post 9-11 Policing: The Crime Control—Homeland Security Paradigm Taking Command of New Realities"

EXECUTIVE SUMMARY

The September 11th attacks on the United States redirected priorities with a suddenness perhaps unprecedented in the American police experience. Homeland security, the constant threat of terrorism on our shores, concern with weapons of mass destruction, and security-related intelligence demands surged to the forefront of state and local policing. Requirements and implications of the Patriot Act, homeland security funding, and equipment and training distribution issues have penetrated the law enforcement enterprise at all levels. With no time for preparation, law enforcement repositioning to confront these demands and issues has been paralleled by 9-11 fallouts, including military (reserve) mobilizations that skim police manpower, material expenditures for overtime and color alert mobilization, and heightened concern for preservation of civil liberties.

September 11th impacts and demands intensified the urgency of pre-9-11 police priorities, harnessing new technologies, most notably information technology, and within this realm, interoperability capacities being most obvious. Palpable concern exists that new and still evolving homeland security requirements not be met at the expense of considerable gains in community policing and the restoration of public trust, meticulously crafted in recent years. Similarly, crime prevention and control—the core missions of law enforcement—though currently somewhat muted, remain the dominant concern in the world of law enforcement.

Suffusing this panoply of change is state and local budgetary stress. Many police agencies must address expanding missions in flat or diminishing resource environments. Productivity and asset-leveraging challenges are already evident and are likely to dominate functioning for the foreseeable future.

THE POST 9-11 POLICING PROJECT

The International Association of Chiefs of Police (IACP), the National Sheriffs' Association (NSA), the National Organization of Black Law Enforcement Executives (NOBLE), the Major Cities Chiefs Association, and the Police Foundation joined in 2004 to conduct a project to help position state, local, and tribal agencies to proactively manage a changed and continually changing police environment. Four objectives were pursued:

- **Objective 1: Profile High Impact Changes**. Identify and prioritize the forces and demands, currently evident and emerging, that are redirecting the police mission and roles.
- **Objective 2: Capture Best Practices**. Assemble information on successful policy, program, and resource deployment responses that agencies have undertaken to address changing conditions, missions, and roles.
- **Objective 3: Craft Promising Practices**. Surface or develop policy, program, and resource deployment ideas considered promising for addressing changing conditions, mission, and roles.
- **Objective 4: Package and Disseminate Practices**. Blanket the police community with user-friendly Action Briefs that summarize the best and promising practices information and ideas.

The partners regard this project as an essential effort to address the continuing need for up-to-date change management strategies for American law enforcement.

THE EVOLVING PARADIGM—THE POST 9-11 MODEL

From the totality of project work—Roundtables, CEO Survey, and Literature Review—an outline of post 9-11 policing emerged:

- **The Terrorism Dimension**. During the final years of what might be called pre-9-11 policing, the late 1990's through most of 2001, law enforcement was characterized by a strong sense of direction and clarity. Crime was in decline. Community policing had broad acceptance and support. Public trust was strong. That balance was shattered on September 11, 2001. While not yet universal within law enforcement, or felt with consistent intensity, there is recognition that for the first time since WWII, policing is being conducted, domestically, in a time of war; the United States faces a foreign threat within its own borders.
- **Shifting Eras and Mission Reconfiguration**. Domestic security obligations have rapidly augmented the pre-9-11 mission. Traditional pre-9-11 responsibilities such as community service and crime control are not and cannot be ignored. These remain the primary expectations of citizens and elected officials. Law enforcement's commitment to and belief in the now established crime control and community policing model remains firm. Yet, by the pressure of events and evolving professional concern, there appears to be a transition beyond the Community-

Oriented Policing (COP) model of the 90s to a domestic security model. To some, a homeland security focus should be the next evolution of community policing.

- **Federally-Led Response**. The federal government has taken the lead in our national response. But state and local agencies are moving forward, forming new and strengthening existing regional arrangements, improving interoperability and information exchange and capability, engaging in various forms of terrorism response training, patrolling differently and experimenting with a rich mixture of operating strategies. Dissatisfaction with unfolding federal programming is readily apparent with distribution and targeting of funding and the terror alert system being most prominent.

- **A Leadership Imperative**. Though not specifically mandated, federally, locally, legislatively, or by policy directive, chief law enforcement executives recognize a moral and professional imperative to aggressively confront potential terrorism in their communities.

- **Readying for Action**. The numbing and confusing immediate impact of 9-11 on the collective police psyche has lifted and responses are clarifying. Terrorism prevention and response planning and programming is surfacing in many law enforcement agencies. Much of it is regionally networked and information and intelligence focused. The field is poised for a more aggressive response.

- **Business as Usual Mindset**. The previous observation notwithstanding, a mindset issue seems to exist. A belief is often shared that "terrorism is just a big city (or eastern) problem" and "nothing is going to happen in small town, rural America."

- **The Financial Paradox**. A tightening resource situation parallels the expanding post 9-11 mission. Law enforcement leaders must educate citizens, government leaders, and especially legislators—those with financial powers—about domestic security issues, dangers, and financial requirements in order to ready an effective response.

- **Federal-Local Crime Control Partnerships**. State and local law enforcement is not experiencing withdrawal of federal crime control resources to any measurable degree, which was expected as agencies such as the FBI reoriented for the war on terror. Some suggest an identifiable shift in resources in the reverse—from local and state agencies to federal task forces, mainly Joint Terrorism Task Forces (JTTFs).

- **Federal-Local Homeland Security Partnerships**. Intensified collaboration with DHS is required to better tailor funding strategies and formulas to state and local law enforcement needs. This is likely to occur as law enforcement mobilizes its assets and gains consensus on required and potentially effective strategies.

- **Patriot Act**. State and local law enforcement support is solid for reauthorization of the Patriot Act. Revisions are favored with regard to reimbursement of costs incurred by local governments to detain suspected terrorists, to respond to color code changes, and to expand the definition of domestic terrorism to include violations of American Indian jurisdiction. Concern with singling out persons based solely on country of origin has been expressed. There is a strong sense of need to broaden understanding of the provisions of the Act beyond law enforcement professionals.

- **Preserving Public Trust**. There is widespread concern that the monumental public trust accomplishments of the past decade or so will erode as homeland security priorities take center stage. This concern is linked to diminishing resources and erosion of federal funds for community policing officers, school resource officers, and other staples of policing.
- **Changing Leadership Requirements**. Leadership requirements are changing to cope with new missions and issues. New knowledge and better practices information are required to balance homeland security augmentations and retain the integrity of traditional core missions. Law enforcement executives are engaging more federally, regionally, and locally; trying to sort out changing expectations and regain the stability of the pre-9-11 years, in a post 9-11 environment.
- **Promising Practices**. Finding state and local homeland security programs worth replicating is exceedingly difficult, attesting to both the need for innovative strategies and the rudimentary level of development work to date. The field is particularly anxious to assemble the assets required to address terrorism, most importantly prevention assets.
- **Issues Hierarchy**. The issues that are most critical to law enforcement CEOs today are:
  - Budget/Funding
  - Homeland Security and Terrorism
  - Recruitment, Retention, Staffing
  - Crime and Disorder
  - Crime Prevention
  - Public Trust

Judging by forces of change discussions at the Roundtables, and correlate impacts and responses, homeland security towers above all others. Note also, however, that the resource shortage issue overarches and suffuses the policing environment in its entirety.

MANAGING NEW REALITIES—BUILDING HOMELAND SECURITY CAPACITY

Every project initiative demonstrated and reinforced the preoccupation of law enforcement professionals with homeland security issues, their intellectual readiness to frame priority domestic security questions, tackle the answers, and their thirst for a "game plan." For these reasons our promising practices phase concentrated on homeland security considerations.

Four promising practice briefs have been produced:

- Intelligence Led Policing: The New Intelligence Architecture
- Threat Assessment: Fundamentals and Guidelines
- Multi-Jurisdictional Partnerships for Meeting Regional Threats
- Engaging the Private Sector to Promote Homeland Security

Individually and collectively, the briefs focus on the prevention factor of the Prevention—Preparedness—Consequence Management homeland security equation, honoring a call from the field. The documents attempt to summarize best current thinking in the respective subject areas, recognizing that work was done in a rapidly changing development environment. Operating models and hosting jurisdictions are referenced to direct readers to sources for further inquiry.

A PORTFOLIO OF CAPACITY BUILDING ESSENTIALS

The project identified 37 issues and needs to be addressed to begin to build a body of policies, programs, and practices that state, local, tribal, and special jurisdiction police require to meet the homeland security new reality. Issues and needs of groupings are:

- Leadership
- Prevention and Preparedness
- Technology and Intelligence
- Resources
- Community and Citizen Engagement
- Organizational Transformation
- Externals

These capacities are linked by their concentration on prevention, reflecting an articulated choice of law enforcement CEOs to focus on the still unmet needs on the prevention side of the domestic security/terrorism equation. Consequence management, also vital, has already been treated extensively, though more remains to be done on this side of the security equation as well, including building and refining collaborations.

CAPACITY BUILDING PRINCIPLES

Developed as an extension of the Post 9-11 Policing Project by the IACP governing body as part of its Taking Command initiative, the following principles are recommended for guiding capacity building work:

- <u>**Terrorism is Local**</u>. Terrorism occurs/will occur locally, in the streets and neighborhoods of America. Accordingly, local law enforcement is the front line for protection and response.
- <u>**Bottom-Up Engineering**</u>. Priorities, asset design and development, and funding formulas should be engineered from the ground up—from communities, towns, and cities.
- <u>**Prevention is Paramount**</u>. The need to focus on and value the prevention dimension of the Prevention—Preparedness—Consequence Management equation is a transcending capacity building requirement.
- <u>**Non-Competitive Collaboration**</u>. Priorities, asset design, development, and funding formulas must be fashioned non-competitively, by all first-response agencies and governing bodies at all levels.
- <u>**Community Policing—Crime Control—Homeland Security Nexus**</u>. Federal homeland security resource allocations and distribution must balance these integrated needs to be effective in any one and all areas.
- <u>**Recognizing Diversity**</u>. Priorities, asset design and development, and funding formulas must consider the material differences among law enforcement agency sizes, resources, clientele, and cultures.
- <u>**A Permanent Place at the National Table**</u>. The Department of Homeland Security, Federal Bureau of Investigation, and Joint Terrorism Task Forces, among other federal entities, must engage state and local law enforcement in policy making more intensely and in more meaningful ways.
- <u>**Urgency**</u>. Four years have elapsed since 9-11-01. Urgency must drive developmental activities.

BUILDING ON EXISTING CRIME CONTROL ASSETS AND INFRASTRUCTURE

Homeland security programming should be incorporated into the totality of the police mission as seamlessly as is possible. Many, probably most, terrorism-engendered issues simply have not been dealt with before. Accordingly, state, county, municipal and special clientele law enforcement agencies have no choice but to develop and adapt new concepts and practices. Substantial infrastructure and a historical and contemporary body of "intellectual property" are in place in virtually every agency to meet development challenges. While first-time inventions seem required, existing crime prevention and control concepts and strategies, regional arrangements, intelligence-led policing, investigations and patrol capacities, and community policing and problem solving programming and skills are among the infrastructure capacities that should and will be exploited and fine-tuned to address domestic security issues successfully in coming years.

Applying Contextual Themes of Administration to Future Criminal Justice Issues

III

Parts I and II explored the past history of administration and the contemporary applications of the evolving contextual themes of criminal justice administration. Here we begin a view toward the future, with the future defined as *from this moment on*. We can learn from the past, but we cannot change it. We can apply what we learn from the past to present endeavors and in planning for the future; however, the present is only the space of time between the past and the future. With this view in mind, Part III will begin with a discussion of the application of the last of the five contextual themes. Subsequent chapters will cover special issues that criminal justice administrators are facing now and in the foreseeable future.

Applying Client-Oriented Service to the Administration of Criminal Justice Agencies

11

■ Introduction

This chapter will explore the theme that is guiding administrators now and into the foreseeable future. The fifth theme, Client-Oriented Service, started in the latter part of the 20th century and has continued into this century. The application of this theme to contemporary and future criminal justice agencies is where we begin in this chapter. To set the stage, historical key milestone concepts from Chapter 4 will provide a starting point for the discussion of the application of Client-Oriented Service.

- Importance of employee-customer contacts

  1987, *Moments of Truth*, Jan Carlzon

- Focus on customer service

  1983, *In Search of Excellence*, Thomas Peters and Robert Waterman

In the 1960s, attention was on the Open Systems concept, and in the 1970s, the focus was on social equity. In the 1980s, the focus of administrators moved to the people being served—or to the "clients," as they were called in the private sector. Peters and Waterman's best-selling publication, *In Search of Excellence*, spotlighted how successful private businesses were customizing services to the desires of their clients.

Several years after the publication of this book, Peters produced a training video, "Excellence in the Public Sector." In the training video, Peters visited five public sector agencies to demonstrate how the excellence qualities found in the private sector could be transferred to the public sector. One of the five agencies he visited was the New York City Department of Juvenile Justice (DDJ). DDJ provided pretrial detention for 5,000 children each year and aftercare services for 1,000 children. Many of these juveniles were arrested and detained while waiting for a court appearance.

The organization challenge was to provide a system of services for detained juveniles whose stay varied from a few days to many months and also to maintain supportive aftercare services. For years, the agency had major organizational problems, a poor reputation, and low success in the rehabilitation of juvenile offenders. Peters showed how getting criminal justice employees to work with juvenile detainees and parolees as "clients" or "customers" proved beneficial. Viewing the detainees as customers with certain needs for specific services changed the juvenile justice agency into a successful enterprise with a good reputation for reducing juvenile offender recidivism (Peters, 1989).

Jan Carlzon wrote about his experience in taking over a failing airline corporation and making it successful by concentrating on the service of employees when they came in direct contact with the customers. He called these contacts "the moments of truth." He found these moments much more important in establishing the reputation of the corporation than high-profile advertising and public relations campaigns. This approach, developed in the private sector, became a major factor in the public sector administration.

■ Client-Oriented Law Enforcement Service

As discussed in Chapter 10, a prime concern in the public sectors during that period was Social Equity. This concern was a result of the growing citizen distrust of the government, in general, and the police (as the most visible representatives of the government), in particular. In Chapter 9, the importance of crime prevention was discussed as an Open Systems concept. The importance of prevention was based on research that revealed that the police seldom discover a crime in progress. When they do apprehend offenders, it is usually as the result of information provided by the public. In preventing crime and in apprehending criminals, public cooperation is of prime importance. If the public does not trust the police, gaining their cooperation will be difficult.

During the 1960s and 1970s, a growing number of citizens viewed the police as too professional; they seemed to be more an occupying army. The only contact that many citizens had with the police was when radio car officers responded to calls-for-services. These contacts were often emotionally charged and cast officers in the role of enforcers. Public dissatisfaction with police services could be seen in ballot measures that reduced tax support for law enforcement. Crime increased and police services were stretched to the limit. Police service became (in most cases) reactive rather than proactive. Public trust of the police continued to diminish.

In demonstrating the need for public trust in police work, the author as a professor asks students to envision someone they do not trust who has authority over them. The students are asked if they would do what that person ordered them to do. The students respond in the affirmative because of the power that this authority figure has over them. Then the students are asked if they would volunteer information to this authority figure they do not trust, for example, information that would help the authority figure be successful. The students respond, "No way." They are not inclined to help this authority figure be successful; in fact, they hope that he or she fails. The students are then asked to think of the police in this light. If the police are viewed as only authority figures not to be trusted, the public will not come forward with the information needed to apprehend criminals and will not cooperate in prevention efforts.

As discussed in Chapter 5, there was a realization that law enforcement, in the effort to become professional, had strayed from the early American philosophy of a shared community-police responsibility. This became a major topic of discussion in the 1970s and 1980s. As a result, the attention of police administrators shifted to key milestone publications and other business world research that was aimed at gaining client support and trust. For example, the author, as a police administrator, modified Jan Carlzon's "moments of truth" definition to fit law enforcement as described in the next section.

"Moments of Truth" in Policing

Any time that the public comes into contact with the police and judge (form an opinion about) the quality of service that they are receiving, that is where the real values and missions of policing comes through. That is the "moment of truth" that creates trust and support.

It is the patrol officers who respond to calls-for-service, the traffic officers who write citations, and the 9-1-1 telephone operators who are the first contact that most people have with the criminal justice system. Proper selection, training, and motivating of these personnel are of prime importance for police administrators in promoting Client-Oriented Service.

Peters and Waterman's emphasis on decentralizing service (to be "closer to the customer") was another factor in what became know as community policing. The police movement toward a client-orient concept started in the 1970s (and even earlier in some agencies) and moved through a number of approaches in the 1980s and 1990s. The evolution of concepts through this period demonstrates how the fabric of each contextual theme is designed from many attempts, modification, and enhancements.

Table 11–1 displays the evolution of policing modes over several centuries. The evolution of policing was discussed in Chapter 6 but is shown here in relationship to the evolution of administrative themes and concepts. The enlightenment of the Open Systems period, and the pressures of the social equity period, caused police administrators to seek better methods of promoting public trust. The development of Client-Oriented Service went through a number of stages.

Table 11–1	Evolving Modes of Policing and the Contextual Themes Model
Policing mode	**Administrative concepts**
Watch & Ward (1700s)	
Watchman (1800s)	Peel Principles
Professionalism/legalistic (1900s)	Pendleton Act
	Organization function
	Employee relations
	Open systems
Service-oriented (1970–)	Social equity
Team policing (1970s)	Client-oriented
COP/POP (1980/90s)	
PAC (2000s)	Eclective prospective

■ Evolutionary Stages of Client-Oriented Service in Law Enforcement

Community-relation and press-relations programs were a product of the 1970s (and, with some agencies, the 1960s) and the first step in the evolution of Client-Oriented Service. Police administrators implemented community relations programs aimed at enhancing their public image. Another way of defining these programs was to "get the public to like the police." Community relations and press relations officer positions were created to facilitate this approach. Because police work is of much interest to the press (and to the public, as indicated by the many television and movie productions relating to "police work"), the media has a key position in shaping public opinion. There is a natural conflict between the press and the police. The press wants all the information and the police have to restrict the release of some information that may jeopardize the investigations or prosecutions. Consequently, most agencies of any size selected and trained certain personnel to function as liaisons with the press.

Community relations officers were specially trained to present their agencies in the best possible light. Some larger agencies hired public relation firms to assist in developing community relations programs. Departments used public displays, demonstrations, lecture, and television and radio messages to inform citizens about police operations, crimes, and crime prevention. Community relations officers were available for speeches at community meetings and social gatherings.

A problem with this approach was that it often neglected Carlzon's "moments of truth" concept. It was not high-profile community relations programs that formed public opinion but, rather, the direct interaction of employees with the public being served.

Team Policing was the next step in the Client-Oriented Service approach. Started in Los Angeles in the early 1970s (by then Chief Edward M. Davis), this approach took Peters and Waterman's decentralized "close to the customer" concept and applied it to policing. Davis also incorporated the "territorial imperative" idea from a best selling book of the day by Robert Ardrey (1966). Ardrey's idea was that all living organisms, from ants to humans, have a special territory that they protect and proclaim as "their turf."

Davis used these concepts in deploying employees into Basic-Car Districts, in which officers were responsible for specific districts. The people in those districts became "their people." Davis put it this way: "If the policeman is white and the people he serves are black, he may think at first, 'I don't like black people very much,' and the black people may think at first, 'We don't like white cops very much.' Yet he's their protector, and he knows that they are depending on him; and if they sit down and rap together about how to protect the area, pretty soon the whiteness and the blackness disappear, and it become Us, a feeling of unity" (Davis, 1978, p. 136).

These Basic-Car Districts were groups of census tracts that were combined to conform to what community members felt were their neighborhoods. The districts were formed into Teams, which led to the development of Team Policing. The Los Angeles Police Department was divided into 80 teams. Each team was headed by a lieutenant who had the authority and responsibility for patrol, traffic, and detective services in that team area. He or she was the "chief of police" for that territory under the concept of decentralization and bringing the service "close to the customer." Decisions that previously had to be made at central command were now delegated to the local team commander.

Basic-Car District officers established **Neighborhood Watch** programs, and Chief Davis can be credited with this concept. Davis had Basic-Car District officers develop "block captains" who provided their homes for neighborhood watch meetings, combining both the concepts of "territorial imperative" and getting "close to the customer." This approach involved gathering of neighbors to meet periodically with their Basic-Car District officers and share quality of life-related concerns. These meeting served to exchange information that could reduce and prevent crime, help the police customize their services to neighborhood needs, and promote a cooperative interaction between the police and the public. As discussed in Chapter 5, Team Police came to an abrupt end because of political and financial reasons after less than a decade of operation. However, it served as a foundation for **community policing** and started the Neighborhood Watch Program that has continued into the 21st century.

Community-Oriented Policing (COP) was the next evolutionary approach, and Lee Brown, then the Chief of Police of the Houston Police Department in Texas, can rightfully be called the father of this concept. As implemented in Houston, organizationally it was focused on the decentralizing of patrol functions. The Neighborhood Watch concept from Davis's Team Policing was incorporated as a major component. Even though his COP revolved mainly around the patrol functions, Brown made it a philosophy throughout the department.

The philosophy was not a new concept. In fact, it was a return to Sir Robert Peel's 1830s principles for the London Metropolitan Police. The Peel Principles of Policing (below) can rightfully be called the "holy grail" of modern law enforcement.

Sir Robert Peel's Policing Principles

1. *To prevent crime and disorder, as an alternative to their repression by military force and by severity of legal punishment.*

2. *To recognize always that the power of the police to fulfill their functions and duties is dependent on public approval of their existence, actions and behavior, and on their ability to secure and maintain public respect.*

3. *To recognize always that to secure and maintain the respect and approval of the public means also the securing of willing cooperation of the public in the task of securing observance of laws.*

4. *To recognize always that the extent to which the cooperation of the public can be secured diminishes, proportionately, the necessity of the use of physical force and compulsion for achieving police objectives.*

5. *To seek and to preserve public favour, not by pandering to public opinion, but by constantly demonstrating absolutely impartial service to law, in complete independence of policy, and without regard to the justice or injustices of the substance of individual laws; by ready offering of individual service and friendship to all members of the public without regard to their wealth or social standing; by ready exercise of courtesy and friendly good humour; and by ready offering of individual sacrifice in protecting and preserving life.*

6. *To use physical force only when the exercise of persuasion, advice and warning is found to be insufficient to obtain public cooperation to an extent necessary to secure observance of law or to restore order; and to use only the minimum degree of physical force which is necessary on any particular occasion for achieving a police objective.*

7. *To maintain at all time a relationship with the public that gives reality to the historic tradition that the police are the public and that the public are the police; the police being only members of the public who are paid to give full-time attention to duties which are incumbent on every citizen, in the interests of community welfare and existence.*

8. *To recognize always the need for strict adherence to police-executive functions, and to refrain from even seeming to usurp the powers of the judiciary of avenging individuals or the state, and of authoritatively judging guilt and punishing the guilty.*

9. *To recognize always that the test of police efficiency is the absence of crime and disorder, and not the visible evidence of police action in dealing with them.*

Source: Reith, C. (1948). *A Short History of The British Police.* New York: Oxford University Press. pp. 64–65.

Many contemporary police departments have adopted portions of these principles into their mission and value statements. The "Management Principles of the Los Angeles Police Department" (which the author was involved in drafting) offers an example of how law enforcement has incorporated these principles into client-oriented policing. These principles can be found in **Appendix 5**. The focus shifted from the number of arrests to "preventing crime and disorder." The measure of effectiveness became "the absence of crime and disorder, and not the visible evidence of police action ("1" and "9" of Peel's Principles). The heart of Peel's Principles ("7") states that the "police are the public and that the public are the police; the police being only members of the public who are paid to give full-time attention to duties which are incumbent on every citizen, in the interests of community welfare and existence." This philosophy became the theme of community-oriented policing.

Chief Lee Brown added the "**fear of crime**" to client-oriented policing. Brown pointed out that there is often more fear of crime than actually justified by the amount of crime. Furthermore, it is often the fear of crime that causes communities quality of life to deteriorate. This fear often causes people to move to other neighborhoods. **Appendix 6** is a survey of a large inner city area that will be discussed later in this chapter under the topic of evaluating client-oriented effectiveness. It is mentioned here because it demonstrates how the fear level can be greater than justified by the crime. In the survey, residents were asked which crimes they feared most. Although they mentioned robberies and gang violence as crimes they feared most, many residents did not list these as crime they or their families had recently experienced. It was found that their fears were based on what they heard from others, what they became aware of through the news media, and via visual indicators such as graffiti. Lee Brown made reducing fear of crime a part of the community-oriented policing effort. This effort included providing facts and rumor control through neighborhood watch meetings and media releases.

Brown called his program Neighborhood-Oriented Policing (NOP). His philosophy was to change the police officer from enforcer to an officer who would provide Client-Oriented Service. He described his philosophy:

> *The more desired perception is for the officer to be viewed as someone who can provide help and assistance, someone who expresses compassion through emphasizing and sympathizing with victims of crime, and someone who can organize community groups, inspire and motivate groups, and facilitate and coordinate collective efforts and endeavors of others (Ottmeier & Brown, 1988, p. 13).*

In addition to Peel's Principles, community policing incorporated a number of other approaches. One approach came from the milestone 1973 **Kansas City study** that measured proactive, reactive, and controlled patrol beats. This study found that when randomly applied, none of these tactics significantly affect criminal activity. From this, directed patrol developed, which focused officers on specific crime problems during the time they were not responding to calls-for-service. With community policing, these specific crime problems were to be related to the neighborhoods being patrolled (Kelling, Dieckman, & Brown, 1974).

The **Broken Windows theory** (Wilson & Kelling, 1982) was another concept that became part of community-oriented policing. In 1982, the concept was published as an analogy to describe the relationship between disorder and crime. A broken window left unrepaired shows others that no one cares about the property, causing a chain reaction of events that deteriorate neighborhood quality of life.

W. Skogan later contributed to this theory, describing what he referred to as "contagion proposition." He wrote that certain disorders generate more disorder unless quickly controlled. Current levels of disorder can produce future crime problems, fear of crime, victimization, and residential dissatisfaction (Skogan, 1996).

Problem-Oriented Policing (POP) is a concept attributed to Herman Goldstein (1979). The concept incorporates the idea that law enforcement attempts to reduce crime problems should take on a more scientific approach. It should involve proactive policing strategies that focus on the identification of underlying causes of problems, then select solutions to prevent a problem from recurring. This approach stemmed from the directed patrol concept of the Kansas City study, providing yet another example of the evolution of client-oriented policing. The concept was further related to a number of underlying issues:

1. Traditional police responses to community problems had proven ineffective.

2. These responses had generally been reactive, and police rarely had made serious attempts to anticipate and head off community problems.

3. In attempting to deal with community problems, the police generally had looked only to themselves and had rarely enlisted the aid of other community institutions and resources.

4. The police response to the problems they confronted had been characterized by an over-reliance on law enforcement.

5. Traditional measures of police performance had overemphasized numbers (arrests, tickets, response time in minutes, etc.) without regard to whether these quantitative measures reflected the quality of police service.

6. Because police and community situations and problems vary so greatly, no hard-and-fast set of rules had been devised to guide performances in all situations.

7. The fiction that police officers do not exercise discretion should finally be abandoned because even in the most rigid law enforcement–oriented police departments, officers exercise great discretion.

8. Like other professionals' discretion, police discretion should be acknowledged and structured in ways that more directly address the problems they are expected to confront.

9. Because police hold such broad authority, they must be held closely accountable for exercising it in ways that best serve to address community problems (Eck & Spelman, 1987).

Throughout the history of law enforcement, selective enforcement has occurred. As discussed in Chapter 6, the police have never been provided the resources to enforce all the laws. This is because of the general public's fear of a "police state," where the police are equipped to enforce laws and regulations not supported by the majority. Consequently, the police have always had to focus their limited resources where they thought they were most needed. POP brought forward the Open Systems concept of thinking "outside the box." It also incorporated the idea of a "Big Y, little x" approach (discussed in Chapter 8), in that it encouraged discretion but applied measures of control in ensuring that the efforts of employees met community needs.

A major component of POP is known by the acronym **SARA** (scanning, analyzing, responding, and assessing).

Scanning is the clustering of incidents into meaningful units. It is another word for the traditional first step of problem solving, gathering the facts. The information gleaned can be divided into units by behavior, location, persons, time, and events.

Analyzing is often considered the heart of the problem-solving model because any mistakes made here can lead to misguided responses. Determining the cause of problems is most important to developing a resolution. Analysis includes identifying the magnitude of the problem, all the persons or groups involved or impacted, identifying all the possible causes of the problem, and constructing a number of approaches from which to choose.

Responding is the approach that is most effective once the plan of action is clearly defined. It may be simple (such as playing "elevator-type music" on the public address system to encourage gang members not to congregate at a certain location) to quite involved (such as evicting tenants involved in drug trafficking from public housing). A Web site has been created whereby various policing agencies can exchange responses to like problems.

Assessing is evaluating the effectiveness of the response. Traditional methods for evaluating include numbers of arrests, reported crimes, response times, citizen complaints, field interviews, calls-for-services, and clearance rates. More nontraditional and insightful methods include:

- Reduced instances or repeat victimization
- Decreases in related crimes and incidents
- Neighborhood indicators, which can include increased profits for businesses in the target area, increased usage of the area, increased property values, less loitering and truancy, and fewer abandoned cars
- Increased citizen satisfaction regarding the handling of the problem (determined through surveys, interviews, focus groups, electronic bulletin boards)
- Reduced citizen fear related to the problem (Office of Community Oriented Policing Services, 2001)

Community policing has become more of a generic term that combines both community-oriented and problem-oriented policing. It is considered a department-wide philosophy that emphasizes the need for partnership with the community. It includes proactive problem-solving efforts in order to promote neighborhood quality of life and prevent and reduce those factors that cause crime. It involves strategic and tactical elements that include fixed assignment of officers to a particular shift or time and the decentralization of decision making to the level at which the officers meet their "clients." In summary, this approach (that has taken policing into the 21st century) involves:

- Decentralizing services to specific neighborhoods
- Empowering employees and giving them responsibility and authority for specific neighborhoods
- Empowering residents and having them share responsibility and authority for neighborhood quality of life
- Applying problem-solving approaches
- Evaluating success based on achieving goals that are mutually set by residents and employees

Table 11–2 compares the differences between what has been called "traditional policing" and community policing. The comparison reveals the different approaches that are involved in contemporary policing. These approaches are an important part of the Eclectic Perspective approach to criminal justice administration.

Police Accountability to the Community (PAC) is a term that the author has introduced to describe the evolution of client-oriented policing in the first decade of the 21st century. The evolution of policing reminds us that no approach is static. The community policing mode evolved from Team Policing and was further enhanced by problem-oriented policing. No approach can be considered the final answer. Each approach is part of the continuing effort to find better methods of policing in an ever-changing environment.

To forecast the future of policing, one should reconsider the elements of social dynamics because policing is influenced by social change. It is useful here to revisit Alvin Toffler's "three waves" of social dynamics, discussed in Chapter 4 (Toffler, 1980). In retrospect, we can see that the 2000s have not produced a working society completely devoted to information and technology, as Toffler predicted. Rather, information and technology have become the "physical element" that we depend on (as land and energy were in the preceding periods of history). The "minds" of the employees and customers have become the important human element whereas muscle and dexterity where of prime importance in the past. As discussed in Chapter 6, the elements of successful enterprise for the future appear to be:

Historical paradigms	Vital physical elements	Vital human elements
Service	Information and technology	Minds

Service has emerged as the major theme of today's occupations. What is service? It is tasks that our ancestors did for themselves that we now pay others to do for us. Today, most working people have specialized jobs and pay others to cook their food, make and clean their clothes, create their leisure time activities, and, yes, provide their policing.

The trend for the immediate future of policing, as in the past, will be influenced by social dynamics. Members of today's society hire others to do many

Table 11–2	Traditional vs. Community Policing: Questions and Answers	
Question	**Traditional policing**	**Community policing**
Who are the police?	A government agency principally responsible for law enforcement.	The police are the public, and the public are the police. The police officers are those who are paid to give full-time attention to the duties of every citizen.
What is the relationship of the police force to other public-service departments?	Priorities often conflict.	The police are one department, among many, responsible for improving the quality of life.
What is the role of the police?	To focus on solving crimes.	To take a broader problem-solving approach.
How is police efficiency measured?	By detection and arrest rates.	By the absence of crime and disorder.
What are the highest priorities?	Crimes that are high value (e.g., bank robberies) and those involving violence.	Whatever problems disturb the community most.
What, specifically, do police deal with?	Incidents.	Citizens' problems and concerns.
What determines the effectiveness of police?	Response times.	Public cooperation.
What view do police take of service calls?	Deal with them only if there is no real police work to do.	View them as a vital function and a great opportunity.
What is police professionalism?	Responding swiftly and effectively to serious crime.	Keeping close to the community.
What kind of intelligence is most important?	Crime intelligence (study of particular crimes or series of crimes).	Criminal intelligence (information on the activities of individuals or groups).
What is the essential nature of police accountability?	Highly centralized; governed by rules, regulations, and policy directives; accountable to the law.	Emphasis on local accountability to community needs.
What is the role of headquarters?	To provide the necessary rules and policy directives.	To preach organizational values.
What is the role of the press liaison department?	To keep the "heat" off operational officers so they can get on with the job.	To coordinate an essential channel of communication with the community.
How do the police regard prosecutions?	As an important goal.	As one tool among many.

Source: Malcolm, K. (1988). "Implementing Community Policing." Washington, DC: Department of Justice, National Institute of Justice, U.S. Government Printing Office. November: 8–9.

things our ancestors did for themselves. It follows that people expect the tax-financed police to provide services that result in crime-free and peaceful neighborhoods. Consequently, when the contemporary community-oriented police officer requests today's working community members to attend neighborhood watch meetings, their response may be different than just a decade ago. When people today are asked to participate in crime prevention efforts and (as suggested by some COP programs) to get involved in being the "eyes and ears" of the police, the response is more likely to be, "What do we pay taxes for?" With many people working long hours and traveling long distances to work, they may resent the idea of "partnering" with the police to protect their neighborhoods. They are more inclined to spend their non-working hours involved in personal "quality-time" activities.

This is not to say that community policing is outmoded. Most crimes are not solved by the police apprehending the perpetrator in the act. Rather, most crimes are solved because some community member provides the police with information that leads to the arrest of the violator. Retaining public trust so that the public provides the information needed to bring criminals to justice is still of prime importance. The philosophy of community policing remains essential in gaining and maintaining public trust.

Additionally, the police continue not to have the resources to enforce all the laws. This has resulted in selective enforcement throughout history. Selective enforcement is placing limited resources to work on selected problems. It is the selection of these problems in which today's public wants to be involved. Problem-oriented policing is a more current form of selective enforcement, which involves local community members in determining how limited police resources will be deployed.

The recent trend of public demand for more customized services and products impacts policing. Additionally, "home rule" continues to be an important element in the way our society wants to be governed. This is why nationally we have more than 17,000 separate police departments. There is a growing feeling among members of our service-minded public that they no longer have time to be a "partner" in helping to deliver the community services. They do, however, want to be involved in specifying what services they receive and how these services are to be customized to their neighborhood needs.

In the past, as part of community-oriented policing, the police could rationalize their failure to cope with some crime problems by arguing that the public should be held accountable as part of the police-community partnership. This approach somewhat negated the fixing of responsibility and gave law enforcement an excuse for not fulfilling their mission. Today's trend is for the public to be involved in defining what problems are impacting neighborhood quality of life and then holding the police accountable for solving these problems. This trend may be called Police Accountability to Community (PAC) or "making a "PAC" with the community to solve specified community/policy problems.

CompStat, the recent policing approach developed by Lee Brown of the New York Police Department (which has won wide acclaim for reducing crime), is a prime example of this trend. This computer-driven statistical approach provides a means for individual neighborhoods to establish which problems are to be solved:

- Determine specific objectives for each patrol area with public input.
- Apply innovative tactics, rapid placement of personnel and other resources to specific problems.
- Employ relentless follow-up and assessment (Maple, 1999, p. 246).

In a 2005 article regarding the Los Angeles Police Department's use of Comp-Stat (Gascon, 2005, pp. 34–43), the importance of clients (referred to as "stake-holders") involvement in defining local problems was emphasized. The police are then held accountable for creating and implementing plans for solving the problems specified by the clients.

People employed in specialized jobs are demanding customized quality-of-life services for which they want to hold the providers accountable. Additionally, the threat of terrorism is causing police agencies to redeploy some of their limited resources from community-oriented activities to Homeland Security functions. These trends are requiring the police to redirect their client-oriented policing approach from a police/public partnership to a more PAC approach of policing. This approach has the public involved in establishing what community problems are to be addressed by the police, but the police are held accountable for solving them. There is a "PAC" between the community and the police, wherein the police are held accountable for solving community-defined problems specific to individual neighborhoods.

The PAC approach, as with other changes, began to materialize several decades earlier. During the later part of the 1980s, the author, as chief of the Santa Ana Police Department in California, was privileged to be linked to other police chiefs throughout the country through a program at the Harvard University Kennedy School of Government. The major purpose of this program was to focus the agency's personnel and other resources on resolving specific public safety problems. Additionally, the emphasis was on working more closely with the community and other governmental organizations to resolve these problems.

Surveys were taken to determine specific problems of concern to individual neighborhoods. Once specific problems were identified, responsibility for solving these problems was assigned to specific police administrators. The author, who had recently worked in the private sector of a large financial institution, was aware of how private businesses assigned responsibilities and rewarded employees. Following the private sector example, police administrators could be rewarded for solving specific neighborhood problems with a yearly bonus of up to 7.5% of their salaries.

Similar approaches were being taken by other police executives involved in the Harvard University project. During this period, Lee Brown left Houston, Texas, to take over the New York Police Department. It was as superintendent of the NYPD that Brown implemented CompStat. CompStat was enhanced by William Bratton when he became superintendent of the New York Police Department. Bratton, more recently, implemented this concept in the Los Angeles Police Department. This approach of determining specific neighborhood problems, holding assigned police administrators accountable for solving them, and using computer geographics to monitor progress has become a common approach to policing in the first decade of the 21st century.

Client-Oriented Service in Courts and Corrections

Most of the discussion of Client-Oriented Service has related to law enforcement. Perhaps because law enforcement is the most visible criminal justice component to the public, it has been involved in the majority of community-oriented changes. As discussed in Chapter 6, courts and corrections are still functioning under the "just deserts" philosophy mandated by legislation. Even though they are called "correctional institutions," rehabilitation has been considered less important in protecting the public than "warehousing" criminals. Nevertheless, a number of client-oriented efforts are being made in these two branches of the criminal justice system.

During the client-oriented development period, a **community prosecution approach** emerged. Prosecutors across the country began to view their roles as more than just the efficient handling of cases. This resulted in prosecutors working with citizens and the police to identify the crimes of most concern to their communities and those that were having the most impact on local quality of life. Prosecutors then focused their limited resources towards the prosecution of conditions that were most important to their communities. With this approach, prosecution efforts partner with other agencies and resources in the community to provide more domestic tranquility. This can include civil remedies such as restraining orders to reduce community disturbances, nuisance abatement for gang offenders, trespass statute prosecutions, and health and safety enforcement (Cole & Kelling 1999, pp. 124–137).

An example of this approach is a community prosecution program in Buffalo, New York, which involved fifteen agencies in a "Save our Streets" task force. The task force included the district attorney's office, the police department, probation services, the U.S. Marshals, and the U.S. Attorney's Office. The program, coordinated by the prosecutor, targeted houses suspected of drug use and harboring criminal activity (Grant, 1999). In Washington, DC, the U.S. District Attorney has partnered with the Metropolitan Police of the District of Columbia and other private and public agencies to enhance the prosecutorial function. The prosecutor's office assigns attorneys to assist the police in criminal investigations, in the review of arrest warrants, and with the presentation of arrested cases in court. One of the major advantages in this partnership is the increased flow of information among the community, police and the prosecutor's office (Metropolitan Police District of Columbus, 2005).

In recent years, **community-based corrections** programs have developed. Correctional agencies are forming mutually beneficial partnerships with the police aimed at enhancing community safety. This is related to the community policing movement to make better use of community resources in reducing crime and disorder. Community-based corrections involves a number of noninstitutional approaches, including:

1. Efforts designed to divert accused offenders from the criminal justice system or jail prior to prosecution,
2. Sentences and programs that impose restrictions on convicted offenders while maintaining them in the community, and

3. Efforts designed to smooth the transition of inmates from prison to freedom (McCarthy, McCarthy, Jr., & Leone, 2001, p. 1).

Protection of the public is an important consideration in returning offenders to the community. Corrections is sometimes criticized for high recidivism rates and properly preparing offenders to remain crime-free is a worthy goal of community-based corrections. **Figure 11–1** shows the escalating punishments model to controlling the behavior of probationers under the community-based correction approach.

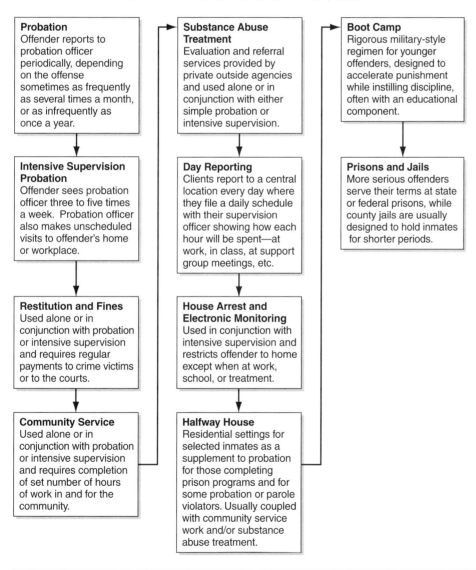

ESCALATING PUNISHMENTS TO FIT THE CRIME

Probation
Offender reports to probation officer periodically, depending on the offense sometimes as frequently as several times a month, or as infrequently as once a year.

Intensive Supervision Probation
Offender sees probation officer three to five times a week. Probation officer also makes unscheduled visits to offender's home or workplace.

Restitution and Fines
Used alone or in conjunction with probation or intensive supervision and requires regular payments to crime victims or to the courts.

Community Service
Used alone or in conjunction with probation or intensive supervision and requires completion of set number of hours of work in and for the community.

Substance Abuse Treatment
Evaluation and referral services provided by private outside agencies and used alone or in conjunction with either simple probation or intensive supervision.

Day Reporting
Clients report to a central location every day where they file a daily schedule with their supervision officer showing how each hour will be spent—at work, in class, at support group meetings, etc.

House Arrest and Electronic Monitoring
Used in conjunction with intensive supervision and restricts offender to home except when at work, school, or treatment.

Halfway House
Residential settings for selected inmates as a supplement to probation for those completing prison programs and for some probation or parole violators. Usually coupled with community service work and/or substance abuse treatment.

Boot Camp
Rigorous military-style regimen for younger offenders, designed to accelerate punishment while instilling discipline, often with an educational component.

Prisons and Jails
More serious offenders serve their terms at state or federal prisons, while county jails are usually designed to hold inmates for shorter periods.

Figure 11–1 Court and Corrections Community Approaches.

The National Institute of Justice funded a study of 14 police-corrections partnerships in the interest of assisting criminal justice administrators implement such approaches. The researchers categorized the partnerships into five categories (Parent & Snyder, 1999):

1. **Enhanced-Supervision Partnerships**

   This was the most common type of partnership and sought to increase the detection of offenders violating probation or patrol conditions by conducting joint supervision activities. Unannounced home visits by probation, parole, and police officers were used as a means of increasing supervision. In a Boston project called "Boston's Operation Night Light," homicides and gang violence was greatly reduced.

2. **Fugitive-Apprehension Units**

   In this approach, correction and police personnel jointly sought to locate and apprehend offenders who had absconded from parole and probation officers.

3. **Information-Sharing Partnerships**

   With this approach, procedures were implemented that increased the exchange of information. Shared database and regular meetings to discuss correctional populations under community supervision within geographic boundaries were examples of partnerships in this category.

4. **Specialized-Enforcement Partnerships**

   Joint efforts with relevant community agencies, specialized-enforcement partnerships were formed to enhance collaborative problem-solving efforts related to the concerns of individual communities.

5. **Interagency Problem-Solving Partnerships**

   Corrections and the police jointly identified mutual problems with their local communities, prioritized strategies and implemented mutually beneficial approaches. These partnerships provided opportunities not available to individual agencies. For example, police officers often were unable to keep gang members from associating with other gang members, whereas a probation or parole officer enforced disassociation as a condition of release. In these partnerships, social equity protections must be maintained. The police, for example, must resist any temptation to circumvent Fourth Amendment rights, by using the probation or parole officers to make searches for which the police have no probable cause.

The Manhattan Institute issued a report recommending a "radical rethinking" of probation. Prepared by probation practitioners, it emphasizes community justice approaches to probation with recommendations summarized as follows:

1. Put public safety first.
2. Supervise probationers in the neighborhood, not the office.
3. Require probation officers to spend more time supervising those offenders who are most at risk.

4. Enforce violations of probation conditions quickly and strongly.
5. Develop partners in the community by:
   - Creating a system that has meaningful participation from victims and the community,
   - Developing partnerships with neighborhood groups, schools, business, and the faith communities to bring offenders into an environment that has pro-social supports,
   - Establishing cooperative partnerships between probation, police, and other criminal justice agencies,
   - Partnering with human service, treatment, and nonprofit agencies to provide enhanced services to assess, diagnose, treat, and supervise offenders, and
   - Creating a comprehensive education campaign to make citizens aware of the crime problems, the steps being taken to address the problems, and communicating the message that their involvement is desired.
6. Establish performance-based initiatives using information-based decision making.
7. Require leadership from the top:
   - In the final analysis, leadership is the most important ingredient for success.
   - It flows from individuals who are risk-takers, willing to enthusiastically embrace a new narrative for their field and the practice of probation (Manhattan Institute, 1999).

As with law enforcement administration, courts and correctional administrators have a number of challenges and barriers in moving traditional organizations toward more client-oriented approaches. Some of these challenges and barriers are discussed in the next section.

■ Administrative Challenges Associated with the Client-Oriented Approach

Resistance from within agencies and external economic, political and social factors must often be confronted by criminal justice administrators in implementing client-oriented approaches. Careful long-term planning efforts involving all levels of the organization, as well as elected officials and community members are required. Following are some of the issues specific to implementing client-oriented approaches.

Organizational structures need to become more organic and flat (discussed in Chapter 7). They must make allowances for an unsteady and ever-changing environment. They must reduce levels of authority to facilitate communication and the delegation of the decision making to its most client-oriented level.

The assignment of personnel to fixed geographic and time assignments must be evaluated in light of historical experience. The philosophy of community policing, for example, is to bring the police and the public into a partnership and to promote an ownership of specific neighborhoods.

The long-term assignment of officers to a particular shift and time is encouraged. However, it must be remembered that in the early years of "professionalism" in law enforcement, police officers were removed from fixed beats and assigned to rotating watches to eliminate corruption. Assigning officers to specific beats resulted in some becoming too familiar with the local public. This led to favoritism, gratuities, and bribery. Of course, during that time, the "spoils system" and the selection of unqualified, untrained, and underpaid personnel contributed to the corruption.

As discussed in Chapter 5, more misconduct was associated with officers being assigned to morning shifts (Rodney King incident) or special units (Rampart scandal) for long periods of time resulting in undesirable subcultures developing. This is where the Eclectic Perspective can sound "warning bells" that serve as reminders that proper controls must be put in place to prevent these types of undesirable situations from occurring.

A good rule of thumb in law enforcement is that patrol officers should have at least half of their time available for proactive activities (**Figure 11–2**). Answering calls-for-service is certainly an important part of a patrol officer's duty and their response time in emergencies can contribute to public faith in police service. However, community policing requires adequate time for crime prevention and problem-solving activities.

Additionally, time is required to help build community partnerships and public trust. Police administrators should evaluate the workload of their patrol officers to ensure time for proactive activities or community policing will not prevail.

Even the geographical location of the police department has something to do with the number of officers available. East Coast departments traditionally have more officers in relationship to the population than West Coast departments. The reason goes back to the advent of the automobile. As our country developed from east to west, the first police departments were in the east and foot beats were the common mode of policing. Officers were hired so that most every few blocks had a "watchman" to cover that area as their beat. These cities continued to hire in this manner as the population grew.

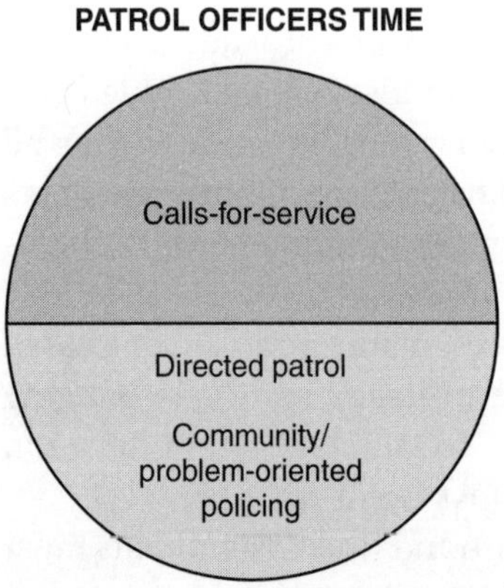

PATROL OFFICERS TIME

Calls-for-service

Directed patrol

Community/
problem-oriented
policing

Figure 11–2 Patrol Time Necessary for Reactive Policing.

By the time that the country had expanded to include what we now call the West, the automobile had become commonplace. Consequently, as western police departments were created, they were developed around the concept of officers patrolling in vehicles and able to cover larger areas than when on foot. This is why, at the beginning of the 21st century, the New York Police Department had more that 40,000 officers for a population of 5 million and the Los Angeles Police Department had less than 10,000 officers for a population of 3 million.

Returning more officers to foot beats for face to face contact with the public is a desirable goal in community policing. For most West Coast cities to do this would require the doubling of the size of their departments. Conversely, East Coast cities still have more officers per capita and are more able to support community policing with time for proactive police activities and more foot beats. History also should remind police administrators that the public tends to reduce financial support for policing when crimes decrease and also when public trust of the police diminishes. It is an unfortunate reality that when the criminal justice system can be considered successful because of a decrease in crime, the public/political response is usually a decrease in tax support. Without proper resources the police are forced to retreat to a reactive mode resulting in an increase in crime.

Without the proactive attributes of community policing, one can predict that crime will increase as it has in the past. When crime reaches a critical level, the public can be expected to respond by providing tax dollars to hire more officers as they did in the 1980s with the "War on Crime." The problem with this "knee-jerk" response is that the police lose too much ground in fighting crime during these tax deduction periods. It takes years to regain this loss once crime goes up and the police are given additional resources. An Open Systems outlook suggests that administrators must continually educate elected officials and the public to the need for continual and adequate financial support if policing is to be effective.

Having enough personnel is also vital to implementing client-oriented approaches in the courts and corrections. As previously discussed, the criminal justice system has never been financed to comprehensively confront the crime problem. Many additional prosecutors, defense lawyers, judges and probation/parole officers, as well as custodial personnel are needed to implement many of the aforementioned concepts. For example, the case loads of probation and parole officer must drastically be reduced if proactive client-oriented methods are to be applied. The important factor in being able to provide Client-Oriented Service is being proactive rather that reactive. This takes an adequately number of trained personnel. Convincing (and continually reminding) the public and elected officials of this factor is an important task for all criminal justice administrators.

Crime may rise as a result of community policing. The author, as a consultant and practitioner, has observed a number of police administrators face political and public criticism after implementing community policing because of a perceived rise in crime. These phenomena also can cause like challenges for court and correctional administrators. What really occurs in these situations is a rise in reported crime. Each year, crime is measured by comparing reported crimes (FBI Uniform Crime Report) with actual crime (Bureau of Justice Statistics National Crime Victimization Survey). The comparison shows that less than half of all crime is actually reported (National Crime Victimization Survey, 2005).

Many crimes go unreported because of a distrust of the police. If a Client-Oriented approach successfully gains the trust of a community that previously has had much distrust for the police, more victims will come forward and report crime that heretofore may not have been reported. The result can be a noticeable increase in reported crime for the initial years following the implementation of community policing. The Eclectic Perspective administrator would do well to prepare the elected officials and the public for the likely increase in reported crime before it becomes a political issue.

■ Measuring the Effectiveness of Client-Oriented Service Organizations

Establishing and measuring Client-Oriented service goals and objectives is yet another challenge facing criminal justice administrators. In Chapter 8, employee evaluations were reviewed. Here, contemporary concepts are discussed as they apply to evaluating the overall accomplishment of the organization, as well as employees. Traditionally, criminal justice administrators have relied on arrest rates, crime rates, clearance rates, and response time to evaluate police performance. Recent trends focus on holding individual employees (from the line employee to the top executive) accountable for solving neighborhood quality of life issues. For example, "fear of crime" (as introduced by Lee Brown) has been added to the list of community factors to be measured.

Goals and objectives must be established that relate to the needs of the community and the abilities of the organization. This often is a delicate balance, which is influenced by economic and political factors.

Management by Objectives (MBO) is an approach credited to Peter Drucker, the well-known management consultant in the 1950–1970s. His approach fits well in measuring client-oriented goals and objective. Drucker observed that people work hardest when they have a clear objective in mind and can see a direct relationship between their efforts and the accomplishment of that objective. He proposed MBO as a means of obtaining higher work standards and greater productivity while applying stricter accountability (Drucker, 1954). Determining community needs and developing them into quantifiable and time-bound objectives, then holding employees accountable for achieving these objectives, is an important part of measuring the effectiveness of Client-Oriented efforts.

Using an Open Systems approach to establishing standards and performance indicators is important in not only measuring annual objectives but in making "midcourse" adjustments when necessary. **Figure 11–3** provides a graphic picture of this approach. In establishing realistic objectives, knowledge of current inputs, processing, and outputs is necessary.

The author, as a new police chief involved implementing the previously discussed **Matrix Community-Oriented Policing** (MiCOP), initiated a program to establish new goals and objectives (see Relative Publication at end of this chapter for more details). Through a number of personnel and community meetings, the mission statement was established. In an effort to ensure that all department members knew and understood the department mission the following actions

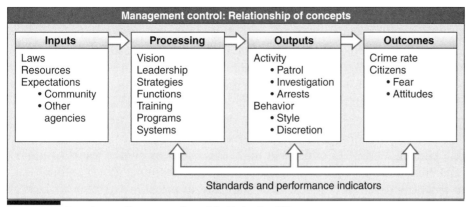

Figure 11–3 Open Systems Management Control for Evaluating COP.

were taken: (1) the mission statement was incorporated in recruit, roll-call, and ongoing training programs; (2) it was included in all promotional examinations; (3) it became a part of the awards and commendation program; and (4) it became the focus of all personnel evaluation reports (Roberg & Kuykendall, 1993).

As part of setting goals and objectives, a survey was developed to determine community and employee opinions. *Input* from public meetings and interviews with those elected by the community as their representatives were also used. All 1,000 members of the department were interviewed in small groups by the executive officers. Every employee also was asked to fill out a questionnaire that asked, among other things, what changes they would like to see implemented in the department, and which practices they would like to see remain in place.

Responses to the survey produced over 200 items that were distributed to the employees in a second questionnaire asking them to rate each item in order of importance. From this process, the 20 most critical issues were selected. Managers were then assigned to task forces with groups of employees to develop ways to resolve these issues. The implementation of these recommendations then became objectives for which all administrators and their employees were held accountable.

Next, the five geographic divisions of the city were surveyed to determine the major policing concerns of individual neighborhoods. Major concerns involving specific crimes, gangs, drugs, vagrants, prostitution, and traffic were defined by individual neighborhoods and resolving them became the focus of yearly objectives set by all employees, line personnel to the top executives.

Factors were established to measure the accomplishment of the objective. These evaluation factors were:

- Specific crime of concern to individual neighborhoods
- Traffic accidents relating to specific neighborhoods
- Response time for life-threatening incidents, and for lesser incidents as they were of concern to specific neighborhoods
- Community satisfaction as established by yearly surveys
- Commendations and sustained personnel complaints
- Employee satisfaction as established by yearly surveys of all employees

Important to the Client-Oriented Service evaluation process is that success is not just based on the quantity of work (e.g., number of arrests, traffic citations, and crime) but must include qualitative measures which are more difficult to evaluation. **Appendix 6** provides one example of a community survey developed by the author for this purpose. Note that questions about what crimes are of most concern are followed by questions about what crimes the person taking the survey had actually been exposed to. Often the comparison of the answers to these questions shows more *fear* of crime than actual victimization. This is a method of measuring the fear of crime that may be reduced by rumor control and factual media coverage. Additionally, it is important that once the "baseline" survey has been taken, it is repeated periodically to measure progress (or lack of progress) in achieving objectives. The National Office of Community Oriented Policing Services provides a suggested community survey formats that may be tailored to the needs of individual agencies (Office of Community Oriented Policing Services, 2006).

Mail-in surveys are a low cost method of surveying (especially if combined with regular mailings such as utility bills), but low response rates make them less desirable in establishing overall community opinion. Interviews are more reliable but often cost-prohibitive. The author found college student volunteers from a local university very helpful. In a mostly Spanish-speaking part of town, the author gained the help of members of a state Hispanic police officers association and their spouses in conducting the interview. A side benefit of this arrangement was that the off-duty officers, who conducted the interviews in "street clothes," said they were able to gain insight into these communities "in a way they never could while in uniform."

In the city where the author was police chief, he was able to reward managers with a yearly bonus for achieving objectives. **Appendix 7** shows a portion of a personnel evaluation form currently being used by the city of Rock Island, Illinois where yearly community quality of life objectives are set between employees and their supervisors. Police officers and other employees then can receive up to a 3% (above cost-of-living increases) increase in salary for achieving these objectives. This type of evaluation and reward process, common in the business world for years, in now becoming more prevalent as part of the Police Accountability to the Community (PAC) approach.

The Police Executive Research Forum suggests using **21 statistical indicators based on seven performance dimensions** to measure the overall effectiveness of police agencies (**Table 11–3**). These measurement factors reflect a comprehensive understanding of the goals and objectives required of a client-oriented service criminal justice agency.

Most of the discussion of measurement of Client-Oriented Service has related to law enforcement. Here the focus is on evaluating such service in the courts and corrections. The *National Sourcebook of Criminal Justice Statistics* (2005) provides some useful information in evaluating the effectiveness of prosecutors and the courts. Information such as how many cases of particular types are prosecuted, how many are plea-bargained, how many go to trial and the trial outcome, the number of judges who are sanctioned or recalled, and convictions rates of prosecutors are just a few facts that are available in national, as well as state and

Table 11–3	Statistical Measures of Police Organizational Performance	
Performance dimensions	**Statistical indicators**
Reduce criminal victimization	Reported crime rates Victimization rates
Call offenders to account	Clearance rates Conviction rates
Reduce fear and enhance personal security	Reported changes in levels of fear Reported changes in self-defense measures
Guarantee safety in public spaces	Traffic fatalities, injuries, and damage Increased utilization of parks and public spaces Increased property values
Use financial resources fairly, efficiently, and effectively	Cost per citizen Deployment efficiency/fairness Scheduling efficiency Budget compliance Overtime expenditures Civilianization
Use force and authority fairly, efficiently, and effectively	Citizen complaints Settlements in liability suits Police shootings
Satisfy customer demands/achieve legitimacy with those policed	Satisfaction with police services Response times Citizen perceptions of fairness

Source: Adapted from Moore, M., Thacher, D., Dodge, A. & Moore, T. (2002). *Recognizing Value in Policing: The Challenge of Measuring Police Performance.* Washington, DC: Police Executive Research Forum.

local government publications. Tying these facts to client-oriented goals and objectives is necessary for proper measurement of results.

The Client-Oriented Service approach in corrections focuses on community safety. Community-based corrections involves programs designed to provide various forms of education, vocational, psychological, and social assistance to enable offenders to be integrated back into the community and remain crime-free. Yet, approximately 60–65% of those granted probation or parole commit new crimes or have their release revoked within one to two years (Maguire & Pastone, 2000). Measurement of recidivism rates is just one way of measuring the effectiveness of client-oriented approaches. As with law enforcement, measuring public fear of crime and domestic tranquility is yet another.

Wrap Up

Evolutionary components of Client-Oriented Service in law enforcement

- Community-relation and press programs
  - Team policing
  - Neighborhood watch
- Community-Oriented Policing (COP)
  - Return to the Peel Principles
  - Kansas City study
  - Broken Windows theory
  - Fear of crime
- Problem-Oriented Policing (POP)
  - SARA
- Community policing
  - Combining COP and POP
- Police Accountability to Community (PAC) policing
  - Diminishing police-public partnership
  - CompStat
  - Matrix Community-Oriented Policing (MiCOP)

Client-Oriented Service in the courts and corrections

- Community prosecution approach
- Community-based corrections

Administrative challenges associated with the Client-Oriented Service approach

- Crime may rise as a result of community policing

Measuring the effectiveness of Client-Oriented Service organizations

- Management by objectives (MBO)
- 21 statistical indicators based on seven performance dimensions

CHAPTER ACTIVITY

Go to the Internet and locate the problem-oriented policing (POP) Web site. Think of a POP problem and investigate what SARA approaches to this problem have been tried by various agencies.

REVIEW QUESTIONS

1. How do the concepts of Peters and Waterman and Jan Carlzon apply today?

2. Describe the evolutionary stages that the Client-Oriented Service concepts have gone through to bring us to what is considered the best approach today. Do you think that these concepts will continue to be considered the best in the future?

3. What are some of the hazards of implementing Client-Oriented Service? As an administrator, how would you overcome them?

4. Discuss some of the Client-Oriented Service approaches of court and correction administration.

5. Imagine that you are a criminal justice administrator and have been assigned to develop and implement a criminal justice entity of your choice (for example, a community-based correction program). What Client-Oriented Service concepts would you consider in fulfilling this assignment?

REFERENCES

Ardrey, R. L. (1966). *Territorial Imperative: A Personal Inquiry into the Animal Origins of Property and Nations.* New York: Atheneum.

Cole, C., & Kelling, G. (1999). Prevention through Community Prosecution. *The Public Interest,* Fall, pp.124–137.

Cronkhite, C. (1988). Santa Ana's Reorganization—Matrix Community Oriented Policing. *The Journal of California Law Enforcement,* April, pp. 17–21.

Davis, E. M. (1978). *Staff One: A Perspective of Effective Police Management.* Englewood Cliffs, NJ: Prentice Hall.

Drucker, P. (1954). *The Practice of Management.* New York: Harper.

Eck, J. E., & Spelman, W. (1987). *Problem Solving: Problem-Oriented Policing in Newport News.* Washington, DC: Police Executive Research Forum.

Gascon, G. (2005). ComStat Plus. *Police Chief. International Association of Chiefs of Police,* May, pp.24–26.

Goldstein, H. (1979). *Problem-Oriented Policing.* New York: McGraw-Hill.

Grant, H. (1999). Buffalo Weed and Seed Initiative. In *Promising Practices to Reduce Juvenile Gun Violence.* Washington, DC: Office of Juvenile Justice and Delinquency Prevention.

Kelling, G., Dieckman, T. D., & Brown, C. E. (1974). *The Kansas City Preventive Patrol Experiment: A Summary Report.* Washington, DC: The Police Foundation.

Maple, J. (1999). *The Crime Fighter.* New York: Doubleday.

McCarthy, B., McCarthy, B., Jr., & Leone, M. (2001). *Community-Based Corrections* (4th ed.). Belmont, CA: Wadsworth/Thomson Learning.

Maguire, K., & Pastone, A. (2000). *Bureau of Justice Statistics Sourcebook of Criminal Justice Statistics*. Albany: The Hindelang Criminal Justice Research Center, State University of New York at Albany.

Manhattan Institute. (1999). Broken Windows Probations: The Next Step in Fighting Crime. *Civic Report,* 7, August, pp.37–42.

Metropolitan Police District of Columbus. (2003). "Community Prosecution." Retrieved March 2006, from http://wysiwig://20/http://mpoc.oc.gov/info/comm./commpros.shtn

National Crime Victimization Survey. (2005). Washington, DC: Department of Justice.

The National Sourcebook of Criminal Justice Statistics. (2005). Washington, DC: Department of Justice.

Office of Community Oriented Policing Services. (2001). *Problem Solving Tips: A Guide to Reducing Crime and Disorder Through Problem-Solving Partnerships.* Washington, DC: Department of Justice.

Office of Community Oriented Policing Services. (2006). *Conducting Community Surveys.* Washington, DC: Department of Justice.

Ottmeier, T. N., & Brown, L. P. (1988). Role Expectations and the Concept of Neighborhood-Oriented Police. In *Development of Neighborhood Oriented Policing.* Arlington, VA: International Association of Chiefs of Police.

Parent, D., & Snyder, B. (1999). *Police-Corrections Partnerships: Issues and Practices.* Washington, DC: National Institute of Justice.

Peters, T. (1989). *Excellence in the Public Sector.* Boston: Enterprise Media Inc. [videotape].

Roberg, R. R., & Kuykendall, J. (1993). *Police & Society.* Belmont, CA: Wadsworth.

Skogan, W. (1996). *Disorder and Decline.* Berkeley: University of California Press.

Sparrow, M. K. (1988). *Implementing Community Policing.* Washington, DC: U.S. Government Printing Office.

Toffler, A. (1980). *The Third Wave.* New York: Bantam Books.

Wilson, J., & Kelling, G. (1982). The Police and Neighborhood Safety. *Atlantic Monthly,* March, pp. 32–35.

Wrap Up

■ RELEVANT PUBLICATION

Matrix Community-Oriented Policing was discussed in this chapter as an element in the evolution of community policing. This article about the Santa Ana Police Department's development of Matrix-COP provides one example of the many approaches to community-oriented policing. (Cronkhite, C. (1988). "Santa Ana's Reorganization—Matrix Community-Oriented Policing." *The Journal of California Law Enforcement*. April, pp. 17–21).

Santa Ana's Reorganization—Matrix Community-Oriented Policing by Clyde Cronkhite

The purpose of this article is to outline the concepts behind the recent reorganization of the Santa Ana Police Department—a reorganization that came about with the hiring of a new police chief and in an effort to energize the Community-Oriented Policing Program.

The Santa Ana Police Department has nearly 600 employees and serves a population of approximately 250,000 (daytime population over 400,000). Santa Ana is the county seat of Orange County, one of the fastest growing areas of Southern California. The city's multi-ethnic population includes a broad spectrum of socio-economical residential areas plus major retail and manufacturing business communities.

The reorganization involved the following five steps:

1. Institutionalizing the department Mission statement.
2. Establishing measurements of accountability for the Mission.
3. Assessing the needs of the community.
4. Assessing the needs of the employees.
5. Reorganizing to meet the needs of 1 through 4.

Institutionalizing the Department Mission Statement

The Mission was developed as a statement through a number of management meetings and retreats. It documents the department's values and provides focus for agency efforts and application of resources.

The Mission of the department is as follows:

". . . to ensure the safety and security of all of the people of our city by providing responsive and professional police service with compassion

and concern. Our Mission is accomplished within the moral and legal standards of our community through a partnership of the community and members of the department."

Next, an effort was made to ensure that all employees knew and understood the Mission. This was accomplished by the following:

- Incorporating it into the recruit, roll call, and ongoing training processes.
- Including it in promotion examinations.
- Making it a part of the awards and commendation system.
- Focusing on it in all personnel evaluation reports.

To further the indoctrination of the Mission, the chief of police and managers randomly asked employees at inspections, roll calls, and individual meetings their interpretation of the meaning of the Mission. All employees were expected to know and to be able to intelligently discuss the Mission.

A slogan contest was held for all employees with a prize of $200 for the slogan that best exemplified the Mission. The winning slogan was "Partners with the Community" which will be displayed on all patrol cars, in police community newsletters, and on public relations billboards throughout the city.

Establishing Measurements of Accountability for the Mission

Measurements had to be agreed upon so that all employees, from the officer in the radio car to the chief of police, could be held accountable. Through a series of meetings, the managers agreed upon the following measures after discussion with employees:

- *Part one crime*—recorded monthly by team, area, and watch.
- *Traffic accidents*—recorded monthly by team, area, and watch.
- *Response time for life threatening incidents*—recorded monthly by team, area, and watch.
- *Community satisfaction*—established in a yearly survey by area and by monthly accounts of commendations and sustained personnel complaints.
- *Employee satisfaction*—established in a yearly survey of all employees. This is a measure for which all supervisors and above are held accountable.

Fiscal year goals were established for each of these measures. These goals are reflected in all personnel evaluation reports. The managers (lieutenants, nonsworn mid-managers and above) have a yearly bonus, which is up to 7½ percent of their salary. The five measures are incorporated into the rating for their bonus. The managers share in this bonus in much the same way that a private corporation gives bonuses when their company makes a profit.

The success measure for all employees is not the quantity of work (number of arrests, and citations) but rather the positive impact they have on these five factors. This approach encourages working closely with each other and with other city agencies and is intended to strengthen external and internal partnerships.

Assessing Community Needs

The department was viewed as a corporation with the city council/city manager being the board of directors and the community members as the shareholders. A survey form was developed (along with input from public meetings and interviews with individual council people) to determine the direction that the community wanted the department to take. The result of the surveys showed that the community wanted special emphasis on the following:

1. Gang activity
2. Street drug activity
3. Prostitution
4. Vagrancy violations
5. Traffic accidents

"Attack Teams" were developed under the leadership of the area commanders (lieutenants). The focus of these Attack Teams is on the five areas of concern to the community. Because of a tight budget, the resources used to finance the Attack Teams come from salary savings and narcotic asset forfeiture money.

Each area commander is given a budget from these funds to "hire" off-duty officers to work outside their regular job hours and to concentrate on positively impacting these five areas. The emphasis is on long-range problem solving.

Assessing the Needs of the Employees

Employees, of course, are the most valuable resource and their job satisfaction is of prime importance. Consequently, all employees were interviewed: managers individually, and supervisors and below in groups of 15. Also, every member of the department was asked to fill out a questionnaire which asked the following three questions:

1. What would you change about the department?
2. What do you not want changed?
3. What should we be doing that we're not doing now?

The response to these questions produced over 200 items that were then distributed back to the employees in a second questionnaire that asked them to rate each item. Through this process, the 20 most important items emerged. These top 20 included a need for more parking space for personal vehicles, more training, and more proactive police work. Managers were assigned to oversee task forces of department employees who were given the opportunity to resolve each of these 20 issues. Their recommendations were published and subsequently implemented.

Reorganization

On July 1, 1988, the Santa Ana Police Department was reorganized. The reorganization focused on the following aspects: achieving the Mission, long-term problem solving, and satisfying the needs of the community and department employees. A key factor was to involve more management and sworn personnel in the Community-Oriented Policing Program for which the Santa Ana Police Department had gained national recognition. Additionally, the five areas of primary concern to the community as established by the community survey were given special emphasis.

A focus of the reorganization was to resolve specific public safety problems and to work more closely with the community and other governmental organizations to resolve these problems. Under the new organization structure, all four captains and seven of the lieutenants share primary responsibility for the Community-Oriented Policing Program instead of one captain and four lieutenants, which had been the case under the prior organization.

The reorganization-called Matrix Community-Oriented Policing (MiCOP) facilitates the accomplishment of the Mission by arranging the department into specialized forces which are capable of attacking problems from different perspectives (Figure 1). All forces share the responsibility for overall success of the Mission but achieve this success through various approaches. MiCOP is a three-dimensional organizational structure approach in which many functions interact to share responsibilities in resolving public safety problems.

First, it is based on the concept that one-dimensional structures are destined to fall; three-dimensional, multi-strength entities, however, provide stability. Second, problems are best solved by attacking them from many overlapping approaches.

In this structure, each employee is held responsible for achieving the Mission in a particular geographical area, for a specified period of time. These responsibilities, however, overlap, providing each area of the city with several forces of the department working to provide service in a matrix effort approach.

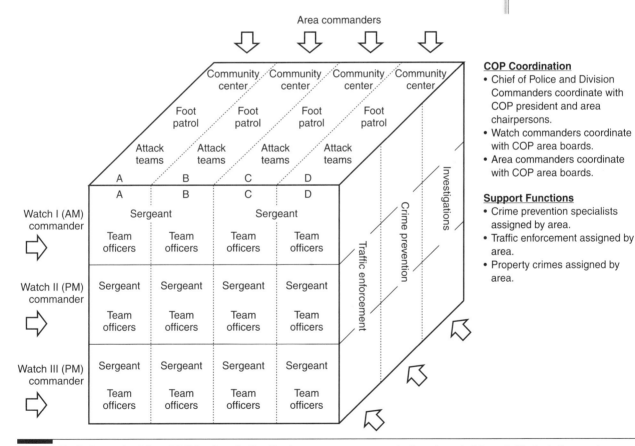

Figure 1 Matrix Community-Oriented Policing Organization Structure (Santa Ana P.D. Reorganization; refer to the Relevant Publication in Chapter 11).

Divisional Responsibility

Under MiCOP, the divisional commanders (captains) are responsible for their respective divisions on a 24-hour basis. They are accountable for achieving the Mission and, along with the chief of police, coordinate with the Community-Oriented Policing president and area chairpersons.

Watch Responsibility

The watch commanders (lieutenants) are responsible for citywide policing on a shift-by-shift basis. They are responsible for achieving the Mission with special priority on responding to calls for services, short-term problem solving and coordinating with the Community-Oriented Policing citywide Executive Board. Their goals are rapid response and resolution of problems of immediate and short-term nature.

Each watch sergeant is responsible for supervising the accomplishment of the Mission in one of the four areas of the city during their watch. Each area has two team territories. Patrol officers are assigned to team territories in which they are responsible for achieving the Mission.

Team officers also attend neighborhood meetings in their territories that are arranged by the area personnel. It is their responsibility to deal with issues on an incident-by-incident basis with focus on rapid response and immediate incident resolution.

Area Responsibility

Each area commander (lieutenant) is responsible for a fourth of the city designated as areas A through D. The area commanders are responsible for these areas on a 24-hour basis. They are accountable for achieving the Mission with special emphasis on long-term problem solving. They coordinate the Community-Oriented Police programs, the community centers, the footbeat program and the Attack Teams.

At the heart of the Community-Oriented Policing program is the community center. One center is located in each of the four areas and is staffed by a sergeant and a number of police service officers who coordinate local neighborhood policing.

Each footbeat is made up of approximately six officers. Additional officers normally assigned to a watch and team will rotate into each area commander's footbeat program for a six-month period. By doing so, these officers gain experience in long-range proactive problem solving and are directly involved in the community center efforts. They bring to the area footbeat program a fresh understanding of the short-range problems in their team territories and take back to their watch a broader understanding of neighborhood issues. This rotation strengthens the matrix approach.

The area commanders have at their disposal funds from salary savings and narcotic asset forfeiture to finance the Attack Teams. The Attack Teams place special focus on the gang problems, street drug problems, prostitution, vagrancy violations, and traffic accidents and use as their resources the "hiring" of off-duty officers.

The efforts of the Attack Teams are not just to make arrests but to develop and implement long-term solutions to these five areas of community concern. They coordinate with other city departments to improve neighborhoods and traffic flow, educate the public, remove graffiti, initiate civil court actions that curtail conditions that cause crime, and develop other innovative ways to provide safe and secure neighborhoods.

Related Responsibilities

Investigative, traffic, and crime prevention activities are likewise divided into specific area and time frame responsibilities. Those who manage and supervise these responsibilities are held accountable for achieving the Mission accordingly. Additionally, these managers and supervisors coordinate with the appropriate components of the Community-Oriented Policing structure in carrying out their responsibilities.

Summary

An essential ingredient of the reorganization is the strong participation of neighborhood and business groups within the community. Neighborhood watch meetings are still effective in some areas. In other areas, special crime issue meetings (grid meetings) are more successful, especially in minority communities inhabited by new arrivals to the city. Tailor-made approaches for individual neighborhoods are necessary.

Another important component of the reorganization is putting the majority of the department (not just a few community relations employees) in direct contact with, and making them directly responsible to, the community they serve.

The basic idea is to focus the resources of the department toward definite goals for which each employee is held accountable. Employees are given the latitude to experiment and create effective methods of achieving these goals. No pretense is made that this organizational structure is perfect. It is felt, however, that it does meet the realities of today's policing demands.

Continual fine tuning and enrichments will be forthcoming and the results of this reorganization will be closely evaluated over the next year.

Criminal Justice Administration and Diversity in the 21st Century

12

■ Introduction

Diversity historically has been an important factor in American society. The Statue of Liberty symbolizes a welcoming of people of diverse backgrounds to the United States. America is often referred to as a "melting pot." This metaphor, however, suggests the fusion of different types of people into one. The very image of a melting pot comes from the iron works factories, where various types of metals are melted at high temperatures, mixed together, and then cooled into one substance.

Diversity, however, means allowing for difference. The "salad bowl" metaphor provides a more realistic image of what we thrive for in the United States. A salad allows a diversity of ingredients to be mixed yet maintains the originality of each ingredient. Allowing people to maintain their cultural and racial differences yet live peacefully together is a mainstay of the American way of life. Embracing differences has enriched American society with various types of entertainment, food, art, fashion, architecture, and many other facets of life that we enjoy.

The Constitution of the United States is a protector of diversity, although it has not always been interpreted as such. It is intended to provide a collective environment in which individuality can be maintained within a united society. The criminal justice system is held responsible for protecting the rights that preserve diversity. This is a vital concept that every criminal justice administrator must incorporate in their duel tasks of achieving the mission of their agency and satisfying the needs of their employees.

■ Diversity

Race and ethnicity are usually the focus of discussions regarding diversity. Until the mid-1900s, most immigrants to the United States were European: German, Irish, Italian, Scottish, Russian, and Polish, to name just a few. Many spoke different languages and certainly many had very different cultural backgrounds. This diverse population of European immigrants formed what today we call the *majority*.

As mentioned in Chapter 10, many of the arriving immigrants settled first in the poorer areas. These poorer areas have been of concern to criminal justice practitioners because of the high crime rates. Certainly, most people who live in poor areas are not criminals. However, poor areas cultivate more criminals and more people who live in these areas become victims of crime. History reminds us that these poor urban areas have been the breeding grounds for crime for centuries. However, a century ago these poorer areas were populated by European immigrants, the forefathers of today's majority. This is an important historical perspective. This perspective provides an understanding that it is not a particular race that is most associated with crime but, rather, people living in the poorer areas.

Figure 12–1 and **Figure 12–2** illustrate how many of our major cities remain segregated. These segregated areas are the areas of the higher crime rates. Review of the 2000 census finds little change from years ago despite growing ethnic and racial diversity in the nation. Researchers base these figures on a segregation index. The index ranges from 0 to 100, providing the percentage of groups that would have to move to achieve even residential patterns. Overall, the least segregated areas tend to be those with the smallest Hispanic and African-American population. Similarly, Asian segregation remains high and has shown very little change in the past several decades (Lewis Mumford Center, 2001).

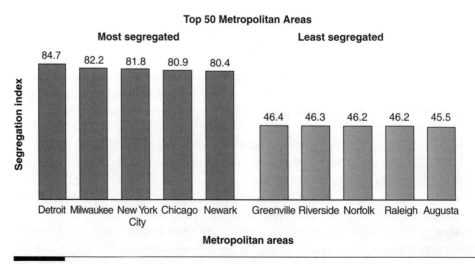

Figure 12–1 White-Black Segregation.

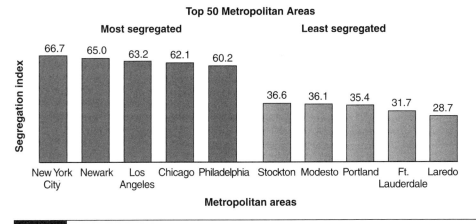

Figure 12–2 White-Latino Segregation.

The consequences of poverty (poor job opportunities, education, and health care) relates to increases in delinquency and crime. Given the higher rates of poverty experienced by ethnic and racial minorities, the segregation of minorities promotes high crime areas (Massey, 2004, pp. 7–8).

A guiding principle should be that it is the consequences of poverty (lack of education, employment, health care, and the like) that have a strong correlation to crime. Perpetuating minority status and segregation promotes crime-ridden poor areas. These areas not only have high crime but also a high rate of crime victims. These are the areas that require a large percentage of criminal justice resources. This is an important perspective that criminal justice administrators must ensure that their employees understand. Educating employees regarding this subject is an important responsibility of today's criminal justice administrator.

Diversity Issues in Today's Multicultural Society

Preparing employees to serve in a multicultural society is a prime task for today's criminal justice administrator. Understanding the terms, differences, and compositions of multicultural communities is important to every criminal justice employee. A term that is most often associated with multicultural communities is *minorities*.

Minority groups are subordinate groups who have significantly less control over their lives than do dominant or majority groups (Schaefer, 2007, pp. 5–6). In fact, the term subordinate group is a more meaningful definition than *minority* because at least one group often placed in this category outnumbers the *majority*. Women are considered minorities within affirmative action categories but constitute 51% of the population. It is for this reason that *subordinate group* has become the term of choice.

Some characteristics that signify that a person or group comes within the subordinate classification are:

1. They experience unequal treatment and have less power over how they live than the majority of people.

2. They share physical or cultural characteristics that distinguish them from the majority of people.

3. Membership in their group is usually not voluntary and they are often born into their group.

4. They usually have a strong sense of group solidarity and sometime form an "us versus them" approach to life.

5. They generally marry others from the same group because of their solidarity (adapted from Wagley & Harris, 1958).

Defining Subordinate (minority) Groups

There are a number of types of subordinate groups that make up today's society.

Racial Groups

Racial groups are socially set apart from the majority because of obvious physical differences. Societies define what is obvious, but in the United States it usually refers to skin color and facial shapes and includes blacks, Native Americans (or American Indians), Arabs, Japanese, Filipinos, Hawaiians, and other Asian peoples. It should be recognized that race can make one a minority, depending on geographical location. For example, whites (Caucasians) are the majority in the United States, whereas in some other countries they are the minority.

A mistaken notion that race is biological has helped promote discrimination between races. Biologically, there are no pure, distinct races. Blood type, for example, cannot distinguish racial groups with any accuracy.

There is no one gene or DNA that can be identified with a particular race. Additionally, interbreeding has caused mixing of the races throughout history. Scientists maintain that the proportion of African Americans with white ancestry is between 20 and 75%. Despite the wide range in these estimates, the mix between blacks and whites today is a fact of life (Schaefer, 2007, p. 13). As Maya Angelou said, "We are more alike than unalike." **Figure 12–3** depicts ethnicity in America, from the 1800s to what it is projected to be in 2100.

Ethnic Groups

Ethnic groups are differentiated from the majority because of cultural differences such as language and food preferences. Hispanics are considered an ethnic group in the United States even though they are often recognized by skin color. Hispanics or Latinos include Mexican Americans, Cubans, Puerto Ricans, and other Latin Americans. Hispanics can be either black or white. For example, dark-skinned Puerto Ricans who may be mistaken for blacks in California may be viewed as Puerto Ricans in New York neighborhoods where many have settled. Ethic groups also include many who are now considered the majority such as Irish Americans and Polish Americans.

Jewish people come within the ethnic group classification because of their long history of being segregated from a host society. They are excluded from the religion category because culture is a more important defining trait for Jewish

United States Past and Future

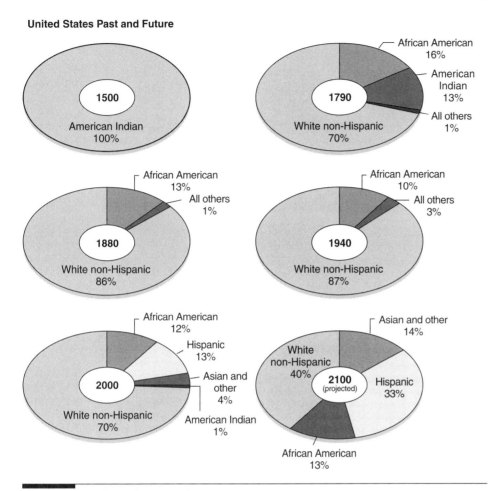

Figure 12–3 Race in America, Past and Future.

people worldwide. Jewish Americans share a cultural tradition that goes beyond theology (Schaefer, 2007, pp. 10–11). **Table 12–1** provides a picture of the number and percentage of racial and ethnic groups in the United States.

Religious Groups

Religious groups that are associated with religions other than the dominant faith is another basis for minority status. Protestants outnumber members of other religious faiths in the United States. The largest minority religion is the Catholic religion. Examples of other religious minorities are the Church of Jesus Christ of Latter-Day Saints (Mormons), the Amish, Muslims, and Buddhists. **Table 12–2** shows membership in many of these minority religions in the United States. Persons of the majority faith can often be stigmatized. For example, the followers of Islam became stigmatized after the 9/11 attacks and "hate crimes" against them increased significantly. This is an example of how the criminal justice system becomes involved in matters relating to religious groups.

Table 12-1	Racial and Ethnic Groups in the United States, 2000	
Classification	Number in thousands	Percentage of total population
Racial groups		
Whites (includes 16.9 million white hispanic)	211,461	75.1
Blacks/African Americans	34,658	12.3
Native Americans, Alaskan Native	2,476	0.9
Asian Americans	10,243	3.6
Chinese	2,433	0.9
Filipinos	1,850	0.7
Asian Indians	1,679	0.6
Vietnamese	1,123	0.4
Koreans	1,077	0.4
Japanese	797	0.2
Other	1,285	0.5
Ethnic groups		
White ancestry (single or mixed)		
Germans	42,842	15.2
Irish	30,525	10.8
English	24,509	8.7
Italians	15,638	5.6
Poles	8,977	3.2
French	8,310	3.0
Jews	5,200	1.8
Hispanics (or Latinos)	35,306	12.5
Mexican Americans	23,337	8.3
Central and South Americans	5,119	1.8
Puerto Ricans	3,178	1.1
Cubans	1,412	0.5
Other	2,260	0.8
Total (All Groups)	281,422	

Note: Percentages do not total 100 percent, and subheads do not add up to figures in major heads because of overlap between groups (e.g., Polish-American Jews or people of mixed ancestry, such as Irish and Italian).

Cults or sects claiming to be associated with a religion often become the focus of criminal justice action. The confrontation with the Branch Davidians in Waco, Texas, in which several federal law enforcement officers were killed (as well as many members of the sect), is a prime example of how traumatic these incidents can be. Freedom of religion is one of the founding principles (a *right*) of the U.S. government and the protection of this right is a major responsibility

Table 12-2	Minority Religions in the United States

Churches with more than a million members

Denomination name	Inclusive membership
The Roman Catholic Church	67,820,835
Southern Baptist Convention	16,267,494
The United Methodist Church	8,186,254
The Church of Jesus Christ of Latter-Day Saints	5,599,177
The Church of God in Christ	5,499,875
National Baptist Convention, U.S.A., Inc.	5,000,000
Evangelical Lutheran Church in America	4,930,429
National Baptist Convention of America, Inc.	3,500,000
Presbyterian Church (U.S.A.)	3,189,573
Assemblies of God	2,779,095
Progressive National Baptist Convention, Inc.	2,500,000
African Methodist Episcopal Church	2,500,000
National Missionary Baptist Convention of America	2,500,000
The Lutheran Church—Missouri Synod (LCMS)	2,463,747
Episcopal Church	2,284,233
Greek Orthodox Archdiocese of America	1,500,000
Pentecostal Assemblies of the World, Inc.	1,500,000
Churches of Christ	1,500,000
African Methodist Episcopal Zion Church	1,432,795
American Baptist Churches in the U.S.A.	1,424,840
United Church of Christ	1,265,786
Baptist Bible Fellowship International	1,200,000
Christian Churches and Churches of Christ	1,071,616
Orthodox Church in America	1,064,000
Jehovah's Witness	1,029,092

Note: Most recent data as of 2006. Membership reporting year ranges from 1992 to 2004.

Source: "Membership Statistics in the United States" in Yearbook of American and Canadian Churches, 2006 edited by Reverend Eileen W. Undner, Ph.D. Copyright © 2006 by National Council of the Churches of Christ in the USA. Reprinted by permission. http: //www.ncccusa.org

of the criminal justice system. This right separates the United States from many countries.

Gender Groups

Males have had a history of being the social majority, whereas females, although the majority by number, have been relegated to a position of the social minority. Women are placed in this subordinate group classification because of their history of being subjected to prejudice—they are physically distinguishable, and group membership is involuntary. Women who also fit into one or more of the other categories can suffer additional jeopardy. Being a female is certainly a factor in crimes such rape, and sensitivity to the **gender** factor is important in investigating related crimes.

Great strides have been made in recent years to overcome gender discrimination, but bias in this category remains an area of concern. For example, although police officers nationally are at near parity racially, the number of female officers remains low. As discussed in Chapter 10, law enforcement was male-dominated until the 1960s. Consequently, it remains behind other criminal justice professions where physical strength is not thought to be a factor. However, progress is being made with now more than 300 female police chiefs. It is a prediction of the author that in the next 20 years most large police departments will have female police chiefs. Police chief positions were dominated by male Caucasians until the 1970s. Male minorities (particularly African Americans and Hispanics) have attained many of these positions in recent years. In the future, the author forecasts, it will be women who become the chief executives in many large police departments.

The same protections that apply to gender apply to homosexuality. Currently, this may be the most sensitive area of discrimination in the criminal justice system. Administrators must ensure that gay persons have the same rights and protections as all other persons. What has been discussed as sexual discrimination holds true for gay persons. The prohibitions against sexual harassment apply equally to homosexuals as well as heterosexuals.

■ Understanding Racism, Prejudice, and Discrimination

It is a task for every criminal justice administrator to prevent racism, prejudice, and discrimination. Understanding the differences and the consequences is important in carrying out this task.

Racism is a belief that certain races are inherently superior to others. In the previous definition of *race*, it can be concluded that race is socially constructed and not biological. Race is primarily based on obvious physical difference. Adolf Hitler promoted the belief that the Jewish "race" was inferior and had to be eliminated. He institutionalized this belief in the Nazi form of government, resulting in massive segregation and eventual genocide. The institutionalization of this belief in the Nazi society promoted many to do unto "them" what they would not do to "us." In other words, to persecute and even kill Jewish people (them) became acceptable to many German citizens, who considered the persecution and killing of "their own kind" (us) as unethical.

Ensuring that this never occurs again is an important responsibility of the criminal justice system. It is important to recognize that racism has infected American society throughout its history. At the time that the founding fathers were institutionalizing these "rights for all people," most people owned slaves. The slaves were considered an inferior race and treated as property rather than as human beings. When slavery was abolished (which took a civil war), segregation became common. In World War II, blacks were allowed to fight for the United States but had to do so in segregated units. Separation in living, eating, transportation, and education was supported by the American government. It is important to remember that the criminal justice system was the arm of the government that enforced the laws and regulations that supported the racism and segregation of that time.

In the hundred years from Reconstruction to the Civil Rights movement, more than 400 laws were passed at state and local levels to perpetuate segregation in education, entertainment, freedom of speech, health care, housing, marriage, transportation, and work (Flack, 2004). It was not until the Civil Rights movement of the 1960s that actions were taken to do away with segregation. In the landmark 1954 *Brown v. Board of Education* case, the U.S. Supreme Court ruled that "separate but equal" facilities, including educational ones, were unconstitutional. This set the stage for doing away with the caste system that had segregated blacks from whites for most of America's history. The images made famous in the movie *Mississippi Burning* reminds us of the federal law enforcement actions necessary to overcome a state government still committed to segregation.

Prejudice and **discrimination** are often given the same definition; however, the difference between these two closely related words is important. Prejudice is a negative attitude or belief toward an entire category of people. Discrimination is negative behavior that excludes all members of a group from certain rights, opportunities, or privileges. So, prejudice is not necessarily expressed in behavior. It may not be possible to eliminate an employee's prejudice because of an upbringing that has implanted such an attitude. It is of paramount importance, however, to prohibit discrimination. Even if it is not possible to change the beliefs of some employees, those employees should not be allowed to behave in a manner that discriminates. Discrimination (negative behavior) is often the result of one's prejudice, but not always, as will be discussed.

Types of Discrimination

The different types of discrimination are important in understanding some of the conditions that impact today's multicultural society. Some may say that denial of opportunities or rights does not exist because they see minorities holding jobs, driving cars, owning homes, and going to college. An understanding of how discrimination is perceived by those "on the receiving end" begins with a knowledge of the different types of discrimination that exist (Schaefer, 2007, pp. 88–92).

Relative versus Absolute Discrimination

Relative discrimination is defined as the conscious experience of a negative discrepancy between what is expected and what is actually accessible. Before even the poorest had access to television, many poor were not aware of "how the other half lived." With television, everyone has visual access to the "good life" and what they are not privileged to have becomes a feeling of relative discrimination. **Absolute discrimination**, however, is actually being denied a fixed standard of living below which no one is expected to exist.

Total Discrimination

Total discrimination is a term that social researchers, and a growing number of criminologists, use to view discrimination from a "total perspective." As shown in **Figure 12–4**, this view includes past as well as current discrimination. Past discrimination includes previous denial of educational, job, health, and other opportunities. Those that take this view argue that it is not enough to focus on current opportunities. Past practices that interfere with current opportunities must be considered. For example, a minority person may not have been provided proper educational opportunities as a child because of past discrimination. When that person applies for a job as an adult (a job that does provides for equal opportunities for qualified applicants) they may not be able to successfully compete because of past discrimination.

In the criminal justice system, the *rule of law* holds that everyone is responsible for their actions (with certain exceptions such as legal insanity). Past discriminative is not a legal excuse. However, an Eclectic Perspective criminal justice administrator will support activities that eliminate current discrimination as a means of preventing future crime.

Institutional Discrimination

Institutional discrimination is the denial of equal rights and opportunities to groups or individuals that results from the normal operations of a society. From this perspective, discrimination can take place without an individual intending to deprive others of privileges and even without an awareness that others are being deprived.

A few examples include:

- Standards for credit risks work against many minorities because of lack of conventional credit references. Low-income areas often have higher insurance costs.
- IQ testing favors middle-class people because the questions included on these examinations relate to middle-class experiences.
- Hiring practice often require several years' experience at jobs that have only recently been opened to members of subordinate groups.
- Many jobs automatically eliminate persons with criminal records including drug offenses, which disproportionately favors the majority population.
- Criminal justice system employees, from patrol officers to judges, are predominately of the majority and consequently do not understand life in poverty areas (Ture & Hamilton, 1992).

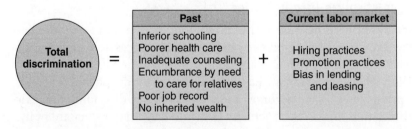

Figure 12–4 Total Discrimination.

It is the latter factor that should be of most concern to criminal justice administrators. Proactive approaches regarding this disparity will be discussion later in this chapter.

As the population in the United States becomes more diverse, more examples of institutional discrimination come to the forefront. In the aftermath of the 9/11 terrorist attacks, Homeland Security procedures were institutionalized. Screening of airport security eliminated many employees from subordinate groups resulting in an occupation that was overwhelmingly minority to one that is 61% white (Alonso-Zaldivar & Oldham, 2002, p. A18).

In the 2000 U.S. presidential election, 1.4 million African Americans were denied the right to vote. This was not because they were black as this would clearly be racist and illegal. It was because they had felony convictions, and 12 states have laws prohibiting such persons from voting. These laws prohibit voting even after completion of a sentence. It should be noted that the philosophy of criminal justice in this country is that once a person completes their sentence, their "debt to society is paid." Currently, 13% of the nation's black male population is precluded from voting by such laws (Human Rights Watch, 2002).

Economical Discrimination

This type of discrimination involves what is often referred to as the informal or underground economy. This economic condition consists of transfers of money, goods, or services that are not reported to the government. Those who promote the informal or underground economy do so because they do not have to pay taxes and often hire employees from subordinate groups at below legal minimum wages. According to the Dual Labor Market Model, many minorities are relegated to informal economy jobs. Those employed under these conditions are usually not provided safeguards against fraud or malpractice that victimizes workers. There are also fewer, if any, of the fringe benefits of health insurance and pensions that are common in regular jobs. Most of these jobs are menial and jobs that the dominate members of society do not want to do. **Figure 12–5** provides a comparison of median income by race, ethnicity, and gender.

The author once lived in a beach community that resisted development for many years. Finally, economics forced the community to open up to tourists. Hotels, restaurants, and many other businesses that accommodated tourists developed rapidly. Those businesses required workers to do menial job such as dish washing, room cleaning, and fast food preparation. These were jobs that the "locals' did not want to perform. People from Mexico (where wages are a fraction of what they are in the United States) were glad to take these jobs. Many were undocumented and willing to suffer poor employment and housing conditions because of their lack of citizenship. Greedy landlords in the less desirable part of town soon began to rent to these people, putting 10–20 in houses built for single families. These new arrivals were usually family-oriented and very responsible. However, in time, they bore children who grew up in these densely populated poor areas. Many of these youth grew up feeling "disfranchised" from the general society because of lack of education and job opportunities. Gangs, drugs, and other crime dramatically increased and these areas became a prime focus for the police. This is just one example of the part informal economy plays

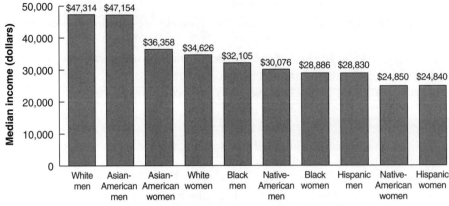

Even at the very highest levels of schooling, the income gap remains between Whites and Blacks. Education also has little apparent effect on the income gap between male and female workers. Even a brief analysis reveals striking differences in earning power between White men and other groups in the United States. Furthermore, the double jeopardy is apparent for African-American and Hispanic women.

Note: Median income is from all sources and is limited to year-round, full-time workers over 25 years old. Data for White men and women are for non-Hispanics.

Note: Data released in 2005 for income earned in 2004.

Figure 12–5 Comparison of Income by Race, Ethnicity, and Gender.

in the development of crime ridden, poorer areas that become challenging for the criminal justice system.

■ Protecting Diversity as an Administrative Responsibility

The Social Equity responsibility of the criminal justice system was the subject of Chapter 10. Also in that chapter, the responsibility of the criminal justice system to ensure *justice* and *domestic tranquility*, as prescribed by the Constitution, was reviewed.

In Chapter 11, the Client-Oriented Service theme was introduced as the trend that has taken us into the 21st century. All of these factors point to a responsibility to protect the rights and to embrace the diversities of all people. This is an essential component of the mission of all contemporary criminal justice agencies. Consequently, another important responsibility of criminal justice administrators is to implement organizational efforts that will carry out this part of the mission. To emphasize, the two most important tasks of an administrator are to (1) *carry out the mission of the agency* and (2) *satisfy the needs of the employees*. Therefore, protecting and embracing diversity is a task that externally applies to the public and internally to employees.

Establishing trust between the police and the minority community is essential. Most crime (that is solved) is solved through information supplied by the public (not through observations of officers). The public normally will not volunteer information unless they trust the police. The "competencies necessary" to effectively interact with minority groups, established from recommendations made by a number of police administrators, are listed here. Some items apply to all personnel, whereas others are primarily for line and staff commanding officers (PERF, 2001, p. 100). These competencies are:

- the ability to communicate with residents in their primary language;
- an understanding of cultural issues relating to police and public safety;
- a respectful approach to relationships with residents;
- the ability to be fair and provide equal treatment;
- the willingness to examine assumptions about links between race/ethnicity and crime in the jurisdiction, in order to bring stereotypes to light;
- interpersonal skills and a sincere interest in engaging with the community;
- the willingness to focus community outreach activities on traditionally underserved populations; and
- a departmental approach to human resources that conveys the same respect for diversity that the department is trying to convey to the community at large.

Recommendations for effective ways for minority communities to get involved with the police include (PERF, 2001, p. 101):

- engaging in dialogue about solutions, rather than about blame;
- encourage minorities to apply for employment with the police department, and supporting those who go through the process;
- developing a broad community understanding of professional police practices (perhaps through contacts with national and state police organizations), in order to form an objective standard by which to judge police actions; and
- acknowledging police officers who promote positive police-community relationships with awards or other commendations.

Learning about the differences in cultures should be important to criminal justice administrators in working with minority communities as well as with minority employees. From one coast to the other, we find cultural differences. For example, if someone grows up on the East Coast and builds a house, a fence probably will not be built. If that same person moved to southern California and built a home without a fence, they would be thought of as "odd" by their neighbors. Legal actions might even come into play to force a fence to be built.

Now, picture the cultural difference between people from various countries. For example, Hispanic and Asian employees are less apt to want to talk about their attributes even when competing for promotions. It is thought to be egotistical in some cultures. The author, when responsible for overseeing the selection of a technology vender to implement a police automation system, found that Chinese businessmen conducted themselves differently from American businessmen. The Chinese offered expensive gifts to the selection committee and often engaged in long periods of silence during negotiations. The gifts that were considered proper in their culture were not in ours. The Chinese often contemplate in silence where Americans fill most periods of time with some type of conversation.

Asian people often refrain from eye contact, as it is disrespectful in their culture. In our culture, it can be thought of as a sign of not telling the truth. Addressing a child before addressing their parents in some Asian cultures is very disrespectful of the parents. These are just a few examples of cultural differences that can distort communications with minority community members as well as employees. **Figure 12–6** provides a "model of cultural learning" that can be helpful.

Achieving criminal justice employee parity with the ratio of subordinate groups is of prime importance in protecting diversity. **Figure 12–7** compares the ratio of minority races in law enforcement as compared to the national population. As can be seen, law enforcement officers are relatively close to parity with the national population; however, there remain a number of individual criminal justice agencies that are considerably out of balance in regards to parity with the composition of their communities. This does not mean that hiring standards should be lowered; it means that more attention must be given to attracting candidates from subordinate groups. The current trend of client-oriented service requires criminal justice employees to understand the multicultural facets of the communities they serve. "Walking in the shoes" of community members provides insight that one can never fully appreciate through training or even education.

Figure 12–8 shows a gender gap in law enforcement hiring that should be of concern. **Targeting** candidates from subordinate groups who are underrepresented should be part of recruitment programs. Targeting includes identifying the underrepresented candidates and determining where they can be contacted to at-

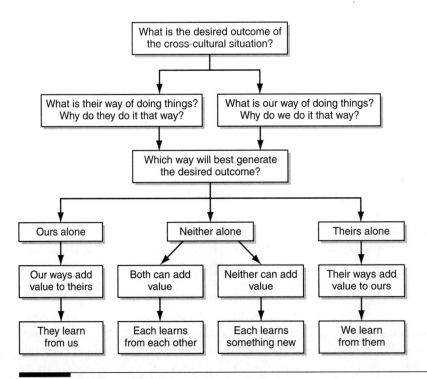

Figure 12–6 Cultural Learning Model.

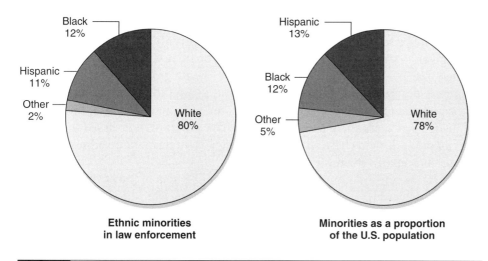

Figure 12–7 Minority Hiring in Law Enforcement.

tract them to the job. The Client-Oriented Service approach of gaining public trust certainly plays an important part in recruiting. If desirable candidates are living in neighborhoods that do not trust the police, recruiting candidates will be difficult. No one really wants a job that they can not be proud of when it comes to their family, relatives, and friends.

The author has found that enlisting the assistance of criminal justice employees, community leaders, and celebrities from the various groups can be of help. The Police Executive Research Forum (PERF) recommends targeting (PERF, 2001, pp. 71–72):

- Universities and colleges that attract minorities.
- Military personnel, as many are from minorities and will be looking for employment after release from service.
- Current minority police officers to recruit and offering recruitment bonuses.
- Religious organizations that have large minority congregations.

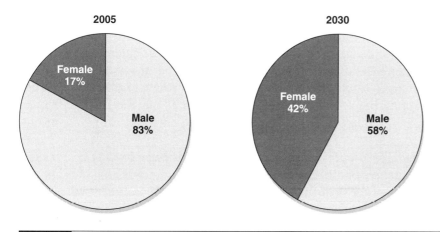

Figure 12–8 Gender Hiring in Law Enforcement.

Additionally, spotlighting administrative positions held by subordinate group members helps in showing job advancement opportunities. Promotions should not be given to subordinate group candidates who do not meet the qualifications for the job. However, targeting qualified subordinate group candidates for promotions is desirable. For example, the author, as a police administrator, would target qualified minority and female officers for "adjutant" position. Most criminal justice managers and executive officers have adjutants who assist them with administrative duties. These adjutants gain important insight into administrative duties that prepares them for promotions.

Education and training of employees is another area of importance. Recommendations regarding racial and cultural understanding education and training are (PERF, 2001, pp. 80–84):

- To be integrated into a wide range of curricula in recruit and ongoing education. Although individual courses may be necessary, making the information a part of the everyday job is important.
- Racial profiling preventive education should be ongoing as a means of helping personnel understand and address a complex issue without being accusatory.
- Police and community perspectives must be incorporated into the education and tailored to agency- and community-specific needs, concerns and experiences. Local minority community leaders should be involved.

Educating employees to the cultural difference in their communities is essential. **Table 12–3** is an example of material provided in one department that explains communication and cultural differences of people living and working in that agency's communities. Insight into cultural difference can certainly enhance the efforts of criminal justice employees. For example, the author (while a police administrator) found that traditional neighborhood watch meetings were difficult to arrange in the Hispanic areas. Cultural research found that many residents were unaccustomed to having meetings in their homes. In Mexico, where they came from, meetings usually were held at their local churches or in community areas. With this cultural insight in mind, neighborhood watch meetings were arranged by blocking off public streets, setting up a public address system, and calling the meeting to order. This approach met with great success.

Communicating in the predominant language of a particular minority community is sometimes difficult. A number of police departments with large Hispanic communities teach basic street Spanish to all new recruits as part of the academy training process. The related publication at the end of this chapter describes a "Point-Talk" card that can be helpful in communicating in various languages.

Providing opportunities where employees (and pre-employees) become acquainted with people of other races and ethnic backgrounds is an important approach. If people of the majority groups grow up in an environment where they have no contact with other groups, they can sometimes form stereotypes and prejudice based on lack of personal experience. If such a person becomes a police officer, for example, and is assigned to an inner-city poor, minority area

Table 12–3 Cultural Awareness Material

The ten dimensions of culture: comparing cultural norms and values

Aspects of culture	Mainstream American	Other cultures
1. Sense of self	— Informal — Handshake	— Formal — Hugs, bows, handshakes
2. Communication and language	— Explicit, direct — Emphasis on content-meaning found in word's meaning	— Implicit, indirect — Emphasis on context-meaning (found around words)
3. Dress and appearance	— "Dress for success" ideal — Wide range acceptable	— Dress seen as a sign of position, wealth, prestige — Religious rules
4. Food and eating habits	— Eating as a necessity—fast food	— Dining: a social experience — Religious rules
5. Time and time consciousness	— Linear and exact time consciousness — Value on promptness (time = money)	— Elastic and relative time consciousness — Time spent on enjoyment of relationships
6. Relationships, family, friends	— Focus on nuclear family — Responsibility for self	— Focus on extended family — Loyalty and responsibility to family
7. Values and norms	— Individual orientation — Independence — Preference for direct confrontation of conflict	— Group orientation — Conformity — Preference for harmony
8. Beliefs and attitudes	— Egalitarian — Challenging of authority — Individuals control their destiny — Gender equity	— Hierarchical — Respect for authority and social order — Individuals accept their destiny — Different roles for genders
9. Mental process and learning style	— Linear, logical, sequential — Problem-solving focus	— Lateral, holistic, simultaneous — Accepting of life's difficulties
10. Work habits and practices	— Emphasis on task — Reward based on individual achievements — Work is necessity of life	— Emphasis on relationships — Rewards based on seniority — Work has intrinsic value

Source: http://www.lapdonline.org

(where crime is high), they may jump to the misguided conclusion that crime is related to race rather than to social conditions. Providing opportunities for such people to get to know at least one person of another background helps to provide the understanding that "we are all more alike than different." The author, as a college professor, has developed programs that pair up white students who are studying to become police officers, which minority students for at least a semester of mutual projects. This has promoted a better understanding of cultural differences that help prepare students to have successful careers in law enforcement. Programs of this type should be provided for criminal justice employees who have never had the opportunity to "mix interculturally."

Educating the minority community to culturally different laws is another important approach. Cultural differences can sometimes lead to unintentional violations of law by minority community members. For example, in some countries from which Hispanics migrate, one continues to drive to a nearest legal aid location after a traffic accident. This is because the police often imprison both parties until the party that was negligent can be determined. Leaving the scene of an accident in the United States constitutes a violation of "hit and run" laws. Discharging firearms into the air during holidays (such as New Year's Eve) is an acceptable custom is some countries; here, it usually is against the law and particularly dangerous in urban areas. Some child-rearing customs in other countries amount to "child abuse" violations of law in this country.

A principle of the American criminal justice system is that "ignorance of the law is no excuse." Consequently, educating minority members to such laws should be an important part of police-minority community efforts. The author, while a police chief in a city with a large Hispanic population, found that aggressive resistance from arrestees often led to violent confrontations. These confrontations were found to be related to the cultural experience of a number of Hispanic arrestees who came from foreign communities where being "proned" (placed face down with hands bound) was a prelude to being shot in the head by a "killing squad." The common practice of the police in this country, on felony arrest, is to "prone" and handcuff arrestees. This was resisted by arrestees who perceived this to be a life or death situation. Getting the "word out on the street" that their lives were not in danger from local police unless they resisted with deadly force became an active program. Communicating this throughout the minority community had a positive impact on resisting arrest situations.

Education programs should inform citizens of what they are expected to do when lawfully arrested, as well as how they should respond when questioned by the police. The minority public must be assured that quality policing includes protecting constitutional rights. Information can be disseminated through community meetings, mass media, personal contacts, and citizen-police academies. Citizen-police academies are especially beneficial in communicating information, promoting mutual understanding, and gaining minority community trust.

Court and Corrections Practices that Affect Diversity

Thus far, this chapter has covered issues that, for the most part, related to policing (however, many have some applications to the other criminal justice fields). Chapter 10 included a discussion of the unequal number and causes of minorities that come to the attention of the criminal justice systems (Tables 10–1, 10–2, and 10–3). Here we continue this discussion and deal with some of the court and corrections practices that administrators should examine as sources of bias relating to minority relations.

Prosecution and Sentencing Practices. In Chapter 6, the recent "get tough on crime" approach was discussed. Mandatory minimum sentences, truth-in-sentencing, and guidelines for sentencing have been created to eliminate disparity, promote certainty, and establish proportionate punishment (U.S. Sentencing Commission, 2004). The impact on these practices on ethnic groups has been well documented (Crawford, Chiricos, & Kleck 1998, pp. 481–511). Additionally, an indirect effect between race and ethnicity and extra-legal factors (e.g., gender and employment status), legal criteria (e.g., offense seriousness and prior record), and context-based measures (e.g., racial composition and crime rate) has been found (Spohn & Holleran, 2002, pp. 329–358).

Ethnic and racial disparities have been found to be most prevalent in drug offense sentencing. "Drug quantity thresholds of crack cocaine (a drug used and sold predominantly by blacks) at the federal level lead to sentences that were disproportionately longer, given the harm differences produced by crack and cocaine. Not surprisingly, the lengthy sentences of drug offenders at the state and federal level has led to an unprecedented number of racial/ethic minorities in the nation's prisons" (Hawkins, Meyers, & Stone, 2003). Other studies show that black and Latino women are convicted of and sentenced for drug offenses at a much higher rate than are white women (Lapidus et al., 2005).

A study of state level court dispositions resulted in three major findings. First, racial disparity is most notable during the decision to deny bail and for defendants charged with violent crimes. Second, ethic disparity is most prevalent during the decision to grant a non-financial release and for defendants charged with drug crimes. Third, when there is disparity in the treatment of black and Latino defendants with similar legal characteristics, Latinos receive the less beneficial decisions (Schlesinger, 2005, p. 170).

Mandatory life imprisonment laws for persons convicted of a third violent felony—"Three Strikes" laws—also have been found to be disproportionately affected racially and ethnically. Higher rates of arrests and more extensive prior records of blacks than whites led to the high prosecution rate of blacks under the "three strikes" legislation. Studies show a disproportionate number of black males impacted by this law (King & Mauer, 2001). Other research reports disparity in plea-bargaining when it comes to minorities (Kautt & Spohn, 2002, pp. 1–36).

In *Images of Color, Images of Crime*, the sentencing impact on minorities is summarized as follows:

> *Whether it is racial and ethnic stereotypes or higher rates of involvement in crime that lead to racial and ethnic disparities in prosecution and sentencing practices, the impact of such practices on people of color has a lasting, profound effect. Incarceration has a devastating effect on offenders who are removed from their families and communities, as well as on family members who must now find the means to provide emotional and economic support to loved ones. For example, family members must now assume the responsibility of raising children of incarcerated offenders, often with minimal*

government support.—The effects of punitive and often hidden practices by the legal systems go beyond affecting individual offenders but, rather, extend to large segments of the U.S. population (Rodriguez, 2006, p. 243).

Practices and Programs in Corrections. Prosecution and sentencing practice have an impact on the corrections system that is mostly beyond their control. However, a number of noteworthy programs have been implemented in the corrections field. *Reentry programs* result from collaboration between corrections and community agencies to develop multiagency strategies to help reintegrate offenders to the community. These programs have identified and provided ways of developing skills needed by minority offenders to lead crime-free lives upon returning to their communities (Case & Fasenfest, 2004, pp. 24–39). *Restorative and community justice efforts*, including sentencing circles, conferencing, and victim-offender mediation programs, are being applied to more minority probationers and parolees. Mandatory drug treatment programs for offenders reentering society are particularly beneficial for minorities because of the disproportionate drug arrest rate for blacks and Latinos.

The purpose of this chapter was not to provide detailed information about programs and approaches to serving multicultural communities. Rather, it was meant to explore why criminal justice administrators need to pursue advancements in this area. We have discussed evidence of disparities and inequities in criminal justice services to subordinate groups. Criminal justice practitioners and scholars continue to debate the reasons for these disparities. Whatever meaning one arrives at, it is clear that disparity exists in the handling of subordinate groups in the criminal justice system. From the "get tough on crime" perspective, a high rate of traffic stops of minorities is justified because those minorities stopped are more likely to be involved in crime, particularly drug-related crime. Critics argue that this is "which came first, the chicken or the egg" reasoning: ethnic and racial stereotypes are used to justify more stops, which result in more arrests, which, in turn, are used to justify higher rates of traffic stops.

The truth probably lies somewhere between these extremes. Additionally, conditions vary from community to community. Whatever the conditions may be, the involvement of criminal justice administration must be recognized. From establishing goals, policies, and procedures to overseeing the actions of employees; protecting diversity is a major challenge for all criminal justice administrators—now and in the future.

KEY CONCEPTS AND TERMS

- Relative discrimination
- Absolute discrimination
- Total discrimination
- Institutional discrimination
- Economical discrimination
- Subordinate (Minority) groups
  - Racial
  - Ethnic
  - Religious
  - Gender
- Types of discrimination
  - Relative
  - Absolute
  - Total
  - Institutional
  - Economical
- Administrative responsibility to protect diversity
  - Establishing community trust
  - Educating and training of employees

CHAPTER ACTIVITY

Interview someone who has a different racial or ethnic background than yours (a fellow student, for example). Seek to determine different views and customs that relate to his or her background. Figure 12–3 contains subjects that you may use to make comparisons. What insight did you gain from this interview that would assist you in providing criminal justice service to a community made up of people with backgrounds similar to the person you interviewed?

REVIEW QUESTIONS

1. Why is diversity important to the American way of life? How and why is protecting diversity an important responsibility of criminal justice administrators?

2. Why does the term "salad bowl" better describe today's approach to diversity than the term "melting pot"?

3. Evidence is presented in this chapter that segregation still exists, particularly in poor inner-city areas. What do you think are the causes and what can be done about it?

4. Discuss why "subordinate group" is a more accurate term than "minority." What is the difference between "race" and "ethnicity"?

Wrap Up

5. Discuss the various types of discrimination. Can discrimination be unintentional?

REFERENCES

Alonso-Zaldivar, R., & Oldhan, J. (2002). New Airport Screener Jobs Going Mostly to Whites. *Los Angeles Times*, September 24, p. A18.

Case, P., & Fasenfest, D. (2004). Expectations for Opportunities Following Prison Education A Discussion of Race and Gender. *Journal of Correctional Education*, p.55–57.

Crawford, C., Chiricos, T., & Kleck, G. (1998). Race, Racial Threat, and Sentencing of Habitual Offenders. *Criminology*, p.36–37.

Cronkhite, C. (1997). Criminal Justice Multicultural Services in the United States: Breaking the Cultural and Language Barriers. *Crime and International Magazine*, July, pp. 111–113.

Flack, S. (2004). Jim Crow Legislation Overview. Retrieved October, 2006 from http://www.jimcrowhistory.org.

Hawkins, D. R. S., Myers, S. L., Jr., & Stone, R. (2003). *Crime Control and Social Justice: The Delicate Balance*. Westport, CT: Greenwood.

Human Rights Watch. (2002). *Losing the Vote: The Impact of Felony Disenfranchisement Laws in the United States*. Washington, DC: Human Rights Watch.

Kautt, P., & Spohn, C. (2002). Crack-ing Down on Black Drug Offenders? Testing for Interactions among Offenders' Race, Drug Type and Sentencing Strategy in Federal Drug Sentences. *Justice Quarterly*, pp.19–21.

King, R. S., & Mauer, M. (2001). *Aging Behind Bars: Three Strikes Seven Years Later*. Washington, DC: The Sentencing Project.

Lapidus, L., Luthra, N., Verma, A., Small, D., Allard, P., & Levington, K. (2005). *Caught in the Net: The Impact of Drug Policies on Women and Families*. NY: American Civil Liberties Union.

Lewis Mumford Center. (2001). *Ethnic Diversity Grows, Neighborhood Integration is at a Standstill*. Albany, NY: Lewis Mumford Center.

Massey, D. (2004). Reparations Segregation and Stratification: A Biosocial Perspective. *Dubois Review*, pp. 1–3.

PERF (Police Executive Research Forum). (2001). *Racially Biased Policing: A Principled Response*. Washington, DC: Police Executive Research Forum.

Rodriguez, N. (2006). The Nexus Between Race and Ethnicity and Criminal Justice Policy. In *Image of Color, Image of Crime* (3rd ed.). Mann, C. R., Zatz, M. S., & Rodriguez, N. (Eds.). Los Angeles: Roxbury.

Schaefer, R. T. (2007). *Race and Ethnicity in the United States* (4th ed.). Upper Saddle River, NJ: Pearson/Prentice Hall.

Schlesinger, T. (2005). Racial and Ethnic Disparity in Pretrial Criminal Processing. *Justice Quarterly*, 22, 2, June, pp.170–173.

Spohn, C., & Holleran, D. (2002). The Effect of Imprisonment on Recidivism Rates of Felony Offenders: A Focus on Drug Offenders. *Criminology*, 40, pp. 329–358.

U. S. Sentencing Commission. (2004). *Fifteen Years of Guidelines Sentencing: An Assessment of How Well the Federal Criminal Justice System Is Achieving the Goals Of Sentencing Reform*. Washington, DC: U.S. Sentencing Commission.

Wagley, C., & Harris, M. (1958). *Minorities in the New World: Six Case Studies*. NY: Columbia University Press.

Wrap Up

■ RELEVANT PUBLICATION

The article summarizes and expands on several concepts in this chapter. (Cronkhite, C. [1997]. Criminal Justice Multicultural Services in the United States: Breaking the Culture and Language Barriers. *Crime and International Magazine*, July, pp. 111–113).

Criminal Justice Multicultural Services in the United States: Breaking the Culture and Language Barriers by Clyde Cronkhite

Urban areas in the United States today include a wide variety of cultures and languages and this variety has spread to most suburbs and many rural areas. The criminal justice system, particularly law enforcement, is responsible for providing equal service to all people in all communities, yet an increasing segment of the public comes from different cultures and speaks different languages from those responsible for providing these services. This article explores the challenges of providing criminal justice service to multicultural communities and describes some methods to enhance such service.

Challenges

Newcomers to the United States may adhere to customs that can cause social friction and may even be classified as crime. This phenomenon can better be understood by considering a cultural difference that exists between people who live on the west and east coasts of the United States. Someone reared on the west coast who moves to the east coast might build a house with a fence around the property or the back yard. It is customary to build such fences on the west coast, particularly in Southern California. East Coast residents are more inclined to let their properties blend together without dividing fences. Building such a fence in the east might cause neighborhood friction and the person doing so might be considered an "outsider." The opposite could happen if one did not fence property in Southern California.

Now imagine the difficulty one can face when moving to the United States from another country in some examples of customary activities of new arrivals which might result in criminal prosecution.

- A person from some countries south of the U.S. may not stop when involved in a traffic accident. In the country they came from, it may be customary to drive on and find an attorney because to stop means automatic incarceration. In the USA, such conduct would be "hit and run," a violation of law.

- Some home healing practices acceptable in other countries, such as placing hot coins on certain skin conditions, may be considered child abuse in the United States.
- Discharging firearms into the air to celebrate certain holidays may be an acceptable custom in some countries but is a violation of law in the USA.

Other customary activities, which are not illegal, still may cause community friction that results in the police being summoned.

- In some countries south of the U.S., it is customary to have parties in the front yard and play music loudly so that the neighbors can share in the enjoyment of the event. In many U.S. communities, parties are generally held privately in the backyard or inside.
- In some foreign communities, meetings can be held in the street by groups at any time. This activity would interfere with traffic flow in most U.S. cities and such activity would require a special permit if allowed at all.

Other examples include activities that may cause friction, specifically between the police and the public in multicultural communities.

- In some foreign countries, the only time a person is handcuffed is prior to execution by government or rebel "killing squads." If an immigrant from such a community is handcuffed by an officer in the United States, he or she may react violently.
- To touch or pat a person on top of the head, as is sometimes done to children in the U.S., is considered a taboo in some Asian religions and may produce violent reactions by parents or relatives.
- In some Asian homes, talking to family members before addressing the man of the house is a personal insult and to look someone in the eye is disrespectful in some Asian cultures.

Customs change over time as new arrivals from different cultures with different values are assimilated into the general population of the United States. In the past, immigrants from European countries shaped most values and customs in the U.S. People brought to the U.S. as slaves from Africa and most Asians had their customs suppressed. Today more than 85 percent of the legal immigrants are from Pacific Rim countries and they bring with them new and different values.

A number of statements and public reactions to them will illustrate the impact that both time and the varying cultural composition of U.S. society has on values, customs and laws.

1. Slavery is appropriate.
2. Only males should vote.
3. Murder should be punishable by death.
4. Any woman should be able to have an abortion on demand.
5. Married men should be able to have a mistress.
6. Men should have the final authority in the home.

Today most people would certainly disagree with the first two statements, but early settlers in the United States did not, and their descendants fought America's bloodiest conflict over the issue of slavery. Currently, the majority supports capital punishment; several decades ago the opposite was true. The right to an abortion is an issue provoking fierce debate, although abortion is legal; several decades ago, doctors and patients in such an operation were arrested for a felony. Most people reared in the United States today would disagree with the last two statements about the relations between the sexes. However, many immigrants would agree with these statements, as they are acceptable in the cultures from which they come, and a large segment of the U.S.-born population acts as if they were the norm here.

Law Enforcement Initiatives

No policing agency is financed to enforce all laws, so selective enforcement occurs. Today's enlightened law enforcement agencies are sensitive to cultural changes that indicate where individual community values want policing resources placed. The cultural composition of individual communities certainly has an impact on these values. Because of the ever-changing composition of communities in the U.S., some progressive criminal justice agencies have begun providing basic information to new arrivals as to what conduct can result in the police being summoned to resolve social conflicts and/or to make arrests. Education and training provided to some criminal justice practitioners by their agencies sensitizes them to the cultural differences in the communities they serve.

Languages certainly present a challenge to today's criminal justice practitioner. Children attending public schools in most large cities in the U.S. speak more than 50 different languages. It may be possible to require criminal justice practitioners to speak another language: the LAPD, for example, requires all police recruits to master "street level" Spanish during Basic Training. But how does the criminal justice system cope with multiple languages? A Chinese community, for example, may have three different languages while many more are spoken in other Asian neighborhoods.

One solution is a language center that provides quick response 24 hours a day to criminal justice practitioners. One such private sector language center serving the criminal justice system today in the United States and Canada provides access to 140 languages within 45 seconds, 24 hours a day, seven days a week. The idea for the language center originated in the early 1980s with a research group called Forum 2000. Forum 2000 consisted of several hundred criminal justice practitioners and futurist researchers who tracked trends with the objective of enhancing a knowledge base that would facilitate criminal justice services. As the Los Angeles Police Department was preparing to handle the 1984 Summer Olympics, Forum 2000 members proposed a language center concept to facilitate communications between the police and Olympic participants.

A card with an array of international flags—each was given a number—was designed. The card could be shown to a non-English-speaking person who would point to the flag of his or her country. The number beside the chosen flag was used to identify the language to be interpreted when calling the language center. The language center housed interpreters who were available around-the-clock to Olympic participants as well as the police.

Jeffrey Munks, then a police officer, developed the concept into a business called Communication and Language Identification Language Line (CALL). He utilized interpreters from the Monterey, California area where several prominent language institutions are located. In 1989 this business was acquired by AT&T and became the Language Line Services. The "flag card" evolved into a card that today represents the most requested of 140 languages. The country flags have been replaced with a message that tells non-English-speaking persons to point to his or her language and the corresponding number identifies the language to be translated. The card divides the languages into global categories such as Middle East, Asia, and Europe to assist in quickly identifying the type of translation required.

Once the language to be translated is identified, a telephone call to the 800 telephone number connects the caller to a translator. Within 45 seconds, the service provides contact with an interpreter who can translate the desired language. The communication method can involve passing the telephone handset back and forth between the interviewer and interviewee, using a speakerphone, or using an extension handset.

The translators work out of their home or business. A computer tracks which translators are on duty at what time and in which locations. Police agencies can have crime report forms and special instructions, such as Miranda Rights, made available on the interpreter's computer monitor so that translations can be customized to the user's needs.

Many 911 communication centers in the United States and Canada are users of the AT&T Language Line. A growing number of police departments and other criminal justice agencies use this service when interviewing non-English-speaking witnesses and suspects and the service is used by officers on patrol as well as by detectives. The service is also used by judges and other courtroom personnel to ensure equal justice and protection of individual legal rights when confronting language differences.

Another device that helps overcome language barriers is "Point Talk." Point Talk cards are made available to police officers in the languages most prominent in their communities. Point Talk uses a side-by-side presentation format to display words and phrases in English and, next to it, the language into which the same words and phrases have been translated.

The card starts at the top of each language column, with the most common information required: "give me your . . . driver's license, I.D., registration" and so on. Other statements are for gaining information from victims and the card also includes directions for the arrested person/suspect such as "empty your pockets," with the last statement in the language column proclaiming "I have just arrested you." The statements on the card are designed to elicit certain body language and/or facial expressions as the user points to a word or phrase. Consequently, the user is often able to communicate the essence of an entire paragraph.

This service, started by law enforcement practitioners, has become an important factor in breaking the culture and language barriers for many components of the justice system as well as fire departments, hospitals and other emergency service providers. In addition to oral communication, the service is planning to provide assistance in translating written correspondence, which law enforcement agencies are finding helpful as criminal activity becomes more international. All Language Line services are now available globally and accessible to criminal justice agencies throughout the world.

Conclusion

The 1990 Census showed that the United States is home for nearly 20 million foreign-born residents, of which 7.3 million are from Pacific Rim countries. This foreign-born population encompasses 32 distinct cultural groups and uses well over 50 different languages. Since the non-native population has doubled with each census since 1970, the year 2000 census could show a doubling of these figures. A 1992 forecast projected that by the year 2040, the nation's estimated population of more than 350 million will include 34.5 million Asian and Pacific Islander residents, an increase from 1992 of nearly 400 percent. Some experts forecast that the birthrate for Hispanics and Asian Americans will outpace that of other cultures, contributing to a demographic turnaround in which the current majority will become the minority by the year 2010.

Criminal justice agencies in the United States have the duty of providing equal service to all people, regardless of customs and language differences. Today, criminal justice agencies are breaking the culture and language barriers through the use of technology, research and a more community-oriented/culturally sensitive approach to providing service. They are informing newcomers to the U.S. of those cultural activities that may result in criminal justice intervention. They are also educating criminal justice practitioners to cultural differences that influence their interaction with foreign-born members of the communities they serve. These recent developments in translation are examples of useful tools to assist enlightened criminal justice agencies to break culture and language barriers in an effort to provide equal justice to all.

13

Criminal Justice Administration and Professional Ethics in the 21st Century

■ Introduction

Every member of the criminal justice system is involved in a vital and noble "profession." When the oath of office is taken by employees, they accept a responsibility to carry out the will of the majority of all people and to protect the rights of all people. As summarized in the Preamble to the U.S. Constitution, members of the criminal justice system are to "ensure justice" and promote "domestic tranquility."

With these responsibilities, law enforcement personnel are given powers of arrest and the power to use force when justified. Judicial personnel are given the power to remove from society those found guilty of crimes. Corrections personnel have the power to imprison and carry out the order to put offenders to death. Criminal justice personnel have the power to deprive people of their liberty within the limits set by the U.S. Constitution and the courts. They are a reminder that we do not live in a complete democracy. In our republic form of government, each individual gives up some liberties so that the majority can have maximum freedom in a complex society.

Members of the criminal justice system play an important role in preserving the delicate balance between maximum freedom and individual rights. With these responsibilities and powers, the people of our country expect criminal justice employees to have strong professional ethics.

◼ Criminal Justice Professionalism

All criminal justice employees have several elements in common:

- They have discretion—the power to make decisions that can deprive others of life, liberty, and property,
- They have the duty to enforce the law,
- They must accept that their duty includes the duty to protect the constitutional rights that are the cornerstone of our legal system, specifically, due process and equal protection, and
- They are public "servants," meaning that their salaries are paid by the public (adapted from Pollack, 2007, pp. 6–7).

Discretion is an important power that allows the police to decide who and when to arrest; prosecutors who to charge; judges who to convict; and correction officers how to punish. Citizens demand that those who make these decisions adhere to a higher standard of ethics. Even in the private lives of criminal justice professionals, citizens expect higher standards than they expect of most others. For example, if a criminal justice employee gets drunk, abuses their spouse, does not pay their bills, or commits even a petty theft, the incident will most likely be headline news. If they don't live exemplary lives, how can they be trusted to make ethical decisions in carrying out their public duties?

Principles of Public Service Ethics

1. *Public service. Public servants should treat their office as a public trust, using the power and resources of public office only to advance public interests and not to attain personal benefit or pursue any other private interest incompatible with the public good.*
2. *Objective judgment. Public servants should employ independent objective judgment in performing their duties, deciding all matters on the merits, free from avoidable conflicts of interest and both real and apparent improper influences.*
3. *Accountability. Public servants should ensure that government is conducted openly, efficiently, equitably, and honorably in a manner that permits the citizenry to make informed judgments and hold government officials accountable.*
4. *Democratic leadership. Public servants should honor and respect the principles and spirit of representative democracy and set a positive example of good citizenship by scrupulously observing the letter and spirit of laws and rules.*
5. *Respectability. Public servants should safeguard public confidence in the integrity of government by being honest, fair, caring, and respectful, and by avoiding conduct creating the appearance of impropriety or which is otherwise unbefitting a public official.*

Source: Adapted from Josephson Institute of Ethics, *Preserving the Public Trust.* Available at http:// www.josephsoninstitute.org.

Criminal justice administrators are expected to ensure that these professional and ethical qualities are manifested in all their employees. When the police chief, state attorney, judge, and warden take their oath of office, they are held accountable to the people for instilling and maintaining these qualities within their public organization. This is why criminal justice administrators can lose their jobs if their employees are unprofessional and unethical. With this in mind, we will now explore the meaning of **professional ethics**.

What is a profession or a professional? **Profession** can be defined as, "An occupational category requiring a state-granted license, and generally involving greater conceptual input than manual labor, i.e., the learned professions: law, medicine, theology, and higher learning" (Dictionary of American Criminal Justice, Criminology, & Criminal Law, 2005, p. 207). A person employed in a profession can be considered a **professional**. Schmalleger and Smykla (2006) have described professionalism in the corrections field as:

> *Commitment to a set of agreed-upon values aimed toward the improvement of the organization while maintaining the highest standards of excellence and dissemination of knowledge. In addition to having knowledge and skills, professionals must present humanistic qualities: selflessness, responsibility and accountability, leadership, excellence, integrity, honesty, empathy, and respect for coworkers and prisoners.*

It should be remembered that a major undertaking at the beginning of the 20th century was to make the criminal justice system more "professional." In fact, the pursuit of professionalism was the driving force behind the development of the contextual themes of criminal justice administration (see Chapter 1). Here, a century later, the pursuit of professionalism is still a major issue. A century of experience has fostered a different perspective. Today, from an Eclectic Perspective, professionalism includes all five of the contextual themes. At the beginning of the 20th century, professionalism meant being more effective and efficient through specialized Organization Functions approaches. Today, as then, professionalism requires standards; however, professionalism in the 21st century includes a humanistic approach with the community as well as with employees.

Professions require standards and usually an advanced level of education. Certainly, members of the judicial law profession meet this definition. However, what about the police and corrections officers? Let us explore the law enforcement and corrections fields of criminal justice in regard to professionalism.

■ Standards for Law Enforcement and Corrections

Most law enforcement agencies and some corrections agencies have state boards that set **standards** for entry-level employees. In 1967, the President's Commission on Law Enforcement and the Administration of Justice (LEJA) recommended that a Peace Officers Standards and Training (POST) commission be established in every state. Today, most states have commissions that have set standards for recruit training. A number of states have developed standards for special duties (i.e., detectives, juvenile officers), supervisors, and even police executives. These types of standards must be established for all law enforcement agencies to meet the qualifications of a true profession.

Accreditation has become an important process in professionalism. In 1979, four law enforcement agencies (the International Association of Chiefs of Police, The Police Executive Research Forum, The National Organization of Black Law Enforcement Executives, and the National Sheriff's Association) established the Commission on Accreditation for Law Enforcement Agencies (CALEA). The program is voluntary. Costs can range from $6,000 for small departments to $25,000 for larger agencies. Standards numbering from 500 to 700 have to be met depending on the size of the agency. More than 500 agencies have undergone the process by which they demonstrate that they meet these standards. Some states have established their own standards and a process of accreditation, including California, Colorado, Idaho, Kentucky, New Hampshire, New York, and Washington. Although accreditation is optional, it provides for a professional status with other benefits, including fewer lawsuits and citizen complaints, stricter accountability within the agency, and lower liability insurance costs. In fact, some cities require that their police departments become accredited because a growing number of municipal liability insuring companies require it.

In 1978, the American Correctional Association pioneered correctional accreditation. In 1999, they developed a national Commission on Correctional Certification and an online Corrections Academy. Just as accreditation provides the opportunity for facilities to be recognized, certification provides a means for correctional staff to be recognized as professional correctional practitioners.

All three criminal justice branches require employees to take an **oath of office**. Exploring these oaths can provide insight into the professional standards required in the various occupations. These ethical standards have been incorporated into the oaths of office for police officers in most every state. Some departments call their ethical standards "core values statements." The FBI Core Value Statement reminds us that "Rigorous obedience to constitutional principles ensures that individually and constitutionally we always remember that constitutional guarantees are more important than the outcome of any single interview, search for evidence, or investigation." It is important to remember that protecting individual rights did not become a part of an officer's sworn duty until the latter part of the 20th century. (The author, as a consultant, has found a few policing agencies that still have not included this important duty in their oath). Also note that the FBI Core Value Statement recognizes that unchecked power can become corrupt: "Respect for the dignity of all whom we protect reminds us to wield law enforcement powers with restraint and to recognize the natural human tendency to be corrupted by power and to become callous in its exercise."

Federal Bureau of Investigation Value Statement

Core Values

The strategic plan for accomplishing the FBI's mission must begin by identifying the core values which need to be preserved and defended by the FBI in performing its statutory missions. Those values are: rigorous obedience to the Constitution of the United States; respect for the dignity of all those we protect; compassion; fairness; and uncompromising personal and institutional integrity. These values do not exhaust all the goals we wish to achieve, but they encapsulate them as well as can be done in a few words. Our values must be fully understood, practiced, shared, vigorously defended, and preserved.

Observance of these core values is our guarantee of excellence and propriety in performing the FBI's national security and criminal investigative functions. Rigorous obedience to constitutional principles ensures that we always remember that constitutional guarantees are more important than outcome of any single interview, search for evidence, or investigation. Respect for the dignity of all whom we protect reminds us to wield law enforcement powers with restraint, and to recognize the natural human tendency to be corrupted by power and to become callous in its exercise. Fairness and compassion ensure that we treat everyone with the highest regard for constitutional, civil, and human rights. Personal and institutional integrity reinforce each other and are owed to the nation in exchange for the sacred trust and great authority conferred upon us.

We who enforce the law must not merely obey it. We have an obligation to set a moral example which those whom we protect can follow. Because the FBI's success in accomplishing its mission is directly related to the support and cooperation of those whom we protect, these core values are the fiber which hold together the vitality of our institution.

Source: FBI Website: http://www.fbi.gov.

Appendix 8 provides the Corrections Code of Ethics recommended by the American Corrections Association. It is important for criminal justice administrators to ensure that the oath of office is thoroughly discussed with new employees and that employees *sign a copy for their personnel file.* Signed copies document the accountability that employees have to these ethical standards.

■ Educational Requirements for Law Enforcement and Corrections Employees

In addition to standards, a profession should have educational requirements, and law enforcement and corrections are most lacking in this area. This is despite the fact that August Vollmer first introduced the idea of college requirements for police officers in 1917 (see Chapter 6). In 1973, the National Advisory Commission on Criminal Justice Standards and Goals recommended that "Every police agency should, no later than 1982, require as a condition of initial employment the completion of at least 4 years of education (120 semester units or a baccalaureate degree) at an accredited college or university" (Police, 1973, p. 369). This report commented on the fact that the undergraduate degree of the 1970s was equivalent to the high school diploma at the beginning of the 1900s. The high school diploma requirement was set for police officers as part of the professionalism effort of the early 1900s, but police agencies failed to keep up with the times. The report stated, "Police, in their quest for greater professionalism, should take notice [of upgrading educational requirements]" (Police, p. 367).

Most law enforcement agencies still have not set a college degree as a hiring requirement. Research finds that officers with higher education have higher motivation, are better able to utilize innovative techniques, display clearer thinking, have a better understanding of the world, and are overall better able to perform today's policing duties (Hayeslip, 1989, pp. 49–63). Educated officers have been found to be less authoritarian, less conservative, and less rigid and legalistic (Dalley, 1975; Finchenauer, 1975, Taylor, 1983). Kenney and Cordner (1996, pp. 277–306) further report that:

> . . . *college-educated officers will have a better understanding of the police role in general, of the importance of the police in society, and an improved sensitivity to the problems and differences in the community they police.*

In another research publication, Carter, Sapp, and Stephens (1989, p. 162) state that:

> *In sum, it is argued that a college-educated officer has a broader comprehension of civil rights issues from legal, social, historical, and political perspectives. Moreover, these officers have a broader view of policing tasks and a greater professional ethos, thus their actions and decisions tend to be driven by conscience and values, consequently lessoning the chance of erroneous decisions.*

Even the U.S. Supreme Court ruled that police officers could be required to have college educations, in *Davis vs. Dallas* (1985). Even today, most criminal justice agencies barely have the time and finances to *train*, let alone *educate*. Establishing university level education requirements can have a positive impact on the performance of all criminal justice employees.

So why is education still not a requirement? Some still believe educated officers are more likely to become frustrated with their work and that limited opportunities for advancement will cause them to quit. These critics further argue that police work requires mostly common sense or street sense, which is not something that you learn in college (Worden, 1990, pp. 565–592). This argument sometimes comes from older police chiefs, who did not receive higher education. Some fear that formal education requirements will prompt discrimination suits from minorities who do not possess such an education.

Other critics believe that a college education would cause unions to seek higher pay for such requirements. Today, many departments are willing to pay (and many already do) more for college educated employees. In August 2006, the magazine *Police Chief* accumulated substantial recent data supporting education in law enforcement. The data provides further evidence that officers with college degrees have fewer citizen complaints and are more adept at community-oriented policing than those without degrees (Mayo, 2006, pp. 20–40).

Progress is being made, particularly at the supervisory and management levels. A growing number of police departments require postgraduate degrees for higher-level administrative positions. The American Correctional Associations Certification program now requires applicants to meet the educational requirements of the category within which they seek certification. For example, the category of correctional executive requires a college degree; correctional managers and supervisors require an Associate's degree; and correctional officers require a high school diploma.

At the hiring level, much needs to be done. A growing number of states do include college education requirements in their hiring standards for peace officers. Most colleges and universities of any size offer criminal justice–related degrees. Those with college degrees are finding that it often gives them an advantage in the hiring process. It is important that criminal justice administrators strive to make it a requirement if criminal justice employment is truly to be a profession.

Understanding Professional Ethics

The status of professionalism within an occupation requires a high level of ethics. As discussed at the beginning of this chapter, citizens expect a very high level of ethics from those in criminal justice. But what is ethics? This section will focus on this subject.

Ethics is defined as the study and analysis of what constitutes good or bad behavior (Barry, 1985). However, as we study and analyze the subject, we find that it has many interpretations. For example, Dr. Sam S. Souryal, a well-known expert on ethics, provides the following definition for corrections officers:

> *Ethics has come to mean behaviors as they relate to a profession. Thus, there are medical ethics, legal ethics, and correctional ethics. All corrections professionals must follow basic ethical guidelines. Ethics boils down to making a choice between right and wrong, and doing what is right. In general, you can use your conscience as a guide. If you use sound reasoning, act in good faith, do your job fairly and honestly, respect the rights of others, and follow the rules and regulations of the agency, you will avoid most ethical problems (Souryal, 1998, p. 9).*

As Whisenand (2005, p. 41) defines it, ethics in policing is concerned with moral duties and how we should behave regarding both ends and means. Police work is an intrinsically practical service enterprise that judges its employees and actions only in terms of the effective use of power and the achievement of results.

Within these definitions, two views emerge: the study of and the behavior or duty to do good. Using these two views, we will define ethics as a *study* of what is considered as good and a *behavior* that is considered as good. Ethics has several branches, which can be adapted for law enforcement. **Normative**, **applied**, and **professional ethics** are described here:

- Normative ethics determines what ought to be done in normal situations (for example, normally a traffic citation should be given when a person violates a traffic law).
- Applied ethics is the application of ethical principles to a specific issue (for example, should a traffic citation be given in the situation in which the violator is a relative of the citing officer?).
- Professional ethics is applied to certain professions or groups (for example, the policy of the policing agency is not to accept gratuities) (Pollack, 2007, p. 10).

An important point here is that *ethics reflects what a society or a subset of a society sets as good behavior*. The author, as a professor, uses Nazi Germany's extermination of millions of Jewish people during the Holocaust as an example of this point. German prison guards stated that they were "just following orders." The inhuman treatment and killing was thought to be the right thing to do because it was institutionalized as such by the ruling power. In the minds of those carrying out these atrocities, what they were doing was "ethical." Slavery and, more recently, segregation were considered ethical in the history of the United States because they were approved of and supported by the government and the majority of the citizens.

The core values of the FBI include the recognition of "the natural human tendency to be corrupted by power and to become callous in its exercise." Because of the troublesome social situations that criminal justice professionals deal with, it is possible for some to become callous and cynical. This condition can foster the "us" versus "them" attitude. This condition can cause the mistreating of criminals and prisoners to be justified within the ethical framework of a subgroup. The author, as a police administrator, has had to deal with situations in which subcultures have developed within organizations that have promoted this type of behavior. Offending employees sometimes can become so immersed in the "ethical beliefs" of their subculture that they believe what they are doing is "corrective justice" or "noble justice."

Corrective justice, or **noble justice**, is defined as "corruption committed in the name of good ends, corruption that happens when police officers care too much about their work. It is corruption committed in order to get the bad guys off the street . . . the corruption of police power, when officers do bad things because they believe that the outcomes will be good" (Crank & Caldero, 2000). It is unfortunate that some popular television programs and movies portray this type of conduct as acceptable. The FBI "Core Values" show that this behavior is certainly unacceptable misconduct that can lead to termination and criminal prosecution. It is the duty of Eclectic Perspective administrators to prevent these situations from occurring.

Ethical and moral often are considered to have the same meaning. Even Abraham Maslow intertwined the two terms when he provided the "Profile of the Ethical Person" (**Appendix 9**). Maslow's profile is included here as a comprehensive list of ethic and moral attributes. The list, however, includes a number of attributes that are socially constructed (responding to challenges, seeming practical and shrewd, for example), whereas others are more of a moral nature (do not do mean things, love the world).

There is a difference between the two terms. *Morals* or morality refer to what one considers good conduct. So morals are individually constructed where ethics are socially or organizational. For example, many of those committing the Holocaust atrocities must have known their acts were morally wrong but thought they were ethically justified because of the ethical standards set by the ruling regime. Understanding the difference between morally right and ethically just is paramount in promoting professional ethics. *Ethics* refers to what *is believed to be right* by a society or an organization (or subset thereof).

There has always been a scholarly debate between whether knowing what is right is learned or something with which humans are born. Whether learned or inherent, most people know right from wrong, unless mentally incompetent. Morality is often used to refer to the whole person or the sum of a person's actions in all areas of life. It is sometimes referred to as what a person does when no one is looking. It is also referred to as the Golden Rule of "doing to others as you would have them do unto you."

Moral duty is frequently referred to in criminal justice codes. In the study of ethics, there are several types of moral duties:

> *General duties refers to those actions that an individual must perform in order to be considered moral. They include being truthful and considerate.*
>
> *Imperfect duties are general actions that one should do but without specific guides as to how and when. Generosity, for example, is thought of as good and moral but how generous should one be. Donating one dollar or thousands of dollars to a charity, where is the line of generosity drawn?*
>
> *Superogatory duties are commendable actions that are not required of a normal person. For example, a Good Samaritan who jumps into a river to save a drowning person, risks their life. This risking of one's life is not a general duty that would be expected of everyone. However, for a lifeguard or a police officer who has accepted the public duty to protect lives, this would not be superogatory, but rather a professional duty (adopted from Pollock, 2007, pp. 13–14).*

Values must be understood as part of what is moral. Values are what one believes to be desirable, of worth, and important. Moral values are those beliefs that relate to goodness that one places above all other.

Members of the criminal justice profession, especially administrative personnel, should be aware of their values, as should all employees. A worthwhile exercise is to rank each of the general values listed here according to one's individual beliefs. Add additional values as needed. Promoting moral values is essential to maintaining **professional ethics** and therefore should be of importance to criminal justice administrators.

Freedom

Peace of Mind

Honor

Religious Faith

Character

Learning/Knowledge

Success

Friendship Security

Recognition

Wealth

Tranquil Environment

Love

Social Acceptance

Family

Good Disposition

Respect

Power

Health

Sense of Humor

Criminal Justice Professional Ethics as a Component of Social Ethics

A number of terms have been discussed as elements of Professional Ethics. **Figure 13–1** displays these terms within the context of Social Ethics. This perspective is important in understanding professional ethics.

Social Ethics is what a society deems to be the right thing to do. It is within this overall concept that the other elements of ethics fit. For the purpose of this textbook, we are referring to social ethics in the United States. Again, we must be reminded that social ethics of our country has changed throughout history and the Bill of Rights has only recently applied to *all* people.

Where social ethics reflect the ideals of the society as a whole, morals and values relate to the individuals within the society. Again, morals are what individuals know to be the right thing to do and values are those attributes that they feel most important. Ideally, social ethics and corrective justice reflect the morals and values of the individuals who compose the society. With the concept in mind, the American social ethics should reflect the morals of "treating others as one wants to be treated." **Social justice** includes the concepts of equality, impartiality, and fairness. Justice "differs from benevolence, generosity, gratitude, friendship, and compassion" (Lucas, 1980, p. 3). It is something that we have the right

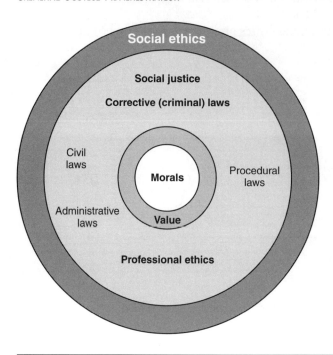

Figure 13–1 Components of Social Ethics.

to have rather than something for which we should feel grateful. It is to support those ideals that are significant to what we hold as social ethics.

In the United States, there are civil laws that protect individuals from "private wrongs." These are behaviors that only need be proven by a preponderance of evidence in a civil court. Also, there are procedural laws, whereby the courts can set standards for policing procedures ("Laws of Evidence") that ensure that individual rights are protected. Additionally, there are administrative laws, which are rules and regulations set by administrative bodies.

Corrective justice (criminal law) encompasses those human behaviors that society deems critical enough that imprisonment can be applied to enforce "the right" behavior. For example, if a person would fail to financially support their elderly parents when they are in need, it would be considered socially unethical. However, it has not been deemed behavior that requires some form of punishment. If, however, a person physically assaults their elderly parents, this behavior has been deem an assault and classified as a crime for which one can be punished.

Criminal laws, from traffic violations to those requiring capital punishment, have been institutionalized to provide maximum freedom for all within a complex society. Some laws can be regarded as *mala in se* (intrinsically wrong), such as murder and rape. These are laws that most everyone agrees are wrong. Other laws can be referred to as *mala prohibita* (legislated to be wrong), such as drug and vice crimes. They are often more difficult to enforce because not all agree they are wrong. However, they reflect the will of the majority through voting or elected officials. Some of these types of crimes are referred to as "victimless crimes." This is an erroneous concept because, under our legal systems, when a certain behavior has been legislated as wrong (as a reflection of the will of the *majority*) all of society becomes the victim.

This is where the criminal justice systems come into the equation, and its employees are sworn to uphold the will of the majority by enforcing laws and regulations. Additionally, their oath requires them to protect the rights of *all* people in carrying out their duties.

Professional criminal justice ethics encompass the standards and requirements that dictate what is the right behavior. This is where all the standards and requirements previously discussed in this chapter come into play.

■ Fostering Professional Ethics

So far in this chapter, the concepts and importance of professional ethics have been discussed. We have defined professional ethics as doing the right thing within our profession—but what is "the right thing"? In this section, we delve into the meanings of what is good behavior, how to judge what is right and wrong, and approaches to institutionalizing professional ethics.

Defining Ethical Behavior

In defining what is ethical, it is helpful to define what is unethical. In Chapter 8, the police officer's *Slipper Slide* (Figure 8–5) provides some examples. **Unethical behavior** can be placed in several categories. **Corruption** is generally defined as misuse of authority to do or not do something for others for some form of personal or group gain (typically, a bribe). **Misconduct** means nonconformity with obligations, departmental rules, and standards (e.g., abusing medical leave, sleeping on duty, and demonstrating culpable incompetence as assessed under internal disciplinary procedures and sanctions). **Crime** refers to serious offenses committed while on duty (e.g., excessive force, burglaries, thefts, selling drugs, murder, or manslaughter). **Civil rights violations** generally involve violations of constitutional rights (e.g., not following *procedural laws* during street interviews and station interrogations such as advising of rights and illegal search and seizures).

Immoral behavior is yet another category of unethical behavior and may not fall within the above categories. In discussing the difference between ethics and morals, examples were given where behavior may be accepted as *socially ethical* but still be immoral (the Holocaust example). This behavior involves not "treating others as one would want be treated." To put this into more understandable terms, it might be said by a corrections officer that they would never like to be treated as a prisoner. But this concept means that if one were to end up as a prisoner, how would they expect to be treated. The situation of lying to one who is being interrogated by the police is a sensitive area when discussing what is moral and ethical. Once we are untruthful to another person, and he or she becomes aware of this, the element of distrust becomes a condition that impacts any further relationship. However, the police can legally tell a person being interrogated a lie to provide a condition where a guilty person might be more inclined to confess. However, police can never *entrap* a person, meaning causing a person to commit a criminal act that they had not intended to do. Consequently, "legal untruths" during interrogations can be considered something that has been defined as ethical. Morally, if we were the one being interrogated, we should feel we are "being treated as we would treat others" as long as we were not induced to commit a criminal act. Being untruthful is an area of moral sensitivity that, within our *professional ethics*, must be used with caution.

How do we determine ethical behavior? A number of guides have been developed and incorporated into approaches used by criminal justice administrators. Ethical dilemmas can occur in all criminal justice functions, and at all levels. The following situations are offered as examples at administrative levels.

A police chief is invited to dinner at a very expensive restaurant by a local businessman who pays for the dinner and an expensive theater ticket for a performance later that night. Additionally, the businessman offers to contribute a substantial amount of money to the police department. The department has a policy that police officers are not to take free meals or coffee at local businesses.

A district attorney is presented with a case by the local police that is certainly based on probable cause. However, winning a conviction in court is not "a sure thing." The district attorney is up for reelection and knows that this case will draw media attention. Losing the case may reflect negatively on his office and influence his chances for reelection. The district attorney has the discretionary power to decide to prosecute or not.

A warden of a state prison is approached by the governor of his state. The governor indicates he would appreciate special privileges for a newly committed prisoner who has been convicted of illegal political contributions. These are special privileges (such as a more comfortable cell and added visitation and telephone rights) not given to other prisoners.

In facing these ethical dilemmas, administrators must understand that their decisions, if unethical, will soon be known by their employees. As will be covered in the next chapter in the discussion of leadership, integrity is important in leadership as employees are guided by what their superiors do. "If they (the boss) can be unethical, why can't I?"

Guides for Confronting Ethical Dilemmas

There are a number of guides that have been developed to assist in making ethical decisions. The following analytical five steps are thought processes and actions that may be taken when clarifying an ethical dilemma:

1. Review all of the facts. Make sure that one has all the facts—not future predictions, not suppositions, not probabilities.
2. Identify all of the potential values of each party that might be relevant.
3. Identify all possible moral issues for each party involved. This is to help see that sometimes one's own moral or ethical dilemma is caused by the actions of others. For instance, a police officer's ethical dilemma when faced with the wrongdoing of a fellow officer is a direct result of that other officer making a bad choice.
4. Decide what is the most immediate moral or ethical issue facing the individual. This is always a behavior choice, not an opinion. For example,

the moral issue of whether abortion should be legalized is quite different from the moral dilemma of whether "I should have an abortion if I find myself pregnant." Obviously, one affects the other, but they are conceptually distinct.

5. Resolve the ethical or moral dilemma (Pollock, 2007, pp. 24–25).

A number of police departments (the Chicago Police Department, for example) provide several additional guidelines as part of their recruit training, referred to by the acronym **ACT**:

- Identify **A**lternatives. You always have more than one choice—to do it or not to do it, for example. What other choice might you have?
- Project the **C**onsequences. What will happen with each choice? For example, making an illegal arrest would force you to then lie on an official police report and could lead to committing the crime of perjury in court.
- **T**ell Your Story. Make your choice and be ready to *tell* why you made that choice:

Bell, Book, and Candle
- The **Bell**—Do any warning bells go off as I consider my choices? This goes along with our definition of *morals* as knowing the right thing to do.
- The **Book**—Does my choice violate any laws, written codes, religious beliefs, department orders, rules, or regulations?
- The **Candle**—Will my decision be able to withstand the *light of day or the spotlight* of publicity? What will my loved ones and their shareholders think?

It is the candle that the author has found to be particularly useful in preparing employees to make ethical decisions. Reminding employees that he or she should always picture their loved ones or shareholders (those they feel personally important in their lives) looking over their shoulder before they choose a course of action. As a police administrator, the author has had to criminally prosecute a few employees for such unethical conduct as keeping drug money seized during an arrest. A subculture had been allowed to develop within a narcotic enforcement unit that made it "okay" to take such funds from "them." When the officers were discovered and were spotlighted by the news media, the embarrassment to their loved ones (shareholders) was even more of a punishment than the loss of their jobs and going to prison. Their children, who had been proud that their parent was a police officer, now saw them portrayed by the media as "bad guys." Preventing these situations is a critical task for every criminal justice administrator.

Discipline in Promoting Professional Ethics

In Chapter 8, discipline was defined as *a state in which an organization's members behave in ways that best serve its goals and purposes*. A "well disciplined" organization is a desirable state and not of a negative nature. Discipline involves both positive (prevention) and negative (punishment) administrative actions.

Administrators should prevent unethical behavior and when it occurs it means that they have failed in one of their major tasks. Here we will focus on *positive* approaches.

Some of the basic organization functions discussed in Chapter 7 apply in preventing unethical behavior. All employees should be required to read and sign the oath of office and the code of ethics. This provides a standardized means of holding employees accountable.

The concept of *inspection and control* (also discussed in Chapter 7) is important in fostering ethics. Criminal justice administrators have an obligation to develop procedures to ensure that unethical practices do not develop.

Methods to Reduce Police Corruption

Internal affair units
Independent civilian oversight agencies
Overt recording devices (videocameras in cars)
Covert high technology surveillance
Targeted integrity testing
Randomized integrity testing
Drug and alcohol testing
Quality assurance test (customer service monitors)
Internal informants
Complaints profiling
Supervisor accountability
Integrity reviews
Mandatory reporting
Whistleblower protection
Compulsory rotation in corruption-prone sections
Asset and financial reviews
Surveys of police
Surveys of public
Personnel diversification
Comprehensive ethics training
Inquisitorial methods (fact-finding rather than due-process emphasis)
Complaint resolution
Monitoring and regulation of police procedures (of informants)
Decriminalizing vice
Risk analysis (to see what areas are vulnerable to corruption)

Source: Wood, J. (1997). *Royal Commission into the New South Wales Police Service: Final Report.* Australia: Government Printer.

Control procedures that track and "flag" potential unethical behavior should be implemented. This means keeping track of use of force incidents and citizen complaints even when they are not proven as "sustained" misconduct. Employees who are involved in an *abnormal* amount of "nonsustained" complaints and use of force incidents should be "flagged" for review by supervisors and appropriate remedial support provided where needed. This is a sensitive area and many employee unions resist this type of tracking, arguing that employee actions should not even be considered questionable if not proven as misconduct. The Chicago Police Department, for example, has abandoned a number of attempts to set up such a program because of the employee organization's resistance. Consequently, that department (along with many others) has suffered substantial civil financial judgments because of misconduct that could have been identified years earlier if such a system was in place (Possley, 2006, Section 2.2).

Policy, procedure, and rules statements provide uniform guidelines and standards for ethical conduct and are another important element in preventing unethical behavior. **Appendix 10** lists typical areas were policy should be document. Policies are guides to be followed except in unusual situations where deviations can be justified. They usually involve critical situations such as the use of deadly force and vehicle pursuits. Procedures are statements of how to carry out a duty in the right manner, for example, the correct action to take in stopping a suspected felon and the information that must be recorded to conform to racial profiling information-gathering requirements. Rules are "shall do or shall not do" statements such as negative racial comments are never to be made in any circumstances or the taking of free meals is forbidden. These statements (which should be part of an agency's operating manual) not only provide positive guidelines but support negative disciplinary proceedings if necessary.

Value-based management is another important positive approach. The primary thrust of such a management philosophy is not so much toward prohibitions (rules) that restrain employees, but toward encouraging employees to weigh their actions constantly in light of the high ethical and constitutional values of their profession. Constant reminders of mission statements, the oaths of office, and the **codes of conduct** that employees have sworn to uphold is a vital part of a criminal justice administrator's job. These reminders should include the recognition that individual dignity is vital in the American system and protected by the U.S. Constitution. All people have a right to be treated with as much respect as they will allow and criminal justice employees have a duty to protect this right.

When unethical behavior brings widespread shame on an agency (such as in the Rodney King incident), coping with the aftermath should include value-based management approaches. These incidents are often indications of the need for change within the agency. Change most often is a product of dissatisfaction. People usually are not motivated to change unless their current status is uncomfortable. Employees become more supportive of change when they see it as a means of reducing their dissatisfaction and of improving their feelings of self-worth. Consequently, administrators should consider these incidents as opportunities to instigate change where change is needed. It can be an ideal time to reinstill the values and mission of the agencies. A renewed emphasis on ethics and a rekindling of the client-oriented philosophy should be viewed as essential in enhancing the morale and professional esteem of employees. Some of the approaches that should be taken are:

Re-affirm a belief in the basic mission

Encourage communication and dialogue

Demonstrate a caring about people

Allow for a ventilating of frustrations

Ensure fairness

Develop skills in "active listening"

Keep personnel on the healthy end of the continuum

Continue towards goals of excellence

Get the issues out in the open.

Ethics training should be an ongoing process. The author, as a consultant, has noted many excellent ethical training programs provided by criminal justice agencies as part of their new employee training. However, a number of agencies are somewhat lacking when it comes to ongoing training. Most criminal justice employees begin their careers with high moral standards and ethical beliefs. After years of dealing with stressful, and sometimes aggravating situations, employees can become cynical and become inclined to abandon the idea of "doing the right thing." Criminal justice employees often see human beings at their worst, court actions that conflict with what they perceive as their duty, and media presentations that often provide an unsavory image of what they do. Cynicism can lead to an "us vs. them" attitude, a subculture that supports unethical behavior and what has been called a "working personality" (Skonnick, 1994). Working personalities result in officers enforcing the law according to its letter rather than its spirit. The right to use of force can be abused when unruly and disrespectful suspects are seen as "them" and can be dealt with in unethical ways. Ongoing training is necessary to combat these unethical behaviors. As an example, the State of Illinois requires all employees (including state police, corrections officers, and court personnel) take a mandatory ethics training course and examination via the Internet every year (http://www.etcc.illinois.gov).

Included in the ongoing training should be a reminder that all employees have options if they really feel the profession (and their working environment) is not what they expected when they took their oath of office. Their options are:

• Conform to what the working environment really is
• Try to change the working environment to be what they thought it should be
• Quit and find another occupation
• Accept it as it really is and try to make improvements where possible

We do not live in a perfect world, nor is any profession "perfect." Unethical practices are never to be considered acceptable; however, there are many "gray areas." Most of us enter the criminal justice profession hoping for stability and clear definitions of what is right and wrong. Experience discloses many situations that do not fit our image of what is right. If we really believe (as we should) that the profession is a noble one, there are some realities that we just have to except and really try to make improvements where possible.

Additionally, "keeping personnel on the healthy end of the continuum" is a way of helping to reduce stress-induced cynicism. Daily exercise not only keeps one physically healthy but also helps to promote a healthy outlook on life. Being in control of one's body can support a mental outlook that offsets many of the conditions that cause cynicism.

Criminal justice administrators also should encourage employees to engage in off-the-job activities that promote a more balanced life. If employees engage in activities that take their mind off the job when they are off duty, they are better equipped to return to work and *do the right things* in meeting their professional challenges. The author (as a police administrator) considered police candidates who had various interests outside of criminal justice as good prospects for long-term law enforcement officers. Questions such as "What hobbies do you have?" and "What do you do for fun?" should be standard questions during hiring interviews.

Ongoing training should remind all that the code of silence is unacceptable. The Police Code of Conduct (see the Relevant Publication at end of this chapter) states under Integrity, "A police officer will not engage in acts of corruption or bribery, nor will an officer condone such acts by other police officers." This means that when a police officer accepts this code, he or she gives up any right to be silent regarding misconduct by other officers.

"Ratting" on others is something we grow up with as not desirable. In school, telling on our classmates often resulted in being ostracized by other classmates. This feeling continues into college and eventually into the workplace. However, when one joins a "profession," one is required to protect the ethical standards of the profession by not condoning misconduct by colleagues. This is true of doctors, lawyers, and other occupations. It certainly is true of criminal justice employees. Criminal justice employees must be reminded that misconduct by any other employee "tarnishes the badge" of all employees. When misconduct becomes public it becomes very public. It becomes "big news" because the public expects those to whom they have given criminal justice powers to be above reproach. The professional reputation, respect, and trust of all are damaged. It is encouraging to note that a National Institute of Justice survey found that 83 percent of all officers in the United States do not support the code of silence as part of good policing (Weisburd & Greenspan, 2000, p. 5). This, however, means that 17 percent do!

Aside from not committing an unethical act, not condoning it in others can be accomplished in several ways. One can tell another not to do it. If the unethical act is committed, it must be reported to a higher authority. It takes a lot of courage for an employee to report another employee to a supervisor in person. For those that cannot muster the courage, anonymous reporting is an option. The author, as a police supervisor, can recall anonymous notes in his mailbox that alerted him to provide closer supervision to someone that might be "tarnishing the badge." As a professor, the author has advised criminal justice students who observe fellow students committing crimes that they need to report it. Students applying for criminal justice jobs are sometime disqualified in background investigations that revealed they did nothing when observing a crime being committed. Comprehensive background investigations often involve interviewing college friends, roommates, and other acquaintances. Candidates may be disqualified when those interviewed comment that they remember seeing the candidate condoning criminal activities at parties, bars, and other student gathering places. If they do not have the courage to report it in person the author has advised at least report it to the local "Crime Stoppers" organization. There, they can report it anonymously and have a record of doing so.

One other dimension that should be a part of ethical training is a reminder that "the right thing to do" is more personal than just following professional ethics standards. Good morals are what each individual knows as the right thing to do—treating others as we want to be treated. In the article, "Beyond Ethics: The Case for Compassionate Policing," Miller (1999) urges "police administrators to encourage officers to reach beyond ethics and embrace compassion in their work" as an important approach to client-oriented service.

Of course, criminal justice administrators must apply negative discipline when unethical behavior is observed or reported. One final thought involves the future structure of criminal justice organizations.

The "**Professional Organization Structure**" is compared to the typical bureaucratic police and corrections organization structure in **Figure 13–2**. In a "professional structure," such as the courts and hospitals, professionals are hired to perform their specialty. The administration of the organization is accomplished by people who specialize in administration and management. Doctors and judges typically do not want to supervise and manage, so they have hospital and court administrators to perform these tasks. Organizationally, the administrators are on the same level as the "professionals" and often are paid the same or even less than the professionals. Consequently, the professionals can spend their whole careers specializing in the profession for which they were hired.

One might say that police and corrections work is not as "white collar" as the medical and legal profession. Perhaps a better comparison might be with the airline pilot's profession. Airline pilots are responsible for the safety of passengers. Consequently, they have high standards and must be trained and educated to perform their complicated jobs. They are well paid to perform the jobs for which they are hired and most continue doing this job throughout their careers. The administration of airlines is conducted by employees that earn the same and sometime less than the pilots.

In the bureaucratic structures of police and correction's institutions, one has to excel in rank to be rewarded with increased salaries. A proposal for the future is for police and corrections to move toward professional organizational structures. They should become agencies in which employees can continue to do the criminal justice tasks they enjoy throughout their careers. If they choose to go

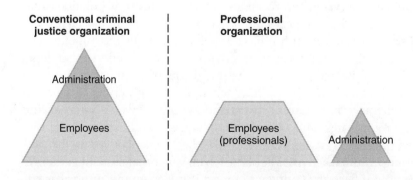

Figure 13–2 Typical Police and Corrections Organization Structure Compared with the "Professional Structure."

into administration, they have that option but do not have to become administrators to gain status and better incomes. The Eclectic Perspective makes one understand that the line personnel of all criminal justice agencies carry out the public missions. They are most important to "ensuring justice" and "domestic tranquility." Their tasks are very complicated and vital to the American way of life. They should be recognized as the professionals they are (with required educational and ethical standards) and receive appropriate status and salaries. This is the status toward which criminal justice administrators must strive if we are to truly be a profession.

A **personal creed** is yet another important component of professional administration. In order for professional administrators to properly lead their personnel, they should have a through understanding of what they as individuals stand for. Combining one's values into a statement that might be compared to the mission or value statement of an organization is a worthwhile endeavor. A personal "mission" statement may be referred to a one's personal creed. Personal creeds should be reviewed for adjustments when administrators are promoted or change assignments to ensure that they focus on personal values that relate to current administrative responsibilities. Students preparing to become professional administrators would do well to create a personal creed as a guide as they plan for their future.

The author has his creed posted where he reviews it daily and also attaches it to other documents, such as to course syllabi, so others can hold him accountable. It is offered below as an example.

Author's Creed

I believe in the efficacy of education, in the dignity of teaching, and in the joy of helping others.

I believe in quality in the classroom, in the home, and in daily life.

I believe in the young, the men and women of a great tomorrow, that whatsoever the young sow, the adult shall reap.

I believe in the diversity of mankind, that differences enrich our lives and that tolerance of differences is essential to a better future.

I believe in humor, in values and ideals, in distinct hopes that lure us on and that searching for the truth makes life exciting and challenging.

I believe that every hour of every day we receive a just reward for all we do and that in every day we should contribute and we should enjoy.

I believe in the present and its opportunities, in the future and its promises, and in the divine joy of living.

Clyde Cronkhite
Professor

KEY CONCEPTS AND TERMS

Professional Ethics

- Professions require standards
  - State required standards
  - Accreditation
  - Oaths of office
  - Codes of conduct

Understanding ethics

- Types of ethics
  - Normative
  - Applied
  - Professional
- Components of social ethics
  - Social justice
  - Corrective or noble justice
  - Professional ethics

Fostering professional ethics

- Unethical behavior
  - Corruption
  - Misconduct
  - Crime
  - Civil rights violations
  - Immoral behavior
- Guides for promoting ethical behavior
  - ACT
  - Bell, Book, and Candle
  - Value-based management
  - Ethics training
  - Professional organization structure
  - Personal creed

CHAPTER ACTIVITY

Select several criminal justice agencies of your choice. Obtain copies of their ethical standards or core value statements. See how they relate to the information discussed in this chapter.

REVIEW QUESTIONS

1. Define "profession." Do you think that criminal justice occupations can be classified as professions? Why or why not?

2. What criminal justice standards, codes of ethics, and other requirements correspond to the basic requirements of a "profession"?

3. What is the difference between ethics and morals? Give examples of what criminal justice administrators can do to ensure the ethical and moral conduct of their employees.

4. Several guides for fostering ethical behavior (such as ACT and Bell, Book, and Candle) were discussed in this chapter. Think of some examples of criminal justice ethical dilemmas. Discuss these dilemmas using one or more of the guides.

5. How is "discipline" an element in maintaining a professional organization? Give examples of discipline approaches that may be applied to ensure professional conduct by employees.

REFERENCES

Barry, V. (1985). *Applying Ethics: A Text with Readings*. Belmont, CA: Wadsworth.

Carter, D. L., Sapp, A. D., & Stephens, D. W. (1989). *The State of Police Education: Policy Direction for the 21st Century*. Washington, DC: Police Executive Research Forum.

Crank, J. P., & Caldero, M. A. (2000). *The Corruption of Noble Cause*. Cincinnati, OH: Anderson.

Dalley, A. (1975). University vs. Non-University Graduated Policemen: A Study of Police Attitudes. *Journal of Police Science and Administration*, 1, pp. 3–5.

Dictionary of American Criminal Justice, Criminology, & Criminal Law. (2005). Upper Saddle River, NJ: Pearson/Prentice Hall.

Finchenauer, J. O. (1975). Higher Education and Police Discretion. *Journal of Police Science and Administration*. December, pp. 22–26.

Hayeslip, D. W., Jr. (1989). Higher Education and Police Performance Revisited: The Evidence Examined through Meta-Analysis. *American Journal of Police*, pp. 8–10.

Kenney, D. J., & Cordner, G. W. (1996). *Managing Police Personnel*. Cincinnati, OH: Anderson.

Local Government Police Management. (2003). International City/County Management Association. Washington, DC: International City/County Management Association.

Lucas, J. (1980). *On Justice*. Oxford: Oxford University Press.

Mayo, L. (2006). College Education and Policing. *Police Chief:* Alexandria, VA: Publication of the International Association of Police Chief. August, pp. 20–40.

Miller, J. (1999). Beyond Ethics: The Case for Compassionate Policing. *The Police Chief*, August, p. 32.

National Advisory Commission on Criminal Justice Standards and Goals. (1973). *Police*. Washington DC: Department of Justice.

Pollock, J. M. (2007). *Ethical Dilemmas and Decisions in Criminal Justice* (5th ed.). Belmont, CA: Thomson/Wadsworth.

Possley, M. (2006). When Cops Go Bad, Everyone Pays. *Chicago Tribune*, October, pp. 2–3.

Schallener, F., & Smykia, J. O. (2006). *Corrections in the 21st Century*. New York: McGraw-Hill.

Skolnick, J. H. (1994). *Justice without Trial: Law Enforcement in a Democratic Society* (3rd ed.). New York: Macmillan College Publishing.

Souryal, S. S. (1998). *Ethics in Corrections*. A "Leaders Guide," a video set training package sponsored and sold by the American Corrections Association of Lanham, MD: (http://www.corrections.com/ACA).

Souryal, S. S. (1992). *Ethics in Criminal Justice: In Search of the Truth*. Cincinnati, OH: Anderson.

Taylor, M. (1983). Police Training: Towards a New Model. *The Police Journal*, pp. 56–59.

Weisburd, D., & Greenspan, R. (2000.) *Police Attitudes toward Abuse of Authority: Findings From a National Study*. Washington, DC: U.S. Department of Justice, National Institute of Justice Research in Brief.

Whisenand, P. (2005). *Supervising Police Personnel*. Englewood Cliffs, NJ: Prentice Hall.

Worden, R. E. (1990). A Badge and a Baccalaureate: Policies, Hypotheses, and Further Evidence. *Justice Quarterly*, 7, September, pp. 565–592.

Wrap Up

■ RELEVANT PUBLICATION

The International Association of Chiefs of Police (Alexandria, VA) is the major law enforcement association in the United States. It has the largest membership of police officers of all ranks in the world. Over the years, it has been instrumental in professionalizing law enforcement. The *Law Enforcement Code of Ethics*, the *Police Code of Conduct*, and the *Canons of Police Ethics*, provide the bases for most ethical standards for police officers in every U.S. state.

Law Enforcement Code of Ethics

As a law enforcement officer, my fundamental duty is to serve the community; to safeguard lives and property; to protect the innocent from deception, the weak against oppression or intimidation and the peaceful against violence or disorder; and to respect the constitutional rights of all to liberty, equality and justice.

I will keep my private life unsullied as an example to all and will behave in a manner that does not bring discredit to me or my agency. I will maintain courageous calm in the face of danger, scorn or ridicule; develop self-restraint; and be constantly mindful of the welfare of others. Honest in thought and deed both in my personal and official life, I will be exemplary in obeying the law and regulations of my department. Whatever I see or hear of a confidential nature or that is confided to me in my official capacity will be kept ever secret unless revelation is necessary in the performance of my duty.

I will never act officiously or permit personal feelings, prejudices, political beliefs, aspirations, animosities or friendships to influence my decisions. With no compromise for crime and with relentless prosecution of criminals, I will enforce the law courteously and appropriately without fear or favor, malice or will, never employing unnecessary force or violence and never accepting gratuities.

I recognize the badge of my office as a symbol of public faith, and I accept it as a public trust to be held so long as I am true to the ethics of police service. I will never engage in acts of corruption or bribery, nor will I condone such acts by other police officers. I will cooperate with all legally authorized agencies and their representatives in the pursuit of justice.

I know that I alone am responsible for my own standard of professional performance and will take every reasonable opportunity to enhance and improve my level of knowledge and competence.

I will constantly strive to achieve these objectives and ideals, dedicating myself before God to my chosen profession . . . law enforcement.

Source: The International Association of Chiefs of Police, originally written 1957, amended 1989.

Police Code of Conduct

All law enforcement officers must be fully aware of the ethical responsibilities of their position and must strive constantly to live up to the highest possible standards of professional policing.

The International Association of Chiefs of Police believes it important that police officers have clear advice and counsel available to assist them in performing their duties consistent with these standards, and has adopted the following ethical mandates as guidelines to meet these ends.

Primary Responsibilities of a Police Officer

A police officer acts as an official representative of government who is required and trusted to work within the law. The officer's powers and duties are conferred by statute. The fundamental duties of a police officer include serving the community, safeguarding lives and property, protecting the innocent, keeping the peace and ensuring the rights of all to liberty, equality, and justice.

Performance of the Duties of a Police Officer

A police officer shall perform all duties impartially, without favor or affection or ill will and without regard to status, sex, race, religion, political belief, or aspiration. All citizens will be treated equally with courtesy, consideration and dignity.

Officers will never allow personal feelings, animosities or friendships to influence official conduct. Laws will be enforced appropriately and courteously and, in carrying out their responsibilities, officers will strive to obtain maximum cooperation from the public. They will conduct themselves in appearance and deportment in such a manner as to inspire confidence and respect for the position of public trust they hold.

Discretion

A police officer will use responsibly the discretion vested in his position and exercise it within the law. The principle of reasonableness will guide the officer's determinations, and the officer will consider all surrounding circumstances in determining whether any legal action shall be taken.

Consistent and wise use of discretion, based on professional policing competence, will do much to preserve good relationships and retain the confidence of the public. There can be difficulty in choosing between conflicting courses of action. It is important to remember that a timely word of advice rather than arrest—which may be correct in appropriate circumstances—can be a more effective means of achieving a desired end.

Use of Force

A police officer will never employ unnecessary force or violence and will use only such force in the discharge of duty as is reasonable in all circumstances.

The use of force should be used only with the greatest restraint and only after discussion, negotiation, and persuasion have been found to be inappropriate or ineffective. While the use of force is occasionally unavoidable, every police officer will refrain from unnecessary infliction of pain or suffering and will never engage in cruel, degrading or inhuman treatment of any person.

Confidentiality

Whatever a police officer sees, hears, or learns, that is of a confidential nature, will be kept secret unless the performance of duty or legal provision requires otherwise. Members of the public have a right to security and privacy and information obtained about them must not be improperly divulged.

Integrity

A police officer will not engage in acts of corruption or bribery, nor will an officer condone such acts by other police officers. The public demands that the integrity of police officers be above reproach. Police officers must, therefore, avoid any conduct that might compromise integrity and thus undercut the public confidence in a law enforcement agency. Officers will refuse to accept any gifts, presents, subscriptions, favors, gratuities or promises that could be interpreted as seeking to cause the officer to refrain from performing official responsibilities honestly and within the law. Police officers must not receive private or special advantage from their official status. Respect from the public cannot be bought; it can only be earned and cultivated.

Cooperation with Other Police Officers and Agencies

Police officers will cooperate with all legally authorized agencies and their representatives in the pursuit of justice. An officer or agency may be one among many organizations that may provide law enforcement services to a jurisdiction. It is imperative that a police officer assist colleagues fully and completely with respect and consideration at all times.

Personal-Professional Capabilities

Police officers will be responsible for their own standard of professional performance and will take every reasonable opportunity to enhance and improve their level of knowledge and competence. Through study and experience, a police officer can acquire the high level of knowledge and competence that is essential for the efficient and effective performance of duty. The acquisition of knowledge is a never-ending process of personal and professional development that should be pursued constantly.

Private Life

Police officers will behave in a manner that does not bring discredit to their agencies or themselves. A police officer's character and conduct while off duty must always be exemplary, thus maintaining a position of respect in the community in which he or she lives and serves. The officer's personal behavior must be beyond reproach.

Source: Reprinted with permission of The International Association of Chiefs of Police, adopted by the IACP in 1992.

Canons of Police Ethics

International Association of Chiefs of Police

Article 1. Primary Responsibility of Job

The primary responsibility of the police service, and of the individual officer, is the protection of the people of the United States through the upholding of their laws; chief among these is the Constitution of the United States and its amendments. The law enforcement officer always represents the whole of the community and its legally expressed will and is never the arm of any political party or clique.

Article 2. Limitations of Authority

The first duty of a law enforcement officer, as upholder of the law, is to know its bounds upon him in enforcing it. Because he represents the legal will of the community, be it local, state or federal, he must be aware of the limitations and prescriptions which the people, through law, have placed upon him. He must recognize the genius of the American system of government which gives to no man, groups of men, or institution, absolute power, and he must insure that he, as a prime defender of that system, does not pervert its character.

Article 3. Duty to be Familiar With the Law and with Responsibilities of Self and Other Public Officials

The law enforcement officer shall assiduously apply himself to the study of the principles of the laws which he is sworn to uphold. He will make certain of his responsibilities in the particulars of their enforcement, seeking aid from his superiors in matters of technicality or principle when these are not clear to him; he will make special effort to fully understand his relationship to other public officials, including other law enforcement agencies, particularly on matters of jurisdiction, both geographically and substantively.

Article 4. Utilization of Proper Means To Gain Proper Ends

The law enforcement officer shall be mindful of his responsibility to pay strict heed to the selection of means in discharging the duties of his office. Violations of law or disregard for public safety and property on the part of an officer are intrinsically wrong; they are self-defeating in that they instill in the public mind a like disposition. The employment of illegal means, no matter how worthy the end, is certain to encourage disrespect for the law and its officers. If the law is to be honored, it must first be honored by those who enforce it.

Article 5. Cooperation with Public Officials in the Discharge of Their Authorized Duties

The law enforcement officer shall cooperate fully with other public officials in the discharge of authorized duties, regardless of party affiliation or personal prejudice. He shall be meticulous, however, in assuring himself of the propriety, under the law, of such actions and shall guard against the use of his office or person, whether knowingly or unknowingly, in any improper or illegal action. In any situation open to question he shall seek authority from his superior officer, giving him a full report of the proposed service or action.

Article 6. Private Conduct

The law enforcement officer shall be mindful of his special identification by the public as an upholder of the law. Laxity of conduct or manner in private life, expressing either disrespect for the law or seeking to gain special privilege, cannot best reflect upon the police officer and the police service. The community and the service require that the law enforcement officer lead the life of a decent and honorable man. Following the career of a policeman gives no man special perquisites. It does give the satisfaction and pride of following and furthering an unbroken tradition of safeguarding the American republic. The officer who reflects upon this tradition will not degrade it. Rather, he will so conduct his private life that the public will regard him as an example of stability, fidelity and morality.

Article 7. Conduct Toward the Public

The law enforcement officer, mindful of his responsibility to the whole community, shall deal with individuals of the community in a manner calculated to instill respect for its laws and its police service. The law enforcement officer shall conduct his official life in a manner such as will inspire confidence and trust. Thus, he will be neither overbearing nor subservient, as no individual citizen has an obligation to stand in awe of him nor a right to command him. The officer will give service where he can, and require compliance with the law. He will do neither from personal preference or prejudice but rather as a duly appointed officer of the law discharging his sworn obligation.

Article 8. Conduct in Arresting and Dealing with Law Violators

The law enforcement officer shall use his powers of arrest strictly in accordance with the law and with due regard to the rights of the citizen concerned. His office gives him no right to prosecute the violator nor to mete out punishment for the offense. He shall, at all times, have a clear appreciation of his responsibilities and limitations regarding detention of the violator; he shall conduct himself in such a manner as will minimize the possibility of having to use force. To this end he shall cultivate a dedication to the service of the people and the equitable upholding of their laws whether in the handling of law violators or in dealing with the law-abiding.

Article 9. Gifts and Favors

The law enforcement officer, representing government, bears the heavy responsibility of maintaining, in his own conduct, the honor and integrity of all government institutions. He shall, therefore, guard against placing himself in a position in which any person can expect special consideration or in which the public can reasonably assume that special consideration is being given. Thus, he should be firm in refusing gifts, favors, or gratuities, large or small, which can, in the public mind, be interpreted as capable of influencing his judgment in the discharge of his duties.

Article 10. Presentation of Evidence

The law enforcement officer shall be concerned equally in the prosecution of the wrong-doer and the defense of the innocent. He shall ascertain what constitutes evidence and shall present such evidence impartially and without malice. In so doing, he will ignore social, political, and all other distinctions among the persons involved, strengthening the tradition of the reliability and integrity of an officer's word. The law enforcement officer shall take special pains to increase his perception and skill of observation, mindful that in many situations his is the sole impartial testimony to the facts of a case.

Article 11. Attitude Toward Profession

The law enforcement officer shall regard the discharge of his duties as a public trust and recognize his responsibility as a public servant. By diligent study and sincere attention to self-improvement he shall strive to make the best possible application of science to the solution of crime and, in the field of human relationships, strive for effective leadership and public influence in matters affecting public safety. He shall appreciate the importance and responsibility of his office, and hold police work to be an honorable profession rendering valuable service to his community and his country.

Source: The International Association of Chiefs of Police

14 Criminal Justice Administration and Leadership in the 21st Century

■ Introduction

Chapter 1 began by defining criminal justice administration as the task of overseeing the fulfillment of the public mission for criminal justice agencies. Administration involves both management and leadership. Management was further defined as making appropriate use of resources (people and equipment) to achieve organizational goals and objectives as efficiently and effectively as possible. In this chapter, the focus will be on leadership.

■ Defining Leadership

Leadership can be defined as the process of getting people willing to work toward some common goal. It involved inspiring rather than requiring people to do their job. The 34th president of the United States, Dwight David Eisenhower, defined leadership as "the art of getting someone else to do something you want done because that person wants to do it."

President Eisenhower made reference to leadership in yet another way when he said, "I would rather try to persuade a man to go along, because once I have persuaded him he will stick. If I scare him, he will stay as long as he is scared, and then he is gone."

Eisenhower's quotes help to understand the difference between leadership and management. Management has more to do with ensuring that resources are used efficiently and effectively. As discussed in Chapter 7, management involves Organization Functions concepts such as Weber's Principles of Bureaucracy, Taylor's "Scientific Management," and Gulick's POSDCORB. Can an administrator achieve an agency's mission by just managing? Can an administrator achieve an agency's mission by leadership alone? The answer to both of these questions is yes. But under what circumstances and for how long? Managing can achieve results in the short term where leadership is required for long term accomplishments. Inspiring and persuading (the two main ingredients of leadership) are required for enduring accomplishments.

■ Historical Perspective of Leadership

In Chapter 8, a number of concepts were discussed that relate to the question of when managing alone will suffice, and when leadership is required. These concepts are reviewed here as they relate to leadership. The process of motivating employees to achieve objectives that support the agency's mission was discussed. Motivation was described as the "force within an individual that initiates, directs, and sustains a particular behavior." So motivation is a personal emotion and varies from employee to employee.

Maslow's Hierarchy of Human Needs (Figure 8–4) provides insight into the concept that what motivates people differs at the various levels of human needs. At the lower levels, just having an income and job security may be enough to do what the "boss demands." Employees many respond to McGregor's Theory X type of manager because the major focus of their life is on just surviving. However, as one advances up Maslow's Hierarchy of Human Needs, he or she is concerned more with social and ego needs. This is where McGregor's Theory Y (Table 8–2) approach is needed and leadership begins to be a requirement. An employee who is motivated by social, ego, and self-actualization needs requires some "selling," as Hersey and Blanchard called it in their *Situational Management* approach (Figure 8–4). They need to be convinced that achieving objectives that support the agency's mission will satisfy their motivational needs.

Vroom's Expectancy Theory points out that what employees expect as rewards is at the heart of motivation. LeBoeouf's Greatest Management Principle (GMP) simply stated is "what gets rewarded is what gets done." However, what rewards varies among employees? Rewards may range from praise, salary, to feeling of accomplishment or acceptance. For one employee, having a job that provides more time with their family might be rewarding, whereas for another, the possibility of promotion or a salary increase might be a motivating factor.

It is an essential task of a leader to determine what motivates their employees and relate their motivational needs to achieving the goals of the agency. Remember, as discussed in Chapter 1, the two major responsibilities of an administrator are (1) accomplishing the agency's mission and (2) satisfying the needs of the employees. These responsibilities require both management and leadership skills if long-term results are to be achieved. Eclectic Perspective administrators will realize that leadership is required both internally with employees and externally with other agencies, elected officials and members of the community. Inspiring and persuading others to achieve the agency's mission is the major task of all criminal justice administrators.

As with many other aspects of administration, the concepts that bring us to where we are today regarding leadership involve many years of development. From **Max Weber's concepts** in the early 1900s to Jim Collin's more contemporary finding in the first few years of the 21st century, a number of building blocks of leadership have been documented. We will begin the exploration of these building blocks by going back to the basic concepts of Max Weber.

Weber distinguished among three forms of leadership within his bureaucratic organization: traditional, **legal-rational** and **charismatic** (Weber, 1947 from his early writing in German):

- Traditional is established through customs and sanctity of traditions such as royal lineage of kings.
- Legal-rational stems from one's formal position in an organization and from the legal responsibilities and duties that are attached to that office such a police chief, warden or district attorney: they are given the position to oversee, to be an administrator.
- Charismatic is a form established by the personal appeal of an individual such as John Kennedy, Winston Churchill, and Martin Luther King.

It is the latter two that relate to criminal justice leadership. As discussed in Chapter 10, in the republic form of government, the majority (through the U.S. Constitution) afford certain government positions authority to carry out the will of the people. Every member of the criminal justice system receives certain authority and responsibilities. When the sheriff, chief public defender, and chief probation officer take the oath of office to oversee their respective agencies, they receive what Weber called legal-rational leadership authority. As discussed in Chapter 7, these chief executive administrators then can delegate authority (and responsibility) down the chain of command, within the bureaucratic organization. From this perspective, all the way down to the line supervisor, each administrative position received this legal-rational authority. However, does this provide each administrator with the ability to inspire and persuade? The answer is no. It does not even ensure that recipients have the ability to manage, only that they are placed in a position with some power of authority. Now let us explore the meaning of power and authority as they are related to being in a position to lead. Even if one can inspire and pursue, they can not carry out their mission without power and authority. Five sources of power and authority in social relationships have been identified as the following:

- Reward power stems from the ability to give people something of value in exchange for their loyalty and willingness to cooperate (e.g., monetary rewards, promotion, and assignments).
- Coercive power comes from the ability to take away or threaten to take away something of value to the individual for failing to comply or cooperate (e.g., desirable assignments, promotions, and income).

- Legitimate power relates to the belief that the person exercising the power is doing so lawfully and rightfully, generally in connection with their position of accepting authority (e.g., the police captain has the authority to deploy his or her personnel to various locations under their command).
- Referent power relates to a person's identity or psychological attachment to an individual or group, or value of importance to that individual or group (e.g., the power of a police SWAT team commander because of the team's prestige).
- Expert power stems from a recognized skill or knowledge which is a value in the organization (e.g., the deputy district attorney has special abilities to handle certain criminal cases [French & Raven, 1959, pp. 150–167]).

This list was more recently expanded to the ten forms of influence as shown below in Yukl's Forms of Leadership Influence (**Table 14–1**). Although reflective

Table 14–1	**Yukl's Forms of Leadership Influence**

1. Legitimate request. A person complies or is influenced by another's request because the person believes that the agent has an "official right" to make the request.

2. Instrumental compliance. A person complies or changes his or her behavior based on an agent's promise (implicit or explicit) to help the person obtain a desired objective or outcome.

3. Coercion. A person complies or is influenced because of the agent's threat (implicit or explicit).

4. Rational persuasion. A person complies or is influenced because the agent has convinced the person that compliance is the best possible way for the person to obtain his or her goals or objectives.

5. Rational faith. A person complies because of his or her belief in the system of authority or leadership, without any explanation being made by the agent requesting the compliance.

6. Inspirational appeal. A person complies because the agent has convinced him or her that compliance is necessitated by some superordinate goal.

7. Indoctrination. A person complies because he or she has been subjected to a process of internalizing the values sought by the agent.

8. Information distortion. A person complies or is influenced by information provided by an agent which is distorted or falsified, but which nevertheless persuades compliance.

9. Situational engineering. A person complies or is influenced because his or her attitudes and/or behavior is affected because the agent is manipulating the person's social or physical environment.

10. Personal identification. A person complies or is influenced because the agent has let the person participate in the decision-making process, which has increased the person's identification with the final decision.

Source: Adapted from Yukl, G. (1981). *Leadership in Organizations*. Englewood Cliffs, NJ: Prentice Hall. pp. 12–17. Adapted by permission of Prentice Hall, Upper Saddle River, NJ.

of the previous discussed factors, the ten are further refinements of conditions that support power and authority. They are indicative of the evolutionary changes that impact leadership. The Eclectic Perspective administrator must be sensitive to these changes and be flexible enough to "mix and match" the correct leadership style to the current organization and social conditions.

Regarding Weber's third form of leadership, charismatic authority, Weber went on say "such authority is short-lived. In its pure form, charismatic authority has a character specifically foreign to everyday routine structures. The social relationships directly involved are strictly personal." Weber believed that to create stability in the organization, charismatic authority needs to be channeled into the mechanics of the bureaucratic structure in the form of legitimate authority based on legal and rational grounds. He felt that charismatic authority, with its reliance on personal relationships, creates inconsistent policies based on personal "whims" and often breaks down. He wrote that over time, the charismatic leader has to institute normal legalistic aspects of bureaucracy, namely (1) a set of written rules that persist over time and that are adhered to, (2) clearly identified administrative officials with their authority specifically defined and limited, and (3) a hierarchical organization with publicly known operational lines of authority (Weber, 1961).

In more contemporary terms, what Weber said was that no matter how charismatic a leader may be, without the ability to manage and "mix and match" the evolutionary concepts of administration to the situation at hand, success will be short lived. There are occasions when a charismatic leader has been "at the right place, at the right time" and inspired a nation or an organization to achieve. However, without the knowledge and ability to apply the concept of administration, their achievements were brief. Such people, if insightful enough to realize their administrative shortcomings, will hire (or delegate to) a person who has the administration talents they are lacking.

A warden or district attorney, for example, who is charismatic and has a persuading rapport with the public, may be able to operate for a time. However, today's organizational environment still embraces the legal-rational authority concept. A charismatic sheriff, for example, who is not adept at administration can be kept in power by political party organizations because of his or her vote-getting power. However, in time the rational rules of organization come into play in carrying out the public mission of the agency. The lack of ability to manage resources by these persons will soon be recognized by the voters and by their employees.

A 2006 *Corrections Today* magazine issue was devoted to "Leadership and Staff Development" in correctional institutions (*Corrections Today*, 2006). In an included article, Michael Kenney states "Leadership is not charisma." **Table 14–2**, from this article, shows a comparison of approaches that demonstrate the differences between being charismatic and being a leader. Kenney concludes by stating "The truth is, real leadership is hard, calculating and effective. It is not glamorous nor for the faint-hearted. It can be gut-wrenching during the difficult times and euphoric when success is achieved, but it is never dull and certainly is not safe.—Leadership required some skills and natural gifts, but, in the final analysis, it is mostly hard work, an open mind and perseverance. Real leadership

Table 14–2	Comparison of Charisma and Leadership
Charisma	**Leadership**
Stirs emotions	Produces actions
Seeks popularity	Seeks integrity
Lessens with time	Strengthens with time
Emphasizes individual success	Emphasizes team success
Is fragile	Is enduring
Is neat—paints a pretty picture	Is messy—tackles difficult issues
Plays it safe	Is willing to take risks
Avoids conflict	Accepts conflict
Needs a crowd	Knows loneliness

Source: Kenny, M. (2006). "Lead at Any Level." *Corrections Today*. August, p. 19. Reprinted with permission of the American Correctional Association, Alexandria, VA.

does not tolerate needy egos or people full of themselves, but is reserved for those who embrace humility, sacrifice and team success" (Kenney, 2006, pp. 18–19).

This is not to infer that a charismatic personality is not important. It certainly is an attribute that can assist in achieving goals. The relationship between charismatic personality and the ability to achieve goals was tested by Judge and Bono using a five-factor model of personality (**Figure 14–1**). In their study they sampled 223 Midwestern community leaders and found that agreeableness (likeable, friendly, good rapport) was the strongest predictor of what they termed "transformational" leadership. This was the personality trait most closely related to charisma and the factor that was most effective in achieving goals. Extroversion and openness were also positively related (Judge & Bono, 2000).

Others have argued that charisma is not a trait that resides in a person but is a behavioral phenomenon. This view sees charisma as based on follower's perceptions of leader behavior. Leaders first evaluate the talents and needs of subordinates. They then expose the weaknesses of the status quo within the organization, followed by the formulation of new goals (Conger, 1999, pp.

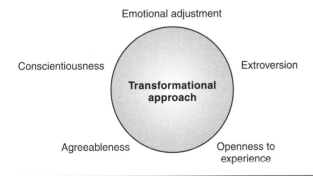

Figure 14–1 Five-Factor Model of Personality.

Table 14–3	Importance of Both Leadership and Management Skills
Skill Area	**Rating by Police Chief Executives**
1. Motivating personnel and maintaining high morale	8.7
2. Developing subordinates into an effective team	8.6
3. Relating to the community	8.4
4. Organizing agency personnel and functions	8.0
5. Administering internal discipline	7.9
6. Maintaining internal review and control	7.9
7. Communicating with all levels within the agency	7.9
8. Establishing and communicating objectives and priorities	7.8
9. Forecasting, planning, and implementing activities	7.8
10. Resolving employee relations problems	7.7
11. Budgeting and fiscal management	7.7
12. Utilizing advanced technology	7.2
13. Coordinating agency activity with other organizations	7.2
14. Securing and managing grant-funded projects	6.2

Source: National Advisory Commission on Criminal Justice Standards and Goals (1976).

145–179). This concept will be explored further in the subsequent discussion of change agent leadership. Follower-centered research has also found that followers who report having charismatic bosses also exhibited a higher need for leadership. This research concluded that these employees were more dependent on rather than empowered by their charismatic leader (De Vries, Roe, & Tailliey, 1999, pp. 109–133). This supports the concept of "different strokes for different folks" and reminds us that the Eclectic Perspective administrator must provide leadership tailored to the needs of employees and the situation at hand.

It is important to remember that to be successful an administrator must be both a leader and a manager. **Table 14–3** rates various leadership and management skills for chief executives. Even though motivating personnel is at the top of the list, organizing, control, planning, budgeting, and other management skills are rated highly.

■ Assessing Leadership versus Management Traits

The Management and Leadership Grid has become a standard method of assessing leadership and management traits (**Figure 14–2**). Blake and Moulton (1964) first created this concept by naming leadership behavior associated with quadrants of an Ohio State leadership study in 1964. During the next 25 years they enhanced their concept into a grid that could be used for study and assessment. In the grid, "Concern for Production," which relates more to management

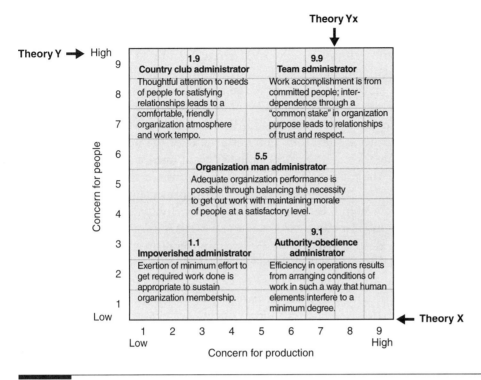

Figure 14–2 Blake & Mouton's Leadership/Managerial Grid Compared to McGregor's Theory X & Y plus "Big Y and Little x Theory."

traits, is placed on the horizontal coordinate. "Concern for People," which can be related more to leadership, is placed on the vertical coordinate. Figure 14–2 compares the grid to the earlier discussed Theory X and Y as well as "Big Y and Little x theory."

The concept is that administrators fit in one of four quadrants or the central part of the grid depending on their traits and behaviors. The traits and behaviors used in these quadrants (as adapted from Gaines et al., 2003, pp. 196–198) are defined as:

Team Administrator (9.9). These administrators fall in the upper-right, or team, quadrant and are strong in both consideration and structure. The team manager accomplishes work through committed people. They are high in concern for both people and production. They are high in both leadership and management abilities. There is a "common stake" in the organization's mission, which leads to a relationship of trust and respect on which true authority is based. This is the ideal type of administrator and one that should be able to achieve both requirements of good administrators—that is, to accomplish the mission and satisfy the needs of the employees.

Authority-Obedience Administrator (9.1). These administrators are overly concerned with the tasks, often disregarding the needs of their employees. They are sometimes called Task Managers and "Theory X " managers as discussed in Chapter 2 and Chapter 8. They are high in concern for productivity and low in concern for people and more associated with management skills than leadership skills. This type of administrator, because of their uncaring attitude, frequently have motivational problems with their employees. They are sometimes effective for short-range objectives but most often experience insurmountable difficulties in the long term.

Country Club Administrator (1.9). Country Club administrators are primarily interested in remaining friends with employees regardless of how they produce. They pay thoughtful attention to the needs of employees and try to make them happy. (Happy employees, however, are not always the most productive.) They are high in concern for people but low in concern for productivity. They are not good managers since they show little care for the principles of management. Neither are they good leaders as they do not inspire and pursue employees to carry out the mission of the agency. Even though they care about their employees, motivational problems often occur because employees see that the organization goals are not being met and the productivity that can promote employee satisfaction is lacking.

Impoverished Administrator (1.1). The impoverished administrators are not overly concerned about goals or people. They exert only the minimum amount of effort necessary to get required work done so that they can remain in their positions. They are more a bureaucrat than a leader and usually little is accomplished under their command. Both low concern for people and production are indicators of this type of administrator. Motivational problems often develop because employees become frustrated about not having any direction and are lacking in means of job satisfaction.

Organization Man Administrator (5.5). This type of administrator tries to balance the necessity to produce organizational results while maintaining the employee morale at a satisfactory level. Instead of being "painted" as black or white, they are gray. They often can survive in the bureaucratic organization but are not willing to exert the maximum effort and go for the highest levels of productivity. Employee motivation is often reflective of this middle ground.

Behavior Profiles

Questionnaires that assess where administrators fit on the grid can be purchased and administrated. However, the results of self-administered assessments are questionable. Administrators answer the questions according to their own perceptions of what they are. It was Dore Schary who said "The true portrait of a man is a fusion of what he thinks he is, what others think he is, what he really is and what he tries to be." The questionnaires should also be administered to the employees of the person being evaluated to determine where their "subordinates" place their "superior" on the grid. The Eclectic Perspective administrator would be wise to have their employees assess them periodically as there is usually a "gap" between what the boss and the employees think. Sometime "the truth hurts" but can be valuable feedback, particularly when trying to make organizational changes.

One of the consulting companies that provides these type of assessments divide behaviors that contribute to or detract from leadership into four **DISC** categories: **Dominance, Influence, Supportiveness,** and **Conscientiousness. Table 14–4** shows how these four categories relate to various personal behaviors and conditions in which one works best. This can help the Eclectic Perspective

Table 14–4   DISC Factors

Tips for Recognizing DISC Behaviors

	D Dominance	I Influence	S Supportiveness	C Conscientiousness
Makes decisions	Quickly	Emotionally	Deliberately	Analytically
Questions	What?	Who?	Why?	How?
Responds well to:	• Quick results • Being in charge • Making decisions • Fast pace • Challenges	• People • Recognition • Personal connections • Optimism	• Providing good service • Clear instruction • Cooperation • Stability, loyalty	• Order, accuracy • Set standards • Systematic approaches • Sufficient time
• Responds poorly to:	• Losing control • Slow results • Being questioned or overruled • Close supervision	• Rigid schedules • Loss of approval • Rejection • Unfriendly co-workers • Pessimism	• Unexpected change • Loss of security • Lack of support • Confrontation	• Criticism • Inconsistencies • Lack of or changing standards • Required socializing
• Mottos	"Tell it like it is." "Just do it."	"People are more important than things."	"Don't rock the boat."	"It's all in the details."

Remember . . . EVERYONE demonstrates ALL FOUR behaviors.

Working with Identified DISC Behaviors

D Dominance	I Influence	S Supportiveness	C Conscientiousness
• Communicate briefly and to the point • Avoid small talk • Stick to the topic • When practical, let them initiate action • Demonstrate your competence • Be confident	• Be informal and friendly • Listen • Publicly recognize accomplishments • Use humor • Acknowledge feelings • Offer variety and creativity • Write down instructions	• Avoid unnecessary changes • Share information • When change is unavoidable, explain fully and ease into it • Express sincere appreciation • Provide a non-threatening environment • Clearly define responsibility and authority	• Demonstrate your dependability • Be specific about expectations • Avoid displays of emotion • Express value of high standards • Recognize accomplishments privately • Be businesslike and task-oriented

Remember . . . DISC describes a particular behavior—not a personality.

Source: Printed by permission of owner: TSS Consultants, Group, Inc.

administrator better understand their weaknesses and strengths. Additionally it can help identify which type of leadership behavior best fits various administrative challenges. This approach recognizes that no one person fits exactly into any of the four categories. The idea is to provide a means for administrators to know themselves, recognize the needs of their employees, and adapt strategies to meet various challenges. By knowing in which category they are the strongest and weakest, administrators are better able to "mix and match" their strengths that are most predictable behaviors for successful results. Following are some examples adapted from the DISC categories (2001, p. 7):

Dominance behaviors are adept at shaping the environment by overcoming opposition that will interfere with desired results. They are able to get immediate results and can make quick decisions. They want power and authority and welcome challenges. They sometimes become too "task oriented" and need to increase their attention to the needs of their employees. This type of leader is often successful at making critical changes in a timely manner.

Influence behaviors are more adept at making changes by persuading others. They are people oriented, make favorable impressions and generate enthusiasm. They like to be popular and view people and situations with optimism. They do concentrate on the task and develop systematic approaches to successfully complete them. They usually take more time to have the task completed. They probably are not as effective in handling timely and critical tasks as those with Dominance and Steadiness behaviors.

Steadiness behavior focuses on cooperating with others within existing circumstances to carry out tasks. They perform in a consistent and predictable manner, demonstrate patience and help others. They tend to calm excited people and create stable, harmonious work environments. The can react quickly to change and work comfortably in unpredictable environments such as organic organizations discussed in Chapter 7. They tend to need colleagues of similar competence and sincerity and need to be encouraged to be creative.

Conscientiousness behavior places emphasis on working carefully within existing circumstances to ensure quality and accuracy. They respond best to directions and think analytically using systematic approaches to achieve tasks. They perform best in environments that have clearly defined performance expectations and are proud of and want recognition for their specific skills. They are good managers and function best in what was described as the mechanistic organization in Chapter 7, They need time to plan carefully and should learn to respect people's personal worth as much as their accomplishments.

These means of assessment are useful in studying leadership traits as well as for administrators to assess their own behavior patterns. Additionally, they can be used in the selection of administrators for assignments that present special challenges.

Traits Associated with Leadership

Whether traits associated with leadership are learned or are traits with which one is born, has been an ongoing discussion. Stodgill (1974) has listed traits that are often associated with leadership as follows:

Communication Skills

Decisiveness

Emotional Control

Flexibility

Industriousness

Integrity

Intelligence

Interpersonal Skills

Intuition

Motivation

Persistence

Responsibility

Self-confidence

Sincerity

Supportiveness

Vision

Everyone seems to agree that most of these traits can be learned, but at what stage of life is not known. Intelligence capacity is often associated with what one is born with but acquiring knowledge is something that is learned. The Eclectic Perspective administrator should assess the traits that they have and the traits that are needed for leadership positions to which they aspire. Going into a leadership position and hoping to learn the traits needed to be successful in the position will probably lead to failure. Insightful administrators know their strength and weaknesses and avoid taking positions for which they are "not the right person."

Emotional Intelligence is a concept that describes leadership traits that work well with the current client-oriented service approach. This concept focuses on social analysis, which Daniel Goleman defines as "being able to detect and have insight about people's feelings, motives, and concerns." Leaders must anticipate and deal with aspects of human behavior in making decisions. Goleman (1995, p. 118) explains Emotional Intelligence as:

- Self-Awareness—Emotional awareness, accurate self-assessment, self-confidence
- Self-Regulation—Self-control, trustworthiness, conscientiousness, adaptability, innovation
- Motivation—Achievement, commitment, initiative, optimism
- Empathy—Understanding and developing others
- Social Skills—Influence, communication, conflict management change catalyst, building bonds, collaboration and cooperation, team capabilities

Empathy is probably the most crucial human relations skill in the 21st century according to this concept. Goleman defines empathy as "understanding others, developing others, service orientation, leveraging diversity, and political awareness" (Goleman, 1995, p. 118).

Listening and learning "when one is kicked in the behind" is another important trait. Fulton J. Sheen wrote, "When you are getting kicked from the rear it means you are in front." Jonathon Lazear (1992) further commented:

> *Many of us are in positions of responsibility. We have a number of people who report to us, who may in turn have substantial numbers of people reporting to them. There is nothing intrinsically wrong with being a leader. But leaders need to know how to take the heat – they need to know how to listen. Work-addicted men are notoriously poor listeners, and that leads to big problems. Powerful men, men who people follow and look to for inspiration and leadership, need to know whom they are leading, and why. What can the leader expect from those he leads? Are the expectations appropriate? A leader needs to know not just that he's being kicked from behind, but why.*

Being able to deal with the "**digital nervous system**" is another essential trait that Bill Gates, CEO of Microsoft, describes in his book *Business at the Speed of Thought* (Gates, 1999). The "digital nervous system" involves rapid activity and responses both outside and within the organization. He points out that leaders must determine how informational technology can best be obtained, applied and managed for organizational processes and relations with customers. This correlates with one of the three Elements of Successful Enterprise – "information and technology" (discussed in Chapter 6).

Comments from an article titled "The Compstat Process: Performance on the Pathway to Leadership" emphasizes how CompStat (discussed in Chapter 11), the computer-digitized "Strategic control system," is an essential part of today's police leadership (DeLorenzi, 2006, pp. 34–38):

> *When commanders gather and use accurate and timely intelligence, devise effective tactics, and relentlessly follow up on tasks, they have an opportunity to showcase and further develop their leadership skills, abilities, competence, and initiative. Therefore, they should be encouraged to strive toward the responsibilities that go along with the command rank and assignment. The Compstat podium should be a place where new and hopeful supervisors and officers aspire to stand someday. The Compstat process, when used effectively for accountability and problem solving, can be a means for developing potential leaders and promoting cooperative and creative leadership.*

Leadership during chaos was certainly an approach exemplified by the handling of the September 11, 2001, New York terrorist attack. As described in an excerpt from the *New York Times* describing the emergency response at the World Trade Center (Wayne & Kaufman, 2001):

> *There is no Harvard MBA course, no corporate strategy session, no business celebrity memoir that can prepare a chief executive to lead a corporation, and thousands of employees, when 110 floors fall out*

from under them. And in the hours that have passed since the collapse of the World Trade Center, many of the nation's chief executives registered the strange sensation of living in a world that they, always so capable, always so sure, had never encountered.

Chaos can occur in all criminal justice fields. The courts can suddenly become inundated because of mass arrests and corrections institutions are subject to prison riots. For example, during the 2005 hurricanes Katrina and Rita, the Louisiana Department of Public Safety and Correction officials were credited with exemplary leadership by their timely and efficient evacuation of inmates from low-lying parish and municipal jails to state institutions. Accolades were given for leadership throughout the department that "was selfless, even heroic, and responsive to the opportunities that arose" (Laborde, 2006, pp. 50–53).

From the experiences of these kinds of events, a number of recommendations have been developed for leadership during such chaos:

- Be calm
- Communicate
- Take care of your people
- Get back to business as soon as possible
- Maintain critical communications
- Have an incident command plan
- Be prepared to retreat
- Deal with post-event stress and physical conditions (Thibault, Lynch, & McBride, 2007, pp. 65–67)

This adds to the list of essential traits for Eclectic Perspective criminal justice administrators.

The CEO Concept of Leadership

Another concept of leadership is to view the criminal justice executive as a CEO (Chief Executive Officer). In the private sector, a CEO reports to a board of directors. He or she must also be mindful of the shareholders and the employees. The success of the CEO directly relates to his or her relationship with these three important entities. The criminal justice administrator, like the CEO, often reports to some type of public board. A police chief, for example, usually reports to a city council or a police commission. The chief also must be mindful of the employees and the members of the community (shareholders).

Ideally, the criminal justice administrator must gain and hold the support of all three "pillars" (**Figure 14–3**). In reality, administrators often have to make decisions that are not popular with at least one of these entities. In doing so, it is important that he or she has the full support of the other two "pillars." Before making decision that may weaken support from one of the "pillars," the Eclectic Perspective administrator will make sure that solid support from the other "pillars" is in place. The author, as a consultant and an administrator, has

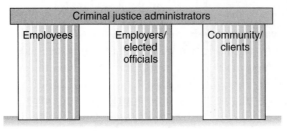

**Three Pillars of Support
for Criminal Justice Administrators**

Figure 14–3 Three Pillars of Support.

observed administrators survive significant criticism from one of the three when they were well supported by the other two. When chief executive administrators lose the support of two of the three, even with strong support of one, they generally lose their jobs.

When chief criminal justice administrators are first hired, they need to be sensitive to the elected officials "pillar" because they are often in a probationary period where the elected officials can fire them at will. The growing trend of 4- to 5-year contracts is providing more job stability for new administrators; however, gaining the support of those who hired them is of immediate importance. From the beginning, developing the support of the employees is probably most important. Today, many employee representative organizations ("unions") have strong political ties and even contribute to the election campaigns of elected officials. The author has observed situations where the employees have caused elected officials to reverse their once strong support for the administrator. For the long term, building community support is also very important. With strong community support, often adverse political pressure can be avoided because of the administrator's popularity with the public.

The importance of maintaining the support of these three "pillars" has changed over the years. When criminal justice administrators had civil service protection, they were less concerned with what the elected officials thought of them. Remember the Pendleton Act of 1883 was meant to eliminate political interference in the hiring and firing of public employees (discussed in Chapter 1 and Chapter 2). With civil service protection, many criminal justice administrators became "untouchable." FBI Director J. Edward Hoover and Los Angeles Police Chief William Parker were very outspoken leaders of their time and were feared by many politicians (discussed in Chapter 6).

In the latter part of the 20th century, the protective support for criminal justice administrators changed with the public and elected officials wanting more control over their criminal justice executives. Consequently, today most criminal justice administrators again serve at the will of the elected officials or have multiyear contracts that must be approved for renewal by elected officials. As a result, most successful criminal justice executives are much more reserved in their public appearances than was prevalent during the Hoover/Parker days. Wise administrators make sure their elected officials get credit for the accomplishments of their criminal justice agencies.

William Bratton, the New York Police Commissioner during the 1990s, serves as an example of this change in leadership style. As commissioner, he gained national recognition for reducing crime in New York. The then mayor of New York felt that Bratton was getting too much credit and media attention, which led to Bratton resigning. Bratton went on to become the chief of police of the Los Angeles Police Department, where he successfully applied what he had learned from past experiences.

Bratton also serves as an example of what is hopefully a trend to hire "secondhand" criminal justice administrators. The position of chief administrator of a criminal justice agency requires exceptional leadership qualities. A number of large cities are providing $200,000 or more a year salaries for top police executives. However, in recent years, the average time for a police chief to serve in many cities is less than four years. The author, as a police chief, found serving in that position much different than serving as an administrator at a lower level. The author went from being a deputy chief in a large city (responsible for policing a section of the city with 2,000 employees servicing 800,000 residents) to being a police chief in a 250,000 population city with 1,000 police personnel. As a "second level" police administrator, one has to respond to all three "pillars" but is still "buffered from heavy politics of public office."

It is the top executive administrator who bears all the responsibility for the actions of his or her department. He or she may delegate but remains responsible for carrying out the mission of the agency (discussed in Chapter 7). The author often described the job of police chief as "being a politician but making sure you do not appear to be one." Knowing how to politically inspire without detracting public attention from the elected officials is an essential attribute of today's Eclectic Perspective administrator. Nothing really prepares you to understand the role like the experience of being a top executive.

Traditionally, many top criminal justice executives are selected from lower level administrative jobs where they have performed well. Some lack the experience to successfully serve in the political environment into which they have been appointed. Conversely, some are selected for executive positions because they have performed well in that position elsewhere. They may not be right for the particular political and organizational situation for which they become responsible. In the private sector, a number of CEOs have been selected for new jobs because they were successful CEOs in another corporation—only to fail in their new top positions because their successful leadership style in their prior job was not the right "fit" for the new job.

This is why William Bratton serves as a good example of a top police executive who has learned from problems experienced as a prior police commissioner. He has been able to convert this experience into valuable insight that can help him better serve as police chief in another large city. Those selecting top criminal justice administrators would do well to consider "secondhand" administrators who have valuable experience (even though these experiences may have resulted in them having to resign, as in Bratton's case) that may make them the "right fit" for the new position.

An article entitled "Leadership Takes on a Variety of Styles" by Walter Wood, Executive Director of the Alabama Department of Youth Services, begins with the statement, "Leadership styles take on many forms depending on the circumstances of a given situation. They may be 'maintenance' styles geared toward keeping an already efficiently operating facility or organization on the right track. Or they may be more dramatic in scope" as needed when changes are required (Wood, 2006, p. 8). The article goes on to tell how he selected a top executive to make changes, who immediately took charge of the organization and determined where the weak areas lay and which organization members could be depended on to lead.

"Change most often is a product of dissatisfaction: people usually are not motivated to change unless their current status is uncomfortable. Employees become more supportive of change when they see it as a means of reducing their dissatisfaction and improving their feeling of self worth" (Barry & Cronkhite, 1992, p. 79). Situations of corruption, excessive force, and other conditions that bring "front page" media coverage, not only cause a loss of public trust but also cause employee dissatisfaction. Employees can become ashamed of the agency for which they work. Under these conditions they are more open to changes that will improve the image of the agency and their repetition as an employee. These situations should be seen as an opportunity to make changes when changes are needed. These situations often generate the search for a leader who can "cure the organization illness." This type of leader is often referred to as a **change agent**.

■ Change Agent Leadership

The process of change can be viewed in three stages: Unfreezing, changing, and refreezing.

Unfreezing. As previously stated, a key factor in the unfreezing phase of change is a discomfort with the old behavior. Certain leadership approaches are required. Rearranging the environmental context that supports the current behavior is often necessary. This might include removal of reinforcements for the current behavior, inducing guilt or anxiety about current behavior, making employees feel more secure about change by reducing threats or barriers to change, removing employees from the environment that supports current behavior, and physically changing the environment in which the person is behaving.

Changing to a new behavior pattern. After unfreezing old behavior, the desired alternative behavior is introduced. This is where Hersey and Blanchard's "selling" approach comes into play as described in their "situational management approach" discussed in Chapter 8. Change agent leadership recognizes that experiences of success with a new behavior are critical at this point. "Celebrating small wins," as Peters says, is important in ensuring that employees gain a sense of achievement in performing the new behavior.

Refreezing. The final phase involves stabilizing and integrating the new behavior. This is where Michael LeBoeuf's Greatest Management Principle (GMP) of "what gets rewarded is what gets done" needs to be put into practice. GMP and the methods of rewarding that were discussed in Chapter 8 are needed to institutionalize the change (Swanson, 1993, pp. 666–667).

Selecting the right type of leader to be the change agent as someone from inside or outside the organization is an important decision in making changes.

Internal Change Agents: Pluses and Minuses

An **internal change agent** can have insightful knowledge about the formal, as well as the informal organization and an awareness of where support and resistance to change may be. This knowledge is essential in implementing strategies for change. These administrators have internalized the values and attitudes of the organization, which can help in reshaping the direction of the agency. Conversely, internal people may owe allegiance to certain people in the organization who may be major resisters to change. Additionally, they may be viewed by the employees as "part of the old school" and not accepted as someone who can lead them to change. An internal agent would be wise to gain the assistance of some external experts such as management consultants to assist in making changes.

External Change Agents: Pluses and Minuses

Here the pluses and minuses are reversed. The **external change agent** can come without "internal baggage" and without the favoritism in treating employees. Additionally, he or she may be more favorably looked upon as someone new and more likely to make constructive changes. They may bring new ideas and vision that is needed to cause productive changes. External agents are usually selected because there is a critical need for change, and special experience and abilities not found in the agency, are needed. The drawback of an outside person is that most often they do not have a true understanding of the organization, especially the informal forces. This may also be true regarding community and political matters.

The external change agent would be wise to make an early effort to gain the trust of certain individuals or groups who can provide the insight they may be lacking. For example, union representatives as well as retired supervisors may be of assistance in this regard. Sometimes, a person working in another agency under the same governmental structure can assist in providing insight. Finding someone who the line employees trust, and who will provide honest feedback to the new administrator can be of great assistance

■ Contemporary Eclectic Perspective Leadership

Inspiration and persuasion have been described as essential ingredients of leadership. The process of applying these ingredients involves what D. Richards calls "winning the minds of others." To win minds, the objective is to convince people and to make them understand the purpose of what is to be done. They must intellectually understand the why, where, and when no matter how complicated the task. To inspire them and gain a long-lasting commitment, one has to win their hearts. The medium for winning minds is information and the medium for winning hearts is emotion, according to Richards (2002).

Shared leadership is another contemporary approach worthy of exploring. Shared leadership is not a new concept and is sometimes referred to as: participative management, job involvement, participative decision-making, dispersed leadership, open-book management, and industrial democracy. The practices of Total Quality Management (TQM), discussed in Chapter 8, falls within this category. The basic concept involves any power-shared arrangement in which workplace influences are shared among individuals who are otherwise hierarchical unequals (Kim, 2002, p. 231–241).

The three elements of successful enterprise discussed in Chapter 6 (being service oriented, making use of information and technology, and utilizing the minds of employees and customers) should be recalled at this juncture. Many years ago, before the advent of instantaneous global news, few people had access to timely information. Employers, elected officials, and other leaders where respected for having access to information that most people did not. They were seldom doubted because "they were in positions that should know." Today with radio, television, and Internet communication, there is not a matter of importance that is not made available to the general public in minutes, if not seconds.

Today most everyone has access to massive amounts of information. Therefore, most everyone has opinions. Today, leaders must be accustomed to being "second guessed" and "Monday morning quarterbacked," because their employees and clients have opinions about how things should be done. Unfortunately, the general public is often subjected to "confetti information." That is headlines, by-lines, sound bites, and the like. The average television coverage of any news event is less than one minute. Consequently, many opinions are based on partial information. This can certainly be seen in criminal cases that receive mass media coverage. What the public receives is a fraction of the information that a trial jury must consider in making a verdict. This also holds true as to the opinions of employees about the administrative decisions made in their agencies.

Regardless, administrators must realize that the involvement of the employee, as well as clients (the public), is an important factor in today's administration. Shared leadership includes involving employees and the community in the decision-making process. Under the Client-Oriented Service theme, with problem-oriented and CompStat approaches discussed in Chapter 11, shared responsibility is required. This does not mean that administrators are not held accountable for the overall results. It does mean involving employees and the community in deciding what needs to be done. The Matrix Community-Oriented approach (discussed in Chapter 7) and the personal evaluation forms that require mutual agreements between the employee and supervisor on yearly objectives (discussed in Chapter 8) are examples of this approach. Additionally, having employees thoroughly understand and sign their oath of office and code of ethics (discussed in Chapter 13) as a means of promoting professional ethics, is another method of ensuring shared responsibilities.

Shared leadership can "help make employees feel more valued and supported by their organization, more committed to its objectives, can cultivate better labor-management relations, and may even promote greater productivity." It also "promotes communication at all levels and helps bridge the traditional schism between management and the line officers" (Wuestewald, 2006, pp. 48–55).

In 2001, Jim Collins published *Good to Great* and subsequently wrote *Good to Great and the Social Sectors* (2005). Collin's followed what Peters and Waterman did in 1982 with their *In Search of Excellence* and Peter's subsequent production of a video and training booklet on *Excellence in the Public Sector* (discussed in Chapters 4 and 8). Collins and his research crew searched through Fortune 500 companies to find those that had followed a "good to great" achievement path in the stock market over the 15-year period, leading up to the 21st century. They identified 11 such companies (Abbott, Circuit City, Fannie Mae, Gillette, Kimberly-Clark, Kroger, Nucar, Philip Morris, Pitney Bowes, Walgreen's, and Wells Fargo). These companies were compared with like companies that were not as successful. The researchers identified particular leadership attributes that correlated to the success of the businesses. **Figure 14–4** shows five levels of leadership that were identified. The term "**Level 5 executive**" refers to the highest level in a hierarchy of executive capabilities and is the level that Collins' writes about. (Most of the qualities in the remaining four levels have been previously discussed in this chapter).

The key findings regarding these Level 5 leaders were:

- Level 5 refers to a five-level hierarchy of executive capacities, with Level 5 at the top. Level 5 leaders embody a paradoxical mix of personal humility and professional will. They were ambitious, to be sure.
- Every good-to-great company had Level 5 leadership during the pivotal transition years.
- Level 5 leaders set up their successors for even greater success in the next generation, whereas egocentric Level 4 leaders often set up their successors for failure.
- Level 5 leaders displayed a compelling modesty, were self-effacing and understated. In contrast, two thirds of the comparison companies had leaders with gargantuan personal egos that contributed to the demise or continued mediocrity of the company.

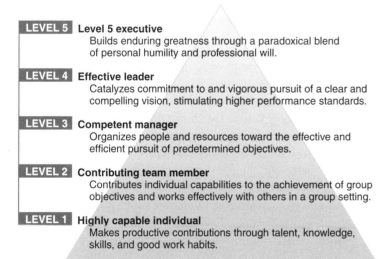

LEVEL 5 **Level 5 executive**
Builds enduring greatness through a paradoxical blend of personal humility and professional will.

LEVEL 4 **Effective leader**
Catalyzes commitment to and vigorous pursuit of a clear and compelling vision, stimulating higher performance standards.

LEVEL 3 **Competent manager**
Organizes people and resources toward the effective and efficient pursuit of predetermined objectives.

LEVEL 2 **Contributing team member**
Contributes individual capabilities to the achievement of group objectives and works effectively with others in a group setting.

LEVEL 1 **Highly capable individual**
Makes productive contributions through talent, knowledge, skills, and good work habits.

Figure 14–4 Collins' Leadership Hierarchy.

- Level 5 leaders were fanatically driven, infected with an incurable need to produce sustained results. They were resolved to do whatever it takes to make the company great, no matter how big or hard the decisions.
- Level 5 leaders displayed a workman-like diligence—more plow horse than show horse.
- Level 5 leaders looked out the window to attribute success to factors other than themselves. When things went poorly, however, they looked in the mirror and blamed themselves, taking full responsibility. The comparison CEO's often did just the opposite—they looked in the mirror to take credit for success, but looked out the window to assign blame for disappointing results.
- One of the most damaging trends in recent history is the tendency (especially by boards of directors) to select dazzling, celebrity leaders and to de-select potential Level 5 leaders.
- I (Collins) believe that potential Level 5 leaders exist all around us if we just know what to look for, and that many people have the potential to evolve into Level 5.
- Larger-than-life celebrity leaders who ride in from the outside are negatively correlated with going from good to great. Ten of eleven good-to-great CEO's came from inside the company, where the comparison companies tried outside CEOs six time more often.
- Level 5 leaders attributed much of their success to good luck, rather than personal greatness.
- We (Collins and researcher) were not looking for Level 5 leadership in our research, or anything like it, but the data was overwhelming and convincing. It is empirical, not an ideological, finding (Collins, 2001, pp. 39–40).

Earlier in this chapter, we discussed the change in leadership style from the days of LAPD Chief Parker and FBI Director J. Edgar Hoover, who were very outspoken and often the focal point of their own success. Collins' work correlates with what has happened to today's successful criminal justice leaders who are less at the forefront, more modest and self-effacing, and much more willing to allow others to take the credit.

In Collins' 2005 *Good to Great and the Social Sectors,* he finds both similarities and differences in leadership. He wrote, "First, the good to great principles do indeed apply to the social sectors, perhaps even better than expected. Second, particular questions crop up repeatedly from social sector leaders facing realities they perceive to be quite different from the business sector" (Collins, 2005, p. 3). Collins synthesized the questions regarding the differences into five issues that form the framework for his 2005 social sector monograph. These five issues are discussed here as adopted from Collins' research and correlated with concepts previously discussed in this textbook:

Issue One: Defining Great— Calibrating Success without Business Metrics. Great leaders are Open Systems minded (discussed in Chapter 9) and continually focus on inputs and outputs. Collins writes, "The confusion between inputs and outputs stems from one of the primary differences between business and the social sectors. In business, money is both an input (a resource for achieving greatness) and an output (a measure of greatness). In the social sectors, money is only an input, and not a measure of greatness" (2005, p. 5).

Collins gave the New York Police Department as an example by describing a CompStat (discussed in Chapter 11) review meeting where command officers are held accountable for problem-oriented objectives, which they have agreed to achieve. Collins describes a captain "sweating at a podium in the command center." Collins writes, "He stands before an overhead map with a bunch of red dots, showing a significant increase in robberies in his precinct. In a Socratic grilling session reminiscent of Professor Kingfield in *The Paper Chase,* the questions come relentlessly. "What is the pattern here?" "What are you going to do to take these guys out?" According to *CIO Insight* magazine, 75 percent of commanders found themselves ejected from their positions for failing to reduce crime in their precincts. "If, week after week at the Compstat meetings, we found precinct commanders not performing to standards," explained Commissioner Bratton, "we had to find someone else to do the job" (p. 4). How the business concept of being held accountable to Client-Oriented Service objectives is being applied to criminal justice agencies has been discussed throughout Chapter 4 and Chapter 11 of this text. This concept is an essential part of today's leadership trends.

Issue Two: Getting Things Done Within A Diffuse Power Structure. Here, Collins finds how different public sector (as contracted with the business sector) leadership is by writing; "In executive leadership, the individual leader has enough concentrated power to simply make the right decisions. In legislative leadership, on the other hand, no individual leader—not even the nominal chief executive—has enough structural power to make the most important decisions by himself or herself. Legislative leadership relies more on persuasion, political currency, and shared interest to create the conditions for the right decisions to happen. And it is precisely this legislative dynamic that makes Level 5 leadership particularly important to the social sectors" (p. 11).

Collins goes on to say, "Social sector leaders are not less decisive than business leaders as a general rule; they only appear that way to those who fail to grasp the complex governance and diffuse power structures common to social sectors" (p. 10).

Issue Three: First Who—Getting the Right People on the Bus, within Social Sector Constraints. Here Collins confronts the civil service protection issue that is not a factor in the business world. He writes, "Business executives can more easily fire people and—they can use money to buy talent. Most social sector leaders, on the other hand, must rely on people underpaid relative to the private sector or, in the case of volunteers, paid not at all. Yet a finding from our research is instructive: the key variable is not how (or how much) you pay, but who you have on the bus" (p. 15).

Collins goes on to point out how important the hiring and screening, and promotion process is in the public sector (discussed in Chapter 8).

Issue Four: The Hedgehog Concept—Rethinking the Economic Engine without a Profit Motive. In Collins' *Good to Great* (2001), he wrote about the **Hedgehog Concept** and its importance to Level 5 leaders. The essence of the Hedgehog Concept is to attain clarity about how to produce the best long-term results, and then to exercise relentless discipline to stay on that track. The concept was that great companies understood three intersecting circles about keeping on this "track"— (1) what you are deeply passionate about, (2) What you can be the best in the world at, and (3) what best drives your economic engine (p. 17). The reader may recall that the research of Peters and Waterman, in their *In Search of Excellence* (discussed in Chapter 4 and Chapter11), found successful businesses were at their best when they "stuck to the knitting," meaning sticking to what they were best at doing.

Collins goes on to say, "Social sector leaders found the Hedgehog Concept helpful, but many rebelled against the third circle, the economic engine." He found this puzzling. "Sure, making money is not the point, but you still need to have an economic engine to fulfill your mission" (2001, p. 17). Consequently, Collins changed the third "circle" to "What Drives your Resource Engine" (**Figure 14–5**). Successful criminal justice administrators, even though not out to make a profit, must cultivate funding that will provide the resources necessary to achieve their mission.

Issue Five: Turning the Flywheel—Building Momentum by Building the Brand. Collins' **Flywheel Concept** is that in the "great" companies he found no exceptional innovation, no lucky breaks but rather a continual, forward movement which he likens to a "flywheel. "Pushing with great effort—days, weeks and months of work, with almost imperceptible progress—you finally get the flywheel to inch forward. But you don't stop. You keep pushing and with persistent effort, you eventually get the flywheel to complete one entire turn." Then, at some point—breakthrough! Each turn builds on previous work, compounding your investment of effort. The flywheel flies forward with almost unstoppable momentum. This is how you build greatness" (p. 23). He relates this to his "Hedge-

The Hedgehog Concept in the Social Sectors

Circle 1: **Passion** - Understanding what your organization stands for (its core values) and why it exists (its mission or core purpose).

Circle 2: **Best at** - Understanding what your organization can uniquely contribute to the people it touches, better than any other organization on the planet.

Circle 3: **Resource engine** - Understanding what best drives your resource engine, broken into three parts: time, money, and brand.

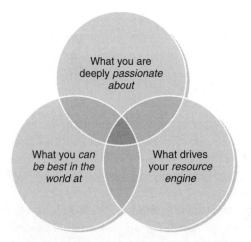

Figure 14–5 The Hedgehog Concept in the Social Sectors.

hog Concept" (Issue 4 above) in that by staying committed to the mission over an extended period—the organization delivers better and better results, which creates stronger commitments and in turn a better organization, which enables even better results. Employees, the community, elected officials (previously discussed as the **Three Pillars of Support**) are affected by this momentum. When they see tangible results—"when they can feel the flywheel beginning to build speed—that's when most people line up to throw their shoulders against the wheel and push" (p. 24).

Collins goes on to state, "Yet despite the differences between business and social sector economics, those who lead institutions from good to great must harness the flywheel effect. Whereas in business, the key driver in the flywheel is the link between financial success and capital resources, I'd like to suggest that a key link in the social sectors is brand reputation –build upon tangible results and emotional share of heart—so that potential supporters believe not only in your mission, but in your capacity to deliver on the mission" (p. 25). Collins cites, as public brands examples, the NYPD, the United States Marine Corps, and NASA.

In summary, Collins describes Level 5 leaders as "ambitious first and foremost for the cause, the organization, the work—not themselves—and they have the fierce resolve to do whatever it takes to make good on the ambition. They display a paradoxical blend of personal humility and professional will" (p. 34). The Relevant Publication at the end of this chapter provides an interview with Collins in which he discussed his research as it relates to law enforcement leadership.

Ken Blanchard has recently published a book, *Leading at a Higher Level*, in which he and his associates research the qualities of outstanding leaders of today. This publication focuses on "servant leadership" as "when people lead at a higher level, they make the world a better place, because their goals are focused on the greater good. Making the world a better place requires a special kind of leader; a servant leader" (Blanchard, 2007, p. 253). Blanchard goes on to list what these leaders do to SERVE:

S—See the future
E—Engage and develop people
R—Reinvent continuously
V—Value results and relationships
E—Embody the values

Blanchard's findings correlate with Collins' research and are of importance to criminal justice administrators. Today's successful criminal justice administrators are leaders who exemplify the qualities for what SERVE stands for.

Throughout this chapter, many concepts of leadership have been discussed. When reviewing recent findings such as those of Collins and Blanchard, the reader should be able to see many of the same elements that have evolved over time. Even though leadership styles have changed to fit social and political conditions, the fundamental concepts of inspiring and persuading employees, the public, and the elected officials while properly managing resources has been the mainstay of successful leadership.

Wrap Up

KEY CONCEPTS AND TERMS

- Historical perspective
  - Max Weber's concepts
  - Maslow's concepts
  - Vroom's concepts
- Management and leadership approaches
  - Charismatic leadership
  - Legal-rational leadership
  - Assessing leadership vs. management
  - DISC (dominance, influence, supportiveness, conscientiousness) assessment
- CEO concept of leadership
  - Three Pillars of Support
- Change agent leadership
  - Internal vs. external change agents
- Contemporary approaches
  - Shared leadership
  - Level 5 executive
  - Hedgehog concept
  - Flywheel concept
  - SERVE Leadership

CHAPTER ACTIVITY

Identify several top executives of current criminal justice agencies (from news items, publications, Web sites). Compare their leadership traits with those discussed in this chapter.

REVIEW QUESTIONS

1. What is the difference between leadership and management? Can an administrator survive as one and not the other? If so, under what conditions?

2. Relate some of the older leadership concepts such as those of Max Weber to the "art and science" of criminal justice administration today.

3. If you were an administrator today, where would place yourself in the Leadership/Management Grid (Figure 14–2) and the DISC categories (Table 14–4)?

4. List some of the leadership qualities discussed in this chapter. Do you think that they are learned or are traits that one is born with?

5. How are some of the contemporary research findings regarding leadership (such as those in Jim Collins's *Good to Great*) related to the task of today's criminal justice administrator?

REFERENCES

Barry, R. J., & Cronkhite, C. L. (1992). Back to Basics. *Sheriff,* March–April.

Blake, R., & Mouton, J. (1964). *The Managerial Grid.* Houston: Gulf.

Blanchard, K. (2007). *Leading at a Higher Level.* Upper Saddle River, NJ: Prentice Hall.

Collins, J. (2001). *Good to Great.* New York: HarperCollins.

Collins, J. (2005). *Good to Great and the Social Sectors.* New York: HarperCollins.

Conger, J. (1999). Charismatic and Transformation Leadership in Organization: An Insider's Perspective on These Developing Streams of Research. *Leadership Quarterly,* 10, p. 102.

Corrections Today (2006). Alexandria, VA: American Correctional Association. August.

DeLorenzi, D. (2006). TheCompStat Process: Managing Performance on the Pathway to Leadership. *The Police Chief,* September, pp. 36–38.

De Vries, R. E., Roe, R. A., & Taillieu, T. C. B. (1999). On Charisma and the Need for Leadership. *European Journal of Work and Organizational Psychology,* 1, p. 81.

French, J. R., & Raven, B. (1959). The Bases of Social Power. In *Studies in Social Power.* Ann Arbor, MI: Institute for Social Research.

Gaines, L. K., Worrall, J. W., Southerland, M. D., & Angell, J. E. (2003). *Police Administration* (2nd ed.). New York: McGraw Hill.

Gates, B. (1999). *Business at the Speed of Thought.* New York: Warner.

Goleman, D. (1995). *Emotional Intelligence.* New York: Bantam.

Judge, T. A., & Bono, L. E. (2000). Five-Factor Model of Personality and Transformational Leadership. *Journal of Applied Psychology,* p. 5.

Kenney, M. (2006). Lead at Any Level. *Corrections Today:* August.

Kim, R. (2002). Participative Management and Job Satisfaction: Lessons for Management Leadership. *Public Administration Review,* p. 62

Lazear, J. (1992). *Meditations for Men Who Do Too Much.* New York: Simon & Schuster.

Personal Profile System. (2001). A Plan to Understand Yourself & Others Produced and Published by TSS Consulting Group, Gurnee, IL

Richards, D. (2002). *Convincing Minds and Winning Hearts.* Louisville, KY: Brown Herron.

Stodgill, R. M. (1974). *Handbook of Leadership.* New York: Free Press.

Swanson, C., Territo, L. & Taylor, R. W. (1993). *Police Administration: Structures, Processes, and Behavior.* New York: Maxwell Publishing Company.

Wrap Up

Thibault, E. A., Lynch, L. M., & McBride, R. B. (2007). *Proactive Police Management* (7th ed.). Upper Saddle River, NJ: Pearson/Prentice Hall.

Wayne, L., & Kaufman, L. (2001). Leading in Turbulent Times. *New York Times*, September.

Weber, M. (1947). *The Social and Economic Theory of Organization*. London: Oxford University Press.

Weber, M. (1961) Power and Bureaucracy. In Kenneth Thompson & Jeremy Tunstal (Eds.), *Sociological Perspectives*. Middlesex, UK: Penguin.

Wood, W. (2006). Leadership Takes on a Varieties of Styles. *Corrections Today*, August, p. 8.

Wuestewald, T. (2006). Shared Leadership: Can Empowerment Work in Police Organizations? *The Police Chief*. January, pp. 48–55.

■ RELEVANT PUBLICATION

The latter part of this chapter reviewed recent findings by Jim Collins. Presented here is a three-part interview with Collins in which he discusses his findings as they relate to law enforcement leadership. The interview was published in the newsletter of the Police Executive Research Forum. From Good to Great in Policing—A Conversation with Jim Collins. Parts I, II, and III. *Subject of Debate*, a newsletter of the Police Executive Research Forum: *20*, 7 (July, 2006), 8 (August, 2006), and 9 (September 2006).

From Good to Great in Policing—A Conversation with Jim Collins by the Police Executive Research Forum

Jim Collins is the author of Good to Great, *published by Harper Business in 2001. Collins' book details his research results on how some companies make the leap from good to great. The factors essential for greatness, Collins discovered, include a culture of discipline and a Level 5 leader. Level 5 executives are able to sustain greatness through a seemingly disparate blend of personal humility and unwavering resolve to do the right thing—for the company and not for themselves, irrespective of constraints.*

Recently, Collins, produced a monograph, Good to Great and the Social Sectors. *PERF's Chuck Wexler talked with Collins about his new publication.*

CW: In the monograph you've written, you say that social service leaders "face a complex and diffuse power map." And I thought that was very true of police chiefs. Do you agree?

JC: Yes. That's a very important consideration, when you look through the lenses of the social sector. A "power map" shows you how 100 points of power are allocated throughout an organization. In a business, if you're a Sam Walton, 100 points of power are all in your hands. He can do whatever he wants with Wal-Mart. Even in a publicly traded company, the CEO still has immense power and can make most of the decisions.

But when you move into community leadership, the distribution of the total points of power can be extremely diffuse. Some of them are in political hands, while others are governed by the economics of the region. There are also government agencies and maybe activist groups that have some of the power.

So if you're a police chief, there are points of power that are out of your control. For example, there are unions. The mayor may have a tremendous amount of power—and that is a reality in making decisions.

In policing, leadership has to have a different flavor. Chiefs still have to be Level 5 leaders, but they have to be much more nuanced in how they assemble the points of power needed to get things done. I refer to this as "legislative leadership," as opposed to the "executive leadership" of an entrepreneurial CEO.

When you are a legislative leader like a police chief, you have to find out where the sources of power are—both visible and invisible—that you can draw upon to get things done, even if you personally don't have the raw power to make things happen.

You may have to draw on the power of shared interests, of shared languages, of coalitions, or of threats or opportunities. A chief needs to have both legislative and executive skills to be effective. And there is a sharp distinction between the two.

CW: This would mean that no individual has enough power to make executive decisions by himself or herself. New police chiefs can have a false sense of power. They may think that just because they're in the position of police chief and they come from a paramilitary organization, people will automatically do what they say.

So the various power bases you talk about—the mayor, city council, and the public—can be a real eye-opener for a new chief. The very beginning of a chief's tenure can be very dangerous. They face a really steep learning curve, right away when some kind of crisis hits.

And given what you've talked about, the Level 5 qualities aren't necessarily learned until a police chief has reached the very top. So there's a danger there. Some chiefs will self-destruct in their first year and then have trouble regaining authority. Because they're not used to—as you have put it—that whole business of "legislative authority."

JC: We've seen the same problem with business leaders who, for example, become university presidents. They don't last very long if they come in and try to lead the university the way they've led the company. They won't survive because of the structural differences—the power differences between the two kinds of organizations.

Being a legislative leader doesn't mean being indecisive. In fact, in this case, it's the ability to get the decision done that matters. The leader may make a decision fairly quickly. But the amount of time it takes to go from making that decision to winding up all the forces needed to make the right things happen may be quite a bit longer than when you have the power of decision right in your hand.

So I think you're right. That danger period is quite a bit longer in legislative settings. Lyndon Johnson was the master of working the Senate. When he first got there, he spent a great deal of time just studying the Senate and its power map. He would observe and figure out how the Senate really worked, in terms of its real power structure, so he could get things done.

CW: Because a chief's tenure is so short, and it takes so much time to build up that legislative base, making changes in policing is very difficult.

Many of the changes you might want to make as a chief you can't make, until you've developed that power base.

JC: If you try to get too far in front of what you need to do first, you may be trying to do the right things, but you may not be able to get them done, and you may in fact be undermining your own strength. You have to get all of the necessary bases of power lined up before you make the changes. You have to do it stepwise. You can't connect all the dots at once, right away.

CW: The difference in policing, I think, is this: Sometimes you feel like it's a hockey game, where the puck is dropped, and the skaters are skating down the ice. They all know their roles. But sometimes there has to be a decision, and it has to be made now, before you've built up the necessary power base. It has to be made right away.

JC: Well, that suggests that luck plays a little bit of a role early in a chief's tenure. You need to have the time to establish that legislative base in the community. But if you happen to have a high-profile event early on and you don't yet have the base, that can be a difficult environment to be in.

Part 2

CW: You wrote about the "Stockdale paradox" in your book. As I recall, Admiral Jim Stockdale was held in a Vietnamese prison camp, where he was tortured repeatedly. He faced countless other constraints on what he could do and say. Still, he never lost faith that he would prevail. But he was also a realist—he had the discipline to confront the most brutal facts.

This lesson is very useful for police chiefs. Very often, they find all sorts of problems coming at them simultaneously. Did you think that people in the social sector can learn from the Stockdale paradox?

JC: Yes. Most people in the social sector face some very serious systemic constraints. They may face limits in funding and constraints on their decisions. As a result, if you're in the social sector, you have to deal with what are sometimes really oppressive constraints.

That's where the Stockdale paradox comes into play. Police officers need to be able to say, yes, we have limits in funding. Yes, there may be certain political constraints, too. There may be constraints in what we'd ideally like to do. But the reality is, if we allow those constraints to become prison bars, if we allow those to depress us, we'll never be able to produce outstanding results. What's needed is to recall the other side of the Stockdale paradox, which states that even in the face of great restraints we can still have outstanding results.

The ability to confront the restraints is what's critical. If we ignore the restraints—try to pretend that they are not there—it's like a rock climber who's trying to pretend that gravity isn't there. But on the other hand, if you say that gravity will prevent you from making any progress, that's equally debilitating.

My own view is that the Stockdale paradox is even more important in the social sector, because of the magnitude, the reality, and the complexity of the constraints that social sector leaders face.

CW: There are times when everything seems the worst—the media is on top of you, the community is upset with you, the rank and file is upset with you, and your boss is upset with you, because all of these other factions are upset with you. And the reason they are upset is because you've made the right decision, which is the right thing to do.

When I think about police chiefs, I think about this question: Do they want to be popular, or do they want to do the right thing? Those who do the right thing are going to face challenges from time to time.

JC: I would cite as an example the position of the school superintendent. There may be a lot of points of power in the community: school board, teachers, parents, and whoever controls the funding from the state or the city. There are also the teachers' unions. But as you're working with all that, you still need to protect your principals so they can do great work. That's part of being a great superintendent. You really want to give a long runway to your outstanding school principals, so that they have enough time to work on a program that's able to reach a momentum of results.

That's something you've got to make happen. But on the other hand, you have pressures from, say, a school board that wants to see instantaneous results, or members of the community who say, I have a specific need, or I have a specific program I want to be introduced, or I want something done for my child. They will try to insert themselves into school policy—telling the principal what he or she ought to do.

This is a classic situation where you have points of power that are at odds with what the leader really has to do to produce the best results. That's part of what the legislative leader does really well—she manages those brutal realities. And sometimes they do find themselves at odds; that's the nature of a complex multi-power system. You're dealing, ultimately, with individual interests and with sources of power.

Individual interests can take many forms. People who say, "I want my home protected" are a prime example. But they don't want to pay more in taxes for policing. So now that leaves the police on the horns of a dilemma.

CW: I'd like to move on to the topic of hiring: you're characterizing the interview process as less than ideal.

JC: The only way to know a person is to have worked with them.

CW: I agree with you 100 percent. But since so much of your book is devoted to the issue of who you hire, have you gotten any insight, short of working with someone, on how you can predict if someone is going to be the right person and the right fit?

JC: There are several things that you would want, in the business sector as well as the social service sector. Ideally, you would want to have access to people who have actually worked with the person you're considering. That would give you a sense of what they're really like to work with. It's much more powerful than an interview.

But even beyond that—and this is different than hiring a police chief: I'm thinking more now of people who are already on the force. That story of Roger Brayton in his science department [included in Collins' book] is very illustrative. What Roger understood is that once you reach a certain point, there is going to be somebody who is on the bus, and there is not much you can do to get them to get off the bus. I would imagine that there is some element of this structural problem of getting people to leave the bus in policing.

Do you have some challenge in this area—how to get people off the bus—in policing?

CW: Oh, absolutely. If police chiefs were sitting in this room here, they'd say that their biggest challenge relates to the fact that they want to have a great staff. And to do that, they may have to transfer some personnel to new positions or in other cases move ineffective personnel along. But too often they face constraints like civil service rules or in some cities political considerations. It's a huge issue.

JC: So the objective reality is that this issue isn't going to go away any time soon. It's even true in volunteer environments, where it's very hard to fire somebody who's not getting paid.

This is why the window between hiring and quasi-permanent status is critically important. I'd guess that in police work there is some window like this for new police officers, early on?

CW: Some departments have them. Certainly, at the initial hiring level—yes. The standards for hiring and retaining police officers are sometimes not as high as we would like. Shifting personnel to new positions doesn't happen as often as it should.

Police chiefs walk into a new job, and are handed what is basically a deck of cards. They may wonder to themselves about at least one staff member: How is it that this person got so far in this organization? I don't think police chiefs are unique in this respect, by the way.

JC: What this speaks to is the fact that there may be some objective sort of hurdle that prevents you from changing people—or at least you can't change them quickly. What you need to remedy this situation—where you have these constraints—is an increased amount of rigor in regard to who makes the early assessments during the window between the hire and permanent employment.

Part 3

This portion of the interview addresses a basic question for police departments: Should a department be run like a business, or is it a unique sort of organization that cannot fit within the confines of the usual business model?

JC: The process of changing the composition of the people on the bus—and changing the culture on the bus—is a much longer process in the social service sector than in a business corporation. The way you do it is not by trying to get all of the people off the bus. Instead, you think about the people whom you allow to stay on the bus through that early-assessment mechanism.

You also need to think about moving the people on the bus to different seats—one that is a better fit for them, or in a less-critical path. Sometimes, if you're not in a position to address whether or not the person should be on the bus, you still have flexibility about the seat issue. This is an area where leaders in social service organizations need to manage carefully.

CW: That is a very key point. I have seen police chiefs who take it upon themselves to move someone from a key spot. Sometimes this decision has a positive impact. It sends a powerful message to the entire organization.

JC: And then you have to grapple with the legislative nuances of a social service organization, because shifting someone to a different seat is a little bit like moving someone from a key committee seat in the Senate. If you anticipate that this might happen, you should do your legislative spadework up front, because you're dealing with a complex-power reality.

CW: A person can come in as a new police chief and think that just because they have the authority, they can make changes in their staff. But if they haven't done the work to build up enough legislative support beforehand, they're going to be undercut.

JC: It may be possible for the chief to act on his own. But if there is a diffuse and complex power map, it is dangerous to act without understanding what that power map is. One university president put it this way, "I realize that I have a certain number of silver bullets. I can fire some of these bullets, and I'm expected to. But the number I've been granted is limited. Maybe I don't have 100 silver bullets. I have six. So I have to be very choosey about when I fire my silver bullets."

CW: Here is a big question in the world of policing. For years, we would look at the business model and say, "We need to make this police department run more like a business." When I finished *Good to Great*, I said, well there are a lot of principles here that apply to policing.

Then when I read your monograph, that said to me: There are a lot of lousy businesses. But there is still the belief that police departments have to adopt business principles—the inference being that the business model is better than the social-service model.

And I think you dispel this notion that the business model is always better. Is this correct?

JC: That's right. Most businesses are average, just by definition. So if you take a lot of the principles of average businesses and export them into policing, you're exporting principles of averageness. We wouldn't want to do that.

What I'm focusing on isn't one model versus another—it's about what separates great from good. It's like a ratio. At the top of the ratio are the great companies, and at the bottom of the ratio are the good companies. If you're looking at the ratio between the two, the word "companies" just cancels out. All you're looking at are the two words, "great" and "good."

What we really need is to do is embrace the principles and discipline of greatness—disciplined people, disciplined thought, and disciplined action. This is a principle that the great businesses embrace, and the average ones don't. Any truly great group or institution is going to need the discipline that's required for greatness, along with the ability to be rigorous in assessing its output. The output is primary.

For policing, one output is measured in crime rates. The positive output is a reduction in crime rate. Everything else is an input. The money budgeted is an input, for example. The rotation of officers on cases is an input.

This single measure of effectiveness lets you keep the crime rate as your principal target and on that basis, make decisions, and figure out where your efforts should go. Then, you truly understand why and how you're making these decisions.

These principles hold true for any great organization. It requires disciplined people who ask: What do we mean by great results? And how do we know if we're improving with these results? What's our baseline? How can we know if we're doing better, as we embrace the sort of discipline that compels us to be better?

As I say in my book, this is what leads to disciplined action. We have to stick with that and continue to hold ourselves responsible for achieving results. That whole notion of a culture of discipline—of disciplined thought and action—is a universal way of thinking about any kind of activity.

I stress this because I think there is a certain arrogance in the business community. They seem to be thinking: Businesses are the best kinds of organizations. We know how to make money. We're efficient. It's almost as if they're looking down on their social sector colleagues, and are ready to tell their colleagues how to do it right.

If I'm a social-sector leader, I may resent that, thinking: You don't understand the realities I face. You don't have a legislative map to deal with. You have an executive map. You don't have the same community pressure that I have. You don't have a police officers' union. There are just so many things that you, as a business person, don't have to cope with. So that makes your life simple.

As a social sector leader, I might resent your attempt to impose your model for running an organization on me. Second, thinking about two different models for getting work done creates a divide—between people in the business world versus people in the social service sector.

The implication is that there is a "business way of thinking" and a "non-business way of thinking." My purpose in writing the monograph, *Good to Great and the Social Sectors* was to build a bridge across that divide. The idea is that greatness connects the two as a common bridge. Both sides are looking to find the factors that go into creating greatness.

Criminal Justice Administration and Cutting-Edge Issues in the 21st Century

15

■ Introduction

This final chapter is devoted to "cutting-edge" issues. These are the issues that are at the forefront of criminal justice administration as this textbook is being published. They are of major importance today and will be, most likely, important in the foreseeable future.

■ The Administration of Homeland Security

Homeland Security was discussed in Chapter 10 as an example of the importance of preserving the delicate balance between individual rights and public safety. It is discussed here as a topic that certainly demonstrates how an issue that was not critical in the past can suddenly become of "cutting-edge" importance. Most criminal justice textbooks published a decade ago had no mention of terrorism and especially of homeland security. The attack of September 11, 2001, propelled this topic to the forefront where it will remain for many years to come.

Client-Oriented Service has been the driving administrative theme through the later part of the 20th century and into the 21st century. Neighborhood policing as well as court and corrections community-oriented programs have provided a united direction in the criminal justice field. The commitment to crime prevention and quality of life issues through shared criminal justice and public partnerships is currently shifting. It is shifting to position of less partnership and more accountability to specific community needs. The major theme of client-oriented service, however, has prevailed and is one of the reasons cited for the notable decrease in crime throughout the nation. The advent of homeland security has had a significant impact on this united direction, particularly in regard to law enforcement.

The International Association of Chiefs of Police (IACP) 2005 report "Post-9/11 Policing: The Crime Control-Homeland Security Paradigm," documents the impact as follows:

- *The Terrorism Dimension.* During the final years of what might be called pre–9/11 policing, the late 1990s through most of 2001, law enforcement was characterized by a strong sense of direction and clarity. Crime was in decline. Community policing had broad acceptance and support. Public trust was strong. That balance was shattered on September 11, 2001. While not yet universal within law enforcement, or felt with consistent intensity, there is recognition that for the first time since World War II, policing is being conducted as if the United States faces a foreign threat with its own borders (p. ii).
- *Shifting Eras and Mission Reconfiguration.* Domestic security obligations have rapidly augmented the pre–9/11 mission. Traditional pre–9/11 responsibilities such as community service and crime control are not and cannot be ignored. These remain the primary expectations of citizens and elected officials. Law enforcement's commitment to and belief in the now established crime control and community policing model remains firm. Yet, by the pressure of events and evolving professional concerns, there appears to be a transition beyond the Community-Oriented Policing (COP) model of the 1990s to a domestic security mode. To some, a homeland security focus should be the next evolution of community policing (p. ii).
- *Preserving Public Trust.* There is widespread concern that the monumental public trust accomplishments of the past decade or so will erode as homeland security priorities take center stage. This concern is linked to diminishing resources and erosion of federal funds for community officers, school resource officers, and other staples of policing (p. iv). (Available at the IACP Web site.)

The concerns expressed by law enforcement officials are reminders of the Eclectic Perspective approach that criminal justice administrators must have in confronting today's volatile environment. Using the metaphor of the administrator as a juggler (used throughout this book), the focus has been on the client-oriented service theme. The emergence of homeland security can not detract from the importance of Client-Oriented Service; however, attention to other themes and related concepts are required. Homeland security has become an additional task for law enforcement.

Homeland security is not just a large city problem. The aim of terrorism is to intimidate a population in furtherance of political or social objectives (FBI, 1987). The 9/11 attacks in New York, being in a large city, may make some feel it is only a large city problem. It should be realized that a similar attack in a small town could cause a greater intimidation impact because the general population would then feel "it can happen anywhere." Consequently, homeland security has become an additional task for all law enforcement administrators.

Domestic tranquility, as ensured in the Preamble to the Constitution, is a responsibility of law enforcement and protection from homeland terrorism certainly fits within this responsibility. However, most criminal justice agencies have not received funding for additional personnel to fulfill this responsibility. There has been new funding for related training and equipment but almost none for personnel. This situation calls for the Eclectic Perspective criminal justice administrators to refocus on Organizational Functions theme concepts relating to efficiency and "doing more with less." Many agencies have to reallocate personnel from community-oriented, pro-active crime prevention activities to homeland security duties (**Table 15–1**).

In addition to innovative changes (see the Relevant Publication at the end of Chapter 7), revisiting some of the basic management "principles" such as POSDCORB may be required. Employee Relation theme concepts for rekindling the devotion of employees to the overall mission when faced with redeployment and long hours of work may be called for. The inspiration and persuasion of leadership certainly is required both internally and externally. This brings us to the Open Systems theme and the concepts of connecting and making use of "outside" resources. One of the major criticisms with the emergency response to the 9/11 terrorist attacks was lack of coordination between the responding agencies. Preplanning as to command and control, communication, and other joint operations requires planning in advance. Educating elected officials, as well as the public, is required in gaining appropriate financial support and understanding as to the tasks that must be accomplished. Remembering Social Equity responsibilities discussed in Chapter 10 is of paramount importance.

The Police Executive Research Form (PERF) surveyed 250 police chiefs after 9/11 and provided some general administrative guidelines:

- *Prevention.* Local police can and will play a critical role in gathering intelligence information on possible terrorists. Community policing networks can be useful in this regard (caution must be taken here as discussed in Chapter 10).
- *Critical Incident Prevention, Preparation, and Response.* Plans must be coordinated with other local, state and federal agencies (this is where the Organizations Functions concept of Planning in POSDCORB comes into play along with an awareness of the Open Systems concepts of "inputs" and "outputs").
- *Aftermath.* Law enforcement must be prepared to work with local leaders to stabilize communities traumatized by terrorist attacks. Local police play a crucial role in reducing fear, as well as preventing and responding to hate crimes. (Neighborhood trust and relationships that should be in place through Client-Oriented Service approaches are needed. The Social Equity concepts relating to protection of the rights of all people are particularly important here [adopted from Police Executive Research Forum, 2001].)

| Table 15–1 | Law Enforcement Homeland Security Reallocation of Resources Since September 11, 2001 |

State and Local Law Enforcement Responses

Part A. In response to the threat of terrorism since September 11, 2001, our agency's *allocation of resources* to various operational law enforcement responsibilities (listed below in alphabetical order) has been affected as follows:

% indicating more or much more resources of State law enforcement and Local law enforcement

	SP	HP	BI	Small	Medium	Large
1. Airport security	38.1%	25.1%	29.2%	4.4%	20.0%	44.9%
2. Border security	28.6%	18.8%	16.7%	4.4%	0.0%	6.7%
3. Commercial vehicle enforcement	47.6%	75.1%	30.4%	11.1%	15.0%	23.7%
4. Community policing	14.3%	25.0%	16.7%	22.2%	30.0%	35.6%
5. Drug enforcement and investigation	15.0%	25.0%	20.9%	22.2%	25.0%	26.2%
6. Forensic science/crime lab services (including DNA)	35.0%	18.8%	25.0%	—	—	—
7. Investigation of high-tech/computer crime	50.0%	33.3%	45.8%	11.1%	35.0%	36.4%
8. Investigation of local agencies (use of force, corruption, etc.)	10.0%	0.0%	8.3%	—	—	—
9. Operational assistance to local agencies (assisting with investigations, etc.)	75.0%	43.8%	41.7%	—	—	—
10. Port security	33.3%	25.0%	29.2%	4.4%	0.0%	20.4%
11. Preventive patrol	71.5%	62.5%	25.0%	28.9%	50.0%	49.2%
12. Responding to calls for service	42.9%	50.0%	21.7%	24.4%	25.0%	25.4%
13. Security for critical infrastructure (state capitol, power plants, etc.)	90.5%	93.8%	66.7%	22.2%	65.0%	73.7%
14. Security for special events and dignitaries	95.2%	100.0%	56.5%	20.0%	50.0%	72.2%
15. Intelligence gathering, analysis, and sharing	95.3%	93.8%	87.5%	15.6%	65.0%	80.5%
16. Terrorism-related investigations	76.1%	50.0%	83.3%	11.1%	30.0%	71.l%
17. Traditional criminal investigation	5.0%	6.3%	12.5%	26.6%	10.0%	15.3%
18. Traffic safety	14.3%	37.6%	4.2%	26.7%	30.0%	16.1%

Source: National Institute of Justice. (2003). *The Impact of Homeland Security on State Law Enforcement.* Washington, DC: Office of Justice Programs, Grant No. 2003-DT-CX-004.

■ Criminal Justice in a Global Society

In Chapter 9, the need for an Open Systems approach was discussed. As this theme developed in the 1960s and 1970s, the emphasis was on reaching beyond the confines of one's own organization. It meant moving away from the earlier "closed system" approach to public service. In the 21st century, the Open Systems approach must expand even further to include a consideration of inputs and outputs that interconnect with other countries. As previously discussed, protection of our communities from terrorism is now a required task.

As with most of the contextual administrative themes discussed in this book, the public sector has followed the business world in developing new approaches to administrating. Today, most businesses of any size must be tuned in to global trends that impact their enterprises. So it is with criminal justice. Many crimes today are intertwined with international interests: drug distribution, art theft, money laundering, and organized crime (especially the "Russian Mafia") to name but a few. Illegal smuggling of immigrants, women, and children for prostitution and cheap labor, weapons, and even nuclear material is now termed *transnational crime.*

International travel allows for quick escape of criminals to other countries. Extradition agreements and coordination through the International Criminal Police Organization (Interpol) is now commonplace. Criminal justice agencies in more than 170 countries now work through Interpol. War-torn countries such as Bosnia, Kosovo, and Haiti now involve civil policing along with the peace-keeping military forces. A number of criminal justice administrators from the United States are involved in overseeing the special needs in these countries struggling to institutionalize a more democratic way of governing (Perito, 2002).

As adapted from Thibault, Lynch, and McBride (2007, pp. 476–477), some factors that demand international criminal justice cooperation are as follows:

- Means of travel that facilitates offender's mobility,
- Technologically advanced worldwide electronic transactions that facilitate transfer of illegally obtained funds and profits to overseas financial businesses,
- Transparency of national boundaries, making it more difficult to detect criminals "on the move" globally,
- Lack of agreement and uniformity as to definitions of crime and punishment for certain crimes especially when they may be construed as political in nature, and
- Through technology, criminals are able to victimize individuals and organization without physically entering the countries of the victims.

In addition to variations in definitions of crimes, adjudication processes often differ. Some countries do as the United States and rely on professionals such as judges, whereas others such as England emphasize a role for laypeople in adjudications. Still others, such as Germany, prefer a mixed bench, wherein professional judges and laypeople sit together to judge the facts of a case (Reichel, 2005, p. 282). The sentencing and punishment practices of various countries should be of interest to criminal justice administrators, as the United States has the highest imprisonment rates and is one of the few countries that still supports capital punishment (**Figure 15–1**).

Comparison of our system with criminal justice systems in other countries provides some interesting "food for thought." Even though we imprison more than in other countries, Figure 9–3 in Chapter 9 shows that only about a fifth of those arrested receive prison sentences. Also discussed in Chapter 10 was the fact that most prisoners in federal prison are there for drug violations. When the author, as a college professor, brings this information up in class for discussion,

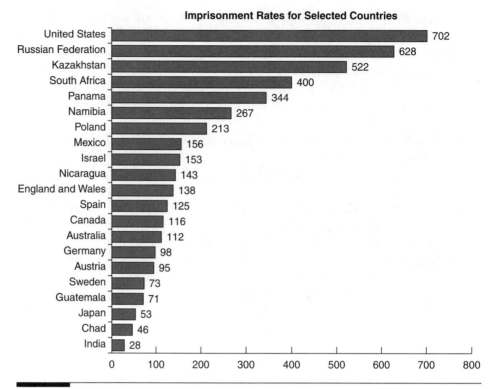

Figure 15–1 Global Imprisonment Rates.

students often express that many of our drug laws should be done away with, as such laws are nonexistent in many other countries. To this, the author has to remind the students that our criminal justice system is to enforcement the will of the people (the majority). Even though there is much coverage in the media about efforts in various states to legalize marijuana (and some municipalities have made possession of a small amount a citable infraction), most voters continue to reject such proposals. The Federal Drug Enforcement Act still lists marijuana as a "substance one" drug with a penalty up to life imprisonment. In 2005, the U.S. Supreme Court in *Ashcroft v. Raich* upheld this federal law, ruling that "Federal authorities may prosecute sick people who smoke pot on doctor's orders." This ruling was a response to some states that have legislated approval of marijuana use for some medical conditions in spite of federal laws. The Court went on to say in this case that state medical marijuana laws don't protect users from a federal ban on the drug (http://www.medicalj.org/raich63.htm).

Regarding how the general public feels about legalizing marijuana, the yearly Gallup Poll provides some insight:

> Although a majority of Americans have consistently opposed the idea of legalizing marijuana, support has slowly increased over the years. In 1969, only 12% of Americans supported making marijuana legal, but in 1977, roughly one in four endorsed it. Support edged up to 31% in 2000, and now (2005), about a third of Americans say marijuana should be legalized (http://www.mpp.org/USA/news/10585.mpp).

This means that about two-thirds of the population still supports keeping marijuana illegal. This issue is discussed here under globalization, because review of what is occurring in other countries should remind criminal justice administrators of their duties under our form of government. We are under oath to enforce the laws as we serve under a system that is governed by the "rule of law." It is also important to remember that in our country (as in many other countries) criminal justice administrators have a great deal of discretion as to how they apply their resources. In our country, however, there is no discretion when it comes to upholding the constitutional rights of *all* people. As discussed in Chapter 11, the current trend of Police Accountability to the Public (PAC) requires criminal justice administrators to keep abreast of the neighborhood problems with which the communities they serve are most concerned. Also, as discussed in previous chapters, the criminal justice system has not been able to (and probably never will be able to) financially support enforcement of all the laws. Therefore, criminal justice administrators in our country must customize the services they provide to best meet the interests of their individual communities, within their limited resources.

Another aspect of having a global perspective is learning from the success and failure of criminal justice approaches being tried throughout the world. The author, on a recent visit to Russia, was informed by their criminal justice administrators of the tremendous increase in crime in that country since their move to "democratize the previously communist form of government." The author was able to share with them our experience (discussed in Chapter 11) of how reported crime often increases as the public becomes more trusting of their police. Also, how countries (and organizations) often experience chaos for a period when allowed to indulge in the new-found freedoms of a more democratic approach. Criminal justice administrators who have taken over agencies that were administrated in a very authoritative manner, often experience employee chaos when they attempt to apply a more Theory Y (discussed in Chapter 8) approach. The informal organization structure that exists under authoritarian administration often develops informal leaders and power bases that become threatened in the new democratic environment.

Today's Eclectic Perspective criminal justice administrators must keep informed of global changes that affect their spheres of responsibilities. Additionally, comparisons of administrative and criminal justice trends on a global scale can provide valuable insight into overseeing today's criminal justice agencies. Most law enforcement administrators, for example, belong to the International Association of Chiefs of Police (IACP), which has chapters in most countries. A number of court and corrections institutions also have international organizations and provide global contacts for criminal justice administrators.

■ Impact of Technology on Criminal Justice

Crimes involving computers and related technology are impacting all facets of the criminal justice system. Theft of electronic value (software, hardware, and digitized "money"), identify theft, computer hacking, and other so-called white collar crime is a part of everyday law enforcement. Criminal justice administrators are responsible for preparing their agencies to protect the public from these crimes. Training and the hiring of experts in the field is an added facet of administrating today's criminal justice agencies.

Using technology to expand the capacities of criminal justice agencies to better serve the public is yet another administrative task. CompStat, the computer analyses approach to holding Police Accountable to the Community (PAC), discussed in Chapter 11, is just one current technological advancement that impacts law enforcement administration. Some other areas for consideration are:

- **The Digital Sherlock Holmes.** Computer modus operandi correlations and analysis is now a part of everyday criminal investigations. Connecting identities and modus operandi factors nationally, and even globally, is now a reality. The Federal Bureau of Investigation (FBI) is in the process of changing the Uniform Crime Report to the National Incident-Based Reporting System. Once implemented (will require reporting agencies to have computerized their reporting to the FBI), access to almost all information contained in a crime report will be available on-line to all authorized law enforcement personnel (Bureau of Justice Statistics, 2000).
- **The Instant Cop.** Command and control communications systems that reduce police dispatch time and decrease the time it takes to access formations saves value "manpower" time. For example, where years ago it took many minutes to check for "wants and warrants," it now takes seconds thereby increasing the time the police have to perform other tasks.
- **The Automated Criminal Justice Administrator.** Using computers to assist in assigning, deploying, and evaluating personnel is now an essential part of administration. From CompStat to Manpower Allocation systems, decisions of administrators are assisted by computers.

Regarding the use of computers in making decisions, the limitations of computers should be understood. The author, in lecturing on the subject, tells the story of the computer expert who was afraid to fly in airplanes. With the threat of terrorist bombers, he became more frightened. So, being a computer programmer, he devised a program to analyze the threat and recommend remedies. He programmed into his computer the question, "How can I reduce the risk of getting on an airplane where there is a terrorist with a bomb?" The computer's reply was, "Carry your own bomb because the statistical odds of *two* bombs on a given plane are remote." Now there is statistical logic to this answer but definitely something is missing. Missing is what is often called "right-brain" thinking. Computers are "left-brain" thinking and although there are reports that scientists are getting closer to producing computers that think like humans, computers will continue to be extraordinarily fast "beancounters." Computers are excellent at taking massive amounts of information and reducing that information to a size with which humans can deal. However, they are not reliable to make decisions. As an example, today's national fingerprint identification systems can go through millions of fingerprint cards in a very short time, but only narrow the search down to perhaps 10–50 possibilities. It is then up to human experts to make the final identification. It is good for criminal justice administrators to appreciate what tasks computers should and should not be relied on to perform.

Today's criminal justice administrators do not necessarily have to be computer experts; however, they do need have a working understanding of computer applications as well as the related benefits and pitfalls. To select automated systems and ensure that vendors deliver what they promise, a criminal justice administrator must know what computers can and cannot do.

Computers can be applied to most all areas of criminal justice if funding is not a problem. As previously discussed, funding is always a problem. Consequently, it is an administrative task to determine which computer applications will provide the greatest benefits with the funds available. In making this determination, using the minds of members of the agency is important. Figure 5–1 in Chapter 5 shows a police department as part of an Open Systems environment. The following were shown as general law enforcement outputs:

- Prevent criminality (e.g., reduce the causes of crime)
- Repress crime (i.e., reduce the opportunities for criminal actions)
- Apprehend offenders
- Recover property
- Maintain public order
- Regulate noncriminal conduct (e.g., enforce traffic and sanitary codes)

Police administrators are involved in setting the overall goals regarding outputs and approving related yearly objectives. As a system, the police agency reacts to certain external input (increases in crime, requests for services, traffic, and population). To function properly, the police agency system requires feedback subsystems that continually measure the outputs (objectives such as the reduction of crime by 10 percent). This measurement (called the "test of correspondence" in Figure 5–1) is often made by comparing crime and arrest statistics, as well as by gauging community support through records of citizen complaints and news media reactions. Based on these measurements, various interventions (personnel reallocations or budget requests, for example) can be made to enhance internal processing to improve on the desired outputs. Today, feedback systems are most often computer assisted.

The system approach can be useful in identifying the types of computer applications most helpful in meeting a police agency's objectives. **Figure 15–2** shows an **Evaluation Matrix** system that involves the minds of those administrators and employees who are in positions to have the knowledge to make appropriate evaluations. On one axis of the matrix various computer systems under consideration are listed. On the other axis, the agency's objectives, activities, interventions, and goals are described (derived from the systems view of the agency as shown in Figure 5 1, in Chapter 5). Using a scale of 0–10, the various administrators and personnel responsible for these functions can evaluate the proposed systems. The figure shows hypothetical scores for the types of computer systems commonly

Scoring	Output						Process	Control of feedback subsystem				Total score
10 = Direct 9 8 7 = Strong 6 5 4 = Indirect 3 2 1 0 = No impact	1. Prevention	2. Repression	3. Apprehension	4. Recover property	5. Maintain public order	6. Regulation of noncriminal conduct	Line, support, and administrative functions	Adjustments			Output goals	
								Resource allocation	Community relations	Budget	Level of effectiveness desired	
Automated wants and warrants system	4	6	10	3	2	8	8	4	3	0	0	48
Automated M.O. investigation system	3	5	10	8	2	0	7	5	2	0	0	42
Command and control system	7	7	8	6	9	6	9	9	5	0	5	71
Automated manpower allocation system	7	7	7	6	6	6	8	10	4	7	9	77

Figure 15–2 Evaluation Matrix for Computerized Law Enforcement Applications.

used in law enforcement agencies. This evaluations process can assist in making decisions that balance the most important needs with budget restraints.

Some general guides in using computers to maximize resources are as follows:

Inputs to computer system should be obtained as close to the sources as possible. Because the success of solving crime depends on information, the sooner information is available to others through "mainframe computers" the better the chances for success. For example, "wireless" laptop computers can allow for crime reports to be made at the crime scene and transmitted to mainframe computers immediately. Inputs directly from traffic citations, traffic reports, field interview cards, field logs, communication logs, booking reports, and other "at the scene" reports should be an objective. Additionally, eliminating as many paper reports as possible should be another goal.

Processing should result in computers cross-referencing and eliminating duplication and manual files. A "rule of thumb" should be that no data should ever have to be entered twice. The data that is entered at the original point of entry (the crime scene, for example) should never have to be reentered again as the incident goes through the criminal justice system. Any subsequent reporting (including the booking form, vehicle impound forms, property form, follow-up investigation reports, filing complaints, court reports, and prison forms) should be programmed so that the original information is carried forward by computers and only corrections and additional information need be added. In this way, the computer can save a great deal of time and duplicated effort.

Output information should be at the "fingertips" of the users. The police officer, the detective, the administrator, the court officials, and corrections personnel should be able to access any and all information at a moment's notice. Just as entering information as close to the source as possible is essential, making the information accessible to the users in a timely manner is equally important.

Larger agencies often have planning and even automation sections that are responsible for the automated systems. Again, using the concept of involving the minds of administrators and personnel, a "Task Force" approach is advisable. **Figure 15–3** shows such an approach. An administrative review committee should be established to oversee, monitor, and guide the development of new automated systems. The committee helps to ensure that the systems meet the needs of the agency's operating components, and its recommendations enable the chief administrator to make decisions regarding these automated systems. The committee members should include the executive administrators from the agency plus representation from the jurisdictions central data processing agency if there is one involved.

The administration review committee can evaluates all requests for automation systems, using the evaluation matrix approach. When a request is deemed to have merit, the committee authorizes the automation information section to study the feasibility to implementation and, based on study results, makes recommendations to the chief administrator. When an application is approved, a task force can be formed and assigned to the automation section. Because the committee members have responsibility for the major divisions of the agency, its members can facilitate assignment of personnel to the task force.

The task force should include automation and planning personnel as well as personnel involved in the function to be automated. For example, if a computerized modus operandi system is to be developed, detective personnel should be on the task force. When the system is implemented, the "user" personnel on the task force will return to their regular assignments and help train their colleagues in the system's use. Using these task force members as trainers helps overcome user resistance to a new system. During the system development stages, the

Figure 15–3 Automation Task Force Concept.

"user" task force members can provide valuable firsthand knowledge of the functions being computerized. After implementation, the task force can be disbanded, reducing the number of persons permanently assigned to automation and planning functions.

Criminal justice administrators should promote information sharing between their agencies and the public. Field officer time can be enhanced by having certain minor crimes reported by victims via the Internet. Many criminal justice agencies have websites that provide useful information to the public. A few departments, such as the Los Angeles Police Department, have developed blog sites where the public can exchange information with the police.

Cybercrime is another facet of technology that criminal justice administrators must prepare their agencies to combat. The National Institute of Justice (NIJ) conducted an assessment of the needs of state and local law enforcement in combating electronic crime and cyberterrorism. As a result of the survey, the following list of critical needs was developed:

- Public awareness
- Adequate data and reporting
- Uniform training and certification courses
- Onsite management assistance for electronic crime units and task forces
- Updated laws
- Cooperation with the high-tech industry
- Special research and publications
- Management awareness and support
- Investigative and forensic tools
- Structured computer crime units (Stambaugh, et al., 2001)

Regarding technology, the following are additional areas that the Eclectic Perspective criminal justice administrators should consider:

- Wireless private secure networks can link all criminal justice personnel anywhere in the world.
- Video game technology can be used in creating revolutionary criminal justice training.
- Pod use should involve 12.3 households in the next decade, making it possible for almost everyone to have access to criminal justice assistance anywhere, anytime.
- Cell phone video will be carried by most everyone in the near future and can be used by citizens to "catch criminals in the act." Build-in time and geolocation readouts can facilitate legal venue and statute of limitations requirements. Conceivably, digital accounts of a crime could be sent to the police anonymously and provide probable cause to arrest without the testimony of the witness. Also, there are a growing number of situations where citizens have used digital cameras to record incidents of police brutality.
- Surveillance cameras can vastly expand the "eyes" of the police. England has 150 surveillance cameras in use and many large cities in the United States, such as New York, Chicago, and Los Angeles, are following this trend.

- Satellite photography could be used to photograph metropolitan areas every few seconds and images digitally stored, ready to be enlarged to what can now be seen from helicopters hovering overhead. Helium floating pads are being manufactured that will support remote viewing cameras that are much less expensive than the cost of deploying helicopters.
- Holography could replace "mug shots" with 3-D images that could be used for suspect identification and lineups (author's research and Thibault, Lynch, & McBride 2007, p. 479).

Whatever the future brings, the Eclectic Perspective criminal justice administrator will need to keep abreast of technological developments to ensure that beneficial advances will be used to provide better service. Technology can increase efficiency by reducing the time spent in performing routine tasks at all levels of the organization—from line personnel to the top executive. Dr. William L. Tafoya, writes in the forward to a textbook by Raymond E. Foster that can assist administrators in this regard:

> "Police Technology is *a clarion call that announces a move in the direction of a new, positive era for American policing in the near-term future—A number of chapters discuss cutting-edge issues: major incident and disaster response, the Internet (still not fully exploited), geocoding, and wireless, for example. A chapter on crime analysis has also been included. This is evidence of the author's understanding of the importance of integration. That is, the value-added benefit of augmenting one capability with another. That a chapter, not merely a closing page, addresses emerging technologies reflects the forward thinking of the author"* (Tafoya, 2004).

It must be understood that technology is not a panacea for achieving criminal justice missions. However, technology advances can provide valuable tools that may greatly assist administrators and will continue to play an important role in all facets of criminal justice administration.

■ Maintaining the Decreasing Crime Trend

Figure 10–3 shows the crime rate in the United State over the past 100 years. The crime rate remained steady through the first half of the 20th century. In the 1960s, it began to rise and continued to rise (with brief periods of decrease) to more than 600 percent over a 30-year period. In the early 1990s, it began to decrease and by 2004 had dropped to the level it was at in the mid-1970s. Unfortunately, recent statistics provide evidence that crime may again be on the rise (**Figure 15–4**). The Police Executive Research Forum (PERF) recently published a report titled "A Gathering Storm—Violent Crime in America," which provides some alarming information:

> *For a growing number of cities across the United States, violent crime is accelerating at an alarming pace. The Federal Bureau of*

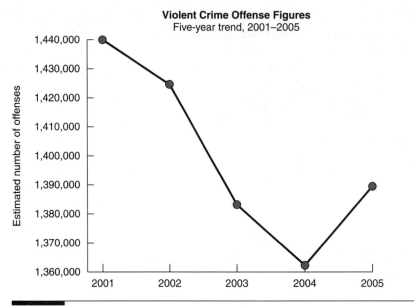

Figure 15–4 Recent Violent Crime Trends.

Investigation's (FBI) annual Uniform Crime Report (UCR) for 2005 reflects a significant increase in violent crimes throughout the country compared to 2004 figures. Nationwide, the United States experienced an increase in three of the four violent crime categories: homicide (3.4%), robberies (3.9%) and aggravated assaults (1.8%). This rise in violent crime was experienced in all areas of the country. The FBI statistics reflect the largest single year percent increase in violent crimes in 14 years (this includes the largest single year increases in 14 years for homicide and robbery, and the largest single year increase in aggravated assaults in 13 years). Importantly, statistics provided to the Police Executive Research Forum (PERF) from numerous cities reflects that the rise in violent crime is continuing into 2006 (PERF, 2006, p. 1).

If one were to ask, "What is the most important task of the criminal justice system?" the answer would simply be to reduce crime. Some of the reasons for the recent increase in violent crimes will be discussed subsequently. First and most important is to determine what caused crime to decrease and how criminal justice administrators can continue the downward trend of the past thirteen years. As with most criminal justice concerns, many of the factors affecting crime are outside the direct control of criminal justice administrators; however, even outside factors should be of concern to the Eclectic Perspective criminal justice administrator. The Open Systems approach involves supporting conditions outside of the organization that can assist in achieving the agency's mission. What follows is a review of some of the most prominent theories about why crime has decreased.

Poverty

Figure 15–5 and **Figure 15–6** show an interesting correlation between poverty and crime. In Chapter 10 the correlation among crime, poverty, and the disenfranchised was discussed. Throughout our history, areas of poverty have the highest crime rates, particularly violent crimes. They also have the most victims of crime. A hundred years ago, these areas were inhabited by many ancestors of today's majority

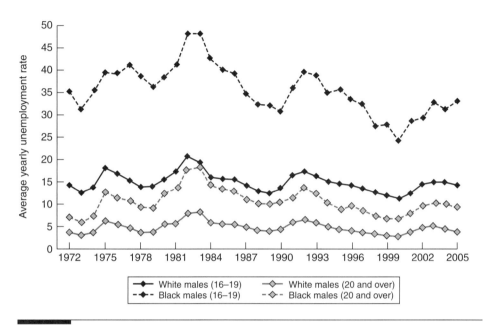

Figure 15–5 Unemployment Rates by Race.

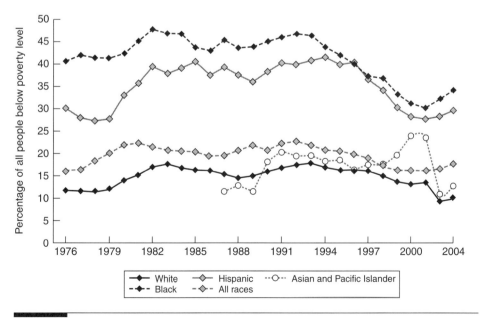

Figure 15–6 Percentage of Population Below Poverty Level.

white population, who were then new arrivals in our country. Today, these areas are populated by blacks, Hispanics, and Asians. This should disprove any connection of race and crime. Crime is most prominent in areas of poverty, and areas of poverty are most often populated by the minorities of the time.

Of course, poverty and unemployment are related to the economical health of the country. The 1990s was a period of strong economical growth in our country resulting in a decrease in unemployment and poverty. Criminal justice agencies usually prosper during these periods with increases in personnel and other resources. This also can contribute to a reduction in crime. The Eclectic Perspective criminal justice administrator will be wise to keep abreast of economical indicators as so goes the economy, so goes crime and tax revenue to support criminal justice agencies.

Incarceration

Figure 15–7 shows a strong correlation between imprisonment rates and crime. In Chapter 6, the most recent sentencing trends of "warehousing" and "just deserts" were discussed. The trend is based on a philosophy that previous rehabilitation approaches failed so imprisonment is the only answer. When an offender is behind bars, she or he cannot commit crime. New prisons were built, but currently most are nearing the capacity limits (Bureau of Justice Statistics, 2006).

As previously discussed, drug offenders make up the majority of the prisoners in federal institutions. Drugs often have been associated with other crimes and the incarceration of drug offenders may be having an impact on commission of other crimes. As harsh as "imprisonment is the answer" sounds, statistics do support continuing a "hard-line" approach, especially with violent offenders. This is an area where the various components of the criminal justice system need to work together and criminal justice administrators need be involved.

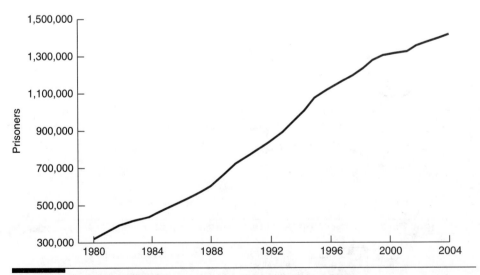

Figure 15–7 Imprisonment Rates.

Community Policing

In Chapter 11, the criminal justice administrative theme of Client-Oriented Service was discussed. This theme, beginning in the 1980s and continuing to the present, also has a correlation with the decrease in crime. It was the 1990s, when this theme became widespread among policing agencies, crime began to decrease. The Client-Oriented Service philosophy is based on the concept that the police must have the trust and support of the majority of the population if they are going to be successful in their mission. The theme is really a return to Sir Robert Peel's Principles that American law enforcement first adopted in the 1800s. The heart of the principles stated that "the police are the public and that the public are the police. The police being only members of the public who are paid to give full-time attention to duties which are incumbent on every citizen, in the interests of community welfare and existence." Under the American form of government, the police are kept at a minimum so that they can not become a military force that can circumvent the will of the majority.

As the police became more technologically proficient in the 1960–1970s, they seemed more distant to the public. The "crime fighting" police, patrolling in vehicles, responding only when called. The "partners with the community" concept seemed to fade and people began to lose trust in the police. Crime increased and it was the realization that community trust and support for the police were important in controlling crime. This realization caused law enforcement to become more client-oriented. As discussed in Chapter 11, most criminals are apprehended because of information provided by community members, not by the police catching the criminal in the act. If people do not trust the police, they will not come forward with needed information. Situations where crime initially increased when community trust in the police improved were discussed in Chapter 11. What occurs is that crime that would not have been reported to the police when they were not trusted, is reported, sometimes giving the false impression that actual crime in increasing. These situations, however, evened out over time.

Reported Crime

One of the theories about the decrease in crime is that less crime is being reported. This theory is not supported by the client-oriented service approach. If anything, reported crime should have risen. An important indicator as to what percentage of crime is being reported can be found in the U.S. Department of Justice's National Crime Victimization Report (NCVR). This is a report that criminal justice administrators should be mindful off and compare with the FBI's Uniform Crime Report (UCR). The NCVR surveys a statistical sound number of households each year to determine how many have experienced some type of crime. Since the NCVR began in 1972, it has revealed that less than twice the number of crimes occurred as reported to the police in the UCR (Bureau of Justice Statistics, 2005). As crime decreased since the early 1990s, according to the UCR, it had decreased by nearly the same rate in the NCVR. This should dispel the theory that the decrease in crime is because less crime is being reported.

With the Client-Oriented Service theme, law enforcement community policing efforts embraced the "broken window" concept, which was discussed in Chapter 11. It will be recalled that this concept was the brainchild of the criminologists James Q. Wilson and George Kelling. Wilson and Kelling argued that crime is the inevitable result of neighborhood disorder. If a window is broken and left unrepaired, it will start a chain reaction of neighborhood deterioration. Relatively minor problems such as graffiti, public disorder, and panhandling are the equivalent of broken windows, and are the forerunners of more serious crime. A best-selling book, titled *The Tipping Point* (2000), spotlights the New York Police Department's application of this concept as a prime example of how focusing on minor situations can be the "tipping point" that results in major ramifications. The book cites the application of this approach by then Chief Superintendent Bratton and Mayor Giuliani as a community policing effort that substantially reduced crime (Gladwell, 2000, pp. 141–151).

It should be noted that Bernard E. Harcourt challenges the claim that the "broken window" approach reduces crime. In his 2001 book, *Illusion of Order: The False Promise of Broken Windows Policing*, he disagrees with the research upon which the approach is based as well as the reported success of the New York Police Department. He shows some evidence that there is a lack of empirical research to support the approach and points out that many other cities that "were not applying this approach" had as great a (and in some case a greater) decrease in crime as did New York (Harcourt, 2001). This argument, however, fails to consider that many of the other cities experiencing reduction in crime were applying various other Client-Oriented Service approaches.

Within the community police approach came the Police Corps program as part of the Violent Crime Control and Law Enforcement Act of 1994 and provided $200 million to help the police fight crime. This act created the Office of the Police Corps and Law Enforcement Education administrated by the U.S. Department of Justice. Besides financing college education for qualified Police Corps candidates, it provided funds to local police departments to hire these Police Corps graduates. The goal was to infuse law enforcement with 100,000 additional officers. Although this goal was not fully met, a great deal of additional officers were added to the ranks of police departments across the nation (Police Corps, 2000).

As discussed in Chapter 11 (Figure 11–7), police departments need enough officers so only half of a patrol officer's time is spent in responding to calls-for-services. The other half is needed for proactive community policing efforts such as Problem-Oriented Policing (POP), Neighborhood Watch activities and crime prevention approaches. The additional officers provided through the Police Corps program, plus more local tax revenues, certainly enhanced the law enforcement service abilities. Currently, even though the "community partnership" concept has shifted more toward a Police Accountability to the Community (PAC) concept (discussed in Chapter 11), the need for adequate personnel to resolve the problems of local communities is necessary. Logically, the local police should not be held accountable for taking care of community problems if they do not have adequate resources. Logic, however, is not always a product of social interactions. Unfortunately, the "war on crime" and the financial support that came with it is now all but a memory. Federal funding for the Police Corps program has all but disappeared as crime has diminished. This is an important factor for Eclectic Perspective criminal justice administrators to realize. When crime goes up (and it can be said that the criminal justice system is failing), the system is usually "rewarded" with an infusion of financial support. During the 1980s and early 1990s, when crime was on the rise, crime was on the agenda of every politician running for office. When crime decreases (and it can be said the criminal justice system has been successful), instead of being rewarded, criminal justice agencies usually have reductions in their budgets. The tragedy is that when resources decrease, criminal justice agencies fall farther and farther behind in supporting their missions. When crime goes up to a critical level, and citizens and elected official become alarmed, they want immediate criminal justice intervention. During these periods, criminal justice agencies often are given mandates to hire large number of personnel in short periods of time in order to reduce crime. Because it takes intensive and lengthy hiring and training efforts (as discussed in Chapter 8), it takes considerable time to bring the agencies up to a level where they can again successfully carry out their mission. If rushed, background investigations of candidates and proper training can suffer. Several police departments such as the Los Angeles Police Department can trace some of their corruption scandals to personnel who were not properly screened when hired under these conditions (Rampart Scandal, 2000, for example). Within the Open Systems concept (discussed in Chapter 9), criminal justice administrators must continually keep their public and elected officials aware of the need for continual support so that crime that has been reduced does not increase.

At the beginning of this section on "Continuing the Decreasing Crime Trend," PERF information was cited that indicates crime is on the increase once again. A recent PERF newsletter states, "This up-tick in violent crimes also seems to coincide to the downward crash of federal funding to local policing." The buildup of the Department of Homeland Security (DHS) and all it entails has diverted most of what had been devoted to local policing. Remember when so many chiefs used to describe their department's programming as "community policing" just to qualify for federal funds? This all has a familiar ring to it, with today's moniker being "homeland security" (Myers, 2006, p. 2). As discussed in Chapter 11, many resources that once were deployed for community police efforts are being diverted to homeland security tasks. If the client-oriented service approach is diluted because of other tasks, an increase in crime may occur as was the case in the 1950s and 1960s when the police focused on "cold war" and the "enemy within" (discussed in Chapter 3 and Chapter 10).

Other Theories Regarding Decrease in Crime

The previous three theories have been discussed in some detail as they present the strongest evidence of being linked to the decline in crime. Many other theories have been put forward and a few deserve some mention.

"Crime Prone" Age Group Decline

The shrinkage in the relative size of the 15- to 24-year-old age group (known as the "crime prone years" as most crime is committed by persons in this age group) may account for a modest portion of the decline in the crime rate. However, the decrease was not in the minor communities where many coming from other countries were within this age group or were having children that grew into this age group. Additionally, the arrest of persons in this age group continued to rise during the years of declining crime (Conklin, 2003, pp. 143–150).

Gun Laws

Stricter gun laws for the possession, carrying, and use of firearms enacted during the 1990s may have had some impact on violent crimes as well as longer imprisonment sentences for those using firearms. This, however, does not explain the fall in burglaries, motor vehicle thefts, and other property crimes (Conklin, 2003, p. 196).

Abortion

Abortions became more prevalent after the 1973 Supreme Court ruling in *Roe v. Wade*. By 1980, the number of abortions per year reached 1.6 million (one for every 2.25 live births). Steven Levitt and John Donohue published a paper in 2001 relating the increase of abortions to the decrease in crime. Their theory was that more unwanted babies were not being born. Their position was that unwanted babies have more of a chance of growing up to become criminals. They argued that abortions during the 1970s and 1980s eliminated many unwanted children who would have reached the "crime prone" years in the 1990s, thereby contributing to the decline in crime during this period. Interestingly, their study shows that the few states that legalized abortion before the Supreme Court allowed it nationwide had a decline in crime before the other states that did not (Levitt & Dubner, 2005, pp. 115–125). The introduction of "birth control" medication also may fit within this theory.

During a recent discussion by the author with students, several brought up the idea that the proliferation of "CSI" forensic crime investigation television dramas may be having an impact on crime. As unrealistic as these programs are, they make it appear that criminals are no match for forensic science. Perhaps these programs are preventing would-be criminals from a life of crime because of the "you're going to get caught no matter" themes of these programs.

All of these explanations of why crime has decreased should be of interest to the Eclectic Perspective criminal justice administrator as crime reduction is a major task for which they are responsible. Determining and perpetuating the factors that have caused crime to decrease should be a top priority.

■ Looking Beyond the Cutting Edge Vanguard Concepts

In these final pages we will attempt to look beyond the cutting edge and discuss concepts that should be on the minds of criminal justice administrators as they prepare to create a better future. In Chapter 6, Enzer's formula states "the future equals the extension of the past, plus the uncertainty introduced by conditions not under human control, plus the uncertainty introduced by human choice." The main idea of this textbook has been that the past history of administration provides building block themes on which the future of criminal justice administration can be structured. Studying the past is a means for preparing for the future.

Part III of this textbook began by defining the future as "from this moment on." The future is something we can change and that is an exciting concept. The future has yet to be created and who gets to create it? Creative people do! The future will be created by those who:

- Take an educated look at the past and learn from it,
- Take an intuitive look at the present and compare it with the past,
- Design a realistic image of what they want the future to be, based on their knowledge of the past and the present, and
- Use this image as a guide to creating a better future for themselves and for their profession.

Note that the word realistic was emphasized. Enzer's formula for the future recognizes the uncertainties. The Eclectic Perspective criminal justice administrator should recognize what is beyond his or her control in forming goals and objectives. One can develop a "grand plan" for which financial and political support is unrealistic, and waste valuable time trying to create something that is not achievable.

By reviewing the concepts related to the five contextual administrative themes that have been discussed throughout this book, the following factors come to the forefront and should be given high priority in preparing for the future.

Vanguard Organization Functions Concepts

The Organization Functions theme includes several "forefront" concepts. First, it may be wise to remember that the concepts within this theme are often called principles. In Chapter 2, Herbert Simon reminded us in his 1946 paper, "The Proverbs of Administration," these concepts should be viewed as "**guides**" (or as Simon put it, "proverbs") and not principles. Today's organic organizations require administrators that can "mix and match" these concepts to meet changing environments.

The concept of **authority and responsibility** (discussed in Chapter 7) is as important in the future as it was in the past. The people (majority) give up some of their freedoms for the good of social accord. They give to those "sworn to uphold the law" authority to enforce their laws and regulations. With this authority comes a responsibility to the people to use this authority within the limits provided by the U.S. Constitution and to protect the individual rights provided by the Bill of Rights.

When criminal justice administrators take their oath of office they receive the authority and responsibility to carry out the public mission of their agency.

As O. W. Wilson reminded us in Chapter 5, "Although he [the administrator] may free himself of the actual performance of the tasks involved, a superior officer cannot rid himself of an iota of responsibility for their accomplishment." This holds true as the tasks are divided (Division of Work) and assigned down the Chain of Command in the organization. It is this concept of authority and responsibility that ties all of this together.

In Chapter 7, Garth Morgan reminded us that "We are shifting from a world dominated by bureaucratic-mechanistic principles into an electronic universe where new organizational logics are required." However, even though contemporary administrators must be more flexible and oversee more organic organizations, they still use many of the founding principles such as those encapsulated in the acronym POSDCORB.

Vanguard Employee Relations Concepts

The several concepts within the Employee Relations theme also should be considered in the "forefront." As discussed in Chapter 14, administrators must provide leadership that inspires and persuades employees to willingly carry out their professional duties. Today's leaders display modesty and empathy for their employees (and their clients). Empathy comes from feeling what others are feeling. The importance of hiring criminal justice employees with varied backgrounds and interests was discussed in Chapter 8 as a means of having employees who can better empathize with various members of today's society. This holds true for administrators and those preparing to become administrators. As a professor, the author encourages criminal justice students to get involved in as many college and community activities as possible, take courses in a variety of subjects outside of criminal justice, and get to know students from other backgrounds as a way of developing the empathy they will need as criminal justice professionals.

Even though today's administrator strives to be a "people person" and provide Theory Y type of leadership, the "Big Y, Little x" concept discussed in Chapter 8 should be remembered. Because administrators cannot relinquish their overall responsibilities, they must provide some inspection and control (a little x). As Luther Gulick reminded us in his 1937 *Papers on the Science of Administration*, "Control consists in seeing that everything is carried out in accordance with the plan which has been adopted, the organization which has been set up, and the orders which have been given . . . control is in a sense the consequence of command in action" (discussed in Chapter 5).

Another timely concept is Michael LeBoeuf's **Greatest Management Principle (GMP)**, "What gets done is what gets rewarded" (Chapter 8). Finding out what rewards motivate individual employees and relating them to the agency's mission will remain an important task for all administrators.

Making criminal justice employment a true profession is an important task for all criminal justice administrators. Requiring a four-year degree, having employees sign the oath and value statements as contracts (the violation of which is grounds for discipline) and requiring ongoing ethics training are all important efforts in fostering quality employees for the 21st century.

Vanguard Open Systems Concepts

An essential Open Systems concept today and into the future is for administrator to coordinate with the other members of the criminal justice system; their social, political, and economic environment; and with the "global society." In addition to being sensitive to the needs of their employees, they must relate well to the needs of the "two legs" of the Three Legs of Support model that are outside of the organization. As discussed in Chapter 14, community support and political support are essential to the success of an administrator. Additionally, building a "professional network" with other criminal justice administrators is a productive means of exchanging ideas and sharing support.

An important element in shaping the opinions of those outside the organization is the media. Today's media is big business. The television and radio news media, for example, now have hourly and around-the-clock coverage. To stay in business, these networks must provide information that holds the attention of the viewer or listener. What holds most people's attention is action, and criminal justice events are prime fodder for action news coverage. Unfortunately, many people only want a quick review of a news event and most news programs limit coverage to a minute or less for each event. This often results in what is sometimes called "confetti news." The public often form opinions based on "bits and pieces" of information rather than on all the facts. The public can form opinions as to the guilt of a person based on the "confetti" information they received via a news broadcast. Contemporary criminal justice administrators must consider this reality and prepare themselves and their employees to plan their news statement to meet the constraints of "confetti news." In Chapter 11, the importance of press relations officers was discussed as one method of confronting this reality.

Another important issue that involves the news media is video coverage of news events that can be used in criminal justice prosecutions. News videos of riots and looting have been used in recent years as evidence to convict offenders. News videos of police pursuits and use of force situations have supported the police against false claims. Keeping a good working relationship with the news media is an important part of being a criminal justice administrator in today's world.

The entertainment media is also of importance as it often shapes the image of criminal justice practitioners for the public. These "law and order" television programs and movies have an impact on criminal justice employees. Chief William Parker of Los Angeles (discussed in Chapter 6) became close friends with a television producer in the 1950s and 1960s. The relationship resulted in *Dragnet* and *Adam 12*, popular television shows that depicted the Los Angeles Police Department in a favorable light. These programs enhanced the public image of the department and helped recruit many new police officers for that department. The more recent *NYPD* television program had a similar effect for the New York Police Department.

During the 1960s, the author remembers police officers suddenly not wearing their hats when they got out of patrol cars (the wearing of hats was a procedural requirement at that time). This was apparently because the two actors that played the parts of Los Angeles police officers on *Adam 12* were not wearing their hats, which interfered with the hairstyles of the day. At about this same time, there were several television programs in which the actors playing narcotic officers wore blue jeans, black T-shirts, and tan leather jackets. Suddenly, narcotic officers were wearing this apparel. These are examples of how entertainment can impact the self-images of police officers. Using the media to assist in achieving agency missions as did William Parker is something that progressive criminal justice administrators might consider.

Vanguard Social Equity Concepts

It is important to remember that the Social Equity theme is unique to the public sector and is one that separates the criminal justice field from all others. It should be acknowledged also that our Constitution was not really applied to all people until the latter part of the 20th century (and there remain areas of discrimination in our country). It is only within the last 40 years that the oath of office of most police officers contains a duty to protect the rights of all people. For example, as discussed in Chapter 10, the Federal Bureau of Investigation's value statement now contains "constitutional guarantees are more important than the outcome of any single interview, search for evidence, or investigation." This responsibility to maintain Social Equity separated American criminal justice from the justice systems in many other countries. Maintaining this concept is one of the most important duties of today's criminal justice administrators.

How pressure to provide public safety has resulted in violations of individual rights as it did in the 1960s and 1970s was discussed in Chapter 10. Current and future criminal justice administrators must not let the pressure of terrorism overshadow their duties to protect individual rights. History has shown that the people, through their vote, their elected officials, and the court, will impose sanctions on those who do not protect individual rights.

A current situation that will no doubt continue for years to come involves those disenfranchised from the society at large. A contemporary criminal justice challenge involves a disenfranchised segment of society, those who are often referred to as "the homeless." Most cities have a concentration of "homeless" in slum areas or areas close to social welfare agencies. There are people who are economically without means needed for proper shelter and food; however, there is a growing population of people who live "on the street" because of addiction or mental conditions.

In the 1960s and 1970s, in a response to a decrease in tax revenues, many state institutions for the mentally ill and those addicted to drugs (including alcohol) were closed. This created a population of addicts who lived on the street as "homeless." This population continues to increase today and has become a real Social Equity issue. On the one hand, people living and doing business in the areas populated by these "homeless" often complain to the police that their public safety and community tranquility is threatened. They complain that the "homeless" sleep, defecate, urinate, and beg on their streets and property, thereby degrading the general wellness in the neighborhoods. On the other hand, civil right activists will defend the rights of these "homeless" to do as they please citing constitutional guarantees.

Criminal justice administrators often find themselves in the middle of this conflict between individual and public rights. The author, as a police administrator, was placed in this position in several cities. He was involved in an approach, although not without controversy, that is being used in several large cities today. For several months, each homeless individual was contacted by a "team" which included the beat officer and a social worker. Each contact was documented. Every individual was informed about and offered shelter, food, and other needed assistance. They were also informed that if they did not take advantage of these offerings by a certain date, trespassing and various health laws were going to be enforced. A "tent city" that provided food, shelter, and sanitary facilities was created nearby. By the deadline, if the "homeless" had not removed their belongings (often cardboard boxes in which they slept), these items were picked up by city workers and deposited at the "tent city" where the owners could retrieve them. The aforementioned laws then began to be enforced. This resulted in a returning of the streets to the residents and business owners, and city parks again became places that families could enjoy. Such actions involve difficult Social Equity issues that many criminal justice administrators will face in their careers.

Homeless Court Programs should be offered. Most of the crimes attributed to people who are homeless are public disturbance offenses such as drinking and urinating in public, trespassing, begging, and blocking public access. In San Diego, California, a courtroom was set up and run outside of the regular courthouse. The defense and prosecution established guides for pleas and alternative sentencing to facilitate the resolution of these types of cases. Plea bargain arrangements held defendants responsible for their offenses and recognized that many offenses were a result of social conditions. Alternative sentencing involved services were offered on site. Involvement in activities that helped to move participants off the streets and through programs, toward self-sufficiency, became part of the court dispositions (Binder, 2001, pp. 14–17).

Corrections planning in reducing the homeless population has been established in such states as Massachusetts, Illinois, Ohio, and Minnesota. Most inmates are eventually released back into society. Corrections programs to offset housing barriers and lack of benefits for those reentering society are being established under such names as Project Return and Transitional Housing for Ex-Offenders (Community Shelter Board, 2002).

The rights of the disenfranchised are just one example of the Social Equity issues that will continue to face criminal justice administrators in the future.

Vanguard Client-Oriented Service Concepts

The importance for the criminal justice system to have the trust and support of the community has been stressed throughout this text. The government structure of our country requires this relationship. The criminal justice system should never be so powerful that it can force compliance of laws that the majority does not support. Most crimes are solved because of information provided by the public. If the public does not trust those that represent criminal justice, they will not come forward with such information. The Client-Oriented Service theme came about to revitalize this relationship and maintaining this approach is a major responsibility of today's criminal justice administration.

Peel's Principle (Figure 11–2) of a police-community "partnership" is shifting more toward a Police Accountability to Community (PAC) relationship. Community members are viewing the criminal justice functions as a service to which they have a right. Many in the general population no longer feel that they have the time to "partner" with their police in meetings and crime prevention efforts. They are, however, willing to voice their opinions as to which services they want the criminal justice system to provide for neighborhood domestic tranquility. Those in the criminal justice system, particularly the police, are now being held accountable to their individual communities to provide such services. Just as the general public wants customized transportation, entertainment and other commercial offerings, they want criminal justice services customized to their local needs. This does not mean crimes are not to be dealt with appropriately. It does, however, recognize that the public has not provided the criminal justice system with the resources to enforce all the laws all the time. Therefore, the criminal justice administrators must focus his or her limited resources toward the criminal justice conditions that are of most concern to their individual communities (their clients).

Looking "over the cutting edge," environmental threats may become as much a of concern to the public as the threat of terrorism now is. In 2006, a former vice president of the United States produced a motion picture titled *An Inconvenient Truth*, which received nationwide interest. In it, Al Gore presented evidence of a global warming threat that, if true, could be disastrous to all mankind. If the majority becomes concerned about such things as the amount of carbons released into the atmosphere by individuals they may call on the police to enforce laws to combat such conditions. The traffic officers now enforce laws relating to vehicle exhaust emissions, however, they may not envision that guarding the public again environmental violations might become part of their daily duties. Becoming "environment protection cops" may not be in the thoughts of most law enforcement officers today but it may be in the future.

History reminds us that at the beginning of the 20th century the "horseless carriage" appeared. Within a decade there were millions of motor vehicles and traffic accidents and congestion became a problem. The police were called on to enforce laws to combat these motor vehicle problems. At first the police resisted, taking the position that they were "crime fighters" and traffic was not a problem that involved police work. A century later, traffic is a major criminal justice responsibility with more people dying in traffic accidents then as a result of criminal law violations. The Eclectic Perspective criminal justice administrator will do well to be prepared for the many changing demands of their clients in the future.

Integrating the community with criminal justice agencies is a necessary concept for success in the future. Just as Client-Oriented service has become the theme of today's community policing, so this concept is important to the other criminal justice fields. Court prosecution and the need to focus on local community concerns were discussed in Chapter 11. Community support also is needed in community-based corrections programs. When released offenders are granted entry into work programs or furloughs, the public can do a great deal to ease their acceptance back into the community (Petersilia, 1998, pp. 3–9). Community-based programs generally have better success rates compared with institution-based programs. One reason for this difference is the impact of interacting with community residents (Minnesota Probation Standards Task Force, 2003).

Wrap Up

KEY CONCEPTS AND TERMS

- Homeland Security
  - Impact on Client-Oriented Service
  - Preserving public trust and protecting individual rights
- Criminal Justice in a Global Society
  - Open Systems theme expansion
  - Americans differ from other countries (drug example)
  - Learning from other countries (rise in crime and public unrest with democratization)
- Impact of Technology
  - Digital Sherlock Holmes
  - Instant cops
  - Automated administrators
  - Evaluation matrix
  - Cybercrime
- Maintaining decreasing crime trend
  - Povery
  - Incarcaration
  - Community policing
  - Reported crime
- Vanguard Contextual Theme Concepts
  - Guides rather than principles
  - Important concepts for each contextual theme

CHAPTER ACTIVITY

Enforcing environmental protection laws was discussed as a possible future task for law enforcement. Research publications and the Internet for indications of other trends that may be of concern to criminal justice administrators in the future.

REVIEW QUESTIONS

1. As a criminal justice administrator, what contextual themes concepts do you think most important if you were assigned to develop the Homeland Security strategy for your agency?

2. Discuss some of the technological advances that can be used by criminal justice administrators in achieving their missions.

3. Why do you think crime decreased in recent years? What can criminal justice administrators do to ensure that this downward trend continues?

4. What global situations relate to criminal justice administration? How does the situation of people's reaction to newfound freedom, as mentioned in this chapter, relate to criminal justice administration?

5. How would you approach the "homeless" issue as a criminal justice administrator. What contextual themes concepts do you think are most important that relate to this issue?

REFERENCES

Binder, S. R. (2001). The Homeless Court Program: Taking the Court to the Street. *Federal Probation*, 65, pp. 65–67.

Bureau of Justice Statistics. (2000). *Effects of NIBRS on Crime Statistics*. Washington, DC: Bureau of Justice Statistics, Department of Justice.

Bureau of Justice Statistics. (2005). *National Crime Victimization Survey (NCVS)*. Washington, DC: Bureau of Justice Statistics, Department of Justice.

Bureau of Justice Statistics. (2006). *Correction Populations in the United States*. Washington, DC: Bureau of Justice Statistics, Department of Justice.

Community Shelter Board. (2002). *Preventing Homelessness: Discharge Planning from Corrections Facilities*. Columbus, OH: Community Shelter Board. Retrieved November 2002 from http://www.csb.org

Conklin, J. E. (2003). *Why Crime Rates Fell*. New York: Person Education.

Cronkhite, C. (2000). American Criminal Justice Trends for the 21st Century. *Crime & Justice International*, July/August, pp. 9–13.

Federal Bureau of Investigation. (FBI). (1987). *Terrorism in the United States*. Washington, DC: Federal Bureau of Investigation.

Gladwell, M. (2000). *The Tipping Point*. New York: Little, Brown and Company, Time Warner Book Group.

Harcourt, B. E. (2001). *Illusion of Order: The False Promise of Broken Windows Policing*. Cambridge, MA: Harvard University Press.

International Association of Chiefs of Police, (2005). *Post-9/11 Policing: The Crime Control-Homeland Security Paradigm*. Retrieved August 13, 2007 from http://www.theiacp.org.

Levitt, S. D., & Dubner, S. J. (2005). *Freakonomics: A Rogue Economist Explores the Hidden Side of Everything*. New York: HarperCollins.

Myers, R. (2006). Putting the "Home" Back in Homeland Security. *Subject to Debate*. October, p. 3.

Minnesota Probation Standards Task Force. (2003). *Minnesota Probation: A System in Crisis*. St. Paul: Minnesota Probation Standards Board.

National Institute of Justice. (2003). *The Impact of Homeland Security on State Law Enforcement*. Washington DC: Office of Justice Programs, Department of Justice. Grant No. 2003-DT-CX-004.

PERF. (2006). *A Gathering Storm—Violent Crime in America*. Washington, DC: Police Executive Research Forum.

Perito, R. M. (2002). *The American Experience with Police in Peace Operations*. Clementsport, NS: Canadian Peacekeeping Press.

Petersilia, J. (1998). A Decade of Experimenting with Intermediate Sanctions: What Have We Learned? *Federal Probation*, p. 62, pp. 3–9.

Police Corps. (2000). Office of the Police Corps and Law Enforcement Education, U.S. Department of Justice. Washington, DC.

Police Executive Research Forum. (2001). Local Law Enforcement's Role in Preventing and Responding to Terrorism, Washington DC: Police Executive Research Forum.

Rampart Scandal, An Independent Analysis of the Los Angeles Police Department's Board of Inquiry Report. (2000). Los Angeles. Retrieved February 1, 2002, from: http://www.usc.edu/dept/law/faculty/chemerinshy/rampart_final rep.html

Reichel, P. L. (2005). *Comparative Criminal Justice Systems*. Upper Saddle River, NJ: Pearson/Prentice Hall.

Tafoya, W. (2004). Foreword. In Raymond E. Foster, *Police Technology*. Upper Saddle River, NJ: Pearson/Prentice Hall.

Thibault, E. A., Lynch, L. M., & McBride, R. B. (2007). *Proactive Police Management* (7th ed.). Upper Saddle River, NJ: Pearson/Prentice Hall.

Stambaugh, H., Beupre, D. S., Icove, D. J., Baker, R., Cassaday, W., & Williams, W. P. (2001). *Electronic Crime Needs Assessment for State and Local Law Enforcement*. Washington, DC: National Institute of Justice.

Wrap Up

■ RELEVANT PUBLICATION

This chapter concludes with an article by the author, which should serve as a reminder of many of the themes and concepts discussed throughout this text and how they relate to criminal justice administration in the 21st century (Cronkhite, C. (2000). American Criminal Justice Trends for the 21st Century. *Crime & Justice International*, July/August, pp. 9–13).

American Criminal Justice Trends for the 21st Century by Clyde L. Cronkhite

As we approached the new millennium, many predications pertaining to the future of criminal justice have been made for the 21st Century. Now that we have crossed the line into the year 2000 (although technically the 21st Century does not begin until 2001) it is an ideal time to assess where we are and where we are going. Crime is down, the economy is up, and community-oriented service seems to be the major theme of criminal justice agencies.

For consideration, this article presents trends that apply to three criminal justice areas: individual vs. public rights, the professionalization and privatization of the practice, and the future of service-oriented concepts and practices.

Individual vs. Public Rights

Under the Constitution the practice of criminal justice must support the delicate balance between individual rights vs. public rights. As our society becomes more multicultural, this balance becomes more complex. The practice of criminal justice is a continuing reminder that citizens have agreed to give up some individual rights to facilitate public order. Figure 1 shows how public support and consequently, political support, changes over time in regards to this issue. Prior to and during World War II, the general mood of the public was more on the side of public rights. A measure of this mood can be seen in how the public (and politicians) feel about capital punishment. Figure 2 shows the executions over the past 60 years and is reflective of the public/political support for capital punishment.

During the 1930's through the 1950's, executions were at an all time high. During the 1960's to 1970's, the mood of the public changed to a more "individual rights" stand as reflected in the civil unrest incidents that occurred across the country. Executions decreased and came to a stand-still with the nationwide moratorium in the 1970's. With this mood swing, the Courts put forth a number of procedural laws (Figure 3) that restrained the action of the criminal justice system and were meant to sensitize criminal justice practitioners to the rights of individuals.

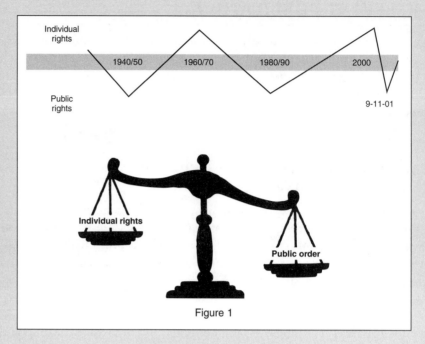

Figure 1

During the 1980s and 1990s there was a return to a more "public rights" attitude by the general public with a subsequent rise in support for the death penalty. There was even an erosion of some of the procedural laws by the Court, such as the softening of *Miranda* rights rule and search and seizure restrictions.

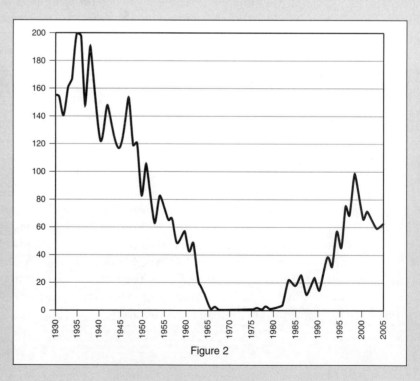

Figure 2

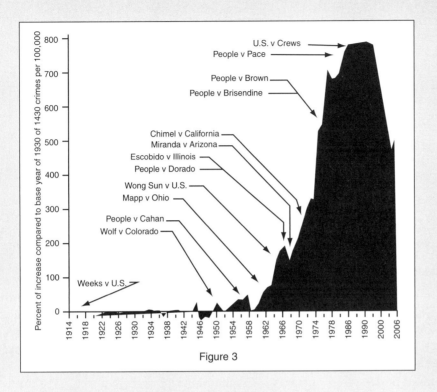

Figure 3

As we enter the new millennium there is evidence of a shift back toward individual rights as exemplified throughout the country by civil rights movements against the police for individual rights violations. There is also a definite movement against the death penalty, with Illinois being first to enact a moratorium. The New Hampshire House recently voted to eliminate the capital punishment in that state and there is a growing death penalty reform movement in the nation's capitol. The significance of this trend for the criminal justice system is that it may signal a return to increasing restrictions upon of criminal justice practitioners.

Professionalization and Privatization of the Practice

The "War on Crime" mood of the nation in the 1980s produced many recommendations for professionalizing the criminal justice system, particularly the police. These recommendations included better selection, training, education, and pay. Most states have now established peace officer standards for selection and training, have adopted codes of ethics, and have raised pay to a competitive level.

The 1967 President's Commission on Law Enforcement and the Administration of Justice voiced the belief that "the ultimate aim of all police departments should be that all personnel with general enforcement powers have baccalaureate degrees." Despite this, higher education requirements today are still almost nonexistent among law enforcement agencies.

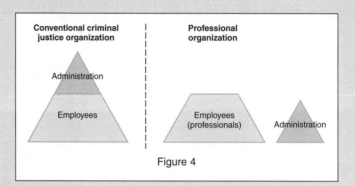

Figure 4

However, the enactment of the Crime Control Act in the late 1990s promises some hope of increased educational standards with the financing of Police Corps programs in a growing number of states.

If more highly educated employees are going to be hired and retained by criminal justice agencies, their working environment must become more challenging and rewarding. Promotion to administrative positions within the ranks has been the predominate means of reward for many agencies. One trend worth exploring is the reorganizing of criminal justice agencies into the professional model set by hospitals and universities (figure 4). In these professional organizations, the majority of employees (physicians and professors) are hired for their expertise and education, and can spend an entire career practicing in their field with substantial rewards in pay and recognition. The airline industry (with the pilots being the "professionals") is another example of this type of organization. With higher selection, education, training standards, and employees becoming experts in their fields, less supervision and management is required. Not only can administrations be smaller but, on a comparable level with the professional employee, employees can follow rewarding and challenging career paths that corresponds with their interests and talents.

With regards to privatization, current statistics (figure 5) show that there are more than twice as many private police as public police, and there are a number of prisons and prisoner transportation functions that have been turned over to private companies. This trend could indicate a growing loss of faith in the public practice of criminal justice. The significance to criminal justice agencies is one of capitalizing on this trend. For example, the police should support the hiring of private police for new business and industrial complexes to reduce an increase in calls-for-service for public police. Further, they should coordinate with the private police to make them an extension of policing efforts, as law enforcement is currently attempting to do with the public as part of community-oriented policing (COP).

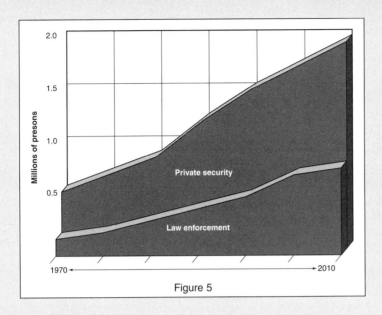

Figure 5

Future of Service-Oriented Concepts and Practices

Figure 6 shows an evolutionary progression of theories and concepts that the criminal justice system has experienced during the past 100 years. Moving from the political model of the 1800s to a legalistic model that emphasized efficiency and effectiveness during most of the 1900s, we have seen in recent years more attention to service. Community/problem-oriented service has at present become the hallmark of policing.

As we enter the 21st Century, what will be the trend? Judging from our past history, it will be an evolutionary enhancement of current practices. The criminal justice system currently exists in a service-driven society. We live in a society of people who pay for others to do many things they used to do for themselves. Working couples now hire others to make and clean their clothes, supply some of their meals, and care for their children. It should

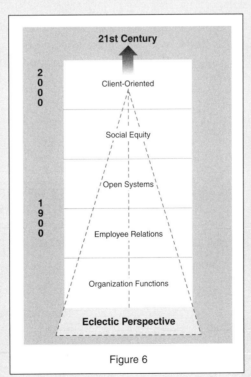

Figure 6

follow that the public expects their tax-financed criminal justice system to provide them with both protection from criminals, and neighborhood peace and tranquility.

Consequently, when the community-oriented police request the average working couple to attend neighborhood-watch meetings, to participate in crime prevention efforts and, as advocated by some COP programs, to get involved in being the eyes and ears of the police, the response may be "what do I pay taxes for?" With many couples working 8 to 10 hours, traveling to and from work and child care centers, they may prefer to spend non-working hours with their families rather than performing services they expect the police to provide.

This is not to condemn COP efforts. Research supports that most crimes are not solved by the police catching a criminal in the act. Rather, most crimes are solved because someone supplied the police with information that lead to the arrest of the perpetrator. If the public does not trust the police because they feel alienated from them, they will not provide the information the police need to do their job. COP can improve public trust in the police.

Additionally, the criminal justice system does not have the resources to enforce all laws. Consequently, the police engage in selective enforcement. Selective enforcement is placing limited resources to work on selected problems. It is in the selection of these problems that the public should be involved.

Selective enforcement, along with the growing emphasis on the police doing more with less, resulted in the development of problem-oriented policing (POP). POP is concerned primarily with identifying and solving community problems (often, but not necessarily, with input from the community.) In contrast, community-oriented policing is concerned with establishing a working partnership with the community, which may include problem-solving.

ELEMENTS OF SUCCESSFUL ENTERPRISE

Historical Periods	Physical Elements	Human Elements
Agriculture	Land	Muscle
Industrial	Energy	Hands
Service	Information/Tech	Mind

Figure 7

An emerging trend (emanating from COP/POP and the emphasis on service) might be called community-accountability policing (CAP). The current New York Police Department's COMPSTAT effort (which has wide acclaim for reducing crime) is one example. It is an effort to enlist the public in determining the problems to be solved but holds the police responsible for solving these problems.

During the early days of community-oriented policing some criminal justice agencies focused more on public relations than on crime control and neighborhood tranquility. Some responded to the increase in crime with "it's not the police's responsibility, the police can't cure crime, it is a social responsibility." Although there certainly is some truth to this, the current trend finds the public expecting the police to provide a service of crime reduction and neighborhood peace. The public does not expect to be partners in providing this service but does want input into what problems the police focus on in each community.

This article has attempted to discuss several areas that the academician and practitioner may want to explore further in creating a better criminal justice system as we enter the 21st Century.

Milestones and Relationship to Contextual Themes

Year of milestone	Title and author	Theme/ period
1887	"The Study of Administration" Woodrow Wilson	1
1890	*Politics and Administration* Frank J. Goodnow	1
1912	"Principles of Scientific Management" Frederick W. Taylor	1
1918	"The Movement for Budgetary Reform in the States" William F. Willoughby	1
1922	"Characteristics of Bureaucracy" Max Weber	1
1926	"The Giving of Orders" Mary Parker Follett	1, 2
1926	*Introduction to the Study of Public Administration* Leonard D. White	1
1936	"Public Administration and the Public Interest" E. Pendleton Herring	1
1937	*Papers on the Science of Administration* Luther Gulick and Lyndall Urwick	1
1937	"Report of the President's Committee on Administrative Management" Louis Brownlow, Charles E Merriam, and Luther Gulick	1
1938	*The Functions of the Executive* Chester I. Barnard	1, 2
1938	"Informal Organizations and Relation to Formal Organizations" Chester I. Barnard	1, 2
1939	*Reorganization of the National Government* Lewis Meriam	1, 2

(continues)

Year of milestone	Title and author	Theme/ period
1940	"Bureaucratic Structure and Personality" Robert K. Mertton	1, 2
1940	"The Lack of a Budgetary Theory" V. O. Key Jr.	1
1941	"The Hawthorne Experiments" F. J. Roethlisberger	2
1943	"A Theory of Human Motivation" A. H. Maslow	2
1944	"Planning and Planners" Lilienthal, David	1, 3
1945	*Big Democracy* Paul Appleby	2, 3
1945	*The Social Problems of an Industrial Civilization* Elton Mayo	2
1946	"The Proverbs of Administration" Herbert Simon	1, 2
1947	"The Science of Public Administration" Robert Dahl	1, 3
1947	*Hoover Commission Report* (first)	1
1949	"Power and Administration" Norton E. Long	1, 3
1949	"The Cooptative Mechanism" Philip Selznick	2, 3
1955	*Hover Commission Report* (second)	1, 3
1957	"The Individual and Organization" Chris Argyris	2
1957	"The Human Side of Enterprise" Douglas M. McGregor	2
1959	*The Motivation to Work* Frederick Herzberg	2
1964	*Integrating the Individual and the Organization* Chris Argyris	2
1966	"Organizations and the System Concept" Daniel Katz and Robert L. Kahn	3
1966	*The American System: A New View of Government in the United States* Morton Grodzins	3
1966	"The Road to PPB: The Stages of Budget Reform" Allen Schick	1
1967	"Organizations of the Future" Warren Bennis	3*
1967	*Inside Bureaucracy* Anthony Downs	3

Year of milestone	Title and author	Theme/ period
1967	*Organization in Action* James D. Thompson	3
1968	Public Administration in a Time Dwight Waldo	3, 4
1969	"Administrative Decentralization and Political Power" Herbert Kaufman	3, 4
1969	*The End of Liberalism* Theodore J. Lowi	3, 4
1971	"Toward a New Public Administration" H. George Frederickson	4
1971	"The Public Service in a Temporary Society" Frederick Mosher	4, 5
1971	"The Recovery of Relevance in the Study of Public Organization" Todd R. LaPorte	4
1972	"The Self-Evaluating Organization" Aaron Wildavsky	3, 4
1973	*Implementation* Jeffrey Pressman and Aaron Wildavsky	3, 5
1974	*The Intellectual Crisis in American Public Administration* Vincent Ostrom	4, 5
1977	*Public Administration: A Synthesis* Howard McCurdy	4, 5
1977	"The Zero-Base Approach to Government Budgeting" Peter Pyhrr	1, 4
1980	*Managing Public Systems: Analytic Techniques for Public Administration* Michael White, Ross Clayton, Robert Myrtle, and Gilbert Siegel	3*
1981	*The New Science of Organization* Alberto Ramos	4, 5*
1981	*An End to Hierarchy and Competition* Frederick Thayer	5*
1981	*Representative Bureaucracy and the American Political System* Samuel Krislov & David Rosenbloom	4, 5
1982	*In Search of Excellence* Thomas J. Peters and Robert H. Waterman	5
1983	*Understanding Intergovernmental Relations* Deil S. Wright	5*
1984	*Organizational Illusions* A. W. McEachern	5*
1986	*Organization Theory for Public Administration* Michael M. Harmon and Richard Mayer	5*

(continues)

Year of milestone	Title and author	Theme/ period
1987	*Moments of Truth* Jan Carlzon	5
1987	*Thriving on Chaos* Thomas J. Peters	5*
1989	*Public Administration: Understanding Management, Politics, and Law in the Public Sector* David Rosenbloom	5*
1989	*Organizational Behavior* David Cherrington	5*
1990	*Public Administration* Jeffrey Straussman	5*
1990	*Organizational Behavior and Performance* Andrew Szilagyi and Marc Wallace Jr.	5*
1991	*Preface to Public Administration: A Search for Themes and Direction* Richard Stillman	5*
1992	*Public Administration: Concepts and Cases* Richard J. Stillman II	5*
2001	*Good to Great* Jim Collins	5*
2002	"The Missing 'X-Factor's: Trust" Tom Peters	5*
2005	*Good to Great and the Social Sectors* Jim Collins	5*
2006	*Images of Organization* Gareth Morgan	5*
2007	*Leading at a Higher Level* Ken Blanchard	5*

*Eclectic perspective contributors

Small Police Department

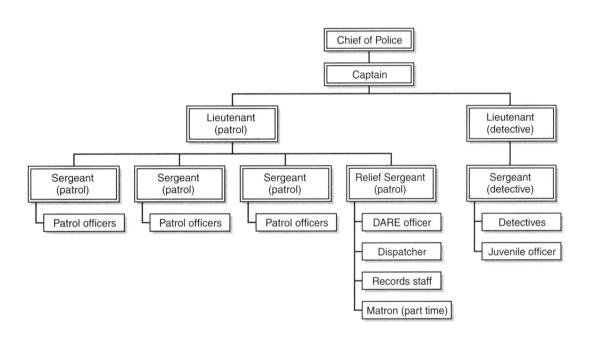

Yonkers Police Department Organization Chart

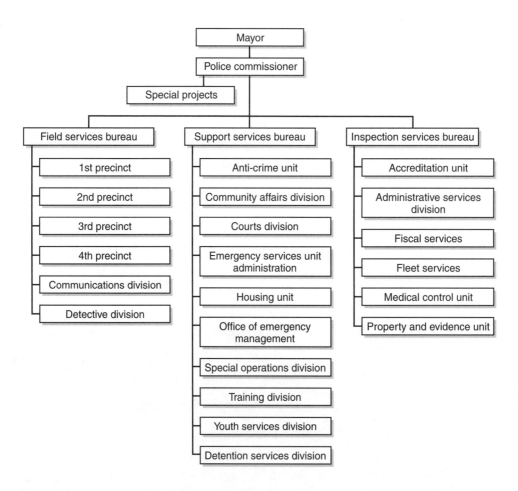

Mayor
Police commissioner
Special projects

Field services bureau
- 1st precinct
- 2nd precinct
- 3rd precinct
- 4th precinct
- Communications division
- Detective division

Support services bureau
- Anti-crime unit
- Community affairs division
- Courts division
- Emergency services unit administration
- Housing unit
- Office of emergency management
- Special operations division
- Training division
- Youth services division
- Detention services division

Inspection services bureau
- Accreditation unit
- Administrative services division
- Fiscal services
- Fleet services
- Medical control unit
- Property and evidence unit

Source: http://www.yonkerspd.com

Texas Department of Criminal Justice Organizational Structure

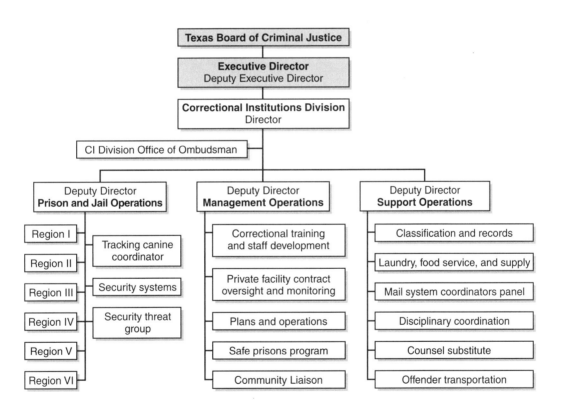

Source: http://www.tdcj.state.tx.us

Appendix 3A

California Police Officer Standards and Training (POST) Requirements

Minimum content and hourly requirements
Regular Basic Course (RBC)—standard format

Domain number	Domain description	Minimum hours
01	Leadership, professionalism, and ethics	8 hours
02	Criminal justice system	4 hours
03	Policing in the community	12 hours
04	Victimology/crisis intervention	6 hours
05	Introduction to criminal law	6 hours
06	Property crimes	10 hours
07	Crimes against persons	10 hours
08	General criminal statutes	4 hours
09	Crimes against children	6 hours
10	Sex crimes	6 hours
11	Juvenile law and procedure	6 hours
12	Controlled substances	12 hours
13	ABC law	4 hours
15	Laws of arrest	12 hours
16	Search and seizure	12 hours
17	Presentation of evidence	8 hours
18	Investigative report writing	40 hours
19	Vehicle operations	24 hours
20	Use of force	12 hours
21	Patrol techniques	12 hours
22	Vehicle pullovers	14 hours

Domain number	Domain description	Minimum hours
23	Crimes in progress	16 hours
24	Handling disputes/crowd control	12 hours
25	Domestic violence	8 hours
26	Unusual occurrences	4 hours
27	Missing persons	4 hours
28	Traffic enforcement	22 hours
29	Traffic accident investigation	12 hours
30	Preliminary investigation	42 hours
31	Custody	4 hours
32	Lifetime fitness	40 hours
33	Arrest methods/defensive tactics	60 hours
34	First aid and CPR	21 hours
35	Firearms/chemical agents	72 hours
36	Information systems	4 hours
37	People with disabilities	6 hours
38	Gang awareness	8 hours
39	Crimes against the justice system	4 hours
40	Weapons violations	4 hours
41	Hazardous materials awareness	4 hours
42	Cultural diversity/discrimination	24 hours
	Minimum instructional hours	599 hours

Source: http://www.post.ca.gov/training/workbooks-current.asp

Appendix 3B

Illinois Law Enforcement Training and Standards Board Basic Police Training Curriculum

Administrative units		400-Hours
Academy director's administrative time		2
Course orientation		2
Examinations		10
Critiques and instructional evaluation		5
Graduation		2
	Subtotal	21
Law		
Case preparation and courtroom testimony		4
Civil rights and civil liability		2
Criminal offenses in Illinois		14
Illinois vehicle code and bail rule		18
Juvenile law and processing		8
Laws of admission		2
Laws of arrest, search, and seizure		16
Rights of the accused		2
Rules of evidence		3
Use of force		4
	Subtotal	73
The police function and human behavior		
Child abuse		2
Communication in the police environment		8
Crisis intervention/disturbance calls		6

Administrative units		400-Hours
Crowd behavior		4
Dealing with variant behavior		4
Domestic violence		4
Gangs		2
Police citizen relations		6
Police ethics		4
	Subtotal	40

Patrol		
Crimes in progress		7
Crime prevention		1
Drug enforcement		4
Fundamentals of report writing		12
Homeland Security orientation		1
Patrol procedures		14
Vehicle stops and occupant control		12
	Subtotal	51

Patrol investigation		
Crimes against persons		5
Crimes against property		2
Crime scene identification		12
Custody arrest, booking, and detention facility procedures		2
Fingerprinting—rolled impressions		2
Fundamentals of investigation		6
Identification procedures		1
Interview and interrogation		4
Motor vehicle theft		4
Service calls		2
	Subtotal	40

Traffic		
Field sobriety testing		24
Hazardous material		8
Traffic crash investigation		16
Traffic direction		1
	Subtotal	49

Police proficiency		
Control and arrest tactics		32
Firearms: orientation and safety		2
Firearms: weapons care and maintenance		2

(continues)

Administrative units		400-Hours
Firearms: training		12
Firearms: night shooting		4
Firearms: shotgun		4
Firearms: record firing		4
Firearms: decision making and situational shooting		8
Initial medical response		18
Law enforcement driving		12
Physical skills and personal fitness		24
Tactical communications exercise		4
	Subtotal	126
Basic police training curriculum total hours		400
Integrated exercises (expanded curriculum only)		40
Course enrichment (expanded curriculum only)		40
Expanded curriculum total hours		480

Maine Criminal Justice Academy Basic Corrections Training Program

Unit of instruction	Hours
1.0.0 Introduction to corrections	
1.2.0 Roles of a corrections officer	1
1.3.0 The criminal justice system	2
1.4.0 History and philosophy of corrections	3
1.5.0 Ethics and values in corrections	2
2.0.0 Security in corrections	
2.1.0 Principles of security	2
2.2.0 Security in non-secure settings	3
3.0.0 Safety and emergencies in corrections	
3.1.0 Escape prevention and response	1
3.2.0 Principles of fire sources, explosives, and suppression	2
3.3.0 Principles of hostage incidents	2
3.4.0 Principles of disturbance control	1
4.0.0 Legal issues in corrections	
4.1.0 Constitutional law	3
4.2.0 Maine statutes	3
4.3.0 Correctional standards	1
5.0.0 Supervision and human relations in corrections	
5.1.0 Patterns of inmate behavior	6

Unit of instruction		Hours
5.2.0	Interpersonal behavior and skills	6
5.3.0	Supervision of inmates	4
5.4.0	Principles of inmate discipline	1
5.5.0	Sexuality in a correctional setting	2
6.0.0	**Special management inmates**	
6.1.0	Supervision of special needs inmates	3
6.2.0	Supervision of juvenile inmates	1
7.0.0	**Done in "A" or "B"**	
8.0.0	**Done in "A" or "B"**	
9.0.0	**Inmate classification**	
9.1.0	Principles of classification	1
10.0.0	**Administrative and operational skills**	
10.1.0	Basic medical situations	4
10.2.0	Unarmed self-defense	6
10.3.0	Report writing	4
10.4.0	Record keeping	1
10.5.0	Principles of decision making	2
10.6.0	Courtroom demeanor	1
10.7.0	Principles of investigations in corrections	2
10.8.0	Communications equipment and techniques	1
10.9.0	Training methods	2
10.10.0	Stress management	3
	Total	76
	Orientation, testing, graduation	4
	Total hours	80

Source: http://www.state.me.us/dps/mcja/training/basic_corr/curriculum.html

Example of Employee Evaluation Form

Seattle Police Department **Daily Observation Report Form**	Phase II DOR #:
	Date:
	Unit:
	Rotation:

Student's Name: Last, First, M.I.   Serial #   FIO's Name: Last, First, M.I.   Serial #

Rating Instructions: Rate observed behavior with reference to the Standardized Evaluation Guidelines and numerically score on scale below. Comment on any behavior you wish, but specific comments are required on ratings of "3" or less, and "6" and above. Check the "N.O." box if not observed. If the student fails to respond to training, then reference FTG 1.43.6 "NRT."

	Rating scale							N.O.	N.R.T.	T.T.
Appearance										
1. General Appearance	1	2	3	4	5	6	7			
Attitude										
2. Acceptance of feedback-FTO/Program	1	2	3	4	5	6	7			
3. Attitude toward police work	1	2	3	4	5	6	7			
Knowledge										
4. Knowledge of department policies and procedures reflected in field performance	1	2	3	4	5	6	7			
5. Knowledge of revised Code of Washington reflected in field performance	1	2	3	4	5	6	7			
6. Knowledge of Seattle Municipal Code reflected in field performance	1	2	3	4	5	6	7			
7. Knowledge of domestic violence (DVPA) laws and procedures reflected in field performance	1	2	3	4	5	6	7			
8. Knowledge of basic case law regarding detention, arrest, search, and seizure	1	2	3	4	5	6	7			

(continues)

	Rating scale							N.O.	N.R.T.	T.T.
Performance										
9. Driving skill: normal conditions	1	2	3	4	5	6	7			
10. Driving skill: moderate and high stress conditions	1	2	3	4	5	6	7			
11. Orientation/response time to calls	1	2	3	4	5	6	7			
12. Report writing: accuracy/organization	1	2	3	4	5	6	7			
13. Report writing: grammar/spelling/neatness	1	2	3	4	5	6	7			
14. Report writing: appropriate time/appropriate form used	1	2	3	4	5	6	7			
15. Field performance: stress conditions	1	2	3	4	5	6	7			
16. Investigation skill	1	2	3	4	5	6	7			
17. Interview/interrogation skill	1	2	3	4	5	6	7			
18. Self-initiated field activity	1	2	3	4	5	6	7			
19. Officer safety: general	1	2	3	4	5	6	7			
20. Officer safety: suspects/suspicious persons/prisoners	1	2	3	4	5	6	7			
21. Control of incident/persons: verbal skills	1	2	3	4	5	6	7			
22. Control of incident/persons: physical skills	1	2	3	4	5	6	7			
23. Problem solving/decision making	1	2	3	4	5	6	7			
24. Radio: appropriate use of codes/procedures	1	2	3	4	5	6	7			
25. Radio: listens/comprehends/transmissions	1	2	3	4	5	6	7			
26. Computer: appropriate use/sends and receives messages/accesses information	1	2	3	4	5	6	7			
Relationships										
27. With other department members/supervisors	1	2	3	4	5	6	7			
28. With citizens in general	1	2	3	4	5	6	7			
29. With groups of orientation other than own	1	2	3	4	5	6	7			
30. With suspects, complainants, witnesses or victims	1	2	3	4	5	6	7			

Minutes of Remedial Training Time (Explain Training and Students Understanding.)

Mesa Police Department—Field Training Officer Program

Daily Observation Report (DOR)

A Daily Observation Report (DOR) is completed on the Officer in Training (OIT) by the Field Training Officer (FTO) after the end of each shift. Good performances as well as poor performances are documented each day. OITs use this daily documentation to improve their skills on a daily basis. FTO Administration Officers review all of the DORs to stay abreast of the progress of the OITs. The DOR is reviewed and signed by the OIT, the FTO, and the FTO Sergeant and then filed in the OIT's Workstation File.

Mesa Police Department Field Training Program Daily Observation Report No. _____ Phase

OIT's Last Name, First Initial, Emp#: _____ Date: /
FTO's Last Name, First Initial, Emp#: _____

Rating Instructions: Rate observed behavior using the scale below. Comment on the satisfactory performances of the day. Comment on any behavior you wish, but a specific comment is required for rating "NO" if not observed. If trainee fails to respond to training, circle "NRT" and comment.

1, 2, & 3 are below SOLO officer standards
4 is performance at an acceptable level
5, 6, & 7 are superior by FTO program standards

List any Remedial Training Time to the right of the category.

Reason for no evaluation (sick, working another detail, etc.)

Appearance										
1.	1	2	3	4	5	6	7	NO	NRT	1. General appearance
Attitude										
2.	1	2	3	4	5	6	7	NO	NRT	2. Acceptance of feedback FTO/FTO program
3.	1	2	3	4	5	6	7	NO	NRT	3. Attitude toward the job
Knowledge—Reflected in field performance										
4.	1	2	3	4	5	6	7	NO	NRT	4. Dept. policies/procedures
5.	1	2	3	4	5	6	7	NO	NRT	5. Criminal, traffic, & city statutes
6.	1	2	3	4	5	6	7	NO	NRT	6. Codes of criminal procedure
Performance										
7.	1	2	3	4	5	6	7	NO	NRT	7. Driving skill: normal & stress conditions
8.	1	2	3	4	5	6	7	NO	NRT	8. Orientation/response time to calls
9.	1	2	3	4	5	6	7	NO	NRT	9. Routine forms: accuracy/completeness
10.	1	2	3	4	5	6	7	NO	NRT	10. Report writing: organization/details
11.	1	2	3	4	5	6	7	NO	NRT	11. Report writing: grammar/spelling/neat
12.	1	2	3	4	5	6	7	NO	NRT	12. Report writing: appropriate time used
13.	1	2	3	4	5	6	7	NO	NRT	13. Field performance
14.	1	2	3	4	5	6	7	NO	NRT	14. Investigative skill
15.	1	2	3	4	5	6	7	NO	NRT	15. Interview/interrogation skill
16.	1	2	3	4	5	6	7	NO	NRT	16. Self-initiated field activity
17.	1	2	3	4	5	6	7	NO	NRI	17. Officer safety
18.	1	2	3	4	5	6	7	NO	NRT	18. Control of conflict: voice command

(continues)

Performance (*cont.*)										
19.	1	2	3	4	5	6	7	NO	NRT	19. Control of conflict: physical control
20.	1	2	3	4	5	6	7	NO	NRT	20. Decision making
21.	1	2	3	4	5	6	7	NO	NRT	21. Radio: appropriate use codes/procedures/listens/ comprehension
22.	1	2	3	4	5	6	7	NO	NRT	22. DXT: appropriate use and performance
Community Policing Categories										
23.	1	2	3	4	5	6	7	NO	NRT	23. Community policing/problem solving
24.	1	2	3	4	5	6	7	NO	NRT	24. Courtesy/relationships

Total Minutes of Remedial Training Time Today (Note Specific Remedial Plans on page 2) _____

Daily Written Documentation to Support Field Trainer's Observations of the Day:

Remember to:

1. Set the stage/scene
2. Consider verbatim quotes
3. Critique performance
4. Use lists as appropriate
5. Report facts, avoid conclusions
6. Check spelling, grammar, etc.
7. Think remedial
8. Consider your audience
9. Do not predict

Source: Mesa Police Department, http://www.cityofmesa.org/police/fto

The Management Principles of the Los Angeles Police Department

Here are the *Management Principles of the Los Angeles Police Department*. These principles form the basis of policy and guide the organization's effort:

Principle I: Reverence for the Law: The main thrust of a peace officer's duties consists of an attempt to enforce the law. In our application of the law we must do it within the legal spirit so clearly set forth by the framers of the Bill of Rights which was an original part of our Constitution. That bill has as its purpose elevating the rights of each citizen to a position co-equal with the state which might accuse him. Its purpose is to provide for an enforcement of the law with fundamental fairness and equity. Because of the Bill of Rights, the dignity of the individual person in America was placed in an almost sacred position of importance.

A peace officer's enforcement should not be done in grudging adherence to the legal rights of the accused, but in sincere spirit of seeing that every accused person is given all of his rights as far as it is within the powers of the police.

In the discharge of our enforcement of criminal statutes, the peace officer must scrupulously avoid any conduct which would make him a violator of the law. The solution of a crime, or the arrest of a lawbreaker, can never justify the peace officer's committing a felony as an expedient for the enforcement of the law.

We peace officers should do our utmost to foster a reverence for the law. We can start best by displaying a reverence for the legal rights of our fellow citizens and a reverence for the law itself.

Principle II: Crime Prevention Top Priority: The basic mission for which the police exist is to prevent crime and disorder as an alternative to repression by military force and severity of legal punishment. When the police fail to prevent crime, it becomes important to apprehend the person responsible for the crime and gather all evidence that might be used in a subsequent trial.

Principle III: Public Approbation of Police: The ability of the police to perform their duties is dependent upon public approval of police existence, actions, behavior, and the ability of the police to secure and maintain public respect.

Principle IV: Voluntary Law Observance: The police must secure the willing cooperation of the public in voluntary observance of the law in order to be able to secure and maintain the respect and approval of the public.

Principle V: Public Cooperation: The degree of public cooperation that can be secured diminishes, proportionately, the necessity for the use of physical force and compulsion in achieving police objectives.

Principle VI: Impartial Friendly Enforcement: The police seek and preserve public favor, not by catering to public opinion, but by constantly demonstrating absolutely impartial service to the law without regard to the justice or injustice of the substance of individual laws; by readily offering individual service and friendship to all members of society without regard to their race or social standing; by the ready exercise of courtesy and friendly good humor; and by readily offering individual sacrifice in protecting and preserving life.

Principle VII: Minimum Use of Force: The police should use physical force to the extent necessary to secure observance of the law or to restore order only when the exercise of persuasion, advice, and warning is found to be insufficient to achieve police objectives; and police should use only the reasonable amount of physical force which is necessary on any particular occasion for achieving a police objective.

Principle VIII: Public Is the Police: The police at all times should maintain a relationship with the public that gives reality to the historic tradition that the police are the public and that the public is the police; the police are the only members of the public who are paid to give full-time attention to duties which are incumbent on every citizen in the interest of community welfare.

Principle IX: Limit of Police Power: The police should always direct their actions strictly toward their functions and never appear to usurp the powers of the judiciary by avenging individuals or the state, or authoritatively judging guilt or punishing the guilty.

Principle X: Test of Police Effectiveness: The test of police effectiveness is the absence of crime and the presence of public order. It is not the evidence of police action in dealing with crime and disorder.

Principle XI: People Working with Police: The task of crime prevention cannot be accomplished by the police alone. This task necessarily requires the willing cooperation of both the police and the public, working together toward a common goal.

Principle XII: People Working with People: Since the police cannot be expected to be on every residential or business block every hour of the day, a process must be developed whereby each person becomes concerned with the welfare and safety of his neighborhood. When people are working with other people in their neighborhood, they can effectively reduce crime.

Principle XIII: Managers Working with Police: Only line police officers perform the tasks for which police were created. They are the operating professionals. Supervisors and managers exist to define problems, to establish objectives, and to assist line police officers in the accomplishment of the police mission.

The evaluation of a manager should be based on the improvement and excellence of his subordinates in the achievement of organizational goals. The life blood of good management is thoroughly systematic, two-way circulation of information, feelings, and perceptions throughout the organization.

Principle XIV: Police Working with Police: For many reasons, some specialization of work is necessary. Specialization should be created only when vitally necessary. When specialization is created, organization should be adjusted to ensure that the specialists and generalists who serve the same citizens work closely together on the common problems in as informal an organizational structure as possible. This will tend to ensure a unity of effort, resources, and the effective service to a common goal.

Principle XV: Police Working with Criminal Justice System: It must be recognized that the police and the people alone cannot successfully resolve the problems of crime. The criminal justice system as a whole, in order to properly serve the public, must operate as a total system with all of its various elements working together. The close cooperation of the police with prosecutors, courts, and correctional officers is necessary in order to ensure the development of a safer community.

Principle XVI: Police/Press Relationships: One of the first and most fundamental considerations of this nation's founders in drafting the Bill of Rights was to provide for a free press as an essential element of the First Amendment to the Constitution. They recognized that a well-informed citizenry is vital to the effective functioning of a democracy. Police operations profoundly affect the public and therefore arouse substantial public interest. Likewise, public interest and public cooperation bear significantly on the successful accomplishment of any police mission. The police should make every reasonable effort to serve the needs of the media in informing the public about crime and other police problems. This should be done with an attitude of openness and frankness whenever possible. The media should have access at the lowest level in a department, to personnel who are fully informed about the subject of a press inquiry. The media should be told all that can be told that will not impinge on a person's right to a fair trial, seriously impede a criminal investigation, imperil a human life, or seriously endanger the security of the people. In such cases, the minimum information should be given which will not impinge on the four areas and we should merely state that nothing more can be said.

In all other matters in our relationship with the media dealing with current news, every member of the department should make every reasonable effort consistent with accomplishing the police task in providing the media representatives with full and accurate material.

Principle XVII: Management by Objectives: In order to effectively deal with the most important problems, objectives must be established. The establishment of objectives and the means used to ensure that they are reached must include the participation of those involved in the task. The setting of an objective has very little meaning without the participation of those involved.

Principle XVIII: Management by Participation: Since employees are greatly influenced by decisions that are made and objectives that are established, it is important for them to be able to provide input into the methods utilized to reach these decisions. Employees should be encouraged to make recommendations which might lead to an improvement in the delivery of police services and assist in the furtherance of the department's meeting its objective.

Principle XIX: Territorial Imperative: Police work is one of the most personal of all personal services. It deals with human beings in life-and-death situations. The police officers and the people they serve must be as close as possible, and where possible must know one another. Such closeness can generate the police-citizen cooperation necessary for the involvement of the whole community in community protection. Organization of assignments should ensure that the same police and the same citizens have an opportunity to continuously work for the protection of a specific community. Strength through interacting together and working together on common problems can be enhanced through officers and the people feeling at home with one another in an atmosphere of mutual cooperation. This may be described as a utilization of the territorial imperative.

Principle XX: Openness and Honesty: For police-public cooperation, there must be respect of the police by the public. This is best ensured by optimum openness of the department in its operations. A general feeling and reality of openness must pervade the police organization. Above all, the police officer must be consistently open, honest, and trustful in all matters. A combination of honesty and openness will effectively develop respect in the community for the police and make it possible for citizens to come to them with problems and information. Where this trust does not exist because of a lack of honesty or openness, the channels of communication between the police and the public are clogged and the police must desperately struggle on alone.

Survey of the Residents

Quality of Life

Q1. On the whole, how do you feel about this development as a place to live on a scale from 1 to 10?

1   2   3   4   5   6   7   8   9   10

very dissatisfied ⟵――――⟶ very satisfied

Q2. Would you recommend this development to any of your friends if they were looking for a place to live?

- Yes
- Maybe
- No
- Don't know

Q3. How willing are people living here to get involved in community programs to improve the neighborhood?

- Very willing
- Somewhat willing
- Somewhat unwilling
- Very unwilling
- Don't know

Q4. In general, in the past year would you say this development has become a better place to live, gotten worse, or stayed about the same?

- Better
- Worse
- About the same
- Don't know

Q5. What do you think this development will be like a year from now? Will it be a better place to live, gotten worse, or stayed about the same?

- Better
- Worse
- About the same
- Don't know

Crime in General

Q6. How safe do you feel in this neighborhood on a scale of 1 to 10?

1   2   3   4   5   6   7   8   9   10

very unsafe ⟵⟶ very safe

Q7a. Overall, what would you say is the **most serious** crime problem in your neighborhood?

- Burglary or break-ins
- Robbery or mugging
- Drugs
- Vandalism/graffiti
- Gang violence
- Car thefts
- Breaking into cars
- Other
- Don't know
- Refused to answer

Q7b. Overall, what would you say is the **second most serious** crime problem in your neighborhood?

- Burglary or break-ins
- Robbery or mugging
- Drugs
- Vandalism/Graffiti
- Gang violence
- Car thefts
- Breaking into cars
- Other
- Don't know
- Refused to answer

Q7c. Overall what would you say is the **third most serious** crime problem in your neighborhood?

- Burglary or break-ins
- Robbery or mugging
- Drugs
- Vandalism/Graffiti
- Gang violence

- Car thefts
- Breaking into cars
- Other
- Don't know
- Refused to answer

Q8. Who do the people in the neighborhood feel is committing most of the crime?

- Residents of Nueva Maravilla
- Non-residents
- Don't know
- Refused to answer

Exposure to Crime

Q9. This past year, has anyone damaged or defaced the building where you live in this community, for example, by writing on walls, breaking windows, setting fires or anything like that?

- No
- Yes—How many times did this happen? _____
- Don't know
- Refused to answer

Q10. This past year, has anyone broken into or somehow illegally gotten into your home?

- No
- Yes—How many times did this happen? _____
- Don't know
- Refused to answer

Q11. This past year, has anyone stolen anything from you or someone in your household in your neighborhood? Something like a bicycle, clothing, tools, money, a purse or wallet?

- No
- Yes—How many times did this happen? _____
- Don't know
- Refused to answer

Q12. This past year in your neighborhood, has anyone taken money or other belongings from you or from other members of your household by force? For example, did someone use a gun or knife, or in any other way force one of you to give them something that did not belong to them?

- No
- Yes—How many times did this happen? _____
- Don't know
- Refused to answer

Q13. This past year, has anyone used violence against you or a member of your household in an argument or quarrel, or in any other way attacked or assaulted one of you in your neighborhood?

- No
- Yes—How many times did this happen? _____
- Don't know
- Refused to answer

Q14. This past year, in your neighborhood, has anyone tried to sell you or members of your family drugs?

- No
- Yes—How many times did this happen? _____
- Don't know
- Refused to answer

Q15. This past year, in your neighborhood, have you been a victim of gang violence?

- No
- Yes—How many times did this happen? _____
- Don't know
- Refused to answer

Q16. This past year, in your neighborhood, has your car been broken into or stolen?

- No
- Yes—How many times did this happen? _____
- Don't know
- Refused to answer

Q17. This past year, in your neighborhood, have individuals loitered or trespassed on your property?

- No
- Yes—How many times did this happen? _____
- Don't know
- Refused to answer

Q18. This past year, in your neighborhood, have you observed CDC property stolen.

- No
- Yes—How many times did this happen? _____
- Don't know
- Refused to answer

Source: Conducted by Clyde Cronkhite. Used by The Los Angeles County Housing Authority, 1990–1992.

Example COP Employee Evaluation

Goals and Objectives From the Last Appraisal

Refer to the last appraisal for this employee. List each goal that had been set and indicate whether you achieved, failed to reach, or exceeded that goal. Explain any situations or conditions that may have affected attainment. Disregard if this is the first appraisal for this employee.

Goal 1:

Goal 2:

Goal 3:

Goal 4:

Goal 5:

Goal 6:

Goal 7:

Goal 8:

Recommendation

No action   Step increase   Pay for performance

Score	Percent increase
700–749	0.50%
750–799	1.00%
800–849	1.50%
850–899	2.00%
900–949	2.50%
950+	3.00%

Current score: 0

Employee's Current Annual Pay
Current Maximum Pay for Employees
Classification

Comments:

Source: Permission to reprint from the Rock Island Police Department, Illinois.

Appendix

8

American Correctional Association Code of Ethics

Preamble

The American Correctional Association expects of its members unfailing honesty, respect for the dignity and individuality of human beings and a commitment to professional and compassionate service. To this end, we subscribe to the following principles.

Members shall respect and protect the civil and legal rights of all individuals. Members shall treat every professional situation with concern for the welfare of the individuals involved and with no intent to personal gain.

Members shall maintain relationships with colleagues to promote mutual respect within the profession and improve the quality of service.

Members shall make public criticism of their colleagues or their agencies only when warranted, verifiable, and constructive.

Members shall respect the importance of all disciplines within the criminal justice system and work to improve cooperation with each segment.

Members shall honor the public's right to information and share information with the public to the extent permitted by law subject to individual's right to privacy.

Members shall respect and protect the right of the public to be safeguarded from criminal activity.

Members shall refrain from using their positions to secure personal privileges or advantages.

Members shall refrain from allowing personal interest to impair objectivity in the performance of duty while acting in an official capacity.

Members shall refrain from entering into any formal or informal activity or agreement which presents a conflict of interest or is inconsistent with the conscientious performance of duties.

Members shall refrain from accepting any gifts, service, or favor that is or appears to be improper or implies an obligation inconsistent with the free and objective exercise of professional duties.

Members shall clearly differentiate between personal views/statements and views/statements/positions made on behalf of the agency or Association.

Members shall report to appropriate authorities any corrupt or unethical behaviors in which there is sufficient evidence to justify review.

Members shall refrain from discriminating against any individual because of race, gender, creed, national origin, religious affiliation, age, disability, or any other type of prohibited discrimination.

Members shall preserve the integrity of private information; they shall refrain from seeking information on individuals beyond that which is necessary to implement responsibilities and perform their duties; members shall refrain from revealing non public information unless expressly authorized to do so.

Members shall make all appointments, promotions, and dismissals in accordance with established civil service rules, applicable contract agreements, and individual merit, rather than furtherance of personal interests.

Members shall respect, promote, and contribute to a work place that is safe, healthy, and free of harassment in any form.

Source: Adopted August 1975 at the 105th Congress of Correction. Revised August 1990 at the 120th Congress of Correction. Revised August 1994 at the 124th Congress of Correction.

Profile of the Ethical Person

Delight in bringing about justice.

Delight in stopping cruelty and exploitation.

Fighting lies and untruths.

They love virtue to be rewarded.

They seem to like happy endings, good completions.

They hate sin and evil to be rewarded, and they hate people to get away with it.

They are good punishers of evil.

They try to set things right, to clean up bad situations.

They enjoy doing good.

They like to reward and praise promise, talent, virtue, etc.

They avoid publicity, fame, glory, honors, popularity, celebrity, or at least do not seek it. It seems to be not awfully important one way or another.

They do not need to be loved by everyone.

They generally pick out their own causes, which are apt to be few in number, rather than responding to advertising or to campaigns or to other people's exhortations.

They tend to enjoy peace, quiet, pleasantness, etc., and they tend not to like turmoil, fighting, war, etc. (they are not general fighters on every front), and they can enjoy themselves in the middle of a "war."

They also seem practical and shrewd and realistic about it, more often than impractical. They like to be effective and dislike being ineffectual.

Their fighting is not an excuse for hostility, paranoia, grandiosity, authority, rebellion, etc., but is for the sake of setting things right. It is problem-centered.

They manage somehow simultaneously to love the world as it is and to try to improve it.

In all cases there is some hope that people and nature and society can be improved.

In all cases it is as if they can see both good and evil realistically.

They respond to the challenge in a job.

A chance to improve the situation or the operation is a big reward. They enjoy improving things.

Observations generally indicate great pleasure in their children and in helping them grow into good adults.

They do not need or seek, or even enjoy very much, flattery, applause, popularity, status, prestige, money, honors, etc.

Expressions of gratitude, or at least of awareness of their good fortune, are common.

They have a sense of noblesse oblige. It is the duty of the superior, of the one who sees and knows, to be patient and tolerant, as with children.

They tend to be attracted by mystery, unsolved problems, by the unknown and the challenging, rather than to be frightened by them.

They enjoy bringing about law and order in the chaotic situation, or for the messy or confused situation, or in the dirty and unclean situation.

They hate (and fight) corruption, cruelty, malice, dishonesty, pompousness, phoniness, and faking.

They try to free themselves from illusions, to look at the facts courageously, to take away the blindfold.

They feel it is a pity for talent to be wasted.

They do not do mean things, and they respond with anger when other people do mean things.

They tend to feel that every person should have an opportunity to develop to his highest potential, to have a fair chance, to have equal opportunity.

They like doing things well, "doing a good job," "to do well what needs doing." Many such phrases add up to "bringing about good workmanship." One advantage of being a boss is the right to give away the corporation's money, to choose which good causes to help. They enjoy giving their own money away to causes they consider important, good, worthwhile, etc. [They take] pleasure in philanthropy.

They enjoy watching and helping the self-actualization of others, especially of the young.

They enjoy watching happiness and helping to bring it about.

They get great pleasure from knowing admirable people (courageous, honest, effective, "straight," "big," creative, saintly, etc.). "My work brings me in contact with many fine people."

They enjoy taking on responsibilities (that they can handle well), and certainly don't fear or evade their responsibilities. They respond to responsibility.

They uniformly consider their work to be worthwhile, important, even essential.

They enjoy greater efficiency, making an operation more neat, compact, simpler, faster, less expensive, turning out a better product, doing with less parts, a smaller number of operations, less clumsiness, less effort, more foolproof, safer, more "elegant," less laborious.

Source: Malsow, A. H. (1971). "Metamotivation [Table 1]." *The Farther Reaches of Human Nature.* New York: Viking Penguin. Used by permission of Viking Penguin, a division of Penguin Books USA, Inc.

Examples of Policy Statement Topics

Personal conduct

Employee conduct
Management/employee relations
When to take police action
Employee-public contact
Employee conflict of interest
Relationships between department employees

Community relations

General provisions
Individual dignity
Role of the individual officer
Equality of enforcement
Responsiveness to the community
Openness of operation
Interpersonal communication
Training in human and community relations

Community affairs

News media relations
Public information
Labor relations
Liaison with criminal justice system
Consular and diplomatic relations

Law enforcement operations

The nature of the task
Police action based on legal justification
Alternatives to physical arrest, booking, or continued detention
Called-for services
Preliminary investigation
Reporting incidents motivated by hatred or prejudice
Civil disputes
Field supervision
Command responsibility at police situations
Crime scene supervision
Follow-up investigation
Informants
Conduct of undercover officers
Undercover officers posing as members of the news media
Department response to impending riot
Police action on school campuses
Police contacts with the clergy
Use of firearms
Hostages
Officers surrendering weapon
Barricaded suspects
Use of chemical agents
Use of nonlethal control devices
Deployment in anticipation of the commission of a crime
Uniformed personnel at planned arrest and search warrant service
    operations
Traffic enforcement
Vice enforcement
Narcotic enforcement

Source: Printed with permission of the Los Angeles Police Department.

Compendium of Criminal Justice Themes and Related Key Concepts

Academics and practitioners have voiced concerns that there is a need to bring together the many theories and concepts of administration into a structure that facilitates learning and application. This text introduced the Contextual Themes Model of criminal justice administration as such a structure. The Contextual Themes Model is meant to provide a structure in which the important administration themes, theories, and concepts are assembled for current and future application. In this Compendium, the key concepts, extrapolated from this text, have been assembled as reminders for criminal justice students, practitioners, and academicians of the variety of theoretical tools that can be applied to contemporary issues.

In the August 2006 issue of *Scientific American*, Philip E. Ross described how experts in various fields assimilate major amounts of data. The article documents that people can contemplate only five to nine items at a time. However, by "packing hierarchies of information into *chunks*, they get around this limitation." This concept is called the "chunk theory." By remembering concepts through key terms that can be placed into five to nine categories, large amounts of information can be mentally retained (Ross, 2006, pp. 64–70). This is the way models such as Maslow's Human Needs Hierarchy and McGregor's Theory X and Theory Y categories (discussed in Chapter 8) bring to mind a variety of concepts. The Contextual Themes Model uses this concept.

The concepts and terms, which should serve as reminders of concepts discussed throughout the text, are categorized under related historical contextual themes. After completing the text, the reader should be able to recall the details of the various concepts using the key terms as reminders. For example, the student may be asked to write about what concepts an administrator should consider implementing into criminal justice agencies or entity within an agency. The student can approach the assignment by going over each of the contextual themes and deciding what concepts within each theme should be considered and why.

The criminal justice administrator should be able to use this approach to review the many administrative concepts that are available for consideration. Then, through an Eclectic Perspective, he or she should be able to "mix and match" appropriate concepts to contemporary challenges. If the reader is unclear about any term or concept, they should consult the index for pages to review.

Organization Functions

- **Major milestone publications and related terms**
  - POSDCORB
    1937, "Notes on the Organization," Luther Gulick
  - Principles of bureaucratic organizations
    1922, "Characteristics of Bureaucracy," Max Weber
  - Scientifically find the best way to do the job
    1912, "Principles of Scientific Management," Frederick Taylor
  - Public service is the business end of government
    1887, "The Study of Administration," Woodrow Wilson
- **Basic terms and concepts**
  - POSDCORB (planning, organizing, staffing, directing, coordination, reporting, budgeting)
  - Line-item, capital, PPBS, and zero-based budgeting
  - Principles of organization
    - Authority and responsibility
    - Unity of command
    - Scalar chain
    - Control (inspection and control, span of control)
    - Division of labor
      ~ Vertical
        > Executive officers
        > Middle managers
        > First-line supervisors
      ~ Horizontal
        > Operations
        > Auxiliary/service
        > Administrative/staff
- **Contemporary terms and issues**
  - Mechanistic (Tall) vs. Organic (Flat) systems
  - Matrix Community-Oriented Policing (MiCOP) organization structure
  - Recent Eclectic Perspective approaches that make bureaucratic organizations more flexible

Employee Relations

- **Major milestone publications and related concepts**
  - Maintenance vs. satisfying factors
    1959, "Motivation to Work," Frederick Herzberg
  - Organizations need to be altered to fit individual needs.
    1957, "The Individual & Organization," Chris Argyris

- Theory X and Theory Y
  1957, "The Human Side of Enterprise," Douglas McGregor
- Hierarchy of Human Needs
  1943, "A Theory of Human Motivation," A. H. Maslow
- Guides, not principles
  1941, "The Proverbs of Public Administration," Herbert Simon
- Motivating employees increases productivity
  1941, "The Hawthorne Experiments," Elton Mayo
- **Basic terms and concepts**
  - Hiring
    - Recruiting and selecting
    - Training
    - Employee evaluations
  - Supervision
    - Define
    - Duties
    - Responsibility of all administrators
  - Motivation
    - "Big Y, little x" Theory
    - Greatest Management Principle (GMP)
    - Expectancy theory
    - Z theory
  - Discipline
    - Positive vs. negative
    - Investigating
    - Penalties
    - Employee Bill of Rights
  - Stress
    - Good vs. bad
    - Causes
    - Remedies
    - Suicides
- **Contemporary terms and issues**
  - Leadership
    - Define
  - Historical Perspective
    - Weber's concepts
    - Maslow's concepts
    - Vroom's concepts
  - Sources of power
  - Charismatic leadership, pros and cons
  - Assessing leadership vs. management
    - Managerial grid
    - DISC assessment

- Leadership traits
  - Basic traits
  - Emotional intelligence traits
    - ~ Empathy
    - ~ Listening
  - Digital nervous system traits
  - Chaos traits
- CEO concept of leadership
  - Three pillars of support
  - "Second-Hand" leaders
- Change Agent Leadership
  - Internal vs. internal agents
- Contemporary approaches
  - Winning minds and hearts
  - Shared leadership
  - Level 5 leadership
    - ~ Modesty, self-effacing, and understated
    - ~ Attribute success to factors other than themselves
    - ~ Hedgehog concept
    - ~ Flywheel effect
    - ~ SERVE concepts
- Professional ethics
  - Trusted and noble responsibilities
  - Principles of public ethics
  - What is a *profession* or a *professional*?
  - Professions require standards
    - ~ State required standards
    - ~ Accreditation
    - ~ Oaths of office
    - ~ Codes of conduct
  - Higher education
    - ~ Reasons it should be required
    - ~ Reasons it is not required for police and corrections
  - Understanding ethics
    - ~ Defined
    - ~ Difference between ethics and morals
    - ~ Types of ethics
      - > Nominative
      - > Applied
      - > Professional
- Components of Social Ethics
  - Social justice
  - Corrective (criminal) justice
  - Civil justice
  - Professional ethics
  - Values
  - Morals

- Guides for promoting ethical behavior
  - Five steps
  - ACT
  - Bell, Book, Candle
  - Authority—responsibility concept
    - ~ Inspection and control
    - ~ Tracking potential unethical behavior
    - ~ Policies, procedures, and rules statements
    - ~ Value-based management
    - ~ Ethics training to combat
    - ~ Cynicism
    - ~ Code of silence
    - ~ Compassion as an element of Client-Oriented Services
    - ~ Professional organization structure
    - ~ Personal creed

Open Systems

- **Major milestone publications and related concepts**
  - Bureaucracy is outdated (or is it?)
    1967, "Organizations of the Future," Warren Bennis
  - Refocusing on Organization Functions in time of economic cut-backs
    1966, "The Road to PPB: The Stages of Budget Reform," Allen Schick
  - The need for Open Systems organizations
    1966, The Social Psychology of Organizations, Daniel Katz & Robert Kahn
- **Basic terms and concepts**
  - Homeostasis
  - Negative entropy
  - Requisite variety
  - Equifinality
  - System evolution
- **Contemporary terms and issues**
  - Total Quality Management (TQM)
  - Deming's Fourteen Points for the transformation of management
  - Consensus Model vs. Conflict Process Model
  - Crime-Control Model vs. Due Process Model
  - Crime prevention as an Open Systems approach
    - Use of the media
    - Preventing victims
    - Use of volunteer citizens
    - Local legislation and review of building permits
    - Triangle of crime
  - Other Open Systems approaches
    - Coordination with private police
    - Reducing youth crime
    - Biochemistry, nutrition, and genetic factors in reducing crime
    - Coordinating community efforts

- Global prospective
  - Americans differ from other countries (drug example)
  - Learning from other countries
- Decreasing crime trend factors
  - Poverty
  - Incarceration
  - Community policing
  - Other possible factors
    ~ Reduced reporting
    ~ Shrinking youthful population
    ~ Stricter gun laws
    ~ Legalization of abortions

Social Equity

- **Major milestone publications and related concepts**
  - Refocusing on Organization Functions in times of economic cut-backs
    1977, "The Zero-Based Approach to Government Budgeting," Peter Pyhrr
  - Public sectors responsibility for individual rights
    1971, "Toward a New Public Administration: The Minnowbrook Perspective," H. George Frederickson
- **Basic terms and concepts**
  - Difference from private sector (cost factor)
  - Became part of the oath in the 1970s
  - Constitutional guarantees part of mission
  - Republic form of government
    - Majority rule
    - Rule of law
  - Responsibility to preserve balance
    - Needed to be sensitive to public attitude shifts
  - "Us vs. Them" mentality
  - Liable for violations of rights
  - Federal government oversight powers
  - Homeland Security protecting individual rights
  - Bias in the criminal justice system
  - Racial profiling
  - Problems from underrepresentation of minorities as criminal justice employees
- **Contemporary terms and issues**
  - "Salad Bowl" vs. "Melting Pot" concepts
  - Major cities remain segregated today
  - Subordinate (minority) groups
    - Racial
    - Ethic
    - Religious
    - Gender

- Understanding
  - Racism
  - Prejudice
  - Discrimination
- Types of Discrimination
  - Relative vs. absolute
  - Total
  - Institutional
  - Economical
- Administrative responsibility to protect diversity
  - Establishing community trust
  - Parity in hiring
  - Educating and training of employees
  - Understanding and supporting diversity regarding employees
  - Educating of minority communities
  - Related court and corrections practices

Client-Oriented Services

- **Major milestone publications and related concepts**
  - Importance of employee-customer contacts
    1987, *Moments of Truth*, Jan Carlzon
  - Focus on Customer Service
    1983, *In Search of Excellence*, Thomas Peters and Robert Waterman
- **Basic terms and concepts**
  - Police
    - Community-relation and press programs
      ~ Need public trust
      ~ Enhancing law enforcement image
    - Team policing
      ~ Total decentralization
      ~ Neighborhood watch
    - Client-Oriented Policing (COP)
      ~ Return to the Peel Principles
      ~ Kansas City study
      ~ Broken Windows Theory
      ~ Fear of crime
    - Problem-Oriented Policing (POP)
      ~ SARA
    - Community Policing
      ~ Combining COP and POP
    - Police Accountability to Community (PAC) policing
      ~ Diminishing police-public partnership
      ~ CompStat
      ~ Matrix Community Oriented Policing (MiCOP)
      ~ Impact of Homeland Security

- Courts and corrections
  - Community prosecution approach
  - Community-based corrections
  - Broken Window probation approach
- **Contemporary terms and issues**
  - Administrative challenges
  - Organic organizational structures
  - Problems with fixed geographic assignments
  - Additional person needs
  - Impact of Homeland Security and rising crime
  - Measuring the effectiveness
  - Management by Objectives (MBO)
  - Seven performance dimensions

Eclectic Perspective

- **Major milestone publications and related concepts**
  - SERVE concepts
    2007, *Leading at Higher Levels*, Ken Blanchard
  - Enhanced bureaucracy to allow more flexibility
    2006, *Images of Organization*, Garth Morgan
  - Application of the five "great" leadership approaches in the public sector
    2006, *Good to Great and the Social Sector*, Jim Collins
  - Five successful leadership approaches that make companies "great"
    2001, *Good to Great*, Jim Collins
  - Use of "Digital Nervous System"
    1999, *Business of Thought*, Bill Gates
- **Basic terms and concepts**
  - Administration approaches
    - Involves both leadership and management
    - Involves establishing
      ~ Missions, goals, and objectives
      ~ Efficiency and effectiveness
      ~ Synergy
  - Administrative viewpoints
    - "Juggler" metaphor
    - "Len" that reflects past to present
    - Ability to "Mix and Match"
    - Importance of keeping abreast of business trends
    - Contextual Themes of the past can prevent current malfeasance
- **Contemporary terms and issues**
  - Reminders from the past for the future
    - Organization Functions
      ~ Guides, not principles
      ~ Authority and responsibility relationship

- Employee Relations
  - ~ Leadership (inspire, persuade, modesty, empathy)
  - ~ "Big Y, little x" concept
  - ~ Greatest Management Principle (GMP)
  - ~ Promoting professionalism
- Open Systems
  - ~ Two "outside" legs of the Three Legs of Support Model
  - ~ Media consideration
- Social Equity
  - ~ Protecting individual rights
- Client-Oriented Service
  - ~ Maintaining public trust and support
  - ~ Peel Principles remain as "Holy Grail"
  - ~ Shift to police accountability to public
  - ~ "Environmental Protection Cops"
  - ~ Integrating the community and criminal justice agencies

Prominent names in the history of criminal justice administration

- **Police**
  - Sir Robert Peel
  - Leonhard Fuld
  - August Vollmer
  - O.W. Wilson
  - William Parker
- **Corrections**
  - Zebulon Reed Brockway
  - Mary Belle Harris
  - John Augustus
  - Alexander Maconochie
- **Courts**
  - Arthur T. Vanderbilt
  - A. Leo Levin
  - Edward B. McConnell

Note: Figures are noted with an italicized page locator; tables are noted with a *t*. **Index**

Figure Credits

Chapter 6

Figure 6–1: U.S. Department of Justice. http://www.ojp.usdoj.gov.

Chapter 8

Figure 8–2: Reprinted by permission of *Harvard Business Review*. An exhibit from "One More Time: How Do You Motivate Employees," by Frederick Herzberg (January/February 1968). Copyright © 1968 by the Harvard Business School Publishing Corporation; all rights reserved.

Figure 8–4 (left): Adapted from Hershey, P. & Blanchard, K.H. (1977). *Managing Organizational Behavior*. Englewood Cliffs, NJ: Prentice Hall.

Figure 8–4 (right): Maslow, Abraham. (1941). A Theory of Human Motivation. *Psychological Review*, 50.

Chapter 9

Figure 9–1: Harrison, M.I. (1987). *Diagnosing Organizations: Methods, Models, and Processes*. Newbury Park, CA: Sage Publications, Inc. Copyright ©1987 by Sage Publications, Inc. Reprinted with permission of Sage Publications, Inc.

Figure 9–2: Adapted from the U.S. Department of Justice. *Compendium of Federal Justice Statistics*. (1989). Washington, DC: Bureau of Justice Statistics, 1992, p.3.

Figure 9–3: Derived from Rainville, G. & Reaves, B. (2003). *Felony Defendants in Large Urban Countries, 2000*. Washington, DC: Bureau of Justice Statistics.

Figure 9–4: Estimated based on figures from *A National Justice Research in Brief*. (1991). Washington, DC: U.S. Department of Justice. 2005 figures from http://www.ojp.usdoj.gov/bj.

Chapter 10

Figure 10–3: Data from author's research and national crime statistics documents.

Figure 10–4: United States Department of Justice, Bureau of Justice Statistics. http://www.ojp.usdoj .gov/bjs/glance/tables/exetab.htm.

Chapter 11

Figure 11–1: DiAsclo, W. (1997). *Seeking Justice: Crime and Punishment in America*. New York: Edna McConnell Clark Foundation. Used with permission of the Edna McConnell Clark Foundation.

Figure 11–3: Roberg, R.R., Kuykendall, J., & Novak, K. (2002). *Police Management*. Los Angeles, CA: Roxbury Publishing Company. Printed with permission of the publisher.

Chapter 12

Figure 12–1: From "Ethnic Diversity Grows, Neighborhood Integration Lags Behind." Reprinted by permission of John Logan, Brown University. http://www.s4.brown.edu.

Figure 12–2: From "Ethnic Diversity Grows, Neighborhood Integration Lags Behind." Reprinted by permission of John Logan, Brown University. http://www.s4.brown.edu.

Figure 12–3: Schaefer, R. T. (2007). *Race and Ethnicity in the United States*. (4th ed.). Upper Saddle River, NJ: Pearson/Prentice Hall. Printed with permission of the publisher.

Figure 12–4: Schaefer, R. T. (2007). *Race and Ethnicity in the United States*. (4th ed.). Upper Saddle River, NJ: Pearson/Prentice Hall. Printed with permission of the publisher.

Figure 12–5: DeNavas-Walt, Proctor, and Mills 2005; for Native Americans, author's estimate based on Bureau of the Census, 2003b.
Figure 12–6: Hoecklin, L. (1994). *Managing Cultural Differences*. Wokingham: Addison Wesley.
Figure 12–7: Estimates by the author based on the U.S. Bureau of Justice Statistics.
Figure 12–8: Estimates by the author based on the U.S. Bureau of Justice Statistics and the National Center for Women and Policing.

Chapter 14

Figure 14–1: Haberfeld, M.R. (2006). *Police Leadership*. Upper Saddle River, NJ: Pearson/Prentice Hall. (Adapted from Judge & Bruno, 2000). Printed with permission of the publisher.
Figure 14–2: Based on concepts from Blake, R. & Mouton, J. (1964). *The Managerial Grid*. Houston, TX: Gulf Publishing Company.
Douglas, M. (1957). The Human Side of Enterprise. Management Review. November.
Figure 14–4: Collins, J. (2001). *Good to Great*. New York: HarperCollins Publishers, Inc. Printed by permission of the publisher.
Figure 14–5: Collins, J. (2005). *Good to Great and the Social Sectors*. Boulder, CO. Printed with permission of the author.

Chapter 15

Figure 15–1: Figure developed from International Centre for Prison Studies. November 29, 2002. World prison brief. Data available at http://www.kcl.ac.uk/depsta/rel/icps/worldbrief/world_brief.html.
Figure 15–4: http://www.ojp.usdoj.gov/bjs/glance/tables/corr2tab.htm.
Figure 15–5: U.S. Department of Labor, Bureau of Labor Statistics. Data available at http://www.bls.gov/data/home.htm.
Figure 15–6: U.S. Bureau of the Census, Current Population Survey, Annual Social and Economic Supplements. Poverty and Health Statistics Branch/ HHES Division. Washington, DC: U.S. Bureau of the Census; U.S. Department of Commerce. Available at http://www.census.gov/hhes/income/histinc/histpovtb.html.
Figure 15–7: http://www.ojp.usdoj.gov/bjs/glance/tables/corr2tab.htm.